Extraordinary Lives

www.readersdigest.co.uk

Published in the United Kingdom by Vivat Direct Limited
(t/a Reader's Digest), 157 Edgware Road,
London W2 2HR

Printed in Portugal
ISBN 978 1 780 2012 7

Extraordinary Lives

Contents

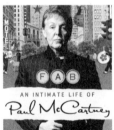
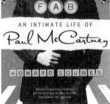

Things I Couldn't Tell My Mother
Sue Johnston

The relationship with your mother is perhaps the most precious and fraught of any woman's life, but Sue Johnston always seemed to be disappointing hers—especially when she quit a steady job to go into acting. When she began writing her story, Sue set out to record 'all the big things, and all the small things. Everything I wanted to tell my mother but felt I never could'. The result is an honest, poignant and often very funny memoir by one of Britain's favourite actresses.

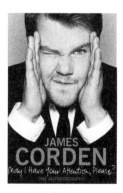

May I Have Your Attention, Please?
James Corden

As far back as he can remember, James Corden only ever wanted to entertain. But it wasn't easy getting there. *May I Have Your Attention, Please?* is the story of how it all happened, and how he found nation-wide fame as an actor, television writer, producer and presenter, and created the lovably loud Smithy in the award-winning *Gavin & Stacey*. This warm, cheeky and hilarious story of one of our most popular comedy stars tells what it's like to try, try, and try again, and to get there in the end.

Elizabeth Taylor
by J. Randy Taraborrelli

If ever there was an American princess, it would have to be the actress with the sapphire-blue eyes—pampered, beautiful, beloved Elizabeth. By the power of her personality, the drama of her life, and the example of her philanthropy, she has seduced us, charmed us and inspired our admiration. Indeed, because we've been so transfixed for decades by her talent and her beauty, we sometimes lose sight of what she has truly done.

'Elizabeth' by J. Randy Taraborrelli

Prologue

Even with all the star treatment accorded her over the years, the truth is undeniable: it has never been easy being Elizabeth Taylor. Gentle and caring at her core, while often appearing to be petulant and self-consumed, she is a complex woman who has usually been misunderstood—not only by others, but, it would seem, by herself as well.

In trying to understand Elizabeth's life, one must first turn to her childhood. Born into an affluent family, young Elizabeth possessed an engaging quality and stunning beauty. From the beginning, her mother, Sara—a former actress—believed her daughter to have the makings of a great star. So, from the time Elizabeth was about two, Sara endeavoured to create in her the ultimate image of dignity, grace and beauty. With the passing of the years, nearly every aspect of the young girl's behaviour would be carefully considered and altered. Her speech. Her posture. Her gait. It was as if Sara were a director, coaching the promising new star of a landmark movie.

Sara even orchestrated how her daughter would interact with others: if a broad laugh was too much, it would be replaced with a shy giggle. As a result, Elizabeth's early life became a training session for succeeding in a business at which her mother had only found marginal accomplishment. For Elizabeth Taylor, perfection became the only option. Anything less would be considered failure.

Part One
Childhood

Sara Viola Warmbrodt was born on August 21, 1896, in Arkansas City, Kansas. For all her time on this earth, she would be quite a character, a memorable presence not only in the life of her daughter, Elizabeth, but in the lives of nearly every person she would touch over the years. Sara was an actor, whose first successful show, *The Sign on the Door*, went to London in 1924. After it closed, four less successful theatrical productions in New York followed. By the time she was thirty, Sara began considering her options. It was at just that time that Francis Taylor—a man whom she had dated casually back in Arkansas City—came back into her life.

Francis Lenn Taylor was born on December 28, 1897, also in Arkansas City. He had dropped out of high school and worked as an apprentice in an art gallery owned by his beloved, if also demanding, uncle, Howard Young, in St Louis. When Francis turned twenty-one, his uncle gave him the opportunity to work at a gallery in New York that he had opened there—the Howard Young Gallery—which specialised in eighteenth- and nineteenth-century European paintings.

Francis and Sara were married in 1926. Then Sara made the fateful decision to leave show business. 'I gave up my career when I married Daddy,' she once said (referring to Francis). Francis was to manage a branch of the Howard Young Gallery that was about to open in London, and he and his new wife settled into a suite at the luxurious Carlton Hotel, paid for by Howard Young.

For the next two years, Francis and Sara would travel all over Europe in first-class style—Paris, Berlin, Vienna and Budapest—thanks to Howard Young's generous underwriting of such excursions. In the process, they would traffic with the powerful and affluent of the art world and acquire from them old masters for the Young Gallery.

When Sara became pregnant at the end of 1928, the couple

decided to take root in London. Howard leased a lovely nineteenth-century cottage for them at 11 Hampstead Way. With its beautifully manicured gardens and pathways and its gorgeous views of verdant Hampstead Heath, it was an enchanted place.

In June 1929, Sara gave birth to their first child, a son named Howard (after his great-uncle). With the addition of the baby, the Taylors' home was suddenly too cramped, with just two bedrooms. The couple did have a nurse, a cook and a driver, after all. Howard solved the problem by purchasing a larger eighteenth-century home nearby, known as Heathwood, at 8 Wildwood Road, again overlooking the heath. Landscaped with aged trees and colourful wildflowers, the redbrick home came complete with a large kitchen, stately dining and living rooms, pool and tennis court.

Howard was a stunning baby, with large, expressive blue eyes, wavy blond hair and perfectly placed features. He was his daddy's boy, though. Sara believed a father and son should share a special bond. Therefore, while she was an affectionate mother, she would often abdicate parental duties to Francis. It was as if she saw the raising of her first-born as an opportunity to further shape her husband into an even fuller, more responsible man. However, such devotion to Francis's betterment would not last for ever. Things would change dramatically, beginning on February 27, 1932 — the day Sara gave birth to a daughter.

THE NEW TAYLOR baby girl was named Elizabeth after both her grandmothers and Rosemond after her paternal grandmother's maiden name. By the time she was one month old, she was the most gorgeous baby, with unusually bright, lavender-blue eyes, and even a double line of eyelashes.

With the birth of her daughter came a sea change in how Sara lived her own life. It was as if she saw Elizabeth's birth as a challenge to mould a life from the moment it began. She enrolled her in singing and dancing lessons before she had reached the age of two. By three, Elizabeth knew how to curtsy, shake hands, speak to adults . . . and, as she put it, 'be a lady'.

Following Elizabeth's arrival, Sara seemed to lose all desire to make Francis the ideal gentleman. Although most husbands would have been relieved to not have to hear opinions about their grooming habits and clothing choices, Francis was not one of them. He had actually come to rely on Sara's pointed criticisms. However, after Elizabeth entered their home, the Sara he had known began to drift away from him.

ELIZABETH TAYLOR lived in and around London, England, for the first six years of her life, years she recalls as being 'the happiest days of my childhood'. No wonder. She and brother Howard enjoyed a privileged life, with servants at their beck and call, but not really because of anything Francis had done to ensure their security. In fact, the Taylors' situation was an unusual one, because the family had been, in a sense, adopted by two wealthy men. The first was Francis's uncle, Howard Young. The other was a family friend named Victor Cazalet.

Victor and Howard virtually seeded the Taylor family's prosperity, allowing them to remain unaffected by the worldwide depression. Francis fully understood what motivated Howard to subsidise his family: he was a pushy relative who wanted to coax his nephew into a successful life. He was domineering and tough—much like Sara—and never let Francis forget that he was in charge. Francis understood that much, and learned to live with it. However, he never quite understood what kind of relationship Victor Cazalet had with Sara. Were they having an affair? Many people in their circle suspected as much. Others were certain that Victor, unmarried with no children, was homosexual. From all accounts, Francis never knew for certain what was going on. 'Over the years, I heard a lot of stories about Sara, suggesting that if Howard ever dropped the ball, Victor would pick it up and continue to support the family,' said a family friend. 'Yet, despite such manoeuvrings, everyone seemed to get along just fine. They were able to coexist, and I think it was Sara who was really controlling everyone in her midst—not Howard, not Victor, and certainly not Francis.'

The friend continues: 'There were discrepancies as to who was paying for Elizabeth's and Howard's private schooling. It was thought that Victor paid for their education. Sara just kept mum about it, saying it was a private matter. I later learned she got money from *both* men for those educations and then let them each think he was responsible for the schooling. That was the kind of woman she was, savvy but also manipulative.'

'My family was held hostage by those men,' Francis Taylor told his friend Marshall Baldrige many years later. 'There's not much I could do about it. They were bigger ... and stronger, too.'

Sara had style and grace to spare. A thin but shapely brunette, she shimmered when she entered a room. She had impeccable taste, scrutinising every decorating detail of the homes in which she and her family would live — fabric, paint, wallpaper — making sure everything was of the highest quality. She was also the consummate party giver, hosting carefully choreographed evenings of dining and entertainment in the family home. Conversations at dinner were always spirited, about politics, the arts, music and current events. At such gatherings, the Taylors mixed with celebrated figures, such as Winston Churchill and Sir Anthony Eden. But despite her worldliness, Sara craved a greater sense of purpose. Her interest in Elizabeth's future became the primary focus of her life.

By the time she was four, Elizabeth truly was lovely, her alabaster complexion offset by dark curls and luminescent blue eyes that, in a flattering light, seemed violet. Also, there was a vibrancy about her. She wasn't like other children. She had something other tots didn't possess, a precociousness that wasn't cloying or irritating. Her glowing youth and cameo-like beauty were often the subject of attention. 'People would stop me in the streets,' Sara had said, 'and they would tell me, "That child should be in pictures. Why, she's the spitting image of Vivien Leigh!"'

IN THE SPRING of 1939, the American embassy in London sent a notice to all citizens of the United States residing in Britain, warning them that a war was about to break out, and that they should return to America as soon as possible. It was not an easy decision for the Taylors to make.

Marshall Baldrige recalls, 'Francis did not want to go. But Sara had decided that the family should move to California. At the same time, Howard decided that the gallery should move to America. "I guess I have to go, but I want you to come with me," Francis told me sadly. "I need your support. Sara and Howard will completely destroy me in America." I didn't want to leave London, my family. "Francis, I just can't go," I told him, "but maybe one day I will meet you there." He had tears in his eyes. I felt awful. I knew that I was throwing him to the wolves.'

On April 3, 1939, Sara, Elizabeth and little Howard (along with a nanny) sailed to America aboard the SS *Manhattan*, but without Francis. He stayed behind to wrap up loose ends with the business.

It was during that eight-day journey to the United States that a Hollywood film called *The Little Princess*, starring eleven-year-old Shirley Temple, was shown as part of the activities schedule for passengers. Sara took her children to see the movie in the ship's theatre. Elizabeth, seven years old, hadn't seen many films in London and was excited to go to this one.

If any child ever had star quality on the screen, it was Shirley Temple. She is easily the most famous child star of all time. Elizabeth, as she has recalled it, sat in the dark theatre, watching the young curly-haired star with awed fascination. She could sing, dance, act . . . She truly was a wonder. When the lights came up, Elizabeth Taylor turned to her mother: 'Mummy,' she whispered urgently, 'I think I might want to be an *actress*. A movie star!'

AFTER ARRIVING in New York, Sara Taylor, her children and their nanny boarded a train to Pasadena, California, where Sara's father lived. Sara had loved Southern California when she worked in the theatre there years earlier and, with her heart now set on some kind of show-business career for Elizabeth, she felt that settling near the entertainment capital of Hollywood made the most sense. The Taylor family showed up at the doorstep of Sara's father's house on May 1, 1939. Elizabeth and Howard were enrolled in the private Willard School, outside Pasadena.

In December, Francis followed his family to America.

'As soon as Francis arrived,' recalls Francis's friend Stefan Verkaufen, 'the family settled in Pacific Palisades, California, in an expansive home leased for them by ... Who else? Howard Young, of course. A year later [in 1941], Howard bought the family a home in Beverly Hills. It was then that I received an excited telephone call from Francis, telling me that he had relocated his art gallery to the nearby Beverly Hills Hotel. It was a prime location, one of the most famous hotels and a virtual crossroads of the world, with potential clients from all over the globe. He was very excited. He also said that he and Sara were getting along better and that he was happy to see her again.'

Once ensconced in Beverly Hills, Sara enrolled Elizabeth in singing and dancing lessons, and Elizabeth continued with her riding lessons. Then Sara arranged an important 'audition' of sorts for Elizabeth with Hedda Hopper, one of the leading gossip columnists in show business.

'It was one of the most painful ordeals I have ever witnessed,' Hopper later recalled. She said that Elizabeth was 'clearly terrified, but I felt that the mother was never going to rest until this child was famous. She wanted to have a glamorous life through her child; I had seen too much misery in child stars. Let a child be a child, that was my motto. And I told Sara Taylor just that.'

Sara Taylor continued her networking in Hollywood, hoping to meet someone who might be able to assist her in making her daughter a star. Sara also continued as the consummate dinner-party and cocktail-hour hostess. Because people gravitated towards her anyway, it wasn't difficult for her to find her place in Beverly Hills society and even assist Francis in securing affluent clients for his art gallery.

It happened to be at Francis's place of business that Sara met Andrea Cowden, wife of J. Cheever Cowden, chairman of Universal Pictures. Cowden had come into the gallery to examine the

Augustus John paintings that Francis had on show there. Sara and Andrea hit it off immediately, and Sara invited the Cowdens to the Taylor home for tea.

The afternoon tea party—in February 1941, just before Elizabeth's ninth birthday—was a great success. Sara told J. Cheever how much time and energy she had devoted to seeing her daughter become a star in show business. Then she brought out Elizabeth. Years later, Andrea Cowden would recall, 'She was the most beautiful child I had ever seen. She did not walk; she danced. She was so merry, so full of love for every little thing, whether it was a person, an animal or a flower. At that time, you didn't know what she'd be, but you knew she'd be something.' J. Cheever was impressed enough to offer to sign Elizabeth to a contract at Universal.

The deal was signed on April 21, 1941: a hundred dollars a week for five months, the money to go to Sara—not Francis, incidentally—on Elizabeth's behalf.

By the end of the summer of 1941, Elizabeth Taylor was on a sound stage at Universal Studios, making her first 'short' film, a sixty-minute trifle, first called *Man or Mouse* but soon renamed *There's One Born Every Minute*. In it, Elizabeth portrayed a misbehaving little brat. But then she was dropped by Universal two weeks after she finished the film. The executives didn't think her performance qualified as one that suggested a new star in the making. 'The kid has nothing,' noted Universal's casting director, Dan Kelly, in an oft-quoted memo. 'Her eyes are too old. She doesn't have the face of a kid.'

Everyone in the Taylor household was disappointed by the surprising turn of events. But Sara and Elizabeth had now been given a taste of the movie business, and it was all they needed to whet their appetites for more.

In 1943 the Taylors received the horrifying news that Victor Cazalet, a major in the British army by this time, had been killed in a plane crash. Of course, all the Taylors were devastated. It would be many months before either Sara or Francis would be able to reconcile their close friend's sudden and tragic passing.

It would be in the same year as Cazalet's death that Elizabeth would get her next break. Metro-Goldwyn-Mayer staff producer Sam Marx recalled the story in a documentary about Elizabeth: 'I was an air-raid warden in Beverly Hills. One of the other air-raid wardens in the unit was Francis Taylor. In addition to being an air-raid warden, I was a producer at MGM. He knew it, and he began talking to me about his beautiful daughter. I was starting a film called *Lassie Come Home*. In it was a charming little girl named Marie Flynn, and for that reason I had no need for any other girl. So I wasn't being very nice to Francis in putting him off. Then, when the first rushes came in, I found that the girl was a head taller than Roddy McDowall. In those days, you couldn't have the girl be taller than the boy. So we had to take her out of the part. MGM had just made a film [in which] there were seven charming little girls. The casting office agreed to get them to my office at five o'clock. And then I remembered Francis Taylor.

'I called him at his gallery and told him what was going on. He reported that his daughter was in Pasadena with her mother [visiting Sara's father] and possibly would get to the studio, but he wasn't sure. At five o'clock the casting director ushered in the girls. I started looking them over, when my secretary called from outside and said another girl had just arrived. Elizabeth, with her mother. She walked in and was wearing a blue velvet cape. Her blue eyes, the dark hair, the cape—it was like an eclipse of the sun, blotting out everybody who was in the office. We never even *thought* to make a test.' Elizabeth had won the role.

It would be on the set of this film that Elizabeth would meet one of her lifelong friends, Roddy McDowall, who was the thirteen-year-old star of the movie. 'On her first day of filming, they took one look at her and said, "Get that girl off the set. She has too much eye make-up on, too much mascara,"' Roddy once recalled. 'So they rushed her off the set and started rubbing at her eyes with a moist cloth. Guess what? They learned then that she had no mascara on. She has a double set of eyelashes. And the wonderful thing about Elizabeth was that she was so totally unaware of her beauty. At a place—MGM—that was full of gorgeous women, she did stand out. She was the most beautiful child I had ever seen.'

'I had a great imagination,' Elizabeth recalls, 'and just slid into being an actress. It was a piece of cake.' She only had four scenes in the movie—less than ten minutes of screen time. Still, on the strength of that one film appearance, MGM signed her to a seven-year contract.

As if to reaffirm the correctness of their decision regarding Elizabeth's talent, the studio then loaned her to 20th Century Fox for one film, *Jane Eyre*. She received no credit and was only seen in the film for less than three minutes as a friend of Jane's—but they were three minutes that exhibited the on-screen magic that would be hers for the rest of her career. In the movie, young Elizabeth even had a death scene that was so poignant and real, it is worth repeated viewings. A staggering amount of wisdom was apparent in her acting.

NATIONAL VELVET was one of thirty pictures released by MGM in 1944. It was one of only four films given the Technicolor treatment, evidence of the importance of the production to the studio. Pre-production would take almost two years, and with a beautifully written script based on the beloved novel and a cast that included Mickey Rooney, one of the studio's most important stars, the only thing remaining was the casting of the film's central character, Velvet Brown. If producer Pandro S. Berman was unsure who would portray the twelve-year-old girl who disguises herself as a fifteen-year-old boy in order to ride in the Grand National steeplechase, there were two people on the lot—Sara and Elizabeth—who were absolutely sure of who would play that part: Elizabeth Taylor.

Looking back on *National Velvet* today, Elizabeth believes she got the role in that movie by 'sheer will-power'. She told Director Pandro S. Berman that she totally identified with the main character, she had the appropriate English accent, she could ride horses—what else did he need? The problem was that Berman felt

Elizabeth was too slight in build to pull off the notion that she could masquerade as a boy. She was just a little girl, after all, and she looked like one. But 'I am going to play that part', the youngster said with steely determination.

In *National Velvet*, Elizabeth would appear opposite Mickey Rooney, who played the role of the young wanderer who winds up training a horse named The Pie for the Grand National steeple-chase. She has recalled, 'The first time I ever had to cry [on film] was in *National Velvet*. The horse was supposed to have colic, and of course, he was Velvet's life. When the character Mickey played said he didn't think the horse would live, Velvet cries. I knew the scene, and it hadn't worried me in the slightest. Anyway, when we rehearsed the scene, Mickey put his arm round me and said, "Honey, you know in this scene you have to cry." And I said, "Yes, Mickey, I know." "Well," he said, "you should think that your father is dying and your mother has to wash clothes for a living and your brother is out selling newspapers on the street and he doesn't have shoes and he's cold and shivering and your little dog was run over." It was meant to make me cry. Instead, I started to laugh. I didn't have the heart to say anything to him. When I did the scene, instead of imagining my father dying and my mother doing the laundry in a snowy stream, all I thought about was the horse being very sick . . . and the tears just came. But how generous of Mickey to try to help me.' (Of course, Elizabeth is entitled to her own memory about her first screen cry, but the truth is, she was called upon to cry in both *Jane Eyre* and *Lassie Come Home*.)

National Velvet is as irresistible today as it was when it was made more than sixty years ago. It was released nationally on January 26, 1945 and was an immediate hit, grossing over $4.25 million. The film's reviews and Elizabeth's personal notices were glowing. '[She imbued] the character with such a sweet, fragile charm that not even a splendidly restrained Mickey Rooney could steal scenes from her,' enthused the *New York World-Telegram & Sun*. MGM rewarded Elizabeth with a lucrative long-term contract, establishing her as one of its top child actresses.

BY THE AGE of thirteen, Elizabeth Taylor had become a major movie star, thanks to *National Velvet*, earning a salary of $300 per week — not much today, but at the time a reasonable amount to pay a child actress. Sara earned about ten per cent of that amount as her daughter's chaperone and acting teacher.

Elizabeth was not like other actresses there who constantly subjugated themselves to the irascible studio boss. In fact, she wasn't fond of L. B. Mayer at all: she thought him a hypocrite. She would point out that he constantly encouraged all the children at the studio to think of him as a benevolent father and come to him with their problems. 'But just try to get an appointment with the man. It will simply never happen.'

When she was about fourteen, Elizabeth could no longer contain her feelings about the much-feared studio boss. She and her mother were having a meeting with Mayer about a newspaper article that suggested Elizabeth was being considered for a role in a musical. Sara told Mayer she thought Elizabeth would need more singing and dancing lessons. For no reason anyone could think of, Mayer suddenly blew up at her. He began swearing at her, calling her a stupid woman and berating her. He reminded her that he had pulled her and her daughter 'from the gutter'. As he went on, Sara just sat before him with her eyes closed, apparently trying to remain centred and calm, as her Christian Science background would have dictated during such a crisis. However, Elizabeth couldn't take it. She stood up and yelled at him, 'Don't you dare speak to my mother like that. You and your studio can just go to hell.' Mayer stood up and shouted, 'You can't talk to me that way, young lady.' She countered with, 'I most certainly can. You can take your studio and you know where to put it.' Then she stormed out of the office. Sara stayed behind and tried to smooth things over with Mayer. Elizabeth never set foot in L. B. Mayer's office again. It's amazing, in retrospect, that Mayer continued to give her work. 'He must have needed me badly,' she has said by way of explanation.

Though just a petite five foot two — Elizabeth fibbed to the press and added two inches to her height—she appeared taller and more willowy on screen than in person. She also, of course, had the bluest, most expressive eyes. They were the focal point of a face that seemed sculpted from marble. The entire picture was framed by dark, luxurious hair. Everywhere she went, heads turned.

One of the challenges Elizabeth faced at MGM concerned the schooling she received on the lot, where the studio had its own little red schoolhouse for the child stars. It was, as she recalls it, 'a ridiculous way of schooling us. Between takes you had to study for a minimum of ten minutes.' There have been stories reported about the young thespian's lack of interest in her studies and her decision that the world of movies was the only one about which she needed to know.

Though she was now making a good deal of money, she didn't know how to keep track of it. So poor was she at maths, she had to count by using her fingers when she was seventeen. Her reading and spelling skills were also weak. Still, the studio pushed her along in its school system, passing her from one grade to the next.

Despite her fame and popularity, the young Elizabeth Taylor would become an extremely antisocial teenager, not knowing how to mix and relate to people—mostly adults—who did not make their living in front of movie cameras. She often wondered what it might be like to go to a regular school, to be able to have friends who were not actors, who did not always seem to be performing for cameras even in their personal lives. She felt isolated, which probably prompted her interest in pets. MGM certainly made a lot of her fascination with small animals: countless photos were taken of Elizabeth with a golden retriever named Monty; a spaniel called Spot; a cocker, Twinkle; a cat she named Jeepers Creepers; not to mention her horses, King Charles and Prince Charming. Of course, it's entirely possible to speculate that Elizabeth felt that she could better relate to her pets, considering the circumstances of her life at the time. Or . . . perhaps she just liked animals.

Nothing became more important to Elizabeth Taylor than her career, because it was all she had and all she felt that distinguished her. A note to her mother, written when the actress was a teenager, illustrates this point. 'I've done a lot of thinking,' Elizabeth wrote, 'and I realise that my whole life is being in motion pictures. For me to quit would be like cutting away the roots of a tree—I'd soon become dead and useless. I also like to think maybe I have brought happiness to a few people, but more than anything I would like to have made you happy. But I'm afraid I haven't succeeded very well. I'm not going to stop trying, though.'

A Date with Judy was the 1948 film that marked the first time Elizabeth, then sixteen, wore make-up on screen and had, as she puts it, 'a leading man who wasn't four-legged'. Robert Stack, twelve years her senior, played her love interest in that film and gave her her first 'adult' on-screen kiss. 'I think in real life I got my own first kiss about two weeks before,' she told Barbara Walters. 'I was in a panic that I'd be kissed on the screen before I was kissed in real life, and that would have been a terrible humiliation.'

Though she enjoyed her career, Elizabeth, for years to come, would be conflicted about it. Francis once told Stefan Verkaufen, the Viennese art dealer who was very close to the Taylors and who had by this time moved to Los Angeles, that late one night, Elizabeth approached both her parents as they were preparing for bed. She complained that she was sick and tired of making movies and that she just wanted to be a regular child. Sara took her daughter's cry for help as a sign of ingratitude. 'But you're *not* a regular child,' she told her. 'You have a responsibility, Elizabeth. Not just to this family, but to the country now, the whole world.'

Elizabeth looked to Francis for help, but the only way for him to be there for his child would have been to stand up to his wife, and apparently he couldn't bring himself to do it. Instead, he held his tongue, not saying a word. Elizabeth fled from the room, crying.

When recounting this upsetting story, Francis told Stefan that it was painfully clear to him that Elizabeth's feelings for him had come into focus with that exchange. 'I could see that she'd lost all respect for me that night,' he told Stefan. 'It was as if a dagger had pierced my heart.'

Years later, Elizabeth would blithely state, 'You know, my *real* fathers were Benny Thau [an MGM executive] and Jules Goldstone [her agent].' How sad that she would end up feeling that way, especially considering her father's understandable problems and his utter inability to address them. He wouldn't have hurt her intentionally for the world. Yet he had done just that, and she would never forget it.

Part Two

Finding Her Way

By the time Elizabeth was about sixteen, Sara had become preoccupied with her daughter's social life—her dating life, specifically. As much as she wanted Elizabeth to remain a little girl, Sara also wanted her to be viewed by the public as popular and desirable. She wanted Elizabeth to date—or perhaps it would be more accurate to state that she wanted people to *think* Elizabeth was dating.

Despite her formidable image, Elizabeth was actually extremely naive when it came to romance. All she wanted was to fall in love and have the kind of head-over-heels experiences she'd acted on the screen. Indeed, when it came to matters of the heart, a film's fantasy was her only frame of reference. She wasn't going to be finding boyfriends on her own, that much was clear. It was at Sara's urging that MGM set Elizabeth up on her first date, when she was sixteen. It was to be with an all-American football player, the handsome Heisman Trophy winner Lieutenant Glenn Davis, just out of West Point. Tall, with reddish brown hair, he was all muscle and swagger. As soon as Sara met the twenty-three-year-old Davis, it was true love—even if Elizabeth seemed shy and ambivalent.

At this time, the summer of 1948, Elizabeth was making *Little Women*, Louisa May Alcott's autobiographical account of her life with her three sisters in Concord, Massachusetts, in the 1860s. During filming, she and Glenn saw each other from time to time.

When Elizabeth told a reporter that she and Davis were 'engaged to be engaged', it became a big story and no one questioned it at the time, not even Davis.

In September, the affable Davis was shipped off to Korea. He left Elizabeth with a little gold football round her neck and his picture on her dressing table to help keep their 'love' alive. She promised to wait for him.

In February 1949, the Taylor family went to Howard Young's winter home at Star Island, Florida, where Elizabeth would celebrate her seventeenth birthday. It was at Young's, during a dinner party, that she met William Pawley. At twenty-eight, he was more than ten years her senior. With coal-black hair and penetrating eyes, he had the chiselled face of a Hollywood actor, complete with pencil-thin moustache. He was gregarious, funny, unfailingly polite and wealthy as well. Elizabeth was infatuated with him.

However, in March 1949, Glenn Davis was granted leave from his tour of duty and wanted to see Elizabeth. She had no problem going to meet Glenn Davis upon his arrival in Florida and acting as if she anticipated a happy future with him. As she saw it, none of it was real anyway.

As expected, the scene at the airport turned into a mad one, with photographers jostling to get the best photographs of MGM's winsome star with the all-American boyfriend she had missed so much, and Elizabeth put on the expected show of chirpy, girlish emotion at the very sight of the slack-jawed Glenn. The next day, photos of the two were published in newspapers all over the country.

When Glenn figured out what was going on, he turned round and went back to Los Angeles feeling betrayed and hurt—and with a ruby and diamond engagement ring in his pocket. As it happened, he had intended to ask Elizabeth to marry him. But once they were away from the panting press, he found that she was distant and totally uninterested in anything he had to say. She had changed. The scene was over.

At the end of May 1949, Elizabeth and Sara were house guests of the Pawley family in Florida. The day after they arrived,

William presented Elizabeth with a three-and-a-half-carat emerald-cut solitaire diamond ring—for which he had paid $16,000. Now they were officially, and quite suddenly, engaged. MGM organised a press conference to announce the engagement, and during it, Sara reminded reporters that Elizabeth had never really been engaged to Glenn Davis, which was true. Still, these sudden romantic experiences must have seemed a tad disposable for Elizabeth: out with one boyfriend and in with the other, and without much consideration for either of them. In retrospect, it was not a good impression to make on a naive seventeen-year-old.

Elizabeth's engagement to Pawley ended a few months later when he tried to persuade Elizabeth to give up her career for him. Elizabeth told the press that it had to end because she was about to start two new movie projects—*The Big Hangover* and *Father of the Bride.*

AS A SUITOR, men didn't come much better than Nicky Hilton, or at least that's how it seemed at first blush. Twenty-three-year-old Conrad Nicholson Hilton, Jr, was the son of the millionaire hotel owner Conrad Hilton and one of the wealthiest and most eligible bachelors in Los Angeles. Elizabeth, at seventeen, was introduced to Nicky, as he was called, on the set of *A Place in the Sun* and began dating him in the autumn of 1949. She was swept off her feet by his charm, magnetism, Texan drawl and rakish good looks. Six feet tall, with brown hair and eyes, broad shoulders and a reed-thin waist, he was, as Elizabeth later put it, 'spectacular in every way'.

In late winter of 1950, after a brief courtship, Nicky asked Elizabeth to marry him, and she accepted. That was also the month she graduated from high school.

A primary reason why Elizabeth wanted to marry at just eighteen was that she was absolutely frantic for some distance from Sara. Marriage seemed a good way to win her freedom. Marriage also represented an outlet for Elizabeth's urge to explore her sexuality. She was still a virgin. As she later wrote, 'I had always had a strict and proper upbringing. The irony is that the morality I learned at home required marriage. I couldn't just have an affair. I was ready for love, and I was ready for lovemaking.'

Just as her marriage was being discussed, Elizabeth was in the midst of filming Vincente Minnelli's *Father of the Bride*. Elizabeth finished the movie just hours before her engagement to Nicky was announced. As if to further blur the distinction between reality and fiction, MGM then decided to delay the film's release to coincide with Elizabeth's wedding, over which the studio took complete charge. MGM's wardrobe mistress, Helen Rose, created Elizabeth's $3,500 bridal gown, a gift from Louis B. Mayer. Ceil Chapman designed her trousseau, and Edith Head her many honeymoon outfits . . . all of which were presents to their star from the studio. Was it any wonder that young Elizabeth had such trouble distinguishing between her film career and her real life?

In the days before the wedding, Elizabeth became ill and depressed, much as she would in years to come when she had to appear on the set of a movie she didn't want to do. Many of her relatives felt that she believed she was making a mistake, but she knew it was too late to change her mind. Therefore, on May 6, 1950, the Church of the Good Shepherd in Beverly Hills was filled with MGM executives, movie stars and Hilton hotel executives for the wedding of eighteen-year-old Elizabeth Taylor.

'I closed my eyes to any problems,' Elizabeth recalled, 'and walked radiantly down the aisle.' The excitement and anticipation she felt was evident on her face.

In truth, though she put on a brave face for the world, privately Elizabeth was scared. 'I was terrified,' she later recalled. 'There was a big reception, and for the first time in my life, I had two glasses of champagne. Then the time came to leave and I had a third glass. I wanted to run, I was so scared. I really had no idea what was coming.'

For their honeymoon, the newlyweds would embark on a three-month vacation to the south of France on the *Queen Mary*—but not right away. Mother's Day was just round the corner, and Elizabeth had never been away from Sara on that special day, so

Nicky would have to wait it out before he would be able to honey-moon with his new wife. Finally, the Hiltons boarded the *Queen Mary*, where they were properly ensconced.

The next day, Elizabeth woke up still a virgin. Nicky hadn't slept with her in the intervening week, and then they spent their first night on the cruise at a bar, drinking. It would actually be two more nights before the marriage was consummated. 'Then came disillusionment,' Elizabeth later recalled, 'rude and brutal. I fell off my pink cloud with a thud.'

The story of Elizabeth's honeymoon with Nicky has almost become the stuff of legend. The way he gambled and drank while in Monte Carlo, leaving his bride alone and sobbing until the wee hours of the morning, has been told numerous times. Indeed, people who saw them on their honeymoon have recalled Nicky's belligerent behaviour towards his new wife. He was suddenly angry at her and jealous of the attention she generated, and after the honeymoon it became clear that he was an alcoholic with seri-ous drug and gambling problems. He and Elizabeth had violent quarrels. While they were out on the town one evening, witnesses watched him give her a forceful shove that sent her reeling back-wards. She stumbled and fell, landing with a shattering impact that knocked the wind from her. 'That'll teach you,' he said, standing over her. Then he walked away, not even looking back at her on the floor, where she lay sobbing.

After seven months, the Hiltons separated. They divorced in February 1951. Elizabeth, who was making about $2,000 a week, did not ask for alimony. 'I don't need a prize for failing,' she remarked at the time.

Failure. It was a word Elizabeth wasn't used to having applied to her. Her mother had been pushing her towards excellence for so many years that the idea of not succeeding at something was enormously upsetting. It filled her with the most intense feelings of inferiority, of worthlessness. She would never forget the way it made her feel, and she would often think back on this time as the beginning of all of the heartache in her life.

Even in one of her first appearances before the camera, the face that would one day be heralded as the most beautiful in the world shows all signs pointing in that direction.

Sara Taylor poses with three-year-old Elizabeth and five-year-old Howard who, at this stage, was actually the 'looker' in the family.

Elizabeth at thirteen with King Charles, the thoroughbred who appeared with her in 'National Velvet'.

Elizabeth and Howard as teenagers. Throughout her life, her beloved brother would remain Elizabeth's most trusted confidant.

Mr and Mrs Conrad Hilton, Jr. Never would Elizabeth have dreamed that 'Nicky' would turn out to be a wife batterer.

Elizabeth with her sometimes troublesome but always loyal mother, Sara.

1950s glamour. Even dressed in a simple man-tailored shirt, as she is here on the set of 'Giant', Elizabeth's beauty dazzles.

Elizabeth and her second husband, British actor Michael Wilding. She was twenty years younger than Wilding. The marriage would last for four years.

The marriage to Michael Wilding produced two sons. Michael Howard Wilding was born on January 6, 1953. Then, on February 27, 1955, Elizabeth's twenty-third birthday, Christopher was born.

Elizabeth thought that her third husband, Mike Todd, was one of the two loves of her li (the other being Richard Burton). With their daughter, Liza, born on 6 August 1957.

Richard Burton in a rare publicity photo from the late 1950s. In 1961 he was cast in 'Cleopatra' as a replacement for Stephen Body. It was a decision that would change the course of his life.

Though Elizabeth and Richard were both mar ried, they could not resist each other. Within weeks of working together on 'Cleopatra', the were having a complex and often painful affe

In 1966, Elizabeth and Richard filmed what is arguably their best movie, 'Who's Afraid of Virginia Woolf?' Elizabeth would win an Oscar for her work.

Following her second marriage and divorce from Richard Burton, Elizabeth took John Warner as her sixth husband (in her seventh marriage) on December 4, 1976.

Elizabeth and Larry Fortensky, her seventh husband, in Gstaad in late 1994.

With her children and their spouses in May 2000. At the age of sixty-eight, Elizabeth was honoured as Dame Commander of the Order of the British Empire.

Not surprisingly, her perceived failure at being a good wife took its toll. By the time she began work on *Father's Little Dividend* (the sequel to *Father of the Bride*), she had lost twenty pounds, become a chain-smoker, and was suffering from high blood pressure, colitis and an ulcer.

It would actually take years before Elizabeth would hint at the horror she experienced as Nicky's spouse. Because she wanted to maintain some privacy, she didn't even tell the judge all the details when he asked why she was divorcing Nicky. She just said that he had been 'mean' to her and had called her mother derisive names.

Many years later Elizabeth finally revealed a secret she had kept for almost half a century: the final beating she endured as Hilton's wife had caused a miscarriage. 'I left him after having a baby kicked out of my stomach,' she said sadly. 'I had terrible pains. I saw the baby in the toilet. I didn't know that I was pregnant, so it wasn't a malicious act. It just happened. He was drunk. I thought, "This is not why I was put on earth. God did not put me here to have a baby kicked out of my stomach."'

AFTER HER MARRIAGE to Nicky ended, Elizabeth was angry . . . at herself, at Nicky, at fate, and at everyone around her, including her parents. In fact, she was now more argumentative than ever with Sara. Elizabeth was in full-fledged rebellion mode and would seemingly do anything she could think of not only to horrify Sara but also to assert her independence from her. Elizabeth was definitely changing. For instance, she had in the past employed colourful language in expressing herself. But now she was swearing more than ever, and out of anger rather than just to shock others. Even more disturbing, she had started drinking alcohol. Though she suffered terrible stomach problems as a result of the stress in her life—and she was on a strict diet of baby food!—she refused to rest. She seemed to be careering out of control.

Once Elizabeth was divorced from Nicky, MGM decided to cast her in the film *Ivanhoe*. While she was in London making that film, Elizabeth began to date charming matinée idol Michael Wilding.

He was a major star in his native England, a sophisticated man who was listened to and respected in the intellectual, theatrical circles in which he spent his time. As they got to know each other, Elizabeth remembers feeling that Michael was the kind of man who could 'take care of me, make me feel good about things, about the world'. His conversation was witty and, to a twenty-year-old, profound. In her eyes, he became infallible.

At the time, Michael Wilding, twenty years Elizabeth's senior, was married to actress Kay Young, but they were separated. With his receding hairline and tweed suits, he certainly seemed more the fatherly type than the lover. He suffered from epilepsy, a closely guarded secret at the time because of the stigma attached to the condition, and this very likely was at the root of his timid demeanour and cautious nature in public settings.

Elizabeth and Michael dated throughout the summer of *Ivanhoe*, and he helped her tremendously by lending emotional support during what turned out to be a very difficult production for her. Based on the classic novel of the Crusades by Sir Walter Scott, *Ivanhoe* was just the kind of historical, Technicolor epic that MGM did better than any other studio. Elizabeth was unhappy with the script, though, because there were two leading ladies in the film — she and Joan Fontaine — and only one got the hero in the end. And it wasn't Elizabeth. To add to her unhappiness, because she was in London making this movie, she was unable to attend the wedding of her brother, Howard, to Mara Regan. Howard had just received his Army induction notice and wanted to be married before he was shipped off to war.

WHEN ELIZABETH returned to Los Angeles, she telephoned Michael Wilding in London to ask if he might want to come to the States to visit her. He agreed to do so, and the two spent the winter months of 1951 in California dating and getting to know each other. On December 12, Wilding was granted a divorce. That night, he and Elizabeth were dining at Romanoff's restaurant in Los Angeles when he pulled from his pocket a sapphire and diamond ring. He intended it to be a simple token of his feelings—a commemoration of his new freedom and a commitment that he was interested in pursuing a future with her. However, when he went to put the ring on her right hand, she snatched it from him and put it on her left hand, third finger. 'That's where it belongs,' she told him, beaming. Then she kissed him and said, 'Now, that makes it official. Or shall I spell it out for you? Will you marry me?'

On February 21, 1952, Elizabeth and Michael were married in a brief ten-minute service in Westminster at the Caxton Hall Register Office. She had ultimately decided not to give her parents enough warning to allow them to make the trip abroad, explaining to a Taylor relative that she didn't want them present 'because I know they aren't supportive of me and Michael, and I'm just not going to put up with it from them'.

The Wilding marriage started out on an easy and romantic note, but the peace would not last long. In the summer of 1952, Elizabeth learned that she was pregnant. As soon as the studio heard, it placed her on suspension: she would not be paid for pregnancy leave. Around this time, Wilding rejected the studio's script for *Latin Lovers*, and he, too, was placed on suspension. Compounding matters, leaving England had cost him just about every cent he owned: the British tax department billed him the equivalent of about $100,000. The couple was now living on Elizabeth's savings.

Her pregnancy also marked the first time her weight had become an issue. She'd always been thin, but with her pregnancy she gained fifty pounds. She'd lose most of it when the baby was born, but her figure was never quite the same, and neither was her appetite. From this time onwards, the scales would be one of her greatest foes.

Her first child, Michael Howard Wilding, was born by Caesarean section on January 6, 1953. The middle name of Howard was in honour of her brother, who had returned home from Korea in time for the birth. The baby was beautiful, with dark curly hair and deep blue eyes. Elizabeth was thrilled, saying that the newborn had given her a new sense of purpose. 'I've never felt so important in my life,' she said.

The studio, eager to capitalise on the publicity of motherhood for one of its biggest attractions, arranged for Elizabeth to begin giving interviews as soon as she returned home from the hospital. 'We brought a nurse from the hospital to take care of little Mike,' she told a reporter from *Screen Life*. 'But she will leave as soon as I finish my next picture [*Rhapsody*]. I intend to take care of him all by myself.'

DESPITE THE CHILD they had together, Elizabeth's marriage to Michael was in trouble after the first couple of years. There were myriad problems, not the least of which was that Michael had begun to take his wife's illnesses less seriously than he had in the past. By this time, Elizabeth had all sorts of health issues, including a sciatic nerve problem that kept her wheelchair-bound for days at a time. Michael joked that she used hospitals as if they were resorts. However, he was serious when he said that he believed that there were underlying reasons for Elizabeth's poor health — even if he wasn't sure what they were at the time.

'If she gets a cold,' he recalled, 'she reacts so violently, she's almost dead from pneumonia. She stubs her toe, it's broken. She bumps into something, she ends up in a cast. It makes no sense. No person is that fragile.'

Michael believed there was some subconscious reason for his wife to find ways to prolong her physical despair. It's possible that, on some level, Elizabeth realised that being terribly ill was one way to control her life. When she was sick, she didn't have to make movies she didn't wish to make — and was also absent from any of the complex responsibilities of her personal life. Being ill also got her the attention of her mother, and she knew that this interest from Sara was focused on her well-being instead of on her career. On some level, it must have made her feel loved.

As Michael stopped caring about Elizabeth's physical problems, their communication began to sour and even, at times, became violent. While they were dining with Frank Sinatra one evening, she insulted Michael about his wardrobe. He told her to shut up.

She went to slap him, but he seized her wrist in midair and gave it a sharp twist. Elizabeth screamed out in pain. 'You broke my wrist! If I have to miss a day of filming because of this, I'll sue you!' Wilding was indifferent to her outburst. 'Oh, screw you, Elizabeth,' he said before walking out of the restaurant and leaving her with Frank.

Elizabeth even tried to compel Michael to rise — or sink, as it were — to the level of a Nicky Hilton by inciting him to anger. One morning, he was doing a crossword puzzle and not paying attention to her. 'She snatched the paper from my hand and threw it into the fire,' he remembered. '"So much for you and your stupid games," she said, adding, "Go on, hit me, why don't you." I told her, "I've never gone in for hitting hysterical females." She moaned, "Oh, God, if only you would. At least that would prove you are flesh and blood instead of a stuffed dummy."'

Despite their marital problems, the couple did not abandon the relationship, determined to make it work for the sake of their young son. By the summer of 1954, Elizabeth was again pregnant. At this time, they decided to purchase an estate in Beverly Hills, close to producer David O. Selznick's home, funded by her savings.

Elizabeth's second child, Christopher, was born on her twenty-third birthday, February 27, 1955. By that time, she and her husband were barely speaking. In fact, the Wildings' marriage was so clearly devoid of passion that sleeping in the same room had become a laughable concept. Though he had his choice of guest rooms, Michael chose to sleep in the living room, on a big violet-coloured divan, while Elizabeth occupied the master bedroom. She would cry herself to sleep, heartbroken that another marriage was about to end for her.

The summer of 1956 found Elizabeth restless to find entertainment outside her crumbling marriage. On 30 June, Kevin McClory, an assistant to movie producer Mike Todd, invited her to join Todd and a group of his friends for a weekend of sailing on the *Hyding*, a 117-foot yacht that Todd had chartered. She was happy to go, Elizabeth said, eager to escape the degenerating situation at home.

Todd seemed unable to keep his eyes off her in her pink toreador trousers and pale blue sweater. As the ship headed out into the open sea, Elizabeth felt seasick, 'and since I've never been shy about complaining, I'm sure I carried on a bit'. Todd heard that she was unwell and suggested she have a cocktail to treat her symptoms. After he escorted her to a bar in the ship's cabin, the two were seen in animated conversation. As the day wore on, Elizabeth and Mike enjoyed each other's company while she continued to drink champagne. She knew then that she would be moving on from Michael Wilding.

In July 1956, MGM announced that the couple were separating. Elizabeth tried to convince herself that the marriage was not a complete failure, since it had lasted more than four years and produced two children. But she knew it had truly ended long before the world was told of its demise. 'The marriage with Michael had become the relationship for which we were much more suited—brother and sister,' she later observed. 'He was one of the nicest people I'd ever known. But I'm afraid in those last years I gave him rather a rough time, henpecked him, and probably wasn't mature enough for him.'

OF COURSE, amid all the personal upheaval in her life, there was Elizabeth Taylor's astonishing movie career. Important as many of her films may have been, it has to be said that a great many of them were inferior projects that she only made either because she was forced to do so by the studio or because she needed the money. In truth, it's not from those movies that one really learns much about Elizabeth, other than her growing ability as an actress in a succession of bad films. 'Don't ask me about acting,' she would say. 'Someday I hope to be really good. I've always been an intuitive actress as opposed to an instructed one. I have no technique. I just try to become the other person, by forgetting myself completely. I've been good so few times, but I'd like to be good always.'

That said, Elizabeth was a unique and great movie star, no matter the ratio of good films to bad in her career. By the early 1950s, her talent and box-office appeal, not to mention her breathtaking beauty, had caught the attention of other movie studios. One such was Paramount, who contracted with MGM for Elizabeth to appear in *A Place in the Sun*, based on Theodore Dreiser's popular novel *An American Tragedy*. (MGM had previously loaned her to Warner Bros in 1947 for its film version of the stage hit *Life with Father* and would let that studio have her again in 1956 for *Giant*.)

It was in *A Place in the Sun*, under George Stevens's direction, that Elizabeth finally rose to the challenge of her craft. In fact, she has said that she really didn't take acting seriously until she did this movie. Playing opposite Montgomery Clift, her performance as the beautiful, wealthy Angela Vickers was inspired. When Academy Award time rolled round, the film received nine nominations, including Best Picture, Clift for Best Actor and Shelley Winters for Best Actress. It wound up with six Oscars. Despite her own Oscar snub, Elizabeth had arrived as an actress, her performance hailed by critics as being the equal of Winters's.

Montgomery Clift became one of Elizabeth's best friends during this time. He was handsome, with a shock of dark brown hair, piercing blue-grey eyes, sensuously full lips and a strong jawline. Taylor and Clift were achingly beautiful, and their love scenes were so convincing that they will for ever rank as classic examples of young love on the silver screen.

Despite the closeness of their personal relationship, Clift's sexual orientation kept him from giving himself to her. They got along so well, it seemed unfair that he preferred men over women. If Monty, as he was called by his friends, had been heterosexual, there's little doubt that he and Elizabeth would have married. 'We really loved each other,' Elizabeth once told Barbara Walters, 'in the fullest sense of the word.'

On May 12, 1956, Monty left a gathering at the Wildings', which had also been attended by actor Rock Hudson. On his way down a treacherous canyon road, Monty had a terrible automobile accident. Elizabeth arrived on the scene to find her friend bloodied almost beyond recognition. His teeth had been knocked down his throat, preventing him from breathing. Without a moment's hesitation, Elizabeth plunged her hand down his windpipe to clear the blockage. While she was at his side, photographers arrived on the scene. 'If you take one picture of this man in this condition,' she told them through her tears, 'I swear to God, I will not pose for another photo, ever!' Rock Hudson recalled it this way: 'She prevented the photographers from taking Monty's picture by the foulest language I have ever heard. And then six of us formed a line to hide him.' The paparazzi backed off. 'His head was so swollen it was almost as wide as his shoulders,' Elizabeth later said of Clift's injuries. 'His eyes had disappeared. His cheeks were level with his nose . . . and it was like a spoon had gouged a big chunk out of his mouth and teeth.' She accompanied Monty to the hospital, not about to leave his side. The incident showed people another side of her personality. Though she could be tremendously self-absorbed, she could also be a good and loyal friend, as she would demonstrate countless times in the future.

In 1956 Elizabeth appeared in the Warner Bros film version of the best-selling Edna Ferber novel *Giant*. Her co-stars were Rock Hudson and James Dean, both of whom she developed a deep feeling for. It was on that set, in Marfa, Texas, that she and Hudson became close friends; the two spent a great deal of time together, drinking and partying. 'We used to sit up all night talking about everything,' she has said. 'We had no secrets from each other, ever, all through the years.' Of course, as we now know, Hudson was gay and closeted, his entire life and career an emotional complication for him.

The film is an epic in every meaning of the word, and would wind up garnering nine Oscar nominations. Although Elizabeth demonstrated a wide range in her acting, going from nubile teenager to handsome, sixtyish, matronly grandmother, she once again came up empty at Oscar time, while her co-stars Hudson and Dean were both nominated for Best Actor. Although nominated, *Giant* failed to gain the Best Picture Oscar. That would go to Mike Todd for *Around the World in 80 Days*.

ELIZABETH HAD NEVER met anyone quite like Mike Todd. A good-looking guy with a firm, square jaw and jet-black hair, he had lean cheeks beneath steady brown eyes. His skin was ruddy, described by one magazine as 'like a rock granite quarry, after a dozen years of being battered by rainstorms'.

It wasn't his appearance that set Todd apart, though. It was his unquenchable spirit. He loved his life and lived it to the fullest, and after so many years with the dour Michael Wilding, Elizabeth couldn't help but be attracted to someone like him. She would find that he had a brilliant mind, always with a project in the offing or a great idea in development. He was also a man of unquestionable integrity, she would learn: his word was his bond. He was also a powerful and self-sufficient man, very much, it could be said, unlike her own father. It looked like Elizabeth couldn't go wrong with Mike Todd, even if he was twice her age.

If there's one thing Mike offered Elizabeth that no other man before him could, it was his scathing, even mischievous, wit. Elizabeth likes to tell the story of the time, before the world knew they were a couple, when Todd took her to a dinner party and introduced her as 'Tondelayo Schwarzkopf'. The hostess couldn't take her eyes off her. Finally she said to Elizabeth, 'I have to tell you, you look a lot like Elizabeth Taylor . . . only heavier.' Todd got a kick out of that and slapped Elizabeth on the rump. 'See, I told you you were getting fat,' he said.

Todd, who had amassed quite a fortune, had just finished making the epic *Around the World in 80 Days* when he met Elizabeth. Based on Jules Verne's 1873 novel, Todd's film was in many ways a reflection of himself—a big, brassy, colourful, larger-than-life epic. At a cost of $6 million, a paltry amount by today's standards but quite a sum for its time, the film went on to gross in excess of $42 million. In addition to a Best Picture Oscar, it would earn four others.

Mike Todd was like Elizabeth: always moving forward, never taking the time to reflect on the past. As his biographer Art Cohn wrote: 'He is reborn each day without knowledge of the past. He has no yesterdays, no reminiscences or regrets. What is done is done for; he must start clear at each moment.'

The day after MGM announced Elizabeth's separation from Wilding, Todd said he wanted to meet her at MGM. He was late arriving, and she sat in the canteen sipping a Coke and steaming about his tardiness. When he finally showed up, he grabbed her by the hand and dragged her to an empty office without saying a word. He then sat her down and proceeded to tell her how much he loved her and how determined he was to make her his wife. He would not take no for an answer.

'Don't horse around,' he finally concluded. 'You know you're going to marry me.'

Elizabeth expressed surprise. 'If this was what getting swept off your feet was like,' she said later, 'well, I must admit, as much of a brute as I thought he was, I was still quite flattered.'

Mike treated his raven-haired beauty not only to expensive gifts but also to a whirlwind life that included private planes, yachts, fancy automobiles and extravagant estate living with Picassos and other works of fine art. He was also a passionate lover, giving her the kind of powerful intimacy and connection that had been missing from her life with both of her previous husbands. When she wanted tenderness, he was as gentle as a puppy in spite of his out-ward roughness. But his gentleness could never be mistaken for weakness. 'Mike was strong, which was very good for me,' she once observed. 'I will get away with murder if I can, and I loved it when he would lose his temper and dominate me. I would purr because he had won.'

It's interesting that Elizabeth sought such dominance, especially since she had felt so manipulated as a child star. But still, as her mother's daughter, she would never allow herself to submit to any such mastery. The predictable result in her life—from Mike Todd onwards—would be, for the most part, chaos. 'Every woman should have a Mike Todd in her life,' she wrote in her 1987 memoir, *Elizabeth Takes Off.* 'My self-esteem, my image, everything soared under his exuberant, loving care.'

'He was a very rebellious guy who went against the grain and he taught her to be that way,' observed the columnist Liz Smith. 'She was quite different after meeting Mike Todd. He said, "Audacity makes the star", and she began to live that motto. They had big fights, and they made up and fought again. Then they made up again and he would spoil her with presents. After Mike, she would always have relationships that had a lot to do with fighting and making up.'

In November 1956, Elizabeth fell and hurt her back. She'd experienced spinal problems in the past, but after the accident matters became much worse. She was forced to undergo a four-hour operation. 'Three discs were gone,' she later recalled. 'They cut away all the dead bone, right down to the nerve centre. They took bone from my hip, my pelvis and from a bone bank and made little matchsticks and formed clusters that finally calcified and became one long column, six inches long.' She was in tremendous pain for, as she put it, 'longer than I can remember. I was in a hospital bed for two months and had to learn to walk all over again.'

On February 2, 1957, a barely recovered Elizabeth married Mike Todd, at the beachfront estate of Todd's friend Fernando Hernandez. Mike was forty-nine, Elizabeth twenty-four. Of course, Sara and Francis were present, as were Howard and Mara. In fact, Mara was one of Elizabeth's attendants, the other being Debbie Reynolds. Debbie was married to Eddie Fisher, Mike's close friend and also one of his best men, along with Michael Todd, Jr. At this time, Debbie, Eddie, Elizabeth and Mike were inseparable; their close friendship was well known by all.

Six months later, on August 6, 1957, Elizabeth gave birth to a girl, whom she and Mike named Elizabeth Frances and nicknamed Liza. When doctors said Elizabeth should not have any more children, Mike gave them permission to perform a tubal ligation on her. Elizabeth later said she was very upset by the decision, calling it 'a huge shock to me'.

Meanwhile, her film career soared. In 1957, MGM hoped to replicate the success of *Gone With the Wind* by putting into production the big-budget Civil War epic *Raintree County*, in which she would co-star with Montgomery Clift. Elizabeth had to take Monty under her protective wing just to get him through the picture, due to his many emotional and physical addictions. Not even the best plastic surgeons were able to restore his face to what it was before his accident. Only a glimmer of his former beauty remained. Although it fell short of *Gone with the Wind*, *Raintree County* earned Elizabeth an Oscar nomination as Best Actress.

IN MARCH 1958, Mike Todd was selected by the Friars Club of New York as Showman of the Year. A dinner was planned in his honour at the Waldorf Astoria Hotel on the twenty-second. Elizabeth has always said that she was bedridden with bronchitis and was therefore unable to accompany him. She had arranged time off from *Cat on a Hot Tin Roof*, which she'd just begun two weeks earlier, in order to recuperate. Her director, Richard Brooks, says that Mike told him that she was actually feeling better and was going to go with him to New York. Brooks says he convinced Todd that the movie's insurance carrier would be upset that Elizabeth had taken time off the film but was well enough to go on a trip to New York. So it was decided that she would not go. Whichever way it happened . . . she didn't go with Mike.

Feeling on top of the world, Mike soared off in *The Lucky Liz*, his private plane, into dark and stormy skies. He had kissed Elizabeth goodbye numerous times before leaving, in a manner that could only be described as desperate. 'I'm too happy,' he told her, according to her later recollection. 'I'm afraid something's going to happen because I'm too happy.' Elizabeth would say that when Mike left, she had a vague but nonetheless disturbing feeling, a premonition of danger.

There was pouring rain, with thunder and lightning, throughout the night—'very Macbethian', she has recalled—and as the hours passed, her fever increased. Mike had said he would call at six in the morning, when his plane was set to land in Albuquerque for refuelling. However, the call never came. Elizabeth's instincts would prove to be painfully acute: Mike had been in a fiery plane crash en route to the East Coast.

'I'm sure Mike conned those pilots into taking that plane up,' said his friend the Hollywood columnist James Bacon. 'No self-respecting pilot would have taken the plane up in that kind of weather. The next morning at seven, my phone rang. It was the Associated Press bureau chief in Albuquerque. He said, there's a plane down here that's crashed and everybody's dead. Mike Todd's plane. So I had to call up Dick Hanley, Mike's secretary, and Rex Kennamer, Elizabeth's doctor, and the three of us converged on her home. We told her.'

Elizabeth recalled, 'All I could do was scream "No, no, no!". I ran downstairs, frantic, out of my mind, and all through the house and out into the street, screaming and crying in my nightgown. I fell to my knees in the middle of the street. Screaming, "No, no. Not Mike. Dear God, please, not Mike." Rex picked me up and carried me into the house. That's all I can remember because he knocked me out with a hypodermic needle.'

Elizabeth, just twenty-six at this time, was truly inconsolable. Her mourning was so great that her very life appeared to be in jeopardy as she repeatedly declared she would never be able to live without Mike. Her director, Richard Brooks, came to visit her. 'Dick [Hanley] took me up to her bedroom, where she was in a state of absolute screaming nerves,' he later told Peter Lawford.

Her friend Shirley MacLaine recalled, 'I went over there just after Mike died, and Sydney Guilaroff [Elizabeth's friend and hairdresser] was there, feeding her vodka and helping her to the bathroom. She was shrieking and screaming.'

Of course, Sara, Francis and Howard were at Elizabeth's side during this ordeal. Photographers who were staked outside Elizabeth's home waited to take candid pictures of the grim-faced Taylors as they came and went from the house.

In the next few days, Elizabeth became obsessed with trying to figure out what she was doing the very moment Mike lost his life. Had she been awake? Asleep? In her grief, she took pills to sleep, pills to stay awake, pills for depression, pills for anxiety . . .

The very wealthy and eccentric Howard Hughes, who was a stockholder in TWA, heard of Elizabeth's loss and lent her a TWA jet, complete with crew, so that she could fly to Chicago in privacy for the funeral. Elizabeth had to be restrained by her brother, Howard, lest she literally hurl herself onto the casket. A mob of perhaps 10,000 people pushed forward as the grieving young widow, dressed in black with dangling diamond earrings, was escorted from the funeral to her limousine. They shouted out her name, took photos, pushed and shoved for a better view of her. There was never a private moment for Elizabeth, even in grief.

At the cemetery, when the graveside service was over, the crowd descended upon Elizabeth and Howard as they tried to make their way back to their waiting car. They began ripping at Elizabeth's clothes as Howard shouted at them to 'Get back! Get back!' Finally, when brother and sister got in, the mob 'swarmed like insects all over the car, so you couldn't see out of the windows', Elizabeth later recalled. Then they began rocking it back and forth. Inside, Elizabeth began to scream at the top of her lungs, like a caged animal. It was a terrible scene.

As her car finally pulled past the fanatical crowd and out of the cemetery that day, it stopped for a moment at a nearby intersection. Elizabeth spotted a young girl standing at the kerbside, holding a single wilted rose and looking appropriately mournful. Elizabeth lowered the darkened window. As soon as it went down, a myriad of hands bearing floral offerings waved in her direction — it was as if they had come from nowhere. Undaunted, Elizabeth seemed transfixed as she leaned out and pointed to the girl. The little girl's mother excitedly led her to the waiting car. Elizabeth ignored her and took the girl's flower, locking eyes with the child. 'You're sweet,' she said quietly. 'It's you I'll try to remember.'

ELIZABETH ALMOST didn't make Mike Todd's funeral. She got the courage to do so from an unlikely source — Mike's best friend, Eddie Fisher. The two had been inseparable. Eddie considered

Mike a father figure, and even named his son (born just three weeks before the plane crash) after him. When Elizabeth began dating Mike, the couple continued to enjoy the company of Eddie and his wife, Debbie Reynolds. Eddie had been emotionally devastated by the sudden loss of his good friend and was one of the few people in Elizabeth's life who truly grasped the deep impact his death had on her. Shortly before Todd's funeral, Eddie's limousine passed the throng of reporters and fans outside the Todd estate. He had arrived to escort Elizabeth to Chicago.

The night before, he had come to the same home to find Elizabeth wandering in a daze, appearing drugged and confused. He and Debbie explained the plans that had been made for the trip to Chicago. Elizabeth at first said she was unable to go, contending that her children needed her. Reynolds offered to stay behind to look after them, and Taylor was left with little reason to avoid the event. So it was agreed. Elizabeth and Eddie would fly together, and Debbie would remain in Los Angeles.

On the flight to Chicago, Elizabeth clung to Eddie, the turbulence reminding both just how they had lost the man so dear to them. They could identify with each other's pain better, perhaps, than anyone else they knew. They both loved Mike. Talking about him was a way of keeping him alive in their hearts. It was also a way for Elizabeth to keep her soul from going into complete atrophy because, as she put it, 'I knew that with each passing day, I was getting harder inside, building a resistance to love. I was afraid I would never love again, and then Eddie came into my life and I began to think, maybe . . .'

James Bacon succinctly put it this way: 'Eddie Fisher performed the most dangerous duty known to man: he dried a widow's tears.'

Edwin John Fisher, with his meticulously combed dark brown hair and somewhat foxlike face, was born in 1928 in Philadelphia, the son of Russian Jewish immigrants. From those humble beginnings, he rose to the top rung on the pop music ladder before he was old enough to vote. With an easy smile and an ingratiating demeanour, he was considered 'cute' and a snappy dresser. He was a genuine teen idol by 1954—having sold more than eight million records—when he met America's girl next door, Debbie Reynolds, a five-foot-two, eyes-of-blue, energetic and wholesome entertainer. Fans overwhelmingly approved of their relationship, which was covered in detail by all the movie magazines.

Eddie and Debbie were wed in 1955. Despite the birth of their daughter, Carrie, during their first year together, the marriage was in trouble almost from the beginning. Still, they muddled through and were inspired by the marriage of their close friends Elizabeth and Mike—that is, until Mike died. Eddie was so sad about his friend's death that Elizabeth's heart went out to him. Since the source of their mourning was the loss of the same man, a bond grew. Within about five months, both began to consider the unthinkable. Could the two of them be a couple?

It didn't take long for the tempestuous Liz-Eddie-Debbie triangle to make international news. Editorials denounced Elizabeth; fan magazines encouraged readers to boycott her films. The press seemed to forget that she was a recent widow and now painted her as a calculating home wrecker. In just a few months, Elizabeth's status had changed from sainted widow to shameless hussy.

One evening, shortly after deciding to unveil their forbidden love, Elizabeth and Eddie left Musso and Frank Grill in Hollywood. The press flashbulbs were clearly accompanied by a sound that was brand new to Elizabeth: the unmistakable grumble of a disapproving public.

'Shame on you,' one said.

'Whore!' yelled another.

Eddie recalled that the two huddled together, ducking into the black sedan. As the driver headed off, Elizabeth looked back at the angry mob. 'Oh, dear Lord,' she said, 'what have we done?'

INTERESTINGLY, despite the imbroglio in which she found herself, Elizabeth's career as one of the world's leading actresses did not suffer. By the end of the 1950s, she was one of the most beautiful and sought-after women in film. Everything about her promised excitement. Bad publicity, good publicity, triumphs, tragedies . . . It all blended together to create a Hollywood personality the public could not get enough of. The film version of *Cat on a Hot Tin Roof*—in which she played a woman with a voracious appetite for sex—was a box-office success; she was nominated for another Oscar for her work in it, this time losing to Susan Hayward (in *I Want to Live*). Elizabeth's success, despite the affair with Eddie, only emboldened her to believe that she could do no wrong, even when she was very wrong in what she was doing.

Six months after the affair started—and a month shy of the one-year anniversary of Mike Todd's death—Debbie filed for divorce for the third time in her marriage to Fisher. When it was finally granted, custody of the couple's children and a large financial and property settlement were Debbie's. It had been acrimonious, though, and by the time all of the mudslinging was over, Debbie truly loathed Eddie—and the feeling was mutual.

With Eddie's divorce at last finalised, he and Elizabeth were free to marry after a suitable, and legally directed, waiting period. First, though, Elizabeth wanted to convert to Judaism. She says that her decision to do so was not influenced by Eddie; she had first wanted to convert when she was married to Mike Todd, who was also Jewish. At the formal religious conversion ceremony, her parents were at her side as witnesses in full support of her decision. Her Jewish name would be Elisheba Rachel.

Elizabeth and Eddie were married on May 12, 1959, in a Jewish ceremony. She wore green chiffon and looked radiant. Mike's son was best man. At just twenty-seven, Elizabeth had now been married four times. Eddie and his new bride then sailed off to Spain for their honeymoon. 'When Elizabeth loves, she loves better than any woman in the world,' he said. 'She gives more love than any human being I have ever known in my entire life. Gives more and takes more, and that's love and loving.'

So devoted to Eddie was Elizabeth that she would rearrange her schedule so that she could sit ringside at his nightclub appearances. Towards the end of the show, Eddie would acknowledge friends and family. Afterwards, he would walk towards Elizabeth's side of the stage. 'Liz! Liz!' the audience would chant. 'Oh, have I left anyone out?' he would ask.

Finally, he would point to her and say, 'I am honoured to be graced with the presence of the most beautiful woman in the world, my wife, the light of my life, Mrs Eddie Fisher.' Held in a large halo by a blue–white spot, Elizabeth would stand and allow the audience's approval to wash over her. Then Eddie would swell into full voice for his finale, 'That Face', which he would dedicate to Elizabeth. However, Eddie's encore number was eerily prophetic: the Rodgers and Hammerstein song of lost love from *South Pacific*, 'This Nearly Was Mine'.

Alas, it took Elizabeth just a few months to come to the conclusion that she had made a big mistake. Eddie was not Mike, nor did he have the older man's strength, determination and know-how in the care and handling of a complicated woman like Elizabeth Taylor. She finally had 'an epiphany', she said: their mutual grieving over the terrible loss of Mike Todd was what had actually brought her and Eddie together, not any true feelings of romance.

Those who remember Elizabeth on the set of *Suddenly, Last Summer* recall seeing her and Eddie constantly entwined and demonstrative of their affection for each other. In retrospect, their passionate display seems more like an act, played strictly for the crew. Offstage, but not always in private, her obvious contempt for the man she chose to replace Mike Todd would today probably be considered spousal abuse, with her hurling withering epithets at a cowed Fisher.

Despite the emotional tumult with Eddie at this time in her life, Elizabeth's work on *Suddenly, Last Summer* is captivating just the same. She would be nominated for an Academy Award for it. Critics noted that even at a time in her life when she seemed out of control, she managed to pull herself together for the film. It's because acting remained her great passion, and when she loved a role, as she did in this film, she would give herself to it completely. It was a sanctuary from the chaos of her jumbled world.

ELIZABETH TAYLOR'S next movie, *Butterfield 8*, was one she did not want to make. She had just agreed with producer Walter Wanger to star for 20th Century Fox in the epic *Cleopatra*, for a million dollars. Legend has it that Wanger called Elizabeth and related the offer through Eddie Fisher, who had answered the phone. As a joke, Elizabeth supposedly replied, 'Sure, tell him I'll do it for a million dollars.' Her salary for *Cleopatra* was astronomical for the times, the most any actor had ever been paid.

Still high from that achievement, she was brought back to earth with a thud when she learned that she still had one more film to do for MGM. She'd thought her deal with them had expired. It hadn't. The studio demanded that she make *Butterfield 8* — based on John O'Hara's novel — for only $125,000. *Cleopatra* would have to wait. Eddie was given a small part in the film, not for his acting ability so much as for his ability to babysit the star. It was, he says, 'the worst job of my life, trying to deal with my hellion of a wife'.

While Mike Todd had had the wherewithal for the conflict she so desired, Eddie did not. His supplication at her feet filled her with rage. She became abusive during the making of *Butterfield 8*, trying to spur him into anger to get a rise out of him so that he might prove to her that he really was a man. It never worked. Instead of engaging in battle, Eddie was unfailingly sweet, which only infuriated her all the more. She couldn't help but connect his avoidance of the sparring bouts she would instigate with the weakness of her father. 'Wimp!' she would shout towards Eddie as he headed away from the growing tornado that was Elizabeth Taylor.

Production began on January 4, 1960, in New York. Eddie did what he could, but in the end, Elizabeth was determined to have a terrible time, and so she did . . . as did everyone else.

Despite all the melodrama that had surrounded the making of *Butterfield 8*, Elizabeth was terrific in it. As always, it was her talent that would redeem her, and there was now another level of humanity to it. In a 1975 interview, her *Cat on a Hot Tin Roof* director, Richard Brooks, said that in his view her work had been enhanced by the experience of Mike Todd's death: 'What it did, mainly, was it helped her grow up. Death and anguish were things she'd read in a script and she could emulate from other performances or from being told about. But when Todd died, it was something happening to her. She used everything in her life from that moment on—the joys as well as the sorrows.'

Part Three

Her Destiny

With *Butterfield 8* out of the way, Elizabeth Taylor was finally free to make *Cleopatra*. The day scheduled for the beginning of principal photography was September 28, 1960. An eight-acre outdoor lot at Pinewood Studios, fifteen miles northwest of London, had been majestically re-created as the ancient city of Alexandria. Peter Finch had been cast as Julius Caesar, Stephen Boyd as Mark Antony.

On 13 November, Elizabeth's health took a turn for the worse. She had woken with a terrible headache. So bad was the pain that a doctor had to be summoned. Before long, Elizabeth was checked in to a hospital, suffering from spinal meningitis.

After a week in the hospital, Elizabeth, Eddie and the children abruptly took off for Palm Springs, where she would recuperate, leaving those invested in *Cleopatra* in London to wonder if she would ever return to the set. By this time, $7 million had been spent on the film, and Elizabeth had stepped before a camera only a handful of times, giving the studio about twelve minutes of usable footage for its millions. Her absences had already cost the production's insurer millions of dollars. Therefore, 20th Century Fox made the decision to shut down the production, as if they had any other choice with its star an ocean and a continent away.

MARCH 4, 1961, was a date Elizabeth would never forget. She, Eddie and the children were in London, staying at the Dorchester Hotel. She was ready finally to begin work on *Cleopatra* and would shortly be leaving for Rome. On this day, though, something in her body had gone very wrong, and she collapsed. She was found on the floor, suffocating, her face turning blue. By sheer coincidence, down the hall from Elizabeth's room, a bachelor party was being given for a medical student. The hotel operator figured that a doctor would be at that party and made a call to the room. Sure enough, a noted anaesthetist was there. He ran down the hallway to Elizabeth's room, where he found her on the bed, nearly unconscious. He tried to dislodge the congestion in her throat with his finger, but to no avail. Then he pushed his finger against her eye, pressuring it to ensure that she would not go into a coma. She woke up instantly, took one look at him, hurled an epithet at him, and passed out again.

Elizabeth was immediately transported to the London Clinic. There, an emergency tracheotomy was performed. While she was on the operating table, though, she says she woke up. Looking at the doctors and nurses, she tried to speak. However, the air from her lungs just went out through the gaping hole in her throat. A nurse saw the terror in her eyes and leaned over to comfort her. Elizabeth managed to ask for a piece of paper and a pen. She wrote, 'Am I still dying?' Then she lost consciousness again.

By this time in her life, Elizabeth had had colitis, three Caesarean sections, a tonsillectomy, anaemia, a crushed spinal disc, bronchitis, meningitis, phlebitis, a broken leg, double pneumonia, and three vertebrae replaced in her spine, and she wasn't even thirty. After the tracheotomy, though, she didn't seem to have the will to go on. In fact, Eddie was told that she was dying.

It appears that Elizabeth was not totally unaware of the possibility that something in her mentality may have been responsible for her illness. In 1965, in her first memoir, she would write, 'When I became sick with pneumonia, I think it was my subconscious which let me become so seriously ill. I had been hoping to be happy, pretending to be happy. But there was something deeply desperate inside me and my despair became so black that I just couldn't face waking up any more.'

When the news got out that Elizabeth was in her final days,

thousands gathered in front of the hospital to hold vigil for her. There were prayer services all over the world. The possibility that she might die was major news; some news outlets even erroneously reported that she *had* died—much to her later glee.

Of course . . . she recovered. One day, she just looked up at Eddie and, because she couldn't speak, her eyes did the talking for her: *I'm alive*, they seemed to say. *I can't believe it. How wonderful!*

For the next week, Eddie sat at her side, watching over her. She seemed so fragile lying in her bed, her arms stuck full of needles, her body connected to all sorts of beeping machinery. She looked so young and innocent without her make-up, nothing at all like the hellion she'd been with him in recent months. Sympathy for her surged up in Eddie. He was so moved and frightened, there were times he would put his head on her breast and sob. He did love her, no matter what she thought of him.

'I remember wondering: without her anger, what would she be?' he recalled years later. 'It occurred to me that I'd never known her when she wasn't angry. At me. At the studio. Her mother. Mike, for dying and leaving her. Without her anger to keep her going, I wondered if she would just fall limp and be . . . nothing. I just didn't know.'

When she left the hospital to go back to Hollywood on March 27, Elizabeth credited Eddie's devotion for her return to—not good, but reasonable—health. She would stay in California for a six-month recuperation before resuming work—finally—on *Cleopatra*.

That year, Elizabeth had received an Oscar nomination for Best Actress for her work in *Butterfield 8*. She had already received three previous nominations but had lost each time. However, she had garnered such worldwide sympathy in recent months that winning the prized statuette her fourth time round seemed a foregone conclusion. At the awards show on 17 April, Yul Brynner had the happy task of announcing that, indeed, Elizabeth had won the Academy Award. What a victory for her and her mother, Sara, who was in the audience with Francis.

When Elizabeth's name was called out as the winner, she

appeared genuinely stunned. The applause was thunderous. Eddie helped her to her feet and escorted her to the top of the stairs leading to the stage. After kissing Eddie, Elizabeth, resplendent in a white Dior gown, her tracheotomy scar clearly visible, made her way unsteadily to the podium. Once there, she stood shaking as the audience of 2,500 rose as one, roaring its approval. Despite all that had happened to her in her life—and all she had done to provoke the public's confusion and even its scorn—she was still the beloved icon, one of the world's greatest stars, and this truly was her shining moment. Finally, in a soft, whispery voice, she said that she didn't know how to express her gratitude, except to say, 'Thank you. Thank you with all of my heart.' She turned, walked shakily across the wing to the backstage ladies' room—and fainted.

IT WAS SEPTEMBER 25, 1961, the first day of principal photography on the newly revamped production of *Cleopatra* at Cinecittà Studios outside Rome. The Roman forum site had been constructed at Cinecitta, while the Alexandria set, which would be utilised later, was built on a private beach at Anzio, some 35 miles away. This day had certainly been a long time coming, with so many writers, directors and producers having careered in and out of the project that it had become difficult for industry trade publications to keep track of the players. By this time, Peter Finch was out of the cast as Caesar, replaced by Rex Harrison. Stephen Boyd was also replaced as Mark Antony by Richard Burton. (Both Finch and Boyd left the production to fulfil other commitments.) A big problem, though, was that the script remained unfinished. Four-time Oscar winner Joseph Mankiewicz had replaced Rouben Mamoulian as director. Mankiewicz had done what he could to rewrite the script on his own, but now he and a team of writers would be forced to do the best they could with what they had, scripting the rest of the movie on the spot.

Even when Elizabeth Taylor was not being filmed for a star turn in one of her movies, she had a way of making the smallest incidents of her life memorable. Her entrance onto the set of *Cleopatra* on the first day of shooting is a good example. Wearing a full-length black mink coat, Elizabeth walked with purpose onto the busy set, aware that all eyes were riveted upon her. She was followed by two hairdressers, two costume designers, a seamstress, secretary, assistant and a press agent. With her jet-black hair in an elaborate upswept style, her eyes heavily circled with black eyeliner, she was certainly ready for her close-up as monarch of the Nile. She walked past her co-stars, Rex Harrison and Richard Burton, without so much as a glance in their direction. Her attention was focused on her director, Joseph Mankiewicz. She stood before him. Taking her in head to toe, he bowed. She extended her hand, palm down. 'Are you ready, my queen?' he asked. He took her hand and kissed it.

'I was *born* ready, dear sir,' she said. She then dropped her mink to the floor, where it fell behind her. Elizabeth took one step forward, a vision in gold brocade, sequins and beads.

For a few seconds, Joe appeared stunned. 'My dear, you leave me breathless,' he told her.

'Of course I do,' she said.

Elizabeth's deal for the movie contained some of the most startling concessions given to an actress up to that time. In addition to her million-dollar fee, she also got $3,000 a week in living expenses, plus food and lodging, and first-class round-trip airline tickets to the movie's locations for herself, three other adults and her three children. She required two penthouse suites at the Dorchester in London, plus a Rolls-Royce Silver Cloud limousine at her disposal at all times. Elizabeth also demanded that the movie be shot in Todd-AO rather than 20th Century Fox's own trademark widescreen process, CinemaScope, so that, as owner of that company (she had inherited it from Mike Todd) she would derive royalties from its use; expansive sets had to be built to fill this widescreen process, which accounted for a lot of the movie's budget. She would also receive ten per cent of the film's gross receipts. In the end, Elizabeth would make a fortune from this movie — more than $7 million, and in the early sixties that was *a lot* of money.

After greeting director Joseph Mankiewicz on that first day of filming, Elizabeth stood in place as people swarmed busily about her. A make-up artist applied powder to her face while a hair-dresser fussed with her coiffure. Meanwhile, her co-star Richard approached. Once he was standing next to her, he leaned in and breathed on her neck. 'You're much too fat, luv,' he said, his voice a soft murmur, 'but you do have a pretty little face.'

Elizabeth might have been insulted had the comment been made by anyone other than Richard Burton. However, coming from him, in that intoxicating Welsh accent of his, it somehow seemed like a compliment. She couldn't help herself. She had to laugh. It erupted from her in the way a good laugh always did, like a horse's whinny, loud and shrill, and full of joy. 'Why, the nerve!' she said, punching him on the shoulder. She then hurried over to Eddie Fisher and sat on his lap, as if to send a message to Richard that she already had a husband, thank you.

THE MOVIE INDUSTRY had never seen anything quite like Richard Burton—and to this day, no one has really replaced him in the business. He was a one-of-a-kind actor, his sheer presence filling the screen like no other. Certainly, few people expressed themselves like Burton, with his Welsh accent so musical in tone, his voice clear, rich and distinctive. He was smart and witty, sexy and passionate. He was an object of desire for most women with whom he crossed paths. His face was angled and, usually, serious. He had tousled brown hair, piercing blue–green eyes and a rugged frame, though he was no more than five foot nine.

To know Richard Burton was to either love or hate him; there was usually no grey area when it came to one's reaction to him. However, friend and foe alike agreed that on his good days, he was an electrifying man filled with a zest for life, love and work. He was a smart, mostly self-educated scholar who spoke four languages and had such an amazing memory that he could recite nearly any passage of Shakespeare. However, there was always a profound sense of anguish about him. On his bad days, he was sullen and depressed, a dark person who could be cruel to even his closest friends. In the end, there was always something tragic about Richard Burton—which may be one reason he remains so vividly alive in the memories of everyone he touched in his lifetime.

He was born Richard Walter Jenkins, Jr, on November 10, 1925, in Pontrhydyfen (pronounced *Pont-reader-ven*), Wales, the twelfth of thirteen children. He never knew his mother; she died giving birth to his youngest sibling. His father was fifty when Richard was born. He was a hardworking coal miner whose backbreaking job yielded little money to support his large family, so Richard was shipped off to live with his oldest sister, Cassie, and her husband. At school, Richard spoke only Welsh until aged about ten. In high school, the young man was taken under the wing of a teacher, Philip Burton, who brought the seventeen-year-old into his home and taught him drama and literature and English. Richard changed his last name to Burton in honour of his teacher.

He began doing theatre in England in 1943. In 1948 he made his British film debut in the Welsh yarn *The Last Days of Dolwyn*. It was on the set of this film that he met eighteen-year-old blonde Welsh actress Sybil Williams. He would take her as his wife in 1949, after which she gave up her career as an actress.

During his rapid climb to stardom, Richard was rarely faithful to Sybil. He especially fancied actresses, and there would be plenty on his list of conquests, such as Tammy Grimes and Zsa Zsa Gabor. Sybil accepted Richard's infidelity as part of their life together. She looked the other way, though she wasn't happy about it. From a practical standpoint, Sybil had to consider the well-being of her two daughters, Kate and Jessica. Kate Burton would grow up to become a successful actress. Sadly, Jessica was diagnosed as both autistic and schizophrenic. She would be institutionalised on and off from the age of six, a heartbreaking situation neither Sybil nor Richard would ever be able to reconcile themselves to.

The real challenge that faced Richard, though, was that he was an out-of-control alcoholic. When sober, he was a delight, kind and generous, a good and loyal friend. After a few drinks, however, he often became belligerent and difficult.

In 1952, Richard left London for Hollywood. His first US film, *My Cousin Rachel*, earned him his first Academy Award nomination. Burton was then cast in the biblical epic *The Robe*. It turned out to be 1953's top-grossing film and earned Richard his second Oscar nomination. More movies followed. By 1961 he was starring in the Broadway hit *Camelot*. He would leave that show in order to make *Cleopatra*.

Richard arrived in Rome with his wife, Sybil, their daughter Kate, and Roddy McDowall (who would play Octavian in *Cleopatra*). The contingent checked in to a villa about two miles away from the Fishers.

Elizabeth had first met Richard years earlier at the home of actor Stewart Granger in Los Angeles, when Granger and his wife hosted a Sunday brunch. Richard was in attendance with Sybil. Elizabeth was there with Michael Wilding. Her first impression of Richard, as she has recalled it, was that he was an egotistical lout. She barely paid attention to him. Instead, she sat in a deck chair by the pool, reading a book. Every now and then she would notice Burton as he recited Shakespeare in a big, booming voice or gave a long oration about some political matter, commanding the attention of everyone present.

The two would only have a couple of brief exchanges in the next few years, one at a cocktail party hosted by Tyrone Power, another at a chance meeting in a restaurant. Yet whenever Elizabeth happened upon Burton, he was always at peak emotion, as she would put it, 'giving a lecture about something or singing a bawdy song that was completely inappropriate. I thought, My goodness, does the man ever shut up?'

Publicly, Burton's view of Elizabeth was not exactly flattering either. 'All this stuff about her being the most beautiful woman in the world is absolute nonsense,' he said after first meeting her. 'She's a pretty girl, and she has wonderful eyes. But she has a double chin and an overdeveloped chest and she's rather short in the leg.'

Everyone knew, though, that what Richard said publicly was often part of his act of bravado. Privately, he would say that in the first seconds he laid eyes upon her on the set of *Cleopatra*, he was, this time, really taken by her. She was shorter than he remembered, but also slimmer and more curvaceous. More than anything, he loved her laugh. It was genuine and irresistible. 'I will never forget that first laugh,' he'd say.

It was at this time, as she was preparing to make *Cleopatra*, that Elizabeth decided that she wanted to adopt a child with Eddie. Because she'd had a tubal ligation after her third baby, she was no longer able to bear children. Elizabeth and Eddie agreed that their marriage was in trouble, and they thought that adopting a baby might help to salvage it.

She and Eddie had asked a friend of theirs, Maria Schell, to assist them in adopting a baby of Swiss, German or Austrian descent. They explained that they hoped to bring into their family a child who was ill or disadvantaged so that they might share with him or her their good fortune. She told people that she had a strong, nagging feeling that there was a child 'out there somewhere' who needed her.

Indeed there was. In the small village of Mering, Germany, thirty miles north of Munich, a hardworking but impoverished couple were raising two young daughters in a one-room apartment. When the wife discovered she was pregnant again, it was, she recalled, 'a great shock to us. There was certainly no more space in our one room for another child, and we wondered where the extra money for food and clothes would come from. [The baby] was born prematurely,' she said. 'For the first few months of her life, this tiny baby struggled for her life in a hospital for premature children in Augsburg.'

The couple was told that their new daughter would have to spend months in the hospital, but they did not have the money to pay for her care. After four months, they became desperate. 'Then, in August 1961,' the child's mother said, 'I saw an ad in *Heim und Welt* [*Home and World*]. It said: "I seek for my acquaintance to adopt a very young boy or girl."' The couple decided to answer the ad, and were asked if the baby could be brought to Munich.

They took their daughter, whom they had named Petra, to a hospital in Munich and left her there with the understanding that Elizabeth would soon visit her. They then went back to Mering. However, in a few days, they received more devastating news. Doctors in Munich had discovered that the baby had a congenital hip injury that had gone undetected by the medical staff in Augsburg. The injury would take time and lots of money to treat. 'My heart was breaking as I realised that there was no hope for Petra's adoption now,' recalled her mother. 'But then word reached us from Rome: Miss Taylor had seen the baby, and though she had been warned not to adopt her because of her injury, she told Maria Schell that she wanted her not in spite of her injury, but *because* of it.'

That night, the couple decided that they would give their baby to Elizabeth. 'It was as if it was prearranged by some power greater than us,' said the child's mother. 'We felt that it was meant to be.'

They knew they had made the right decision when, three days later, they received a letter from Elizabeth. Elizabeth wrote that if money was needed for the child, 'I have plenty of it to give.' She had been told, she said, by doctors that she could not have any more children, and she 'longed for another. Not only do I have the money,' she added, 'I also have the love to give, and I so want to give it.'

The paperwork for Elizabeth and Eddie's adoption of the nine-month-old baby was finalised in January 1962.

Elizabeth later recalled, 'She was covered with abscesses, suffering from malnutrition, had a crippled hip—and I just loved her. She didn't cry, and she didn't laugh. She had very dark eyes. She watched everything, and I held her, and I bathed her, and I changed her for three days, and finally she started giggling, and finally she would cry when she wanted her bottle. This funny little introverted person responded so much to love. I was hooked by the end of a few days. The German officials wanted me to have a "perfect baby". To me, she *was* perfect.'

The child would be renamed Maria in honour of Maria Schell. In years to come, Elizabeth would spend a small fortune on corrective surgeries for Maria. Though the child would spend agonising years in body casts, she would grow to be healthy and happy.

ELIZABETH TAYLOR and Richard Burton began their celebrated affair in much the same way they would conduct their relationship for the next twenty years: fearlessly, carelessly, passionately . . . and publicly.

From the outset, Taylor and Burton had one thing in common at their core: they were two people who had grown accustomed to living their lives on their own terms. No doubt, as they would both insist, they didn't mean to hurt their loved ones in the process of fulfilling their hearts' desires, but if feelings had to be hurt and hearts had to be broken, they eventually decided, so be it. 'I knew that what I was doing, loving Richard, was wrong,' she wrote in her autobiography. 'But I couldn't help loving Richard. I don't think that was dishonest. It was a fact I could not evade.'

Between September 1961 and January 1962, Elizabeth filmed her scenes in *Cleopatra* as Richard concentrated on his. They weren't scheduled to appear on camera together until the third week in January, but by that time they had got so close—with luncheons and dinners together and then late-night partying—that many on the set had begun to speculate that something was going on between them. Since Sybil Burton had been dividing her time between Rome and London, and Eddie between Rome, New York and California, they were not around to prevent their spouses from spending plenty of time together.

Elizabeth has a memory of a night she, Eddie, Richard, Sybil and Roddy McDowall went to dinner after a long day at the studio. As the party rose to leave the restaurant, Elizabeth and Richard were so tipsy that they had to hang on to each other just to walk. 'Oh, we're a bloody mess now, aren't we?' she said with a cackle of a laugh. 'See, Eddie? It's all your fault. You should have made us leave sooner.'

Elizabeth's reaction to Richard that night: 'I absolutely adore this man.'

The first day that Elizabeth, almost thirty, and Richard, thirty-six, would work together in front of the camera on *Cleopatra* was January 22, 1962. The events of that day would foreshadow the dysfunction in their relationship, with Richard showing up for rehearsal so hungover from the previous night's drinking binge that he could barely walk

'I need a cup of coffee,' Burton said, trembling.

When someone handed him a cup, Richard was so jittery he couldn't even raise it to his mouth without spilling the coffee all over himself. 'Oh, you poor dear,' Elizabeth said as she helped him steady his hand. 'Let me help you.' As she held the cup for him, he gingerly sipped from it. 'Thank you, my dear,' he said weakly.

One may have thought that Elizabeth would have been aghast that a co-star would show up for work in seemingly no condition to perform. In the past, she would never have allowed such an unprofessional display without making a big issue of it. However, such was not the case on that morning with Richard. Rather, she was drawn to him because of what she perceived as a tantalising conflict in his personality. He was strong, very much unlike her father. Yet he had an extreme vulnerability—very much *like* her father. 'That endeared him to me,' she recalled. 'I thought, he really *is* human. He was so vulnerable and sweet and shaky that with my heart, I *cwtched* him.' (That's Welsh for 'hugged' him.)

In their first moment on screen together, Elizabeth, as Cleopatra, whispers to Richard's Mark Antony, 'To have waited so long, to know so suddenly. Without you, this is not a world I want to live in.'

'Everything that I want to hold or love or have or be is here with me now,' Burton, in character, responded.

When they embraced and kissed, the electricity was almost palpable. They filmed the scene a few times. The final time, they held the kiss so long that some observers began to feel uncomfortable. 'Cut!' Joseph Mankiewicz said. They continued kissing. 'I said, cut!' he repeated.

They broke their embrace and, after a few self-conscious moments, walked their separate ways.

About a week after they finally began working together, Richard and Elizabeth were on a beach in Torre Astura, where an elaborate replica of the royal palace had been built. The day began at noon, and the weather was not making production easy on anyone. At one point, Elizabeth and Richard were called to the set, extras were being placed, and cameras were about to roll, when a torrential downpour fell and everyone scattered. Richard grabbed Elizabeth's hand and pulled her towards the plaster façade of a palace wall. Opening a tremendous door, they entered and closed it behind them. Hank Lustig, a jeweller from London, had flown in to present some pieces to Mankiewicz for the production and had sought shelter in the same spot. Above their heads were about six storeys of scaffolding with leaky wooden planks — not the best place to stay dry.

'Have you lost your mind?' Elizabeth asked Richard. 'We'll get drenched here. Do you know how long it takes to get this make-up done if it gets wet?'

Richard climbed a painter's ladder and reached into a bucket. From it he retrieved an open bottle of wine. 'Well, it's already wet, isn't it?' Burton said as he took a swig and handed the bottle to her.

Lustig slipped behind a piece of equipment as Elizabeth and Richard passed the bottle back and forth. He recalls, 'They spent the next twenty minutes peering through cracks in the façade or peeking out the door. They laughed almost the entire time, or at least, mostly, she did. It was like they were children, hiding from their parents.'

At one point, a suspicious silence led Lustig to check if the two had left. They hadn't. They were passionately kissing.

When the rain subsided, the calls for the two stars had built to near pandemonium. It was decided that it would be best for Elizabeth to depart first so that they wouldn't be seen leaving together. She fluffed her outfit and gathered herself to go. She started out, then turned back to Richard. 'You truly are a horrible, horrible man.'

'If I was twice as awful,' he said, 'I'd be perfect for you.'

She smirked before stepping back into the real world.

BY THE END of the third week of January 1962, Elizabeth and Richard had worked together for about five days on the set of *Cleopatra*. One morning, Richard walked into the make-up trailer at Cinecittà and made a startling announcement. Chris Mankiewicz happened to be present. 'Gentlemen,' he said in stentorian tones, 'last night I screwed Miss Elizabeth Taylor in the back seat of my Cadillac.' His proclamation met with awkward silence.

One might imagine that the consummation of such an important, life-changing relationship in the lives of two people like Elizabeth and Richard would have occurred in some exotic and wildly romantic location. However, from all accounts, it does indeed seem that he had his way with her in the back seat of his Cadillac.

It didn't take long before Louella Parsons, the Hollywood reporter, was reporting that the ever tempestuous actress was in the midst of yet another torrid affair that could possibly lead to the dissolution of not only her marriage but someone else's as well. More than a thousand reporters swarmed onto the *Cleopatra* location, all after the big story that Elizabeth was involved in a romance. Within days, the story got to Eddie, who was in New York on business. He telephoned Elizabeth to ask her to hold a press conference and deny any kind of romance with Richard Burton.

'I'm sorry, Eddie, but I can't,' she told him.

'Why?'

'It's just not the right time,' she said, being guarded.

'Thanks a lot,' Eddie said before slamming down the phone.

By the time Eddie got back to Rome a few days later, it seemed as if everyone on the set of *Cleopatra* knew what had been going on behind his back. He couldn't help but notice the way people averted their eyes when he walked into a room.

That night, Eddie and Elizabeth had a quiet meal and some

uneasy conversation before retiring for the evening. As they lay next to each other, Elizabeth drifted off almost immediately. Suddenly, the phone rang. Eddie picked it up quickly, so as not to have it awaken her. It was Bob Abrams, a friend of his who had come to Rome to visit him. 'There's something you need to know,' Bob said, according to a later recollection. 'Elizabeth and Richard are having an affair.'

Coming from Bob, Eddie knew it was true. Just as he hung up the phone, Elizabeth stirred. 'A friend just called me to tell me that you and Richard Burton are having an affair,' he said. 'Is it true?'

Elizabeth exhaled deeply, as if to suggest an imminent confession. 'It's true,' she said, her voice nearly a whisper.

The two then lay in bed, side by side, staring at the ceiling and not saying another word about it.

ONCE IT WAS CLEAR on the set of *Cleopatra* that Elizabeth and Richard were involved, there was simply no way for it to be concealed from the press. Finally, after about a week of indecision as to how to handle things, Elizabeth made a choice. 'I had to be with Richard,' she said many years later. 'I knew it was wrong. I knew it would hurt people. But I also knew what I had to do. God help me, I had to be with Richard.'

'It was decided by Joe [Mankiewicz], Walter [Wanger] and Roddy [McDowall] that someone had to do something about Sybil,' a friend of Burton's in London recalled. 'They liked her very much and felt it was wrong for her not to know what was going on with Richard. Roddy, it was decided, would be the bearer of bad news. He screwed up his courage, flew to London, and told Sybil that Richard was having an affair with Elizabeth. She reacted by slapping him across the face.'

Once the Burton-Taylor romance was out in the open, Richard seemed to feel he had licence to behave as inappropriately in public as he liked where Elizabeth was concerned, and she seemed to be a willing participant in the torture he inflicted upon Eddie Fisher. One night, Burton showed up unexpectedly at a dinner party at the Fishers' villa in Rome, Eddie recalled. When confronted by Eddie, Richard became belligerent. 'Why don't you just go home to your own wife?' Eddie shouted at him. '*She's* your woman, not Elizabeth. Elizabeth is mine.'

'They're *both* my women,' Richard shouted back. He could barely stand, and the aroma of liquor surrounded him. He turned to Elizabeth. 'Are you my woman?' he demanded. 'If so, come here and prove it.'

The moment hung as both men watched her, waiting for her next move. Guests present at the Fisher villa were uncomfortable, stunned by Burton's audacity. Elizabeth stood motionless for a moment, her eyes locked on Richard. Then she moved towards him, holding her glass of champagne. With all eyes on her, she leaned into this man who seemed to have a hypnotic effect on her, and she pressed her lips against his.

Humiliated in front of his guests, Eddie stepped past the kissing couple in the doorway and went outside. Richard was the first to break. He turned to walk out, past Fisher. Richard halted a moment, turned to Eddie, and said, 'Keep her warm for me, won't you?' Then he was gone.

Elizabeth, feeling the eyes of the crowd on her, gathered herself a bit, then whirled round and glided towards a grand marble staircase. She tipped her champagne glass high, taking one last big gulp before plopping the empty glass on a butler's tray and floating up the stairs.

EDDIE MADE UP his mind that the only thing he could do to salvage what little dignity he had left was to get as far away from Elizabeth and Richard as possible. He planned to drive to Milan, where he would sort out his jumbled thoughts and twisted emotions. Before he left, he decided to have a little chat with Sybil Burton. It was February 17, 1962.

'You know, they are having an affair,' Eddie told Sybil. Of course, she already knew. 'I know,' she said simply.

'What are you going to do about it?'

'Nothing,' she said. 'Richard has been having affairs for years, and he always comes back to me. Trust me. I know my husband.'

Eddie laughed in her face. 'Clearly, you don't know my wife. We are talking about *Elizabeth Taylor* here. She wants your husband, and I can tell you from experience that she's a woman who *always* gets what she wants. Your marriage? It ain't gonna recover.'

The two stared at each other, a silence hanging between them. Sybil began to sob and ran from the room.

Eddie left the Burton villa and took off for Milan. The problem, though, was that he was as obsessed with Elizabeth as she was with Richard. He stopped three times along the way to call her, but he couldn't locate her. Finally he tracked her down at her secretary Richard Hanley's apartment. Very upset with him, she told him that Sybil had appeared unannounced at the studio and confronted her and Richard. The argument turned so volatile that no one was able to work after it. The production had to be cancelled for the day. 'And it's all your fault,' Elizabeth said angrily.

After she hung up, Richard told Elizabeth that it was over between them. It was too difficult for everyone concerned, he said. He told her that she should just go back to Eddie and he to Sybil. Besides, he said, Elizabeth was too combative a person. He was used to more passivity from a woman. After all, 'Syb' had put up with a lot from him, he pointed out, probably more than Elizabeth could ever tolerate. It was better, he said, if he and Elizabeth now cut to what he called 'the inevitable conclusion' of their romance.

'But Richard, no!' Elizabeth protested. Unfazed, Richard turned and walked out of the door.

By the next morning, everyone at Cinecittà had heard that Elizabeth had had some kind of breakdown over Richard. Walter Wanger went to her villa to see if he could be of assistance. When he arrived, Elizabeth was in her bedroom, being tended to by her physician, Dr Kennamer. About an hour later she appeared, looking distraught. 'I feel dreadful about this whole thing,' she said, her hands trembling. She poured herself a brandy and sank into a chair. 'I don't know what to do,' she said.

She seemed out of it, slightly loopy. After a few minutes with him, she rose and excused herself. After some time, Wanger went upstairs to check on her. 'I'm fine,' she said from the other side of a closed door. 'I've taken some sleeping pills. But perhaps I should eat before I doze off,' she added weakly. Wanger went back downstairs to see about her lunch. The meal was prepared. A maid took it to Elizabeth.

Five minutes later, the maid's screams reverberated through the house. 'Miss Taylor has taken too many pills,' she cried out. 'I can't wake her!'

Pandemonium erupted. An ambulance was called. A snitch in the household called the tip in to a newspaper. By the time Elizabeth got to Salvator Mundi International Hospital, the paparazzi were present. She had her stomach pumped; she survived an overdose of sleeping pills. Maybe it was accidental. However, the reports were that she had swallowed thirty pills, so maybe not. The studio issued a statement that said that she had suffered from a stomach ailment. The public bought it.

ON APRIL 2, 1962, it was announced that Elizabeth and Eddie Fisher were divorcing. Stewart Wilson and Victor Zellman were the accountants whose task it was to iron out a settlement with Eddie. Wilson met Elizabeth in Rome. Also at the meeting was Mike Todd, Jr, who was president of the Michael Todd Company, founded by his father.

Elizabeth came swirling into the room in a white caftan with matching turban, in full Cleopatra make-up. She was in between scenes for the movie, smoking a cigarette from a diamond-encrusted cigarette holder. 'So, boys, what do I have to do to end it with Eddie?' she said.

'Give him money,' said Stewart Wilson.

'How much?'

'A lot,' said Wilson. 'He's saying he wants millions.'

Elizabeth took a deep drag from her cigarette. 'I cannot *believe* that I have to pay this man money,' she said. 'How is it that the *wife* has to pay the *husband*? Eddie Fisher had a career long before I came along.'

'He says his career was ruined because of you,' Todd said.

'It's easy to blame Elizabeth Taylor for every damn thing that happens to every damn person in Hollywood, isn't it?' Elizabeth said. She then decided that she would give Fisher a million dollars if he would sign the divorce papers. 'Tell him that. And then when he gets up off the floor, have the papers ready for him to sign and a cheque ready to give him.'

'But Elizabeth—' Todd began.

She held her hands up and said she didn't want to hear another word about it. 'It's worth it to me to end this,' she concluded. Then she extended her hand to shake theirs, thanked them, and told them that the meeting was over. With that, she left the room.

The next day, Elizabeth's attorney in Los Angeles presented Eddie with the offer. He turned it down. (Later, Eddie insisted that no such offer was extended or rejected.) Stewart and Victor had to go back to Elizabeth and give her the bad news. This time Richard was with her.

'You've got to be kidding me,' Elizabeth said when told the news. Richard sat in a chair, looking amused.

'He said he wanted more,' said Stewart Wilson.

'Well, he's not getting more,' Elizabeth said angrily. 'And, in fact, now he's not getting the million, either.'

'Unbelievable,' Richard said. 'Taking money from a woman.'

'That's what *I* said yesterday,' Elizabeth remarked. 'Tell him to get a job. How about that? Try working. Like the rest of us.'

By the time the final decree was handed down, Eddie would end up with roughly half a million dollars—a significant amount of money in 1964, if not now. It's difficult to understand why Elizabeth still, to this day, holds such hostility towards Eddie or exactly when her animosity started. When she wrote her first book in 1965, she still seemed to have some warm feelings for him. 'I was not a very healthy girl,' she wrote. 'Poor Eddie. What hell that must have been for him.'

It's become accepted wisdom over the years that Eddie's career ended as a result of the adverse publicity concerning Elizabeth, Richard and Debbie, but that's not really true. When he got back to the States after leaving Rome, he put together a new act, which opened to rave reviews in Los Angeles. The tour took him to Las Vegas, Chicago and Philadelphia before he made his successful opening at the Winter Garden Theater on Broadway on October 2, 1962. Though he made no direct mention of Elizabeth, the new act was nothing if not autobiographical, with songs such as 'You Made Me Love You' and 'What Kind of Fool Am I?'

THOUGH THERE WAS no way for them to recognise it at the time, it's clear now that Elizabeth and Richard's extramarital affair was a sign of the times. Society was seeing a change occurring in sexual mores, and the *Cleopatra* stars were nothing if not a reflection of those changes.

'According to the code of ethics today, I *was*, I suppose, behaving wrongly because I broke the conventions,' Elizabeth wrote in her 1965 memoir, *Elizabeth Taylor*. 'But I didn't feel immoral then, though I knew loving Richard was wrong. I felt terrible heartache because so many innocent people were involved. But I couldn't help loving Richard.'

Meanwhile, in Rome, the Italians joined in a chorus of condemnation about the illicit relationship between the two married stars. Even Pope John XXIII entered the fray: 'We like to call Rome a Holy City. God forbid it becomes a city of perversion.'

The most damning blast of all, however, came from *L'Osservatore della Domenica*, which was published weekly in Vatican City. It said, in part, 'The trouble is, my dear lady, you are killing too many [marriages]. When will you finish? And your poor children, those who are your true children and the one who was taken from an honest situation. Don't these institutions think before handing children to somebody? Was it not better to entrust this girl to an honest bricklayer and a modest housewife rather than you, my dear lady, and to your fourth husband?'

Elizabeth finished reading that article and sat frozen. She couldn't believe that the Vatican had questioned her right to adopt Maria. One thing she could always say about MGM: as much as she hated the studio, it had protected her from this kind of publicity. Now, alone at 20th Century Fox, she had even managed to tick off the Pope!

THE DAY AFTER the Vatican's vicious attack on her, Elizabeth had to film one of the most memorable scenes in *Cleopatra*. In it, the queen, holding her son, Caesarion, makes her triumphant entrance into Rome. If she is accepted by the Romans and they acknowledge Caesarion as Julius Caesar's only child and heir, the Roman and Egyptian empires will merge and she will be the most powerful woman in the world. Otherwise, she will be banished and her life will lie in ruins. A throng of Romans would be portrayed by thousands of Italian Catholic extras. Grand in scope, this scene would become one of the most expensive ever filmed.

It was ironic that Elizabeth found herself in much the same situation as her royal character, due to all the negative press of late. Would the army of Italian extras accept her and go about the business of creating the scene at hand? Or would they, antagonised by the Vatican's position, jeer at her rather than cheer for Cleopatra?

When Elizabeth got to the studio, she was informed that there'd been a bomb threat against the production. The presence of security guards on the set, disguised in togas, only served to heighten the suspense. Elizabeth feared that one of the extras in that scene might have a gun and shoot her. 'I don't think I can do it,' she told Richard.

In costume as Mark Antony, Burton said, 'Don't worry. I'm here, luv. The police are here. It will be fine.'

The wardrobe Elizabeth had to wear for the scene was impossibly heavy: the fifteen-pound headdress was two and a half feet high. Years later she would recall, 'I thought, well, in front of the children and my mother and father, I mustn't look afraid. So I got into my costume, which seemed to weigh hundreds of pounds, and crawled up on the [three-storey-high] Sphinx, feeling totally trembly.'

According to the script, as she made her way beneath the Arch of Titus, Cleopatra was to be greeted by the chants of her constituency. The extras were told to wave and shout, 'Cleopatra! Cleopatra! Cleopatra!'

'Richard was out of the shot,' Elizabeth recalled, 'but I was supposed to look at him. Mother, Dad and the kids were standing next to him.'

The moment Joseph Mankiewicz yelled, 'Action', the fifty-foot-high Sphinx, with Elizabeth and the youngster atop it, began to lurch forward. As instructed, she sat atop the monstrosity, not moving a muscle. A frozen and regal glare played on her face, and she stared ahead at Caesar.

As Elizabeth made her way through the crowd, the extras did as they were told: 'Cleopatra! Cleopatra! Cleopatra!'

However, as the scene continued, Elizabeth noticed that the chanting slowly began to change: *'Leez! Leez! Leez!'*

The thousands of extras seemed to forget they were in a movie. Now, in their eyes, atop that Sphinx sat not Cleopatra but Elizabeth Taylor.

The sound echoed throughout the cavernous set as the extras screamed and shouted and applauded and blew kisses at her. *'Baci! Baci! Baci!'* they shouted—which means 'kisses' in Italian.

For Elizabeth, this was not only a moment on the set of a movie unlike any other in her long career, it was a moment in her life like no other as well. Obviously, these Italians did not agree with the Vatican's position on Elizabeth—their sympathies were with her. 'The tears were pouring down my face,' she recalled. Joseph Mankiewicz had to stop the scene as Richard and everyone else present—her parents, her children—came forward to surround Elizabeth, all crying. Mankiewicz handed her a bull-horn. *'Grazie! Grazie!'* she said to the crowds.

Sara couldn't believe what she'd just seen. She and Francis had come to be with Elizabeth during this difficult time, and she was glad that they had decided to do it. She would tell the story for years; it would become one of her best tales. To say that she was proud of her daughter would be an understatement.

The filming of that scene impacted on everyone who witnessed it, including Richard Burton. Never before had he known of a woman who could command such adoration. His presence at such a jaw-dropping display of adulation would be the catalyst for his new commitment to a life with Elizabeth Taylor. She had to be his . . . and he would do whatever necessary to have her.

WITH THEIR SPOUSES GONE, Elizabeth and Richard were finally free to be together. Of course, Elizabeth was happy about that, but she was stung by the position the Vatican had taken against her and concerned that the natural mother of Maria might hear about the controversy and have second thoughts about having given her daughter to Elizabeth. She sent her a telegram. 'She cabled her assurances that her love for Petra was as strong as ever,' recalled the woman, 'and that she would do her utmost to continue to provide the best for the child. She was so worried that she later wrote me to say that she would fly to Mering to reassure me of her devotion to Petra. It was not necessary. Her heart spoke for her.'

Maria's natural mother might have been satisfied, but the press couldn't help but criticise Elizabeth's mothering skills. To be fair, she faced challenges as a mother that most women of her time could never relate to, largely as a consequence of her career. However, she continued to dedicate as much of herself as possible to her children, and it wasn't easy for her to have the children she did bear.

'When I was pregnant with Liza, it was only a few months after my back operation,' she has recalled, 'and the doctors thought the pressure from the embryo would push the newly formed bone [in her back] right out and cripple me. They decided the baby should be aborted. I said, "Not on your nelly." So they fixed my back brace with elastic gussets over my stomach to make room for Liza.'

The back brace pushed the baby up into Elizabeth's ribs and even moved her heart a couple of inches, causing her to lose consciousness from time to time. She was therefore put on the heart drug digitalis, but in time the medicine began affecting the baby's heartbeat. Ultimately it was decided to take Elizabeth off the medicine for twenty-four hours, risk her going into a coma, and then deliver the baby, if possible. The baby was born by Caesarean section and, they thought, stillborn.

She didn't breathe for fourteen long minutes.

They told Todd that the baby was gone, though Elizabeth would be fine. This was when the doctors suggested that she not have any more children and asked if they could perform a tubal ligation, and Todd agreed to it. While all of this was going on, the baby began to breathe. She would live — and thank goodness for it, Elizabeth would say, because Liza was a part of Mike that continued in his stead.

Still, as much as Elizabeth cared for Michael and Christopher Wilding, Liza Todd Fisher and Maria Taylor, they were obviously affected by their mother's indiscretions and bad publicity. It's not as if she were unaware of the ramifications. 'I've been married too many times,' she admitted in 1965. 'How terrible to change children's affiliations, their affections — to give them the insecurity of placing their trust in someone when maybe that someone won't be there next year.'

Indeed, one day Eddie Fisher was present in their lives. The next day he was gone, replaced by someone the children knew as 'Uncle Dick'. Liza, who was about five, once asked one of Elizabeth's friends, 'Did you see *Around the World in 80 Days*? My first daddy made that. My second daddy made a movie also. And Richard, maybe my next daddy, makes movies, too — lots of them — as does my only mommy.' Richard never wanted Liza to call him Daddy, even after he and Elizabeth married. He wanted her to know that her father was Michael Todd, 'and he was a very wonderful man, and don't you ever forget it'.

As youngsters, the Taylor children were well adjusted and, for the most part, had fun. Sometimes they would meet Elizabeth for lunch at the studio; she loved those times most of all. They watched, wide-eyed, as she filmed some of her scenes in the colourful Cleopatra garb. A break in filming gave them an hour together. They would have a light meal and, as they ate, laugh and talk about whatever interested them at the time. Then Michael, Chris and Liza would return to the villa with their governess, while Elizabeth went back to work in front of the cameras. 'I try to get as much time with them as I can,' Elizabeth explained in an interview. 'I know I am doing a lousy job, but as God is my witness, I am trying to be as good a mother as Elizabeth Taylor can be.'

It's interesting that Elizabeth did not treat her children the way that her mother, Sara, had treated her in terms of being critical and judgmental. It was as if she'd made a decision to be much more accepting of their faults than Sara had ever been of hers. In fact, many people in her life felt that she might have been a little too permissive. No one, however, has ever heard of any of Elizabeth's children complaining about her treatment of them.

IT WAS DURING their Easter break in 1962 that Elizabeth learned about a side of Richard she hadn't seen in a man since her marriage to Nicky Hilton: his violent side. During the three-day break, Elizabeth and Richard decided to drive to Porto Santo Stefano, about a hundred miles north of Rome. Though the weekend started off pleasantly enough, it soon took a tragic turn.

According to Burton's diary entry, he rented a two-seat Fiat sports car so that he and Elizabeth could make the drive. Once at their small villa in Porto Santo Stefano, they frolicked on the beach, drinking and having fun, thinking that they had ducked the photographers who followed their every move and that they were alone. However, as Richard recalled, 'We found out soon enough that every bush—and there were hundreds of them—contained a paparazzo. We were thoroughly trapped.'

He wrote that, at that point, the weekend was ruined for them. Feeling like caged animals, they took out their frustration by drinking 'to the point of stupefaction and idiocy'. The more they drank, the more paranoid they began to feel.

The two began talking about love and death, and Elizabeth, in a dramatic moment, said that she was prepared to kill herself for him. 'Here and now,' she said, slurring her words. 'I'll do it, Richard. That is how deeply I love you.' They were both light-headed from brandy, vodka and champagne, and Richard laughed. It made no sense, yet, in their mutual haze, it somehow made all the sense in the world.

Elizabeth left the room and appeared a moment later with a bottle of sleeping pills. 'I'll do it,' she said. 'I'll do it now, for you.' Again, Richard laughed her off, thinking, he would later say, that she was threatening to off herself with vitamins. He knew she had a flair for the dramatic.

'Don't be ridiculous! Good Lord,' Richard flamed, 'I left a perfectly good woman to be with a lunatic!'

Elizabeth reached to open the bottle of pills. Richard swatted the container from her hand, sending it flying. When she went to retrieve it, he lost control. 'It didn't begin as a bar-room brawl, but it certainly ended as one,' he later told a friend.

His hazy memory of that night resumes hours later, when he came to and staggered into the bedroom. There he found Elizabeth sprawled on the bed, her head hanging off the side of the mattress, her mouth agape. She was out cold. He shook her repeatedly but couldn't wake her.

The sight of the empty pill bottle from earlier that night sobered him up quickly. 'I wasn't even sure she had taken them,' he said later. 'It would have been just like her to flush them down the loo and wait for me to find her.' He couldn't take that chance, though. He loaded her into the car for a hair-raising drive to Rome and back to Salvator Mundi Hospital. The doctors, after pumping her stomach, told him she had taken a large dose of sedatives. For the second time in four months, Elizabeth Taylor had apparently decided that life was not worth living.

When she awoke, Elizabeth had two black eyes. Her face was swollen almost beyond recognition. Three weeks would pass before it would finally return to its natural beauty. During that time, she was unable to work on *Cleopatra*. The studio said she was injured when the chauffeur had to stop her limousine unexpectedly.

ON JUNE 23, 1962, Elizabeth Taylor filmed her final moments in *Cleopatra* on the stunningly beautiful island of Ischia, in the Bay of Naples. The production had seemed to drag on endlessly: 632 days had passed since it began at Pinewood.

Though it was costly and epic in size (and, at more than four hours, in length as well), the general consensus about *Cleopatra*— when it was finally released a year later, on June 12, 1963, in New York—was that it was not a very good movie. While it was photographed beautifully, it's a big brute of a film that in the end topples over under its own weight.

Ultimately, the only reason to watch *Cleopatra* is to see just how stunning Elizabeth looks in it in her many lavish costumes. She's a regal vision, her eyes heavily made up, her complexion flawless. From this point on in her career, Elizabeth had final authority over all her costumes, hairstyles and make-up. She would also have final say over the director chosen by the film's producer, as well as the right to veto the script if she didn't like it.

However, her acting in *Cleopatra* seems unexpressive and dull. She received the worst reviews of her career, so vicious that they are not even worth memorialising here.

Another reason to watch the movie is to see Elizabeth and Richard work together for the first time, in hope of discerning some sense of magic between them. Surprisingly, considering their private lives, they have little chemistry on the screen. The two act as if they've never even met; their scenes of passion fall flat. Perhaps because there was such sexual tension between them offstage, they had to suppress their true emotions and, in doing so, ended up muting their performances.

In the end, *Cleopatra*—which had been budgeted at $2 million— would cost almost $50 million to make (about $150 million in today's currency). It is still considered the most expensive movie ever made. However, it has had a long life, and it did manage to break even in 1966. With $430 million in earnings in today's money, *Cleopatra* now rests at an impressive number thirty-seven in the list of all-time box-office moneymakers.

By August 1962, Elizabeth Taylor and her new lover, Richard Burton, were at her home, Chalet Ariel, in Gstaad, Switzerland—a playground for notables such as the Aga Khan, Joan Crawford and many others. Given its glittery reputation, it's surprising to find that Gstaad is basically just a lovely one-street village. In the centre of town, which is free of traffic bylaw, there are expensive restaurants, shops, hotels and bars. It feels like a magical place, especially in the winter months, when the town is blanketed by rolling drifts of snow.

Elizabeth paid half a million dollars for her sumptuous sixteen-room chalet in Gstaad. Built mostly of warm oak, Ariel sat on a crest overlooking the majestic scenery and, off in the distance, Céligny, where the Burtons lived.

With the production of *Cleopatra* over, she had time to consider the past few months of her life. However, in their first week there, she and Richard had one of their blazing rows. It's unknown exactly what the disagreement was about, but it must have been a big one because it caused Elizabeth to reconsider some of her recent choices where Richard was concerned. 'I wrote Richard a letter that said that we were destroying too many lives,' she recalled. 'We should part.' She left the note for him on his pillow. Hours later, without any kind of emotional display, he left. Before he left, he told her, 'I just wanted to take care of you.'

'I can take care of myself,' she said through her tears.

Despite her unhappiness, her mind was set, and she would not contact him. As the days turned into weeks, she became morbidly sad. 'I'd never seen her like that,' said a woman who knew Elizabeth very well in Gstaad at this time. 'I think she had made up her mind that Richard was out of her life. She said she doubted that she would ever see him again, and she said she knew it was for the best.'

When Richard left Elizabeth's chalet, he drove off to his own home, a much more modest one, in Céligny. There he joined Sybil and his daughters. Meanwhile, just one mountain range away,

Elizabeth was still trying to get through the days. 'I was dying inside and trying to hide it from the children with all kinds of frenzied activity,' she recalled. 'Their sense of loss was almost as great as mine.'

Then, one day, Richard called. He wondered how she was doing, he said. He missed her and wanted to have lunch with her. If she had only slammed the phone down with an indignant *'How dare you interrupt my solitude,'* her life would have been a different story. However, it wasn't meant to be that way. 'Yes,' she said, she would love to see him again.

The two arranged to meet that afternoon at Château de Chillon, a medieval castle where tourists dine while taking in the breathtaking view of Lake Geneva. Elizabeth and Richard arrived at exactly the same moment. He looked tanned, rested and sober, but a bit nervous.

They took each other in, and in unison they chirped, 'Well, you look marvellous,' before bursting into laughter. Elizabeth and Richard then enjoyed a quiet, if awkward, luncheon. With many people, the truth of how they feel comes forth when they have had too much alcohol. Not so, Richard. His greatest truth was revealed when he was sober, when he could dig deep within to bare his soul, as he did during this lunch. 'I love you,' he told Elizabeth, according to his recollection. 'But what scares me about you is that I think you are too selfish to be in a real marriage.'

Elizabeth was stung by his observation. For once, Richard didn't mean to hurt her; he was simply being honest. He explained that he'd been so reliant on Sybil for so many years, she'd become his rock. She put aside her career for him and their children. She would do anything for him, he explained. 'She put up with bloody hell from me,' he said.

At last, the truth of why Richard was so reluctant to leave Sybil had come forth. Sybil had been his greatest salvation, the woman upon whom he could most depend. She'd always been there for him, even when he didn't deserve it. He couldn't bear to lose her. The irony of it all didn't escape Richard. 'I know you, Elizabeth, because I am you,' he told her. 'I'm a selfish bastard. I've always been my own greatest concern, and I've never been able to abandon that notion, and neither can you, dear.'

'But I would do it for you, Richard,' Elizabeth said.

'I'm not certain you could do it for me, luv,' Richard told her. 'Tolstoy put it best: "Everyone wants to change humanity, but no one is willing to change themselves."'

The subject was dropped. However, Elizabeth would not be able to forget Richard's summation of her. Was he correct? Was she so selfish that she couldn't survive in a loving marriage? On the one hand, it bothered her that he felt this way about her. But on the other, she admitted that his assessment of her was probably accurate. Of course she was selfish. She was accustomed to having the world spin round her desires. However, there was something about Richard that made her want to . . . *change*.

After their meal, they didn't even kiss. They would see each other a couple of times a week for the next few weeks before Elizabeth made what she would recall as 'the most alone, mature and unpopular decision of my life'. She would be there for Richard whenever he called, and for whatever reason. If he wanted to talk in person, she would be there. If he just wanted to speak on the telephone, that was fine, too. If he wanted to have sex with her, she would be there for that as well. In return, she would require nothing from him — absolutely nothing.

Elizabeth believed that her decision was a mature one, born out of what she felt was 'an unselfish love for Richard'. She just wanted him to be happy, she said, and if that happiness was with her, fine. If it was with Sybil? She would live with that as well.

IT WAS NO SURPRISE that, as a nod to the public spectacle of their lives together, Elizabeth would be paired with Richard for another film. While 20th Century Fox may have thought that the publicity that surrounded their personal shenanigans was to the detriment of *Cleopatra*, MGM held no such reservations.

Richard was scheduled to make a film for the studio with

Sophia Loren, called *The VIPs*. Without even knowing what it was about or seeing a script, Elizabeth said that she would like to be in the film with Burton instead of Sophia Loren. Of course, no studio was going to resist, and it was ironic that Elizabeth ended up at MGM again, considering all the bad blood between her and the studio.

In December 1962, Elizabeth and Richard checked in to adjoining suites at the Dorchester Hotel in London, where the movie was to be filmed. While making *The VIPs*, the couple also spent a great deal of time at Richard's favourite pubs in London. They would start the morning with Bloody Marys, continue with a few bottles of champagne, then their brandies . . . and by that time, it was just noon.

Burton spent weekends with Sybil and their daughters, while Elizabeth stayed at the Dorchester, counting the hours until his return. He told more than one reporter that he had no intention of leaving his wife and marrying Elizabeth. Though Elizabeth's hands would shake with anxiety when she read such reports, she didn't push Richard or question him or make demands of him. When he returned from visiting his family, Richard would be very upset and often in tears. 'He's more miserable when he's with them than he is when he's with me,' Elizabeth reasoned to Roddy McDowall. 'But this is what he wants, I suppose.'

On some days, Sybil would show up on the set and act as if she and Richard were happy, helping to make decisions about wardrobe. On other days, Elizabeth would be the one making the decisions, and she would veto Sybil's. It was a confusing time for everyone.

Finally, in the spring of 1963, Richard Burton came to a difficult decision. He would leave Sybil. Of course, Elizabeth was elated. He had made his choice, and it was to be with her.

The question, as she now saw it, was whether the two of them could make their relationship work without the heartache and angst that had been its hallmark from the very beginning, over a year earlier.

THROUGHOUT THE SUMMER of 1963, Elizabeth and Richard remained in London. As Elizabeth put it, 'We got to know each other away from the constant anxiety of making a movie together.' Then, in September 1963, they arrived in Mexico, where Burton would go before the cameras in John Huston's film of Tennessee Williams's play *The Night of the Iguana*. When they arrived at Mexico City's airport, there was such a mad crush awaiting them that Elizabeth refused to get off the plane until security dispersed the crowd. 'Don't be ridiculous,' Richard said. 'We'll get through as best we can. This is our life, so get used to it.'

'Get used to it?' Elizabeth said, her voice raised to a screech. 'I've been doing this for twenty-five years, buster!'

The two exited the plane cursing and hollering at each other — followed by seventy-five pieces of luggage carried by airport personnel. It was the perfect scene for the paparazzi. The next day, 'Liz and Dick' (as they were usually called by the media) were on the front page of every newspaper, smiling, scowling, cursing and posing. 'We always give the people exactly what they want, don't we?' Elizabeth later joked with Burton. Then, to a writer, she said, 'My best feature is my grey hairs. I have them all named. They're all called Burton.'

'They were both very funny, and I think this is something people really have missed about them,' said their friend the columnist Liz Smith. 'You didn't have that kind of ribald humour coming from a Hollywood couple at that time, and I don't think you've seen it since.'

The Night of the Iguana was a tough shoot; everyone was miserable from the heat and the awful, crawling creatures, though the cast was a good one that included three leading ladies for Richard: Ava Gardner, Deborah Kerr and Sue Lyon.

While in Mexico, Elizabeth had six-year-old Liza with her. Maria was in a clinic in Europe, recovering from surgery on her hip. The boys — Michael, eleven, and Christopher, nine — were with their father, Michael Wilding, in Los Angeles, where they were going to start school.

Elizabeth and Richard were ensconced in a lovely four-storey compound called Casa Kimberly in Puerto Vallarta. Spread out over 22,000 square feet, it had ten bedrooms, eleven bathrooms, three kitchens and a huge swimming pool. Richard eventually bought the estate for $40,000, and it would remain one of the Burtons' homes for the next decade.

Lucille Wellman was a close friend of Ava Gardner's who visited her in Puerto Vallarta. 'My first night there, Ava and I went to dinner with [screenwriter] Meade Roberts and Richard and Elizabeth Taylor. Elizabeth looked marvellous in a white, flowing caftan and matching turban, with the longest dangling diamond earrings I had ever seen. I found her to be completely charming and guileless. She was aware of the effect she had on people, I think, and she did whatever she could to dispense of it quickly. Richard was the same way. They seemed to get along well; they were very happy—at least, that was my perception.'

According to Wellman, Elizabeth put her head on Richard's shoulder and said, 'I wonder if this man will one day be my husband.'

'If we don't kill each other first,' Richard said with a warm smile.

Elizabeth looked at him lovingly. 'But what a way to go, darling,' she said. 'What a way to go.'

He kissed her on the lips.

In 1963, Elizabeth's family came to visit for Christmas: her parents, Sara and Francis; her brother, Howard, his wife, Mara, and their five children; the Wilding boys; and even Maria, who was now out of the clinic. The occasion marked a turning point in Elizabeth's relationship with Richard. She had never been more content. She knew he felt as if he had a real place in her life, and his love for her seemed to grow with each passing day. Indeed, she had devoted herself to him, and he knew it. 'He began to fall for her in a way that he hadn't before, and she for him,' said his brother Graham Jenkins. 'I think it was at Casa Kimberly that their true love was born. She saw another side to him, and he of her. Now they were one.'

Part Four
'Liz and Dick'

By the beginning of 1964, Sybil Burton had filed for divorce from Richard, citing abandonment and cruelty. When her attorney noted in the paperwork that Burton had 'been in the constant company of another woman', *Newsweek* called it 'the throwaway line of the decade'. The million-dollar settlement Richard gave her nearly bankrupted him, but he agreed to it because he felt so guilty about leaving her.

Elizabeth felt that Sybil's decision to divorce Richard was the best way to start 1964.

Elizabeth's and Richard's friends and family were fairly exhausted by their wild personal adventures and tempestuous romance. For those in their inner circle, it was almost anticlimactic when the couple decided to charter a plane and secretly marry in Montreal on March 15, 1964. For Elizabeth, though, this was a marriage she wanted more than anything else in her life. 'I didn't have butterflies for this one,' she said, 'because I knew beyond all doubt that it was right.' Richard was nervous enough for the two of them. Ronald DeMann, Elizabeth's hairdresser at the time, recalled that Burton—who was by this time starring in *Hamlet* in Toronto en route to Broadway—was so nervous on the plane ride that 'he drank himself silly'. Elizabeth said to DeMann, 'I don't know why he's so nervous. We've been sleeping together for two years.'

Despite his nerves, it was clear that Richard truly loved Elizabeth. 'I fell in love at once,' he had said. 'She was like a mirage of beauty of the ages, irresistible, like the pull of gravity. She has everything I want in a woman. I think of her morning, noon and night. She will be my greatest happiness—for ever, of course.'

'The two of us act like we're seventeen-year-olds,' Elizabeth said at the time. 'My favourite time is when we're alone at night and for hours we giggle and talk—about, maybe, books, world events, poetry, the children. We love to watch old movies on TV to regenerate our souls. Sometimes I wake up in the morning with my eyes absolutely swollen shut from crying at some wonderfully old movie the night before.'

Elizabeth and Richard were married in the Ritz-Carlton Hotel's bridal suite in Montreal by a Unitarian minister. It was Elizabeth's fifth wedding, and she was only thirty-two. Richard was thirty-nine. Of course, Elizabeth was late for the ceremony, causing Richard to ask in his own inimitable fashion, 'Isn't that fat little tart here yet? I swear to you, she'll be late for the last bloody judgment.'

When she did arrive, Elizabeth looked beautiful in a low-cut canary-yellow gown designed by Irene Sharaff that was patterned after the gown Elizabeth wore in her first scene with Richard in *Cleopatra*. At her neck was a $100,000 emerald brooch, which had been a gift from Richard during the filming. His wedding gift to her was an emerald and diamond brooch from Bulgari. He would later give her matching earrings and a bracelet. The jewels are sometimes referred to as the Grand Duchess Vladimir Suite.

Richard's agent, Hugh French, who attended the ten-minute ceremony, recalled, 'When the minister pronounced them man and wife, the loveliest of smiles appeared on both their faces. It was so very apparent that they were thrilled, that they took the vows very seriously.'

'I truly believe in my heart that this marriage will last for ever,' said the now five-time bride. 'I know I have said that before, but this time I really do think it is true.'

After their return to Toronto, Richard got back to the business of *Hamlet* and performed in the show that evening. He received six curtain calls. Finally, he stepped towards the front of the stage and said, 'I would like to quote from the play—act three, scene one: "We will have no more marriages."' It brought the house down.

AFTER TORONTO, the next stop for the play was Boston, and after Boston, Richard took his star turn in *Hamlet* at the Lunt-Fontanne Theater on Broadway in April 1964. During his Broadway run, Richard's reviews were stunning. Indeed, he was the toast of the town during this time, and Elizabeth happily basked in the glow of his stardom. It was almost as if she didn't have a career herself—she never mentioned it. 'I was totally devoted to Richard,' she recalled, 'and not for a second did I regret it. I was so proud of him. I was never as happy as I was during that early time in my marriage to Richard.'

The Burtons were staying at the Regency, and their time there, with Elizabeth's children, was happy. The couple was more kind and loving to one another than ever in the past. 'We were a real family,' Elizabeth said dreamily. 'It was picture perfect.'

There were times, though, when Richard's drinking was a problem. After having as many as four Martinis before going onstage, he would sometimes have trouble retaining his lines.

One night in May, Richard completely massacred his 'the play's the thing' speech and was booed by someone in the audience. He was as infuriated as he was hurt. When he got back to the Regency, he found Elizabeth in the parlour, curled up on a couch, drinking a Vodka Collins and watching a Peter Sellers movie on television. 'They booed. Can you believe it?' he roared as soon as he walked into the suite. 'How dare they, those snivelling bastards.'

'How dare *you*, Richard?' she said, looking up at him.

Burton walked over to the television and turned it off. 'What do you mean?' he asked, his temper rising.

'How dare you allow those people to pay those high ticket prices and then show up not able to perform,' Elizabeth said, standing up.

'My drinking has never interfered with my work,' he said.

'Well, we're all in denial about something, aren't we?' she said, remaining calm. 'Now, I'd like to get back to my movie. Please.'

Richard went into the bedroom and undressed. He returned half an hour later in his pyjamas and robe and in bare feet. 'Are you still watching that silliness?' he asked her. He was clearly still angry.

'Oh, be quiet, Richard,' Elizabeth said. 'It's almost over.'

'It *is* over,' he declared. Then, with a thrust of his bare foot, he kicked in the television screen. In doing so, he cut himself so badly that it took Elizabeth more than an hour to stop the blood flow enough to get him to a hospital. It was then that Elizabeth discovered something about Richard that she hadn't known: he had haemophilia. A simple cut could bring on profuse bleeding and severe pain, even though his case was mild.

IN THE SUMMER of 1964, Elizabeth found herself working in a very different venue for her—the theatre. Philip Burton, Richard's mentor, had asked if she would participate with Richard in a literary evening at the Lunt-Fontanne to raise funds for his American Musical and Dramatic Academy. The programme involved the Burtons reading excerpts from the works of D. H. Lawrence, Shakespeare and Elizabeth Barrett Browning. Elizabeth rehearsed for two weeks; she had a tough time with it. She was always very aware of the kind of education she'd had at MGM, and she found herself, in some ways, feeling intellectually inferior. 'I never mind being wrong with Richard because I learn from him and he never treats me like an idiot,' she would later write. 'He makes me feel an intellectual equal of his, which, of course, I am not.'

It's also true that Elizabeth was often afraid of boring Richard. She and a tutor of the children's were walking on a beach in Puerto Vallarta once, and she was talking about Richard and how much she loved him. 'But I'm afraid I'm going to lose him,' she said. 'I think I bore him. I don't think I'm smart enough.' It was a stunning admission.

On the big night, she walked onto the stage, swathed in pleated white silk, with emerald and diamond earrings. It was a starstudded audience. Elizabeth had barely started when she flubbed her lines. 'Oh, I'll have to begin again,' she said apologetically. 'I screwed it up.' From then on, the audience was with Elizabeth as the underdog in the production. Her reviews the next day were generally positive.

Also at this time, Elizabeth was writing a book: *Elizabeth Taylor: An Informal Memoir.* 'Even our fights are fun—nothing placidly bovine about us,' she wrote. 'Our fights are delightful screaming matches, and Richard is rather like a small atom bomb going off— sparks fly, walls shake, floors vibrate.' When writing about the possibility of his cheating on her, she noted, 'I would love him enough to love the hurt he might give me and be patient. I have learned that pride is very bad, the kind of pride that makes you say, "I won't tolerate that."'

At the end of the year, the Burtons filmed their third movie together, *The Sandpiper.* Elizabeth hadn't been in front of a camera in two years, having devoted that time to her husband and his career. But once she was back working on a sound stage, she couldn't have been happier. When the film was released in 1965, it was a box-office smash. If nothing else, it validated the commerciality of its stars because, in truth, the movie suffered from a weak story that an even weaker script could not overcome. Despite brisk ticket sales, the Burtons knew they had made what Elizabeth later referred to as 'a real turkey'.

ARGUABLY, the Burtons' greatest film achievement is their 1966 version of Edward Albee's *Who's Afraid of Virginia Woolf?* The four-character story involves the often poisonous relationship between George, a history professor, and Martha, his wife. The action takes place over a single drunken night when the couple entertains campus newcomers Nick and Honey (played by George Segal and Sandy Dennis).

The play is considered a black comedy, but there is tragedy lurking in practically every line. This is not so much a battle of the sexes as 'total war', as George rhetorically says to his wife late in the play. *Virginia Woolf* today is almost painful to watch, but oddly compelling, the viewer squirming in his seat, wondering what these two bitter, foul-mouthed dipsomaniacs will do or say next to humiliate each other (and their young guests, too).

Elizabeth has said that she had a difficult time imagining herself as the character of Martha, not only because of the age difference between her and the character but also because 'I couldn't imagine myself dominating Richard'. The way Elizabeth explained her character sounded as if she were describing herself: 'Her veneer is bawdy. It's sloppy. It's slouchy, it's snarly. But there are moments when the façade cracks and you see the vulnerability, the infinite pain of this woman inside whom, years ago, life almost died but is still flickering.'

The Burtons' decision to bring Mike Nichols to Hollywood as the director of *Virginia Woolf* was a shrewd one. By 1965, Nichols was *the* director in the Broadway theatre. After a successful career as the partner of Elaine May, writing and performing stand-up, he made his directing debut in 1963 in Neil Simon's hit *Barefoot in the Park*, which earned Nichols his first Tony. With *Virginia Woolf*, he would become as much a presence in films as he had been in New York theatre.

Elizabeth was paid $1.1 million for the film, Richard $750,000. She also received her now standard ten per cent of the profits. In the end, the Burtons cleared more than $6 million on this movie.

'Working together on the film was probably their best experience together in terms of their careers,' says Diane Stevens, who worked for John Springer, Elizabeth's PR man. 'I spent many days on that set, and I can tell you that it was truly a collaborative effort between the Burtons, Nichols and writer-producer Ernest Lehman. For instance, it was Mike Nichols's and Rich Burton's idea that [Elizabeth] lower the key of her speaking voice for greater effect. She was eager to take direction from Burton, never felt insulted when he offered direction to her. I would see the three of them huddled together in a corner, working on ideas.'

For Elizabeth, playing the role of the tormented Martha, a dowdy, blowsy character in her mid-forties, was a challenge unlike any other in her career. She gained twenty-five pounds for the part. The acerbic personality of the character, along with the combative relationship she had with her husband, probably wasn't as much of a stretch for Elizabeth to convey as she said it was in interviews.

Diane Stevens recalled, 'I walked in on a major row during a break in filming the movie. Just as I entered Rich's dressing room, Elizabeth hurled a vase at him. He ducked, and it almost hit me. It crashed into pieces on the floor, and she reached for an empty pitcher and threw *that* at him, without even acknowledging that I had entered the room. "You bastard!" she screamed at him. He ducked again. Then he picked up a fruit bowl and threw it at her. She ducked, and I got the hell out of there. Fifteen minutes later, they emerged holding hands.'

It wasn't just alcohol that was a problem for Elizabeth; it was also her dependency on painkillers. She was in constant pain from her back problems, and she needed the drugs. Diane Stevens tells this story: 'I remember sending a telegram at Elizabeth's direction to doctors Carl Goldman and Victor Ratner in London. It said, "Urgent. Send pink pills at once. Elizabeth." She didn't know the names of the pills she was taking; she only knew she couldn't survive without them. Dr Goldman told me the pink pills were Diconal, one of the most powerful painkillers in the world. She was in agony during *Virginia Woolf*.'

In the end, despite the melodrama that surrounded its making, *Who's Afraid of Virginia Woolf?* is considered a masterpiece by most film scholars. It was nominated for thirteen Academy Awards and won five, including a second one for Elizabeth. Richard would turn in many Oscar-worthy performances for the remainder of his career but would never win the statuette.

As the 1960s were drawing to a close, the inevitability of Elizabeth's approaching fourth decade suggested that her days as an ingénue were past. Leading-lady roles would give way to character parts—though starring character parts, to be sure. She and Richard made movies together during these years, but they also continued with their individual careers.

In retrospect, none of the films the Burtons made during this time did them much justice. Most were bad choices, as if their excessively bad personal habits had caused them also to have poor judgment when it came to choosing scripts.

These movies, no matter how bad, generally turned a profit. Such good fortune afforded the Burtons the wherewithal to continue living the Good Life, which for Elizabeth consisted of wild shopping sprees, especially for precious jewels. Her favourite is the Krupp diamond. 'It had been owned by Vera Krupp,' she has explained, 'of the famous munitions family, who helped knock off millions of Jews. When it came up for auction, I thought how perfect it would be if a nice Jewish girl like me were to own it.'

To see the Krupp up close—33.19 carats, for which Richard paid $305,000 when he bought it for his wife on May 16, 1968—is to behold probably the most amazing diamond in the world. It shimmers, as if it's actually alive, with every colour of the rainbow.

During her years with Richard, Elizabeth received a great deal of eye-popping jewellery from him. Among the most famous was the Taylor-Burton diamond, formerly the Cartier diamond (69.42 carats), for which Richard paid $1.1 million. So large was this stone that Elizabeth eventually stopped wearing it as a ring. Instead, she had Cartier design a V-shaped necklace of graduated pear-shaped diamonds, mounted in platinum, from which it would gracefully dangle.

Later, for a birthday, Elizabeth would receive from Richard a Persian necklace made in 1627 for Nur Jahan, wife of the emperor Jahangir. Richard said he'd wanted to buy her the Taj Mahal, but it was too big to squeeze into their chalet in Gstaad.

Many decades later, Elizabeth Taylor would look back on this time with a sense of appreciation. 'When I think about the sixties,' she says, 'I'm glad that I knew the wildness, glamour and excitement when I was in my prime: the parties, the yachts, and the private jets and the jewellery. It was a great time to be young, alive and attractive. I enjoyed it.'

Probably the biggest regret of this time for Elizabeth was the 1967 Oscar disappointment of *Who's Afraid of Virginia Woolf?* — not that the Burtons both lost when nominated, because, as it happened, Elizabeth won. Because of Richard's vast insecurity, however, neither he nor Elizabeth attended the awards ceremony. Instead, that evening, the Burtons had a few friends over for dinner, never mentioning the Oscars. Elizabeth did not even know she had won until the next morning.

ON NOVEMBER 20, 1968, Richard Burton took an emotional telephone call from Sara Taylor, telling him that Elizabeth's father, Francis, had died. He was seventy-two. He'd not been in good health for some time; he had suffered a stroke in 1965 and another in 1967.

Though Francis had a difficult, challenging life, he had got through it with the greatest of dignity. True, he had not always been the ideal father. However, in more recent decades, Francis was always at his daughter's side when she most needed support: when she lost Mike Todd in the plane crash, when she had her tracheotomy, and in the midst of countless other times of melodrama. Still, their communication was always strained and never quite what either of them truly wanted for each other. But there was always more time — or, at least, that's how it seemed.

Elizabeth and Richard immediately made plans to fly to Hollywood for the funeral. At this time, Elizabeth was in a weakened state, due to a recent operation — a partial hysterectomy, resulting from medical conditions that had developed after the birth of Liza. Francis's death felt to her, as she would recall it, like more than she could bear. She had a complete breakdown, or, as Richard put it, 'she was like a wild animal'.

On the limousine ride to Francis's gravesite, Elizabeth and her mother sat mostly without speaking. At the service, they were pensive, until Elizabeth broke the silence, according to Marshall Baldrige, Francis's trusted friend from London, who was, of course, at the service.

'I should have spent more time with him,' she announced.

Sara said, 'He would have liked that.'

Those few words seemed to affect Elizabeth deeply; her strength and resolve began to crumble. She began to cry.

Her mother looked at her. 'But I'm not crying, dear,' Sara said plainly.

Elizabeth wasn't sure what she meant by her comment.

Sara continued, 'If a man's widow isn't crying, it isn't good form for others to do so. It makes me seem unfeeling.'

'This late in Sara's life, she was still considering public opinion of paramount concern,' observed Baldrige.

Francis was buried in the Sanctuary of Peace section of Westwood Memorial Park. The small golden plaque on the site reads: FRANCIS L. TAYLOR — ALL OUR LOVE — 1897–1968.

BY THE END of the 1960s, it was clear that Elizabeth and Richard had truly begun to plummet to the depths of alcoholism. Their drinking continued in a way that can only be described as out of control. In May 1969, the Burtons left Puerto Vallarta for London for the filming of *Anne of the Thousand Days*, in which Richard was to play King Henry VIII. Richard suffered from insomnia for the entire shoot and started taking sleeping pills. During some weeks, he drank to excess, staying up all night and then arriving late at the studio for work. In other weeks, he stopped and couldn't even stand the smell of vodka.

With Richard, it was one extreme or the other. There was no moderation.

Richard once explained that the reason he drank so much while making movies was 'to burn up the flatness — the stale, empty, flat, dull, deadness one feels after a scene'. He also remarked that the Burtons found their high-profile lifestyle troubling. 'Elizabeth and I both feel unsure of ourselves at a party because no one really wants to know us. They stare as if we are prize animals. We drink to kill the icy isolation.'

Still, despite the complexities of their private lives, there was a great advantage to the couple's working together at this time. From Elizabeth, Richard learned the technique of film acting. As he explained it, 'She taught me subtleties in film-making that I never knew existed, such as the value of absolute stillness and also that my penetrating voice need not be pitched louder than a telephone conversation. She's the consummate cinematic technician.'

Elizabeth felt the same about Richard. 'Working with Richard is working with the absolute pro,' she said. 'He gives you the feeling of antennae — a quivering, positive contact. He can turn emotion on and off in seconds, having it under complete control, yet you sense the latent power all the time. Richard will do anything to put other actors at their ease, even flubbing his own line — anything so the cut in the film will be his fault. He gives so much. He has electricity. He speaks verse like prose, and his prose sounds like poetry.'

In another interview, Elizabeth said of him, 'Richard is just like a well: there's no plumbing the depths. You can't describe a volcano erupting. You can't describe the sound of the wind in the trees when there is no wind.' What she may have been expressing was that he had a volatile temper, and she was capable of matching it, on a daily basis.

BY THE BEGINNING of the 1970s, things were getting worse between Elizabeth and Richard — the drinking, the insecurities, the fighting. Many of their more public arguments have been chronicled in newspapers, magazines and books. Basically, their disagreements were always along the same lines: both would have too much to drink. One would demand something of the other, not get it, and then throw a fit, maybe a fist, and, at the very least, a glass of liquor. As the months turned into years, the temper tantrums between them would leave feelings of resentment that even the passing of time would not be able to erase.

To be fair, despite their problems, it's clear that the Burtons really did love each other and were committed to their relationship, such as it was. Sometimes, they were able to see the light. In March 1970, for instance, they were having dinner with friends when the subject of their drinking came up. Richard pointed to Elizabeth and said, 'Now, there's someone who could never give up a drink.'

Who knows why his statement touched a nerve? Certainly, Richard had said a lot worse about Elizabeth over the years. But for some reason, her temper boiled over. She snapped, 'You know what? I hate your guts.'

'You've had too much to drink, tubby,' Richard said. 'So bugger off.'

From there, the scene got worse. By the time it ended, all the guests had got an earful, and it is doubtful they ever forgot a word of it.

The next day, Elizabeth felt anguish over the breach. 'We're not very nice people, are we?' she asked Richard in front of Dick Hanley and other staff members.

'No, we're not,' Richard agreed sadly.

Elizabeth approached him and embraced him tightly. 'I only know that without you I would have been dead years ago,' she said. 'I do love you, honey.' She melted into his embrace; he kissed her fully on the lips.

There were so many levels of psychological chaos at work within Richard Burton, causing him to drink, that he would have to have been married to a psychiatrist, not a movie star, in order to have been fully understood. He still felt tremendous guilt about leaving Sybil and his daughters for Elizabeth, even after all this time. He was also angry about the way his career had thus far unfolded. Though *Anne of the Thousand Days* had earned eight Oscar nominations, including Best Picture, Actor (Burton) and Actress (Geneviève Bujold), he was again overlooked on awards night. It had been his sixth nomination and his sixth loss.

WHEN ELIZABETH turned forty in February 1972, she tried to be optimistic about the future during star-studded birthday festivities in Budapest (where Richard was filming *Bluebeard*). 'I love my life, and everything is going so well,' she told the press. A photo of her and Burton, taken by Norman Parkinson in Hungary, is quite haunting: both are in luxurious black furs—she with a fur hood and wearing the magnificent Krupp diamond ring. He has his smouldering eyes fixed upon her because she is the only woman for him, no matter the cost to his ego or his emotional well-being. She returns his gaze with an equal measure of affection, yet with a distant, faraway look that conveys both great love and tremendous sadness. By the time she and Richard began work on a TV movie called *Divorce His, Divorce Hers* — their last film together — it was clear that the subject matter was prophetic.

On July 4, 1973, she released the following statement: 'I am convinced that it would be a good and constructive idea if Richard and I are separated for a while. Maybe we loved each other too much — I never believed such a thing was possible. But we have been in each other's pockets constantly, never being apart but for matters of life and death, and I believe it's caused a temporary breakdown of communication. I believe with all my heart that the separation will ultimately bring us back together. I think I shall return to California, because my mother is there, and I have old and true friends there, too. Wish us well during this difficult time.' She ended her statement with a simple plea: 'Pray for us.'

THOUGH THE BURTONS had their share of personal problems, they also had a brood of children to consider: her four, Michael, Christopher, Liza and Maria; and Richard's two, Kate and Jessica. Somehow, they managed to give them as much of their time as possible. The children adored them, and the feeling was mutual. However, Elizabeth and Richard were so consumed by their own lives and careers, is it any wonder they had trouble being good parents? Richard simply didn't have the patience or the selfless temperament it takes to raise children. Somehow, Elizabeth *did* have the ability to be a good, though perhaps not very strict, mother.

Elizabeth's first-born, Michael, was a teenager now and having trouble with his grades in the boarding school he was attending. He kept getting kicked out of one after another, so much so that the Burtons seemed to be running out of educational options for him.

Richard spent hours lecturing the teenager about his scholastic future. But Michael just wasn't interested in discussing his schooling with his stepfather. 'Let's face it,' Burton decided, 'our son is a hippie. His hair lies on his shoulders, and we can't keep him in school. It bothers Elizabeth, too, but she goes round sermonising, "He has the right to wear his hair any length he wants."'

Burton noted that the entire time Michael and Christopher were in Puerto Vallarta, the only reading they did was of comic books. He wasn't going to fret if they refused to read literature. However, he did not approve of their smoking while away at school. Elizabeth was not much help. She said she wasn't going to ruin their spring vacation by 'getting on their backs about stuff that they see us do here every day'.

In October 1970, Michael — then seventeen — married nineteen-year-old Beth Clutter. Burton was unhappy about the marriage. 'The kid has no high school diploma,' he raged. 'He's got no job. What is he going to do, live off us for the rest of his life?'

'He's our son,' Elizabeth said. 'We have to support him.'

Elizabeth gave the newlyweds a Jaguar and a $70,000 London town house as a wedding gift. She also arranged for the couple to receive a monthly stipend.

It was clear that Michael wanted to start his own life as soon as he possibly could, away from Elizabeth and Richard. The marriage, predictably, would not last long, though the couple would have a child in July, named Leyla, making Elizabeth a grandmother at age thirty-nine. She could not have been more thrilled about it. By then, she and Beth had bonded; Elizabeth showed her nothing but kindness and warmth.

At this time, Liza — Elizabeth's daughter with Mike Todd — was having trouble with her studies, but she was a hard worker and determined to pull through. She and Richard were very close.

Maria still had a number of physical problems, with good days and bad days. Elizabeth took time to give special attention to her, as did Richard. Both were concerned at her timidity and hoped she would grow out of it.

Richard remained close to his daughter Kate—though at a distance, due to the divorce from her mother. Because his other daughter, Jessica, was still in a mental hospital, it pained him even to think about her. All he could do was make enough money so she would never have financial worries. Anything else was more than he could handle.

ELIZABETH'S STATEMENT to the press about her separation from Richard Burton generated international headlines. After she released the statement, she flew to California. Meanwhile, Richard, drinking from a bottle of vodka, held a press conference in New York.

'You know, when two volatile people keep hacking at each other, and then occasionally engage in a go of it with physical force, well, it's bound to happen,' he said, seeming in perfectly good nature.

On July 13, 1973, Burton left for Rome to film a new movie with Sophia Loren, called *The Voyage*. So that he would not have to deal with the paparazzi constantly on his tail, Sophia and her husband, Carlo Ponti, offered to put Richard up in the guesthouse of their sixteenth-century villa, about thirty minutes outside Rome.

A couple of days later, Elizabeth got a phone call from Richard. They had earlier organised their schedules so that they would both be making movies in Rome at the same time, and she was about to begin work on *The Driver's Seat* there. Richard felt that a faraway romantic setting might diminish the tension between them. 'We may as well be together here at the Pontis', luv,' he told her. 'It makes no sense to be apart.'

Elizabeth was conflicted as to how to proceed, but she decided to take him up on his offer. On July 20, she arrived in Rome.

Ellen Pallola, who was Sophia Loren's personal assistant at that time, recalled, 'The Burtons started arguing the day Elizabeth showed up at the villa. I heard her say, "You *are* flirting with Sophia. And you're doing it in Italian so I can't understand a word! How dare you?"

'Burton took off with Mr Ponti, enraged. I recall him saying, "That woman came all the way from the United States just to make my life a living hell. And I'm the fool who invited her here."

'Over the course of a week, the two of them caused so much turmoil at the villa that Mrs Ponti finally pulled Mrs Burton aside. She told her, "Elizabeth, you must know that I do not have designs on Richard."

'Mrs Burton said, "Of course I know that. But he is such a flirt, and I'm sick of it."

'"As much as I adore Richard," Mrs Ponti said, "he is not the man for you. There is much too much suspicion. A marriage cannot survive suspicion. You must end this misery."

'"I am,' said Mrs Burton. "Thank you for caring. It's over."'

The next morning, Elizabeth left the villa, leaving Richard behind. Ellen Pallola recalled, 'I helped carry her bags to the car. Before she got into the car, Mrs Ponti embraced her tightly and said, "You know what makes us women, don't you? That we believe love comes before anything else and that we would willingly give up everything for love. You must find your love." Mrs Burton, who was in tears by this time, got into the car and was driven off.'

After leaving Sophia, Elizabeth checked in to a seven-room suite at the Grand Hotel. She was expected on the set the next morning, yet she didn't show up until 5 p.m.

'We waited all day for her,' said the film's director, Giuseppe Patroni-Griffi. 'When she arrived, she was in terrible shape. She said to me, "I never thought I would have as bad a day as I am having today. I thought when Mike Todd died, that would have been the worst day of my life. But *this* is the worst day of my life." I suggested we put work off a few days. "No," she said. "I must work. I must take my mind off things."

'So we were ready to begin. Before we started, she asked to address the cast and crew. She stood before everyone and said, "I am sorry I was late today. That is not like me at all. However, I am having a dreadful day, and I just hope that you will forgive me." Everyone had been aware of the strain her roller-coaster marriage put on her personally. They had expected an aloof yet professional actress that first day of shooting, but she revealed herself as a human being. After her plea for forgiveness, the studio filled with applause. Some came up to her and hugged her. She returned their embraces without hesitation. All the barriers between star and the rest of the cast were brought down, and we went to work.'

EARLIER, in the summer of 1973, when Elizabeth Taylor was in a Los Angeles nightclub, she met a tall, handsome man named Henry Wynberg. He was three years her junior, born in Holland to working-class parents. He'd found work in California as a used-car salesman.

Of the woman he refers to as 'Elizabett', he recalls that the first thing he noticed about her was her great beauty, her silken yellow dress, and the fact that, indeed, she did wear real diamonds. Henry and Elizabeth began dating. 'She started calling me at all hours,' Henry recalled, 'confiding in me about her marriage problems with Burton. Before I knew where I was, I was in deep.'

Wynberg had nothing to do with show business, and perhaps it was precisely for that reason that Elizabeth seemed fascinated by him. The two had an innocent flirtation, nothing more. But then, much to her surprise, Wynberg showed up in Rome when he heard she was having trouble with Burton. He called her at the Grand Hotel to see how she was faring, and she invited him up for a drink. The next thing everyone in her life knew, Elizabeth was romantically involved with Henry Wynberg.

As she filmed *The Driver's Seat*, the couple was photographed all over Rome. It was a very public romance, and that was the way Elizabeth wanted it. She did nothing to hide it. They were photographed on a cliff in Italy, embracing. Fully aware of the photographers behind bushes and trees, she lifted her face to the breeze so that it would blow her hair back in serene undulation. She always knew how to be the perfect subject for a photo, even when she was supposed to be caught unawares; when in the company of photographers, though, Elizabeth Taylor was *never* unaware.

In November, Elizabeth ended up hospitalised at the University of California, complaining of severe stomach pains. It turned out she had an ovarian cyst. Her doctors didn't know whether it was malignant, so they would have to operate. Henry Wynberg took a bed next to Elizabeth's in her room and stayed with her. He wasn't long for that room, however, because as soon as Richard Burton, who was still in Italy filming *The Voyage*, heard about the situation, he was on the telephone to Elizabeth.

At first, Elizabeth was determined not to return his call. That lasted for about a day. Soon she was on the phone, begging him to visit her. She was sure she had cancer, she said, and she was scared. 'I don't want to die alone,' she said, crying. 'Please, can I come home?' The time away from her had been, as Burton recalled in his diary, 'six months of torture, agony'. He told her that he had stopped drinking. He was a different man, and he wanted—no, he *needed*—to see her as well.

The next day, Elizabeth had her surgery. The cyst was not malignant. There was great relief all round. Elizabeth checked out of the hospital and into the Scripps Clinic in La Jolla to recover. Wynberg got his extra bed in her room and started tending to his girlfriend's recovery.

The next weekend, though, Richard Burton had taken Wynberg's place in Elizabeth's room. He had flown in from Italy to claim his wife and had no intention of leaving the States without her. 'The next thing I knew,' Elizabeth recalls, 'he was by my bedside and we were kissing each other and crying. "Please come back with me," he asked.'

'It can all be over without warning,' he said at the time, 'and I can't bear the thought of losing the old girl.' He was determined, he said, to live each day to the fullest with her and never let another petty squabble come between them.

As soon as Elizabeth was released from the clinic, she and Richard took off for Naples, seeming happier than ever. 'Richard and I are together again,' said she, 'and it will be the happiest Christmas of my life.'

Elizabeth's recovery was, as always after any of her surgeries, difficult and longer than expected. Richard was at her side the entire time, showing great patience.

A few months later, the two were off to Oroville, California, a small town about an hour's drive north of Sacramento, where Richard was to begin filming *The Klansman*, a story of racial discord in the South.

Their marital bliss did not last long. They spent an unhappy tenth anniversary in Oroville, fighting and drinking. Unfortunately, whatever epiphany Richard had had when Elizabeth was in the hospital, faded with the passing of a short time. Now he was looking at other women.

'It was brutal,' publicist Dale Olson, who worked on the set of *The Klansman*, recalled. 'The final straw came when Burton presented an eighteen-year-old waitress with a ring and tried to act as if he was having an affair with her. I'm not sure he was, though. I think he was trying to make Elizabeth jealous.'

The girl in question was named Kim Dinucci. Beverly Wilcox was her best friend, also eighteen at the time. She recalls, 'There was no romance with Kim. In fact, Richard gave us *both* rings. We met him in the diner Kim worked in. When I asked about Elizabeth, he said, "'Tis she who is the repository for my heart."

'That night, he asked us to join him for dinner. So there we were, at a restaurant, with Elizabeth Taylor and Richard Burton. Burton started flirting with the waitress. He said, "Now there's a woman I would like to sleep with." Elizabeth said, "Why can't you stifle your little Welsh lusts until I'm out of the way?" It got very tense. Then Elizabeth left.

'After she was gone, Richard turned to us and said, "Would you two like a go of it, back at the motel?" We said no, absolutely not. It was pathetic and very sad.'

As soon as Elizabeth left town, Richard became deathly ill with a fever of 104° and was flat on his back at Saint John's Hospital in Santa Monica. He tried to phone Elizabeth, but she would not take his calls.

In April 1974, the Burtons announced that their reconciliation attempt had failed. They were getting a divorce. Two months later, on June 26, Elizabeth appeared in a courthouse in Saanen, near Gstaad, to finalise the divorce. Richard sent a doctor's certificate from the United States, saying he was too ill to appear.

The judge granted Elizabeth a divorce. She kept $5 million in jewels, even though they had been a joint investment for the couple. Richard, beaten down by the years, said, 'Just let her have them. Who cares?' She also got Casa Kimberly, lots of money, a priceless art collection, and was awarded custody of Maria, whom they had formally adopted as a couple in 1964.

IT WASN'T OVER YET. Indeed, if any of her friends sensed that Elizabeth's relationship with Richard had not ended with their divorce, it was because they realised how attached she had become not only to him but also to the melodrama that had characterised their relationship for so many years. Also, despite her anger with him and disappointment with how their marriage had turned out, she could not easily accept that she had invested so many years into a relationship only to have it fail.

For the following year and a half, Elizabeth had one foot planted firmly in the past—she and Richard spoke on the phone at least three times a week—and the other in the future: she and Henry Wynberg rented a home in Bel Air and began the next phase of their relationship.

In February 1975, Wynberg accompanied Elizabeth to Russia, where she would act in the first Soviet–American coproduction, a remake of the classic children's story *The Blue Bird*, directed by George Cukor.

On August 11, the night of the movie's wrap party, she received a telegram from Richard in Switzerland. He wanted to see her.

Three days later, on 14 August, Elizabeth and Henry arrived in Switzerland. That night, Elizabeth met Richard at a friend's villa for dinner. As soon as she saw him, she rushed into his arms, her face awash in tears. She'd missed him desperately, she said. He told her that he shared her heartache and that he wanted them to return to their romance.

The next day, Henry was on a plane back to the United States, alone. Elizabeth had told him earlier in the day that it was over between them.

Richard later recalled, 'Then for two days (16th and 17th), we circled each other—very wary, very polite. On the third day, we had a fight (18th). Then we knew we were ourselves again.'

Two days later, on August 20, they announced their plans to re-marry.

'I was upset,' said Diane Stevens, who was an associate of their press agent, John Springer. 'I called Elizabeth in Switzerland. "What in the world are you doing?" I asked. "I'm very worried about you."

'"I know, I know," she told me with a tone of resignation. "But I love him and he loves me. Won't you please be happy for us?"

'What could I say? "Of course I am happy for you," I told her. "I just hope you know what you're doing."

'She said, "Honestly, he's changed. He's so different, so loving. He's not drinking as much. I think this time it can work."'

Off Elizabeth went with Richard Burton—again—travelling about the world in a dizzy haze, from Switzerland to Italy to Israel and then South Africa, battling each other and loving each other, as was their way. Somehow, the conflicted lovers ended up in Botswana—and that's where, on October 10, 1975, they were again married. It would be Elizabeth's sixth marriage, to her fifth husband. They exchanged forty-dollar wedding bands.

In November, Richard celebrated his fiftieth birthday. He was sober but looked as if he was dying. His skin was a terrible shade of off-yellow, and it seemed as if he was suffering from tuberculosis. Elizabeth was drinking enough for the two of them; not only was she unhappy about Burton's failing health, she was already beginning to think she had made a mistake in remarrying him. He wasn't the man she had married eleven years earlier, that's for sure.

'I didn't think that their second marriage would last ten minutes,' recalled their personal bodyguard, Brian Haynes. 'But I could see that they seemed to need each other. When he was there, she seemed to hate him. When he was away, she couldn't bear to be without him.'

It was inevitable, perhaps, that Elizabeth would end up on the losing end of any bargain she had made with Richard to be happy 'until death do us part'. In Gstaad, during the Burtons' Christmas sojourn there, Richard met a tall blonde divorcée, Suzy Hunt. She was only twenty-seven. He was drawn to her immediately, much to Elizabeth's dismay. He would pursue this woman, and he informed his wife of his plan.

Hunt's involvement with Richard grew well beyond what Elizabeth had suspected, or at least hoped. Suzy wasn't merely a device to enrage her, thereby enlivening their humdrum marriage. Richard actually had feelings for this woman, or 'girl', as Elizabeth described her.

One evening, when an argument over her husband's new assignation had reached its crescendo, Elizabeth pointed towards the front door and said, 'That's it—I want you out!'

Richard, having expected the demand, said, 'My bag has been packed since breakfast.'

As he started to gather his things, she continued, 'Out of our room. You'll stay in this house.' Richard moved into a guest suite. Elizabeth knew that if he went out of that front door, he might never come back.

Elizabeth's plan to keep her husband close created at least one extremely uncomfortable moment, however, when Suzy picked Richard up at his and Elizabeth's home to go to a dinner party.

Elizabeth watched from the terrace outside the front door of their chalet as Hunt's limousine ground to a halt. Suzy emerged in a floor-length gown and glided up the stairs, not noticing Taylor.

'Stunning,' Elizabeth said, startling her. 'I always loved that dress. I'm so glad it found a good home.'

Suzy was speechless, seemingly overawed by Elizabeth's presence. 'You know, I'm sorry about this whole business,' she told

Elizabeth, according to what she later recalled. 'I never wanted to hurt you, of all people.'

Elizabeth had heard this speech before, but in the past, she hadn't been on the receiving end of it. 'My dear,' she said in a world-weary tone, 'you'll last only six months with Richard. That, I can guarantee.' It wasn't so much a threat as a prediction, based on years of experience.

'Well, perhaps you're right,' replied Suzy, 'but my, what a six months it shall be.'

Elizabeth forced a smile. 'Oh, certainly, dear, for all of us.'

IN JANUARY 1976, Robert Lantz, the agent representing Richard and Elizabeth, met Richard in Switzerland to discuss future projects. After a year of doing *Equus* on Broadway, Anthony Hopkins had left the show, and Tony Perkins had taken the role. Now Perkins's involvement was coming to an end, and Lantz went to see if he could motivate Richard into essaying the part. 'He was in terrible shape,' said Lantz. 'Tired, hungover, not well. He needed a project, something to get him back in the swing. He had a script and said he would read it over. The next morning, he came down the stairs, and I could see that he had not touched a drop of alcohol. He said, "I'll do it. I love the play, and I promise you I will be all right." And I said, "Well, you know, it can change your life if you can pull this off. But do me a favour. Don't let Elizabeth come. It will be a circus if you do." He said he would do his best.'

Richard left for New York to begin rehearsals for *Equus*, and he asked Suzy to join him. Of course, she flew to be at his side. He told friends that now that he was sober (for the time being), he couldn't imagine what had got into him that he'd decided to remarry Elizabeth. 'I don't know,' he said, 'don't even ask me. It's like a huge dream,' he said. 'I remember thinking, What am I doing here? Odd place to be married — in the bush, by an African gentleman. It was very curious. An extraordinary adventure, doomed from the start.'

In February, Elizabeth received a telephone call from Richard. He said that he needed to see her immediately. He was having a difficult time in rehearsals for *Equus*.

'It was very difficult for him to learn the lines,' said Robert Lantz. 'Tony Perkins gave up his last Saturday matinée before the Monday on which Burton was to make his debut. Peter Shaffer [the writer of the show] and I went to the theatre and sat in the last row. The lights went out, and the announcement came over the loudspeakers. "At this performance, Anthony Perkins will not appear." There was a big groan. "He will be replaced by Richard Burton." And the house exploded like at a ball game. Richard came on, and I can truthfully say he gave the worst performance any actor has ever given. I was mortified for him. After it was over, Peter and I went backstage.

'By the time we saw Richard, he had already been given hell by the director. Now he was filled with new motivation. He said, "Robbie, I'm going back to the hotel. I'm going to cancel every appointment. I'm going to rearrange the furniture in the suite so that it resembles the stage, and I'm going to rehearse by myself all day Saturday, Sunday and Monday, and I will appear Monday night as advertised." So Monday night came, and of course, it was a totally sold-out house. He then gave a much much better performance. Brilliant. I knew he could do it if he put his mind to it. But this was a tough time for him, a lot of distractions.'

Indeed, and one more was on her way, at Richard's behest.

PATRICK MCMAHON, who worked for Richard Burton at this time as an assistant, recalled, 'Richard came to the theatre [the Plymouth] in a good mood one morning, which was rare in those days, because he was nervous about the show and feeling inadequate in the role. "Guess what?" he said. "Elizabeth is coming today for lunch."

'Alarm bells went off in my head. Suzy [Hunt] had worked so hard to keep him off the bottle, and even though she hadn't been totally successful, he was drinking far less. The one thing, I felt, that could really throw him for a loop would be Elizabeth Taylor.

No one in the show really wanted her there, but really, how could you keep her away—especially after he had summoned her?'

Morning came and went with no Elizabeth. Richard seemed disappointed, often peering out into the empty theatre in anticipation.

Later in the afternoon, there was a bustling noise in the back of the Plymouth; then the back door opened. From the stage, Richard looked into the empty expanse to see Elizabeth walking down the centre aisle very carefully, as if she were an old woman. She was wearing jeans with a lavender blouse dotted with sequins, her hair in a big bouffant style.

'Oh, *dah-ling*,' she said in a loud voice. She stopped in the middle of the theatre and threw her arms out towards Richard with a theatrical flourish. 'I've arrived! Have you missed me? Why, it's been *hours*!' She then continued down the steps with great deliberation.

She took a seat just outside the orchestra section, with all eyes upon her. 'Oh, don't mind me,' she said with a dismissive hand wave. 'Just go on with your rehearsal.'

After the cast completed the act it had been working on, Elizabeth applauded loudly. 'Bravo!' she exclaimed. 'Bravo!'

'I think the old girl's had a bit too much to drink,' Richard said. He still hadn't even come down from the stage to greet her.

'I heard that, buster,' she said good-naturedly. 'And I'm not drunk. Not yet, anyway. But the day is still young.'

At that, Richard walked down the steps of the stage and to her seat. She rose, seeming unsteady, and the two embraced.

Patrick McMahon recalled, 'The sight of them together, "The Liz and Dick Show", well, it was something to see. The rest of the rehearsal was filled with her comments back up to the stage—all complimentary and exuberant, such as "Oh, my! *Yes!*" or "*Mahvellous!*" or "Perfection! Sheer *perfection*!" and Richard trying to hush her up from the stage. After they finished, Richard walked off the stage and straight to her. He took her by the hand, and the two walked up the steps very gingerly—I mean, you would have thought they were in their nineties—and then out of the theatre, seeming as happy as they could be.'

Alas, their post-marital bliss did not last long, as expected. They returned two hours later in the midst of an argument.

'You know that I hate to drink alone,' Elizabeth said.

'Well, you know better than to encourage me to drink,' he said.

'What the hell has *happened* to you?' she said.

'The fight was loud but also comical, and everyone present enjoyed their banter,' says Patrick McMahon. 'But by this time, I was very nervous. I wanted her out of there. If Suzy showed up, it would have been a horrible scene. As it was, the rest of the day was shot. Richard was disturbed and distracted. I just prayed she would not be back.'

The next day, rather than meet him at the theatre, Elizabeth met Richard at the Lombardy Hotel on East 56th Street. When she showed up, he was waiting for her, with Suzy Hunt at his side, at the hotel's bar. He seemed nervous and not as well as he had been the day before. The truth was that he knew he could not do the show—already tough on him—until he took care of some unfinished business with Elizabeth. It was draining enough, and he couldn't have loose ends with her. 'What's wrong with you, luv?' she asked, concerned.

'I want a divorce, luv,' he said meekly. One hand rose to touch Elizabeth's face. She backed away from it, staring at him for a moment, seeming at a loss for words. 'Why, you sonofabitch,' she finally said, her temper rising from zero to one hundred in no time. 'You dragged me all the way from Switzerland to tell me *that*?'

'I'm sorry, luv,' he said. Then he and Suzy walked away from her, leaving her standing alone in the bar.

She was upset, but not so much that she didn't go to one of his preview performances anyway. After the show, it was chilly backstage between them, as one might expect. The next day, when Richard got back to the theatre, he went to his dressing room and, in a scene right out of *Butterfield 8*, saw a message from Elizabeth, written in lipstick on the mirror. It said simply, 'You are fantastic, luv.' Richard didn't erase it for the entire run of the play.

On July 29, 1976, less than ten months after they were wed for a second time, Elizabeth and Richard were granted their second divorce. She said she wanted some jurisdiction over her own life, and the only way to obtain it was to let Richard go. 'I love Richard with every fibre of my soul. But we can't be together. We're too mutually self-destructive.'

Part Five

Coming to Terms

In the summer of 1976, as the paperwork was being finalised for Elizabeth Taylor's second divorce from Richard Burton, she was invited to a Washington bicentennial reception commemorating the two hundredth anniversary of the United States and honouring Queen Elizabeth II of England. The invitation came about because Henry Kissinger had met Elizabeth and Richard a year earlier in Israel and was enchanted by them. When he heard how terribly unhappy she was at her separation from Burton, he invited her to Washington, where she began attending social and political functions on almost a daily basis. 'She swept into Washington like Cleopatra into Rome,' wrote one reporter at the time. Her escort to most of the functions was Halston, her fashion designer.

When she began to consider her appearance at the bicentennial reception, Elizabeth knew she didn't want to go to the gala alone. British ambassador Sir Peter Ramsbotham suggested that she go with the chairman of the Bicentennial Commission, John Warner. Though she'd met him casually on several occasions, Elizabeth didn't remember him. However, after her date with him at the reception, she'd never forget him.

Republican politician John William Warner, Jr, was six feet tall and silver-haired. Born on February 18, 1927, he became a Navy man, serving during the last two years of World War II and then with the Marines in Korea. He got his law degree from the University of Virginia in 1956. A year later, he became an assistant US attorney in Washington. That same year, he married Catherine Mellon of the Pittsburgh Mellons, whose wealth of more than a billion dollars was derived from oil and banking.

In 1972, Warner became Richard M. Nixon's Secretary of the Navy. Shortly thereafter, in 1973, his marriage ended. With his divorce from Mellon netting him a settlement of almost $8 million, he was living quite comfortably at Atoka Farms, a 2,200-acre estate in Middleburg, Virginia.

In 1976, he took his position with the Bicentennial Commission. He was a distinguished man at the age of fifty, thought of as one of the most eligible bachelors in Washington. He was also a tad . . . dull. 'You never thought of him as being funny or charismatic,' said one person who knew him well at the time. 'He wasn't particularly witty, either. He was just a very nice, even-tempered man with simple tastes.'

Diane Stevens no longer worked for John Springer but had stayed in touch with Elizabeth over the years. She says, 'The romance with John happened very quickly. She went to his estate in Virginia, took a breath of fresh country air, and absolutely loved it. There were farm animals and tractors and horses and motorcycles, which she and John rode. "You would not believe the life John has," she told me on the phone that August. "It's so tranquil, so beautiful, with the most lovely rolling hills. If I never make another movie again and could live here for ever with no stress, I would be very happy." I told her I thought she would miss the pace of her jet-setting life. "Oh, please," she said. "I've been all over the world, and frankly, I'm exhausted. I am absolutely sick of being the main attraction in a three-ring circus. Is that so wrong?"'

Elizabeth had to leave the farm behind to go to Vienna late in the summer to film the movie version of Stephen Sondheim's Broadway hit *A Little Night Music*. She didn't really want to do it but had committed to the part earlier. She had to sing 'Send in the Clowns', which terrified her. 'Every great singer has done it,' she said, 'and now, here comes Chunko.' She gained fifteen pounds during this production.

While Elizabeth was in Vienna, she and John Warner had lengthy conversations about life and love and began forging their romantic relationship by long-distance telephone communication. But Warner slowly revealed himself to be quite the chauvinist. He made it clear that if Elizabeth was to be in his life, she would have to give up aspects of her own. 'That Hollywood stuff and all those jewels will have to go,' he told her. As she got to know him, she realised that he was a lot like her ex-husbands—controlling and manipulative. Rather than run for her life, she began to cling to him and become emotionally attached.

On October 1, 1976, John flew to Vienna, where he asked Elizabeth to marry him and presented her with a ring made of rubies, diamonds and sapphires. At the same time, he said that he would consider running either for governor of Virginia or a seat in the Senate. Warner was an ambitious politician. Did he want an alliance with one of the most famous and sought-after women of her time in order to help secure his political fortune? 'Oh, please,' said one person who knew Warner at the time. 'Of course. Not to say he didn't like her, and maybe even loved her. But anyone who thinks that politics wasn't part of his plan is being naive. John never did anything without an eye towards how it would affect his political career.'

On Saturday, December 4, 1976, Elizabeth married John Warner in an intimate sunset service at his Atoka Farms estate. The fifteen-minute ceremony was attended by only a few close friends and employees of the couple. At this same time, the incumbent Virginia senator William Scott announced that he would not seek re-election. The Warners would spend early 1977 testing the political waters for a possible senatorial candidacy.

Since much of John Warner's Republican constituency was conservative, the question was whether or not the 'wow factor' of Elizabeth Taylor's presence on his arm would outweigh the controversial image of a Hollywood actress who'd been married seven times. As John Warner's wife, her loyalty would be pushed to the extreme on the campaign trail. Could she survive without a limousine at her beck and call and instead travel on a Greyhound bus? Could she survive without her hairdresser, her make-up woman? Could she give of herself in an unselfish manner to someone else's cause, a venture that really had nothing to do with her own career or her own interests?

Shaking hands with people in the 'real world', kissing their babies and making conversation, all the while smiling cheerfully, was a new version of Elizabeth Taylor, one that captivated her public. Her fans were used to Elizabeth running *from* them, not *towards* them. Paparazzi had for years been the bane of her existence. Now she had to accommodate them and smile gamely, rather than risk the wrong kind of picture being published in the press.

Elizabeth would later observe that the discipline she'd depended on as an actress would be key to her success on the campaign trail. Despite any difficulties she may have experienced, there was something redemptive about this time in Elizabeth's life. 'The campaign was harder than anything I'd done in my own career,' she would later say, 'but there was something exhilarating about it.' Indeed, she had to admit that giving of herself in this way felt good and made her feel that she was contributing to something that really mattered. Still, it ate away at her that she wasn't being true to who she was as a woman, as a movie star. She enjoyed what she was doing with John, but on a deep level—as she would later explain—she wished that she could experience that sense of generosity and also preserve her identity as a star.

In the end, John lost his party's vote to run for the Senate. The victory went to his opponent, Richard Obenshain. He would be running against Democratic candidate Andrew P. Miller.

Elizabeth returned to Virginia in July, determined to help John find a place in politics. But then, in a twist as sudden and tragic as any of Elizabeth's plotlines, Richard Obenshain was killed on August 2 in a plane crash. The task of picking a new nominee fell to the seventy-eight-member Republican State Central Committee. They chose John Warner.

For the next three months, Warner would campaign tirelessly, spending more than a million dollars in his bid to convince voters that he would do them proud as their senator. Everywhere he went, Elizabeth was at his side. The days were long and the work gruelling, but Elizabeth was determined that she would see it through.

Finally, on November 7, 1978, John Warner was elected to the United States Senate by less than a one per cent margin. Out of 1.2 million votes, he won by just 4,271. Without Elizabeth, there's little doubt he would have lost. 'I cannot tell you how happy and proud I was of him,' she said, remembering the day John Warner was sworn into office. 'The ceremony marked one of the happiest moments of my life. I had no idea that it also marked the beginning of the end of my marriage.'

'THE PRESSURE to stay youthful and beautiful had been one she'd lived with all her life,' said one friend. 'With the passing of time, Hollywood was losing interest. She was depressed about it, drinking a lot because of it.'

One of the biggest problems in Elizabeth's life until she married the senator had to do with time: she never had any — to think, to review, to assess where she'd been, to contemplate where she was headed. Now, though, there was little else to do in those rolling hills of Virginia. It was then that she began to review some — though certainly not all — aspects of her past.

It could be argued that Warner used Elizabeth when he needed her during his senatorial campaign but then left her to her own devices for the rest of their marriage. Elizabeth says today that when he was elected, she found herself 'in a kind of domestic Siberia'.

On some weekends, she would flee to the East 68th Street digs of her friend and fashion designer, Halston, in Manhattan. During these sojourns, she would hang out with Andy Warhol and Truman Capote at Studio 54 and party with the Liza Minnelli crowd. The tabloid press had a field day, publishing unflattering pictures of an overweight, boozy, obviously miserable Taylor. It was reported that her weight had ballooned to nearly two hundred pounds.

Elizabeth became more depressed than she'd ever been before.

Her only outlet was to eat and drink and take pills to escape her unhappiness. As her weight soared, she continued to eat to dull her pain. By the end of 1979, Elizabeth was in real trouble. Her marriage was just about over—they were living separate lives, his outside the house and hers in it—and her health had seriously deteriorated.

The day that Elizabeth forced herself to look into a full-length mirror after getting out of the bath was one she would not soon forget. As she gazed at her reflection, she realised that not only was she no longer the most beautiful woman in the world, but that she had allowed the circumstances of her life to crush her. It was on that day that she knew she had to accept the truth about herself and deal with it. Somehow.

Once Elizabeth decided that she had to lose weight, she was dedicated to doing it. She decided to recapture some of her career, thinking that if she were motivated to lose weight because of an impending role, she might be more likely to stick to a diet.

She had been saying that she wanted to do something on the stage, a real challenge for her. She reached out to producer Zev Bufman, and the two chose to mount a production of *The Little Foxes*, for which she would be paid $50,000 a week—a pittance considering what she was used to earning, but still more than any other actress had ever been paid to do theatre work.

WHEN LILLIAN HELLMAN'S Gothic drama *The Little Foxes* was first translated from stage to screen in 1941, four members from the Broadway cast were invited to re-create their roles in the film version. Noticeably absent was Tallulah Bankhead, who had been a sensation on the Great White Way—Broadway—as Regina Giddens. Bette Davis, then at the pinnacle of her star power, went after and got the role on screen of the greedy, murderous, beautiful Regina. Now, forty years later, in 1981, Elizabeth, with a string of successful film roles in which she had played strong southern beauties, decided to add Regina to her portrait gallery of wilful femmes fatales.

Her director, Austin Pendleton, remembers his first meeting with his leading lady. 'My first reaction when she walked into the room was that she was a person who has a great appetite for life, for living, for connecting with people. I knew she would have no trouble making the transition from film to stage because so many of her movies were adaptations of theatre pieces—*Cat on a Hot Tin Roof*, *Virginia Woolf*, *Suddenly, Last Summer*—where you had long-sustained narrations, and I knew if she could do that in front of a camera, she could do it onstage, too.'

To begin losing weight, Elizabeth went to a health spa. Over a period of months, she eventually lost forty pounds. She had a goal: to get onstage and not look heavy in her costumes. She felt a responsibility not only to herself, but to the audience that would be paying money to see her. She wanted to look her best for them.

The Little Foxes' pre-Broadway tour had its premiere on February 27, 1981, Elizabeth's forty-ninth birthday, at the Parker Playhouse in Fort Lauderdale, Florida. The show opened at the Martin Beck Theater (since renamed the Al Hirschfeld Theater) on May 7, 1981. The reviews would be mixed, but the audience reception was strong. An hour after the final curtain, when she strode into Sardi's on the arm of John Warner, everyone in the restaurant stood up and began applauding.

Elizabeth appeared for 123 sold-out performances, until September 6. The play was a personal success for her, and for it she was nominated for a Tony. The show then moved on to New Orleans and Los Angeles.

Throughout the run of *The Little Foxes*, John Warner was not really in Elizabeth's life, though they were still married. It was clear to them both that the marriage was over. It became even clearer to Elizabeth when he called her and told her that he had sold the estate and bought an apartment. She would have to find a place for her animals, he said.

She had horses and dogs and cats and nowhere to put them. Certainly she deserved more consideration! She noted that she had even sold the famous Burton-Taylor diamond for $3 million (three times what Burton paid for it) to help defray the costs of Warner's political campaigns. She said she was 'sick' about having parted with it.

The official announcement came on December 21, 1981: John Warner and Elizabeth Taylor were separating. By the beginning of 1982, Elizabeth had moved back to Los Angeles, purchasing the home of Nancy Sinatra, on top of a steep hill in a heavily wooded section of Bel Air, for about $2 million. This beautiful estate, behind stone walls and iron gates, complete with swimming pool and amazing view of LA's wide vista, was to be her last home.

ELIZABETH ARRIVED in London on February 23, 1982, to begin rehearsals for *The Little Foxes* there (which was scheduled to open on March 11). Her first order of business was to visit Richard Burton. She hadn't seen him since 1976, when he'd asked her for a divorce in a New York hotel. Since that time, they had both married other people. Still, when she was taken to the hospital on Christmas Eve 1981, complaining of chest pains, who was the first person she called? Richard. The two commiserated about their ruined marriages, hers to Warner and his to Suzy Hunt, from whom he was now separated. They promised to see each other in February, when Elizabeth would be in London for the opening of *The Little Foxes* and her fiftieth birthday party. That time was now upon her.

There had been a dark flip side in coming to terms with the past for Elizabeth. The more she thought about days gone by, the more she drank to escape the pain of so many memories. In recent years, her drinking had become out of control. She was sinking into a dark abyss.

As she drank, she also took pills—Percodan being her drug of choice to numb the pain, not only in her body but in her heart. 'Drugs had become a crutch,' she would later admit. 'I wouldn't take them just when I was in pain. I needed oblivion, escape . . . I was hooked on Percodan.'

It was in this treacherous environment of alcohol and drug usage that Elizabeth attempted to sort out her past with Richard. Even under the most sober of times, it would have been a challenge to sift through the wreckage of their two marriages and divorces. In the end, the conclusion she finally came to could not have been more depressing: she loved him for no reason other than that she'd always been compelled to do so. And worse, she had to admit that she still felt the same way about him.

On the day that Richard was to arrive in London for a charity performance of fellow Welshman Dylan Thomas's *Under Milk Wood*, Elizabeth called him and reminded him that they'd agreed to see each other. He remembered and said he couldn't wait to see her as well.

ELIZABETH SENT A CAR to collect Richard at the airport and bring him to her Chelsea town house, which had been leased for the run of the play. When he showed up at her doorstep, she was stunned by how he had aged. He was fifty-six, but he looked fifteen years older. He was thin—down from his ideal weight of 175 pounds to about 140—and weak. Not only had all the drink caught up with him, he was in unremitting pain from a damaged nerve in his hip that had made his right arm almost useless. He'd also had back surgery almost a year earlier and had not fully recovered from it.

She thought he looked terrible; her heart went out to him. She suspected he felt the same way about her—after all, she was terribly overweight and seemed out of breath just running to the car to greet him. She had been on the road with *The Little Foxes* for eighteen months and had gained back all the weight she'd lost, and then some.

For a few moments, Elizabeth and Richard took each other in, probably wondering how they—two of the most beautiful and sexy figures of the 1960s—had turned out as they had in the 1980s. They ignored the obvious about each other and made small talk. Elizabeth invited Richard to a birthday party being thrown for her by producer Zev Bufman at a discotheque called Legends.

The birthday party for Elizabeth's fiftieth was difficult. She wore a silver-and-purple harem pants outfit, in which, given her weight, she did not look her best. 'I recently came across a picture taken at my party,' she once recalled. 'It made me shiver. My eyes had disappeared into suet. I'm wearing stage make-up, and I look like a drag queen. I did my best to deny the truth,' she said, 'but my self-image suffered badly.'

Richard wore some sort of mink jacket with slacks. His shoulders were stooped, his posture that of a much older man.

Guests at the party included Tony Bennett, Ringo Starr and Elizabeth's children. Richard did not drink much at first, but Elizabeth, no doubt feeling the pressure of the evening, did not know when to stop. She would later admit that during this time, she could not leave the house without taking at least two Percodans mixed with Jack Daniel's. She felt that the combination of the drug and alcohol made her somehow more talkative and social. 'It gave me false courage,' she would say. 'Then, during the course of an evening—like every four hours—I'd take another two Percodans. And, of course, I had a hollow leg. I could drink anybody under the table. My capacity to consume was terrifying.'

One of Richard's attorneys, Aaron Hill, was present at the party. He recalled that at one point in the evening, Elizabeth approached Richard, a glass of champagne in each hand. She handed one to him. 'Here, darling, a toast,' she said. 'To us.'

Richard took the glass. 'Perhaps you shouldn't, luv,' he said, taking her glass from her as well. She quickly took it back. 'I *said* . . . a toast,' she insisted. Some of the party guests sheepishly gathered round her, seeming embarrassed. 'To us. The greatest damned couple of all time. *Liz and Dick*,' she continued, slurring her words. 'Long may we live . . . to love and torture each other . . . until death do us part . . . *and even then*!'

'Hear! Hear!' someone said as people raised their glasses.

'That was quite a toast, my luv,' Richard remarked.

'You bet it was,' Elizabeth said, clinking his glass. Then she dragged him onto the dance floor. She danced in a seductive circle in her harem outfit, all round Richard, to the pounding disco rhythm of Donna Summer's 'Love to Love You Baby'. Richard just stood frozen in the middle of the floor, stiffly wagging nothing more than his head from left to right.

At one thirty in the morning, Elizabeth took Richard back to her town house. They were both intoxicated. She put him to bed and lay next to him, as she would recall it, until she knew he was asleep. She spent the night staring at his face, trying to divine just what it was about him that had held her captive for so many years. She still loved him, that much she knew. She fell asleep with her head on his chest. In the morning, she woke with a pounding headache, her head on a pillow. He was gone.

That night, Elizabeth felt that she had to see Richard. She knew that he was performing *Under Milk Wood* at the Duke of York's Theatre and decided that she would attend the performance.

While Richard was onstage working, Elizabeth suddenly walked out from the curtain behind him. The audience erupted into applause, but Burton didn't know why until he turned round and saw his ex-wife. Had she intended to sabotage his performance? He looked startled and upset. As the crowd cheered, Elizabeth took a deep bow. 'Oh, thank you all so very much,' she said. After the crowd simmered down, she turned to Richard and, in Welsh, said sweetly, 'I love you.'

'Say it again, my petal,' Richard said. 'And say it louder.'

'I love you!' she exclaimed, again in Welsh. Again the audience cheered, this time on its feet.

After she walked offstage, Richard tried to resume his performance, but he had lost his place in the script. 'I've got the wrong page,' he said, apologising. 'Excuse me. I'm a tad distracted.'

After the performance, Elizabeth and Richard went back to her house. They had a few drinks and a few laughs, and then he went home. Elizabeth felt happier than she'd been in some time and went to bed and slept soundly for the first time in months.

The next morning, though, she woke up to a huge disappointment. Apparently, when Richard had shown up at his hotel the morning after he'd spent the night at her home, after her birthday party, the press had been lying in wait for him. They wanted clarification of his relationship with Elizabeth. Now, those comments were all over the papers. His version of what happened the night of her birthday was not truthful: 'Elizabeth and I went back to her house after her party. Elizabeth said, "Hey, aren't you going to kiss me?" I took her in my arms and kissed her. After we kissed, I pulled her down on the couch . . . for old times' sake.'

After that comment, which suggested that he and Elizabeth had made love, Richard was on a roll. His appearance with Elizabeth had generated interest in him and in *Under Milk Wood*, and he obviously liked the attention. He told the reporters that Elizabeth had to sell the Burton-Taylor diamond 'to support' John Warner. He seemed miffed that she got $3 million for it and asked, 'Why didn't the little bitch sell it back to me?' He said that Elizabeth wanted nothing more than to marry him again but that he refused to do so. 'She's an erotic legend—a black-haired dwarf with a big stomach and overflowing breasts. I love her.' As for her try on the London stage in *The Little Foxes*, he took the opportunity to interfere with her chances with the critics, saying, 'I firmly believe she cannot act onstage. In fact, when it comes to the stage, I always tell Elizabeth that she is a divine joke.'

When Elizabeth read Richard's account of the evening and then his subsequent comments about her, she was crushed. Aaron Hill, Richard's attorney, recalled, 'Elizabeth called me in tears. She said that she couldn't believe the things coming out of Richard's mouth.

'I told her, "Elizabeth, look, he's obviously trying to push you away. He loves you, but he knows that you are poison together." I didn't want to tell her that he'd met someone else in Vienna [Sally Hay, thirty-four years old and the production assistant on the movie he was working on at the time, *Wagner*]. I wasn't sure if she knew or not. But I knew that Richard had become serious about this other woman very quickly.

'"But if he would just give us a chance," she said. "We're older and wiser now." I begged her to leave him alone. I told her that he would continue to torture her with his words and actions until she was either gone from him for ever or she hated him. She said that they had been beating each other up for so long, she didn't know what to think about any of it.' She then asked Hill to meet her at her home to discuss the matter.

When he showed up at Elizabeth's door, her eyes were red from crying. He sat down in the parlour, she across from him.

'So have you talked to Richard about me?' Elizabeth asked, according to Aaron's memory. Her voice was flat and devoid of expression.

'Yes, I have,' Aaron said, lying. 'Elizabeth, he's so very sorry he hurt you. He said he didn't mean a single word of it.'

'But you told me earlier that he was trying to push me away,' Elizabeth said. 'Which is it? Is he sorry, or is he trying to get rid of me?'

'It's *both*, Elizabeth. You have to leave him alone.'

'But he looks so sick,' she said. 'He needs me now more than ever.'

Aaron had no comment. He was struck by her devotion, especially in light of Richard's very cruel public comments.

'So listen. I have an idea,' Elizabeth continued, speaking with confidence. 'Zev [Bufman] and I were talking, and we thought it would be *fabulous* if Richard and I were to do a show together . . . We're thinking of Noël Coward's *Private Lives*. Just think of the *money* we could make. Liz and Dick onstage, for all their fans to see. I would have a chance to keep an eye on him, and . . . Who knows what can happen? Maybe a *third* marriage,' she said with a laugh, but probably not kidding. 'Isn't this a *grand* idea? Tell me you'll talk to Richard and convince him. Promise me.'

Hill promised to talk to Richard about Elizabeth's proposition.

As 1982 CAME to a close, for Elizabeth, the happiest memories of the year probably involved her children. In February, she had married off her adopted daughter, Maria—now twenty-one—to entertainment agent Steve Carson. Maria had grown into a beautiful woman, and with her bluish green eyes, dark hair and full face, she actually looked as if she could be Elizabeth's natural daughter. Now she was working as a model, and her previous handicaps were all but forgotten. (Maria would have a baby in November 1983, naming the child after her beloved mother.)

Later in the year, Michael would marry Brooke Palance,

daughter of the actor Jack Palance. An actor himself, though one for whom commercial success had always been elusive, Michael was heartened by his mother's unwavering support of his career. He'd turned out to be a level-headed, respectable person, getting past his hippie phase with apparent ease.

A year earlier, in 1981, his brother, Christopher, had married Aileen Getty, an oil heiress and grandchild of billionaire John Paul Getty. They would have two children and move to Pebble Beach, Florida, where Christopher would become a stained-glass artist.

Then, in 1984, Liza would marry artist Hap Tivey. Over the years, Elizabeth had done the best she could with her children, despite her own problems, and apparently it was enough, because her children did seem to turn out quite well. As she put it at Maria's wedding, 'God has kept an eye on my children, I think, even during the times when I wasn't able to do so.'

AFTER HAVING SEEN Richard in London, Elizabeth spent the rest of the year obsessing over him. Earlier, in July and at the end of the run of *The Little Foxes* in London, he'd had the audacity to show up backstage with his new girlfriend, Sally Hay. Elizabeth tried to be cordial, but it was difficult. Richard had obviously moved on . . . again. She would not give up hope, though, that maybe they would be together again, somehow.

The good news for her was that he had agreed to star with her in *Private Lives*, which would begin its run on Broadway in the spring of 1983, produced by her newly formed Elizabeth Taylor Theater Company.

Noël Coward's *Private Lives* is a comic gem. The play opens with two newly married couples, Elyot and Sybil and Amanda and Victor, who are honeymooning in the same hotel. The problem is that Elyot and Amanda were once married and, through happenstance, are reunited when they share an adjoining terrace with their new spouses. It's a clever comedy that takes wit and subtlety to pull off. Elizabeth and Richard were a lot of things, but subtle wasn't one of them.

By the second week of March 1983, Elizabeth and Richard were in New York to begin rehearsals for the play. The night before the first run-through, Elizabeth was in a restaurant with her date, Victor Luna, a wealthy Mexican attorney she had recently begun seeing, and Richard and Sally. It was a wretched evening. Her greatest frustration was that she couldn't get Richard's attention. All his focus was on Sally. Elizabeth hated the way he acted when he was with her.

The next day, at that first rehearsal, Elizabeth showed up without so much as having read the play, let alone memorised her lines. As usual, Richard not only knew his lines, but hers as well. Once upon a time, she had found that habit appealing. Now, she just found it irritating.

In his diaries of this time, Richard wrote about the rehearsals for *Private Lives*. On 14 March, he said that Elizabeth was in such bad shape, she couldn't even read the script. He found her to be as 'exciting as a flounder' as she rehearsed, but hoped she would rise to the occasion. He also wrote that she had begun to bore him, which he never would have imagined possible. Twice an hour, he wrote, she would complain to him about her abject loneliness. Though concerned about her, he admitted it would not have bothered him in the least if he had to be replaced in the role.

Private Lives previewed at the Shubert in Boston on April 7 for a limited run, then at the Lunt-Fontanne on Broadway on May 8, 1983. Opening night was a mess. The curtain went up thirty-five minutes late. Then the intermission between the first and second acts was longer than the first act! The next morning, Frank Rich of the *New York Times* wrote a raspberry of a review: '[It has] all the vitality of a Madame Tussaud exhibit.' Burton, though sober at the time, suddenly refused to stick to the script, despite having been the only one to know the show inside out by the first rehearsal. His ad-libs threw off the other cast members.

Though it was savaged by the critics, the show made enough money in advance sales that it had to go on. Elizabeth and Richard downplayed the effect their poor notices had on them. In actuality, though, it was a stressful time. Richard was not used to being panned, and he felt that if Elizabeth hadn't been sharing the stage with him, the show would have been received differently. However, the simple mathematics of the box-office figures made it clear: their fans wanted Liz and Dick together again. If the public only knew what was going on backstage . . .

Richard understood the unspoken—that Elizabeth had designs on him and a possible third marriage—and he was not interested. He was trying to take care of himself, and the less emotional chaos around him, the better. In fact, the combination of the poor reviews and Elizabeth's unpredictable moods led him to want out.

Richard, Elizabeth and two of their associates met at the Laurent Hotel in New York, where Richard was to plead his case. He explained that he needed to be released from *Private Lives*. Elizabeth listened to her ex-husband's pitch, then took a few moments to deliberate.

'Richard, I think it would be very wrong to disappoint our fans,' she told him. 'So I have to say no.' She was not going to let him out of his contract.

For a moment, Richard was speechless. 'Very well, then,' he announced as he rose to leave, his tone deep and theatrical.

He left the meeting without saying a word about his true feelings rather than giving Elizabeth the satisfaction of knowing how angry he was about the matter. Still, his attempts to leave the production had made it clear to Elizabeth that he didn't have the emotional attachment to this project that she did. It was business for him, so she would make it business for her as well. And what better way to clarify that her personal life didn't include him than to present her romantic interest in another man publicly? She had not kept her relationship with Victor Luna a secret, but prior to Richard's attempt to flee *Private Lives*, she rarely mentioned Victor's name. Suddenly, Elizabeth's backstage conversations began revolving round Luna. She even cancelled a few performances, announcing that she and Victor had to go off somewhere to 'recuperate' from another one of her illnesses. This infuriated

Richard, who said, 'This has proved it. I can never get together with that woman again.'

On a few occasions, Elizabeth had her understudy step in to perform. To Richard's horror, people would stand up during those performances and actually leave the theatre. Without Elizabeth in the show, some felt it a waste of time. It was a humiliating experience for Richard.

'She won't let me out of my contract, yet *she* never shows up for work,' he fumed. 'And she's taking *him* with her. Enough is enough!'

Richard summoned Bob Wilson (his secretary) and Ron Berkeley (his hairdresser) to his suite. 'I have an announcement to make,' he said. 'Sally and I are getting married.'

Both men realised that Richard's sudden decision to wed was made out of anger. 'You're only doing this to spite Elizabeth,' Ron said. 'Don't do it, Rich. Not right now.'

'Maybe you're right,' Richard said angrily. 'But I don't care. I'm marrying Sally immediately. So don't try to stop me.'

RICHARD AND SALLY went to Las Vegas and were married on July 3, 1983. Afterwards, he telephoned his brother Graham Jenkins and told him the good news. Graham, not realising that Burton had not yet told Elizabeth, called friends at the BBC to pass the news on to the media.

The next morning, the Fourth of July, Elizabeth opened her news-paper to find that Richard had officially declared his independence from her, again, by marrying someone else. That she had to read about it in the newspaper rather than hear about it from him was, for her, a dagger in the heart. She couldn't believe his cruelty.

To save face, Elizabeth issued a statement saying she was 'thrilled and delighted' for the newlyweds. Soon after, she announced her own engagement to Victor Luna—though, in retrospect, it would seem that she had no real intention of marrying him.

During the course of the Broadway run, Elizabeth would be unable to appear more than a dozen times due to her 'laryngitis'.

The play's audiences attended faithfully, though. But word gets round pretty quickly in Times Square, and attendance soon dwindled. It closed on July 17, almost a month earlier than it was scheduled to end. It hardly mattered: a four-week booking into the Forrest Theater in Philadelphia began on July 20.

The couple's agent, Robert Lantz, recalls, 'It was while we were in Philadelphia that a meal was planned for the newlyweds—Richard and Sally—and the newly engaged couple, Elizabeth and Victor.'

'Look at my ring, Robbie,' Elizabeth said, holding out her hand. 'From my sweetheart, Victor. Oh, Robbie, we are just so happy,' she added, really putting it on, obviously trying to vex Richard.

'Why, it's quite nice,' Lantz said.

Richard inspected the ring as well. 'Hmmm. One carat, I see,' he said dryly. 'You *are* on a diet, aren't you, luv?'

Everyone laughed nervously. Everyone, that is, except Elizabeth.

Robert Lantz recalls, 'Actually, the show they were doing *offstage* was much more entertaining than the one they were doing onstage.'

After stops in Washington and Chicago, the *Private Lives* tour finally ended in Los Angeles, in November 1983. I sat in the audience of their final performance. The show went off without a hitch until the third act, when Elizabeth began throwing biscuits at someone in the first row, as if sharing a private joke with that person. From that point on, it seemed as if all bets were off as Elizabeth followed Richard's lead of not sticking to the script. The two started making up dialogue as they went along. The audience ate up their antics, as if finally being given entrée to the private lives of two celebrities whose fame and notoriety had kept them on tenterhooks for almost a quarter of a century.

Backstage, there was no heartfelt farewell between old lovers, no moment that Elizabeth Taylor and Richard Burton might take with them and remember for the rest of their lives. Though Elizabeth at fifty-one, and Richard, fifty-seven, had each made in excess of a million dollars during the play's run, both were left to wonder if it had been worth it.

Elizabeth went to her dressing room and greeted the usual

smattering of VIPs, thanking them for coming. When they had all been shuttled out, a wardrobe assistant came to fetch her glittering stage costume. Taylor was sitting in the dressing room, staring into a mirror, occasionally tipping back a glass of whisky. Still wearing her costume, she said, 'No need to have this cleaned. It will be burned in a few hours.'

The assistant laughed awkwardly and told Elizabeth how honoured she was to have worked with her. Before going, the wardrobe girl asked, 'Is there anything I can do for you?'

Only the sound of clinking ice cubes was heard for a moment. Then, without moving, Elizabeth said, 'I'm just going to stay here a while. Sometimes miracles happen.'

No one knows if she was waiting for Richard to come and say his goodbyes or whether she hoped for some other 'miracle'. However, as it would happen, after that final show Richard immediately went with his new wife back to Europe, where the two would, he hoped, live a good and long life together. After waiting for about an hour, Elizabeth had little choice but to go her way as well, only alone.

By December 1983, Elizabeth Taylor's friends and family were truly afraid for her life. 'You would be talking to her, and suddenly you would realise that she had passed out with her eyes open,' one intimate recalled. 'She would appear to be dead, her breathing so light. You would call an ambulance. They would rush her to Cedars [hospital], sirens blazing. They would save her.

'The next day, she would be released, drinking from a flask and taking pills in the car on the way home, thanks to all her enablers who surrounded her and refused to tell her no. She'd spend hours on the phone, talking to anyone who would listen about Richard and how he had hurt her but how she would take him back again if he wanted her. Then, again, another scare and back to the hospital, sirens blazing.'

During one of her hospitalisations—this one for colitis—on Monday December 5, she woke to a room full of visitors. Her brother, Howard, was present, as were three of her children, Christopher, Michael and Liza. Also present was her good friend Roddy McDowall and her doctor. At first she was surprised that they had all come to visit at the same time. How nice, she thought. She was happy to see them. However, that feeling didn't last long. Each took a folding chair and put it at her bedside, encircling her. Each then began telling her that they couldn't bear to see what she was doing to herself. They wanted her to get help. Then each read from a prepared paper a litany of transgressions — how she had hurt them, how she had embarrassed them, how she had humiliated herself. They each ended by saying that if she didn't get off drugs, they were certain that she would soon kill herself.

When she looked up at them from her sickbed, she could see the pain in their eyes. It hit her hard that she was the cause of it. Howard said that they wanted to take her to a 'clinic', as he called it, to help her reconcile not only her drinking and drug habits but also her emotional problems. 'Well, I need time to think about it,' Elizabeth said, unsure how to proceed. 'I need two hours.'

After they left her room, she began to ruminate on what they'd told her. She'd always thought of herself as the one to make decisions about her future, and now she was being told that she must do something she wasn't sure she wanted to do. However, she also couldn't imagine living another day in such despair and, worse yet, inflicting it upon her loved ones. She thought about every word they had said to her, and she knew they were right.

In two hours, everyone returned to her room. Elizabeth told them that she would go with them. They checked her out of the hospital and drove her two hours from Los Angeles to Rancho Mirage, a suburb of Palm Springs. There, Elizabeth would be checked into the Betty Ford Center, where she would begin the next chapter of her life.

AT THAT TIME, the Betty Ford Center, founded the previous year by former First Lady Betty Ford, was not widely known. As in Elizabeth's intervention, President Gerald Ford and the four

Ford children had confronted Mrs Ford with her own addiction to alcohol and prescription drugs. After she was treated for chemical dependency at the United States Naval Hospital, she sought to establish a treatment centre that was, at first, to be targeted to women's needs. The Betty Ford Center is comprised of nine complexes alongside a man-made pond in the middle of a desert oasis. Surrounded by rolling sand dunes and verdant hillsides, it soon became a facility for men and women, with half its space devoted to each. Elizabeth put the centre in the news by being the first major celebrity to seek treatment there. After her highly publicised treatment, dozens of celebrities would follow her example — Liza Minnelli, Mary Tyler Moore, Johnny Cash, Robert Downey, Jr, Tony Curtis, and even Eddie Fisher. But in December 1983, Elizabeth was the first.

Elizabeth was dropped off at the front door of the Betty Ford Center, her friends and family not permitted to enter with her or spend a great deal of time saying goodbye. A nurse's aide met her at the door and walked her to a sparse room with two beds — which cost about $150 per night. She had no make-up and no clothes, except for those on her back.

For the next seven weeks, Elizabeth would wear jeans and sweaters or athletic wear. She would rise at 6.30 a.m. for breakfast at seven. She would eat in the cafeteria with the others, do daily chores, and attend meetings similar to Alcoholics Anonymous. Though there are no bars on the windows, no locks on the front doors ('It's your honour that keeps you there,' she would later explain), on that first night she was more terrified, she would admit, than she'd ever been in the past.

The first week was spent detoxifying. She went through terrible episodes of withdrawal, as one can imagine, given the amount of time she'd depended upon alcohol and drugs. It would take a week before she could say the words that marked her first step towards recovery: 'Hello. My name is Elizabeth, and I'm an alcoholic and a drug addict.'

It was in group therapy that Elizabeth finally faced the truth about herself. It wasn't easy for her to speak about her personal problems in front of strangers. As one of the most famous women on the planet, she didn't have the cloak of anonymity that gave others the freedom to be open about their mistakes.

One woman who attended group therapy with Elizabeth recalls, 'She was completely without artifice, totally unpretentious, so much so that when she would casually drop a sentence such as, "That reminds me of the time Eddie and I fought about Debbie", it was a little jarring because you knew exactly who she was talking about. If it took her a few beats to adjust, I can tell you that it took many of us equal time to do the same thing. It's not every day you sit in a room with Elizabeth Taylor and have her cleanse her soul.'

Of course, Elizabeth faced problems the others in her group could never truly understand, try as they might. She'd been a star since childhood, her life often mirroring the film roles in which she'd immersed herself. The fact that she never had a 'real' childhood was something that had bothered her for years, but she said she didn't realise how much of an issue it was for her until it came up during therapy.

'She had been working since the age of nine,' said a friend of hers who has talked at length with her about her recovery. 'Frankly, she felt cheated. She felt, somehow, wronged. She blamed her parents. Why couldn't her father have tempered her mother's ambition so that she could have had a more normal lifestyle? She had to come to terms with the fact that even though her life was not the norm, it was what it was, and she had the privileged life she'd had partially as a result of her mother's persistence and determination. "It certainly wasn't Mother's fault that I drank and ate and took pills once I became a star," she told me. That was *her* choice. It was how she had decided to reconcile her fame, the pressures of her lifestyle, and public image versus her private self.'

Through therapy, she began to clarify in her mind that most of her actions regarding not only Richard but also her other husbands were made under the influence of alcohol and drugs. She'd even tried to kill herself! Now, it was impossible for her to fathom that she had ever thought life was not worth living.

Perhaps the most important element of her treatment at the Betty Ford Center had to do with the cultivation of an inner life. Prior to being admitted to the centre, the most time Elizabeth had ever spent analysing her years on this planet was when she was married to John Warner. She'd come to certain decisions at that time, most having to do with her loss of identity and her need to lose weight in order to once again feel a sense of pride about herself. However, unguided by professional mental-health care workers, any dissection of her life usually led to heavy drinking and taking of medications to dull the pain of bad memories. At the Betty Ford Center, therapists were present to guide her through her tumultuous history and to assist her in coming to terms with it. It soon became clear to her that her unsupervised evaluations of the past were largely responsible for her having become reattached and obsessed with Richard Burton.

Though it was a difficult seven weeks, the time would have a great impact on her. During the next year, Elizabeth would return to the centre for periodic outpatient therapy sessions to gauge her progress. After all, the Betty Ford Center does not offer its patients a quick fix, but rather the tools to maintain their sobriety in the outside world. When a sober Elizabeth Taylor was finally released from the Betty Ford Center on January 20, 1984, she realised that the real work was still ahead of her.

ELIZABETH WAS AT HOME with her daughter Maria in Bel Air on August 6, 1984, when the call came from her publicist, Chen Sam. Richard Burton's longtime associate, Valerie Douglas, had just phoned Chen to give her the most dreadful news, and now she had the terrible task of passing it on to Elizabeth: Richard was dead.

A day and a half earlier, on August 4, he had complained of a headache. His wife of thirteen months, Sally, thinking it nothing serious, gave him a couple of aspirins. Burton went to bed early. The next morning, when Sally woke up, she found her husband's breathing laboured and she had trouble waking him. She called for an ambulance, which took him to a hospital. Apparently, he'd had a brain haemorrhage. Richard underwent surgery, but he did not pull through. He was fifty-eight.

Richard and his brother Graham Jenkins had had a conversation about Elizabeth three weeks before Richard died. Richard had said that he missed Elizabeth 'all the time', but he had come to the realisation that he was too old and ill for her to be able to take care of him. In the end, he was glad that he'd found Sally. 'She knows how to take care of an old man,' he said wistfully. Before they parted, his greatest love was still on his mind. 'You know, Elizabeth and I never really split up,' he told Graham. 'And we never will.'

Elizabeth was crushed by the news of Richard's death. She fainted. When revived, she called Victor Luna and asked him to be with her. 'I knew she would be devastated, shattered,' Luna said, 'but I didn't expect her to become completely hysterical. I could not get her to stop crying. I realised then how deeply she was tied to this man. And I realised I could never have that special place in her heart. For me, the romance was over, and I told her that.'

For the next few days after Richard's death, Elizabeth sat in front of the television, numb and unaware of the passing of time. Her friend Diane Stevens called. She said that Elizabeth told her she was looking through a scrapbook of photos of· her and Richard. 'I'm so sorry about Rich,' Diane told her. 'I know how much you loved him.

'"You were there for so much of it, so, yes, I think you do know how we felt about each other. Most people, I'm afraid, don't get it. My God, the trouble we caused each other," Elizabeth said with a chuckle as she apparently thumbed through the photographs before her. She mentioned that she'd been afraid to feel anything at all for the last couple of days for fear that she would be totally engulfed by waves of sorrow, as she had been when Mike Todd died. However, when she started remembering Richard, she was surprised to find that she actually felt good. "And right now, talking to you," she said, "I only remember the good times."'

No doubt, Elizabeth's grief over Richard's sudden death was eased somewhat by the knowledge that they had finally set things straight with each other. Earlier, in the spring of 1984, when she and Victor Luna were on a vacation in London, they had met Richard and Sally Burton at a London pub. The energy between Elizabeth and Richard was different, somehow, not as charged as it had always been in the past. 'You look wonderful, luv,' he said to her. She told him about her experiences at the Betty Ford Center and, as she later recalled, said that she wished the two of them could have had such therapy back in the sixties, when they were married to each other and living their lives in a style that was totally out of control. Richard had to smile. 'Ah, but then we wouldn't be who we are now, would we?' he mused.

For the rest of their time together that day, Richard had seemed happy. Though he was still drinking, he didn't seem as sickly as he had when he was in *Private Lives*. He looked fit and well. 'Something was different the last time I saw him,' Elizabeth would later observe. 'And I don't think I imagined it, given what would happen in a few months. I just knew my sweet Richard was going to be OK. I knew it in my heart.'

Now he was gone, and Elizabeth had to make a decision about whether she should go to the memorial service in Wales. When she called Richard's widow, it was clear that Sally really didn't want her there. She said that she feared Elizabeth's presence would cause a circus-like atmosphere at the service, and she wanted Richard to be remembered with more dignity on that day. Perhaps, then, Elizabeth said, she could go to the funeral, which was to be in Céligny. No, Sally said. That also would not be a good idea. It was clear that Sally did not want Elizabeth to be a part of any of Richard's services. Elizabeth was heartsick, but in the end, she was determined to abide by Sally's wishes.

At the last moment, Sally called to tell her she'd had a change of heart. Yes, she said, of all people, Elizabeth should be present at the memorial service. However, by then, there was no way Elizabeth could have got to Wales in time. Whether Sally was merely trying to be gracious or whether she actually wanted Elizabeth at the service is something only she would know. However, Elizabeth was determined not to think the worst of her. (Years later, Sally would say she truly did regret telling Elizabeth not to attend the service: 'I wish, now, I hadn't done that'.)

On August 19, about a week after the Welsh memorial service, Elizabeth embarked on a pilgrimage to Pontrhydyfen. As she stepped out of her private jet at Swansea airport, a crowd of about a hundred greeted her with cheers. She looked radiant, dressed in pink and wearing the Krupp diamond, the best of all the jewels Richard had given her. She'd come to visit Richard's family after having visited his grave in Céligny the previous weekend. While she ate dinner that night at the home of Burton's sister, Hilda, and her husband, Dai, a crowd of mourners stood outside their front door, singing old Welsh songs like 'We'll Keep a Welcome in the Hillside'. Over a roast beef dinner, Elizabeth told the couple about her experience when she went to the grave site.

When she showed up at the graveyard in Switzerland, just as the sun was rising, Elizabeth and her daughter Liza were greeted by a group of paparazzi. They had reasoned that Elizabeth would eventually show up, and they got their wish when she finally appeared before them.

However, Elizabeth had arranged to have four bodyguards accompany her. As soon as they arrived, mother and daughter went to Richard's grave, and as they stood before it, each bodyguard popped open a multi-coloured umbrella to shield the two women from the photographers' lenses. As soon as Elizabeth knelt at the grave, she began to cry. She wept for a good fifteen minutes, with Liza trying to comfort her. When it was time to go, the pair walked slowly out of the cemetery, Elizabeth leaning heavily on Liza's arm. Elizabeth would describe her moments at Richard's grave as unusually intimate. 'I couldn't help thinking that it was one of the few occasions ever that Richard and I were alone.'

THE MONTHS AFTER Richard's funeral were very difficult for Elizabeth, as she tried to find her bearings not only in her life after Richard but also without alcohol and drugs. 'Thank God I was clean and sober when he died,' she would later say. 'If not, I wouldn't be here today. I would have totally destroyed myself out of grief.'

In 1984, she began dating Dennis Stein, a wealthy New York businessman her own age. By the end of the year, she was engaged to him and wearing a twenty-carat sapphire ring he'd given her. However, by January 1985, Elizabeth realised that she was about to make a mistake—and fortunately came to her senses. 'Finally, I'm growing up,' she said. Then, with a laugh, she added, 'I think I have figured out that I don't have to marry every man I date.' In the next five years, she would be linked with many interesting men, such as the millionaire financier and publisher of *Forbes* magazine, Malcolm Forbes, and actor George Hamilton.

Part Six

The Glory Years

It seems almost impossible to imagine that in the early 1980s many people didn't know what AIDS was or how it was contracted. AIDS—acquired immunodeficiency syndrome—was first reported in the United States in 1981. It was referred to as a 'gay cancer' by a media grasping for a way to explain it to the masses. Everyone knew what cancer was, and the disease did seem to be striking, for the most part, homosexual men. In January 1985, the world wasn't even clear as to what specific role HIV—human immuno-deficiency virus— played in the passing on of AIDS, or even how it was transmitted.

In those early years of the epidemic, Elizabeth Taylor knew as much about AIDS as anyone else in the entertainment community: that some of her closest friends were dying from it and that much of the world seemed indifferent to their loss. Over the years, many of her gay colleagues had suffered terribly in their private lives as a result of their true selves not being accepted in the entertainment business. She'd known many actors who'd been closeted, such as Montgomery Clift and Rock Hudson, and she had always reached out to them with friendship. As a mother protector to so many gay men, she was confused, hurt and angry when AIDS began to take her loved ones. 'I felt early on that people needed to become better educated about the disease,' she would later say. 'I couldn't sit back and watch this terrible sickness take so many of my friends without wondering if there was something I could do.'

In January 1985, Elizabeth's publicist, Chen Sam, was contacted by two men who were attempting to put together an organisation that would offer assistance to AIDS patients, and they wanted Elizabeth's help. Bill Misenhimer, an AIDS activist, and Bill Jones, a Los Angeles caterer, had a vision that they, along with five other gay men, would call AIDS Project Los Angeles (APLA). They hoped to convince Elizabeth to become chairperson of the first major AIDS benefit, which would be called the Commitment to Life Dinner, and the proceeds of which would benefit APLA. In meeting with Misenhimer and Jones, Elizabeth learned that celebrities were shunning the disease as if it didn't exist. No one wanted to be identified with this 'gay epidemic'. 'I was so angry,' she would recall. 'The attitude that people had, the bigotry! It incensed me.'

She began polling her friends to see what support she could get. Frank Sinatra turned her down when she asked him to become involved with the dinner, telling her that it was one of her 'lame dog causes' and that it would hurt her to become involved in it. She got a similar response from Nancy Reagan when, in January 1985, she attended President Reagan's second inauguration. 'No one wanted to get into it with me,' Elizabeth said years later. 'I noticed that my calls weren't being returned. I must say, *that* was a first in my life.'

At about this same time, Rock Hudson was undergoing secret treatment for AIDS in Paris. Elizabeth knew he was ill, and certainly knew he was gay. But when *Daily Variety* broke the news of Rock's AIDS diagnosis on July 23, Elizabeth was crushed, more determined than ever to spread the word about the disease. Hudson was the first major celebrity to announce that he had AIDS, and that — combined with the public's leap to the conclusion that he was also homosexual — was all stunning information to digest. When he returned to Los Angeles for further treatment, Elizabeth was the first to visit him at the hospital. Seeing him, and coming to terms with the fact that he truly was dying, strengthened her resolve to do something about the disease that would claim his life.

In the summer of 1985, Elizabeth announced plans for the Commitment to Life Dinner. 'No one wanted to come,' she told Whoopi Goldberg years later, in 1993. 'I've never received so many no's in my life. It actually was because of Rock that I was able to get people to come to the dinner. The town said, "Oh, one of our own has been stricken."'

In a couple of years' time, the epidemic would again strike home for Elizabeth when her daughter-in-law Aileen Getty (married to but estranged from her son Christopher), would confide in her that she was HIV positive. Aileen would admit she'd had an unsafe sexual affair outside her marriage in 1984 and through it had caught the virus. Elizabeth's friend Liz Smith recalled, 'Elizabeth said to me, "Liz, this girl is like my own child. She's the mother of my two grandchildren. How can I do anything but everything I can to save her life?"'

Aileen and Elizabeth had always had a special camaraderie, perhaps because they shared such troubled lives. Aileen once said she was 'victimised by my parents, by my legacy, by life. I'd been in seven institutions, I'd had twelve shock treatments, I had seven miscarriages. I was anorexic, a self-mutilator. I'd been there and back.' She also said of her mother-in-law, 'It was easy to talk to her. She taught me that I was still a beautiful person.' (Aileen has remarried and remained close to Elizabeth.)

The Commitment to Life Dinner took place in the ballroom of LA's Bonaventure Hotel on September 19, 1985. It was a huge success, generating more than a million dollars for APLA. Soon after, Elizabeth would join forces with Mathilde Krim, a New York doctor who had established the AIDS Medical Foundation. Dr Krim and Elizabeth, along with David Geffen, Dr Arnold Klein and others, founded amfAR — the American Foundation for AIDS Research. 'We plan to muster the talent of America's brightest researchers to solve the mysteries of AIDS,' Elizabeth said. 'We are prepared to do what it takes to find a cure.'

Two weeks later, on October 2, Rock Hudson died, but with his death came the emergence of a new and reborn Elizabeth Taylor. From this point onwards in her life, she would have a cause that inspired more passion in her than anything else in which she'd ever invested herself.

WHILE THE OCCASIONAL film or TV role kept her from falling into creative atrophy, Elizabeth moved gracefully through this challenging time in her life. She would also branch out, in 1987, with an exciting new business venture that would lift her public profile even higher and generate millions of dollars in the process. She would license her name to a perfume company, the Parfums International division of Chesebrough-Pond's, to market a fragrance that would be called Elizabeth Taylor's Passion. Elizabeth announced the new venture at a press conference in New York on January 14, 1987.

She explained that she would be involved in every aspect of developing the scent. What would it smell like? 'It will have a violet aroma, of course,' she said.

Elizabeth would make appearances in department stores to promote the fragrance, as well as appearing in a lavish advertising campaign. Within a few years, Elizabeth Taylor's Passion would become the fourth largest-selling women's perfume in America, grossing $70 million annually. The fragrance business would enhance Elizabeth's portfolio: her net worth was nearly $100 million by the end of the 1980s.

THE LATTER HALF of the 1980s had seen the rebirth of Elizabeth Taylor as an AIDS activist and perfume business entrepreneur, but she would find that her recovery as an alcoholic and drug addict would not be easy to preserve.

First off, Richard Burton's and Rock Hudson's deaths had taken their emotional toll. Then, there was the tumult of strategising her war against AIDS. On top of all that, her many appearances in conjunction with the perfume business also proved exhausting.

Slowly, over a period of about five years, from 1982 to 1987, the stress in her life contributed to a variety of illnesses—such as osteoporosis, which had begun to affect her pelvis and hips. There were mornings when she would not be able to get out of bed, yet would have a full schedule of personal appearances. Her doctors, wishing to ease her misery, prescribed a variety of medications for her. She began to depend on them, and before she knew it, her drug use was out of control and she was even drinking again.

Meanwhile, Elizabeth was very concerned about her mother, Sara, now ninety-two. In the autumn of 1988, Sara was hospitalised with bleeding ulcers in the Eisenhower Medical Center, which happened to be adjacent to the Betty Ford Center. Margaret DeForest and Eleanor LaSalle, two women from Palm Springs whose mothers were friends of Sara Taylor's, both spent much time with Sara and, in the 1980s and 1990s, with Elizabeth when she would visit her mother in Palm Springs.

'I think what people don't know about Elizabeth is how devoted she remained to her mother,' says DeForest. 'Yes, there was frustration, especially when Sara got into her nineties. They had their share of mother–daughter battles, but they were absolutely in love with each other.

'When Sara went into the hospital with ulcers, it really scared Elizabeth. My mother told me that she thought it was the thing that put Elizabeth over the edge that year—the thought that Sara might die. Then, one morning in October [1988], my mother got a call from Elizabeth. "No one can know this," she told her, "but tomorrow I am going into the Betty Ford Center." She said she was totally addicted to painkillers again because of her osteoporosis. She just wanted my mom to know so that she could help her make certain arrangements at the hospital with Sara.'

Elizabeth checked in to the Betty Ford Center on October 25, 1988. Every day while Elizabeth was there, she and her brother, Howard, would visit Sara in the hospital. One day Eleanor LaSalle showed up with her mother to visit Sara. Elizabeth and Howard were in the room.

'It was a sad scene,' Eleanor said. 'Elizabeth was in a wheelchair because she could barely walk. She was trying to get off painkillers, but she was in excruciating pain. There she was, in the wheelchair, sitting next to Sara, who was lying in bed, quite ill, in and out of a coma. The two were holding hands and whispering back and forth to each other. It took my breath away, it was so moving.'

ELIZABETH'S STAY at the Betty Ford Center in the autumn of 1988 was, in many ways, more difficult than the first time, five years earlier. She was paranoid and disorientated upon her arrival, and it was clear that she was, at the age of fifty-six, suffering now more than ever. As in 1983, she stayed at the centre for seven weeks.

Amazingly enough, Sara Taylor recovered. At ninety-two, she seemed indestructible, leaving the hospital and returning to her home in Palm Springs. Elizabeth was having a more difficult time, and when she left the centre on December 10, 1988, she was off alcohol but not the drugs. She would never be able to get off her medication completely, especially with her osteoporosis, but she was now taking it in a more controlled way.

One day, at Betty Ford, Elizabeth noticed a man with long blond hair and hazel eyes, whose personality she found amusing. He was a tall, thirty-seven-year-old truck driver and construction worker named Larry Fortensky.

Later, Elizabeth would tell one assistant that what most attracted her to him was that he had no idea who she was. Of course, he knew the name Elizabeth Taylor—he just didn't know that she was this woman with whom he was beginning to strike up a friendship.

During subsequent group therapy meetings, he became taken by her demeanour, a mixture of frailty and fortitude. They began having long conversations about life and love as he pushed her about in her wheelchair. There was a spark between them, and they both felt it.

Lawrence Lee Fortensky, born in 1952, was the eldest of seven children, three boys and four girls. He was raised in lower-middle-class Stanton, about an hour south of LA. He dropped out of high school and began working odd jobs as a teenager. By the time he met Elizabeth, Larry had been twice married. His first marriage, when he was nineteen, lasted eighteen months and produced a daughter. A year later, he married again, his wife just seventeen, and began to work in construction, making minimum wage. He was a hard worker who enjoyed getting his hands dirty. One problem that he faced, however, was that he had been a heavy drinker. It had interfered with both his marriages.

For the first year that she knew Larry, Elizabeth thought of him as a good friend and nothing more. One wouldn't think that an iconic film legend and a hardworking day labourer would have much in common. The fact that both of them were trying to stay sober helped to establish a strong bond between them. They also liked to eat, which provided a lot of laughs as Larry took Elizabeth to all the greasy spoons he enjoyed in and around Stanton. Dressed in her black leather jacket and blue jeans with boots, her hair teased in a biker style, she would always be an astonishment to the other diners.

Of course, Elizabeth was also a pampered celebrity, and there was no escaping that side of her, either. During this time, she introduced two new fragrances, White Diamonds for women and Passion for Men. One launch party for the new perfumes was at the New York Stock Exchange. Her date? Saudi arms dealer Adnan Khashoggi. While in New York for the party, Elizabeth stayed at Khashoggi's opulent $25 million apartment on Fifth Avenue. The place had its own Olympic swimming pool, not to mention $30 million worth of artwork.

By contrast, Larry lived in a modest two-bedroom apartment, which he rented. He operated an off-road Caterpillar dirt compactor, making $18.50 an hour. Elizabeth viewed him as a good friend, though, and by early 1989, she was often inviting him to her Bel Air home for the weekend. He didn't feel he fitted in very well, but he liked her, too, and accepted her invitations.

Despite their differences, there was something between Elizabeth and Larry. As their friendship progressed, she found a new level of intimacy with him because they had both been in the same group therapy. Twenty years younger than Elizabeth, Larry was quiet and unassuming—or at least he was in the beginning of the relationship—and also strong and dependable. He was also handsome, with his Nordic features and muscled body. Elizabeth could not stop herself from falling for him.

In the spring of 1989, Larry moved into Elizabeth's home. He came with one suitcase containing two pairs of worn-out blue jeans, three cowboy shirts, a pair of crusty old work boots, tennis shoes, underwear . . . and no socks. 'Now, you'll sleep *here*,' Elizabeth said cheerily. She showed him one of the guest rooms she calls the Yellow Room. He unpacked and made himself at home.

One day, about a month later, Elizabeth's cook came out of the kitchen, carrying a breakfast tray. She saw Larry and felt sorry for him. He seemed so out of place. What was he doing there, anyway? None of the staff knew for sure. Was he Elizabeth's boyfriend? Or just a visitor? 'Here,' said the cook, handing him the tray and putting him to work. 'Why don't you take this up to Elizabeth.'

Instead of being insulted, Larry took the tray and climbed the steps to the master bedroom. He knocked on the door, entered the room, and closed the door. Hours later, he came back out, went downstairs, gathered his belongings, and moved them all into Elizabeth's bedroom. He and Elizabeth had become lovers.

Meanwhile, Larry would keep his construction job. On the days he worked, Elizabeth would wake up at 4 a.m. to have breakfast with him before he left. Then he would have his day, and she would have hers. Finally, at 4 p.m., he would return, sweaty and tired, to his movie-star girlfriend's Bel Air cocoon, where he would then be pampered by her household staff as they exchanged details of their experiences in the outside world. Sometimes, she would meet him at his construction site.

Benny Reuben worked with Larry in early 1990 on a construction site in Studio City, California. He recalls, 'Man, we're working in the hot sun, and at about 2 p.m. a white Mercedes pulls up, and we're trying to see who it is, and the door opens up and it's Elizabeth Taylor.

I'm thinking, What is Elizabeth Taylor doing *here*? I'm looking for the cameras, thinking we're on *Candid Camera* or something. She walks over to Larry and plants a big one right on the kisser. And he says, "Elizabeth, you can't be here without a hard hat." He hands her one, and she puts it on. She turns to us and says, "Hello, boys." Most down-to-earth woman you'd ever want to meet. She brought dough-nuts, coffee. Afterwards, I said, "What the hell, man? Why didn't you tell me you were dating Liz Taylor?" He said, "You didn't ask." She started coming regularly after that. Classy lady, all around.'

At the beginning of 1990, Larry had to prove his mettle. First, Elizabeth's constant companion, Malcolm Forbes, died in February. She was crushed by the loss. Then, a month later, she became deathly ill. Larry learned that if a man wants to be with Elizabeth Taylor, he has to be the kind of person who won't run for the hills when she becomes ill. She contracted a simple infection that advanced into a pulmonary virus, causing her to be admitted to St John's hospital in Santa Monica. It was a terrible time. The doctors told her she was going to die—again! Of course, she lived—but only after a very painful open-lung biopsy.

Larry stayed at the Bel Air home while she was in the hospital, keeping the homestead running in her absence. Truly, Elizabeth was able to depend on him, and his dependability made her feel that she wasn't alone in the world. Somehow, he managed not to feel insecure around her, not to be intimidated by her worldliness and his apparent lack of sophistication. She appreciated that about Larry, and soon she was in love with him. He felt the same way.

Elizabeth's work for amfAR—the American Foundation for AIDS Research—continued to be successful, and by 1990, the charity had collected $30 million, largely due, no doubt, to her involvement. In 1991, she established the Elizabeth Taylor AIDS Foundation, through which she would channel her philanthropic work for AIDS research and care. 'I want to know that all the money that's donated is going to patient care,' she later told the *Los Angeles Times*. 'Whatever it is, I tag it, so it doesn't go into some executive's pocket.'

THE WEDDING INVITATION, which was designed by Cartier, was a simple and classic white card with black type:

Mr Michael Jackson
requests the pleasure of your company
at the marriage of his beloved friend
Miss Elizabeth Taylor
To Mr Larry Fortensky
On Sunday, the sixth of October 1991 at 5 p.m.

A few months earlier, Elizabeth had asked Larry to marry her. He accepted. In the past, when she became engaged, she always received an expensive and eye-popping bauble from her fiancé. Not this time. Instead, she took Larry's grandmother and aunt shopping for new dresses and shoes. In July, Elizabeth and Larry made the announcement that they would marry in October and the ceremony would take place at her friend Michael Jackson's Neverland Valley Ranch. 'After being together for four years, Larry and I decided we wanted to spend the rest of our lives together,' Elizabeth said in a statement released by her publicist. 'Life is good and sweet, and we love each other. I always said I would get married one more time, and with God's blessings, this is it, for ever.'

But how did Michael Jackson fit into this puzzle?

Elizabeth and Michael had been friends since the early 1980s. Michael always said that no one had been a better, more understanding friend over the years than Elizabeth Taylor. She was always available with a warm hug and an understanding ear. After getting to know him, she felt that he was terribly misunderstood. She took him under her wing, as she had so many emotionally wounded people over the years. Because both had been child stars, they understood each other's problems and commiserated about their lost childhoods.

With his kind of money, Jackson could do anything he wanted at Neverland, so he had decided to turn it into his own private amusement park, with a huge Ferris wheel, bumper cars, steam trains and a carousel. There was a zoo with a menagerie of alligators, giraffes, lions and a twelve-foot albino python. There was a games room, a toy room, an arcade . . . all of it allowing Jackson to relive his childhood and also to entertain children there. Its existence would play a part in getting him into trouble in years to come, but in 1988 it was a dream come true for him.

Overlooking the somewhat eccentric nature of what Jackson brought to Neverland, the property itself provided the perfect backdrop for a romantic, storybook wedding. It was verdantly green as far as the eye could see, hills rising and falling in undulated sweeps, reminiscent of the English countryside where Elizabeth was raised. Old-fashioned windmills dotted the landscape. Thousands of trees gently shaded superbly manicured grounds, which included a five-acre man-made ice-blue lake with a soothing waterfall. It would be here that Michael, thirty-three in 1991, would host the wedding of his friend, Elizabeth, fifty-nine, to Larry Fortensky, thirty-eight. Michael would personally plan every detail of the event. He gave his executive assistant, Norma Staikos, a million dollars and told her to do whatever necessary to make the day a memorable one for his good friend Elizabeth and her new husband.

On October 6, 1991, a large white gazebo, festooned with silk swags of green and decorated with daisies and gardenias, was set up near the lake at Neverland. Among the 160 guests present were Quincy Jones, Gregory Peck and Brooke Shields. Former president Ronald Reagan and his wife, Nancy, were also there. Entertainment reporter Liz Smith, the only journalist present, documented the event in her column.

At 5 p.m. Elizabeth's mother, Sara, was escorted in a wheelchair to the front row. Larry then walked down the aisle, wearing a white jacket with black trousers. He met his best man, Elizabeth's hairdresser, José Eber, at the podium. And then came the bride, in a golden ankle-length gown, designed for her by Valentino at a cost of $30,000. She wore yellow roses in her hair and long diamond earrings of her own design, by Cartier. She had rarely been any slimmer, at just 110 pounds.

Michael Jackson was at her right side, an unusual substitute for the long-gone Francis Taylor, especially since her brother, Howard, was alive and present. Jackson looked dapper in a black suit with black gloves, a diamond pin on his collar and gleaming silver boots. Elizabeth's thirty-eight-year-old son, Michael Wilding, Jr, was at her left.

An unlikely marriage took place on this day: a movie star who'd been one of the most famous women in the world for almost fifty years wed a day labourer twenty years her junior, a man she'd met while waging battle with her worst demons at a drug rehabilitation centre. Could such a union last? Who could predict what the future would hold for them? However, in this serene time and very strange place, Elizabeth Taylor was content with the seventh man to take her as his wife. Certainly, if there was one thing she'd learned in her sixty years, it was to enjoy the moment and not look too far into the future.

ON THE FIRST ANNIVERSARY of Elizabeth's marriage to Larry, a long-time assistant went to the elegant Hotel Bel-Air and paid $3,500 for one night in its most commodious space — the Presidential Suite. It's a two-bedroom, two-bathroom, well-appointed accommodation. The formal living room has a wood-burning fireplace and double French doors, which lead to a private garden patio and large outdoor spa. The assistant decorated the suite with fragrant lavender and bouquets of yellow roses. She also ordered an extravagant meal to be delivered that night: beluga caviar to start ($250), and roasted rack of Colorado lamb with Niçoise olives and fig jus ($44 a plate), with chocolate soufflés for dessert ($25 each). It was all to set the stage for the perfect celebration of one year of marriage for her employer, Elizabeth, and her new husband, Larry. That night, Elizabeth and Larry happily left for the hotel to enjoy their evening.

The next morning, when the assistant came downstairs, she was stunned to find Larry lying on the couch in the living room, watching television. The entire household staff was concerned about what might have occurred to cut the romantic evening short. Before anyone had time to do any snooping, however, Elizabeth swept into the kitchen and announced, 'We decided to come home because it was boring.' Then she walked out, as if she just wanted to quell the gossip, once and for all.

Things obviously weren't going well . . .

Of course, it had been expected that there would be adjustments to be made when Elizabeth married Larry, especially considering their divergent stations in life, the huge disparity in their finances, as well as the twenty-year difference in their ages. One of the biggest challenges to their union had to do with her determination to try to remake him. She thought of him as a diamond in the rough and wanted to polish him. She began the work she felt necessary in transforming him not only into the ideal husband but also the perfect social partner.

By this time, she was among the ten richest women in the world, according to *Forbes*, her fortune estimated at $150 million. She was one of the most sought-after celebrities in Hollywood, with a full social calendar that involved Larry as her escort. When she took him to a formal dinner at her friends Burt Bacharach and Carole Bayer Sager's home, he seemed not to fit in with the others there. She didn't even like the way his fingernails looked in comparison to the other men. She made a mental note, as she would later tell it, to make an appointment with a manicurist for him the next day. When Burt asked him about a film, he responded, 'Oh, yeah. I seen that one.' Elizabeth cringed.

It had finally happened. Perhaps it was inevitable. Maybe the only surprise was that it had taken eight marriages to seven men before it had unfolded: Elizabeth Taylor had re-created in her own life the marriage her mother once had with her father. However, there was one difference between what Sara had done back then and what Elizabeth was doing now. Francis wanted to change and welcomed Sara's suggestions. But Larry wasn't nearly as open to Elizabeth's advice.

In February 1992, Elizabeth celebrated her sixtieth birthday with a party at Disneyland with hundreds of guests. The one problem of the day concerned Elizabeth constantly trying to tell Larry how to pose for photographers. 'You mustn't smile so broadly,' she told him in front of several witnesses. 'It causes lines to form round your eyes.' It must have been the proverbial straw breaking the camel's back because Larry snapped—and that was when Elizabeth learned something about him she wasn't aware of in the past: his temper. 'Stop picking at me,' he told her angrily. 'I mean it. Stop it *now*.' He stormed off.

In the intervening months, Elizabeth had Larry's hair restyled in a way she felt better suited him. She even started giving him speech lessons. One of her servants recalled, 'Elizabeth summoned top designers like Valentino, Versace and Armani to customise a wardrobe for him. He soon began to rebel against her attempts to dominate him.'

For instance, he refused to stop smoking in the master bedroom. Elizabeth had given up smoking in 1990 after a terrible bout with pneumonia and had asked him repeatedly not to smoke in the bedroom. He refused to do it. Elizabeth began to wonder why her husband would care so little about her health that he would do the one thing that could cause her problems. Perhaps he viewed it as a way of seizing control. Also, he insisted upon eating in bed, getting crumbs all over the sheets. The more she asked him not to do it, the more he did it. Finally, Elizabeth is a light sleeper; he liked to have the television on all night and refused to compromise his viewing habits. It had been her bedroom for many more years than it had been his, and one day she had his belongings removed from it. It was back down to the Yellow Room for Larry.

Larry continued to fight Elizabeth's domination of him and even used her household staff as his accomplices. 'He wanted to be informed about every telephone call Elizabeth received,' said a former staff member. 'The pharmacist would send over medication on a weekly basis. Larry demanded that we not take her medication up to her until he had counted the pills. If he was not around, we were supposed to hold the medicine downstairs until he returned. We explained to him that he was putting us in a difficult position, and he said, "Look, I'm doing this for her own good." None of us believed that. We knew it was about control.'

Brian Bellows is a friend of Larry's who was invited to a cocktail party at the Fortenskys' to thank some of Elizabeth's wealthier friends for money they donated to the Elizabeth Taylor AIDS Foundation. Larry had invited Bellows and a few other friends of his so that he would, as he told them, have someone to talk to at the gathering. 'I was amazed at how much Larry had changed,' he recalled. 'I hadn't seen him since the wedding. He looked great in his suit with his haircut, but he was quiet and seemed afraid to say or do anything. He was just standing in a corner, drinking a soft drink, not getting into the mix at all.'

Bellows went over to Fortensky. 'What's going on, man?' he said, extending his hand. 'Looks like you're hiding, buddy.'

'Big night for the wife,' Larry explained. 'I don't want to screw it up for her. Plus, I gotta tell you,' he continued, suddenly seeming angry for no apparent reason, 'I'm about to blow, man. I'm about to lose my cool. And if I do, I'm gonna turn this whole damn house on its ear, man.'

ELIZABETH'S MOTHER had not been well in recent years. True to her nature, though, she still wanted to maintain her independence and insisted on keeping her condominium at the Sunrise Country Club in Rancho Mirage, California. One of her friends there recalls, 'From her little home, she had a wonderful view of rolling green golf courses and lovely blue lakes. She just wanted to tend to her rosebushes, be with her friends in her ladies' bridge club, have her life. Living a full life had always been important to her, and she did just that. Elizabeth visited often. However, at the end, she wasn't able to come as much because of her own health issues.

'Sara looked at newspaper photographs of her unwell daughter and said, "Look, she's sicker than I am. I'm the one who should be visiting her, not the other way round."'

Indeed, Elizabeth had not been in good health for some time, and then, in December 1993, things took a turn for the worse when she tripped and fell in her chalet in Gstaad. The accident aggravated the arthritis in her left hip. She began the year 1994 crippled by terrible pain.

Sara had the spirit of a passionate artist whose vision had been successfully realised. The joy of knowing that her ultimate goal had been achieved brought her great joy. Or, as her Palm Springs friend observed, 'Her love for Elizabeth knew no bounds. There were pictures of Elizabeth carefully placed all over her condominium in silver frames. One that she most cherished was of her with Elizabeth at the opening night of *The Little Foxes* in New York, in 1981. In it, Elizabeth is wearing a red shawl, a white gown with a deep, plunging neckline, and, of course, lots of diamonds and pearls. Sara would show it to me and say, "Will you just look at my daughter? Now, if she is not the most beautiful woman in the world, then I don't know who is. Don't you agree?"'

Indeed, Sara Sothern Taylor remained Elizabeth's biggest fan until the very end. She passed away quietly on September 11, 1994. She was ninety-eight. She was buried next to Francis in the Sanctuary of Peace section of Westwood Memorial Park. The small plaque on her burial site reads: SARA S. TAYLOR—LOVING MOTHER, DEVOTED WIFE—1895–1994.

'COME WITH ME,' Elizabeth Taylor said to five members of her household staff. 'Quickly, now. Hurry!' They followed her up the stairs and into her master bedroom. Once they were all inside, Elizabeth closed the door and locked it. 'There,' she said. 'That should keep him out of here. We'll be safe here until he cools off.'

One of the surprising facts Elizabeth learned about Larry Fortensky over the first couple years of their marriage was that he had a temper, or, as one of her household staff put it, 'He had fits of uncontrollable rage.' He was, as he would put it, 'pissed off on a regular basis', and often it had to do with her not putting much stock in his opinion or his advice. Still, he knew what he was getting into when he married Elizabeth. Did he really expect that he would be the one running the household?

It would be an hour before Elizabeth would release her staff from the bedroom. Meanwhile, Larry ranted and raved in the living room—about what, no one was even sure. Elizabeth was adamant that her employees not suffer the consequences of her husband's temper. One day, she walked into the kitchen and happened upon him berating one of her female employees. Elizabeth was alarmed enough to step between them.

'Larry, I don't know how you treat your construction crews, but you will not behave this way to my staff,' she said angrily. 'They are more than employees. They're my family.'

One witness recalls of the incident, 'Larry stormed off and shut himself in his bedroom, where he slept three days straight.'

Larry's temper and inconsideration weren't the only issues in the Fortenskys' marriage. There was Elizabeth's health as well. Earlier, in the winter of 1994, she'd had to undergo a complicated hip replacement operation. Her recuperation continued to be long and difficult all the way into 1995, with Larry at her side the entire time. She would be confined to a wheelchair for much of the time, to her great exasperation.

The two fought about her recovery, and Larry began to feel as Michael Wilding once had, that Elizabeth really didn't want to get better, that she thrived on her illnesses. In June 1995, things got even worse when she had surgery to replace the other hip. There was no way that her marriage would survive a second recuperation.

That summer she decided to end it with Larry. 'I think it's time for you to go,' she told him. 'I'm not happy, and you're not happy.'

Brian Bellows, Larry's friend from Stanton, California, recalls, 'Larry telephoned me and said, "Before you read it in the papers, I want you to know that Elizabeth and I are separating." He sounded very depressed, unhappy. "What the hell happened?" I asked him. "She's set in her ways," he told me. "She's been her own woman for so long, she never really listened to one thing I told her. Guess I can't blame her. She's Elizabeth Taylor. Why would she ever listen to *me*, anyway?"

'My impression was that the two hip surgeries were what ruined that marriage. He said, "She's been hurting for so many years, it's just a place she's used to being in, and I can't handle it." In a sense, I don't think he had what it took to get her through the health issues, and she was unwilling to be helped, I believe.'

In February 1996 Elizabeth filed for divorce, citing 'irreconcilable differences'. She offered a one-sentence statement: 'We were not able to communicate, and I am very saddened that it didn't work.'

With the mention of their failure to communicate, a comment Elizabeth made during her marriage to Richard Burton comes to mind. 'A woman will try and dominate a man,' she said. 'She will try and get away with it. But, really, inside herself, she wants to be dominated. She wants the man to take her. When he doesn't, she begins to needle him. If nothing happens, she goes on needling— until he stops listening. At that moment, she becomes bitter, and he goes deaf. There is no more dialogue.'

Elizabeth was surprised when Larry sued her for $5 million and attempted to invalidate their prenuptial agreement, claiming they were both represented by the same attorney when it was signed. She was angry and probably felt the way she had earlier when Eddie Fisher went after her for money so many years ago.

During the Taylor–Fortensky litigation, Elizabeth's financial documents were produced to provide insight into her wealth. The details of her financial portfolio were stunning. Consider this: her net worth was $608.43 million. Her properties round the world were valued at $127.45 million. Her art and jewellery were valued at $102.77 million. Her stocks and bonds, $274.21 million. Her interest-bearing bank accounts, $104 million. She was also making about $12 million annually from her perfume business. She'd recently cashed in stock in the Hilton hotel chain (acquired through her first marriage) for a profit of $21.7 million. Also, she inherited $8.7 million from the estate of her close friend Malcolm Forbes. Is it any wonder that Fortensky felt he was entitled to more than the $5,000 per month he was to be paid in a divorce settlement?

In the end, Elizabeth did love Larry and decided just to work it out with him. They settled for more than a million dollars. In

November 1996, they were officially divorced. However, the two remained close friends.

IT WAS in early February 1997 when Elizabeth knew something was very wrong with her. She couldn't figure out how to use the telephone. 'And who ever used a telephone more than me?' she later asked, jokingly. She'd been having headaches, loss of memory and dizzy spells, but that morning she knew something was very wrong. She screamed for help. She was taken to a hospital immediately, and after a series of brain scans, she got one of the most frightening diagnoses of her life: she had a brain tumour. It was large, possibly the size of a golf ball, and would have to be removed. This very serious operation was scheduled to occur in two weeks, on Monday 17 February. Ironically, at this same time, American Broadcasting Company was planning a sixty-fifth birthday celebration to honour her, which was to be videotaped before a live audience and later televised. *Happy Birthday Elizabeth: A Celebration of Life* was to be produced at the Pantages Theater in Hollywood, the very day before her operation.

Elizabeth was uncertain whether or not to proceed with the tribute. In the end, though, she decided she would go through with it—postponing the operation by just one day—but only because the audience's contributions, which could (and did) total more than a million dollars, were to be earmarked for the Elizabeth Taylor AIDS Foundation.

In the end, *Happy Birthday Elizabeth: A Celebration of Life* turned out to be a star-studded success, paying homage to one of the greatest film stars of our time, and rendered even more nostalgic by the pending life-or-death operation.

Two days later Elizabeth checked in to Cedars–Sinai Medical Center. As she faced her own mortality, she couldn't help but think about those she'd loved and lost over the years. She realised that she'd taken so much of her life for granted. At the age of sixty-five, she now wished to cling close to her children, all of whom were with her at the hospital, and to her grandchildren and to her friends. She thought a great deal about her father, trying to make sense of her complex relationship with him. She also missed her mother. However, she knew that she was imbued with Sara's indomitable spirit. Anyone who had known both women could see that Sara lived on in her daughter. 'And I have *lived*,' she said at the time. 'If the knife slips while I'm on that operating table tomorrow and I never wake up in this world again, I'll die knowing I've had an extraordinary life.'

Of course, Elizabeth pulled through the delicate surgery. Could anyone have imagined otherwise? She was completely bald after having had her head shaved for the operation, but she didn't care. In fact, she liked it — and even posed for a picture for *Life* magazine.

Elizabeth had faced her own mortality, once again — and had survived it, once again. It wouldn't be over for her, though. There would be more battles to wage.

On February 27, 1998, on her sixty-sixth birthday, she took a fall while preparing for dinner with her son Christopher and his family. She broke her back in the fall and would be in a back brace for two months.

Then, on January 28, 1999, Elizabeth received the shocking news that Larry Fortensky had either fallen or was pushed down a staircase in his home outside Los Angeles. He had landed on his head. His blood alcohol level when he was found was through the roof. Doctors operated on him, but the damage done to his body was so severe — a broken neck and back as well as severe head injuries — that his prognosis was grim: he might never walk, or even move, again. Elizabeth immediately telephoned Larry's daughter, Julie, to comfort her. The two stayed in daily communication for the five weeks that Larry lay in a coma. He emerged from it in March but would never be the same.

Six months later, on August 18, 1999, Elizabeth took another fall and, unbelievably, broke her back — again! This time the pain was almost more than she could bear. It took months for her to heal. Though surrounded by friends and family at the hospital, and then at home, it was difficult for her to keep her spirits up. She had to go through the misery with just moderate use of drugs, lest she become addicted again.

By the end of the year, though, she was making public appearances. When she attended Andrea Bocelli's concert in Los Angeles in November, she was asked how she had survived the year. She responded with typical Elizabeth Taylor candour: 'How did I survive *any* year?' She then let loose with that self-mocking laugh of hers. 'You just do it. You force yourself to put one foot before the other, and you just refuse to let it get to you. You fight. You cry. You curse. Then you go about the business of living. That's how I've done it. There's no other way.'

IN ELIZABETH, the world found a movie star like no other. From *Cleopatra* to *Virginia Woolf*, she breathed life into more than sixty-five characters. Some performances were simply watchable, others brilliant, but all eminently engaging simply because of her star power and charisma. Heavy or thin, young or old, ailing or well, she suffered our condemnation and commanded our devotion in equal measure.

Indeed, if ever there was an American princess, it would have to be the actress with the sapphire-blue eyes—pampered, beautiful, beloved Elizabeth. By the power of her personality, the drama of her life, and the example of her philanthropy, she has seduced us, charmed us and inspired our admiration. Indeed, because we've been so transfixed for decades by her talent and her beauty, we sometimes lose sight of what she has truly done. After years of struggle, she mobilised Hollywood to recognise a health crisis that had only previously been mentioned in hushed tones. Her bravery and passion proved to the world that Elizabeth Taylor had truly become an aware and compassionate member of society, managing to merge the polite façade she and her mother had created in her youth with the purposeful woman she is at her core.

It was during this period of self-discovery that Elizabeth learned she was going to receive an honour even her mother couldn't have expected. At the age of sixty-eight, she would become a Dame, recognised by the British royal family. She received the call in the winter of 2000 from Buckingham Palace: she and Julie Andrews were to be honoured as Dame Commanders of the Order of the British Empire—the female equivalent of a knighthood. Both were born in Britain in the 1930s, though they'd spent their working lives mostly in the United States. The ceremony was set for Tuesday, May 16, 2000.

Along with her twenty-four pieces of luggage, Elizabeth was accompanied to England by an entourage that included her four grown children and their partners; her attorney, agent, hairdresser, and make-up artist; and also her trusted assistant Tim Mendlesen.

On the special day, Julie Andrews was the first to receive her insignia, for services to acting and entertainment, at a ceremony in the ballroom at Buckingham Palace. Next came Elizabeth, who received her Dame Commander's brooch in honour of her services to acting and charity. With her head slightly bowed, Elizabeth accepted the honour as Queen Elizabeth pinned the insignia on her blouse. 'Today doesn't compare to anything else that's happened to me in my life,' she said, nearly overcome by emotion. She looked regal, maybe even more so than the queen herself, in a heavy pearl necklace and Van Cleef & Arpels pearl and diamond earrings that she designed for the occasion. The Krupp diamond from Richard Burton shone brightly from her right hand. With her hair in a bouffant and wearing lavender, she hadn't looked as good and vibrant in some time. Her children surrounded her—the salt-and-pepper–haired Michael, forty-eight, with his wife, Brooke; Christopher, forty-six, and his wife, Margi; Liza, forty-three and Maria, thirty-nine.

It's probably not surprising that there was one man on Elizabeth's mind on this memorable day: Richard. It had been back in 1970 when she and Richard Burton arrived at Buckingham Palace to accept his Commander of the British Empire. Elizabeth had worn a Russian-style fur hat on that day, looking stylish and proud on the arm of her husband. She couldn't help but wonder what his reaction would have been to her own day of honour. As much as

Elizabeth had tried, she'd not been able to get over his death. 'I miss him so much,' she said of Richard. 'Oh, how I wish he was here.'

When she got back to the United States, Elizabeth hosted a small dinner party with some of her closest friends and family members, including her brother, Howard and his wife, Mara. Howard and Mara had been married since 1951 and spent much of their lives together with their children in Hawaii and California. It's difficult to resist the temptation to contrast Howard's sole, long marriage to his sister's track record in that department, but Elizabeth would be the first to say that she always believed her brother had chosen the more sane lifestyle. 'How I admired Howard's disdain for the movies,' she once commented.

On this night, with friends and family surrounding her, Richard was on her mind, as was Mike Todd. She became emotional when talking about them, her eyes filling with tears. 'You know, Mike didn't deserve to die that way,' she said, her voice shaking. Her guests were surprised. It was rare for Elizabeth to bring up Mike's death; she usually only spoke of his life, not his tragic demise. However, the honour she'd received in England had stirred so many memories for her, and, inevitably, when she thought of Richard, she automatically thought of Mike. After all, they were the two loves of her life. 'And why is it that I always have this feeling that Richard Burton is going to walk right through that door at any minute and start giving me hell about something?' she asked one of the guests. Then, with a laugh, she concluded, 'Somewhere, the two of them are probably having drinks, waiting for me to join them. And oh, the hell we shall cause in heaven if, in fact, that's where we end up, which' — she concluded with a cackle — 'I *highly* doubt.'

'It's her desire to live that has pulled her through so many crises in her life,' says her friend José Eber. 'Who knows where that comes from? Maybe it's from actually being at death's door so many times and just realising how precious life is. Or it could be a positive outlook at her very core that pushes her onwards. Or is it her mother, maybe?'

That evening, as she stood before friends and family in her Bel

Air home, Elizabeth Taylor raised a glass of sparkling cider. 'There's a woman who deserves our deepest appreciation,' she began, 'because if it weren't for her, we'd all be somewhere else right now. She taught me how to be a different kind of dame,' she added, prompting raucous echoes of laughter. 'Let's all drink to my mother, Sara Taylor.'

'Hear, hear!' shouted a guest.

'No!' she commanded, bringing the room to a hush. 'Let's drink to two things.'

All eyes were on her. 'To my mother. And forgiveness.'

Editors' Note: On the 23rd March, 2011, Dame Elizabeth Taylor died in Los Angeles at the age of seventy-nine. The double Oscar-winning actress had a long history of ill-health and was being treated for symptoms of congestive heart failure. Her four children were with her when she died at Cedars-Sinai Medical Center.

J. RANDY TARABORRELLI

Journalist J. Randy Taraborrelli was born in 1956 and lives in Los Angeles. He is the author of eleven books, including the best-selling *Jackie, Ethel, Joan: Women of Camelot*; *Sinatra: A Complete Life*; and *Michael Jackson: The Magic and the Madness*. He has also written biographies of Diana Ross, Carol Burnett and Princess Grace. Of Elizabeth Taylor, Taraborrelli says: 'This is a woman who has been . . . defined by hardships. I had never seen any of it chronicled in an empathetic way. So I decided to find the real story.'

Paul McCartney
FAB An Intimate Life
by Howard Sounes

In a few short years, Paul McCartney had become one of the most famous people in the Western World. Even Elvis hadn't been fêted so far and so wide as the Beatles. At home, perhaps only the Queen was more famous and, on October 26, 1965, the boys became the first pop stars to be honoured by Her Majesty as Members of the Order of the British Empire. Some old soldiers sent their military medals back in disgust, while a crowd of over-excited schoolgirls gathered outside the Palace to shriek at the Beatles through the iron gates.

'FAB An Intimate Life of Paul McCartney'
by Howard Sounes

PART ONE: WITH THE BEATLES

I: LIVERPOOL AND HAMBURG

'They may not look much,' Paul would say in adult life of his Liverpool family, having been virtually everywhere and seen virtually everything there is to see in the world. 'They're just very ordinary people, but by God they've got something—common sense, in the truest sense of the word. I've met lots of people, [but] I have never met anyone as interesting, or as fascinating, or as wise, as my Liverpool family.'

Liverpool is not only the city in which Paul McCartney was born; it is the place in which he is rooted, the wellspring of the Beatles' music and everything he has done since that fabulous group disbanded. A predominantly white, working-class city, its people are descended from the working poor of surrounding Lancashire, plus Irish, Scots and Welsh incomers. Their regional accents combined in an urban melting pot to create Scouse, the distinctive Liverpool voice, with its singular, rather harsh pronunciation and its own witty argot; Scousers typically live hugger-mugger in the city's narrow terrace streets built from the local rosy-red sandstone and brick.

Paul's maternal grandfather was a farmer's son from County Monaghan and it's likely there was Irish blood on the paternal side of the family, too. McCartney is a Scottish name, but four centuries ago many Scots McCartneys settled in Ireland, returning to mainland Britain during the Potato Famine of the mid-1800s. Paul's paternal ancestors were probably among those who recrossed the Irish Sea at this time in search of food and work. Paul's paternal grandfather married a local girl and had ten children, the fifth of whom was Paul's dad, Jim.

MUSIC PLAYED a large part in family life. Birthdays, Christmas and New Year were all excuses for parties around the piano and it was Jim McCartney's fingers on the keys. He also played trumpet, 'until his teeth gave out', as Paul says. Jim became semiprofessional during the First World War, forming a dance band in which his older brother Jack played trombone. Jim made up tunes as well, though he was too modest to call himself a songwriter.

It was Jim's luck to have been too young to serve in the First World War and he was too old for the Second. Liverpool's docks were a prime German target during the early part of the war and it was at this desperate time, with the Luftwaffe overhead, that Jim met Paul's mother, Mary. They married on April 15, 1941. The Blitz on Liverpool intensified during the next few months, then stopped in January 1942. Britain had survived its darkest hour, and Mary McCartney was pregnant with one of its greatest sons.

James Paul McCartney, best known by his middle name, was born on June 18, 1942. Two years later, a second son was born, Michael, Paul's only sibling. The boys were typical brothers: close, but also rubbing each other up the wrong way at times.

Paul was three and Mike one when the war ended. Dad resumed a former job at the cotton exchange as a salesman, though it was Mum's work that was more important to the family. Mary McCartney was the NHS in action, a relatively well-paid, state-trained midwife who worked from home delivering babies for her neighbours. In 1946, Mary was asked to take up duties on a new housing estate at Speke, south of the city, and the McCartneys were given a new, three-bedroom corporation-owned house on a boulevard that leads, today, to Liverpool John Lennon Airport.

Paul's new suburban home gave him access to woods and meadows where he went exploring. In the evening, Mum cooked while Dad smoked his pipe, read the newspaper or did the garden. There were games with Mike, and the fun of BBC radio dramas and comedy shows. In 1950, the family moved one mile to 12 Ardwick Road, a slightly less salubrious address but opposite a playing field with swings.

Paul's parents got their first TV in 1953, as many British families did, in order to watch the Coronation of the new Queen, twenty-seven-year-old Elizabeth II. Master McCartney distinguished himself by being one of sixty Liverpool schoolchildren to win a Coronation essay competition. 'Coronation Day' paid patriotic tribute to a 'lovely young Queen' who, as fate would have it, would one day knight him as Sir Paul McCartney. Winning the prize showed Paul to be an intelligent boy, which was borne out when he passed the Eleven Plus exam and was selected for Liverpool's premier grammar school. One of the best state schools in England, The Liverpool Institute, or Inny, had a fine reputation for giving the brightest boys of the city the best start in life.

Paul was impressed and daunted by this new school when he enrolled in September 1953. Going to the Inny drew him daily from the suburbs into the urban heart of Liverpool, a much more dynamic place. Paul went into the B-stream, which specialised in modern languages, and studied German and Spanish. Paul's other favourite classes were art and woodwork, both hobbies in adult life. Before music came into his life strongly, Paul was considered one of the school's best artists; curiously, music lessons left him cold. Although Dad urged Paul to learn to read music, he never learned what the dots meant. 'I basically never learned anything at all [about music at school].' Yet he loved the Inny, and came to recognise the head start it gave him in life. 'It gave you a great feeling [that] the world was out there to be conquered, that the world was a very big place, and somehow you could reach it from here.'

At the Inny, Paul acquired the nickname Macca. Friends Macca made at school included John Duff Lowe, Ivan 'Ivy' Vaughan and Ian James, who shared his taste in radio shows, including *The Goon Show*. In the playground, Macca was 'always going through programmes that were on the previous night,' James recalls. 'He'd always have a crowd around him.' Two more schoolboys were of special significance: Neil 'Nell' Aspinall, who became the Beatles' road manager, and a skinny kid one year Paul's junior named George.

Born on February 25, 1943, George Harrison was the youngest of a family of four, the Harrisons being a working-class family from south Liverpool: Dad drove buses for a living. It was on the bus home from school that Paul and George first met properly. 'I discovered that he had a trumpet and he found out that I had a guitar, and we got together,' George recalled. 'I was about thirteen. He was late thirteen or fourteen. He was always nine months older than me!' As this remark implies, George always felt that Paul looked down on him.

Paul's family moved again, this time to 20 Forthlin Road in Allerton, a pleasant suburb closer to town. The address was a compact brick-built terrace with small gardens front and back. This new home suited the McCartneys perfectly, and the first few months that the family lived here became idealised in Paul's mind as a McCartney family idyll: the boy cosy and happy with his kindly, pipe-smoking dad, his funny kid brother, and the loveliest mummy in the world.

What happened next is the defining event of Paul McCartney's life. Mum was diagnosed with breast cancer. At the end of October 1956, Mary was admitted to the Northern Hospital where she underwent surgery. It was not successful. Paul and Mike were taken into the hospital to say goodbye to her. Paul noticed blood on her bed sheets. Mary remarked to a relative that she only wished she could see her boys grow up. Paul was fourteen, Mike twelve. Mum died on October 31, 1956, aged forty-seven.

His Aunt Joan recalls that Paul didn't express overt grief when told the news. When he did address the fact that his mother had died, Paul did so by asking Dad how they were going to manage without her wages. Stories like this are sometimes cited as evidence of a lack of empathy on Paul's part, and it is true that he would react awkwardly in the face of death repeatedly during his life. It is also true that young people often behave in an insensitive way when faced with bereavement. Over the years, however, it became plain that the premature death of his mother was a trauma Paul never forgot, nor wholly got over.

Paul reacted to the death of his mother by taking comfort in music. He exchanged the trumpet for an acoustic Zenith guitar, wanting to play an instrument that would also allow him to sing. Learning proved challenging because Paul was left-handed and he tried at first to play as a right-hander. It was only when he saw a picture of singer Slim Whitman playing guitar the other way round that Paul restrung his instrument accordingly. Schoolmate Ian James played guitar with greater proficiency and gave Paul valuable lessons.

As to what the boys played, the first real musical excitement for young people in postwar Britain was skiffle, incorporating elements of folk, jazz and blues. Close on the heels of skiffle came the greater revelation of rock 'n' roll. Elvis Presley broke in Britain in May 1956 with the release of 'Heartbreak Hotel'. The singer and the song electrified Paul, and Elvis was his role model, as he was for boys all over the world. Paul began to neglect his school work, and spent his free time practising Elvis's songs, as well as other rock 'n' roll tunes that came fading in and out over the airwaves from Radio Luxembourg, introducing Paul to the charismatic Americans who sat at Elvis's feet in the firmament of rock: Chuck Berry, Jerry Lee Lewis, Buddy Holly, Little Richard and rockabilly pioneer Gene Vincent, whose 'Be-Bop-A-Lula' was the first record Paul bought.

Paul imitated his heroes with preternatural skill but he was more than a copyist. Almost immediately, he started to write his own songs. 'He said, "I've written a tune,"' recalls Ian James. 'So we went up to his bedroom and he sang it.' Created from three elementary chords, 'I Lost My Little Girl' was of the skiffle variety, with simple words about a girl who had Paul's head 'in a whirl'. Paul McCartney had become a singer-songwriter. Now he needed a band.

JOHN WINSTON LENNON was a year and eight months older than Paul, born on October 9, 1940. Like Paul, John was Liverpool Irish by ancestry. Dad was a happy-go-lucky merchant seaman named Freddie. Mum, Julia, was a flighty young woman who dated various men when Fred was at sea, or in prison. All in all, the couple made a poor job of raising their only child, whom Julia passed, at the age of five, into the more capable hands of her older sister Mary, known as Mimi, and Mimi's dairyman husband George Smith, who brought John to live with them in their cosy cottage, Mendips, on Menlove Avenue, just over the hill from Paul's house.

John's childhood was upset again when Uncle George died in 1955. Thereafter, John and Aunt Mimi shared Mendips with a series of male lodgers whose rent allowed Mimi to make ends meet and who, in one case, shared her bed. This was an eccentric start in life, and John grew to be an eccentric character, clever, with a quick wit and an intense stare that was later mistaken for a sign of wisdom—in fact he was just shortsighted. He also had a talent for art and a liking for language. Like many solitary children, John was bookish, more so than Paul, accounting in part for his lyrics being generally more interesting than Paul's. John was mad for rock 'n' roll. In fact, many friends thought John more or less *completely* mad. In researching Paul's life it is remarkable that people who knew both Paul and John tend to talk about John most readily, often with laughter, for Lennon said and did endless amusing things that have stuck in their memory, whereas McCartney was always more sensible, even (whisper it) slightly dull by comparison.

Like Paul, John worshipped Elvis Presley and played guitar enthusiastically, but badly, using banjo chords taught to him by his mum, who was living round the corner with her current boyfriend. Having grasped the rudiments, John formed a skiffle group with his best mate at Quarry Bank High School, Pete Shotton; the band was named the Quarrymen, after their school. The lads performed covers of John's favourite songs at parties and youth clubs, sometimes going weeks without playing, for one of John's signal characteristics was laziness. Indeed, the Quarrymen may well have come to nought had they not agreed to perform at a humble summer fête.

On July 6, 1957, a procession of children, floats and bands made its way through Woolton Village to St Peter's Church field, with the outgoing Rose Queen, a local girl, sitting in majesty on a flatbed truck. The Quarrymen followed on another. Around 3 o'clock the new Rose Queen was crowned, after which there was a parade of children in fancy dress, and the Quarrymen played a few songs.

John was strumming his guitar and improvising lyrics to the Dell-Vikings' 'Come Go With Me'. Paul thought this clever. He had been brought along to the fête by Ivan Vaughan, who knew John and thought his two musical friends should get together. The introduction was made in the church hall, where the Quarrymen were due to play a second set. John recalled: 'We talked after the show and I saw that he had talent. He was playing guitar backstage, doing "Twenty Flight Rock".' Not long after this meeting, Pete Shotton stopped Paul in the street and asked if he'd like to join the Quarrymen. He was asking on behalf of John, of course.

GIRLS STARTED TO FEATURE in Paul's life around this time. A pale, unsporty lad with a tendency to podginess, Paul was no teenage Adonis, but he had a pleasant, open face and a confidence that helped make him personable. Initially, he just buddied around with girls he'd known since primary school; likewise, he knocked about with Forthlin Road neighbour Ann Ventre. 'I'll be famous one day,' he told her boldly.

'Ha! Will you now?' she replied, astounded by that confidence. Like many people who become successful, Paul *knew* at a young age that he would do well.

Confidence is attractive and by the time he was fifteen, Paul had his pick of girlfriends. He lost his virginity to a local girl he was baby-sitting with, the start of what became a full sexual life.

Being in a band was an excellent way to meet girls, but early Quarrymen gigs brought the lads more commonly into the company of the men who operated and patronised the city's social clubs. Small-time though these engagements were, Paul took every gig seriously. 'I think Paul had more desire to be successful than John,' comments Quarryman drummer Colin Hanton. 'Once Paul joined, there was a movement to smarten us up.' Paul was also quick to advise his band mates on their musicianship. 'He could be a bit pushy,' remarks Colin, a sentiment many musicians have echoed.

Paul would cycle over to John's house to work on material. 'John, your little friend's here,' Aunt Mimi would announce when he appeared at her back door. The boys practised upstairs in John's bedroom, decorated with a pin-up of Brigitte Bardot, whom they both lusted after. Mimi preferred them to practise in the front porch, which suited John and Paul, because the space was acoustically lively. Here, Lennon and McCartney taught themselves to play the songs they heard on the radio, sitting opposite each other, trying to prevent the necks of their instruments clashing, and singing in harmony. Both had good voices, John's possessing more character and authority, which Paul made up for by being an excellent mimic. Apart from covering the songs of their heroes, the boys were writing songs, the words and chord changes of which Paul recorded neatly in an exercise book.

During term time, Paul and John met daily in town, which was easy with John now studying at the Liverpool College of Art, which was next door to Paul's grammar school. When Paul slipped out to have lunch with John, his friend Georgie would often tag along. John treated Paul more or less as his equal, but he regarded this boy with condescension. Paul did, too, but he was shrewd enough to see that George was becoming a good guitar player. Ultimately, John was sufficiently impressed to invite Harrison to join the band, but ever afterwards the two senior band members would regard George as merely their guitarist. 'Nobody respected George for the great [talent] he was,' says Tony Bramwell, a Liverpool friend who went on to work for the Beatles (John called Bramwell 'Measles', because he was everywhere they went). The arrival of Paul and George squeezed out most of John's original sidemen.

Despite Paul's drive to make the Quarrymen as professional as possible, they were still rank amateurs. It is also a wonder that their early experiences didn't put them off trying to make a living as musicians. On one occasion, auditioning for a spot at a working men's club, the Quarrymen watched as the lad before them demonstrated an act that was nothing less than eating glass. The boy cut himself so badly he had to stuff newspaper into his mouth to staunch the blood. But Paul's dreams were not quelled; indeed, he seemed ever more ambitious, while the fact that Dad had been down this road already also accounts for Paul's professionalism.

JOHN KEPT IN CLOSE TOUCH with his mother, who was more like a big sister. Julia Lennon attended Quarrymen shows, with the band sometimes rehearsing at her house. Paul was fond of Julia, as he was of most motherly women, feeling the want of a mother himself. On July 15, 1958, as Julia crossed busy Menlove Avenue, she was knocked down and killed by a car. John was seventeen.

In the wake of this calamity, John's friendship with Paul strengthened. The fact that Paul had lost his mother, too, meant both boys had something profound in common. They began to write together more seriously, creating significant early songs such as 'Love Me Do'. But Paul wrote alone as well, composing the tune of 'When I'm Sixty-Four' on the family piano around this time, 'thinking it could come in handy in a musical comedy or something'. Unlike John, whose musical horizon didn't go beyond rock 'n' roll, Paul had wider tastes and ambitions.

The Quarrymen performed only sporadically in the first half of 1959, including an audition for a bingo evening. The first set went well enough, and the management rewarded the lads with free beer. They were all soon drunk, and so the second set suffered. John started taking the piss out of the audience, and the Quarrymen weren't asked back. Added to this, after an altercation that night, drummer Colin Hanton left the band. Steady drummers were hard to come by and his loss was a bigger blow than they realised. John, Paul and George would struggle to find a solid replacement right up to the point when they signed with EMI as the Beatles.

While playing in the band with Paul and George, John maintained a parallel circle of college friends, headed by art student Stuart Sutcliffe. John and Paul were both artistic, but Stu was a true artist. He had a painting selected for the prestigious John Moores Exhibition at the Walker Art Gallery that sold for £65, part of which John and Paul persuaded Stu to invest in a bass guitar. So it was that Paul found himself in a band with John's older, talented and good-looking college friend, someone John grew closer to as he and Stu moved into student digs together. There was naturally some jealousy on Paul's part.

One of the places Paul and his friends hung out in Liverpool was the Jacaranda coffee bar managed by an ebullient Welshman named Allan Williams. Williams had recently begun to dabble in concert promotion and his partner in this enterprise was the London impresario Larry Parnes. Parnes's modus operandi was to take unknown singers and reinvent them as teen idols with exciting stage names: Reg Smith became Marty Wilde, Ron Wycherley was transformed into Billy Fury. While Parnes had plenty of groups in London to back his singers on tours of the south, he wasn't so well provided with backing groups in the North and Scotland. So Williams suggested that John Lennon's group audition for Parnes.

At this juncture they were the Silver Beetles, but they were a band without a drummer. Williams hooked them up with a twenty-six-year-old bottle-factory worker, Tommy Moore. In the end, the Silver Beetles were offered the chance to back a Liverpool shipwright John Askew, who had been given the moniker Johnny Gentle, on a seven-date tour of provincial Scotland. In mid-May 1960, they took the train to the small town of Alloa, Clackmannanshire.

There was only a brief opportunity to rehearse and Johnny explained his act to the boys: he said he came on like Bobby Darin, in a white jacket, and stood at the mike singing covers such as 'Mack the Knife'. Paul was the first to grasp what Johnny required from his backing band: 'He just seemed to know what I was trying to get over. He was one step ahead of John in that sense.' After Johnny's set, the star signed autographs for his girl fans. The Silver Beetles played on and Johnny noticed that the girls were looking over his shoulder at his backing band, as much if not more interested in them than him.

The Silver Beetles soon ran out of cash. Allan Williams belatedly sent money, but not before the boys had been obliged to skip out of at least one hotel without paying their bill. Driving from Inverness to Fraserburgh on May 23, Johnny crashed their van, causing drummer Tommy Moore to bash his face, breaking some teeth. The boys took the injured man to hospital, but Lennon soon had Moore out of bed, telling him, 'You can't lie here, we've got a gig to do!' Tommy played the Fraserburgh show but, not surprisingly, quit the Silver Beetles when they got home to Liverpool.

Broke and drummerless, the boys asked Williams if he had any more work, and were rewarded with perhaps the lowliest gig in their history. Allan had a West Indian friend, nicknamed Lord Woodbine, who managed a strip club. The Silver Beetles were persuaded to accompany Janice, a stripper who would work only to live music. 'She gave us a bit of Beethoven,' Paul recalled. 'We said, "We can't read music, but we can play the Harry Lime Cha-Cha, which we've arranged ourselves," so that's what she got.'

Williams's house band at the Jacaranda upped sticks and left one night, deciding they could do better elsewhere. They eventually called Williams to tell him they'd gone to Hamburg in Germany, which was pulsating with life, the local club owners crying out for live music. Allan and Lord Woodbine went to see for themselves and met a club owner named Bruno Koschmider, who told Williams that his Hamburg customers were mad for rock 'n' roll, but Germany lacked good, home-grown rock bands: he needed English bands. Some time later, Williams persuaded the German to take a young Liverpool act he nominally managed named Derry and the Seniors. They did so well in Hamburg that Koschmider asked for an additional Liverpool act. This time Allan suggested the Silver Beetles.

Paul had just taken his A-levels, with half a hope of going to teacher-training college, an ambition Jim McCartney wanted to hold him to. 'All the families were against them going,' says Williams. 'I sort of described Hamburg as a holiday resort!' Jim McCartney was a particularly hard sell but, if Paul really meant to go, his father knew it would be a mistake to try and stop him.

Before they could go anywhere, the band had to find a new drummer. Approaching nineteen, Pete Best had been thumping the skins for the best part of two years as a hobby. Paul and John watched Pete play at the Casbah, a youth club. Later, Paul called Pete on the telephone: 'How'd you like to come to Hamburg?' he asked.

On August 16, 1960, the Beatles, as they were now finally calling themselves, assembled outside the Jacaranda where Williams was loading his Austin van for the road trip to Germany. As they waited for the off, the boys cut out paper letters spelling 'THE BEATLES' and stuck them to the side of the van. The overburdened vehicle pulled away from the kerb and trundled down the road. Among the small crowd waving them off was John's sweetheart, Cynthia Powell. Further back, not wanting to embarrass her son, was Millie Sutcliffe. As the women wept, the boys were beside themselves with the excitement of what was going to be a great adventure.

LIKE LIVERPOOL, Hamburg is a northern port on a river, the Elbe, which flows into the North Sea, and, like Liverpool, Hamburg was bombed heavily during the Second World War. Bearing in mind the history, it is surprising how well the Beatles were treated only fifteen years after the war.

The boys arrived after dark on August 17, 1960 and parked outside the Kaiserkeller, Bruno Koschmider's underground club in St Pauli, a neighbourhood renowned for uninhibited night-time entertainment. Derry and the Seniors were on stage, blasting out rhythm and blues to an audience of enthusiastic Germans, including Horst Fascher, a former boxer working as a pimp. Horst, or Horsti as Paul called him, became firm friends with the boys, a pal and protector in the rough-and-tumble world of St Pauli.

The next day, Koschmider informed the band that they were playing a former strip joint named the Indra, which he wanted to turn into a club catering to the rock 'n' roll craze.

The Indra had the dimensions and charm of a large shoebox. Further disappointment came when the boys were shown their digs: the Bambi Kino, a fleapit cinema also owned by Koschmider. The Beatles were to be accommodated in the windowless back rooms, without proper toilet facilities or even hooks to hang up their clothes. With the tolerance of youth the boys made the best of it, beginning their Indra residency almost immediately.

The regime was punishing. The Beatles were contracted to play four and a half hours every weeknight, and six on Saturdays and Sundays. Even with fifteen-minute breaks between sets these were musical marathons. 'When the Beatles came they knew about fifteen songs,' recalls Rosi Haitmann, one of Koschmider's barmaids. It was barely enough to fill half an hour, yet the Beatles managed to play nightly at the Indra for the next seven weeks, during which time they enlarged their set. Then Koschmider closed the Indra, because of complaints about noise, and moved the Beatles to the Kaiserkeller to replace Derry and the Seniors.

In a bigger room, the Beatles' lack of experience became more apparent. Koschmider grumbled to Allan Williams, who wrote to the boys advising them to put on more of a show.

The Beatles threw themselves into an increasingly madcap performance. Paul hollered in uninhibited imitation of Little Richard, while John became a character from *The Goons*, singing comic songs, using funny voices, saying any outrageous thing that popped into his head. The crazier John became, the more the crowd liked it. He wore a toilet seat round his neck, even shrieking '*Sieg Heil!*' at the audience, which was forbidden in postwar Germany. The audiences loved it all, sending up beer and cheap champagne, which the boys guzzled greedily.

To stay awake they started taking Preludin, an over-the-counter slimming aid that had an effect similar to that of amphetamines. Drunk on beer and speeding on pills, the boys played on hour after hour, taking requests from their audience, telling jokes, pausing to smoke cigarettes, drink and even eat on stage. Pleased with them, Koschmider extended their contract.

In the small hours of the morning, after most of the patrons had left, the Beatles slowed into a semi-somnolent blues jam, playing for themselves and club workers like barmaids Rosi and Ruth Lallemann. Even though Paul had a girlfriend, Dot Rhone, waiting for him in Liverpool, Ruth says she began to date Paul, though they never actually had sex. There were, however, other German girlfriends. After work, the friends sometimes shared a cab to the beach, where they spent the last days of summer. It was a happy time.

There was a breath of autumn in the air when Klaus Voormann, a young graphic artist, saw the Beatles performing. Delighted by this exuberant music, Klaus rushed home to tell his sweetheart, Astrid Kirchherr. They returned the following evening with their friend from art school, Jürgen Vollmer.

After the madness of the war, the adult survivors rebuilt a Germany that was subdued and conservative. To the generation of Astrid, Jürgen and Klaus, this new Germany seemed dull. They looked to Paris, where Jean-Paul Sartre and Jean Genet led the existentialist movement, and styled themselves 'Exis' in honour of these free-living French intellectuals, though they understood little of existentialist philosophy. It was more a shorthand for dressing in black and adopting bohemian ways.

During a set break, Klaus introduced himself and his friends shyly in broken English. The musicians admired their clothes. John noted Jürgen's floppy haircut, asking if he'd had it done in Paris.

'No, I cut it myself.'

'Funny looking, ain't it, George? Would look good on Paul, though,' said John.

The Exis and the Beatles liked each other immediately. Astrid, Klaus and Jürgen were bright, arty people of the type John and Stu had mixed with at college in Liverpool, while grammar-school boys Paul and George could also relate to them. They took comfort in each others' company, meeting in cafés and bars during the day and nightly in the club, where the Beatles' other German friends, Horsti the pimp and bar girls Rosi and Ruth, looked askance at the interlopers. 'We didn't like them because they were posh,' says Rosi, though she had to admit that Astrid, with her cropped blonde hair and chilly Teutonic manner, had charisma.

Pete Best, however, was excluded from this new friendship, not being quite as sophisticated as the others, while Stu stood apart from the boys for his lack of musical ability, a source of growing frustration to Paul, in particular. 'Paul and George occasionally gave Stuart an angry look, because he must have played some wrong chord,' recalls Jürgen. 'But [we] liked Stuart a lot. He was an artist like us.'

Astrid took pictures and told the Beatles she wanted to conduct a photo session. She posed the boys against fairground machinery in the nearby park. Lacking much English, she manipulated the lads with her hands, tilting their heads this way and that. As she touched Stuart's face, she felt a frisson of excitement. She resolved to learn English as soon as possible.

In emulation of their new Exi friends, the Beatles started to dress differently, acquiring black leather jackets and trousers to replace their lilac stage jackets, the leathers giving them a new, macho look. Astrid took them home to meet Mummy in the suburb of Altona. 'They loved mashed potatoes and steak so Mummy did all that for them, and a nice cup of tea, which they couldn't get in Hamburg.' The Beatles were slightly surprised to discover that Astrid lived in a self-contained flat at the top of her mother's house, decorated mostly in black. Here she slept with Klaus, which would have been unusual for an unmarried couple in Liverpool.

Astrid, however, was falling in love with Stu. Within two weeks of their meeting, she ended her relationship with Klaus and took Stu as her lover, a turn of events Klaus took with laudable maturity.

Paul found that there were many girls eager to sleep with him and his band mates. 'We were used to these little Liverpool girls, but by the time you got to Hamburg if you got a girlfriend there she's likely to be a stripper who knew a thing or two. [It was] quite an eye-opener.' By all accounts, there was a nightly orgy at the Bambi Kino, with George losing his virginity while the others lay in their cots nearby: '. . . after I'd finished they all cheered. At least they kept quiet while I was doing it.'

One of the girls who supposedly slept with Paul during his first visit to Hamburg was a teenager named Erika Wohlers. 'We always sat beside the stage, me and my girlfriends. During the breaks, the group would sit at our table. Paul and I got close to each other [and] had sex for the first time at some point in 1960.' Erika later claimed that Paul made her pregnant.

In October a new club, the Top Ten, opened on the Reeperbahn, showcasing Tony Sheridan, a British singer who later married Rosi the barmaid. The boys went to see Tony's show and sometimes got up on stage with him, playing together with a passion that was partly due to their belief that this was a moment to be seized before the public lost interest in rock 'n' roll.

The owner of the Top Ten, Peter Eckhorn, offered to hire the Beatles after they finished at the Kaiserkeller. A furious Koschmider banned the boys from the Top Ten but they defied him, ruining their relationship. As the Beatles played out their contract, Koschmider resolved to get his own back. The law stated that anybody under eighteen had to leave St Pauli by 10 p.m., a rule the Beatles flouted nightly because George was underage. After a tip-off from the vengeful Koschmider, the police deported Harrison on November 21, 1960. The others carried on as best they could, moving their things over to the Top Ten, where Eckhorn had offered them digs. As they prepared to depart the Bambi Kino, Paul and Pete started a fire in the corridor. It was tiny, of no consequence, but the police arrested Paul and Pete the following morning—the first but not the last time Paul would have his collar felt. The lads were taken to jail for a few hours, before being deported.

PAUL ARRIVED HOME on December 2, 1960, full of stories of his German adventures, but Dad soon brought his son down to earth. Having had his fun, Paul was now expected to get a proper job. The Labour Exchange sent him to an electrical firm where he was set to work coiling cables, though the management soon expressed interest in training him as a junior executive. John and George slouched by and persuaded him to come back to the band. Paul agreed, but held on to his job for the time being.

The Beatles played a memorable Christmas dance at the Litherland Town Hall on December 27, showing how much they'd learned in Hamburg. They gigged virtually daily in January and February 1961, building a Merseyside following. So busy did they become that Paul's old schoolmate, Neil Aspinall, gave up an accountancy course to drive the boys around.

The Cavern, where the Beatles first performed in early February 1961, was a warehouse cellar—three barrel-vaulted storerooms under the pavement of Mathew Street in the middle of Liverpool.

It proved a popular but claustrophobic venue. Deep underground, without air conditioning or a fire exit, the club quickly became stuffy, while condensation caused the limewash to flake off the ceiling and fall like snow. On the plus side, the cellar had good acoustics, and the narrow quarters engendered a sense of intimacy.

Ray McFall, the owner, started to open at lunch time as a place for office and shop workers to come for a snack, with the attraction of live bands on stage. The boys had already played the venue as the Quarrymen; they first performed there as the Beatles on February 9, 1961, and almost 300 times over the next two and a half years. The Cavern became inextricably linked with their rise to fame. They were performing face to face with their public— sometimes they plucked cigarettes from the lips of girls, took a drag, then handed the ciggies back.

The audience was not exclusively female. Boys also liked the Beatles. 'Their sound was different and they were an outrageous lot,' recalls Cavern regular Ray O'Brien. 'Whereas you knew what the other bands were going to do next, you never knew with the Beatles. There was a lot of repartee with the audience.'

For girls, the Beatles were, of course, also objects of affection. 'I used to think Paul was the best looking,' muses Frieda Kelly, who founded the Beatles' fan club. Like most girls, Frieda relished the direct, friendly contact with the boys. Nobody became hysterical: the original female Cavern fans disdained the crazed girls who came later. 'I never screamed,' says Frieda. 'I was a fan, but I wasn't a *maniac*.'

After being deported from Germany, Paul had written to the German police to get permission for the band to return. Agreement came, so long as they obtained work permits. They did so without delay. George had turned eighteen, so there was no further difficulty there.

Paul quit his job and returned to Hamburg with the Beatles in March 1961, gambling his future on the success of the band. This time the Beatles would be playing for Peter Eckhorn at the Top Ten, sleeping in the club attic. Taking the view that they had secured this gig themselves, the boys wrote to Allan Williams informing him that he would not receive a commission. Williams wrote a two-page reply that was by turns indignant, threatening and pleading; he claimed he had a deal pending to book Ray Charles: 'I had thought of you going on tour with him.' The Beatles didn't believe him, or didn't care. They had outgrown Williams.

Paul and John's Liverpool girlfriends, Dot and Cynthia, came over to Hamburg for a visit. John was willing to bed down with Cyn in the band's communal room above the Top Ten, but Paul didn't want to bring Dot into this overcrowded den. The boys were friendly with an older woman at the club, and she kindly allowed Paul and Dot to sleep on her houseboat on the Elbe, a happy and romantic visit culminating in Paul giving Dot an engagement ring.

Paul's relationship with Stu was increasingly strained, however. Paul was now not only proficient on lead guitar, but could turn his hand to playing bass, piano and drums. Stu couldn't even master the simplest of instruments. He was only in the band because he was John's mate.

Paul had recently broken his guitar, after which he had little choice but to play the Top Ten piano during their set. One night, Paul made a rude remark about Astrid, and Stu swung a punch at him. 'They were always fighting,' says Ruth Lallemann. 'You didn't talk about things. You fought.' This particular fight over Astrid was bad enough to signal the end of Stuart's tenure as a Beatle. He quit the band soon afterwards to live with Astrid and study art, remaining friendly with the boys. Indeed, as soon as Stuart left the band Paul seemed better inclined towards him. As neither John nor George wanted to take up Stuart's bass, the job fell to Paul, who needed a new instrument. Stu generously lent him his expensive Höfner and, later, Paul bought the smaller, cheaper Höfner violin bass, which became his signature instrument.

Soon after Stu's departure, the boys were hired to back Tony Sheridan on a recording session for Polydor. The result was a single, 'My Bonnie', released locally in August 1961, a lively cover of the traditional song, 'My Bonnie Lies Over the Ocean'. It made number thirty-two in the German singles chart that year, and remains a very engaging record.

The band returned to Liverpool before 'My Bonnie' was released, finding themselves increasingly in demand on Merseyside, where there were now scores if not hundreds of similar 'beat bands'. One memorable night at Litherland Town Hall, the Beatles and the Pacemakers joined forces. 'We said, "Let's have one band for tonight,"' remembers Pacemakers' leader Gerry Marsden. The musicians swapped instruments: Paul played the town hall piano, the Pacemakers' pianist played sax. 'We had a ball.'

When John turned twenty-one in October 1961, he received £100 as a gift from a well-to-do aunt, an act of such munificence Paul never forgot it, often remarking that nobody had ever given *him* a hundred quid. Still, John used his birthday money to treat him and Paul to a trip to Paris where they arrived dressed in rocker gear, their hair in long, greasy quiffs.

One of the first things John and Paul did when they got into Paris was look up their Exi friend Jürgen Vollmer, who was now working in the city. Jürgen decided they should meet his girlfriend, but she was horrified by these scruffy English rockers. John and Paul weren't going to pull any Parisian women the way they were dressed, so Jürgen took them to the flea market where they bought beatnik-type outfits.

Next they wanted their hair cut like Jürgen's—combed forward over their eyes and cut in a fringe. Jürgen sat Paul down first in front of the mirror, draped a towel over his shoulders, and snipped away at his quiff, changing it into a softer, floppy Left Bank moptop. For a man to wear his hair like this in 1961 was rebellious.

A SHORT STROLL from the Cavern was a branch of NEMS, a local chain of family-owned electrical stores founded by a Jewish-Polish immigrant, Isaac Epstein, whose grandson, Brian, helped to manage the business. Born in 1934, making him only seven years Paul's senior, Brian Epstein found school an ordeal, and was then called up for National Service, a duty Paul narrowly avoided (conscription ended in 1960). Brian was ejected from the military, classified 'emotionally and mentally unfit'. Next he attempted to become an actor, but he didn't do well here, either. Having quit the Royal Academy of Dramatic Art in London, he was blackmailed by a homosexual pick-up in Liverpool: Brian had a taste for rough trade.

During the consumer boom of the late 1950s, the Epsteins opened additional branches of NEMS, selling electrical goods and records. Brian managed these stores and invested a great deal of energy in the record division, adopting a policy of ordering any record any customer requested. He claims in his autobiography to have been ignorant of the existence of the Beatles until a young man walked into his shop asking for 'My Bonnie'.

Epstein placed an order for 'My Bonnie', and when a girl came in asking for the same record, he ordered 200 more and went to the Cavern to meet the band with his assistant, Alistair Taylor, on November 9, 1961. The Cavern MC promptly announced that *Mr* Epstein was in the room, as if that was a big deal. Brian was only twenty-seven, but must have appeared middle-aged to the denizens of the Cavern from the way he dressed and spoke.

Epstein asked the band about 'My Bonnie' and they proceeded to banter back and forth. 'They were extremely amusing and, in a rough "take it or leave it way", very attractive,' Epstein later wrote. 'I will never know what made me say to this eccentric group of boys that I thought a further meeting might be helpful to them and me.' Still, a meeting was scheduled at his office for December 3.

The Beatles approached the date with a mixture of hope and scepticism. After all, what could the manager of an electrical shop do for them? When the appointment came, Brian asked the boys if they'd considered professional management. They talked about how this might work and agreed to meet again. In the meantime, Epstein consulted Allan Williams, who advised him not to touch the Beatles with a bargepole. Not put off, Epstein went to a lawyer and duly presented the four Beatles—that is John, Paul, George and Pete Best—with a contract that bound them to him for five years, during which time Brian would have a hand in every part of their act, taking up to 25 per cent of their gross earnings in commission.

Paul was hesitant, weighing up the pros and cons. Then he said he hoped the Beatles would make it. 'But I'll tell you now, Mr Epstein, I'm going to be a star anyway.'

2: LONDON

When the boys put their names to Brian Epstein's contract, one of the stated aims was to get the band a recording contract. Brian sent 'My Bonnie' to EMI in London, receiving a reply informing him that neither HMV nor the Columbia label wanted to sign his group. It was the first of several slaps in the face. Brian, however, had been corresponding with *Liverpool Echo* journalist Tony Barrow, who composed sleeve notes as a sideline for Decca. This led to Brian securing an audition for the Beatles in London on New Year's Day, 1962.

Paul knew that if he meant to make it in show business he had to go 'down south', even though southerners had a reputation for being unfriendly and condescending. The Beatles headed south, driven by Neil Aspinall in the band's newly acquired van. The lads arrived in the capital late, checking into the Royal Hotel on Russell Square, sufficiently excited about being in London to rush over to Trafalgar Square where they helped usher in 1962.

Fifteen songs from the band's live show had been selected for the Decca audition. Epstein forbade the boys from playing their usual, much more raucous rock 'n' roll set (though they did perform 'Money'), and the result was a sadly lacklustre performance, partly because the musicians were nervous and overtired. Some weeks later, Brian received the decision: 'Not to mince words, we don't like your boys' sound,' executive Dick Rowe told Epstein, ensuring his place in history as one of those hapless souls who let the Beatles slip through his fingers.

Brian returned to London in February 1962 to have the Decca tapes transferred to vinyl at the HMV shop in Oxford Street, with a view to hawking the discs around town. The technician cutting the discs suggested, in light of the fact that Brian's act wrote their own material, he might speak to Sid Colman, who worked upstairs for the music publisher Ardmore & Beechwood.

Brian explained to Colman that he needed a record contract

before a publishing deal. Colman suggested Brian contact his friend George Martin at Parlophone: 'I think he might be very interested.'

A large part of the Beatles' success can be put down to the fact that the boys worked with first-rate people from the start. Naive though he was, Brian was honest and devoted, while the man who was to become their record producer was even more impressive, and without him the Beatles may not have achieved half of what they did.

Born in 1926, the son of a London carpenter, George transformed himself into 'an officer and a gentleman' during the Second World War, in which he served in the Fleet Air Arm. After the war, he used his serviceman's grant to study at the Guildhall School of Music and became head of Parlophone, part of EMI, in 1955, by which time he was known for making comedy records for the likes of Spike Milligan. Success with comedy records was all very well, but they didn't lend themselves to follow-ups, and Martin badly wanted to sign a pop act that would enjoy longevity.

Epstein gave Martin a passionate sales pitch about his wonderful young band and the exciting musical renaissance taking place in Liverpool. The men hit it off. Martin wasn't particularly impressed by what he heard, but he was intrigued by the fact that more than one person in the band was singing, and concluded that Paul had the 'most commercial voice'. At the end of this cordial meeting, Martin suggested that Epstein bring his group into the studio when convenient.

Before they could audition for EMI, the Beatles had to return to Hamburg. Part of the fun of going back to Germany was seeing Stu and his fiancée Astrid again. However, Stu was experiencing a severe deterioration in his health: he felt tired and suffered seizures. On April 10, 1962, the day before the Beatles arrived, Stuart collapsed and died at Astrid's flat. He was twenty-one. John became hysterical when he was told; not so Paul, who tried to console Mrs Sutcliffe: 'My mother died when I was fourteen and I'd forgotten all about her in six months.' If he really did say this, it can be excused as the sort of gauche comment young people make at times of crisis, and of course it wasn't true.

The Beatles stayed in Hamburg to play the Star-Club, the newest, biggest rock 'n' roll venue in St Pauli, which attracted such established American stars as Gene Vincent and Little Richard. The Star-Club was the best venue the Beatles had played; the band correspondingly were more professional-looking now that Brian had got them out of their leathers and into suits and ties. But there was still a loutish element to these young men, as demonstrated by the way they treated their apartment opposite the club: it had to be fumigated when they left.

The Beatles were rescued from their own muck by a telegram. Wired by Brian on May 9, it read: CONGRATULATIONS BOYS. EMI REQUEST RECORDING SESSION. PLEASE REHEARSE NEW MATERIAL. George Martin had met Brian again and was showing a keener interest. He agreed that a contract should be drawn up so that if he liked what he heard when he met the boys, he could sign them forthwith.

IT WAS LOVE at first sight, as George Martin would write of the moment he met the Beatles at Abbey Road Studios in St John's Wood on June 6, 1962. The band performed for him with gusto. Martin wasn't madly impressed by the original songs John and Paul had written, including an early, dirgelike 'Love Me Do'. Still, the boys exuded an energy and charm that gave Martin a warm feeling. He agreed to sign the band for one year, during which time he would have the right to record six titles, with the Beatles receiving a niggardly but then standard royalty of a penny per disc. At least they had a deal and, surprisingly, it was with an EMI label, even though they'd previously been turned down by head office, which led to problems later.

A more immediate concern was that Martin didn't like the Beatles' drummer. He found Pete Best 'almost sullen' and didn't think he kept time well. In truth, Pete had never fitted in. He didn't have the same history with John, Paul and George and often seemed the odd man out, not sharing the same jokes and references. Curiously, this enhanced his image with fans on Merseyside: girls fancied Pete more than the other Beatles.

Change was also to come in Paul's personal life. For two years he had been dating Dot Rhone. Despite doubts she may have had about his fidelity, Dot wore Paul's engagement ring and looked forward to becoming his wife. Paul's family was part of the attraction. 'I loved his dad—he was great,' she told the *Daily Mail* years later.

In early 1962, Dot fell pregnant—'So we started to make plans to get married.' Paul told Dot he was getting the marriage licence and all seemed set fair when Dot miscarried. Paul ended the relationship soon afterwards. 'Deep down he was probably relieved,' she said later. A baby might have cut short the Beatles' career.

The decision having been made to fire Pete, the job of telling him fell to Brian, who called Pete into his office. 'They don't think you're a good-enough drummer,' he told him. As Pete tried to defend himself, the telephone rang. It was Paul calling to check that Brian had plunged in the knife.

Pete staggered downstairs to where Neil Aspinall was waiting. Neil and Pete were close. Curiously, the Beatles' roadie had recently embarked on a relationship with Pete's thirty-eight-year-old mother, with the result that Mo Best had given birth to a boy they named Roag. Neil was astounded to hear that his band had sacked his lover's son, and considered quitting in protest. Pete told him there was no need and, indeed, Aspinall stayed with the Beatles for the rest of his working life, ultimately becoming the head of their corporation. All that time, however, Pete suffered the daily humiliation of being a rejected Beatle, becoming so depressed during the height of the Beatles' success that he tried to gas himself.

Pete's replacement was a short, goofy-looking fellow with a large nose. Ringo Starr's real name was Richard Starkey—Ritchie to family and friends (and referred to as such in this book)—the only child of Richard and Elsie Starkey. Dad deserted the family when Ritchie was three and Elsie did what work she could to make ends meet, including scrubbing floors. Despite their poverty, Elsie made a great fuss of Ritchie. It is worth noting that all four Beatles were blessed with loving matriarchs—Aunt Mimi included—helping imbue their boys with confidence. After school, Ritchie became an apprentice engineer, chucking his apprenticeship to play drums with Rory Storm and the Hurricanes, a local band fronted by an athletic blond lad whose real name was Alan Caldwell. Rory insisted his band also adopt stage names, so Ritchie became Ringo Starr, named after the rings he wore, Teddy Boy-style.

Ringo had sat in with the Beatles more than once and John, Paul and George agreed that he would be the ideal replacement for Pete. Cavern dwellers, however, were indignant when Ringo took the stage with the band the first time: 'Pete for ever. Ringo — never!' they chanted.

With the arrival of Ringo, the Beatles were complete and, on September 4, 1962, they set to work recording their first single. Not yet trusting the Beatles' own material, Martin gave the band a madly catchy tune titled 'How Do You Do It?', written by professional songwriter Mitch Murray. The boys recorded it without enthusiasm, making it clear they would prefer to cut their own songs. The best they had to offer was 'Love Me Do', the slow, bluesy number written when John and Paul were boys and already demonstrated at their first meeting with Martin. They ran through it again with less than satisfactory results, Martin still detecting a weakness in the rhythm section.

When the band returned to the studio six days later to have another go, Ritchie was dismayed to discover that Martin had hired a professional session drummer, Andy White, to take his place. Suspecting he was to suffer the same fate as Pete Best, Ringo sat, stony-faced, while John and Paul taught Andy their material. They then recorded 'Love Me Do', Ringo's mood ameliorating slightly when Martin permitted him to bang a tambourine in accompaniment. Ritchie wasn't fired from the band, but he never entirely forgave George for replacing him on that first session.

When 'Love Me Do' was released on October 5, 1962, it meandered around the charts before reaching number seventeen shortly before Christmas. While this wasn't at all bad for a debut single, it fell short of being a smash hit, possibly because EMI gave the record little promotion: there was resentment that Brian Epstein had got his band in through the back door. Says *Liverpool*

Echo's Tony Barrow: 'It wasn't an important release from EMI's point of view.'

Barrow had started work as a public relations man for Epstein's new management company, NEMS Enterprises. One of his first jobs was to produce a profile of Paul and the other Beatles for the press. He spoke to fan-club secretary, Frieda Kelly, who was dealing with an increasing amount of mail. Girls tended to ask about the same things in their letters. To save time she typed up 'Life-lines' for each Beatle, giving the essential information. Under 'Instruments played', Paul listed 'Bass, guitar, drums, piano, banjo', putting 'Girls, songwriting [and] sleeping' as his hobbies.

Paul didn't specify in his Lifeline what sort of girls he liked. In real life he was dating Rory Storm's sister, Iris Caldwell, a professional dancer. The affair was tempestuous.

After the modest success of 'Love Me Do', and the Beatles' high-handed rejection of 'How Do You Do It?', Martin was anxious to see if the band had what it took to score a hit. He was sure 'How Do You Do It?' would have made number one, as indeed it later did for Gerry and the Pacemakers, whom Brian signed as the second of what became a stable of local acts. The Beatles were unrepentant. 'John just said it was crap,' says Gerry Marsden. 'And I say thank you to John every night on stage for giving me my first number one.' Martin asked the Beatles what they had that was better, to which they suggested 'Please Please Me', a song John and Paul had had knocking around for a while.

'Please Please Me' was brighter than 'Love Me Do', the opening guitar chords creating a big, optimistic sound, while the lyric was frankly sexual in a way adolescents could identify with: trying to get your girl to do what you both wanted, but were scared of in case you fell pregnant like Dot, and now like Cynthia, too. Unlike Paul, John had gone ahead and married his girlfriend, though secretly. The Lennons were expecting their first child in April.

By the end of eighteen takes of 'Please Please Me', George Martin pronounced that the boys had cut their first number one (in fact, it reached number two on the *Record Retailer* chart used by the *Guinness Book of Hit Singles*).

Before they could find out whether George's confidence was well placed, the Beatles returned to Hamburg to play a final stint at the Star-Club, a venue that, like the Cavern, they had now outgrown. It was December. The boys shared Christmas dinner with club friends and, on their last night, Paul persuaded his long-term German girlfriend, Ruth Lallemann, to come to the airport and wave him off. 'He said, "I think it's the last time I come here, because we're going to get big."' The next time Ruth saw Paul would be in London when he was a superstar. All of a sudden, everything was happening very fast.

BACK HOME, the Beatles found they had virtually no free time, as they rushed from club to theatre to recording studio, travelling long distances to fulfil relatively minor engagements. Seeking to capitalise on the success of 'Please Please Me', George Martin called the Beatles back to EMI and asked them to perform their stage show for him, thus creating a complete album. The Beatles recorded ten songs on the day, to which EMI later added the numbers previously released as singles. It opened with John and Paul singing in joyful harmony 'I Saw Her Standing There' and ended with John alone — his voice in shreds — screaming 'Twist and Shout'.

The Beatles' debut album established the convention whereby John and Paul would write and sing most of the songs, with at least two lead vocals reserved for George and Ringo. Here, then, was essentially the sound of the Beatles on stage in 1963, as they would have sounded at the Cavern: four young men having the time of their lives. Entitled *Please Please Me*, to hook fans who'd bought the single, the LP went to number one in May and held the top spot month after month, right up until the band's second LP displaced it. This was sensational.

The original songs on the LP are credited to 'McCartney/Lennon' and published by Northern Songs Ltd, details that would cause Paul more angst than almost anything in his career.

The first two songs the Beatles released had been published by Ardmore & Beechwood, but Brian had been disappointed by the way they had promoted them, so George Martin suggested a new publisher, Dick James. Forewarned that Epstein was dissatisfied with the promotion Ardmore & Beechwood had secured for 'Love Me Do', Dick telephoned a contact at the BBC while Brian was in his office, and talked the Beatles onto the TV show *Thank Your Lucky Stars*. Brian offered Dick the rights to John and Paul's new songs.

The boys wanted a company and Northern Songs was thereby created, in honour of the fact the songwriters were from the North of England. Dick and his partner Charles Silver owned half of Northern Songs, John and Paul were assigned 20 per cent each, Brian the remaining 10 per cent. Furthermore, Northern Songs would be managed by Dick James Music, the publisher taking a 10 per cent commission off the top, which meant that James earned more money than John and Paul did. Under the terms of the deal, all the songs John and Paul wrote for the next three years would go into Northern Songs, with an option for an additional three years. Brian took George Martin's advice that the deal was sound, and it wasn't unfair for its day. So John and Paul signed their songs away to Dick's company. Paul came to regret deeply that he hadn't taken independent legal advice: 'We just signed this thing, not really knowing what it was all about,' he complains now, 'and that is virtually the contract I'm still under.'

Paul's other bugbear is song credits. In the tradition of the great songwriting teams of the past, John and Paul paired their surnames together when they became published writers, styling themselves 'McCartney and Lennon' on *Please Please Me*. This suited Paul, but his business partners didn't think McCartney and Lennon euphonious. 'You'll be Lennon and McCartney,' he was told. 'It sounds better.' Paul agreed to the change, implemented for the Beatles' next single, 'From Me to You', but it came to irk him when Beatles songs he had written entirely on his own, notably 'Yesterday', were credited to Lennon and McCartney.

For the time being, though, there was just the joy of making music and seeing it successful. One morning in the spring of 1963, Paul woke to hear the milkman coming up the garden path whistling 'From Me to You'. It was the moment that Paul felt he'd made it.

SHE WAS A LOVELY-LOOKING young woman, just as pretty as Paul had seen in the papers, for Jane Asher was equally if not more famous than Paul McCartney in early 1963—an actress since she was five years old, a regular panellist on the television show *Juke Box Jury*. On April 18, 1963, two weeks shy of her seventeenth birthday, she was helping review a pop concert at the Royal Albert Hall for the *Radio Times*.

'Noisy' was Jane's verdict of the concert until the Beatles bounded on stage. 'Now these I could scream for,' she remarked. When the Beatles met Jane backstage, they clustered around her, kidding and flirting. After the show, the Beatles and Jane adjourned to the Chelsea apartment of journalist Chris Hutchins, where the boys popped pills and drank up all the wine. Falling into a contrary mood, John made embarrassing sexual remarks until Paul rescued Jane, taking her into the bedroom where they talked of less provocative matters. Paul concluded that a person he perceived initially as a 'rave London bird' was a well-brought-up young woman of whom his mother would have approved. So began the most significant romance of Paul's life to date.

The Ashers lived at 57 Wimpole Street, a tall eighteenth-century town house with a basement music room in which Mrs Asher, a professional oboist, gave lessons, and a first-floor drawing room in which Dr Asher, a psychiatrist, kept a grand piano and, adjacent to that, his consulting room. Everything was wonderfully close at hand, with the Wigmore Hall, for example, where Jane started to take Paul to hear classical music, just around the corner. Jane was more interested in Beethoven than the Beatles when she met Paul.

Paul was welcomed into this stimulating home, akin to his Liverpool family in that the Ashers were another clever, energetic musical clan, but socially a world apart. It was a world Paul was intellectually equal to. Mum would have been proud to have seen her son welcomed into this fine London home, while noticing that Paul was starting to sound different: there was a refinement in his speech from the time he met the Ashers. There was, some say, an element of social-climbing in Paul's relationship with Jane. 'He felt it was important to be in the centre of things,' says Tony

Barrow. 'And that's where Jane Asher came in, to a great extent, being not just the girlfriend, but somebody who could lift him up that social ladder.'

HARDLY A DAY PASSED without a radio or television broadcast, personal appearance, recording session or concert. The Beatles worked like dogs and, as they did so, refined their image. Paul was still instrumental in this, as in so many of the changes the band went through. They visited Dougie Millings, a Soho tailor who dressed many celebrities. McCartney worked with him on designs for new stage suits, and the idea of the round-neck suit came into being. This was a twist on a Pierre Cardin design, a distinctive suit with braided edges, bell cuffs and pearl buttons. Worn over shirt and tie, the suits were light, suitable for stage work, and became an important part of the Beatles' look.

In early August, the Beatles played their last show at the Cavern, with boys and girls queuing down Mathew Street to get into the club. There was a sense of bereavement. 'The best time really to me was the Beatles before they became famous,' says Frieda Kelly. 'As soon as they became famous you knew you'd lost them.'

John and Paul wrote 'She Loves You' on the road. The refrain was banal—'Yeah! Yeah! Yeah!'—but John and Paul's harmonising was irresistible. Released at the end of August, 'She Loves You' went directly to number one.

The Beatles started to live in London full time, all four men initially sharing a flat in Green Street, Mayfair. Paul soon got to know his way around. If he avoided places where fans knew to congregate, he found he could get about without limousines or bodyguards.

One of the addresses Paul visited regularly was Brian's office in Monmouth Street, Covent Garden. NEMS Enterprises had grown quickly in the wake of the Beatles' breakthrough as Brian signed up a roster of other Liverpool artists that included Gerry and the Pacemakers, Cilla Black and Billy J. Kramer. Brian was also in the fortunate position of being able to offer Lennon-McCartney compositions to his artists. Black, Kramer and Tommy Quickly all released Lennon-McCartney songs in 1963, with Kramer achieving number one with 'Bad to Me'. Paul was delighted. 'John and I were a songwriting team and we wrote for everyone. We just knocked them out.' Perhaps the most interesting of these song gifts was to a new band named the Rolling Stones.

The Stones were of an age with the Beatles, both bands led by clever, ex-grammar-school boys infatuated with American music. The musicians met while the Stones were still obscure and became friends, Paul forming a particularly close and enduring association with Mick Jagger and Keith Richards. It was thanks to George Harrison putting in a good word for the Stones that the London-based band got their record deal with Decca.

On September 10, 1963, the Stones' manager, Andrew Loog Oldham, bumped into John and Paul on Charing Cross Road. He explained that he had nothing to record for the Stones' next single. So John and Paul gave the Stones what proved to be their breakthrough second single, 'I Wanna Be Your Man', teaching the band the chords that afternoon. The record went to number twelve, from which point the Stones were in the ascendant, becoming almost as popular as the Beatles themselves. Although it is often assumed the two bands were deadly rivals, their friendship strengthened as they became more famous.

By now the Beatles were a youth sensation in Britain, yet the national newspapers all but ignored them. Most show-business writers considered home-grown pop groups of less interest than American stars. Derek Taylor, correspondent for the *Daily Express* in the North, felt differently. Taylor reviewed a Beatles concert in Manchester for his paper and followed up with a profile of Brian Epstein: the beginning of a long association with the band. Taylor's interest was unique until the Beatles appeared on *Sunday Night at the London Palladium*, a variety show broadcast live from the theatre on national television. Sundays are typically quiet news days and, on just such a quiet Sunday in October 1963, editors were only too happy to seize upon the Beatles' success and the extravagant behaviour of their fans. The next morning's papers presented the Beatles as the stars of a new youth phenomenon that was approved of as part of mainstream family entertainment.

It wasn't only the popular press that had become closely interested in the Beatles. At the end of 1963, William Mann, music critic with *The Times*, wrote a serious appraisal of the Beatles' music that stands as one of the most highfalutin articles about the band ever published. 'The outstanding English composers of 1963 must have been John Lennon and Paul McCartney,' Mann began, going on to explain he found their music fresh and authentically English. It was when the writer came to analyse the songs in academic language that he lost some of his readers: 'the major tonic sevenths and ninths built into their tunes, and the flat submediant key switches . . .' yet Mann was clearly right when he praised 'the discreet, sometimes subtle varieties of instrumentation' on the Beatles' records, and concluded: 'They have brought a distinctive and exhilarating flavour to a genre of music that was in danger of ceasing to be music at all.'

THE TERM 'BEATLEMANIA' started appearing in newspapers in late October, as journalists documented the hysterical fan reaction to the group. When the boys returned to Britain on October 30 from a brief Swedish expedition, hordes of fans screamed in welcome at Heathrow Airport.

By chance, the American television compere Ed Sullivan was passing through that day. Show-business legend has it that on seeing hundreds of girls holding up signs for 'Beatles', Sullivan assumed this was an eccentric, and eccentrically spelled, British animal act. When he was put right, he saw a booking opportunity for his TV show.

All of this served as the build-up to the Beatles appearing in the Royal Variety Show in November, attended in 1963 by Her Majesty the Queen Mother, Princess Margaret and the Earl of Snowdon. The presence of royalty always drew big stars and a large television audience, but tended to inhibit the performers. In being their own cheeky selves, the Beatles proved a breath of fresh air. John introduced their final song, 'Twist and Shout', by asking the audience for help: 'Would the people in the cheaper seats clap your hands?' he said, adding, with a nod to the royal box, 'and the rest of you, if you just rattle your jewellery.' At a time when royalty was treated with greater deference than today, this was considered a daring remark that fell just the right side of insolence.

PAUL MOVED OUT of the Mayfair flat to lodge with the Ashers, using a box room at the top of their house, opposite the bedroom of Jane's brother, Peter, who became a great mate. Paul loved his garret, where he had a piano installed so he could sit and compose new tunes in the style of a jobbing songsmith, though in reality he was an increasingly famous star.

Life at Wimpole Street suited Paul so well he lodged there for the next three years, the sanctuary of the Ashers' home almost as important to Paul as his relationship with Jane, whom everybody in the Beatles' circle liked. 'She was good for him,' affirms Tony Bramwell. 'The Asher family were good for him, too.' Margaret Asher's basement music room also became a cosy den for Paul and John to write in. 'We wrote a lot of stuff together, one on one,' John would say of these sessions. 'Like in "I Want to Hold Your Hand", I remember when we got the chord that made the song. We were in Jane Asher's house, in the cellar, playing the piano at the same time and Paul hits this chord and I said, "That's it! Do that again." In those days we really used to write like that.'

Songwriting sessions such as these—some of the happiest and closest times John and Paul ever enjoyed—were all the more precious for being squeezed between the engagements that still had the Beatles travelling considerable distances every week. With everything else that was going on, the boys found time to record their second LP, *With the Beatles*, released in time for Christmas. The cover photograph, by Robert Freeman, presented the Beatles solemn-faced in black turtleneck sweaters, an indication that, while the Beatles would play the fool on TV, they had ambitions to be taken more seriously. The LP included the closer, 'Money', which had new significance now the Beatles were earning £2,000 a week from touring alone, then a sensational sum. The new album went to number one, with 'She Loves You' relinquishing the top spot on the singles charts only when the Beatles released, 'I Want to Hold Your Hand'.

Not long after, the Beatles met 3,000 fan-club members at a ballroom in Wimbledon. 'They shook hands with all the fans,' noted Neil Aspinall. 'About 10,000 of them, actually, because [the fans] kept going back to the end of the queue and coming round again.' The band then performed in a cage for their protection, which was a first. And, as if being in a cage wasn't strange enough, as they performed the boys were pelted with jelly babies. John had mentioned in an interview that he'd recently been sent a present of the sweets but George had eaten them all—a casual remark that caused girls to inundate the band with what they now presumed were the Beatles' favourite treats. George stalked off stage in protest, already irritated by 'the mania', as he described it. Paul kept on smiling, showing a greater tolerance for all aspects of their success, as he always would.

For Christmas 1963, the boys and other NEMS acts performed songs and took part in pantomime-style skits before sold-out audiences of screaming, jelly baby-hurling young ladies. The screaming had become ridiculous. These were not screams of anguish, but girls enjoying the catharsis of yelling until their faces went red and tears streamed down their cheeks. The Beatles had entertained 100,000 fans in this hysterical fashion by mid-January.

After the briefest of breaks, the group flew to France for a three-week residency at L'Olympia, a Parisian music hall, where they fared badly. The audience reaction was muted and, *sur le continent*, the lads attracted the attention of effeminate boys, rather than over-excited girls. On top of which, the reviews were bad. Not that the Beatles seemed to care as they hung out at the luxurious George V hotel, having parties with girls from the nearby Lido Club.

The Lido girls were ushered away when Jane visited from England, along with Paul's father and brother Mike, who noted that Paul was listening to *The Freewheelin' Bob Dylan*—having previously dismissed folk music as 'rubbish'. Dylan would become an increasingly important influence.

These high jinks at the George V were as nothing, however, compared to the excitement caused by a telegram from the USA. 'One night we arrived back at the hotel ... when a telegram came through to Brian from Capitol Records of America,' Paul recalled. 'He came running into the room saying, "Hey look. You are number one in America."' 'I Want to Hold Your Hand' had gone to number one.

A FEW DAYS LATER, on February 7, 1964, the Beatles flew to New York. The mood on the flight was apprehensive. 'They've got everything over there, will they want us, too?' Ringo asked rhetorically. The drummer's gloom reflected what a struggle it had been to generate interest in the band in the USA. Despite the fact Capitol Records was owned by EMI, the American label declined repeated suggestions from George Martin that they should release the Beatles' singles, Americans having little interest in foreign practitioners of what was, after all, their music. Desperate to get their music out in America in some form, Brian Epstein cut deals with two minor US labels, Vee-Jay and Swan, who released 'Please Please Me', 'From Me to You' and 'She Loves You', without much initial success. Radio stations proved resistant, but slowly things started to change. Curiously, the assassination of President Kennedy in November 1963 may have had some bearing on America taking the Beatles to its heart. In the depressing aftermath of the murder, young Americans looked beyond their country, and heard a fresh, joyful sound coming from England. American DJs began to play imported copies of 'I Want to Hold Your Hand' prior to Christmas 1963, the popularity of the song spreading across the States and into Canada. Capitol released it on December 26 and Vee-Jay rereleased 'Please Please Me' in January. Suddenly, American airwaves were crackling with the happy English sound.

A number of other factors also fell into place. Sid Bernstein, a theatrical agent in New York, had been reading about the Beatles and struck a deal with Brian to present the group at Carnegie Hall. More significantly, Ed Sullivan, who had witnessed the fans' reaction to the Beatles at Heathrow, arranged to have the band appear on his networked television show. Brian accepted a modest fee but insisted shrewdly that his boys get top billing and appear on three consecutive editions. This was good work on Epstein's part, counterbalanced by an example of ineptitude.

Manufacturers in Britain and North America had been approaching NEMS asking permission to produce Beatles merchandise. It soon became too much for Brian to deal with, so he delegated merchandising to his lawyer, David Jacobs. Jacobs sold the rights to merchandise any and all items under the Beatles imprimatur to a couple of young British hustlers, Nicky Byrne and John Fenton, agreeing that they could sublicense to manufacturers in Britain and abroad on a 90–10 split in the entrepreneurs' favour. Fenton expected NEMS to renegotiate but they didn't seem to see what a mistake they'd made and, for the next few months, Fenton and Byrne were free to make a fortune.

The young men set up a US licensing operation named Seltaeb—'Beatles' spelled backwards—to capitalise on the new American interest in the band. Within days, Seltaeb had signed licences for everything from Beatles golf bags to toothpaste, bringing in a revenue of $3.5 million.

As the Beatles' visit to America approached, Seltaeb and their manufacturing partners became concerned that Capitol wasn't doing enough to promote the band. So they took action. 'We had every lift boy in New York saying, "The Beatles are coming—which floor do you want?"' remembers John Fenton. Disc jockeys began counting off the days, hours and minutes to the Beatles' arrival. The irrepressible Murray 'the K' Kaufman on WINS used 'Beatle' as an adjective, and February 7, 1964 became Beatle-Day or B-Day: 'It is now 6.30 a.m., Beatle time . . . They left London thirty minutes ago . . . They're out over the Atlantic Ocean, headed for New York . . . The temperature is thirty-two Beatle degrees . . .'

Announcements went over the air in the New York area that any girl who made it to Kennedy Airport to greet the boys would receive a buck and a Beatles T-shirt. The T-shirt manufacturer bussed girls to the airport to make sure of success.

By the time Pan Am Flight 101 landed, there were thousands of fans at Kennedy screaming for the Beatles. 'Without Seltaeb, the Beatles would have found it a lot harder to conquer America,' says Fenton, with a touch of exaggeration: after a slow start, Capitol Records *had* started to push the band, spending upwards of

$50,000 on promotion, promising to make 1964 'the year of the Beatles'. It all helped to create the day the Beatles arrived in America: the 'turning point', Brian always called it.

A fleet of Cadillacs conveyed the group into Manhattan, where they booked into the venerable Plaza Hotel. Sid Bernstein watched the limousines pull up at the Fifth Avenue entrance amid a scrimmage of fans. Paul paused on the threshold, turned and waved. 'I said, "Wow! He's a good-looking kid." There was a lot [more] screaming for him than the other boys.'

It is hard to appreciate how unusual the Beatles looked to a mainstream American television audience when they appeared on the *Ed Sullivan Show* on February 9. 'We came out of nowhere with funny hair,' Paul reflected. Paul sang lead on 'All My Loving', the first of five songs divided between two spots. An estimated 73 million people across the United States watched on TV, the highest Nielsen rating yet recorded. For many young Americans, this was the moment that ushered in the 1960s; the Beatles would become the soundtrack to their lives, ensuring that all four band members, not least Paul, would command attention and affection in the USA for the rest of their careers.

A WEEK AFTER RETURNING from the USA, the Beatles began work on their first film. Epstein cut a deal with United Artists for them to star in a movie named after a Ringoism: 'It's been a hard day,' the drummer had sighed at the end of another gruelling day, only to notice it was already night, '. . . day's night.' Playwright Alun Owen wrote the script, having had the benefit of spending time with the band on the road, while the director was thirty-two-year-old American Richard Lester, who would shoot quickly in black and white on a low budget: UA wanted the movie in theatres before the Beatles craze passed.

A Hard Day's Night was essentially a musical, but the style in which Lester shot the picture gave it the feel of a documentary, in which four cheeky youngsters are pitched against their over-excited female fans and adult authority figures, who are depicted as comically inept, or out of touch and pompous.

Spending time with the Beatles, Alun Owen had picked up on slang expressions like 'grotty' and 'fab', commonly used by the boys. The first usage of 'grotty' in English was by George in the film, according to the *Oxford English Dictionary*, while 'fab' — an abbreviation of fabulous — had been in common usage but came to be associated with the Beatles. The Beatles' PR man Tony Barrow wrote about the 'Fab Four' in his press releases: 'fab' suited them.

While making the movie, the Beatles were also recording an original soundtrack album, and Paul and John had to come up with new songs. They rose to the challenge with 'Can't Buy Me Love', which went to number one virtually simultaneously in the UK and USA.

At twenty-two, Paul found himself an exceedingly rich young man in a family who'd never had much. Though careful with his money, Paul shared his good fortune around. He handed out gifts, notably a racehorse to his dad, and helped family members financially. Several family members became financially dependent on him, as he helped them buy houses, and in some cases put them on what became known as the 'McCartney Pension', so they never had to work again. This didn't necessarily engender harmony.

These were mostly problems for the future, however. Plans were being finalised for a full-scale US tour. Before this took place, though, the Beatles were committed to play shows in Denmark and Holland, after which they had to schlep halfway round the world to Hong Kong and Australia. All these foreign concerts were triumphs: Britain, Sweden, Denmark, Holland and Australia had fallen to the Beatles. Brian's next campaign would be his biggest: the Beatles' invasion of the United States.

SOMETHING STRANGE had happened in America since their first visit: by August 1964, the Beatles were a focus for nutcases and extremists. '*Beatle worship is idolatry*' read a placard wielded by the ultrareligious in San Francisco. More alarmingly, Ringo received death threats in Quebec from anti-Semites who mistook him for a Jew: for their concerts at the Montreal Forum, Ritchie had a bodyguard sitting beside him on stage. What with the screaming fans, inadequate sound systems, and now the fear that there might be assassins in the audience, the Beatles rushed through their shows, wanting them over with as soon as possible.

It was the sound quality that bothered George Martin most when he came out to record the boys playing the Hollywood Bowl for a live LP: the producer found the challenge of getting a decent recording insuperable. 'It was like putting a microphone at the end of a 747 jet—just a continual screaming sound.'

The Beatles returned to New York, where they met Bob Dylan. Like the Beatles, Dylan was a young man in his twenties from a provincial, working-class, northern town, in his case Hibbing, Minnesota. Dylan was a folk star before the Beatles found fame, his debut album released when the boys were still playing Merseyside dance halls with Pete Best. By the time CBS released Dylan's second album, Dylan and the Beatles were both stars, though of a different order. Girls screamed at the Beatles; Dylan's audiences listened to him in respectful silence, as to a poet.

Both Dylan and the Beatles were singer-songwriters at a time when few artists wrote their own material. As Brian Epstein bestowed Lennon and McCartney songs on acts he managed, so Dylan's manager Albert Grossman gave Bob's compositions to his own stable of artists—notably 'Blowin' in the Wind' to Peter, Paul and Mary. Initially suspicious of folk music, Paul had been very impressed by Dylan's albums, which featured lyrics more sophisticated than anything John and Paul had so far written. Meanwhile, the Beatles had something Dylan didn't have, and wanted, which was chart success. For all these reasons, Bob and the Beatles were curious about one another, and John Lennon asked their mutual friend, journalist Al Aronowitz, to set up a summit meeting.

Aronowitz made the introductions, and drinks were poured. Aronowitz suggested they smoke dope, he and Bob assuming that the Beatles were fellow potheads. As it turned out, the Beatles hadn't smoked pot before. Dylan himself rolled the first joint.

Dylan and the Beatles bonded that night, Bob later taking the boys on a tour of New York. In turn, the Beatles entertained him when he came to England. Both influenced the other. Dylan began to set his poetic songs to rock 'n' roll music, 'going electric', which was a turning point in his career. Conversely, Dylan's influence was heard in the Beatles' lyrics, which became more story-based and at the same time lyrical and mysterious. Try though he might, Paul would never equal Dylan's consistent ability to write lyrics that seem to contain original insight into what it is to be a human being. Dylan at his best is profound. McCartney at his best is a brilliant tunesmith, but he is a mediocre lyricist for the most part.

Still, that first night together in New York had been a truly historic meeting, and the night Dylan and his friends turned the Beatles on to pot. Paul becoming a habitual grass smoker, which would get him into a lot of trouble.

3: YESTERDAY

Paul decided to buy a house for his father, putting Dad on the McCartney Pension and retiring him to a five-bedroom property named Rembrandt in the village of Gayton on the Wirral. Though primarily a home for Jim and Mike McCartney, it would also serve as a Merseyside base for Paul.

There had been no woman of significance in Jim's life since Mary died, so when Jim proposed to Angela Williams, Paul immediately drove up from London to meet her. The initial meeting between the star and his prospective stepmother was friendly. Always good with children, Paul also bonded with Angela's daughter, Ruth, aged five, who became his stepsister when, on November 24, 1964, Jim and Angela were married.

A new LP, *Beatles for Sale*, was released a few days later. It had been recorded on the fly between the Beatles' engagements, and George Martin rates it as one of their lesser works. But there was still much of interest. The inspiration for 'Eight Days a Week', for example, came from a casual conversation Paul had had with his chauffeur on the drive to John's country mansion in Kenwood.

'How've you been?' Paul asked.

'Oh, working hard,' grumbled the chauffeur, 'eight days a week.'

When Paul arrived he told his friend what the driver had said. 'John said, "Right—'Ooh, I need your love, babe . . .'" and we wrote it. We were always quite quick to write.'

The first full year of Beatlemania ended in December with *Another Beatles Christmas Show* at the Hammersmith Odeon. After a break in which Paul took Jane to Tunisia, the Beatles went back into the studio to record songs for their second movie, *Help!* George Martin kept the tape running continuously when the band was in the studio, to capture every precious second of Beatles' sound, with John and Paul's between-songs chatter preserved for posterity as a result. They were still making music together much as ever they had, but now the friends were partners in business, too — big business.

High earners were taxed excessively under Harold Wilson's Labour Government of 1964–70 (50 per cent, rising to 55 per cent in 1965), meaning that most of the Beatles' money went to the tax-man. By floating Northern Songs on the London stock exchange, Paul and John created shares that could be sold tax-free. Figures show that Northern Songs was a rapidly growing business; in its first two years, the company reported six-monthly profits rising from £17,294 to almost a quarter of a million pounds. The flotation was oversubscribed, giving Northern Songs an initial paper value of £1.9 million. The share value then fell below offer price, as speculators took a quick profit, and the Beatles bought shares back, a shrewd move as they doubled in value over twelve months.

At this stage in his career, Paul was more interested in making music and having fun than reading contracts. Having been introduced to marijuana, grass had become part of the Beatles' lives, creating a problem for director Richard Lester when he came to shoot *Help!* in February 1965.

'We showed up a bit stoned, smiled a lot and hoped we'd get through it,' admits Paul. 'We giggled a lot.' It was a fine time to be in London, which had started to 'swing'. The young started to dress differently, women wearing bright make-up and short skirts, pioneered by the designer Mary Quant, while men grew their hair and affected an eclectic mixture of modish, foppish and antique clothing. The trendsetters shopped in boutiques in the King's Road and on Carnaby Street in Soho. They met up at night in such fashionable clubs as the Ad Lib, a penthouse above Leicester Square.

How wonderful it was to be young, good-looking and successful in London at this time, moreover to be loved and admired by people all over the world, the money absolutely pouring in. Paul was informed by his accountant in 1965 that he was a millionaire. He was earning so much he kept fat envelopes of spare cash in his sock drawer at Wimpole Street. He'd bought Dad a house and given his kid brother an allowance, and he'd given Jane some nice bits of jewellery. Now he proved how serious he was about their relationship by taking her shopping for a house.

Paul chose a property in Cavendish Avenue, a quiet residential street in St John's Wood, within walking distance of Lord's Cricket Ground, Regent's Park and, most importantly, the EMI studios on Abbey Road. Paul could also get into the West End easily, while his chosen neighbourhood retained a village-like atmosphere. Paul referred to his new house simply as Cavendish. It is still his London home.

As renovations were made to his new home, Paul remained in his garret in Wimpole Street. One morning, he awoke with a melody in his head that he assumed was a jazz standard that had insinuated itself into his unconscious. Paul went straight to the piano. 'I just fell out of bed, found out what key I had dreamed it in, and played it. It just kept tumbling out. I thought, "Well, this is very nice, but it's a nick ..." It was the only song I ever dreamed!'

Paul played the tune for friends wherever he went, to the extent that it became a joke within the band. Paul was canvassing as many people as possible to see if it really was an original composition, and played the tune one evening at the home of the singer Alma Cogan. At this point there were no words. Alma's mother came in and asked if anybody would like scrambled eggs and this became the working title: 'Scrambled Eggs'.

In May 1965 Paul and Jane visited Bruce Welch of the Shadows at his holiday home in Portugal. The couple flew first to Lisbon, and were then driven the 160 miles south to the Algarve. Paul occupied himself during the drive by fitting words to his tune. The moment they got to the villa, Paul dashed for a guitar like somebody in need of the toilet. 'I could see he had been writing the lyrics on the way down; he had the paper in his hand as he arrived,' recollects Welch.

'Yesterday' was a song of confusion, defeat and regret, emotions one wouldn't imagine Paul had much experience of, and radically different from the upbeat songs that had made the Beatles popular. Here was a ballad more suited to artists like Frank Sinatra or Ray Charles (both would cover it). The words are not brilliant, but the lyric does resonate. Paul has suggested that the song related to the death of his mother, showing how deep that loss ran.

When he got back to London, Paul performed 'Yesterday' for the band and George Martin. 'Ringo said, "I can't really put any drums on." And John and George said, "There's no point in having another guitar." So George Martin suggested, "Why don't you just try it yourself?"'

What made 'Yesterday' distinctively Beatles-eque was George Martin's decision to use a string quartet to lend the song a classical elegance. Arranging this record was a turning point for Martin in his relationship with the band, after which he made an increasingly significant, creative contribution. Partly as a result, Beatles records began to become more interesting.

Around this time, John and George had their first, life-changing acid trip. John and Cynthia and George and his girlfriend Pattie Boyd had been to a dinner party at the home of their dentist who slipped the drug—then unrestricted and little understood—without warning into their coffee. John and George suspected the dentist was trying to get them and the girls into an orgy; the dentist said no, admitting rather that he'd dosed them with LSD. John was furious. George didn't even know what LSD was. It would come to have a considerable effect on the Beatles' music.

The party moved on to the Ad Lib. 'Suddenly, I felt the most incredible feeling come over me,' George recollected. 'It was like a very concentrated version of the best feeling I'd ever had in my whole life.' The Beatles had to take an elevator to the penthouse. 'It felt as though the elevator was on fire and we were going into Hell, but at the same time we were all in hysterics and crazy. Eventually we got out on the top floor, and sat there, probably for hours and hours.' At dawn George drove Pattie, John and Cynthia home to Surrey very, very *slowly*.

The boys couldn't wait to tell Paul. John had always loved *Alice in Wonderland* and here was a drug that could send him down the rabbit hole any time he liked. He urged Paul to take LSD without delay. Paul's reaction highlights an essential difference between him and his friend: 'When acid came round we'd heard that you're never the same. It alters your life. I think John was rather excited by that prospect. I was rather frightened.'

So Paul declined LSD, and kept declining as John and George took more acid trips, growing closer as a result. They were in the LSD club now, and Paul wasn't. It created a rift.

SID BERNSTEIN, who had booked the Beatles for two shows at Carnegie Hall on their first visit to the USA, realised he could have sold those seats many times over. He started talking to Brian Epstein about putting the boys on at Madison Square Garden, which held 17,000 people. Then he saw that even this venue wasn't large enough. 'I'm changing my mind,' Sid told Brian over the telephone. 'I'd like to do Shea Stadium. Fifty-five thousand seats.'

When Brian had digested the data, he expressed cautious excitement. 'I don't want an empty seat in the house, Sid.'

'Brian, I'll give you $10 for every one.'

Neither Sid nor Brian needed to worry. All 55,600 tickets—priced at around $5, plus taxes—sold. Not only would the Beatles at Shea Stadium be the biggest show any act had played, it would be the Beatles' highest-earning single engagement at $180,000, worth about $1.2 million in today's money.

It was a beautiful summer day on August 15, 1965. Late in the afternoon the Beatles boarded a helicopter in Manhattan and were flown out to the gig, everybody crowding the windows to peer down at the horseshoe-shaped baseball stadium. Around a quarter past nine in the evening, the Beatles ran out of the tunnel under the stands, sprinting across the diamond to take their places on the stage. Everybody was seated back in the bleachers, though virtually the entire audience was on their feet, screaming, many girls trying to scale the mesh fence penning them back.

The sound was appalling, essentially relayed via the PA system and blown about with the wind. And, of course, there were no screens to help the fans see the performers. Despite all these shortcomings, almost everybody at Shea had a great time. Among the thousands were Mick Jagger and Keith Richards, who went on to perfect the stadium rock tour with the Rolling Stones in the eighties and nineties.

All the Beatles had a ball. By the time they came to the last song, John was playing the organ with his elbows and laughing his head off, George giggling along with him. Paul remained focused, though even he had to laugh at the end.

After New York, the Beatles played a series of arena concerts across North America, working their way west to California where five days had been set aside for rest and recuperation. The boys hung out with actor Peter Fonda and members of the Byrds, and John and George turned Ritchie and Neil Aspinall on to LSD.

Though he still refrained, Paul did get laid in Los Angeles. The chief point of interest is that Paul was prepared to cheat on Jane. He had just given her a diamond pendant for her nineteenth birthday, and was planning to move into Cavendish with her.

This was also the week the Beatles met Elvis Presley. Elvis had been Paul's number one musical hero as a boy, likewise John, though both had a low opinion of the work Presley had done after being drafted into the army. When the boys entered Elvis's home in Bel Air, the King was watching a mute TV, simultaneously playing electric bass to a record on the jukebox. After some desultory conversation, the boys picked up instruments and played along, Paul sitting on the sofa next to his hero. He wasn't overwhelmed, joking that Brian might be able to find El a job playing bass in one of his Mersey Beat bands. As they left the house after what was a relatively stilted meeting, John quoted from the movie *Whistle Down the Wind*, in which Alan Bates's fugitive character is mistaken briefly for Jesus Christ by a gang of children. 'That wasn't Jesus,' he told the lads, 'that was just a fella.' In later years, Paul put the best perspective on the summit, saying, 'It was one of the great meetings of my life.' It was Elvis after all, the man who had inspired them, his career in decline as theirs was ascendant. 'He was our greatest idol, but the styles were changing in favour of us.'

Elvis's highest-placed single in the *Billboard* chart that year was 'Crying in the Chapel', which reached number three in May. The Beatles scored five US number ones in the same year, the fourth of which was 'Yesterday'. Over the years it would become the most successful Beatles song of all, the first to receive five million airplays in America. And counting.

IN A FEW SHORT YEARS, Paul McCartney had become one of the most famous people in the Western World. Even Elvis hadn't been fêted so far and so wide as the Beatles. At home, perhaps only the Queen was more famous and, on October 26, 1965, the boys became the first pop stars to be honoured by Her Majesty as Members of the Order of the British Empire. Some old soldiers sent their military medals back in disgust, while a crowd of overexcited schoolgirls gathered outside the Palace to shriek at the Beatles through the iron gates.

After smoking a cigarette in the toilets of Buckingham Palace (not a joint, as Lennon later claimed), the Beatles were presented to the Queen in pairs. Paul and Ritchie went up at the same time. 'How long have you been together?' Her Majesty asked politely. In reply the boys sang a snatch of the music hall song, 'My Old Dutch': '*We've been together now for 40 years / An' it don't seem a day too much!*' The Queen looked at the young men with amusement, the beginning of a long and surprisingly warm relationship between Paul and his Queen.

The Buckingham Palace investiture took place during the making of a new album with George Martin, who had quit as head of Parlophone to start his own company, striking a deal with EMI whereby he would continue to produce the Beatles on a freelance basis for a producer's royalty. It may or may not be coincidental that, with his enhanced financial stake in the band, Martin became more involved in the creative process, adding the orchestral touches that are a hallmark of the Beatles' mature work.

THE BOYS had got into the habit of delivering two LPs a year to EMI and, at the end of 1965, the company wanted a Christmas release. So they went into Studio Two at Abbey Road on October 12 with few songs prepared and worked like the devil. Bearing in mind the circumstances in which it was made, *Rubber Soul* is hugely impressive, the best work they had yet done: inventive, fun and exciting to listen to, a true turning point. Together with the album that followed it, *Revolver*, and the singles made at the same time, the Beatles closed the first half of their career, when they had essentially been a good little dance band recording up-tempo love songs with adolescent lyrics, and became a far more ambitious creative unit. As has often been observed, it was as if the Beatles stepped out of the black-and-white world of the early 1960s and began broadcasting in colour.

Paul has made it clear in interviews that two of his *Rubber Soul* songs, 'You Won't See Me' and 'I'm Looking Through You', give a contemporaneous insight into his relationship with Jane Asher. This is intriguing because Jane is one of only a handful of the Beatles' close associates who, apart from a few brief comments, has never told her story. Her silence has inhibited the normally garrulous McCartney, who has said little about his time with Jane, but he has revealed that he wrote 'I'm Looking Through You' at Wimpole Street at a time of tension in the relationship, essentially because Jane insisted on pursuing her acting career, which took her away from London, whereas Paul wanted her to wait at home for him.

When Paul met Jane she was only seventeen, and she had allowed her older, more worldly boyfriend to take the lead. Almost three years had passed and the girl had grown into a young woman with her eyes set on a career as a stage actress. Jane was no longer as biddable as she had been, or as other Beatles partners were.

When Paul was in London recording *Rubber Soul*, Jane was

rehearsing a Bristol Old Vic production of *The Happiest Days of Your Life*, which kept her in the West Country. One can imagine Paul calling Jane's Bristol digs, demanding to know where she was, who she was with, becoming the jealous boyfriend of 'You Won't See Me'. The conflict was serious enough for the couple to separate briefly. They soon patched it up, but Paul was not faithful.

Several women have attested to affairs with the star during his time with Jane, and in his authorised biography in the 1990s, Paul admitted: 'I would go with other girls; it was a perfectly open relationship.' It seems the relationship was more open on his side than hers. Certainly Jane had more reason to be insecure about what Paul was up to. 'You'd go down a club and half the girls on the dance floor would dance right in front of Paul, letting their dresses ride up,' comments the writer Barry Miles, who became a friend.

With investment from Peter Asher, who was now coining it in as a pop star, Miles and art critic John Dunbar (married to singer Marianne Faithfull) opened an art gallery-cum-book store, named Indica, in Piccadilly. Paul started hanging out at Indica. He had a voracious appetite for meeting new people and imbibing their ideas, and Miles and his friends were instrumental in expanding his cultural horizons. 'Through us he met all the art people, like [the art dealer] Robert Fraser,' recalls Miles. Fraser accompanied Paul on a shopping spree to Paris, where he acquired two works by René Magritte. Paul later bought a third Magritte: a picture of an apple that inspired the Beatles' record label. These were relatively cheap in 1966 at two or three thousand pounds each, forming the basis of an extensive art collection.

London's avant-garde set were also a hedonistic bunch, and part of the pleasure of hanging out with his hip new friends was that Paul could smoke pot and get laid. Visiting the Dunbars, Paul struck up a relationship with their attractive nanny, Maggie McGivern, who claims to have conducted a three-year affair with Paul behind Jane's back. Miles notes that Maggie was 'only one of many'.

Another mate was Tara Browne, son of Lord Oranmore, head of the Guinness brewing family, who was due to inherit a fortune when he turned twenty-five. Until then, Tara was living recklessly on credit, roaring up and down the King's Road in his hand-painted sports car. Paul found himself more and more in this moneyed, druggy, fast-paced world of aristocrats, bohemians, writers, artists and beautiful girls. The sun seemed to shine every day during the summer of 1966; English music and youth style was applauded; the England soccer team won the World Cup; and the Beatles' *Revolver* was the soundtrack album of the season.

In these exciting times, Paul must have looked back on the first few years of the Beatles' existence as far less interesting. He certainly seems to have placed a low value on the Beatles' early songs, judging by the fact that he signed away his rights to their first fifty-six tunes in the spring of 1966 for a one-off payment.

Royalty income from the initial Lennon-McCartney songs was paid to the boys via another company they'd formed with Brian named Lenmac Enterprises. In April 1966, John, Paul and Brian agreed to sell Lenmac to the now-public Northern Songs for £365,000, apparently judging it wise to take the cash before these early songs—numbers such as 'She Loves You', 'Can't Buy Me Love' and 'A Hard Day's Night'—became as obscure as skiffle tunes. This was an extremely unwise decision as it turned out, because their early songs proved to be evergreen.

The Beatles returned to EMI in April 1966 to make *Revolver*, the complementary album to *Rubber Soul*, and one in which Paul's new-found interest in avant-garde music came to the fore, notably on 'Tomorrow Never Knows', featuring John's spacy vocal, echoing drums, Indian tambura and tape loops, which seem to make the sound of screaming seagulls. 'Tomorrow Never Knows' is a leap forward for a band that just recently had been yelling '*Yeah! Yeah! Yeah!*', and Paul's tape loops are a large part of what makes it one of the Beatles' 'heaviest' tracks. So it is almost schizophrenic of Paul to have also recorded his first children's song on *Revolver*, the nonetheless delightful 'Yellow Submarine', complete with nautical sound effects. The dark 'For No One', with its lyric about a love that should have lasted years, provides further insight into Paul's troubled relationship with Jane.

As the Beatles began to make increasingly sophisticated music, they wearied of performing to live audiences who would rather scream at them than listen to their songs. Neither did they have the inclination to continue appearing on every TV show that extended an invitation. They decided to produce promotional films to be broadcast in their stead, and started by miming to 'We Can Work it Out', 'Day Tripper', 'Help!' 'Ticket to Ride' and 'I Feel Fine', early versions of the pop video.

WHAT BECAME THE BEATLES' farewell tour began on June 24, 1966, when the band played three shows in Germany. Then they flew to Japan to play the Nippon Budokan Hall, a Tokyo auditorium with special spiritual status: many Japanese considered it a desecration to stage a pop concert there. NEMS received death threats and, when the Beatles arrived, there were street protests.

This difficult world tour became seriously unpleasant in the Philippines, a corrupt police state led by Ferdinand Marcos. With US patronage, Marcos was shaping up to be a fully fledged dictator, while his young wife, Imelda, lived like a queen. Mrs Marcos very much wanted to meet the Beatles and an invitation had been extended to visit the First Family at their palace. Brian declined: the boys had grown to loathe civic receptions of this type. Unfortunately, nobody in the Philippines was brave enough to tell Imelda.

Officials came to the Beatles' suite at the Manila Hotel to remind them they were expected at the Malacañan Palace as honoured luncheon guests. Mrs Marcos and members of the Cabinet, Congress and Senate had assembled in readiness, with their wives and children, many dressed in Beatles costumes. Furthermore, the Filipino people had been informed by television that the party was to be broadcast. Without consulting the boys, Brian Epstein waved the men from the palace away.

The Beatles played their two Manila shows on schedule on July 4. That night, they started to see news reports on television about how they had insulted the nation by standing up the First Family.

When the boys called downstairs for breakfast the next morning, inedible and apparently tainted food was sent up. The newspapers screamed news of the snub. 'I was a little embarrassed,' Mrs Marcos now says, insisting however that she and her husband didn't orchestrate the censure in the press or the way the band was mistreated as they tried to leave the country. She had no idea, for example, that Brian Epstein was having trouble collecting money due for their concerts, or that officials were demanding a tax on the takings.

When the Beatles reached Manila Airport that afternoon, airport staff refused to help with their luggage and switched off an escalator to inconvenience them further. The Beatles and their entourage were jostled, kicked and punched as they made their way to the departure gate. Brian was obliged to hand over $17,000 cash at the last minute, after which their plane was cleared for takeoff.

As the KLM jet climbed into the safety of international air space, the Beatles felt relieved to have got out of the country in one piece. Then they blamed Brian. When they stopped in New Delhi, the band informed Brian they wouldn't tour again once they'd fulfilled the rest of their summer engagements. Epstein took the news badly.

'What will I do if they stop touring?' he asked his assistant, Peter Brown. 'What will be left for me?'

Home again, Paul enjoyed a summer break in advance of the release of *Revolver*. Earlier in the year, John and Paul had given in-depth interviews to Maureen Cleave of London's *Evening Standard*, in which they'd let their guard down. Paul came across as a pretentious young man bent on self-improvement. 'I'm trying to cram in all the things I've missed. People are painting things and writing things and composing things that are great, and I must *know* what people are doing.' He also criticised the US for the plight of its black citizens, contrasting their struggle for civil rights with life in dear old England, 'O sceptred isle!' he said, misquoting Shakespeare, as he often did. It was a habit that could make him appear pompous when reported in print, but may only have been meant playfully in conversation. 'He was a relentless tease,' recalls Cleave.

The journalist's subsequent interview with Lennon at Kenwood had him predicting portentously that 'Christianity will go.' Paul had expressed similar irreligious sentiments but he would never have been so injudicious as to say: 'We're more popular than Jesus now,' as John did in his interview. 'Jesus was all right but his disciples were thick and ordinary.'

Whereas British readers took John's comments as no more than an opinionated young man sounding off, when Maureen's interviews were reprinted in America, readers were hugely offended. Reports reached an already overwrought Brian Epstein that US radio stations were banning Beatles records because of what John had said, while their erstwhile fans were staging ceremonial burnings of the albums. The Ku Klux Klan was promising ominous 'surprises' for the Beatles when they came over. It was therefore in a state of high anxiety that the Beatles flew into Chicago in August 1966.

John apologised if his comments had been misconstrued, indicating that he was a Christian (which was more than Paul was prepared to say), and didn't have any 'un-Christian thoughts'.

The Beatles gave their first concert the next day, Paul scanning the bleachers for a sniper. Though no shots rang out, there were other indications that America's love affair with the band might be waning: there were unsold seats in Detroit—also in New York, where the band played a return engagement at Shea Stadium.

The tour concluded in California, where the Beatles played first to a vast crowd at Dodger Stadium in Los Angeles, an event that descended into a near-riot as fans swarmed over their limousine as they tried to leave the gig. The driver took shelter behind a fence, which fans attacked, beaten back by cops with billy clubs.

The next day, the Beatles flew north to San Francisco for their final show at Candlestick Park, a baseball stadium outside the city. Knowing it was the last show, Paul asked Tony Barrow to tape the concert. It was a futile exercise with the PA equipment as it was and the fans howling. The boys could just about make themselves heard when they performed boot stompers like 'Long Tall Sally', but when they attempted more subtle songs, like 'Paperback Writer', with its harmonised intro, the nuances blew away on the wind. So it was, in a squall of white noise and white light, that Paul retired from his life as a touring Beatle.

4: LINDA

After their gruelling concert tour, the Beatles took time off to pursue independent projects. John went to Spain to act in Richard Lester's film *How I Won the War*; Ringo kept him company. George travelled to India to study the sitar with his new friend, Ravi Shankar.

Since setting up home together in Cavendish Avenue, Paul and Jane had become increasingly aware of their differences. Jane didn't like clubs, she'd only ever had a polite interest in pop, and was not into drugs. She had her own circle of theatrical friends and there were awkward evenings at Cavendish when Paul and Jane tried to mix them. The couple was most *simpatico* on the rare evenings when Jane would cook and they would sit together watching telly.

In January 1967, Jane flew to the United States with the Bristol Old Vic for a four-and-a-half-month tour. There was no way Paul was going to spend four and a half months alone: he was going to have his mates round, pick girls up, drink, take drugs, leave his clothes where he dropped them and the dishes unwashed. He was going to enjoy bachelor life.

Paul also threw himself into work with the Beatles at Abbey Road, where many elements came together to enable the band to take another leap forward in their musical journey. Without concert commitments, the Beatles had limitless time to devote to their work now; their musical and intellectual ideas had expanded greatly. At a time when other artists were creating increasingly sophisticated music, not least the Beach Boys with their *Pet Sounds* album, the Beatles felt pricked to show they were still number one. It was time to record the seminal rock album, *Sgt. Pepper's Lonely Hearts Club Band*.

The band had started work in late November 1966, cutting John's 'Strawberry Fields Forever'. John had returned from filming *How I Won the War* looking radically different. Having had his hair cut short, lost weight and taken to wearing 'granny' glasses, he had transformed himself into a professorial figure, but one increasingly strung out on acid. His new song was a psychedelic look back on his Liverpool childhood, named after the children's home Strawberry Field near Aunt Mimi's house, which stood in walled grounds, a 'secret garden' he'd roamed around as a boy. Paul played the haunting keyboard introduction on a mellotron and John's vocal sent a shiver down the spine as he sang.

Paul looked homeward again with 'Penny Lane', a song he'd had kicking around for a year or so before the Beatles set to work on it in December 1966. He was writing about a place he knew intimately and viewed nostalgically: the landscape of his Liverpool childhood laid out as in a pleasant dream—the buildings, streets, shops and everyday characters he had grown up with.

As with 'Strawberry Fields Forever', George Martin's arrangement of 'Penny Lane' was immaculate, the producer working long hours with the boys to create the equivalent of classical tone-poems. Many rock musicians attempted to combine their music with classical instrumentation in the years ahead, often sounding pretentious. With Martin's help, the Beatles melded pop and classical forms to create music that is natural, honest and enduringly pleasing, and there is no lovelier song in the Beatles' canon than Paul's 'Penny Lane'.

In mid-January, the Beatles started work on the monumental 'A Day in the Life', the inspiration for which is often attributed to the untimely death of Tara Browne, who was killed in December 1966 when his Lotus crashed. News reports of the death—GUINNESS HEIR DIES IN CAR CRASH; A BOY WHO HAD TOO MUCH—are often said to have prompted Lennon to begin work, though Paul doesn't recall a particular connection. Although 'A Day in the Life' is primarily John's song, Paul contributed the idea of the twin passages of *ad libertum* orchestral music, coming before (Paul's) bridge, then again after the last verse, building to the climax. McCartney and Lennon were both now familiar with the leading 'serious' composers of their age—the likes of Berio, Cage and Stockhausen. In the spirit of these innovators, Paul put a radical suggestion to George Martin as to how they might fill twenty-four bars in the middle and end of 'A Day in the Life'.

'He said, "I want a symphony orchestra to freak out,"' recalls Martin, who said the musicians wouldn't know what he was talking about. Instead, he wrote a musical 'shriek': forty-one musicians playing their instruments from the lowest to highest note.

The recording of this remarkable passage of music was organised as a happening, and filmed for posterity. The Beatles came to the session in what was becoming identifiable as flower-power costume (whimsical, colourful and foppish), while George Martin and his orchestra were asked to wear evening dress. The Beatles invited friends, partners and fellow celebrities to take part, including members of the Rolling Stones and the Monkees. After Paul had conducted his apocalyptic ascending chord, the celebrities were asked to emit a final, punctuating *hummm*—later replaced by a crashing E chord, played by Paul and others simultaneously on keyboards, the sound allowed to reverberate on the record until the needle lifted. Thus Paul became a composer of serious orchestral music.

Although it seems obvious now that the double A-side 'Strawberry Fields Forever'/'Penny Lane' was a masterpiece, it was their first single since 'Please Please Me' to fail to reach number one in Britain, kept off the top spot by Engelbert Humperdinck crooning 'Release Me'. Perhaps the new Beatles were too arty for their fans; the two songs did not feature on the *Sgt. Pepper's Lonely Hearts Club Band* LP. George Martin considers the failure to include them 'the biggest mistake of my professional career'.

Four days later, Paul flew to the USA to visit Jane, taking with him a tape of rough mixes of the new songs. They were reunited in Denver, with Paul arriving in time to help Jane celebrate her twenty-first birthday. They spent the next few days together in the Rockies, walking in countryside thick with snow.

Paul then flew home, coming up with a new movie idea as he travelled back across the Atlantic. He had the idea of getting the boys into a charabanc—of the type that traditionally took working-class Liverpudlians to the seaside, jaunts described as 'mystery tours'—and making a film of the Beatles' own Magical Mystery Tour. He jotted the concept down.

PAUL RETURNED TO ENGLAND at a time when the forces of law and order were starting to crack down on the drug culture. In February, police had raided Keith Richards' country home, charging Richards, Mick Jagger and Robert Fraser. While the trio awaited trial, police busted Brian Jones and his friend Prince Stash, the son of the French painter Balthus. They went from the police station to the Hilton Hotel on Park Lane, but the hotel management made it clear that they were not welcome. Stash, a foreigner, didn't know what to do. He took a call from Paul McCartney, whom he knew slightly. 'I'm sending my car right now. You're moving into my house, and if they want to bust you again they'll have to bust me as well,' Paul said. So Prince Stash joined Paul and an artist friend, Dudley Edwards, at Cavendish Avenue, running movies, taking drugs and entertaining what Stash describes as 'harems' of girls, while Beatles fans camped outside, periodically bursting in through the gates 'like cattle breaking through a fence'.

One night in May 1967 Paul, Dudley and Stash drove to the Bag o' Nails, a trendy club behind Liberty's department store. The club was already full of people Paul knew, including Peter Brown from NEMS. Peter introduced Paul to an attractive young American photographer, Linda Eastman. Paul asked everybody back to his place and, half an hour later, Linda found herself inside the home of one of the world's most eligible bachelors.

Linda was born on September 24, 1941 in New York City, the second child of the wealthy Lee and Louise Eastman. She had an older brother, John, and two younger sisters. Dad had worked his way up from a poor immigrant background in the Bronx, where he was born Leopold Epstein in 1910, son of Russian-Jewish parents. Shortly before their first child was born, the Epsteins changed their surname to Eastman; there was no connection with the photographic firm Eastman Kodak, as is often suggested, the name being chosen simply to seem less Jewish. Judaism played little part in Linda's life and she grew to be a tall strawberry blonde, as if inhabiting the WASP name Daddy had chosen. She had a long face that could appear handsome or plain, but she possessed a good, full figure, and a flirtatious manner that attracted men.

Linda had a difficult relationship with her father, who had ambitions for his kids, but Linda didn't fit the pattern. She was not academic, or intellectual; rather, she had a dreamy interest in nature and animals. As she became a teenager, she added rock 'n' roll to her unsuitable interests but she followed her future husband, academic Mel See, to Arizona, where on December 30, 1962, their only child, Heather, was born. Linda loved Arizona but felt she'd been hasty to have a child with a man who now bored her. When Mel was offered a job in Africa in 1964, Linda refused to go with him. She took Heather back to New York, divorcing Mel the following year.

With money inherited from her mother (who died in a plane crash in 1962), Linda was able to rent a nice apartment on the Upper East Side of Manhattan. Working as an editorial assistant at *Town & Country* magazine, an invitation came in one day for a press reception for the Rolling Stones on a boat cruising the Hudson. Linda grabbed her camera. 'I was the only photographer they allowed on the yacht. I just kept clicking away and I enjoyed it, and suddenly I found that taking pictures was a great way to live.'

Lee Eastman was unimpressed by his daughter's new avocation, taking pictures of 'longhairs'. 'My father used to say, "If you want to be a photographer, get trained." Well, I never had the patience. I'm too lazy.' Photographing celebrities requires access, above all, and Linda's talent was her ability to flirt and make friends. One of her first contacts was Danny Fields, editor of the teen magazine *Datebook*, whom she met at the dockside after the Rolling Stones' cruise. Linda also got a date with Mick Jagger.

Over the following two years, Linda notched up approximately twenty lovers, most of whom were famous, including singers Tim Buckley and Jim Morrison. Once, Danny and Linda interviewed Warren Beatty. 'The next day she said, "Guess who I spent the night with?"' It is because of this period in her life that Linda came to be tagged a groupie, but why shouldn't a single woman sleep with the handsome and famous men she met? Yet Linda didn't seem to date any ordinary boyfriends in New York in 1966–8.

A couple of months after photographing the Stones, Linda was commissioned to come to England to take pictures for a book.

Born in 1942, Paul (left) around the age of
seven, with his mother Mary and younger
brother Michael, born in 1944.

A fussy young man with little experience
show business, Brian Epstein, was running
the family record shop in Liverpool when
became the Beatles' manager.

The Beatles playing the Cavern, Liverpool,
February 1961, between their first and
second trip to Hamburg.

The Beatles' first visit to the United Sta
was a sensation. Here they are on the 'E
Sullivan Show', February 1964.

met the teenage actress *Jane Asher* in
3. By 1965, he was lodging with her
lthy and sophisticated family in London's
mpole Street.

In 1971, Paul launched his new band,
Wings, featuring (from top) guitarists
Denny Laine and Henry McCullough, Paul
and Linda and drummer Denny Seiwell.

married *Linda Eastman* at Marylebone
ster Office, London, on March 12, 1969,
before the Beatles recorded their last LP.
s to be a very successful marriage.

Some of the music Wings made in the
1970s wasn't as good as Paul's earlier work.
Some of the outfits and hair styles Paul and
Linda wore were very much of that era.

The McCartneys in their London garden, April 1976. From left to right are thirteen-year-old Heather, Paul, four-year-old Stella, Linda and six-year-old Mary.

McCartney returned to touring in 1989, aged forty-seven, with a show that was f[...] per cent Beatles material.

In the mid-1990s, the three surviving Beatles reunited for the 'Anthology' project, recounting the story of the band for a TV series and book.

Sir Paul McCartney (knighted in 1997) organised two memorial services for his la[...] wife. Here he leads Stella out of St Mar[...] in-the-Fields, London, on June 8, 199[...]

Paul and Heather Mills announced ir engagement in July 2001, outside the usician's London home. Despite a rocky urtship, they married the following June.

In June 2008, Sir Paul returned to Liverpool to help the city celebrate its year as European Capital of Culture. With Yoko Ono at a fashion show at LIPA; his old school.

ce his divorce from Heather Mills Cartney, Sir Paul has spent much of his e in the company of the American Nancy vell. They married on October 9, 2011.

With John Lennon and George Harrison gone, it has fallen to Sir Paul McCartney to carry the Beatles torch to celebrate the greatest band in the history of popular music.

Naturally she wanted to photograph the Beatles. Linda's entrée was Brian's assistant, Peter Brown. And before she knew what was happening, Linda was inside Cavendish looking at Paul's Magrittes.

Art was something she knew about. That, and the fact she had lost her mother early helped create a connection with Paul. That Linda came from money was also attractive, as was the fact she was a motherly woman, actually a single mother.

The next day Linda showed up at the NEMS office. Peter Brown let her come to the *Sgt. Pepper* photo session, which Brian Epstein was hosting at his new home in Belgravia. The Beatles would be there, together with journalists and photographers and a few select disc jockeys. Linda, normally no clothes-horse, dressed very carefully for the occasion, wearing a skirt and a trendy striped blazer. Indeed, she seems to have taken more care with her appearance than her equipment, forgetting to put any colour film in her camera (she had to borrow some). Linda joined in the photo shoot, making a beeline for Paul and crouching at his feet. He regarded her with mild interest as if not sure what to make of her, a moment captured for posterity by one of the other photographers.

That weekend Linda phoned Cavendish and spoke to Prince Stash, who told her, 'Paul's in Liverpool.' She said, 'I want to come over.' So Linda came to Cavendish Avenue and fell into bed with Stash. Yet when Linda flew back to New York, her conversation was not about Prince Stash, but Paul McCartney. She returned home on the same flight as Brian Epstein's partner, Nat Weiss, who recalls that she told him she was going to marry the Beatle. She seemed so determined he didn't doubt her.

At the end of May 1967, Brian Epstein threw a weekend house party at his country retreat in Sussex, to which all four Beatles were invited. Epstein had a grand piano brought down from London so Paul could play. But Paul didn't show. Jane Asher was due back from the USA and Paul had to get the house ready.

Cavendish was in a heck of a state, having served as a bachelor pad for Paul and his mates for the past four and a half months. In the hours before Jane's return, Paul dashed about cleaning and herding waifs and strays out the door. He drove to Heathrow in time to meet Jane, a pack of pressmen closing in. Reporters asked when they planned to marry. 'Not now,' replied Jane, travel-weary and nervous about meeting a lover who had been like a stranger to her for months.

Three days later, *Sgt. Pepper* was officially released. Acclaimed by press and public as a triumph, it went straight to number one in Britain and America, selling more than 11 million copies in the United States alone. *Pepper* has become recognised as the key transition record from pop to the more self-consciously serious form of rock music, perhaps the most significant album in the history of rock. A considerable amount of the credit goes to Paul. Even John conceded in later years, when he usually spoke about Paul with scorn, that '*Pepper* was a peak, all right.' It was also the last time he worked properly in partnership with Macca, 'especially on "A Day in the Life".'

To celebrate, Paul and Jane threw a party that lasted all weekend, then hopped on a plane to Scotland, where Paul had recently bought a holiday home on the Kintyre peninsula, a finger of land trailing in the seas off western Scotland. High Park Farm—a single-storey stone cottage, built in the nineteenth century, with one bedroom, open fires and corrugated tin roof—is only ten minutes' drive from Campbeltown, but Campbeltown itself is 500 miles from London, the last 138 miles of road from Glasgow through wild and mostly empty country. As Paul and Jane headed into the Highlands they entered a seemingly more ancient land, which gave Paul an idea. 'There was a road sort of stretching off up into the hills, you could see it go for miles, and I thought [of] "The Long and Winding Road".' Once local people got over the surprise of seeing Paul about the place, he found that they treated him much the same as anybody else and were in fact quietly protective of his privacy, helping make Kintyre an ideal retreat.

Paul introduced himself to the neighbours. The Blacks were musical, Archie Black loving nothing better than a singsong around the piano. Paul would join in, though Mrs Black's elderly mother was unimpressed when the music went past her bedtime.

One night the old lady stomped on the floor. 'What is that noise?' she asked her daughter when she came upstairs.

'Mother, it's Paul McCartney.'

'I don't care if it's Winston Churchill, I'm not having it!'

The weather was glorious when Paul and Jane visited, so they stayed a few days longer than intended. And, when they had to go, they were able to fly to London; private planes could use nearby RAF Machrihanish, which meant Paul could get back to Beatles business within two hours.

PAUL HAD SUCCUMBED to peer pressure to try LSD when his late friend Tara Browne offered him acid after a night at the Bag o' Nails. Paul's first trip wasn't pleasant, and he felt too exhausted the next day to do any work. Then, during the making of *Sgt. Pepper*, when John took acid by mistake, Paul took him home to Cavendish, where he dropped acid to keep John company. He had a vision of John as 'a king, the absolute Emperor of Eternity', which would seem to betray an unconscious inferiority complex. But when a reporter asked if he had taken LSD, Paul confirmed that he had had no regrets: 'It was truly a religious experience', adding that he hoped world leaders would try the drug. The interview made the front page of the *Sunday People* on June 18, 1967, Paul's twenty-fifth birthday: BEATLE PAUL'S AMAZING CONFESSION: 'Yes—I took LSD.'

Following the police raid at Keith Richards' country house, Robert Fraser, Keith Richards and Mick Jagger were sentenced to six, twelve and three months respectively, though the Stones ultimately won their appeal. There was a feeling that the police were working up to busting a Beatle. Paul's LSD confession was therefore awkward for John, George and Ritchie, who found themselves the subject of unwanted scrutiny about their own drug use.

As it turned out, Paul's drug confessions didn't do the Beatles any serious harm. The boys were still loved by the press and public, deemed fit to represent the nation in *Our World*, a prestigious television broadcast on June 25, featuring contributions from eighteen countries via the new technology of a satellite link-up.

The Beatles would perform a specially written song, John's 'All You Need is Love', live from Abbey Road.

The band was joined by their friends and family. Sitting at the Beatles' feet were Mick Jagger and Keith Richards, together with Pattie Harrison (*née* Boyd, having married George the previous year), Jane Asher, Mike McCartney and other McCartney relations. Presiding over everybody was George Martin, the picture of cool in a white linen suit, who had hired an ensemble of string and brass to perform the introduction to the song, and a collage of background tunes to lend an international flavour to proceedings. The whole thing was so complex, it was bound to go wrong, yet it worked perfectly—John delivered an immaculate vocal, the band played without a hitch, all looked happy as they sent their message of love to the world. Released as a single a few days later, 'All You Need is Love' went to number one in Britain and the USA and embodies all the charm and optimism of the hippie era, as well as the intellectual vacuity of the beaded and bearded. It is the quintessential sound of the summer of love.

IN 1966, THE BEATLES' recording contract had lapsed and while Brian had renegotiated their deal, EMI had temporarily stayed payment of royalties. Then in January 1967, with the new contract in place, the company had paid over a very large sum in back royalties, with much more to come. To avoid punitive surtax legally, the Beatles had established a company, Apple Corps, and embarked on the weird, often comic final phase of their career.

Although Apple was a tax dodge, the Beatles were sincere about creating a company that had the financial clout of a major corporation, but that was run with hippie ideals: creating and selling the groovy things they and their friends were interested in. Apple would be prominent in the music business, its record label based on the Magritte picture that hung in Paul's drawing room, but there would be many, smaller enterprises: Apple clothes, Apple Electronics, a spoken-word recording unit named Zapple, even an Apple school for Beatles children and the children of their friends.

Apple started life in offices at 94 Baker Street, a couple of bus stops from St John's Wood, which made it convenient for Paul. While Apple business was conducted upstairs, the ground floor became the Apple Shop, managed by former Quarryman Pete Shotton, the intention being to sell hippie clothes and other items designed mostly by an attractive young Dutch couple, Simon Posthuma and Marijke Koger. (Marijke regularly visited Paul at Cavendish to give the Beatle private Tarot readings, and they ended up in bed.) Another new face was Alex Mardas, a Greek-born TV repairman whom John believed was an electronics genius, and duly made head of Apple Electronics. 'Magic Alex' was set up in a workshop behind Marylebone Station where he strove to develop such stupendous inventions as light-emitting paint and a spaceship that could be powered by the engine from George Harrison's Ferrari.

Then the boys fell under the sway of another absurd character. The self-styled Maharishi Mahesh Yogi had studied maths and physics at Allahabad University before going into the Himalayas and re-emerging as a holy man whose message for the world was that heavenly bliss could be experienced through 'transcendental meditation' or TM. Pattie Harrison was the first in the Beatles' circle to embrace the Spiritual Regeneration Movement, informing her husband that the Maharishi was giving a talk at the Hilton Hotel. George Harrison obtained tickets and corralled John, Cyn, Paul and Jane into joining him and Pattie at the master's feet. The yogi was a funny little fellow with long hair. The Beatles were amused and impressed by his shorthand route to nirvana, and accepted an invitation to spend a few days with him in Bangor, Wales, where the holy man was to give a series of seminars, starting that bank holiday weekend.

The Beatles arrived in Bangor on August 25. The weather was sunny and there was a holiday mood in the Beatles party, which included Magic Alex, Donovan, Marianne Faithfull and Mick Jagger. In the kerfuffle at the station, Cynthia Lennon was held back by a policeman who mistook her for a fan. 'Tell them you're with us!' John yelled to his wife, but the train left without Mrs Lennon.

Brian Epstein had been in decline since the Beatles' last, unhappy tour. He had become dependent on amphetamines and now slept late, missing appointments. The Mersey Sound was yesterday's music, and Brian's recent signings hadn't made much impact. In January 1967, Brian had merged NEMS with the Robert Stigwood Organisation, allowing Stigwood, a young Australian, to take over part of his company. Brian kept the Beatles, but now that the boys had given up the road they didn't need him on a daily basis. He had successfully renegotiated the band's contract with EMI, but the rumour was that when his own management contract came up in the autumn, the Beatles might drop him.

When the Beatles told Brian they were going to Bangor, he said he would join them after the weekend, which he planned to spend in the country with Peter Brown and Geoffrey Ellis from the office. Brian had arranged for some young men to visit over the weekend, but dinner came and went without the guests arriving. Brian told Pete and Geoff that he was driving back to town and returned home to Belgravia in the middle of the night. Sunday dawned. Brian didn't stir. His staff knocked on his bedroom door, but there was no answer. Eventually they called a doctor, who forced the door and found Epstein dead, surrounded by pill bottles.

The press was on hand to cover the Beatles' weekend with the Maharishi and they clamoured for a reaction. John looked lost. George spoke twaddle about there being 'no such thing as death'. Paul muttered that he was deeply shocked and put his arm around Jane, who looked increasingly like she was in a play she wanted to get out of.

After their manager had been laid to rest, the Beatles convened a series of meetings to decide how they should proceed. Robert Stigwood had an option to take over all of NEMS, and thereby the Beatles, which the boys didn't want. Stigwood was paid off and it was decided that the reins of the band's day-to-day management should be picked up by Brian's assistant, Peter Brown, a member of the original Liverpool 'family'. But Paul doubted frankly that Brown was up to the job. Who was Peter, after all, but a mate of Brian's who used to sell records?

Certainly Paul was the most businesslike during the days ahead, saying, 'We've gotta do something. We'll do *Magical Mystery Tour.*' He led the Beatles back into the studio in September with a renewed sense of purpose, laying down John's mighty 'I am the Walrus', and George's typically insubstantial 'Blue Jay Way', as well as the instrumental 'Flying', all of which would feature in the forthcoming picture.

The Beatles were in a hurry to get these songs down and the film made because they wanted to spend time with the Maharishi at his ashram in the Himalayas. Paul decided *Magical Mystery Tour* could be shot very quickly indeed and handed Peter Theobald, a young film-maker, fifteen pages of notes and told him he had six weeks.

Madly, Paul decreed that the Beatles would start filming the following Monday. His idea was to hire a coach, put the Beatles in it along with a diverse cast of supporting actors, then motor down to the West Country and film an impromptu road movie with musical interludes. Not only did Theobald have no script, no budget had been prepared, the coach hadn't been hired, and no actors had been engaged. Meanwhile, no one thought to consult the relevant trade unions, which then had considerable control over film crews. As far as they were concerned, the whole production would be illegitimate.

The picture was a hoot to make, though. The coach, painted yellow and decorated with hippie decals and the words 'MAGICAL MYSTERY TOUR', reached picturesque Teignmouth, in Devon, where everybody checked into the Royal Hotel. The Beatles hadn't put sufficient thought into the logistics of looking after a cast and crew on location and Paul spent hours making sure everybody had a room for the night—a terrible bore. The following day they drove towards Dartmoor, intending to film at Widecombe Fair, but got stuck on a humpback bridge, causing a traffic jam. They drove instead to the seaside resort of Newquay, in Cornwall, where they stayed for the remaining three days of the tour. Despite the chaos, Paul showed every sign of enjoying himself, riding a tandem on the beach with dwarf actor George Claydon, leading a singsong in a pub, and chatting up female holidaymakers.

When they got back to London, the boys filmed a striptease scene at the Raymond Revue Bar in Soho. To complete the picture, the Beatles needed a studio. As nobody had thought to book Twickenham, they shot the requisite scenes at a disused air-force base at West Malling in Kent, including a wacky car chase and the Beatles miming to John's 'I am the Walrus', the only real point of interest in the whole film, for this was weird and powerful music, performed by Lennon wearing an egghead while his fellow Beatles donned strangely disquieting animal masks.

It was Paul's decision to sell the first rights to the BBC, rather than open the picture in cinemas. The Corporation agreed to broadcast the film on Boxing Day, when it would be guaranteed a massive audience. The problem was that the BBC intended to show what was a colour film in black and white, and they wanted cuts before showing it to a family audience: bare breasts would be covered up.

With this unsatisfactory deal done, Paul and Jane went to Scotland for a few days' holiday. The trip gave Paul and Jane a chance to talk about their relationship.

When Jane had come back from the USA, she had found Paul even more difficult to live with. 'Paul had changed so much. He was on LSD, which I hadn't shared. I was jealous of all the spiritual experiences he'd had with John,' she confided to Hunter Davies, the Beatles' authorised biographer, in one of the very few interviews she ever gave on the subject of Paul. Gamely, Jane went along with him to see the Maharishi, even though she (in common with George Martin) didn't think much of the yogi. She put up with the drug-taking and got along as best she could with Paul's hippie friends.

The couple invited Paul's father and Angie and her daughter Ruth to Cavendish for a family Christmas. Jane opened a special gift from Paul to reveal a diamond engagement ring. He asked her to marry him, and she said yes. The engagement was announced to the press shortly thereafter.

Whatever problems they had had, the couple seemed to have reached an understanding by which Paul would stop being jealous of Jane's career. 'I wanted her to give up work completely,' he told

Davies during a joint interview with his fiancée. 'I know now I was just being silly.'

With Paul and Jane's future apparently settled, the McCartneys sat down on December 26, 1967 to watch *Magical Mystery Tour* on BBC1, as did millions of people across the UK. It was a huge disappointment. The film was plotless and, although apparently meant to be amusing, failed to raise a laugh. Even though there were several good songs, and the film was less than an hour long, it dragged, and the decision to broadcast in black and white robbed it of the modicum of visual appeal it originally possessed. Viewers called the BBC with complaints; others wrote to the newspapers to express how let down they felt. Paul defended the picture to the *Daily Mirror*: 'We wanted to try something different . . . It doesn't mean that we won't go on trying.' Indeed, the remaining months of the Beatles' existence as a working band would be marked by an unswerving, and laudable, commitment to innovation.

The Beatles flew to India in mid-February 1968 for what George Harrison described, with his facility for a phrase, as 'the world-famous "Beatles in the Himalayas" sketch'. The Maharishi's ashram was situated on a fifteen-acre plot of land beside the Ganges, with a large and comfortable bungalow accommodating the yogi, and huts for his followers. The Beatles brought a host of celebrity friends and flunkies with them, including Donovan, Magic Alex, Mike Love of the Beach Boys, and Mia Farrow with two of her siblings. The band members, who had parted with the requisite week's wages in exchange for their stay (a huge sum in their case), moved into their huts with the intention of remaining for two months. Each morning began with a communal vegetarian breakfast, interrupted by monkeys swinging down from the trees to pinch their food. The disciples then met the Maharishi to talk and meditate. After lunch there was more meditation and a rare amount of time for the Beatles to hang out together, think and make music, which was the happiest outcome of the trip. They wrote a lot of songs in India.

George loved the atmosphere, sinking deeply into the Indian spiritual life. When Paul tried to talk to him about the Beatles' next album, Harrison almost bit his head off. 'He would say, "We're not here to talk music—we're here to meditate." All right Georgie Boy. Calm down, man . . .' For her part, Cynthia Lennon hoped for a second honeymoon with John, but found her husband moody and distant, taking himself off to sleep in a separate hut. Ritchie and his wife, Maureen, returned home, fed up with the strange food, the flies, the thieving monkeys and the heat. Paul and Jane followed.

After they had left, John got it into his head that the Maharishi had made passes at some of the girls in the ashram, including Mia Farrow. Lennon confronted the Maharishi, then left the ashram in high dudgeon, denouncing the yogi as a randy conman. This was probably disingenuous on Lennon's part. While he may well have been a charlatan, didn't the yogi have as much right as the next man to try and get laid? Perhaps by throwing his tantrum, John was creating a cover for his own imminent act of sexual betrayal. George Harrison remained loyal to the yogi, and Ritchie and Paul also maintained a long-term respect for the Maharishi and transcendental meditation, which Paul continues to practise.

Back in London, Apple began to sign acts, some of whom proved very successful. Jane's brother Peter introduced James Taylor to the Apple record label, which Peter now helped run. Paul played on Taylor's debut LP, which launched the American star on a long career. Perhaps the most surprising Apple artist was a devoutly religious classical composer named John Tavener. Uncommercial though his music was, John Tavener fitted into the strange world of Apple, which released his oratorio *The Whale*.

Apart from the eclectic nature of the Apple artists, it was striking how often Paul's instincts proved right. Paul gave the band Badfinger a simple but catchy song, 'Come and Get It', and told the group exactly how to record it. It became a top ten hit. Even more spectacular was Paul's success with Mary Hopkin, a Welsh folk singer who was drawn to his attention by the model Twiggy, who had seen Hopkin on the TV talent show *Opportunity Knocks*. Mary was a shy eighteen-year-old with an ethereal voice, and Paul thought he might have the right song for Mary to sing. 'Those Were the Days' was a new arrangement of a traditional folk song.

The teenager found the nostalgic, world-weary lyric hard to empathise with, but 'I kept showing her the way she should sing it and suddenly she got it . . .' said Paul, who instinctively felt he knew best. As with Badfinger, he was right. When Mary sang the song Paul's way, it went to number one in thirteen countries.

John and Paul flew to New York on May 11, 1968 to further promote Apple, appearing endearingly naive. It is almost imposs- ible to imagine a major star today saying, as Paul did, 'We're in the happy position of not really needing any more money, so for the first time the bosses aren't in it for the profit. If you come and see me and say, "I've had such and such a dream," I will say, "Here's so much money. Go away and do it."'

Linda Eastman showed up at their press conference. 'I man- aged to slip Paul my phone number,' she recalled. 'He rang me later and told me they were leaving but he'd like it if I was able to travel out to the airport with him and John. So I went out in their limousine.' Nat Weiss was also in the car. To his mind, this was all part of Linda's relentless campaign to make Paul her husband.

As they flew home from New York, Paul and John were in fact both on the cusp of making momentous changes in their personal lives. Paul was falling in love with Linda but hadn't yet decided to break with Jane. And, just as Jane had stood by Paul during these manic Beatles years, Cynthia had been John's rock. Yet John's eyes were also on someone new.

THERE ARE STRIKING SIMILARITIES between Linda Eastman and Yoko Ono, two strong women who now stride into the Beatles story, elbowing aside the loyal, sweet-natured Englishwomen John and Paul had been with for so long.

Born in Japan in 1933, Yoko came to America as a girl, becom- ing almost as American as Linda. Like Linda's father, Yoko's daddy was a man of wealth, a financier who managed the Bank of Tokyo in New York after the war. The Ono family lived in Scarsdale, the same upstate town Linda grew up in. Even more remarkably, Linda and Yoko both attended, then dropped out of, Sarah Lawrence College. Both women then drifted into bohemian

New York City, to the disapproval of their parents. As Linda became a Manhattan press photographer with friends on the arts scene, Yoko became a conceptual artist. Furthermore, both were now divorcées with young daughters: Kyoko was eight months younger than Linda's daughter Heather.

In 1966, Yoko came to London and, like Linda, made her way straight to the Beatles, coming to Cavendish Avenue to ask McCartney to donate Beatles sheet music as a birthday gift for her composer friend, John Cage. Paul referred Yoko to John Lennon, whom she first met at the Indica in November when she staged an art exhibition. The show consisted of absurdist and humorous works, including 'Ladder Piece'; John gamely climbed a ladder to peer through a magnifying glass at a sign on the ceiling. It read 'YES'. He laughed.

John, with his weakness for twaddle, invited Yoko to lunch at Kenwood, after which she deluged him with invitations to her events. John invited Yoko in return to a Beatles session, and made a clumsy initial pass, which she rebuffed. But when John went to India, Yoko wrote to him regularly.

Cynthia became sick of Yoko's missives and what she saw as the woman's 'determined pursuit' of her husband. Poor Cyn still loved John. She went on holiday to Greece with a group of friends, leaving their four-year-old son, Julian, with a baby sitter. When John found he had Kenwood to himself, he lost no time in asking Yoko over. So it was that Cynthia came home to find her husband and his Japanese lover sitting in bathrobes in her sunroom. Shocked and confused, Cynthia blurted out that she was going for lunch. Would anybody like to join her? John and Yoko declined. 'The stupidity of that question has haunted me ever since,' says Cynthia, who fled by taxi.

A Beatle had fallen in love with a strong-minded divorcée of moneyed American background, a tough, worldly woman who would make a formidable life partner. That describes John Lennon and Yoko Ono as it does Paul McCartney and Linda Eastman. Two men who had been like brothers since school days were falling for almost identical women.

5: WEIRD VIBES

Shortly after returning from India, the Beatles convened at George Harrison's home in Esher to run through twenty-three new songs that became the basis of their next album, *The Beatles*, known as the *White Album* because it was packaged in a plain white sleeve. Gone are the corny songs of Beatlemania. The Beatles were now men making mature, reflective music, the quantity and variety of which sets the album apart as one of their greatest achievements. This musical variety is partly a result of the fact the Beatles were no longer a team. They were increasingly at war with one another, often working individually on their own songs, sniping at each other and with the studio staff who'd served them for years. The format was shaken up; old faces left, new people and new studios were used.

In a way, Yoko Ono is to be thanked for this shakeup in the Beatles' working methods, even if her presence ultimately proved toxic. Yoko went everywhere with John. It soon became clear she was not a docile Beatles partner in the mould of Cyn, Mo and Pattie. Yoko was also unlike Jane, who had a career of her own but was assiduous in not getting mixed up in Paul's work. In contrast, Yoko interfered constantly.

When the band assembled in Studio Two at EMI to begin their new album on May 30, 1968, Paul, George and Ringo were flabbergasted to find Yoko sitting with John, apparently intending to stay there while they recorded. In the past, the Beatles hadn't even liked Brian in the studio. Yoko broke the rules. She intruded, sitting with the boys and, when they began John's 'Revolution', a blues song that referenced the uprisings sweeping the world, Yoko yelped, moaned and squawked along with her lover. Then John suggested Yoko dub a backing vocal instead of Paul, who 'gave John a look of disbelief and then walked away in disgust', recalls studio engineer Geoff Emerick, who'd worked on every Beatles album since *Revolver*, but wasn't enjoying this one. Before long, Yoko was in the control room, venting her opinion. A line had been crossed.

John was allowing this strange woman to meddle with a band that, aside from small disagreements, had hitherto been four friends united against the world. 'It just spoiled everything,' laments Tony Bramwell. 'Yoko caused the split between all of them. George called her the witch; Ringo hated her; Paul couldn't understand why somebody would bring their wife to work.'

It was unheard of for band members to leave London while an album was in production. Yet Paul, George and Ringo now left John and Yoko to fiddle with 'Revolution', and amused themselves elsewhere. Paul went up north to be best man at his brother's wedding. He and Jane seemed happy. 'They could not have been more lovey-dovey,' recalls Tony Barrow. Yet as soon as he got back to London, and Jane returned to the Bristol Old Vic, Paul took another woman to bed: Francie Schwartz, a twenty-four-year-old advertising agency worker from New York who had come to Apple with a movie script. According to Francie, Paul thought Jane had a boyfriend in Bristol, and chose to get even with her by allowing Francie to move into Cavendish while Jane was away. He even invited Francie along to EMI to watch him record 'Blackbird'.

Paul then left on a business trip to Los Angeles. He left a message with Linda Eastman's answering service, saying he could be reached at the Beverly Hills Hotel. Arriving in LA, Paul checked into the pink hotel, taking Bungalow Number Five, which was favoured by Howard Hughes, then hit the clubs. 'He pulled a few slappers [and] by the time we got back to the hotel, there was queues of girls around the block,' says Bramwell.

The next day, after fooling about by the pool with the girls, Paul went to see Capitol Records' chief Alan Livingston, then came back to change. 'And there was Linda!' recalls Bramwell. 'So, immediately, Paul got me to clear away all the birds, and just locked himself in the room with her.' That night Paul attended Capitol Records' sales convention, screening a promotional movie about Apple. Having played the businessman, Paul returned to Linda at the Beverly Hills Hotel, where they spent the next day together canoodling like love birds. 'They were absolutely inseparable,' notes Bramwell. 'She was perfect for him: motherly, big-breasted and she had a *je ne sais quoi*.'

When McCartney got home to Cavendish Avenue, however, he continued his affair with Francie Schwartz. One morning, Paul and Francie were in bed together when there was a knock at the bedroom door. 'Who is it?' asked Paul, for there were always friends floating around the house.

'Jane,' replied his fiancée, who had returned to London to appear in a play.

Paul leaped out of bed, put on some clothes, and led Jane downstairs and into the garden. Francie came to the window to watch them; Paul yelled at her to get back inside. Then Jane left.

A little later, Margaret Asher came to Cavendish and boxed up her daughter's belongings.

A COUPLE OF DAYS after this, the Beatles attended the London premiere of *Yellow Submarine,* an animated feature film based on Paul's children's song, which had turned out better than expected. Although the Beatles had little to do with the project, it had captured the character of the band, their style and wit, as well as the feel of swinging London in exuberant Pop Art images that were attractive and amusing. Beatles partners accompanied the boys to the premiere, including Yoko, but there was no sign of Jane. The reason emerged a few days later when the actress appeared on Simon Dee's BBC show and said her engagement was off. 'Did you break it off?' Dee asked.

'I haven't broken it off, but it's finished,' Jane replied firmly, which was all she had to say on the matter, then and ever more. For his part, Paul seemed surprised by Jane's public announcement, which made him look foolish.

At this stage, Francie was given her marching orders. At least one member of the Beatles organisation believes Paul used Francie as an excuse to end his relationship with Jane: Tony Barrow is also of the opinion that Jane took her breakup with Paul in her stride. 'I think she had realised by then that he was not going to marry her, simply because she was determined not to give up the theatre, and he was determined that she should.'

While this is an interesting hypothesis, it is hard to believe that a relationship that had lasted more than five years, one both partners had expected to lead to marriage, should have come undone without hurt and regret on both sides. Also, Jane's subsequent studied silence on the matter can be interpreted as an indication of how bruised she was.

John now demanded as expeditious a divorce as possible from his wife, relegating Cynthia and their son Julian to his past: he would see little of the boy in the years ahead. Beatles people were scared of talking to Cyn lest it offend John, and virtually the only member of the Beatles family who bothered to contact her after the breakup was Paul. To his credit, he drove over to Kenwood to tell Cyn how sorry he was about the way John had treated her. Paul had hardly behaved better with Jane, and Cynthia believes Paul felt bad about that. 'Paul blamed himself and was heartbroken,' she later wrote, contradicting Tony Barrow. Paul may well have been more honest with an old friend like Cynthia.

It was Paul's habit to dream up songs on the drive to Kenwood, where he and John met to write in the old days and, as he drove to console Cyn, the journey engendered a song, intended to cheer up five-year-old Julian Lennon. 'I started with the idea "Hey Jules", which was Julian, "don't make it bad, take a sad song and make it better." I knew it was not going to be easy for him.' He later changed the title to 'Hey Jude' because it was more euphonious.

Paul perfected the song at Cavendish while John and Yoko were visiting; John interpreted the lyric egocentrically, believing 'go and get her' meant he should leave Cyn for Yoko. Paul muttered that the words weren't right yet.

'Hey Jude' was the first Beatles record released by Apple. The corporation had new offices now, an eighteenth-century town house at 3 Savile Row, a fine address in a classy part of Central London, very much putting themselves on show. They brought a large entourage with them: employees, mates and weird and wonderful hangers-on. Along with Magic Alex, there was Caleb the I-Ching thrower, whose prognostications could make or break an Apple deal, and a House Hippie.

Meanwhile, in the hallowed EMI Studios, where Sir Thomas

Beecham and Sir Edward Elgar had made beautiful music, John was screaming that he wanted to die on 'Yer Blues'; Paul shrieked back at him on 'Helter Skelter'; and George sang about pigs, complete with porcine noises. There was, as George himself would say, 'a weird vibe'. Then Ritchie quit.

Paul had been partly responsible. Dating back to the Quarrymen days, Paul had an unfortunate habit of telling his drummers what to play, and he was quite capable of having a bash himself if they didn't oblige, which pissed Ritchie off. 'Every time I went for a cup of tea, he was on the drums!'

Ritchie went round the band telling his friends individually that he was leaving because he didn't feel he was playing well, and he felt out of things. John replied that he thought it was the other three who were close. Paul said the same, while George had always been justified in feeling ignored by Paul and John. In short, all four Beatles now felt isolated and miserable. It didn't stop them continuing work on the *White Album* in Ringo's absence, with Paul playing the drums on 'Back in the USSR'. Ringo returned shortly thereafter, welcomed back warmly with flowers arranged around his kit, but a line had been crossed: a Beatle had left the band.

When Paul came home from these fraught sessions he found Cavendish in chaos. There was dog crap on the carpets; his dope stash had been plundered; ligger friends camped out in his spare rooms; and women fought like cats for a place in his grubby bed. It was all too much. Paul reached out to the one woman who had made sense to him in recent months.

Finding somebody to look after Heather in New York, where she had just started school, Linda came to London to discover her rock-star boyfriend living in bachelor squalor. Paul was not home when she arrived: he was round the corner recording 'Happiness is a Warm Gun'. Linda went over to Abbey Road and took pictures of the band working. It was late September 1968, almost the end of the Beatles, but the beginning of Paul and Linda's life together.

The Beatles finished the *White Album* with a marathon twenty-four-hour recording session in mid-October 1968. Then Paul travelled to New York with Linda to meet her daughter. One night before the trip, when Linda was speaking on the phone to Heather, she passed the receiver to Paul, who suggested to the little girl that he might marry Mummy. Paul was sincere. The couple formed a tight unit that mirrored John and Yoko. Apart from being his lover, Linda also had the makings of a steadfast lieutenant in the Beatles Wars. 'She watched his back,' Peter Brown comments. 'She was utterly loyal, and looked after his needs domestically and in every other way.' Another quality Paul appreciated was that, having come from money, Linda didn't seem interested in his wealth. She preferred a simple life, as he did, to a degree. So when Paul and Linda came to New York, they stayed at Linda's apartment on East 83rd Street, exploring the city by walking and riding the subway like any other couple.

To help him get about unrecognised, Paul bought an old coat from a thrift shop and let his beard grow. Thus disguised, he mooched about the city, an experience very different from his previous visits. Anything Paul wanted to do seemed possible with Linda, or Lin as he called her. She had bucket-loads of American confidence, which he liked. Both were relaxed and open about sex. They told each other everything about their past (and there was a lot to tell). Lin dug rock 'n' roll in a way Jane never had and, unlike Jane, this American girl wasn't uptight about drugs.

Lin wasn't a committed careerist. She was more than ready to settle down with a man who could look after her daughter. Conversely, there was a hippie chick, go-with-the-flow looseness about Lin that Paul dug, exemplified when they were out walking with Heather. Lin said she had to do an errand on her own, but Heather could lead Paul back to the apartment. So Paul let the little girl take him home. It was such a relaxed and pleasant journey—so different from his normal life—that he found himself singing a happy tune as he walked with the child, a tune that became 'You Never Give Me Your Money'.

When Linda took Paul to meet her father, Lee Eastman didn't go out of his way to make friends. It was his method to challenge new people and Paul seemed intimidated at first. 'Paul was scared to death of him,' states Linda's stepbrother, Philip Sprayregen.

But when Lee spoke condescendingly to Lin at dinner, Paul defended his girlfriend stoutly, took her by the hand and led her out of the apartment. He and Lee got along better after this.

Clearly Paul and Linda were a couple heading for marriage. In any event, they were solid enough to take Heather with them when they returned to England at the end of October 1968.

Adjusting to life in the UK did not prove easy for Linda's daughter. Having suffered the breakup of her parents when she was a toddler, and being taken to New York, where Mom had an ever-changing cast of boyfriends, Heather was now relocated to a foreign country where the people were beastly towards her. The big girls who stood outside Paul's house were the worst, giving Heather and her mommy filthy looks. Children her own age weren't much nicer. In Robinsfield Infants, a private school in St John's Wood, Heather was picked on for being American; nobody wanted to be her friend.

After the period when kids shunned Heather came a second phase when schoolmates took an interest in her because of who 'Daddy' was. Indeed, being brought up in Paul's shadow would blight Heather's life. But there was a good side to having Paul as Dad: he liked children and lived in a cool house, full of interesting things, with plenty of pets to play with. In addition, there was the farm in Scotland.

Linda and Heather fell in love with Kintyre, a wild empty landscape in which Linda could ride for miles, as she had done in Arizona. Paul and Heather both took up horse-riding and rode with her. Best of all, she, Paul and Heather could be alone together away from the press, the fans and the other Beatles.

Admittedly, the cottage was in a poor condition but, one day, Lin said, 'You know, I could make you a great home.' It was exactly what Paul wanted to hear.

BEFORE CHRISTMAS, Paul flew to Portugal with Linda and Heather to visit Hunter Davies, whose authorised Beatles biography had recently been published. During their stay, the couple decided to marry. Lin was now carrying Paul's child, and he enjoyed the ritual of phoning Lee Eastman to ask his permission formally, which the patriarch granted, having adjusted his view of Paul for the better. His daughter's marriage to the Beatle would become a business union between McCartney and Eastman & Eastman, which would advise Paul to their mutual benefit.

The Beatles' winter of discontent, as George Harrison described it, began in the new year when the band, plus Yoko, assembled on a sound stage at Twickenham to realise Paul's new *grand projet*. The Beatles were to 'get back' to their roots by rehearsing, then performing, a new set of songs live on stage, the whole process filmed by Michael Lindsay-Hogg as a movie/TV special to promote the album. It was a typically high-concept McCartney idea with great commercial potential, except the others weren't keen.

Paul called Glyn Johns, who had been working regularly with the Rolling Stones, and he was hired as recording engineer on the project, becoming the Beatles' de facto producer. The Beatles had decided they didn't want George Martin this time, Lennon telling Martin that they didn't want any of his 'production shit' on this new album—a slap in the face Martin took as gracefully as was possible.

Now the Beatles were expected to make music with a virtual stranger while being filmed by a large crew of other strangers on a charmless sound stage outside London, and it was all Paul's idea. It wasn't long before McCartney clashed with his band mates, most seriously with George when Paul tried to tell him how to play guitar on 'Two of Us'. The upshot was that George walked out of the sessions. John, Paul and Ritchie held a crisis meeting, whereby John suggested they might hire Eric Clapton to replace George. Paul *assumed* John was joking. Then they all went over to Esher to tell George they loved him and needed him, and he agreed to come back on the understanding they leave Twickenham, give up the idea of a live performance, and continue their work at Savile Row.

For the past few months, Magic Alex had been working on a new recording studio for the basement of the Apple building, an advanced multi-track facility that would make EMI's Abbey Road look antique. But this bespoke studio facility proved useless. Alex's idea of a sixteen-track system was, ridiculously, to equip the studio with sixteen individual speakers; he'd also built the studio in a room where the boiler was located, meaning they had to turn the heating off to avoid it being heard on their recordings; and they couldn't use the control room because Alex had neglected to cut holes through the wall for the cables. 'It was just hysterical,' says Johns. 'Anyway, we borrowed a bunch of gear from Abbey Road and carried on.'

Once these technical difficulties were resolved, everybody relaxed. The new basement studio had a kitchen next door to serve them with snacks, and four floors of mates upstairs to hang out with. George suggested that keyboard player Billy Preston sit in with them, Billy being an old pal from Hamburg. The presence of a guest had a civilising influence, as did a visit from Linda and Heather. Uncle Ringo let Heather have a bash on his drums, clutching his ears in alarm as she did so, which made her laugh. As Daddy led the boys through covers of old favourites, Heather danced around and around until she fell over, giddy, the Beatles smiling at each other, everybody now in a much better mood.

In playing these old songs, and in their conversation between numbers, the Beatles showed themselves already nostalgic for their past. One of the songs they were working on, 'One After 909', had been dredged up from the cache of 100 or so tunes John and Paul wrote as kids, but had thought too simple to bother with.

Paul had two substantial new ballads, 'Let it Be' and 'The Long and Winding Road', as well as the country blues 'Get Back', lampooning Britons who were saying that immigrants from the nation's former colonies should 'get back' to where they came from. Paul had changed the words to make the song about a character named Jojo in Tucson, Arizona. Fans have long wondered whether the words were a veiled reference to Linda's ex-husband, Mel See, whose given first name was Joseph, and who lived in Tucson. Mel's former partner Beverly Wilk reveals that Mel himself felt the song was about Linda and Paul pushing him away when he tried to have contact with Heather. When Mel tried to contact Heather, Beverly says, 'it was all excuses' as to why he couldn't see his daughter. 'They weren't really nice to him in the earlier years.'

JOHN GAVE AN INTERVIEW to journalist Ray Coleman complaining that Apple was a financial mess and he was down to his last £50,000. 'If it carries on like this, we'll be broke in six months,' he said. The remarks were read with interest by the Rolling Stones' manager, Allen Klein, who set out to persuade Lennon that he could rescue the Beatles.

Klein was an accountant who built a reputation by recovering royalties owed to his pop star clients. He had negotiated a thumping $1.25 million advance from Decca for the Stones and Paul was impressed, but Klein had made no real headway with the Beatles until John's 'six-months-from-bankruptcy' interview.

Paul was furious when he read John's comments: the quote was misleading. John may have been down to his last £50,000 'in readies', as Paul would say, but in reality they were all rich men, despite losing money because of Apple's crazy schemes and day-to-day expenses. Nevertheless, Peter Brown insists that the core business, Apple Records, made money. 'All this about people ripping us off was marginal in the big picture. Also, part of our image was that we had to be cool, nice people—we were artists, and we were treating people with more respect than the rest of the business world.'

Allen Klein was very different from the cool, nice people at Apple. He looked like a truck driver and had a calculator brain. He also had the ability to charm the credulous, which, for all his wit and cleverness, Lennon was. John warmed to a man who told him that he, too, had had a tough upbringing, being an orphan and all; Klein exhibited a wide knowledge of John's music and, cleverly, was attentive and respectful to Yoko, whose influence he discerned.

The meeting they had went so well that John drafted an immediate memo to the chairman of EMI informing him that Klein was authorised to represent John's interests forthwith. With the issuing of this missive, the Beatles' endgame began.

MICHAEL LINDSAY-HOGG claims credit for suggesting the Beatles do a concert on the roof of the Apple building on January 30, 1969, though the whole thing remained unconfirmed until the last minute. 'George was sort of a no; Ringo was on the fence; Paul was, "This is going to be fun." And then John said, "Fuck it, let's do it!" Then they went up on the roof . . . That was the last time they played together.'

The Beatles played for just under three-quarters of an hour that Thursday afternoon, with Billy Preston on the organ, performing all new songs including 'Get Back'. Although intended as a public event, people on the street five storeys below couldn't see the Beatles on the roof, while their music blew about on the wind. Still, a sizeable crowd gathered and the police were eventually summoned by complaints about the noise, as the Beatles guessed they would be. Lindsay-Hogg had a camera set up in the hall to film the officers when they arrived to shut down the gig. By the time Mr Plod emerged on the roof to ask the Beatles to desist, the boys were ready to oblige, having played until their fingers were cold. They ran through 'Get Back' one last time, with Paul and John exchanging happy, comradely looks and Lennon coming up with the perfect ad-lib ending: 'I'd like to say thank you on behalf of the group and ourselves and I hope we passed the audition.'

Producer Glyn Johns attempted to make an album out of the tapes he'd amassed over the past few weeks, including the rooftop concert. 'The whole reason why I came up with the idea for my version of [the record that became] *Let it Be* to be the way it was, was because I had sat and witnessed them having a laugh, basically, and being hysterically funny, and just behaving like normal musicians . . .' Meanwhile, Lindsay-Hogg worked on a rough cut of the film that, like the album, came to be known as *Let it Be*.

Almost as soon as they came down from the roof of the Apple building, however, the Beatles lost interest in the whole project, and started work instead on a new set of songs that would constitute their final album, *Abbey Road*. Before they got too deeply into this, however, Paul took time out to get married.

RAIN WAS FALLING as a mob of 300 fans milled about the entrance to Marylebone Register Office on March 12, 1969. Many of the girls were superfans in their late teens or early twenties who had never outgrown their crush on Paul and had found out that he was getting married. Late, best man Mike McCartney pulled up in a car, his train having broken down, and ran into the building to find Paul, Lin, Heather, Peter Brown and Don Short of the *Daily Mirror* waiting impatiently. There was no sign of the other Beatles. George was at Savile Row, while John and Yoko were being driven to Poole in Dorset to visit Aunt Mimi, whom John had moved to the seaside. He heard about Paul's nuptials on the car radio.

There was a reception at the Ritz Hotel. George and Pattie Harrison showed up late, explaining that the police had chosen this of all days to raid their house in Esher, recovering a small amount of cannabis resin. What with George being busted and Paul getting married, the press had two major Beatles stories on the same day.

By marrying Paul, Linda also became a public figure that day. Her relationship with the British media was complex from the start. Fleet Street always liked Paul, but journalists never warmed to his wife. Almost everybody interviewed for this book who knew Linda personally spoke well of her, yet people in the media who met her over the years found Linda a gauche, abrasive woman lacking charm. Members of the family maintain she never wanted to be in the public eye. Yet that was the life she chose, and the couple manipulated the press from the start.

In her first interview as Mrs McCartney, Linda told Don Short that she wanted to scotch the rumour she was connected to the Eastman Kodak firm, as *The Times* had reported. 'I don't know how that mistake came about except that I am a photographer ...' Linda's friend Danny Fields says the truth is that Linda started the rumour herself to impress people she wanted to photograph. Now she was married to a Beatle, she had a better way to impress the world.

When he saw that Paul had married Linda, John decided to marry Yoko. They flew to Paris, thence to the British dependency of Gibraltar, where a British subject could be married instantly. They did so on March 20.

Having gone to such lengths to avoid the press, John and Yoko then made sure they garnered maximum publicity by staging the first of their so-called 'bed-ins' during a honeymoon in Amsterdam. This was a conceptual happening with a positive if infantile message: at a time of international political tension it was better to go to bed and think peaceful thoughts than make war. In practice, it involved John and Yoko tucking themselves up in the Amsterdam Hilton under signs that read BED PEACE and HAIR PEACE, the latter a reference to their own extreme hirsuteness. When they'd arranged themselves, the press was invited in to photograph and interview the couple.

Paul and Linda watched news coverage of this wacky event on television from their honeymoon suite in New York. It looked for all the world like John and Yoko were trying to upstage them, and in the months and years to come this rivalry became a pronounced feature of their lives, with John and Yoko pitted relentlessly against Paul and Linda.

RETURNING TO LONDON from his honeymoon in the spring of 1969, Paul saw Apple on the brink of disaster. In recent months there had been discussions about bringing in a manager to sort out the mess, and Paul suggested his new American in-laws, the Eastmans. That was rejected by the other Beatles as nepotism. The four Beatles were pulling in different directions. Tony Bramwell says, 'It was like being in the middle of a gigantic divorce.' As in any divorce, the correspondents had their representatives. At the start of February John sent Allen Klein into Apple to conduct an audit. At the same time, Paul persuaded the band to hire his father-in-law's law firm as general counsel, with the result that Linda's lawyer brother John Eastman started going through the Beatles' paperwork. Inevitably Klein and Eastman clashed.

A crisis came when the Beatles had to deal with the issue of the Epstein family wanting to sell Nemperor Holdings Ltd (a new name for the rump of NEMS Enterprises). The Eastmans urged the Beatles to buy Nemperor from the Epsteins, using an advance on EMI royalties, a deal Brian's brother Clive and his mother were inclined to accept. But Klein was against it, saying the deal was an expensive 'piece of crap' and John Eastman a 'shithead', according to Peter Brown, who notes that Paul and his brother-in-law then left the room in a huff. With the enemy out of the way, Klein dripped poisonous words into the ears of John, George and Ringo, saying that if he managed the group there would be a more equitable balance of power, and they would all have more money. The alternative was to let themselves be run by Paul and his in-laws.

John Eastman then wrote a letter to the Epsteins whose tone so infuriated them that they reacted by selling Nemperor to a City investment firm, Triumph. Apple responded by asking EMI to pay Beatles royalties directly to them, with the sad result that Brian's family ended up suing the Beatles.

On top of this, their publisher, Dick James, ignored and increasingly scorned by the Beatles, sold his share of Northern Songs to Sir Lew Grade's Associated Television Corporation (ATV). The mogul now went shopping for additional shares to gain control of the company. Apple resisted this takeover, coming up with a counter-bid, underwritten by Lennon and Klein. Unwilling to get involved in any business deal with Klein, Paul withheld his support, as a result of which the counter-bid failed and Sir Lew gained control of all the songs John and Paul had written since 1962, plus the songs they would write under contract until 1973.

As calamity followed calamity, the Beatles continued to argue over who should lead them forward, pitching Paul and the Eastmans against John, George and Ritchie, who wanted Allen Klein. Although Paul had not signed with Klein (he never did), the other three Beatles now out-voted McCartney, hiring the American accountant, who instigated a reign of terror at Apple; many of the pampered denizens of Savile Row were sent, figuratively speaking, to the guillotine.

While this caused anguish, the office *was* overstaffed, with Apple employees living royally on the Beatles' money. Derek Taylor's press office was particularly profligate. Derek survived the terror, protected as he was by his friend George Harrison, but many others went. Peter Asher who, despite Paul's split with Jane, had been running Apple Records with Ron Kass—who was now fired—read the writing on the wall and quit. The Ashers were in mourning at the time. Jane and Peter's father had been found dead in the cellar of their Wimpole Street house on May 2, 1969. The coroner found that Dr Asher had killed himself with an overdose of barbiturates.

John and Yoko were in a world of their own. Doped up and dressed in white, they floated about London conducting bizarre happenings that were part art events, part peace campaigning, and also clearly a grab for attention. One of their nuttiest ideas was that Apple should send an acorn to every world leader to plant for peace. Apple staff was despatched to the royal parks to gather the acorns, only to find that it was the wrong time of year. Then John and Yoko flew to Canada to conduct their second bed-in for peace in Montreal, demonstrating in the process that John still possessed a genius for music-making. He made a compelling in situ recording of 'Give Peace a Chance'. The song was released on July 4 as a single by a new entity, the Plastic Ono Band, a clear indication that John wanted out of the Beatles.

IT CAME AS a considerable surprise to George Martin when Paul telephoned to say that the Beatles wanted to make one more album. He had assumed his working days with the boys were over.

'My immediate response was, "Only if you let me produce it the way we used to." [Paul] said, "We will." "John included?" "Yes, honestly." So I said, "Well, if you really want to, let's do it." It was a very happy record. I guess it was happy because everybody thought it was going to be the last.'

The old team was reunited in Studio Two at EMI seven years after the Beatles started their recording career in the same room. Remarkably, the boys' last hurrah would prove for many to be their best. In common with the *White Album*, the record that would be named *Abbey Road* had a variety of music, ranging from loose, blues-based rock 'n' roll to sophisticated song suites, yet it was assembled more selectively, creating one immaculate disc that can be played endlessly without sounding stale.

The record didn't get off to a promising start, however. When the band assembled at EMI on July 1, there was no sign of John, who had gone on holiday to Scotland with Yoko, Julian and

Kyoko, and crashed the Austin Maxi he was driving into a ditch. All save Julian needed stitches; Yoko had injured her back.

Without Lennon, the early *Abbey Road* sessions were happy and harmonious. Then John and Yoko appeared, dressed in matching black. Men from Harrods also came with a bed, which they erected in the studio so that the injured Yoko could lie there watching the boys work. 'I thought I'd seen it all,' engineer Geoff Emerick noted in his memoirs. John asked for a microphone to be suspended over the bed so Yoko could make comments on what she heard, and she didn't hold back. 'Beatles will do this, Beatles will do that,' she'd say, omitting the definite article. 'Actually, it's *the* Beatles, luv,' Paul corrected her.

It made sense to name the record *Abbey Road* after the London street where they had made so much wonderful music. Paul came up with the cover concept, sketching a drawing of the Beatles walking across the zebra crossing in front of the EMI buildings. They did so on the morning of August 8, 1969, one of those glorious midsummer days when London basks in sunshine.

How different the Beatles themselves looked from the four boys signed by George Martin in 1962. Seven years on, John resembled an Old Testament prophet, dressed in white with a bushy beard. George Harrison's cadaverous features made him look much older than twenty-six. Ringo had started to take on the flamboyance of a playboy millionaire. Paul was the least changed. Having shaved off his beard, he wore a crisp white shirt and a blue suit, presenting a handsome, mature version of his younger self. Three weeks later he became a dad for the first time (setting aside the paternity claims against him) when, on August 28, Linda gave birth to a daughter they named Mary, after Paul's mum.

Before *Abbey Road* was released, John went to Toronto with Yoko, Eric Clapton and their Hamburg friend, Klaus Voormann, to perform as the Plastic Ono Band. During the trip, Lennon told Allen Klein that he intended to leave the Beatles. Klein begged him not to say anything to the others, because he was renegotiating their contract with Capitol Records. But when the Beatles met in London on September 20, John blurted out his news. Thinking perhaps that John was just shooting his mouth off, no official announcement was made, and the Beatles bumbled on. *Abbey Road* was released and went to number one.

THE MCCARTNEYS were at their farm in Scotland when the Apple press office started to receive enquiries from the United States asking if Paul had died. Fans had begun to see 'hidden signs' that Paul was dead; there was apparently a host of clues on the *Abbey Road* sleeve, including the fact that Paul was walking barefoot across the zebra crossing with a car number plate behind him, the last four characters of which were 28IF. Supposedly this meant he would have been twenty-eight *if* he'd survived a fatal accident that the Beatles had hushed up, replacing Paul with a double so they could continue as a band. The 'Paul is Dead' story grew until, finally, *Life* magazine despatched a reporter and photographer to Scotland to get to the bottom of it.

When the team knocked on Paul's farmhouse door he reacted with fury at what he saw as an intrusion into his privacy, swinging at the snapper, Terence Spencer, who had banged off a picture of him. A few minutes later, Paul realised that a picture of him swinging his fists might be bad PR, so he went after the journalists and made a deal with them. In exchange for Spencer's roll of film, Paul and Linda would pose for another, nicer picture, and he would say a few words. What Paul said was interesting.

'I have done enough press for a lifetime and I don't have anything to say these days,' he told the journalists, in what was a frank insight into his state of mind, adding, 'The Beatle thing is over. We are individuals, all different. John married Yoko, I married Linda. We didn't marry the same girl . . . Can you spread it around that I am just an ordinary person and I want to live in peace?'

The Beatle thing is over! Paul had effectively made the announcement. Yet his comment went almost unnoticed amid the nonsense of his supposed demise.

Over the following months at Kintyre, Paul faced the fact that the band, which had been almost his whole life since school, was defunct. His best friend and partner didn't want to work with him any more; George and Ritchie didn't seem to need him either. Paul had effectively shut himself out of Apple, because of his refusal to work with Allen Klein. There were no plans to make another album or film, or to tour. The only project on the blocks was *Let It Be*, which was his own failed attempt to unite the band. Who knew when that would be released? 'Paul was the most Beatley Beatle of them all,' comments Tony Bramwell. 'He tried [to keep them going] with *Mystery Tour*, and then with Apple. All he wanted to do was keep the Beatles together.'

Paul stayed in Scotland, sinking into depression. 'I nearly had a breakdown,' he admitted years later. 'I wouldn't get up in the morning; and when I did I'd reach for the whisky.' This was grim for Linda. She had a seven-year-old and a baby to look after, with a husband who was depressed and drunk. She later told friends it was one of the most difficult times in her life.

With his wife's support and encouragement, Paul began to think about a post-Beatles career, relying on Linda's advice. They became one of those couples who are so close they are like twins, and though their relationship had its ups and downs, it proved adamantine until death. Shortly before Christmas, the McCartneys returned to Cavendish Avenue, where Paul had a four-track recording machine installed. The first scrap of a song he recorded would open what became his first solo LP: 'The Lovely Linda'. He worked on this homemade album into the new year of 1970. Not only did he write and sing all the songs, he also played all the instruments and produced the tracks, the only other contributor being Linda, who sang shaky backing vocals. Paul's blind spot for his wife's lack of musicality, a symptom of his devotion to her, would characterise and mar his subsequent career.

With Paul shutting himself off from the band, the other Beatles made decisions without him, giving the *Let It Be* tapes to Phil Spector to remix. He recast the songs, adding orchestra and choir to Paul's ballads 'Let it Be' and 'The Long and Winding Road'.

To launch his record, Paul worked with Derek Taylor and Peter Brown on a question-and-answer interview to be given to the press. Paul explained how he'd made *McCartney*, working essentially on his own with Linda harmonising, 'so it's really a double act'. Asked if Allen Klein would have anything to do with his album, McCartney replied, 'Not if I can help it.' Asked if he missed working with the other Beatles, Paul replied, 'No.' Ditto for 'Are you planning a new album or single with the Beatles?' He held back from saying the Beatles were finished, suggesting rather that he was giving the band a rest. Asked about the reasons for his break with the band, Paul cited what has become a music-business cliché: 'Personal differences, business differences, musical differences . . .' As a result, the *Daily Mirror* splashed the story: 'Paul is Quitting the Beatles.'

But the Beatles story doesn't end here. The band would never truly cease to exist as long as there was money to be made from its back catalogue, and everything that Paul was and would do for the rest of his life related to what he had created with the Beatles. But John, Paul, George and Ritchie couldn't continue making music together. The sixties were over. The boys had become men, and Paul had to start a new life.

PART TWO: AFTER THE BEATLES

6: 'HE'S NOT A BEATLE ANY MORE!'

When Paul heard what Phil Spector had done to his *Let It Be* songs—to 'The Long and Winding Road' in particular—he dictated a stern memo to Allen Klein, making it clear that he disliked Spector's embellishments; he wanted the strings, horns and choir reduced, the harp removed, his vocal brought up, and the original piano reinstated. Klein paid not a blind bit of notice, and *Let It Be* was readied for release. McCartney's mood wasn't ameliorated by the critical reception of the *McCartney* LP. Most listeners agreed that 'Maybe I'm Amazed' was *almost* a classic, but *Melody Maker* found 'sheer banality' elsewhere on the album.

Next came the movie *Let It Be*, giving glimpses into the fraught relationships within the band; that and the rooftop concert, which was a joy to behold, helped make the film and album a success— with the LP going to number one on both sides of the Atlantic and

Spector's version of 'The Long and Winding Road' becoming the Beatles' twenty-seventh and last number one single. McCartney would never be happy with it or the LP and, thirty-three years later, he contrived to have the album remixed as *Let it Be ... Naked*.

Paul wanted to make another solo album and, in October 1970, he and Linda took the kids to New York to start work on what became the *Ram* album, working with drummer Denny Seiwell and session guitarist Dave Spinoza. Paul's debut album had been a homemade record; as a result, he was determined to make his second more professional, putting more work into the songs, some of which seemed to express his feelings about the breakup of the Beatles. 'I think he was getting a lot off his chest,' comments Seiwell.

As 1970 drew to a close, Paul put his mind to resolving his relationship with the Beatles, telling a reporter, 'I love them, I really do. But only by being free of each other financially will we ever have any chance of coming back together as friends.'

John Eastman came to Kintyre to discuss the options and Paul reached a momentous decision. They would go to court to ask a judge to dissolve the Beatles' partnership and appoint a receiver to run Apple until a new manager could be agreed. Allen Klein would oppose this, and John, George and Ritchie would line up behind Klein. So Paul would have to sue his band mates. John, George and Ritchie received letters from Paul's lawyers informing them that they were being sued by their own Macca. It came as a profound shock. 'I just couldn't believe it,' said Ritchie.

The writ was issued on the last day of 1970. Paul was in Scotland, his attention diverted by the latest issue of *Rolling Stone*, which carried the first instalment of a two-part interview with John Lennon. McCartney read with horrified fascination how he had taken over the leadership of the Beatles after Brian Epstein died, only to lead the band 'round in circles' while John, George and Ringo had been made to feel like his sidemen. McCartney 'thought he was the fuckin' Beatles, and he never fucking was ... none of us were the Beatles, four of us were,' John growled, and asserted that the movie *Let it Be* was edited to Paul's advantage, with scenes involving him and Yoko cut 'for no other reason than the people were orientated towards Engelbert Humperdinck . . .' This comparison to the middle-of-the-road balladeer cut McCartney most deeply—that, and John's assessment of his first solo album: 'Rubbish,' opined Lennon.

PAUL CAME DOWN to London to attend the opening of his court case on February 19, the first part being an application to appoint a receiver to manage the Beatles' affairs. Inside the Royal Courts of Justice, McCartney's QC listed reasons—including tax offences in the USA—why Klein was not a man to be trusted, and told the judge Paul had never agreed that Klein should represent him. In reply, Klein said he was appealing against his tax convictions and McCartney hadn't complained about the enhanced royalties he'd negotiated for the band: the Beatles' income had increased to £4.3 million a year during his tenure.

The court heard from Lennon, Harrison and Starkey in the form of written affidavits, read aloud by barristers. Paul went into the witness box to tell the court, among other things, of a conversation he had had with Allen Klein in which Klein blamed Yoko for the discord within the band, saying, 'The real trouble is Yoko.' Paul wondered aloud what John would have said if he'd heard that basic truth. He had now.

Leaving the lawyers to get on with the case, Paul and Linda flew to Los Angeles to complete *Ram*. Despite the good work done in New York, Paul had become bogged down, unable to select between the twenty or so songs he had recorded.

The McCartneys were still in LA when Mr Justice Stamp ruled in Paul's favour. 'The appointment of Abkco [Klein's company], without the concurrence of Paul was, in my judgment, a breach of the terms of the partnership deed,' said the judge. Klein had received excessive commission, and McCartney had grounds to distrust the American, whose statements read 'like the irresponsible patter of a second-rate salesman'. The judge appointed an accountant, James Spooner, to manage the Beatles' affairs until a full hearing on the issue of dissolving the partnership, which was McCartney's ultimate goal. Paul had conducted his case well, with the help of a first-class legal team, showing himself to be a formidable courtroom adversary: when he went to law, McCartney usually got what he wanted. That evening, a thwarted John Lennon threw bricks through the windows of Paul's London home.

James Spooner therefore became the Beatles' court-appointed manager, duties he undertook from his desk in the City of London. Spooner tended to agree with McCartney's view that Allen Klein was a crook, while he considered John simply impossible. 'John Lennon was a brilliant man, but terribly tiresome,' he observed, likewise declaring McCartney was correct to sue his band mates. 'They'd have been bust otherwise. Klein ripped them off by taking a percentage off the *gross*, rather than off the net, after expenses . . . They had huge tax liabilities on previous years which nobody had ever told them how to reserve for. But, happily, they were earning a million a year each, so they were able to pay past tax liabilities out of the current and future income.'

More importantly, Paul formally adopted Heather as his daughter. Although a couple of hippies in many respects, there was a traditional parental firmness to Paul and Linda McCartney: 'We explain to Heather that she can't have too much ice cream or that sweets will ruin her teeth—that sort of thing,' Paul said. 'She's going to get the lot when she's twenty-one and I want her to have learned how to cope when that time comes. I don't want her to be a spoilt little brat. We're really quite strict with her in some ways.' Indeed, some observers felt Paul was stricter with Heather than his own natural children. As yet, however, Heather could be measured only against Mary McCartney, who was coming up for two, but Lin was pregnant again.

FOR MANY PEOPLE, *Ram* is one of Paul's best solo albums, with a Beatles sparkle. The cover features a photo Linda took of Paul shearing their Blackface sheep. Inside it is illustrated with a collage of snapshots, many taken by Linda on the property, emphasising the fact that, although they had employed session musicians, this was another homemade McCartney production, one in which all the songs were credited to Paul and Linda McCartney.

This may have been a ruse. Under the terms of the contracts he had signed as a Beatle, any songs Paul wrote until 1973 were owned by Northern Songs and an entity named Maclen Music. By crediting new songs to Paul and Linda McCartney, he clawed back half the royalties. How much writing Linda actually did is questionable and, indeed, Paul's publishers took the view that his wife wasn't capable of being his co-writer, suing him on that basis (the dispute was later settled out of court).

But while many fans loved *Ram*, other listeners wondered what had happened to the man who had been a prime mover in the world's greatest pop band. While it had been ridiculous to suggest in 1969 that Paul McCartney was dead, one might wonder if he'd undergone a lobotomy before leaving the Beatles.

Having released two exploratory solo albums, Paul's next move was to form a band. He intended to develop the group slowly, enjoying the process of playing small shows again and making records in a relaxed collaborative atmosphere. The nucleus of the new group became Paul, Linda and Denny Seiwell, the drummer on *Ram*. As yet Linda didn't play an instrument. Paul was sure she could pick up keyboards, so when they got back to London, Lin went for lessons with Mrs Matthews, an elderly neighbour. The lessons didn't go well. 'Mrs Matthews gave up,' recalls Evelyn Grumi, whose family occupied the apartment over Mrs Matthews' basement flat and was thereby obliged to listen to Linda plonking about on the piano. 'Mrs Matthews said, "She doesn't know her right hand from her left."' So it was that Paul found himself in a band with a woman who could neither sing nor play. As George Martin remarked, 'I don't think Linda is a substitute for John Lennon.'

To be fair, Linda didn't really want to be in the band at all: it was Paul's fancy that his wife should work with him; he found it 'comforting'. Professional sidemen would cover Linda's bum notes. Her value was the moral support she gave Paul. He saw Linda as his career partner now, using her as his link with the world, which is to say that Mrs McCartney was the one who made calls on Paul's behalf, getting information he wanted, screening out people he didn't want to speak to, making the peace with those he'd upset.

Lin was a tough broad who grew tougher during their long marriage.

Still, Paul also felt the need of a more experienced musician in the band, someone he could write with, play with and sing harmony with, as he had with Lennon. He chose Denny Laine, a musician he'd known since the early 1960s. A friendly, easy-going guy with a broad Birmingham accent and a wide love of music, particularly jazz and blues, in 1964 Denny co-founded the Moody Blues, who supported the Beatles on tour and went to number one with 'Go Now'. He knew the Beatles well by this stage. As a result, he was relaxed around Paul, not somebody who would ask a lot of star-struck questions about the Beatles. 'I think that's why Paul wanted me in the band—because he knew I wouldn't bring up all that stuff.'

Confusingly, this meant there were now two men named Denny in the band, both initially paid a retainer of £70 a week. This was a reasonable wage in 1971, but certainly not riches, especially not for Seiwell, who had the additional expense of relocating with his wife from New York. Happy-go-lucky Laine was more relaxed, 'I wasn't looking for anything more to start with, because I knew there would be a deal along the line.'

AFTER A LONG and complicated labour, Stella Nina McCartney was born at King's College Hospital on September 13, 1971. So thankful was Paul that mother and daughter had come through OK, that he imagined a guardian angel with wings standing over the family. It was this image that gave him the name for the new band: Wings.

Wings began recording their first album, *Wild Life*, in London, using up leftovers from Paul's LA sessions. The band had a rocking sound, which was partly Denny Laine's influence. But in the cold light of day there were only two interesting songs on *Wild Life*: 'Tomorrow' and 'Dear Friend'. The latter is sometimes read as a message from Paul to John Lennon, but in truth it could mean almost anything, so insubstantial are the words. By then, John had addressed their broken friendship more eloquently on his *Imagine* album, which he made with help from George Harrison and Klaus Voormann, under the direction of Phil Spector, demonstrating what a difference a professional producer can make. Paul's record sounded amateurish and thin; *Imagine* sounded big as a mountain.

Paul launched Wings with a party at the Empire Ballroom in London's Leicester Square. He showed up in a baggy tartan suit and Lin wore a maternity dress. Paul had cut a sharp figure during the sixties; now he had mislaid his style compass. It would be years until he found it again. Not all seventies fashion was bad, but it is fair to say that Paul McCartney dressed appallingly throughout that decade, wearing ill-chosen clothes and sporting a trendy yet hideous mullet haircut.

Despite the size of the Wings launch party, none of the other Beatles attended, and there were hardly any old faces from Apple. 'This was a fresh start,' says Denny Seiwell, 'and we did not discuss the Beatles.'

PAUL HIRED an additional guitarist for Wings, Henry McCullough, who had played notably with Joe Cocker's Grease Band and was an old friend of Denny Laine's. It soon became clear that Henry didn't quite fit into Wings, which was poppier than both he and Laine wished, with a distinct weakness in the keyboard department. Paul admitted that his wife was 'absolute rubbish' on keyboards, but there was no prospect of replacing her.

On January 30, 1972, news came from Northern Ireland that the British Army had opened fire on a Republican demonstration, killing thirteen people. In the wake of this incident, Paul wrote a protest song, calling for the British to get out of Ireland. John Lennon wrote two songs of his own about Bloody Sunday, both of which shared the simplistic sentiment expressed by Paul in 'Give Ireland Back to the Irish'. It is also possible that Paul wanted to reach out to John again by aligning himself with one of his old friend's pet causes. Certainly, Paul tried hard to remake their friendship in the seventies.

As the song was rush-released, Paul led his fledgling band out on the road for the first time. On the morning of February 8, 1972, the McCartneys, together with their children, the band and the family dogs, headed north on the M1 in an Avis truck and a green van. They reached Nottingham University, where the roadies informed the students' union that they had Paul McCartney outside. Could Wings put on a show? The students didn't believe it until they saw Paul for themselves, at which point the booking was made. So, the following lunch time, Paul McCartney got back on stage to play for a live paying audience for the first time since Candlestick Park. He opened with a Little Richard cover, 'Lucille', after which it was mostly unknown territory. 'We haven't got too many numbers yet,' McCartney told the students. The kids yelled that they didn't mind.

Back in the van, Wings divvied up the takings, mostly in coins and one-pound notes. 'Paul would go, "One for you, one for you, one for you . . ."' recalls Seiwell, adding with some bitterness, 'It was probably the most money I ever made touring with Paul.'

Linda's musicianship still proved feeble, however. On one occasion, when Paul counted the band into 'Wild Life', he was met by silence from his left. Looking over, he saw his keyboardist wife mouthing back that she'd forgotten the chords. The audience didn't care, and neither did Paul. He was having a ball. Wings was a Mom and Pop act. Backstage you were liable to find Mary and Heather McCartney drawing pictures while baby sister Stella (known as Stelly) slept in a makeshift cot in a drawer. Significantly, the band's next single was an arrangement of the children's nursery rhyme 'Mary Had a Little Lamb', because Mary McCartney had a pet lamb in Kintyre.

Being a parent had evidently changed Paul and, when he took Wings on a European tour in the summer of 1972, the band travelled in a brightly coloured double-decker bus, the top deck laid out with beanbags and mattresses for the band and the kids to lounge about on. The idea of this European tour was to get the band some road experience before they attempted anything more ambitious. So the Wings' double-decker trundled up through France into Germany.

Almost all the adults on the bus smoked grass, and for a long tour they needed a regular supply. Rather than risk taking drugs through Customs, the band had dope posted to them from England. One parcel was addressed to Denny Seiwell, care of the Gothenburg Park Hotel, where Wings arrived on August 10, 1972. As the band came off stage that night, Paul, Linda and Denny Seiwell were seized by Swedish detectives. They were ordered to pay a fine totalling £1,000, and allowed to go on their way. But the drug conviction meant Paul was now unable to take Wings to the United States and Japan, as planned. Paul would make similar mistakes again and again during the course of his career.

Shortly afterwards, the McCartneys were in trouble again, this time in Scotland where the police had found marijuana growing in a greenhouse at High Park Farm. Paul was summoned to appear before the sheriff's court in Campbeltown to face charges under the Misuse of Drugs Act.

The following spring, Paul and Lin flew by private plane to RAF Machrihanish, where they met their lawyer Len Murray and John McCluskey QC, the advocate hired to represent them in court on drugs charges. Linda had seemingly enjoyed a joint on the flight. 'She was stoned out of her mind,' notes an unimpressed Murray.

A giggling Linda borrowed McCluskey's bowler hat and wore it throughout the day, as though laughing at the proceedings, which resulted in a nominal £100 fine, at which point Linda tossed her hat in the air for joy. Later, Len Murray said of McCartney, 'I was quite impressed with the way he conducted himself. He certainly never gave the impression of not caring . . .'

Paul and Linda were as one, however; Paul's devotion to his wife was expressed in Wings' new single, 'My Love', recorded at AIR Studios, George Martin's new facility overlooking Oxford Circus. Paul had come to AIR because he wanted to record with an orchestra, and George was the best man for that job.

'My Love' was lifted by Henry McCullough, who bucked against Paul's regimented way of making music and wanted to extemporise. As the orchestra played, Henry tore off the solo of his life. 'It had got to the point where I *achingly* wanted to be the guitar player in the band, instead of learning parts,' says the guitarist, 'and Paul found that way of working a little risky.' The song became a number one hit in the USA. This success was followed by the new album,

Red Rose Speedway, which Paul asked Glyn Johns to produce.

Johns had gone on to become one of the foremost producers in rock, working successfully with Eric Clapton, the Eagles, Led Zeppelin and the Who. To his mind, Wings was not in the same league as these acts. The essential problem for Glyn was that Paul lacked a musical equal. 'While the Beatles existed, John wouldn't let him get away with anything too syrupy. He'd take the piss out of him.' The result was that Wings smoked dope and jammed in the studio to little effect: Johns often didn't even bother to run the tape. He didn't appreciate the sycophantic atmosphere around Paul so he quit *Red Rose Speedway*, describing the album Wings went on to make without him as 'a load of rubbish'.

More mediocrity followed when Paul agreed to take part in a music special for the television arm of Sir Lew Grade's media empire. Grade, the owner of Northern Songs, had been suing Paul over registering his new songs to Paul and Linda McCartney, thereby depriving Grade of royalties if titles were credited to Paul alone. To settle the dispute, Paul agreed that Wings would appear in a fifty-five-minute television special for ATV.

Broadcast on May 10, 1973, *James Paul McCartney* consisted of a series of musical performances, including Beatles songs such as 'Blackbird' and 'Michelle' (a sign of what a hard bargain Grade had driven). Many numbers were presented in the form of short films. For 'Mary Had a Little Lamb', Wings mimed along to a backing track while surrounded by a flock of sheep. The most interesting part of the show was footage of Paul hosting a family party in a Merseyside pub. Jim McCartney was present, a smartly dressed gent of seventy.

The other highlight was a performance of 'Live and Let Die', which Paul had written for the new James Bond film. He cut the record with George Martin at AIR, Martin having written an arrangement for orchestra. It was a perfect Bond theme, a top ten hit on both sides of the Atlantic, and one of the best half-dozen songs of his post-Beatles career, not coincidentally because McCartney was working again with George Martin, one of the few people in the music business whom he respected enough to be guided by. It was also a very modern-sounding song, tailored for the bombastic, pyrotechnically enhanced stadium rock shows of the 1970s, which were just around the corner for Wings.

FOR SOME YEARS, Paul and Linda had been in the habit of driving out of London to enjoy the countryside. One such tour took them to the village of Peasmarsh in East Sussex. Tucked away in the woods, an eccentric circular house was for sale, built in the 1930s. A stream running through the wood led to a nearby waterfall, hence the house's name, Waterfall. The property was accessible only via a private, 300-yard track, and completely hidden by the trees. London was only an hour away by car, with a convenient aerodrome at nearby Lydd. In a break in Wings' 1973 UK tour, the McCartneys bought Waterfall, expanding their landholding by buying additional neighbouring tracts of land and farms, creating an extensive country estate that eventually became their main home.

Paul had so much money washing around that he was looking for investment opportunities. Lee Eastman suggested Paul invest in song-publishing, one of Lee's specialist areas. 'Linda's dad asked me what kind of music I liked. And the first name I said was Buddy Holly.' That spring, the Eastmans bought the Nor Va Jak publishing company, in which were held US rights to Buddy Holly's biggest hits, making Paul the proud owner of 'Maybe Baby', 'Not Fade Away' and 'Peggy Sue', among other classics. The Eastmans went on to acquire more song catalogues for Paul, though the songs he most wanted to own—those he'd written with John Lennon—remained stubbornly beyond his reach.

Aside from publishing, cash and property, Paul owned a valuable art collection and several luxury cars. The other members of Wings were all still being paid a paltry £70 a week, with occasional bonuses—the musicians were under the impression they would be cut in on the band royalties eventually. 'That just never happened,' says Denny Seiwell. By the time the band convened at Paul's Scottish estate to work on the next album, these financial complaints were starting to have a negative effect on morale.

Paul had discovered that EMI operated recording studios in

far-flung countries and had booked Wings into the facility in the Nigerian port city of Lagos for September 1973. In preparation, Wings worked on Paul's new songs in the barn on Low Ranachan Farm, part of McCartney's enlarged Scottish estate. Despite the charming rural setting there were fractious words in the barn. Henry McCullough and Paul came to an impasse on July 14 when Paul told Henry once too often what he should play and, at the end of the day, Henry put his guitar case in his car and drove home to London. He didn't return. Paul continued as if nothing had happened. Denny Seiwell suggested they postpone the trip to break in a new guitar player and Paul refused. Seiwell quit.

Paul had lost two band members in a matter of a few days, but he carried on regardless, flying to Lagos at the end of August. The actual recording sessions for *Band on the Run* were no less fraught than the build-up to the record. Paul discovered that Lagos was not a paradise resort but a dirty, dangerous, disease-ridden city, stickily hot in the monsoon season. The villas hired to accommodate them were alive with spiders, insects and lizards. And the EMI facility in Apapa turned out to be little more than a shed attached to a pressing plant. The next thing Paul knew, he was being mugged during an evening walk with Linda. As Lin screamed at the muggers not to hurt her husband, the men made off with his valuables, including the demo tapes.

When a writer loses his manuscript and is obliged to write again from memory, the writing often comes more cleanly the second time. Forced to remember his songs, Paul laid down a series of minor classics, playing the drums himself and dividing up the guitar parts with Laine. '[We] made the album as though we were just two producers/musicians,' recalls his band mate, emphasising that Paul still made no allusion to the loss of McCullough and Seiwell. The strain of it all got to Paul, though. Halfway through the work he collapsed in the studio. It turned out to be a panic attack.

When Paul returned to London seven weeks later, he had the basis of the best studio album Wings ever made. It seems that Paul's desire to show Seiwell and McCullough he could do without them made him raise his game. Denny Laine found working creatively with Paul a pleasure. 'The thing about Paul is that it was difficult to be his equal as far as the public was concerned, but in the studio we were pretty much on a par.' Paul was also very fair with song credits and the split of publishing income.

That autumn, Paul went into AIR in London to add strings and horns to *Band on the Run*, then staged an elaborate *Pepper*-like photo shoot for the album, inviting a disparate bunch of celebrities to pose with him, Lin and Laine in a jailbreak pose. The resultant cover was fun while the music was good. Here at last was the old McCartney panache, and *Band on the Run* was a deserved number one album in the US and UK, yielding several hit singles.

AN ELEMENT OF ROUTINE creeps into most lives, especially when children are involved. The McCartneys generally spent the working week in London, the kids in local schools and Paul in the studio. At the weekend, they usually drove down to Waterfall, their cottage in Sussex. They visited relatives on Merseyside for Christmas and New Year, then spent a couple of weeks each summer in Kintyre where Heather rode in the gymkhana while Paul and Linda had fun entering their livestock in competition at the annual agricultural show.

For some time now, Paul had been denied a US visa due to his drug convictions. In the spring of 1974, the problem was solved and Paul and Linda began going to the States again. Paul immediately took the opportunity to call on John Lennon, who was stranded in America.

After making the *Imagine* album in England, John and Yoko had moved to New York in 1971, living originally in the St Regis Hotel, then in a Greenwich Village apartment before moving into the Dakota, a grand old apartment building on Central Park West.

The US authorities wanted Lennon out of the country so John's lawyers had advised him to apply for US residency. While his application was in the pipeline, John was permitted to remain in the United States, but warned that he might not be let back in if he left.

In the autumn of 1973, John had left Yoko for their assistant, May Pang, with Yoko's blessing. By March 1974, Lennon and May were living in Santa Monica, California. One night, the McCart-neys called by to say hi. Considering all John had said about Paul over the past few years, the meeting was surprisingly cordial, the ex-Beatles feeling comfortable enough in each other's presence to jam together.

The time was right for a *rapprochement*. John and Paul's contract with Northern Songs had expired, allowing them to benefit from their new songs via their respective publishing companies; both had enjoyed solo success, and John had come round to the view that Paul had been right about Allen Klein. In fact, all the Beatles had turned their backs on Klein and were now suing him. The boys had also agreed sensibly that their faithful retainer, Neil Aspinall, should head up Apple Corps, which he ran successfully until his retirement in 2007. Furthermore, John, Paul and George had con-tributed individually to Ritchie's recent album. In short, they were almost back to being mates. Before he left, Paul gave John some brotherly advice. He told him Yoko missed him and, if he felt the same, he should try and win her back, which is what Lennon did.

Making full use of his new visa, Paul decided to take the family and Wings to Tennessee for a working holiday. Denny Laine was still in the band, but there was a new British drummer, Geoff Brit-ton (who was subsequently let go), and a new lead guitarist, a diminutive twenty-year-old Glaswegian named Jimmy McCulloch.

THE BEATLES' PARTNERSHIP was finally dissolved in London's High Court in January 1975, a quiet end to a long and public war, with Paul the clear victor. He had achieved everything he wanted, plus the satisfaction of knowing that the others had come to the conclusion that he had been right about Klein. And Apple Corps was now in Neil Aspinall's safe hands.

On March 1, 1975, Paul and Linda attended the Grammy Awards, in which Wings were nominated for *Band on the Run*, win-ning two awards on the night: one for Best Pop Vocal Performance by a Group, and another for Geoff Emerick's engineering—a wor-thy winner considering the trying circumstances under which the record had been made.

In commercial terms, Paul had done considerably better than John, George and Ritchie since the breakup of the Beatles. Harrison's career had fallen flat. Lennon had enjoyed chart success, but he didn't tour. After he returned to Yoko and they had their son, Sean, he essentially retired from public life. And Ritchie was never going to be anything but a novelty act.

The *Venus and Mars* album was patchy, but this sort of soft rock was what the market wanted. Paul capitalised by taking Wings on the road in the UK in the autumn of 1975, followed by an Australian tour, all part of the build-up to a major tour of the USA. John might have scorned Paul's material as 'Muzak'—a disparaging reference to the American company that created muted versions of pop hits for public places—but millions of Americans happily tapped their steering wheels to the sound of Wings as they drove to and from their jobs in 1975.

That Christmas, John and Yoko were home with two-month-old Sean and their photographer friend Bob Gruen when the doorbell rang. They were startled. People didn't just come knocking on the front door within the Dakota building: security was tight. John asked Gruen to see who it was. As the photographer cautiously approached the front door he heard somebody singing 'We Wish You a Merry Christmas' outside. Gruen then saw it was Paul and Linda McCartney on the doorstep. The two chief Beatles had another reunion, which, according to Gruen, was a happy occasion: 'They seemed like high-school buddies who hadn't seen each other in a long time.'

FOR THE LAST FEW YEARS, Paul's father had lived as an invalid, nursed by Angie. Jim McCartney rarely left home now. Most of the time he stayed inside, crippled by arthritis. A lifelong smoker, Jim also suffered from bronchitis. When he developed bronchopneumonia, there was tension between Paul and Angie over what should be done. Paul wanted Dad in hospital; Angie insisted she look after her husband at home. 'We had a falling-out as the rest of the family wanted Jim to die in hospital, where his life would have been prolonged by a few painful weeks. But Jim wanted to die in his own bed,' Angie said, 'so I kept him at home. It caused a lot of bad feeling at the time.'

Wings were about to embark on a European tour, starting in Copenhagen on March 20, 1976. Two days before the first show, Jim McCartney died, aged seventy-three. Paul went ahead with a scheduled Wings press conference in London the next day, then flew to Copenhagen to open the tour. He didn't tell the band his father had died and, remarkably, he didn't return home for the cremation on March 22. Paul could easily have hopped over by private plane; Wings didn't have a show that day.

Members of the Beatles had chosen not to attend funerals in the past, such as that of Brian Epstein, for fear their celebrity would attract a mob and detract from the occasion. But to deliberately miss one's father's funeral—especially when father and son had been so close—is strange. Mike McCartney has written in explanation that 'Paul would never face that sort of thing.'

In the aftermath of Jim's death, Paul's relationship with Angie deteriorated. His stepmother went on holiday after the funeral with what seemed to be indecent haste. When Angie subsequently decided to go into theatrical management, and Ruth pursued show-business dreams, there were further clashes, culminating in a blazing telephone row over money. Ruth McCartney has alleged that Paul then stopped the £7,000-a-year pension that had formerly been paid to Jim. Increasingly hard up, mother and daughter moved out of their bungalow into a flat. A deep rift was opening up between Paul and his stepmother and stepsister.

7: THE GOOD LIFE

Paul's status in the USA remained sky-high, having achieved four number one singles and four number one albums in America since 1970. Interestingly, he was yet to score a single number one in Britain, where critics and audiences were more circumspect about his songs, often considering them overly sentimental.

In April 1976, Wings released 'Silly Love Songs' in which Paul made his case plain: he liked writing love songs. If people had a problem with that, it was tough. The single became Paul's fifth US number one, but failed to reach the top of the British charts and was, in fact, mocked at home. 'Silly Love Songs' heralded a new album, *Wings at the Speed of Sound*, which showcased songs sung not only by Paul, but also by his fellow band members, including the third Wings drummer, Joe English, a big, bearded fellow with a surprisingly sweet voice.

Buoyed up by chart success, Paul and Linda dropped by the Dakota on the evening of April 24, 1976 to see the Lennons and watch *Saturday Night Live* on TV, in which Lorne Michaels, the executive producer, jokingly offered to effect a Beatles reunion. He announced that NBC could offer the union rate of $3,000 for the performance of three songs and held up a cheque. John and Paul discussed going down to NBC there and then for a 'laff', but in the end it was too late.

The next night, Paul dropped by again. This time he met a less positive reception. As is often the way, picking up an old friendship can be difficult. At least John seemed to feel that way. He may also have been a tad jealous. John had read that Paul was now worth $25 million and complained to Yoko that they'd never be as rich. 'Paul just kept turning up at our door with a guitar,' Lennon said later. 'Finally I said, "Please call before you come over. It's not 1956, and turning up at the door isn't the same." That upset him, but I didn't mean it badly.' As it was, John and Paul never saw each other in the flesh again after these last Dakota visits.

Paul began his Wings Over America tour in Fort Worth, Texas, on May 3, 1976. It was to be the most successful tour Wings ever gave. The first the audience saw of the star of the evening was when Paul stood spotlit on stage in swirling dry ice, singing 'Venus and Mars'. He segued from this into the faster 'Rock Show', also designed specifically for the arena stage.

Linda sat prettily at her keyboards on a riser, the base of which changed colour during the show, looking happy and relaxed. Denny Laine stood to Paul's left, wielding a fashionable double-neck guitar; guitarist Jimmy McCulloch peeled off his solos; and behind them drummer Joe English thrashed like Animal in the *Muppet Show*. Alongside Joe stood four horn players, featuring Paul's old friend Howie Casey on saxophone, the brass section adding punch to Wings' sound. This was a long way from the university tour of 1972. It was a big, expensive, state-of-the-art rock show with a laser light display during 'Live and Let Die'. 'It was the first time we'd spent enough time on the road to get really good as a band,' says Laine. And the sound quality was good. The technology of the rock show had improved sufficiently to enable everybody in the Fort Worth arena to hear the nuances of Wings' sound.

The highlight of the show came, however, when Paul sat at the piano and played 'Lady Madonna', the first of four Beatles songs in the set. Paul performed only Beatles songs he had written alone—'Lady Madonna', 'The Long and Winding Road', 'Black-bird' and 'Yesterday'—but each held his audience spellbound.

To transport Wings around the USA, McCartney hired a BAC 1-11 passenger jet, the interior transformed into an open-plan rock-star lounge. There was a discotheque in the back for the McCartney children: thirteen-year-old Heather, Mary, almost seven, and four-year-old Stella. Among others, the tour party included the McCartneys' housekeeper Rose Martin, who minded the kids when Paul and Lin were on stage, an ex-FBI man who looked out for potential assassins and kidnappers, and a new road manager, twenty-seven-year-old Londoner John Hammel, who proved so satisfactory that he has stayed by Paul's side ever since, his job description evolving into Personal Assistant.

During the long intercontinental flights, the horn players fell into an extended game of Ten Card Brag, betting nickels, partly because they were not well paid. Paul sat in with the lads, borrowing his stake. The pot of money grew into a large pile of change. 'Here you are, boys—four of a kind,' Howie Casey announced one day, laying down his winning hand. As Howie gathered in his coins, McCartney went berserk, as if he'd been cheated out of a fortune, to the amusement of his sidemen. 'I think it's the winning.

It's not the money,' says Howie, who notes that when he and others grumbled about the wages they were paid, Paul gave them a generous end-of-tour bonus of $10,000. 'That's great, but it would have been better if we'd had a decent [salary in the first place].'

There was a predominantly family vibe on the tour with an official ban on drugs and groupies. That way Linda kept Paul away from temptation, though he showed no signs of straying. 'I never saw [Paul with another woman],' says Denny Laine. Indeed, Denny hardly ever saw Paul without Linda. If Paul walked into a room, you could bet Lin would follow. 'He wanted somebody he could rely on,' says Denny, explaining the attraction. 'She came from money, too, so he could trust she wasn't after his money, [and] the kids went everywhere with them. This was a life he hadn't had much of and really loved.'

AFTER RETURNING HOME from this hugely successful tour, Paul decided to celebrate the life of one of his musical heroes, Buddy Holly, with a luncheon party on what would have been Buddy's birthday, thus also celebrating his ownership of a slice of Holly's publishing. The lunch proved so enjoyable that Paul decided to hold Buddy Holly Week every September, featuring a party plus public events for fans.

A couple of weeks after the first Buddy Holly lunch, Paul took Wings to Venice to play a charity concert and celebrate Lin's thirty-fifth birthday, after which Paul didn't play live for three years. The McCartneys didn't need the money. *Wings Over America* had filled the coffers; McCartney Productions Ltd (MPL) turned over more than £3 million in 1976–7, out of which Paul paid himself a salary of £96,500 — at a time when national average earnings in the UK were less than £4,000. The company cleared a £1.1 million profit. 'In the last two years I have earned more money than I have ever earned in all the boom years [of the Beatles],' the star revealed in a 1977 interview. 'Lee [Eastman] told me that if I got an office and a couple of good people to pay out of my own pocket, I could own my own material.' Lee's advice had proved sound.

In 1977 Paul bought 1 Soho Square, a five-storey Edwardian

town house in Central London. Before MPL moved in, Paul had the building gutted and redecorated Art Deco-style. Other bespoke features included an antique Wurlitzer loaded with Paul's favourite records, valuable artworks and a restored pipe organ on the first-floor landing. There was a penthouse flat at the top of the building, and space in the basement for a recording studio.

The MPL building was Paul's own, better-organised version of the Apple operation at 3 Savile Row, which Apple finally got around to selling in 1976. The Beatles had always been refreshingly public about their place of work and Paul did the same with MPL now. Anybody who was interested could find his new office easily.

Likewise, Paul's Cavendish Avenue address had always been well known to his fans. After his marriage to Linda, the house was transformed into a family home, with a scruffy, lived-in feel, the kids hurtling about followed by their dogs, none of whom seemed house-trained. Linda had taken to growing vegetables in her back garden, which also included a small zoo of animals. The McCartney cockerel woke the whole avenue at dawn.

The McCartneys were less often in St John's Wood nowadays, spending more time in Sussex. In September 1976, Paul began expanding the property, making a planning application for the erection of a stable block and, unusually, for a 70ft observation tower. The tower attracted media attention, not least because it looked like something from a prisoner-of-war camp. In fact, Paul had little personal security and, rather than erecting the tower to watch for intruders, he wanted to be able to look out over the tree canopy.

And the McCartneys' marriage was evidently solid. That Christmas, Linda bought Paul the double bass Bill Black had played on Elvis Presley's Sun sessions, while there was further good news when a live triple album of *Wings Over America* went to number one in the United States.

In the summer of 1977, the McCartneys headed back to Scotland. Denny Laine was living in a cottage on Paul's estate so that he and Paul could write together. One afternoon Paul came over to the house with an idea. 'He wanted to write a song that reminded him of the area,' remembers Laine. 'He already had the

"Mull of Kintyre" title.' The men sat outside Laine's cottage, looking at the scenery: '. . . you didn't have to come up with anything. It was just in front of you.' The finished song was a waltz with good, poetic lyrics. The words are in fact noticeably superior to all Paul's solo work to date, which is explained by the fact that McCartney didn't write them. At least not all of them. While Paul wrote the chorus, Laine says he wrote 'quite a lot' of the rest of 'Mull of Kintyre', meaning that Paul has to share the credit for what may be his best post-Beatles lyric.

The recording of the song was highly unusual, using the services of the Campbeltown Pipe Band. Paul had originally intended the song as an album track, but he had such a good feeling about it he made it a single, shooting a promotional video with the pipe band on Kintyre. At the start of this video, Paul is seen strumming his guitar outside a cottage, with Linda walking down to meet him, new baby James in her arms. In fact, he travelled several miles up the coast to make the video and the cottage is nothing to do with the family. The pipe band members were charmed by the McCartneys, and happily signed away their rights to royalties for a modest one-off payment. Each man got £30 cash on the night of the recording, and another £300 for the video, which they thought generous. Nobody expected what happened next.

Released in mid-November 1977, 'Mull of Kintyre' went quickly to number one in the British charts—the first and only Wings song to do so—then stayed there for what seemed for ever. Paul, who was in the habit of calling MPL to ask about weekly sales, was given astonishing figures: up to 145,000 copies a day were being sold in Britain at a time when a good sale was 20,000. 'Mull of Kintyre' soon sold a million, and kept selling. Not since the Beatles had Paul shifted so much vinyl. All told, 'Mull of Kintyre' stayed at number one for nine weeks, selling over two million copies in the UK, the biggest-selling single in British history up to that time.

IN MAY 1978 Paul attended the London premiere of the musical *Annie*, which the Eastmans had added to MPL's music publishing division. The show became a major hit, further enriching the star.

The Eastmans were also in the process of renegotiating Paul's record deal, with the result that McCartney signed with CBS in America for a $22.5 million advance. The size of the deal reflected his track record in the United States and there were high expectations that he would continue to deliver hits for CBS with Wings.

First, Paul had to re-form the band. This time he delegated the job to Denny Laine, who picked two Englishmen: drummer Steve Holley and guitarist Laurence Juber. Previous versions of Wings failed partly because the musicians felt they were underpaid sidemen. Holley and Juber were essentially hired on the same basis, but the terms of employment were explained more clearly; over iced tea on the lawn of his summer home in East Hampton, Lee Eastman spelled out the deal. 'Basically there was an annual amount paid on a monthly basis and there was a percentage of tour revenue,' says Juber. 'It was certainly reasonable.' As Paul's lieutenant, Denny Laine had an enhanced deal, having finally been given a share in the band's royalties. The Eastmans were also beginning to manage Laine's financial affairs, alongside Paul's, within MPL. Unfortunately, Laine had already got into the position of owing the taxman more money than he could pay.

That summer, Wings convened in Scotland to start work on the new album, *Back to the Egg*, produced by Paul with Chris Thomas, who had most recently produced the Sex Pistols' *Never Mind the Bollocks*. There was an attempt to introduce something of the energy of punk to *Back to the Egg*, the title indicating a return to basics.

Denny Laine suggests Paul was bored dealing with young musicians who didn't know the ropes. Some of the elementary rock band stuff that went without being said between Laine and McCartney had to be spelled out to the new boys. Yet Paul was talking about making a movie with them.

The movie project, which ultimately morphed into *Give My Regards to Broad Street*, began when Paul invited playwright Willy Russell to Scotland to hang out with the group to see if the experience might inspire a screenplay. As others had before, the playwright noticed a sycophantic atmosphere around Paul: 'Paul's fame is such [that] the truth is not told. People would say privately, "Why is he redoing that bass part when it was brilliant four days ago?" And I'd go, "Why don't you say it to Paul?" He would probably be the first to accept that his life would be better if the people around him would have that kind of dialogue with him, but this deference infects everybody.'

Willy had written a play, *Stags and Hens*, about a successful Liverpool musician who returns to Merseyside to take up with an old girlfriend. He thought this might serve as a basis for Paul's movie, supplying a challenging but manageable part for him and a role for Linda. 'What there wasn't, really, was roles for the rest of the band and [the] brief was I had to keep the Wings thing intact.' After a week, Willy went home to think about it further. But there were worrying signs of Paul wanting to rush into his new movie. He summoned Willy and his collaborator Mike Ockrent to Abbey Road to tell them he needed a script post-haste. Willy suggested that the only way they could do a rush job for Paul was to go away somewhere quiet with their families. MPL booked the writers onto a plane to Jamaica, where a villa was put at their disposal. They returned with a screenplay titled *Band on the Run*, in which Paul would play a music star named Jet who, weary with his career, takes up with a scruffy young rock 'n' roll band featuring Linda, Denny, Steve and Laurence. There was a read-through at Waterfall. 'And Paul was, I think, very excited by the possibility,' says Willy.

'I've cleared the slate for two months' time,' he told the playwright, with a sense of purpose.

'But there's been no pre-production,' protested Willy, who knew a movie couldn't be made like this. 'You can't do this like *Magical Mystery Tour*,' he warned, realising he was sounding like 'a suit', as Paul and Linda termed company men.

In April 1979, Paul brought the entire Black Dyke Mills Band down from Yorkshire to play on one track at Abbey Road, but work on the album had been going on for so long that EMI told Paul they needed Studio Two back for other artists. So McCartney had an exact copy built in the basement of the MPL office on Soho Square.

Replica Studio felt like being in the control room at EMI. This was a great extravagance on top of his new movie project, but Paul was richer than ever. In signing with CBS, he had recently been given a sweetener, the Frank Music Catalogue, making Paul the owner of *Guys and Dolls*, and adding rights to a raft of hit shows including *Hello, Dolly!* and *A Chorus Line*, which were all earning him big money. But Paul's luck was about to run out.

EVER SINCE she came to England with her mother, Heather had experienced problems. The primary school kids in St John's Wood made fun of her American accent (which she dropped); then Paul and Linda took her out of school to tour with them, which disrupted her education. When she turned eleven, Heather went to a private secondary school in London where she mixed with the children of other wealthy people. During an argument with her parents, Heather revealed that her schoolfriends had given her advice about dealing with her famous father. 'They'd said, "You've no need to worry about your dad . . . if he gives you any more trouble, you can tell the papers."' So concerned were Paul and Lin that they took her out of the school and moved virtually overnight to their country home in Sussex. The McCartneys' primary home now became Waterfall.

Linda put Mary and Stella into the village primary school, sending Heather to the state comprehensive in Rye. Paul and Linda's decision proved a wise one. Ray Fooks, the headmaster of Thomas Peacocke School, who subsequently admitted Paul and Linda's three younger children to his school, found the McCartneys model parents: 'They made sure that their children were treated like everybody else, and their children fitted in perfectly.'

Around the time of the move to Peasmarsh, the McCartney family all became vegetarian, a diet that now became a way of life and something of an obsession. The epiphany occurred at High Park when the McCartneys were about to sit down to a Sunday lunch of roast lamb. They looked out of their windows at the sheep, and decided that eating the peaceful creatures was wrong. Linda said, 'We just looked at the lamb I was cooking and we couldn't eat it any more. It was a couple of months before I figured out what to do about the gaps on our plates where the chops used to be.'

As the McCartneys settled into life in Sussex, it became clear that Waterfall wasn't large enough to be a permanent home for the family. Paul bought neighbouring Lower Gate Farm to remedy this problem, a 159-acre property costing £250,000 in 1979. Originally the farm had been known as Blossom Wood Farm, a name the McCartneys reinstated. Paul planned to knock down the derelict farmhouse and build a substantial new home in its place.

THERE WAS A BEATLES REUNION that spring, when Eric Clapton celebrated his marriage to George Harrison's ex-wife. After being married to George for eight years, Pattie had left the former Beatle in 1974 for his close friend, three years after which George married his secretary, Olivia Arias. The guests included George, whose friendship had survived the changing of the guard, as well as Paul and Ritchie.

The three Beatles got up on stage and performed 'Sgt. Pepper's Lonely Hearts Club Band', the first time they had played together since *Abbey Road*, all looking happy in each other's company. John Lennon telephoned to tell Eric that he would have been there, too, had he known about the party, creating the tantalising thought that all four Beatles might have played together in the tent. Perhaps a Beatles reunion wasn't so unlikely, after all.

Certainly Paul was sick of Wings. The new album was not the smash EMI and CBS had been banking on. Paul simply moved on. Doing exactly what he had at the end of the Beatles, he went home and made a DIY solo album.

Nevertheless, he went ahead with a series of Wings concerts, starting with warm-up shows at the Royal Court Theatre in Liverpool. While he was on Merseyside, McCartney visited the Liverpool Institute. Paul invited the school's entire complement of boys, plus the girls from the school across the road, to a free first-night show at the Royal Court, a typically generous and sentimental gesture from a man who looked back on his school days with affection. Naturally, Paul's relatives also got tickets.

Paul was always nervous before a concert—a healthy sign—but

with all those eager and familiar faces out front he was more jittery than normal. 'Before we went on Paul said, "Oh Jeez, I don't know if this is gonna go,"' recalls Howie Casey. 'I said, "Paul, this is going to be like the second coming. You just walk on there, and they're gonna go nuts." And they did.' It helped that Paul treated his audience to some Beatles songs, including 'Fool on the Hill' and 'Got to Get You into My Life', which gave Howie's horn section a chance to shine. 'For a long time I was embarrassed to do Beatles songs because it seemed like a cop-out,' Paul said afterwards. 'But that's long gone now. I wrote the songs, after all.'

Eight days before Christmas, Wings played the Glasgow Apollo. To give the Glaswegians a treat, Paul closed with 'Mull of Kintyre' accompanied by the Campbeltown Pipe Band, who were bussed in from Kintyre especially. To keep this a surprise, Paul had the pipe band wait outside the theatre until the last minute. Then they entered in full regalia. 'We formed a semicircle behind Paul on stage,' recalls pipe band drummer Ian Campbell. 'We rehearsed it during the day. He said, "Don't just leave the stage [at the end]. Enjoy the adulation, because this song has been amazing." So he started "Mull of Kintyre", which drove the crowd a wee bit [mad], and then when we came out I thought the roof was going to come off. Honestly, they went insane.'

A major Japanese tour was scheduled to begin in January 1980. Paul hadn't played Japan since the Beatles visited in 1966. He had tried to get a visa but had been denied permission. 'We were supposed to have gone there five years earlier but we got our visas revoked,' explains Laine. 'We'd both been busted in the past.' The problems of drug use were not yet as pronounced in Japan as in Western countries, and the authorities were naturally keen to discourage any growth in the drug culture. As a result, the Eastmans had to work hard to get visas for the band in 1980, and it was made abundantly clear that the authorities wouldn't tolerate any drug use on the tour. But nobody wanted to end up in a Japanese jail, and they didn't want to miss out on what was set to be the most lucrative Wings tour yet. Even the guys in the horn section were getting $1,000 a night, and the longer the tour went on, the richer they would get. 'We knew everybody had to be very responsible,' says Laurence Juber, adding with a hollow laugh, 'or nearly everybody.'

Denny Laine and Steve Holley arrived at Narita Airport ahead of the McCartneys on January 16, 1980, travelling first class on TWA. The band members had all been furnished with multiple-use, first-class tickets good for any TWA flight anywhere in the world for twelve months.

Holley and Laine were processed through immigration before the McCartneys arrived, the officials taking five hours to deal with Laine because of his drug history.

When Paul's flight landed, his party was also processed slowly. Laurence Juber was standing next to Paul as they walked through the Customs hall. A Customs man was opening bags seemingly at random. 'He opened one of the suitcases,' says Juber 'and he pulled out a bag of marijuana. At that point Paul kind of turns white, and people came out from behind hidden doors and escorted him back, and me, too. And Linda and the kids as well.'

Among Paul's shirts the Customs official had found just under eight ounces of marijuana, worth about £1,000. Having made this discovery, the Japanese went through all the luggage again, even taking musical instruments apart in case there were more drugs inside. There weren't. Laurence, Linda and the kids were allowed to leave.

Laine and Holley had gone ahead to the hotel, where they checked into their rooms. Steve took a nap, woken by Linda calling to say that Paul had been arrested at the airport for possession. 'I thought she was joking. I said, "Yeah, good one. I'll see you in the restaurant," and I went downstairs. As soon as the elevator doors opened on the main floor, and the press greeted us with a million flashbulbs, I realised that something had happened.'

Paul had been taken in handcuffs to Kojimachi Police Station, where he was locked in a cell. Paul's tour managers hired an English-speaking Japanese lawyer and contacted Eastman & Eastman in New York. Lee Eastman threw a fit. 'When Paul got busted in Tokyo my father went nuts,' recalls Philip Sprayregen, who explains that his stepfather's rage was partly due to his fear that the bust would jeopardise Paul's chance of a knighthood. 'He said, "My God, my daughter could have been a [lady], and he blew it!"'

John Eastman was despatched to Tokyo to try and rescue his brother-in-law. Meanwhile, Paul went to sleep in his Tokyo cell with his back against the wall, fearing he might be raped.

Paul woke to news that he had a visitor and was shown into an interview room, partitioned by a glass screen, on the other side of which stood the reassuringly urbane figure of Britain's consul to Japan, Donald Warren-Knott. The Warren-Knotts had been getting ready for bed the previous evening when they received a courtesy call from the police to inform them that a distinguished British citizen, Mr *Pori Macatnee*, had been taken into custody. 'We began to talk and to my pleasant surprise he was very relaxed,' says Warren-Knott, who'd feared that such a celebrity might try and demand special treatment, which would have been a mistake. 'Nothing of the sort. He took it quite calmly. OK, he knew the packet had been found. Yes, it was his. And it shouldn't have been there. I don't know whether he intended to use it while he was in Japan. If he did, he'd be very foolish, given the circumstances of his previous arrests.'

Paul had one request. 'He said he was a vegetarian and he would be grateful if we could give any help in making sure that he got a vegetarian diet.' The consul said he would ask the guards.

The shows were cancelled and Wings' equipment was shipped back to the UK. The musicians were told to go home, or anywhere they liked on their round-the-world tickets. Despite the prospect of a free holiday, and the fact that they were all paid, the band members were upset. Says Denny Laine, 'I was disappointed. It meant now we wouldn't be able to go to a lot of places and tour, because once you get busted it's hard to get visas and stuff. It was a letdown.'

There was consternation in the penthouse suite of the Okura Hotel when Linda was informed that her husband could face a prison sentence. She and the kids were virtual prisoners themselves, unable to go downstairs for fear of the press. The children were upset. 'The only one unaware of the situation was little Dee Dee,' Linda said, using the family name for toddler James McCartney, and even Dee Dee kept asking where Daddy was.

Over at Kojimachi, Daddy was getting used to prison life. He was obliged to sleep on the floor on a thin mattress, Japanese-style, rising at 6 a.m. with other prisoners, sitting cross-legged while he was interrogated, given half an hour to exercise and eating a bowl of rice for supper. Watched by Japanese men in uniform, Paul felt like a character in a POW movie. He picked pieces of plaster off the wall and used the flakes to tally his days inside. Paul calculated that his incarceration had exceeded a week. He was starting to smell. The police said he could have a bath in private if he wished. Paul chose instead to bath with his fellow detainees, a tough-looking crew whom he charmed by leading them in a bathtime singalong, including a rendition of 'Yellow Submarine'.

When Linda was given permission to see her husband for half an hour, she took him a welcome cheese sandwich. Although they tried to joke about the situation, this was the longest period Paul and Lin had ever been apart, and it was not certain what the outcome would be.

After John Eastman arrived and started talking with the local lawyer and the presiding magistrate, it became clear that the Japanese didn't want a trial any more than Paul did. The authorities were primarily concerned that the local promoters, and the people who'd bought tickets for the concerts, wouldn't be out of pocket. Refunds were swiftly arranged. 'With that little financial problem out of the way, they wanted to get rid of him as quickly as possible,' comments Donald Warren-Knott.

So it was that after nine nights in a Tokyo cell, Paul was put on a flight to Amsterdam, reunited with his family. The McCartneys disembarked in Holland, then flew by private plane to Lydd Airport and finally drove down familiar country lanes to their house in the Sussex woods. Seldom had Paul felt so glad to be home. It was the end of a draining, expensive and embarrassing experience, one that had damaged his image. But the Japanese bust didn't change him. He came out of the experience with the same cocky attitude. He never explained, let alone apologised, to his band members for the inconvenience he had caused them, while the cover of *McCartney II,* Paul's new solo album, featured a grainy image of Paul by

Linda in the style of a prison mugshot, while inside were photos of Paul pulling faces in impersonation of Japanese officials, with an instrumental track titled 'Frozen Jap'.

IN THE AUTUMN OF 1980, Paul gathered Wings together to rehearse what would become his new studio album, *Tug of War*, which George Martin had agreed to produce. The album proved the death knell for Wings. 'Paul called one day,' says Laurence Juber, 'and said, "George doesn't want to do it as a Wings album, so thanks but we don't need you right now . . ." At that point I saw that the writing was on the wall.' Paul was breaking Wings up, though Denny Laine stayed with him for a little while yet.

Around this time, an unwelcome ghost from the past emerged in the form of Erika Hübers (*née* Wohlers), a Hamburg barmaid who had claimed back in the sixties to have given birth to Paul's child. Although Paul had never admitted paternity, a lump sum had been paid by Brian Epstein to Erika plus maintenance for her child, Bettina, until she was eighteen, on the basis the family wouldn't go public. A couple of weeks before her eighteenth birthday, the *Sunday People* splashed with 'I AM BEATLE PAUL'S SECRET CHILD', naming Erika and Bettina for the first time. The girl had already started cashing in on her supposed link with McCartney by singing in clubs as 'Bettina McCartney, the daughter of a Beatle'. Now she seemed to see a chance for a big payday. Paul didn't comment, but the matter refused to go away.

Another echo of the past came in the form of John Lennon's new studio album, *Double Fantasy*, his first for five years, and a solid collection of simple, muscular rock songs as far as his half of the record went. (Yoko had an equal number of tracks; hers were less impressive.) Once again, John's distinctive voice was on the car radio as Paul was driven up to town, punching through the years with lyrics that had an emotional weight and a sense of personal honesty—qualities too often lacking in Paul's work. *Double Fantasy* sold modestly and received some negative reviews. Still, it was the first time for years that John had made a real effort with his music, challenging Paul as he used to.

McCartney was at home alone at Waterfall on the morning of December 9, 1980 when the telephone rang. His manager, Stephen Shrimpton, informed him that John had been shot dead in New York. When Paul saw Lin's car coming back up the drive from the school run he walked outside to meet her. 'I could tell by looking at him that there was something wrong. I'd never seen him like that before.'

Paul had a session booked at AIR in London. George Martin telephoned to ask if he wanted to cancel. Paul said he would rather come in to work. With the press gathering outside, the London studio looked like a convenient bolthole.

Paul then attempted to do a day's work. 'He was just very, very quiet, and upset, as we all were,' recalls Denny Laine. 'He said to me, "I'm never going to fall out with anybody again in my life" . . . I knew he felt that maybe they didn't make up like they should have done.'

The phone rang. 'Can I speak to Paul McCartney?' said a woman.

'He's busy at the moment. Who's calling?'

'It's Yoko.'

Paul cried as he took the call.

Throughout that short winter day, journalists besieged AIR Studios. It was dark when Paul came down in the lift. As he stepped onto the pavement, journalists clustered around him. Television crews were also present. 'It's terrible news,' Paul said, when asked for his reaction to John's death. He was usually relaxed with journalists but this evening he was distinctly edgy. He was also chewing gum, which gave the unfortunate impression that he wasn't taking the matter as seriously as he might.

'Are you planning to go over for the funeral?'

'I don't know yet.'

'What were you recording today?'

'I was just listening to some stuff, you know. I just didn't want to sit at home.'

'Why?'

Bridling, Paul replied, 'I didn't feel like it,' and concluded the interview, 'It's a drag, isn't it?'

The clip was used prominently in news broadcasts. '"A drag" isn't how the world will see it,' commented an ITN newscaster sternly, highlighting the crassness of Paul's remark. Just as when his mother and his father had died, and when Stuart Sutcliffe passed away, Paul had reacted awkwardly, saying and doing the wrong thing. His partner in the Beatles, his best friend, with whom he'd fallen out and never been fully reconciled, was gone, and Paul had sent him on his way with a stupid comment.

REPORTAGE OF John Lennon's murder was a sensation that lasted weeks. Yoko had her husband cremated privately on December 10, 1980. Mass public memorials were held in New York and Liverpool, while John's songs played constantly on the radio, the singles '(Just Like) Starting Over' and 'Woman' both posthumously going to number one in the USA, as did *Double Fantasy*. John's death also created a huge revival of interest in the Beatles, selling truckloads of the band's albums on a wave of nostalgia.

All the surviving Beatles benefited from renewed sales of their back catalogue, leading to a lucrative programme of repackaging and reissuing. While John's death helped make Paul even richer, it also served to elevate his friend into the company of James Dean and Marilyn Monroe, show-business idols who'd died young and were revered like secular saints. Over the ensuing years, Paul tried to persuade the public that John wasn't a saint, and that it was unfair to label McCartney as a platitudinous balladeer in comparison to Lennon, the intellectual and musical heavyweight. But there was a grain of truth in this characterisation.

Paul kept a low profile during the mourning period. He and Linda visited Yoko at the Dakota briefly, then returned to England where Paul resumed work with George Martin on *Tug of War*. Another old friend joined the team at AIR, Eric Stewart, co-founder of 10cc, whom Paul had known since the Cavern days.

Having started *Tug of War* in London, Paul transferred the work to Montserrat where George Martin had built a studio complex overlooking the sea. Apart from the climate, part of the attraction was that everybody could be accommodated in private villas within a secure compound. Security seemed important after John's death. Paul had worried in the 1960s about being shot by a maniac, when such fears had seemed like paranoia. After all, who'd want to kill a pop star? When Mark Chapman murdered John Lennon, apparently to achieve fame, it became obvious to Paul and other rock stars that there was a real danger of being targeted by a copy-cat killer. The fact that Ringo was coming down to play on *Tug of War* made it doubly important to have good security.

Although Denny Laine came to Montserrat, George Martin recruited new players to work alongside Paul, such as the bass guitarist Stanley Clarke and drummer Steve Gadd, two of the best session musicians in the business. Carl Perkins flew in to play on the likeable 'Get It'. Then Stevie Wonder arrived, who'd agreed to sing on a song McCartney had written inspired by the black and white keys on a piano keyboard, from which he'd created a musical metaphor for racial harmony: 'Ebony and Ivory'. As much a musical genius as McCartney, Wonder admonished Paul during the recording for being out of time with his handclaps, which were not 'in the pocket'. 'And you better believe I got it in the pocket,' recalled McCartney. 'He gets results and he knows what he's doing.'

In April 1981, Ritchie married Barbara Bach at Marylebone Register Office, where Paul and Linda had married in 1969. The wedding reception was at Rags, a West End nightclub, with George and Olivia Harrison joining the Starkeys and McCartneys in a Beatles reunion. The musicians gathered around the piano, Paul leading the company in a singsong. Everybody was having a great time, the kids digging into the star-shaped wedding cake.

Despite the family atmosphere, this proved a particularly challenging afternoon for Paul. Denny Laine chose the day to announce he was leaving Wings, ending a chapter in Paul's career on a not entirely happy note. Denny went off to concentrate on his solo career, which soon petered away into negligible sales and melancholy guest appearances at Beatles conventions. More upsetting, Paul heard some home truths about himself at Ritchie's wedding reception: Neil Aspinall told Paul that Aunt Mimi was upset Paul hadn't called her since John's death. It hadn't crossed Paul's mind to do so: he had known Mimi only briefly when he was a kid. Paul was also thrown by a conversation with Cilla Black, a friend since Cavern days. Paul told Cilla how much he liked her husband, Bobby Willis, who had managed her since Brian died. 'Bobby's a nice bloke,' he told Cilla.

'Ah, but what do you really think, Paul? You don't mean that, do you? You're getting at something,' replied Cilla. It was as if everybody believed Paul spoke with forked tongue.

The weirdest conversation of the day took place in the gents' toilet when Paul found himself standing next to Ritchie himself. 'He said there were two times in his life in which I had done him in. Then he said that he'd done himself in *three* times. I laughed it off. It was affectionate. But now, I keep thinking all the time, what are the two times that Ringo thinks I put him down . . .?'

Paul asked this question in a peevish telephone call to the writer Hunter Davies shortly afterwards. He also complained to Davies about Philip Norman's new book, *Shout!*, a lively history of the Beatles that left the reader with the impression that Paul was a shallow young man compared to the more substantial John. Paul reminded Hunter grumpily that John had hurt his feelings many times, noting that Lennon could be a 'manoeuvring swine, which no one seem[s] to realise. Now, since his death, he's become Martin Luther Lennon.' When Hunter put these injudicious comments into print, they served to do Paul's image further damage.

There was more bad publicity for the star that summer when Angie McCartney sold the story of her relationship with her step-son to the *Sun* — a three-part serial headed 'The mean side of Paul McCartney'. Angie described how she'd tried to make a living as a theatrical agent after Jim died, but soon got into debt. When she wrote to Paul to say she would have to sell her home, he showed little sympathy, and when she tried to get him involved in a charity concert they had a heck of a row, Paul accusing her of using his name. As she sank deeper into financial difficulties there were further unpleasant conversations. 'I was tempted to remind Paul that Jim McCartney had told me in the past that Ruth and I would be looked after for the rest of our lives.' When Angie sold Paul's birth certificate to a Beatles collector some years later, Paul washed his hands of his stepmother.

Many friends knew a different Paul—to the controlling, penny-pinching character described by Angie—as someone capable of spontaneous acts of generosity and, indeed, Paul had been gener-ous with Angie and Ruth McCartney, as he continued to be with other family members. If he suspected he was being taken advan-tage of, however, he could become implacable.

IN THE SUMMER OF 1981, the old issue of who owned the songs Paul and John had written together re-emerged. For the past few years Northern Songs had been in the hands of the mogul Lew Grade, who had given Paul to understand that he would have first refusal if Grade ever wanted to sell. In the autumn, the recently ennobled Lord Grade offered Northern Songs to Paul for £20 million. Paul suggested to Yoko Ono that they put up half the money each but she thought the price too high, and tried to get the company for £5 million. Grade then decided to include Northern Songs in the sale of his much larger organisation, Associated Communications Corps (ACC), which made acquiring the songs much more expen-sive. Even at this stage, Paul would have been wise to enter the bidding for ACC. Instead, he complained publicly about the unfair-ness of what was happening: 'I'm not interested in buying his whole company,' Paul said to *The Times*. 'I just want my songs. Give me back my babies, Lew!' Grade subsequently sold ACC to the Aus-tralian businessman Robert Holmes à Court for £45 million, making him the owner of ATV Music in which Northern Songs was held. In the years to come, the value of the song catalogue would make even £45 million look a bargain. It was a missed opportunity.

As McCartney was unwrapping presents at home with the fam-ily on Christmas Day 1981, the telephone rang. A high-pitched voice asked for Paul. 'Who is this?' asked McCartney gruffly, sus-pecting a female fan.

'It's Michael Jackson.'

Although Jackson and McCartney were fifteen years apart in age, the artists stood shoulder to shoulder in their careers in 1981–2. Both were prodigiously talented stars who'd enjoyed huge success in their youth, both were now working with favourite producers on solo albums: Jackson with Quincy Jones on *Off the Wall*, McCartney with George Martin on *Tug of War*.

They intended to repeat the formula with their next albums— Jackson working with Jones again on *Thriller*, McCartney with Martin on *Pipes of Peace*—and it made sense for the musicians to do one another a good turn by co-writing and duetting on songs for their respective LPs: 'Say Say Say' (and less significantly 'The Man') for *Pipes of Peace*, while 'The Girl is Mine' would find a home on *Thriller*, the most successful album in pop history. By associating himself with a young star, Paul hoped to reach a younger audience, while working with an ex-Beatle flattered the American's vanity.

Jackson came to England in the spring and Paul invited him to the country for the weekend, asking Michael if he would like to go riding. The American said he couldn't because, 'I'm not allowed to get dirty.' Paul did get Michael down to Sussex, and delivered him back to his hotel safe and sound, the American proclaiming that he'd had a great time. During his visit, Paul suggested Jackson might invest in song publishing. 'I'm going to buy your songs one day,' Michael told the older man, cheekily.

Paul brought Jackson into AIR Studios, telling Eric Stewart and his other sidemen that they would have to clear out while Michael recorded: Jacko didn't want to see or talk to anybody bar Paul and Lin, and their four-year-old son, James. Between takes Jackson played on the floor with Dee Dee. The guy was weird, but he sang like an angel.

Paul's other collaboration, the Stevie Wonder duet 'Ebony and Ivory', proved a massive hit in the spring of 1982, reaching number one in both the UK and USA partly thanks to a well-produced video in what was now the video age, MTV having been launched the previous year. *Tug of War* proceeded to the top of the album charts in both territories. This was the high-water mark in Paul's post-Beatles career. He would remain a great star during the decades ahead, but he would never sell as many new albums again.

Paul turned forty in June 1982 and made some changes to his life, taking up jogging around the country lanes in Sussex, and quitting cigarettes (but not dope). He also took up painting, turning one of the old farmhouses on his Sussex estate into an art studio, spending hours creating large colourful abstracts.

Paul also determined to pursue the movie project that had begun life as Willy Russell's *Band on the Run*. The last Russell had heard from Paul on the subject was just before the star went on his ill-fated trip to Japan in 1980. 'Next thing we heard he was making a movie called *Give My Regards to Broad Street*,' says Russell. This was an almost totally different film, borrowing only one or two ideas from Russell's script. Part of the thinking was that Paul would, for the first time, try serious acting, in the sense of being a leading man. One of the first people he consulted was David Puttnam, now Britain's leading film producer, having enjoyed success with *Midnight Express* (1978) and *Chariots of Fire* (1981), for which he collected the Oscar for Best Picture. Like many of Paul's acquaintances, Puttnam was used to McCartney tapping him for advice.

Paul explained his vision for *Give My Regards to Broad Street* to Puttnam over supper with their wives at the Savoy Grill. The film was to be a 'musical fantasy drama in the tradition of *The Wizard of Oz*', the title being Paul's laboured pun on the George M. Cohan song 'Give My Regards to Broadway' and the fact that the dénouement would be shot at Broad Street train station in the City of London. The plot had come to Paul while sitting in his chauffeur-driven car in a London traffic jam: what would happen if the master tapes of his new album were stolen? He had written the screenplay himself, just twenty-two pages.

Puttnam saw flaws from the first page: 'The script started with Paul in the back of a Rolls-Royce complaining bitterly about the emptiness of his life. I said, "Look, on page one you've already got a problem. People see you, see a Roller, and you're *moaning*? They're going to hate you. You've got everything they want, and you're moaning about it."'

Paul disagreed and, worryingly, he seriously underestimated

how much time the project would take. 'My impression was he thought it was something he could do in three months. I remember saying to him, "This is not an album. This is a *massive* commitment." So I did forewarn him.'

As in so many aspects of his career, having flirted with working with professionals, Paul decided to do everything himself, asking Puttnam to recommend a director who'd be a cinemagraphic amanuensis, enabling him to make his own film. Puttnam suggested Peter Webb, a forty-year-old photographer who ran an advertising agency. Webb had made a series of popular adverts and won a BAFTA for a short film. He was ambitious to get into movies, though Webb's memory of his early meetings with Paul is that the star didn't say he wanted to make a movie at first, rather a 'one-hour TV special based on *Tug of War*'. Paul put up the equivalent of half a million dollars and Webb started shooting sequences.

When Lee Eastman saw how much money his son-in-law was spending he decided Paul needed a major studio behind him, with the result that 20th Century Fox bought into a 'Hollywood musical with happy ending'. Peter Webb claims he discovered he was shooting such a picture only when he came home to be told by his baby sitter that Paul had left a message that he and Peter were 'going to the Fox'. The baby sitter assumed it was the name of a pub.

Suddenly, Webb found himself nominally the director of a Hollywood movie, starring Paul McCartney. 'I think he got overexcited,' says Webb. 'Once he was in a movie with a Hollywood studio, then he was a Hollywood movie star.' So, apparently, was Mrs McCartney and other members of the McCartney circle: George Martin, Ritchie Starkey and Eric Stewart were all called upon to play themselves. Having acted in a flick or two, Ritchie noticed something elementary was missing from the production. 'Ringo came up to me,' recalls Peter Webb. 'He said, "So where is the bloody script?"' There wasn't one.

The warning signs that should have prevented the project going further were ignored because Paul McCartney was involved. Having fallen flat on his face with *Magical Mystery Tour*, Paul was heading for another cinematic pratfall.

8: TRIVIAL PURSUITS

The new year of 1983 started badly for Paul when the *Sun* splashed the story of Anita Howarth, a Liverpool typist who claimed the former Beatle was the father of her son, Philip. This was ancient history as far as Paul was concerned, dating back to 1964 when Brian Epstein paid off the girl, though Paul never admitted paternity. Eighteen years later, the *Sun* ran with the tale thanks to one of Paul's former employees, Peter Brown, who revealed it in his memoir, *The Love You Make*.

At the same time Paul's other supposed love child, the German Bettina Hübers, continued to pursue her paternity claim. Her lawyers apparently thought she was entitled to a payoff of £1.75 million, a serious-enough claim for Paul and Bettina both to undergo blood tests. The results cleared McCartney, but Bettina and her mother were not satisfied. They asserted that the test had been fixed—believing Paul had used a stand-in—and requested a second test, which the German judge ordered, telling Paul to pay Bettina £185 a month maintenance until the matter was resolved.

Craving time away from public scrutiny, Paul and Linda bought another holiday home, in Arizona, where Linda had lived with her first husband. After a period when the McCartneys had little to do with Mel, they re-established friendly contact for Heather's sake, and started to visit Arizona regularly, staying forty-five minutes east of Tucson in a desert landscape studded with cacti. The McCartneys bought an isolated tin-roof house used by a Tucson banker as his weekender, painting the buildings pink and turquoise, and installing a heart-shaped swimming pool in the yard.

Like their country retreats in England and Scotland, the ranch was a modest abode, but off the beaten track in an area of great natural beauty. The McCartneys continued their habit of making friends of their neighbours and buying adjacent plots of land as they came on the market, eventually owning 1,000 desert acres.

Paul was in Barbados in early 1984 when he received the good news that the Berlin judge had thrown out Bettina Hübers' paternity claim, after Paul had passed both blood tests. Paul was magnanimous in victory, paying not only his own legal costs but also Bettina's £60,000 costs, on the basis that mother and daughter would be ruined financially otherwise, and hoping they would now have the good grace to fall silent. On the contrary, Bettina took the view that Paul's generosity proved his guilt and continues to argue to this day that Paul tricked the doctors.

A few nights after hearing he'd won the German paternity case, Paul and Linda were sitting on the veranda of their rented beach house with Eric and Gloria Stewart, when they heard a tap at the door. 'Christ, it's the police!' Linda exclaimed. There was marijuana on the coffee table, as a result of which the McCartneys were taken to the police station. It transpired that their butler had informed on them.

The following Monday, Paul and Linda appeared before a magistrate and were fined a nominal $100 each. Paul was furious, complaining to his friends that he and Linda had become targets for harassment. 'This holiday is over,' he told Eric.

The McCartneys arrived at Heathrow on January 17, disembarking to go through Customs before boarding a second, private plane. In the process, an item of luggage was held back. Despite what had happened in Barbados, Linda had carelessly brought some grass back home, a tiny amount but enough to be charged.

The following week Linda accepted a £75 fine, telling the press, 'It is horrible to feel like a criminal when you know you are not.' Be that as it may, the McCartneys had now been in trouble for drugs on six occasions in six countries, a record that cast doubt on their judgment and the example set to their children. British tabloid newspapers mocked the McCartneys. Then, much more damaging allegations were made by their old friend Denny Laine.

In an unremittingly negative series of articles, Laine told *Sun* readers that Paul and Lin habitually smoked two ounces of grass a day and routinely smuggled their stash through Customs. Habitual dope smoking, he suggested, had a detrimental effect on Paul's music. 'That's why Paul's albums take ages and ages to make.' He also described Paul as a tight-fisted, inscrutable man, with few friends, who liked the sound of his own voice and patronised those around him, including his brother. Finally, Denny mocked Paul's complex about his mother. 'He's a mummy's boy who didn't have a mummy after his mother died when he was fourteen. He would be lost without Linda.'

All of this bad publicity formed the backdrop to the completion of *Give My Regards to Broad Street*, the project that had ballooned from a TV special into a multimillion-dollar movie. As a release date approached, executives from 20th Century Fox jetted in for meetings with McCartney and Peter Webb, who had found directing a non-acting leading man 'a problem'. Further complications were caused by the fact that Paul was simultaneously working on a soundtrack album and a theme song, 'No More Lonely Nights'. Celebrity mates were roped in to play, including Dave Gilmour, Ritchie and Eric Stewart. Such a gathering of talent created an album far superior to the movie it rode piggyback on.

There was friction between the McCartneys and Webb at this late stage in the process: the director didn't always feel his work was respected, 'let alone appreciated', by Paul. Webb then suffered a serious personal setback. He says he was 'hospitalised', refusing to clarify whether this was for a mental or a physical problem, with the result that Paul had to direct a final sequence of the picture himself.

There were four major premieres of the film, in New York and LA, followed by Liverpool and London. Before the showing at the Liverpool Odeon, Paul was honoured with the Freedom of the City and a civic luncheon, during which he was reunited with Ann Ventre, the Forthlin Road neighbour to whom he'd once boasted he'd be famous. Although they hadn't seen each other since he left home, Paul recognised Ann instantly, and asked after their old neighbours. The premiere that evening went better than in New York and LA: 'There was applause at the end,' recalls BBC Radio Merseyside broadcaster Spencer Leigh. 'It was evident there wasn't much story, but the musical sequences were OK.'

The London premiere of *Give My Regards to Broad Street* took place at the Empire Theatre, Leicester Square. The audience watched an old-fashioned jukebox musical, the scenes strung together by the thinnest thread of a story: unless he got the master tapes of his new record back by midnight, Paul stood to lose his company. The songs were strong, the musical sequences attractively filmed, and Paul was adequate as a leading man, but the dialogue was witless, the supporting characters ill-defined, the story bereft of interest.

The critics gave the film a unanimous thumbs down. Quentin Falk told readers of the *Daily Mail*: 'this is a truly terrible movie', the blame for which had to rest with Paul. 'His screenplay is relentlessly banal, formless and, most unforgivingly, humourless.' Met with scorn, Paul gave up the film as a lost cause. For his director, Peter Webb, making the picture was 'a damaging experience in every way'. He went back to making commercials.

There was also a financial cost. MPL was obliged to pay back $5 million to 20th Century Fox, as well as meeting a $1.8 million shortfall. Some of the financial damage was offset by the success of the soundtrack album, the rights to which Paul had wisely withheld. It made number one in the UK, while the single 'No More Lonely Nights' was a top five hit in the USA and UK. The single might have done better still—it is one of his best post-Beatles songs—had it not been associated with such a bad film.

All told, this celluloid adventure had been a calamitous mistake, one that Paul would excise from his CV. When Paul came to look back on the picture, he noted that Steven Spielberg required five drafts of every movie script. Paul acknowledged that he should have worked as hard. Unfortunately, he preferred to get by on talent. It is a character flaw that has marred his career.

HAVING WORKED with George Martin since the Tokyo bust, Paul felt the need of a change of producer for his next studio album. George wanted a rest from the demanding Paul, too, and asked Eric Stewart if he would take the helm. Having established that Eric would accept the challenge, Paul invited his friend to Sussex to write, and they swiftly completed eight songs.

Although Eric had gained the impression Paul wanted him to produce the new album, McCartney also hired the fashionable young producer Hugh Padgham, who had enjoyed recent success with Phil Collins and the Police. Tensions soon developed between Padgham and Stewart, who seemed to be competing for the same job, with both men finding they had an even greater problem with McCartney himself.

Privately, Hugh had been worried that the material was on the weak side, but assumed an artist of Paul's stature, working in tandem with someone as experienced as Eric, would improve the songs in the studio. Unfortunately, this wasn't happening.

Eric left, and Hugh found himself alone with Paul. At first it felt like a great honour to be asked to produce the album, but work on *Press to Play* stretched on for an amazing eighteen months, while Hugh discovered that he couldn't tell Paul anything. Paul's charm wore off. He told the same old Beatles stories again and again, until they were boring, and nobody had the courage to tell him he was repeating himself. Also, he seemed obsessed with what the public thought of him in relation to John Lennon. Outside music, Paul's conversation was banal, often confined to what he'd seen on TV.

As the two men struggled to complete this unhappy album, Paul was asked to support a charity concert at Wembley Stadium. Towards the end of 1984, Bob Geldof, leader of the new-wave band the Boomtown Rats, had been shocked by news coverage of a famine in Ethiopia into corralling pop stars together to record a charity single, 'Do They Know It's Christmas?', which surpassed 'Mull of Kintyre' as the best-selling single in the history of the British charts. Afterwards, Geldof organised twin concerts to aid Africa: a British show at Wembley Stadium and a sister show in Philadelphia. Geldof wrote to McCartney asking him to perform 'Let It Be', explaining that 'Beatles' music for some reason evokes more emotional response than any other'. Paul agreed, letting Geldof know that he didn't mind if George and Ritchie were invited to join him on stage.

Geldof called Harrison at his holiday home in Hawaii, asking if he would play 'Let It Be' with Paul. 'He didn't ask me to sing on it [sixteen] years ago, so why does he want me now?' Harrison retorted, his own relationship with Paul at a new low ebb. The men had recently had a ratty telephone conversation during which George accused Paul of boasting to the press about how much money he made, though the reported £20 million a year figure was an exaggeration.

The Live Aid concerts held on Saturday, July 13, 1985 were the most significant live events in popular music since the sixties. Not since the Woodstock Festival had so many first-class rock acts been assembled. David Bowie, Elton John, Queen, U2 and the Who all performed in London, and highlights of the American show included performances by Led Zeppelin, Madonna and Mick Jagger singing with Tina Turner.

There was, however, a serious sound problem as soon as Paul began performing 'Let It Be' on a white grand piano on the Wembley stage. His voice was heard briefly at first, then disappeared; only the piano and intermittent shrieks of feedback were audible. Paul struggled on, apparently willing the audience to help him. Although the stadium audience was made up predominantly of people a generation younger than those who had followed the Beatles originally, the concert-goers recognised the tune and began singing the lyric in his place. When Paul's voice finally came through loud and clear the crowd gave a huge cheer, and sang along enthusiastically until the end; David Bowie, Bob Geldof, Alison Moyet and Pete Townshend adding ragged backing vocals on stage. It was a shambolic performance, but the moment was undoubtedly moving, showing that Paul—despite his advancing years and recent failures—was by common consensus the figurehead of British rock. From then on, Paul's presence would be requested at virtually every large, set-piece music event of the kind, and many such concerts followed.

A few weeks after Live Aid, Paul heard that Michael Jackson had invested $47.5 million of his *Thriller* fortune in ATV Music, making him the new owner of Northern Songs. 'He was absolutely furious,' recalls Hugh Padgham. 'Oh my God, the air was blue.'

THE DAY FINALLY CAME in the spring of 1986 when work stopped on *Press to Play*. The record was finished, for better or worse. Paul's manager, Stephen Shrimpton, was concerned that he couldn't hear a hit on the record, and it may not be a coincidence that Shrimpton left MPL around this time. For want of anything better, Paul finally chose 'Press' as the single to launch this troublesome album, and took a camera crew onto London's Underground to film the promotional video. He rode the Jubilee Line looking happy and relaxed, shaking hands with an elderly lady, receiving a kiss from a girl, encouraging normally dour commuters to smile. As he waved goodbye to his crew and the audience, at St John's Wood station, you had to like the man.

But a strong video wasn't enough to save 'Press' and *Press to Play* itself sold fewer copies than any of McCartney's previous studio albums. When Eric Stewart received a copy, he felt he knew why it had failed. Fragments of their original collaboration were audible, but the simplicity of the demos was buried under eighteen months of overdubs. Eric wished he'd been strong enough in the studio: John Lennon would have challenged Paul and resolved the problem; George Martin could have stood up to him; but Eric had been cowed by Paul's status as a former Beatle, a legacy so enormous it inhibited both the star and those around him. 'Where do you go from there?' asks Eric rhetorically. Paul's answer was to celebrate that legacy.

When *Press to Play* sold fewer than a million copies worldwide—poor by Paul's standards—he hired a new manager, Richard Ogden, who set out a three-year plan to get Paul back in the charts and back on the road.

Part of Ogden's job was managing Linda's career, too, which meant realising her pet projects, mostly to do with photography or vegetarianism, for which she had become a zealot. Having given up eating meat and fish, and wearing leather, Linda expected everybody else to do the same. She even had the temerity to ask the Duke of Edinburgh how he, as the figurehead for the World Wildlife Fund, could defend shooting birds for sport. The Duke muttered in reply that his eldest son was almost a bloody veggie.

Linda's vegetarianism was not so much to do with health as a horror of the slaughterhouse. In this regard, Linda found a like-minded friend in television writer Carla Lane, who became another ally in the cause of animal rights. Carla was a Liverpudlian, slightly older than Paul, but it was her devotion to animals that endeared her to Linda. 'We were each lonely people, really,' observes Carla, noting that although Linda was friendly with Pretenders singer Chrissie Hynde and the model-turned-actress Twiggy, she was not overendowed with friends. Similarly, Paul didn't have many pals. 'I never saw Paul with mates. He was always surrounded by people, but he was usually in charge of them.'

The McCartneys kept approximately nine horses, numerous cats and dogs, sheep, a herd of deer and a pet bullock, not to mention numerous small creatures, including rabbits, fish, a turtle and a parrot named Sparky. Though she meant well, Linda's concern for animals could lead to muddled thinking. She fed her animals a vegetarian diet whenever possible, even to those creatures that were naturally carnivorous. Animals at Blossom Farm lived until they died of old age, the McCartneys spending whatever it cost on vets to keep their ageing animal friends alive. And Linda drew Paul and the children into this way of thinking, the whole family becoming evangelical about animal rights.

In order to create vegetarian versions of the traditional, meat-based meals Paul had been brought up on, Linda used textured vegetable protein (TVP) in her versions of such English staples as Sunday roast and shepherd's pie, serving an elaborate soya turkey at Thanksgiving, and having 'non-meat bacon' imported from the USA so that she and Paul could snack on *faux* bacon sarnies.

To help Linda spread this veggie message, Richard Ogden struck a publishing deal with Bloomsbury, with a writer engaged to help Linda turn her menus into a cookbook, *Linda McCartney's Home Cooking*, which put her in the same business as Jane Asher. (After breaking up with Paul in 1968, Jane had married the artist Gerald Scarfe, still pursuing her acting, but also creating a successful second career as a celebrity cake-maker, publishing a series of best-selling recipe books.)

In the summer of 1987, Paul started recording demos and auditioning for a band he would ultimately take out on the road. He ran down favourite rock 'n' roll songs, including 'Kansas City', 'Lucille' and 'That's All Right (Mama)', which he sang with the pleasure of a middle-aged man reconnecting with his youth. When he played the tapes back, Paul decided he wanted to put them out as an album.

Richard Ogden feared an album of rock 'n' roll covers might be reviewed critically in comparison to John Lennon's 1975 *Rock 'n' Roll* album. When Paul insisted, Ogden had the novel idea of allowing a Russian company to release a Paul McCartney 'bootleg'. Despite being banned in the USSR during the Cold War, the Beatles' music had been hugely popular and, with the rise of the reformist Soviet leader Mikhail Gorbachev, it was becoming easier to get genuine Western records in the USSR. EMI licensed the Russian label Melodya to manufacture 400,000 copies of Paul's rock 'n' roll LP, guessing they would print more and that fans who wanted it in the West could buy Soviet imports, which is what happened when *CHOBA B CCCP* (Russian for 'Again in the USSR'), was released the following year.

Around the same time, the star agreed that EMI should issue a new 'best of' LP, and *Paul McCartney: All the Best* sold strongly in the build-up to Christmas 1987, with Paul appearing on British chat shows to promote it. However, after the flops of *Give My Regards to Broad Street* and *Press to Play*, Paul needed what was in effect a comeback record: he wasn't prepared to step off the merry-go-round as John Lennon had done. To help Paul achieve his ambitions, MPL got the star together with Elvis Costello, a talented singer-songwriter of strong character whom everybody hoped would be able to stand up to Paul, pushing him to do better than his usual 'I love you Linda' material.

Although the original idea was that Costello would co-write and co-produce the new album *Flowers in the Dirt*, the old problems soon re-emerged. Paul wanted to do things his way, and Elvis was pulling in a different direction. 'They were kind of banging heads a little bit,' comments guitarist Hamish Stuart. 'It just didn't work, so Elvis left the building.'

The drummer in Paul's new band was Chris Whitten, who had worked on the *CHOBA B CCCP* sessions. Enlarging the group, Paul hired guitarist Robbie McIntosh from the Pretenders and added keyboard player Paul 'Wix' Wickens, who was 'almost a veggie'; increasingly, the McCartneys had little time for anybody who wasn't. Paul was paying good wages: £1,000 a week as a retainer, £3,000 for when they were rehearsing and recording, rising to £5,000 on the road, generous by industry standards. Paul had learned the lesson of Wings.

Meanwhile, Paul's other, more famous former band was about to be inducted into the Rock 'n' Roll Hall of Fame, an institution co-founded in 1983 by *Rolling Stone* publisher Jann Wenner. Stars were falling over themselves to be inducted at the annual ceremony in New York, and Paul was expected to join George, Ringo and Yoko at the Waldorf-Astoria Hotel on January 20, 1988, when the Beatles' fellow inductees would include the Beach Boys and Bob Dylan, who counted among Paul's musical heroes. But Paul boycotted the event because George, Ritchie and Yoko were suing him over a deal the Eastmans had struck when he signed back with Capitol Records after a brief spell with CBS, winning him an extra per cent royalty on the Beatles' back catalogue. The dispute was settled when Capitol gave all four an extra per cent on CDs, which were replacing vinyl.

Despite not attending the dinner, Paul and Linda had a keen interest in the events in New York and, early the next day, Linda called her friend Danny Fields to ask about the evening. Danny who, aside from his work as a journalist, had a seat on the Hall of Fame nominating committee, had recorded Yoko's speech at the dinner. Linda told Paul to pick up the extension and all three listened as Yoko told the Waldorf that if *her* husband had been alive, he would have attended the induction—as neat a put-down of the McCartneys as she'd ever made.

PAUL TOOK A BREAK in August 1988 to visit Liverpool, where he was shocked to discover his old school had fallen into dereliction. The Liverpool Institute had been closed in 1985 by the City Council;

apparently there weren't enough clever boys in the shrinking city to fill such an elite school. Four years on, Paul was dismayed to see that the Inny had become a ruin.

Paul had been looking for a way to give something back to Liverpool. Following his visit, he decided the school should be the focus for his philanthropy. But what was one to do with the place? The only way to save the building in the long term was to give it a use. George Martin, one of the few people in whom Paul placed unswerving trust, mentioned that he'd been helping an entrepreneur named Mark Featherstone-Witty raise money for a school in London based on the New York School of the Performing Arts depicted in the movie *Fame* — a *Fame* school for Liverpool might be a use for the Inny. Paul was circumspect: he hadn't gone to a school for performing arts. George, a graduate of the Guildhall School of Music, took a different view. He believed there was a place for a formal musical education, and a need to teach young people the essentials of the music business if future Lennons and McCartneys weren't to be ripped off, as Paul felt he had been with Northern Songs. He went some way to persuading Paul, whose primary motivation, though, remained saving the Inny. Canny as ever with money, he didn't propose to buy the place. The hope was that the council, and the charitable trust in which the building was held, would give the premises to Paul if he devised a regeneration plan.

Mark Featherstone-Witty proved to be an ebullient, jokey fellow of forty-two, with a theatrical and slightly posh manner (Paul worried that his double-barrelled name would raise hackles on Merseyside), and a varied CV ranging from acting to journalism to teaching, the last of which had led him to create a number of private educational institutions, including the British Record Industry Trust (BRIT) School in Croydon. Now he wanted a new project.

Although Mark had met many famous people working on the BRITSchool, when Paul walked through the door at MPL the entrepreneur was overwhelmed. 'You are trying to carry on a reasonable conversation, but one half of your mind is saying, "I don't bloody believe it. I'm actually talking to Paul McCartney!" I've seen the same reaction with other people.'

The meeting went well. It was agreed that Mark would approach Liverpool City Council to see if it was feasible to turn the Inny into the Liverpool Institute for Performing Arts (LIPA). Paul pledged £1 million of his own money but initially advanced Featherstone-Witty small sums. 'It was "Let's see what you can do with £30,000." So it was to some extent payment by achievement. Also the payment needed to be matched with a payment from other people. He was never going to be the sole funder.' Still, Paul committed himself to a project that would take up a lot of his time, and require much more of his money over the next few years, while Mark discovered that the charming superstar he met on day one could also be 'a right bastard'.

Released in May 1989, *Flowers in the Dirt* was greeted as a return to form and went to number one in the UK, with Paul appearing on TV shows to promote it prior to his first tour since 1979. Paul was interested in playing to as many people as possible, partly because he and Lin wanted to use the concerts to proselytise vegetarianism and ecology. The tour was arranged to coincide with the publication of Linda's cookbook, with the eighty-one-strong tour party served a meat-free diet backstage. Audiences front of house wouldn't be able to buy meaty snacks, either: MPL banned such concessions, licensing instead the sale of veggie burgers.

Alongside didactic articles about vegetarianism in the tour programme, Paul took the opportunity to tell his audiences his life story. A series of long interview features saw him correcting what he viewed as misinterpretations about the Beatles' history. This was a foretaste of a putting-the-record-straight biography Paul had started to work on with Barry Miles. Miles had come up with the idea of the book, *Paul McCartney: Many Years from Now*, agreeing to let Paul vet the manuscript and, surprisingly, retain 75 per cent of the royalties, meaning it was really going to be Paul's book.

On tour, Richard Ogden urged Paul to perform his greatest hits, which meant Beatles songs as well as the likes of 'Live and Let Die'. Paul drew up a set list that featured fourteen Beatles tunes, approximately half the show, and he had to learn to play many live for the first time, never having performed them on stage. As guitarist Hamish Stuart observes, 'Some of them we knew better than Paul did.'

THE TOUR OPENED in Oslo on September 26, 1989, the first of a run of European arena concerts, after which Paul took his band to North America, returning to England in January 1990 to play Birmingham and London. To interject a brief personal note, the first Paul McCartney show I ever saw was on this tour, at Wembley Arena in January 1990. McCartney's solo career had made little impression on me so far. The Beatles were another matter.

McCartney bounded on stage, chubby and grey at forty-seven, but evidently eager to entertain. His band seemed up for the challenge, too, though Linda sat awkwardly at her keyboard, periodically making V-signs as if impersonating Winston Churchill. When the show opened with 'Figure of Eight', one's spirits sank. Were we to be subjected to a series of mediocre new songs? Thankfully, the friendly opening bars of 'Got to Get You into My Life' followed, the start of a sparkling stream of Beatles songs. To see and hear Paul McCartney perform these iconic songs was genuinely thrilling and, unlike his contemporary Bob Dylan, who deliberately changes his songs live, McCartney and his band were playing these classics like they sounded on the records.

Although London audiences have a reputation for being undemonstrative, people were weeping with emotion, couples were embracing. 'Sometimes it was hard to watch,' says Hamish. '. . . you get drawn in and forget what you're doing.' The crowning moment of the show came in the encore when McCartney picked out the plangent opening chords of 'Golden Slumbers' on a Roland keyboard, going on to perform the complete *Abbey Road* medley.

This spine-tingling moment was the closest one could get in 1990 to experiencing the magic of the Beatles live, and it was perhaps better than seeing the boys in the sixties, in that Paul was performing a complex album piece the Beatles never staged, with state-of-the-art sound equipment. I walked away from the show a convert to Paul McCartney as a live performer.

Off stage, Paul and Linda were coping with a difficult family situation. As noted, Heather McCartney had long found the McCartney name a burden. If she was introduced simply as Heather, people showed little interest in her. 'Then somebody would say McCartney and really emphasise it and I'd just watch their face change.' For a fairly simple person who didn't have a strong idea of herself, or what she meant to do in life, this turned into an identity crisis and, in 1988, the twenty-five-year-old admitted herself to a private clinic in Sussex.

After her treatment, Heather went to the United States to spend time with her natural father, Mel See, whom she called Papa. Although she enjoyed visiting Arizona, Heather soon returned to the family estate in Sussex, which she considered her real home, and here her emotional problems returned. During the early part of Paul's world tour, the press reported that Heather had again been admitted to a clinic. Fortunately, Paul and Linda had arranged the European stage of their tour in such a way that they flew home most nights, meaning they could see Heather almost daily. As Heather got better, her parents felt confident enough to continue the tour farther afield.

Paul played Japan almost exactly ten years after he had been deported. Then it was back to the USA, where MPL had cut a sponsorship deal with Visa. The credit card company paid $8.5 million, which covered most of the tour expenses, further agreeing to run nationwide television ads, which caused Paul's ticket sales to rocket. From selling 20,000 tickets for an average city, there was demand for 100,000, transforming an arena tour into a stadium tour, which Paul capped on April 21, 1990 by playing a record-breaking show before 184,000 people in Rio de Janeiro.

After South America, Paul returned to the UK to perform in Scotland and Liverpool, the latter show staged as a fundraiser for LIPA. Backstage, Paul was reunited with several old boys from the Inny, including Ian James, who'd helped teach him how to play guitar when they were teenagers. When Paul became a star, Ian didn't get in touch 'because I didn't feel it was right somehow, like taking advantage'. He hadn't seen his mate for thirty-odd years when Paul and Linda walked in. 'It was like the king and queen'd arrived,' he recalls. Ian hung back, falling into conversation with Paul's brother, Mike. Then Paul saw Ian and all formality was forgotten: 'as soon as he saw me he came over. We just hugged.' Three decades had passed, but their friendship was somehow unchanged. 'So from that point we've stayed in touch, and I've been to a few things like his office Christmas party . . . Linda would always invite the wife and me. She was a lovely woman.' It is worth emphasising that almost everybody who knew Linda liked her, yet her public image was that of a pushy opportunist.

The tour finally concluded in Chicago at the end of July 1990, by which time Paul had played to 2.8 million people in thirteen countries—the longest and most successful tour of his career to date. By getting back to a Beatles-heavy set list, he had recaptured the attention of a vast international audience, who remained bewitched by the Fab Four. It was a lesson he didn't forget, gradually increasing the Beatles content until he became a veritable Beatles jukebox. The situation was now clear. With John dead, and Paul, George and Ringo locked in almost constant disagreements over money, the next best thing to experiencing the magic of the Beatles was to see Paul McCartney live. It has been true ever since.

THE CLASSICAL COMPOSER Carl Davis, who had met Paul courtesy of Carla Lane, asked if Paul would like to collaborate on an orchestral piece for the Royal Liverpool Philharmonic, for whom he was guest conductor. The idea of creating music with a Liverpool theme appealed to Paul, who began telling Carl his life story, starting with how he'd been born in Liverpool during the Second World War. 'That's good!' remarked Davis, seeing the beginning of an oratorio— a word Paul wasn't familiar with. Davis explained it was a piece of music based on a religious story, sung by soloists and chorus: Elgar's *The Dream of Gerontius*, for example. The outcome of their collaboration—the *Liverpool Oratorio*—was indeed to contain an element of pluralistic religiosity, but had much more to do with Paul's life.

To take on such a project was a surprising departure from rock. In the sixties, Paul had dipped into Berio and Stockhausen, but he had never shown much interest in mainstream 'classical' music: on the contrary, Paul and Linda had walked out of a New York production of *La Bohème* when they were courting because they were bored. Yet an appreciation of classical music often develops with maturity and there is no reason why an innately musical person shouldn't like, understand and indeed make orchestral music as well as pop. This is what Paul proceeded to do.

There was a problem, however. When Paul needed to create music for players who went by notes on a page, he had to employ an amanuensis to orchestrate his music. George Martin had scored 'Yesterday' and the 'Eleanor Rigby' sequence in *Give My Regards to Broad Street*, among other pieces with Paul's name attached, raising the question of how much credit is actually due to McCartney on such projects. Martin has always been content to stand in the background; Carl Davis was a different personality. An American who'd made his home in England, Carl had enjoyed a long and successful career and was used to getting due credit. So Carl was 'very taken aback when he [Paul] said, quite emphatically, that he wanted it to be called *Paul McCartney's Liverpool Oratorio*'.

Work on the oratorio started around the time of Paul's 1989/90 world tour, after which the star had a live album to oversee and other projects to attend to. In addition to these commitments, Paul found time to meet Davis regularly, supplying him with the essential story of the oratorio, humming and playing tunes for it on the piano. It was Carl's task to transcribe these tunes, and do the detailed work of scoring the piece, Paul coming back with comments.

By January 1991, the composers had been working together in this way for two years, with the premiere scheduled for June. During final preparations, a documentary camera team followed Paul, the footage revealing tensions, with Paul overruling his partner in a polite but firm way that must have been difficult for Davis to take. At the same time, Paul was capable of rolling out melodies on the piano that sounded so delightful Davis was scrabbling around for a pencil to note them down before Paul moved on to something else. Davis appeared increasingly frazzled by the experience of working with a man who didn't technically know what he was doing, but knew exactly what he wanted and wasn't to be brooked. After all, Paul was paying for everything.

The premiere was held on a summer evening in late June in Sir Giles Gilbert Scott's Anglican Cathedral, the grandest possible Liverpool venue for Paul's work. It was performed by the Royal Philharmonic Orchestra and Choir, conducted by Carl Davis, and featuring two of the most famous singers in the classical world: soprano Dame Kiri Te Kanawa and bass Willard White.

Beforehand, Paul found time to meet Michael Portillo, the minister with responsibility for Merseyside in John Major's government. LIPA needed public sector backing, so it was important that politicians were onside. Few were immune from the charms of a Beatle, especially those now in middle life who'd grown up with the Fab Four. Paul's ability to attract and win over influential figures in this way helped LIPA considerably.

Paul sat behind his celebrity guests for the actual performance, flanked by Linda and the kids. The first impression of the piece itself was that his *Liverpool Oratorio* was a traditional work. As the story developed, one heard echoes of Edward Elgar as well as the Beatles. The music was varied, the playing and singing excellent. At the end, Paul bounded onto the rostrum to hug Carl Davis, congratulate the singers, and accept the acclaim of his audience, as he would at a rock concert. The oratorio was a success, though it was hard to know how much credit was due to Carl Davis and how much to Paul himself.

Paul had foreseen that critics would mock him for his classical pretensions, but the reviews weren't at all bad. Michael John White in the *Independent on Sunday* noted the 'honest innocence' of the oratorio. Plans were made for further performances with a CD release on EMI Classics, by dint of which Paul crossed the Rubicon from pop to the classical division of the old firm. Classical music would be part of Paul's music-making for years to come.

SHORTLY AFTER the *Liverpool Oratorio* premiere, Lee Eastman died of a stroke in New York aged eighty-one. Over the years, Paul had developed a high regard for his father-in-law's acumen, marking his debt by giving the old man a Rolls-Royce on one occasion.

There were financial ramifications for Linda now her father had died. Philip Sprayregen estimates the value of his stepfather's estate in the hundreds of millions. So long as Lee's widow survived him, most of this wealth was held in trust for Lee's children and grandchildren, with Linda standing to inherit her share as and when Monique Eastman predeceased her. In the meantime, John Eastman took over control of Eastman & Eastman, from the Manhattan office of which he continued to advise Paul. The men were close. Apart from being brothers-in-law, they had worked together since Apple days, and spent their summer holidays together, watching their children grow up. Mark Featherstone-Witty remarks that, along with George Martin, John Eastman was 'one of the relatively few people Paul wholly respected and would listen to'. Unfortunately, Mark's own relationship with Paul was not nearly so good.

Paul had promised £1 million to LIPA, but more than ten times that amount was needed. Under pressure, Featherstone-Witty sent out over 600 letters in Paul's name asking the great and the good for donations including, at Paul's suggestion, Her Majesty the Queen. 'It was like one of those wonderful English exercises, *Write in the style of Paul McCartney to the Queen.*'

Paul also wrote personally to select friends and public figures, including the Prince of Wales. Composing the letter made him feel like he was back at school. His two-page, handwritten missive did have something of the schoolboy about it, signed with an elaborate autograph and a smiley face, as if His Royal Highness would appreciate a Beatle's signature. The prince didn't return any money.

The Queen did send a personal donation, however—a gesture that encouraged others to follow her. Celebrities ranging from Chevy Chase to David Hockney also gave to LIPA. George and Olivia Harrison gave an undisclosed donation, though George, despite being a Liverpool Institute old boy, showed precious little interest in LIPA.

Meanwhile, many ordinary people sent in money, including fans who paid to have their name inscribed on an auditorium chair.

Paul agreed to attend three fundraising lunches, leading EMI to donate £100,000, the biggest cheque yet. At the Groucho Club in London, Paul found himself sitting opposite a familiar-looking gentleman who turned out to be Donald Warren-Knott, formerly British consul to Japan. They had last seen each other through a glass screen in Kojimachi Police Station. 'We both thought it rather [funny],' says Warren-Knott, regretting that his organisation wasn't able to make LIPA a grant. Indeed, at the end of this fundraising drive, Mark Featherstone-Witty had collected only £500,000 in addition to Paul's £1 million pledge, which led to some awkward moments with his lead patron: Paul had started to think about doing something for Liverpool around the time he became forty; in the summer of 1992 he turned fifty, and LIPA still seemed far from being a reality.

As his chief fundraiser continued to try and raise the money required, Paul returned to what he knew best, making rock 'n' roll records. The result, *Off the Ground*, is a tuneful, well-made CD that, like so many releases from the back end of Paul's career, made little impact on any but his die-hard fans, of whom, luckily, there were still many.

Paul then embarked on his New World Tour, so named because he was visiting Australia and New Zealand, places he'd missed in 1989–91, as well as playing shows in Europe and North America.

Having learned how well a Beatles-loaded show went down, Paul drew up a set list that was 50 per cent Beatles material, opening with 'Drive My Car', which got the crowd on its feet, incorporating 'We Can Work It Out', 'Magical Mystery Tour', 'Paperback Writer' and 'Penny Lane' in the main set, along with songs from Wings and his solo career. As in 1989–91, playing Beatles songs on stage with Paul was a thrill for the band members who, in common with their audiences, had grown up with this music.

One element of the New World Tour was to raise funds for LIPA, and Mark Featherstone-Witty got lucky with Grundig. The German electronics company offered £2 million over five years for 'title sponsorship', which meant the Grundig name would have to be used over LIPA on its literature. Mark's excitement at the deal was quelled when Paul told him he didn't want to endorse Grundig. In particular, Paul disliked the idea that Grundig would have its name over the institute. 'I remember him saying, "I don't have my name on it; I don't see why their name should be on it. It's all too commercial."'

Although Paul didn't like endorsing products, it had become commonplace to have a corporate sponsor offset some of the costs of a rock tour, as Visa had in 1990. For this tour, MPL had lined up Volkswagen and it was all but signed when Linda said the McCartneys couldn't associate themselves with the car industry for ecological reasons. This left Richard Ogden scratching around for an eleventh-hour replacement sponsor, when MPL remembered the other German firm that had wanted to link its name with Paul's. A deal was struck whereby Grundig paid MPL to be the tour sponsor, as well as giving a smaller donation to LIPA, without having its name too prominently on the institute.

When Paul reached Australia, his tour changed from an arena to a stadium concert, with the visuals and effects correspondingly enlarged. Not everything worked properly at first, and there were other irritants. Paul had agreed that a special LIPA ticket could be sold at the concerts. Costing the equivalent of $1,000, this was a very expensive seat, and many fans who dug deep assumed that a backstage meeting with Paul was included. When this didn't automatically happen, ticket-holders became angry. When Paul looked out from the stage during his set, he routinely saw banners declaring 'WE LOVE YOU PAUL' and so forth. Now there was a banner complaining about a '$1,000 LIPA SCAM'.

Even worse, not enough LIPA tickets were sold in America: part of a wider problem of not selling out the North American shows. Following the 1989–91 US tour, when Paul had been backed by Visa's television campaign, the New World Tour had been planned on selling out the same vast venues. But there was no national TV campaign in 1993, and there were no takers for the last few blocks of seats in towns like Boulder and Toronto. These seats often meant the difference between profit and loss. Paul blamed Richard Ogden, and Ogden resigned accordingly. Looking back on his six years, he concludes that 'Paul wanted to be the top-permost of the popper-most. The Beatles thing. He never lost that desire. Lost maybe the understanding of how to get that sometimes, but [he] was prepared to listen to someone who could tell him. I had a wonderful time managing him.' He also discovered that if you made a mistake with Paul you were up shit creek.

To balance the books, Paul extended the tour into the winter of 1993 and the tour rolled on, with Paul releasing a spin-off live LP, *Paul is Live*. In November Paul took his band to Japan, then South America, by which time everybody was road-weary.

Playing with Paul had been a joy for his musicians, and the New World Tour had been brightened by the introduction of an acoustic set, yet the main show was the same every night, with Paul sticking to faithful recreations of the Beatles songs as heard on record. By the time they reached Santiago, Chile, for the final show, it was, in Hamish's words, 'a little tired'. They had played to 1.7 million people on five continents, with Paul transforming what looked like a loss-making tour into an earner. MPL turned over £14 million in the twelve months to December 1993, squeezing a profit of £2.6 million on the year. Paul then said goodbye to his band, whom he'd been working with for almost six years, explaining that he was committed to a major new project that would keep him at home in 1994. 'I'm off to be a Beatle now,' he said.

9: PASSING THROUGH THE DREAM OF LOVE

For years the press had speculated about a Beatles reunion. The boys themselves said it would never happen, and indeed how could it with John dead? Yet the impossible now came to pass in a partial sense, thanks to the band's old friend and servant, Neil Aspinall, who ran Apple on their behalf.

Since the sixties, Neil had been collecting footage of the Beatles for a documentary film. He first edited the clips together after the band's breakup, creating a 16mm flick he called *The Long and*

Winding Road, and sent copies to the individual band members for old times' sake. Nothing more was done for two decades, during much of which time the Beatles were arguing between themselves.

When all lawsuits were resolved, around 1990, Aspinall raised the idea of a definitive television history of the Beatles using the old footage he had collected. 'I said to the guys, "We're going to have to interview you,"' notes Aspinall. 'There were varying degrees of enthusiasm for that suggestion.' The three surviving Beatles were like brothers who have grown up and left home, seeing their siblings occasionally, feeling affection but quick to be irritated by them. Relations between Paul and George were particularly prickly. Although the men still saw each other socially, George had a tendency to snipe at Macca in interviews, complaining about him to others, and ignoring Paul's calls. Nevertheless, Harrison now had a compelling reason to work with Paul.

Although he'd made millions, George never earned as much from the Beatles as the two principal songwriters and, while his solo career got off to a promising start in 1970 with the acclaimed triple album *All Things Must Pass*, flop records followed, with George suffering the indignity of being sued successfully over his biggest solo hit, 'My Sweet Lord', which infringed the copyright of the Chiffons' 'He's So Fine'. In 1978, he bailed out his friends in the Monty Python troupe when EMI withdrew finance from the heretical *Life of Brian*: Harrison advanced the Pythons the money to make the picture, which proved a hit, encouraging George to invest in more movies via his company HandMade Films. The result was that HandMade Films was mired in debt by 1989. A Japanese tour with Eric Clapton raised some much-needed cash, but George's best chance of a substantial payday lay with the Beatles.

Ritchie could always do with a little extra. He'd earned far less in royalties than John, Paul and George, and had the least successful solo career, yet he pursued a relentlessly expensive jet-set life.

Hard-working, consistently successful Paul was far richer than George and Ritchie combined, and those close to Paul talk of him agreeing to a three-quarters Beatles reunion partly to give the other two some of what he already had: 'serious money'.

Despite being the Beatle who most needed the favour, Harrison vetoed *The Long and Winding Road* as a title for the documentary project because it was a Paul song, with the result that it gained the unimaginative name of the *Anthology*.

Work began in earnest in 1991, with Paul, George and Ritchie interviewed multiple times over the next few years, and the result is that their appearance varies considerably during the series. Paul proved the most consistently entertaining interviewee. He enjoyed indulging in nostalgia and though he had told his stories until they were worn smooth as river pebbles, they were still good to hear. George was more sardonic in his comments, and exhibited a wry sense of humour, while Ringo unfortunately felt the need to hide behind dark glasses and suffered memory lapses.

WORK ON THE *ANTHOLOGY* reached a peak in 1994, which Paul began by inducting John Lennon into the Rock 'n' Roll Hall of Fame, making Lennon one of the first artists to be inducted as both a band member and a solo artist. Yoko came on stage and Paul hugged her, as if they were great friends.

Apart from honouring John, Paul may have had one or two other motives for helping his former partner into the Rock 'n' Roll Hall of Fame: almost immediately the McCartneys got back to England, Danny Fields started receiving calls from Linda asking when Paul was going to be inducted. There was another reason for Paul doing John's memory a good service, too. Yoko was asked if she had any recordings of songs John had been working on that the other three could complete as a 'new' Beatles record. She gave Paul a demo tape of 'Free as a Bird', an unfinished song from the late 1970s.

The following month, the surviving Beatles reunited discreetly to complete it. To help deal with the fact that they were making music without John, the trio told themselves that Lennon had already recorded his part and then popped out of the studio.

Building the song up from John's scanty demo was a production challenge overseen by Jeff Lynne of the Electric Light Orchestra (ELO), who had joined George in the Traveling Wilburys. When

Lynne had fixed the underlying tape, Paul and George added acoustic guitar to 'Free as a Bird', Paul doubling John's piano part and adding the bass. At times it all 'got a little difficult', as McCartney later conceded.

Two months later, Paul and Ritchie met with George at his home, Friar Park, to talk on camera about the old days, McCartney being careful not to say anything that would upset his touchy friend. The boys tried to recreate the repartee of their early days, but appeared awkward in each other's company, and forgetful. Stories were begun, then trailed off into silence. It was when the men started playing old tunes, like 'Raunchy' and 'Thinking of Linking', that they looked happiest, smiling at each other in enjoyment of their musical youth.

PAUL'S PARALLEL PET PROJECT continued to be the Liverpool Institute for Performing Arts, which was at last under construction, Mark Featherstone-Witty having lined up the necessary £12 million funds. Roughly a third of the money was coming from the European Union, a third from the British public sector, the final third, including Paul's £1 million, from private donations. 'And then we discovered we got the figures wrong,' groans Mark. Putting a new roof on the Inny proved more expensive than expected, prompting a lecture from Paul about financial prudence. He would have to reopen his own chequebook to make sure LIPA became a reality.

Although Paul was keen to raise as much money from others first, his underlying commitment to LIPA shows a generous side to his character that is often overlooked by his critics. There are, in fact, numerous examples of the star being very generous, such as when a call came through in 1994 from Horst Fascher, the German pugilist the Beatles had knocked about with in Hamburg. In recent years, Horst had taken up with a Hungarian girl, who had given birth to their daughter, Marie-Sophie, that February. German doctors warned Horst that Marie-Sophie would not live long because of a heart defect. 'In my angst I called Paul. I thought Paul has better doctors in England,' says Horst, who wept on the phone to one of Paul's assistants. 'After twenty minutes he called me back. I said, "Paul, can you help me?" He was saying, "Horst, whatever I can do for you, I do for you."' True to his word, Paul arranged to have the Faschers flown from Hamburg to London and accommodated while eleven-month Marie-Sophie was admitted to Great Ormond Street Hospital. A team of American surgeons was then flown in to operate on the child. Despite the best treatment, she died thirteen days later. 'Then it came to the payment. Paul said, "I take care of everything. You don't have to [worry],"' says Fascher. 'And he flew us back and all of that.' Horst believed the whole thing cost about $190,000. 'I said, "How can I pay you back?" He said, "Horst, forget it."'

This wasn't an isolated example of Paul's philanthropy. For some time Paul and Linda had backed a campaign to reopen their local NHS cottage hospital in Rye, which had closed in 1990 when a new district hospital opened in Hastings. After Paul and Linda had marched with their neighbours, and donated almost a million pounds to the cause, a new nineteen-bed cottage hospital and care centre was opened in Rye, with a 'Strawberry Fields' day room. In a quieter way, Paul and Lin helped out with many local charitable causes, in Sussex and Kintyre, earning respect and affection in the communities.

Paul was continuing to compose orchestral music, no longer with Carl Davis, but with a friend and colleague of Davis's, David Matthews. As a young man, David had worked as an assistant to Benjamin Britten, whose music Paul enjoyed. It gradually emerged that Paul was working on a piece titled *Spiral*, inspired by his interest in Celtic mythology. Paul had recorded a demo on piano, getting an assistant to transcribe the music. He now wanted to develop the score with Matthews.

Paul was also using other arrangers. A collaboration with the American composer Jonathan Tunick resulted in a piano prelude titled *A Leaf*, and premiered in March 1995 as part of 'An Evening with Paul McCartney and Friends' in front of the Prince of Wales at St James's Palace. The event was in aid of the Royal College of Music. In a varied programme, Paul also performed with Elvis Costello and the Brodsky Quartet. At the end, Prince Charles awarded McCartney an Honorary Fellowship of the Royal College of Music, further assimilating him into the English Establishment and the classical world Paul clearly aspired to join. 'Unlike most people in the rock world, he's ambitious to do new things all the time,' says David Matthews, approvingly.

The Beatles' *Anthology* premiered on ABC television in the United States on November 19, 1995, and five days later in the UK, then in 100 countries around the world. The original series ran to approximately five hours, long by normal standards, but nevertheless perfunctory for such an epic story with so many fascinating characters and incidents. The story was better told in expanded video and DVD releases, the final version stretching to more than eleven hours. Well received, the series remains the definitive televisual history of the Beatles, as Neil Aspinall had set out to make it, even if sensitive parts of the story were soft-pedalled to appease the protagonists. Paul didn't want to go into the whys and wherefores of who broke up the band, for instance, so there wasn't a word about his High Court action to dissolve the partnership.

As with any 'authorised' biographical project, the *Anthology* was a glossing-over of the truth, with key areas of the story ignored. But to hear Paul, George and Ringo talk directly at length about the amazing experiences they had shared was compensation.

A couple of days after the show was broadcast, the first of three double CDs of hitherto officially unreleased Beatles music went on sale. This included what George Martin termed a 'rather grotty' home recording of 'Hallelujah, I Love Her So', 'You'll be Mine' and 'Cayenne', all featuring Stuart Sutcliffe. These tapes had been found recently in a Liverpool attic. Beautifully produced, *Anthology Vol. 1* quickly sold more than two million units in the USA alone. One of those who benefited from the runaway success was Pete Best who, like Stuart Sutcliffe, appeared for the very first time on an official Beatles record. Pete was on tracks recorded in Hamburg in 1961, at the Decca audition in London on New Year's Day 1962, and at EMI that June. As a result, Pete received his first substantial payday from the band who had sacked him, making him a rich man finally at fifty-four.

The *Anthology* project as a whole generated a mountain of money. MPL turned over £6.4 million in what had otherwise been a quiet year, with Paul paying himself £1.9 million, including pension contributions, and the *Anthology* continued to earn the boys millions for years to come. Two further CD sets were to be released in 1995/96, with a VHS box set of the documentaries retailing at £99 in the UK, and an expensive *Anthology* book in the works.

All of this, however, was of little account to Paul, for he now faced the terrifying news that Linda had the same cancer that had killed his mother.

WHEN LINDA FOUND A LUMP under her arm, she went to see her general practitioner, who told her it was nothing to worry about and prescribed antibiotics. She sought a second opinion, receiving the results by telephone at Blossom Farm in December 1995. She rang Paul to tell him she had a cancerous tumour in her left breast.

Before going into hospital to have the lump removed, Linda also confided in Carla Lane. 'We sat in the kitchen and she said, "I have cancer." I went to open my mouth, and she put her finger up and she said, "Shush! I want you as my friend to know, *but we're not going to talk about it.*" I said, "OK."'

Then Linda changed the subject, and rarely spoke of it again.

On December 11, 1995 Linda underwent a lumpectomy—the removal of the cancerous tumour and surrounding tissue, rather than a whole breast—at the Princess Grace Hospital in London. Paul and Linda then retired to Sussex to allow Linda to recuperate. 'The operation was 100 per cent successful,' Paul told the media.

It was a mark of how ill Linda felt that she wasn't with her husband on January 30, 1996 when he stood on stage in his old school assembly hall, now the Paul McCartney Auditorium, to open the Liverpool Institute for Performing Arts. To give Liverpool its *Fame*-type school had taken longer and cost almost £6 million more than the original £12 million budget, with Paul loaning LIPA £1.5 million to help bridge the gap: a loan that became £2 million with tax relief when he declared the money as a gift, bringing his total contribution to £3 million. Despite such munificence, some

Merseysiders grumbled that Paul could have paid for the whole thing himself, part of a surprisingly widespread feeling that the Beatles let the city down. This attitude is unfair. Paul had maintained a home on Merseyside, visited frequently, and rescued the Inny from dereliction. LIPA brought some welcome show-business razzmatazz back to Merseyside, with his close association helping persuade other celebrities to become patrons. Some commentators believe the opening of the institute helped begin a wider regeneration of the city that continued through 2008 when Liverpool became European Capital of Culture. And rich though Paul was, £3 million was not an insignificant amount of money to give away.

On Inauguration Day, Paul gave a passionate speech in which he talked about the tremendous start in life he'd received in this building; now he hoped others would benefit. 'Obviously, one of my feelings now is how proud my mum and dad would have been . . .' he said. Then he stopped, choked with emotion. This public display of feeling was also to do with Paul's underlying concerns about Linda, who was now undergoing chemotherapy, despite the fact that the drugs she was taking had been tested on animals. This went against everything Linda believed in as an anti-vivisectionist.

Despite the feelings of sickness induced by the drugs, Linda continued to work the phones for Paul, calling Yoko to ask her, as a personal favour, if she would let Paul have his name before John's on 'Yesterday' when the second volume of the Beatles' *Anthology* CD series was released in March. John and Paul's joint authorship of the Beatles song book was, however, a principle upon which Lennon & McCartney royalties were divided, and Yoko was reluctant to grant a favour that might set a precedent: if they went through the catalogue deciding which were John's songs and which were Paul's, it might become apparent that, more often than not, Paul's songs made more money. Yoko told Linda she would never allow Paul to have his name before John's, a rebuff the McCartneys took hard, considering the fragile state of Linda's health when she asked the favour.

With Yoko and Paul again at daggers drawn, and George Harrison declining to collaborate with Paul on any more 'new' band songs, the brief *entente* in the Beatles War was at an end. Still, Paul remained on good terms with Ritchie, with whom he had a melancholy new bond. The previous December, Ritchie's first wife Maureen had died of leukaemia at the age of forty-eight, a death that touched Paul and Linda because of their own situation, and because Mo had been an original member of the Beatles family, alongside Cyn, Jane and Pattie. Paul responded to her death by writing a moving song, 'Little Willow', encouraging Mo's children to be strong, rather as he had written 'Hey Jude' to buck up Julian Lennon after John abandoned his family.

Linda still wasn't well enough to be with Paul in June when the Queen visited LIPA. Shortly after this, Linda privately acknowledged how ill she was by making her will, leaving her entire estate in trust to Paul; the income from the trust was to be paid quarterly to Paul until his death, after which it would be shared equally between the couple's four children.

Publicly, the McCartneys maintained an optimistic 'we can beat this' façade, as composer David Matthews recalls: 'She never gave in . . . I think she believed she could overcome it.' Paul and David were working together on *Standing Stone*, a symphonic tone poem intended as a centenary celebration for EMI.

Paul and Linda returned to Kintyre that autumn with Heather, approaching her thirty-fourth birthday, Stella, now twenty-five, and nineteen-year-old James. While Heather seemed fragile, Stella was as robust as Paul himself, whom she resembled strongly in personality and features. James was a quieter person who shared Dad's passion for music. When he took up the guitar, Paul advised his son to have formal lessons, to which the boy retorted, 'You didn't.' Just before the trip to Scotland, Paul and James had recorded a song together, 'Heaven on a Sunday', James trading guitar licks with his father. A true family affair, Linda sang backing vocals. It was one of the last times she would record with Paul.

THE TIME CAME when Paul McCartney's considerable contribution to his country's cultural and economic life had to be recognised with more than an MBE. It was now sixteen years since the

McCartneys' last arrest and, what with Paul's recent meeting with Prince Charles at St James's Palace, and his charitable work with LIPA and his local hospital in Rye, Paul's friends felt it was high time he received a KBE.

Although Paul would always tell friends he didn't expect to be addressed as Sir Paul, as if he hadn't expected the honour, the knighthood was instigated by one of his closest associates, and supported by a campaign of friends. Anyone can nominate friends and colleagues for honours by filling out a Cabinet Office nomination form. Mark Featherstone-Witty did so, suggesting Paul would be a worthy recipient of a KBE. 'Some man rang back, enquiring if I knew that Paul already had an MBE. The implication was that this was enough. I gave him a piece of my mind.' Mark also rallied support from friends and influential music-industry figures, including Sir George Martin, who'd received his KBE the previous year. Their campaign was successful. News that Paul was to be knighted was announced in the honour's list on January 1, 1997.

On March 11, Paul went to Buckingham Palace to be knighted by Her Majesty the Queen, watched by Mary, Stella and James. Lady McCartney, as Lin was now formally addressed, was too ill to attend. Stella burst into tears during the ceremony, and Mary said afterwards, 'It was just like the end of a wonderful film, with the Queen placing the sword on Dad's shoulders.'

FOURTEEN SONGS Sir Paul had been working on during his *Anthology* sabbatical were released in May as the album *Flaming Pie*, after John Lennon's humorous explanation of why the Beatles were so named: 'a man appeared on a flaming pie and said unto them, "From this day on you are Beatles with an A."' This new LP came as a welcome change. Although ambitious, impatient and sometimes overbearing, Paul is essentially a decent, happily married family man. But domestic happiness does not tend to beget great art. Though he agonised over some albums, many of his records had been put out before enough reflection and revision had taken place. *Flaming Pie* was different. The fact that the tracks had been written and recorded over a long period of time gave Paul a sense of perspective, allowing him to cut out weak material. Importantly, he sounded less cocksure, more like a man in his fifties should. There was a substance to *Flaming Pie* that had been missing from Paul's albums for years, the material also having a touch of winter about it, as one expected from an artist reaching an age where loss and regret are as important as love and sex. Bob Dylan released such a wintry album in 1997, *Time Out of Mind*. This was shortlisted along with *Flaming Pie* for Album of the Year at the Grammy Awards. Dylan won, deservedly, but *Flaming Pie* was a strong contender.

The Anita Howarth paternity case blew up again in May 1997, an old story still capable of making front-page news in the tabloids. Anita and her son Philip, now a thirty-three-year-old lighting technician, told their story to the *Daily Mail*. 'There was never any doubt in my mind that Paul was Philip's father,' Anita was quoted as saying, while her son described the paternity issue as an albatross around his neck, causing him to dislike Sir Paul and take comfort in drugs. He revealed that he'd developed a heroin habit as a young man, which had led to petty crime. Anita had then told Philip that Paul *wasn't* his father, thinking this would help him. It did for a while, but when the story blew up again in 1997, Anita admitted to Philip she thought Paul actually *was* his father, but the only way to know for certain was to take a DNA test. Paul didn't take the test, but another man whom Mum thought could be a contender did, with the result that he was proved to be Philip's father. Thus ended the four-decade farce of the Liverpool typist. Like the German barmaid story, it turned out to be completely untrue.

THAT SUMMER, the McCartneys checked into the Plaza Athénée Hotel in New York so Linda could be treated at the Memorial Sloan-Kettering Cancer Center. The news was bad: Linda's cancer had spread to her right breast.

Suddenly, death was all around. The McCartneys were shocked when they heard that musician Jeff Buckley, son of Linda's sixties' lover Tim, had drowned; the McCartneys had befriended Jeff in recent years. Not long after this came the news that George

Harrison had throat cancer, which spread to his lungs. A lifelong smoker, his prognosis was not good. Then Derek Taylor, former Apple press officer, died at sixty-three of throat cancer. When Sir Paul attended the annual Buddy Holly Week luncheon that September without Linda, he appeared worn and tired.

Linda's appearance had also changed, which was evident when she accompanied Paul to Paris in October to watch Stelly's first catwalk show for Chloé. Lin had lost a good deal of hair during chemotherapy and what was left was cut short. She was determined to make the best of her trip, though, applauding enthusiastically during her daughter's show.

That autumn, Linda accompanied Paul to the London and New York premieres of *Standing Stone*. Before the performance at Carnegie Hall, Linda spent time backstage with Danny Fields, who introduced her to a friend of his who had been such a devoted McCartney fan in her youth that when Paul married Linda the girl wore mourning to school. 'So I introduced her saying, "This is Bonnie. She hates you for marrying Paul; she wore black when you got married."'

Linda growled, 'If she still wants him, she can have him.'

The friends then talked until Paul appeared. 'They walked down the hallway at Carnegie Hall and she turned around and waved.' It was the last time Danny ever saw Linda.

Paul and Linda then flew to Arizona to try alternative therapy. While they were at their ranch, Lin invited her ex-husband Mel See and his partner Beverly over for a barbecue. They had got along better in recent years, for Heather's sake, fragile as she was, and now they spent a pleasant evening together on the porch, Paul cooking veggie burgers on the barbecue. Mel and Linda and Paul parted on good terms, Paul giving Mel a painting he had made, titled *Holy Cow*. It was the last time Mel and Linda saw each other.

PAUL AND LIN CAME HOME to England for Christmas 1997, spending the holidays with the children at Blossom Farm. On Boxing Day, Lin felt well enough to host a drinks party for friends and neighbours, including the now-elderly *Goon* star Spike Milligan. Linda was putting on a brave face. In recent months, she'd tried every possible treatment, consulting the most eminent doctors in London and New York, undergoing ultrastrong doses of chemotherapy as well as a bone marrow transplant. She even gave up her lifelong habit of pot-smoking, though it was too late to make a difference. Linda was doomed and she knew it. 'That cancer business,' she said on the phone to Carla Lane, 'it's got a hold of me.'

'Linda, darling, you don't know what's round the corner. Every day they come up with something. Let's have faith.'

'I don't think so,' replied her friend, a tough broad to the end.

The reason for Linda's pessimism was that she had been told her liver was enlarged, indicating the cancer had spread to that vital organ. The situation was all but hopeless. Sir Paul and Lady Linda gathered themselves to travel to Paris to support Stella's second fashion show, then returned to Blossom Farm so Linda could attend to some final details. The cottage Heather was living in on the estate was transferred legally into her name and Linda helped her second daughter Mary plan her forthcoming wedding, after which she wrapped up gifts for family members and friends, making arrangements for the presents to be delivered after her death. She also made her goodbye calls.

Sir Paul and Lady Linda flew to Tucson at the end of March, driving from the airport to their desert hideaway. Neighbours in this lonesome desert community heard that the McCartneys were back, and that Linda was poorly, but nobody made a fuss. Mel See received word that Lin didn't want to see anybody except immediate family; the children were at the house with Paul. It was springtime in the desert, beautifully warm but not yet too hot.

Around the end of the first week in April, Linda's liver began to fail. Doctors warned Paul that his wife had only days left and suggested he warn her that she was about to die. Paul chose not to, believing Lin wouldn't want to know. On the afternoon of April 15, 1998, Paul and Linda went for a last desert ride. Paul had to put a hay bale down for Linda to step on as she climbed carefully into her saddle. The sun was setting as they arrived home, just before 7 p.m. When the sun rose the next day, Linda felt too unwell to get up and spent the day in her bed, a gentle breeze blowing through the house as the sun warmed the tin roof. She slipped into a coma. Night again, the last night. The children told their mother they loved her. She became restless around 3 a.m. Paul got into bed with her and told her they were riding through the Sussex woods: 'The bluebells are all out, and the sky is clear.' By the time he'd finished the story, his wife was dead.

News of Linda's demise began to reach the media almost immediately, with journalists going first to Paul's press officer, Geoff Baker, who deliberately misinformed the callers that Linda had died 'on holiday in Santa Barbara', this being a codeword used within MPL for when Sir Paul was in the USA privately. Reporters descended upon Santa Barbara and began a wild goose chase, the subterfuge giving the family time to get home and scatter Linda's ashes, which they did at Blossom Farm and High Park.

Linda's death was major news, partly because it came as a surprise to journalists, who had gained the impression she was successfully fighting her cancer. Carla Lane heard the news on the radio. It was a shock, followed by another shock three days later when the postman delivered a posthumous gift from Linda of antique glass beads Carla had admired. The children also received gifts.

Six weeks later, Paul led a memorial service for Linda at St Martin-in-the-Fields on Trafalgar Square. Born into a Jewish family, Linda had lived her life without religion. In death she would be honoured in two great Christian churches: in London, then later in the month in New York.

Paul attended personally to the details, selecting the music and briefing everybody who would be called upon to speak, sing or play an instrument. Rain was falling as he led his children into St Martin's on June 8, where a large crowd of press and public had gathered around the steps of the church.

Though Linda had never been popular with the British press or public, her passing had occasioned expressions of respect and even affection, while the bereaved family was naturally to be pitied. Press photographers caught images of Stella leading a distraught Heather, the older sibling's face contorted with grief. The 700 mourners inside the church also included, above and beyond Paul's relations, the first public coming together of the three surviving Beatles since Ritchie married in 1981. There was no Yoko.

When everybody was assembled—George and Ritchie sitting alongside the McCartneys—John McGeachy, who had played pipes on 'Mull of Kintyre', appeared on the balcony, clad in tartan, playing the tune of Wings' greatest hit, the pipes reverberating through the building as he descended into the crypt. The Brodsky Quartet performed arrangements of hymns and songs, including 'The Lovely Linda'. Joanna Lumley read the poem 'Death is Nothing'. LIPA students sang 'Blackbird', which had been Linda's favourite song of Paul's; Carla spoke about Linda's devotion to animals, and everybody sang 'Let it Be', after which Pete Townshend told a light-hearted story about Linda setting her cap at Paul in the sixties. 'At the memorial I said that Linda had once—quite tongue-in-cheek—told me she was going to marry "one of the Beatles",' explains Townshend, adding 'Paul has never been angry with me over this, but did tell me after the memorial that he had pursued Linda, and she had never pursued him.' This was, of course, the opposite of what everybody else said.

Two weeks later, Paul presided over a similar memorial at the Riverside Church in New York, attended by the Eastmans and American friends, but again no Yoko. She wasn't invited.

THAT JULY, Sir Paul presided at the LIPA graduation ceremony, appearing on stage with Mark Featherstone-Witty to present each graduating student with a commemorative pin, shaking the men by the hand and kissing the women. He had committed to do this every year and was good to his word. Behind the scenes, Featherstone-Witty found him a changed man. 'He had lost his greatest companion, and in the meetings we had he was always in tears.'

The McCartney family appeared together in public on September 27, 1998, when Mary McCartney married Alistair Donald, whom she'd met at school in Rye and who now worked in London as a film-maker. The service had been on hold for some time because of Linda's illness, but couldn't be postponed for much longer because, like her mother when she married Paul, Mary was pregnant. Sir Paul walked his daughter down the aisle of the church of St Peter and St Paul in Peasmarsh, having driven her from Blossom Farm in a vintage Hispano-Suiza he had owned since the sixties. James McCartney turned up rock 'n' roll-style swinging a bottle of Jack Daniel's, which a church warden confiscated at the door.

The death of Linda had hit all the family hard. James, the youngest, had been particularly close to Mum and was very upset, while Linda's eldest was bereft. Heather stayed at home much of the time after her mother died, unable to function normally. 'I could see no reason for living any more,' she told *The Sunday Times* a year later. A jittery, insecure woman of thirty-six who'd never married or had children, she lived as a virtual recluse in her cottage on the edge of the Sussex estate with her Airedale dog and two cats.

Living up to the McCartney name had long been a source of anxiety for Heather. She had tried to make her mark as a photographer, like Mum, then as a potter, seemingly soon wearying of both pastimes. Now, less than a year after Mum died, in January 1999, Heather attempted to launch herself as an interior designer, making a rare public appearance at a trade fair in Atlanta, Georgia, to showcase the Heather McCartney Housewares Collection, a range of cushions and other household knick-knacks. Sir Paul sat alongside his daughter as she spoke about her designs, which apparently owed a lot to the experience of going to Mexico with Mel See to meet the Hoichol Indians—not that she mentioned her natural father by name. She referred to Paul as her 'real daddy'.

One of Linda's dying wishes was that Paul should be inducted into the Rock 'n' Roll Hall of Fame in his own right, and that happened in March 1999, when Paul was carried in on a wave of sympathy for his loss. Stella McCartney attended the New York ceremony with her father, wearing a white T-shirt printed with the words 'ABOUT FUCKING TIME!' The following month, Dad became a granddad when Mary gave birth to a son. Sir Paul showed off his grandson, Arthur, at the Royal Albert Hall two weeks later during a rock concert in Linda's memory.

SIR PAUL ATTENDED the Dorchester Hotel in London on May 20, 1999 in support of the *Daily Mirror*'s Pride of Britain Awards, whereby the paper recognised people who had 'made a difference'. He came primarily to present an award in Linda's name to a campaigning vegetarian friend, Juliet Gellatley.

Towards the end of the ceremony, a good-looking blonde woman strode on stage, wearing an eye-catching translucent top. With large, shapely breasts and an inviting smile, she was what Paul might once have termed 'a right little raver'. Speaking in a strong northern accent, Heather Mills introduced a friend of hers, student Helen Smith, who had shown fortitude in coping with the loss of both her legs, an arm and a hand due to septicaemia. Although it was not immediately obvious, Ms Mills was herself an amputee, wearing a prosthetic leg. A slight stiffness in her walk was the only sign of the disability.

Heather travelled to Cambodia after the Dorchester show. When she returned home, she discovered that Sir Paul had left a message for her: 'It's Paul McCartney here. I'd like to talk to you about the charity work.' He meant the Heather Mills Health Trust, an organisation Heather advertised in the back of her autobiography, *Out on a Limb*.

Although Heather tended to talk casually about 'my charity', she hadn't yet registered the trust with the Charity Commission, as organisations with an income over £5,000 are obliged to do. Heather's organisation received a windfall thirty times this amount when, in August, Paul invited her to his office and gave her a cheque for £150,000, which she accepted. But she didn't get around to registering the trust as a charity for a further seven months.

As she left MPL that summer day, Heather noticed Sir Paul admiring her backside. He hadn't looked with lust at a woman since Linda died. He felt guilty doing so, then told himself Linda wouldn't mind. Indeed, he convinced himself that Lin was sending him messages via the wildlife on the Sussex estate: 'You'd ask yourself a question and, like, there'd be like an owl in the valley going *whoo-whoo-whoo*.' In short, he had decided to date Heather Mills.

Born on January 12, 1968, Heather was the middle child of John, a soldier, and Bernice Mills. Her life prior to meeting Paul was eventful and mysterious.

Family life started to fall apart in the mid-1970s when Mum was involved in a car accident. During her convalescence, Heather and her sister Fiona were taken into care. When Mum came out of hospital, the family was reunited, then Mum left home to live with an actor, leaving the children with their father. At ten, Heather was caught shoplifting. Around the time she was thirteen, John Mills was imprisoned for fraud, with the result that the children went to live with their mother. At fourteen, Heather claims she ran away from home to join the fair on Clapham Common; she started sleeping rough. She got a Saturday job with a jeweller, from whom she stole, and was given a probationary sentence for theft.

A precocious sixteen-year-old who dressed provocatively, Heather next found employment in a Soho hostess club, apparently working as a barmaid. In Soho, Heather met her future husband, Alfie, who was ten years her senior. He took photos of Heather for a modelling portfolio, and agents suggested the busty teenager might be suited to topless 'glamour' modelling. By Heather's account, she progressed almost directly to being a more respectable 'swimsuit model'. Alfie and Heather's relationship was tempestuous: 'One Friday she called me and said she'd been asked to go to Paris for some modelling . . . Then she phoned up on Sunday night and said, "I'm not coming back. Bye-bye."'

Heather writes in her memoir that at this stage she became 'the face' of a large cosmetics firm in France. 'I would have to live in Paris for twelve months. I'd be paid £1,500 a day . . . It was the chance of a lifetime.' Alfie has no idea how much of this is true. 'It was difficult to believe anything she said.' Heather's French adventure came to a suitably improbable ending in December 1988 when, by her account, the unnamed boss of her unidentified cosmetics firm fell so violently in love with her that she fled, catching a late-night ferry home to Dover. Heather telephoned Alfie to pick her up. On the assurance that she would see a psychiatrist, to help her stop telling lies, so he says, Alfie married Heather on May 6, 1989. The couple lived in Stanmore, then Hoddesdon, a commuter town in Hertfordshire.

Heather ran a small modelling agency for a while, and had cosmetic surgery on her breasts. Then in 1991, on a Yugoslavian ski holiday, she had an affair with her instructor, Milos, and left Alfie once and for all. He filed for divorce.

Heather now found herself in the middle of a civil war in Yugoslavia and became involved in aid work for war victims, developing a particular interest in people who had lost limbs in land-mine explosions. On trips home to the UK, Heather raised money and resources for these people and resumed her modelling career, which became so successful, by her account, that she was able to buy a flat in the salubrious London suburb of Hampstead. Milos was history, replaced by a well-paid bond dealer.

Heather had resolved to end this relationship, too, when the couple set off for a walk in Kensington Gardens on August 8, 1993. As they crossed Kensington Road, a passing police motorcycle collided with Heather, tearing off her left foot in the accident. Surgeons subsequently amputated all but six inches of the leg below the knee. This was the turning point in Heather's life.

For a single, twenty-five-year-old woman with little education who traded on her looks, losing a leg would appear to be an almost insurmountable calamity, and it seemed that way to Heather at first. Then she pulled herself together in a way that showed tremendous character. The tabloid press was eager to tell the tale of a sexy model turned plucky amputee, so Heather auctioned her story to journalists from her hospital bed. Apart from being photogenic, she proved a good talker. Heather started to appear regularly in the tabloids and on daytime television. The *Daily Star* gave her its Gold Star Award for courage; she met the prime minister, John Major, at Downing Street. The attention Heather now received because of her accident made her a somebody.

Soon Heather was doing bits of broadcasting and writing her autobiography. She courted publicity, talking to journalists about her charity work and her love life, which continued to be eventful. Likened by credulous journalists to fellow land-mine campaigner Princess Diana, Heather became the subject of increasingly improbable articles: she was being nominated for a Nobel Prize;

she planned to ski for Britain in the Paralympics; a Hollywood movie was to be made of her life; a career in politics beckoned. 'By my mid-forties, I want to be Secretary of State for Health,' she announced in 1998. Then something almost as unlikely happened. Heather began to date the greatest living Englishman.

IN AUGUST 1999, after a ten-day romance, Heather was engaged to documentary film-maker Chris Terrill. A week before the proposed wedding day, she called it off, telling her fiancé she was going on holiday to Greece. In fact, she accompanied Paul to America for his summer vacation in the Hamptons. When they returned to the UK, they were inseparable. They tucked themselves up in a quaint hide-away cottage Paul owned in Rye, near the town's old church.

In October, they released a charity record, *Vo!ce*, in which Heather delivered a monologue about limbless people, while Paul played guitar and sang backing vocals. Heather proved herself to be as hopeless a musical partner as Linda. It was, though, typical of Paul to take on the interests of the woman in his life.

Paul had also always been one of the most romantic of men. For Hallowe'en he arranged a tryst with Heather in a London hotel, filling their suite with Hallowe'en lanterns. A few days later, he invited Heather and her sister Fiona to Peasmarsh for a bonfire night party. Blossom Farm had become a shrine to Linda since her demise, so Heather and Fiona were accommodated in a house named Beanacres. *News of the World* photographers caught Heather leaving the property the next day. Clearly they had been tipped off.

Rejuvenated by his relationship with Heather, Paul recorded a new rock 'n' roll album, *Run Devil Run*, over five days at Abbey Road Studios. The set list featured songs Paul had grown up listening to, most of them obscure, with a couple of newly written tracks including the title song. Paul decided to perform these rockers at the new Cavern in Liverpool where Beatles tribute bands performed. On December 14, 1999, Paul with his *Run Devil Run* band played to 300 selected guests while millions watched on the Internet. A rather emotionless event was enlivened by a heckler yelling for 'Satisfaction'. Paul later discovered the heckler was a member of his own family.

A few days later, Paul invited Heather to help the McCartneys usher in the new millennium at Rembrandt, Paul's Merseyside base, where Heather was introduced to his children. '[It was] a difficult situation for everybody,' she later admitted.

After the holidays, Sir Paul took his children to Parrot Cay, a resort island in the British West Indies. The day the children left, Heather flew in. During a walk along the beach, Paul told Heather that pirate relics could sometimes be found under the rocks. Coming to a likely stone, he suggested she turn it over. Heather did so, discovering that Paul had been out on the beach earlier and had scratched a heart with their names in the sand underneath. 'I stood there shaking my head in disbelief. This man was too much.'

Stories emerged in the press that Heather Mills might not be an ideal girlfriend for the star. Her ex-husband Alfie told the *Sunday People*: 'Marrying Heather was the biggest mistake of my life.' Other sources suggested that during her time in Paris, Heather had actually kept rich Arabs company, including the arms dealer Adnan Khashoggi. Heather had been a 'party girl' said a fellow model, who claimed to have introduced her to a seamy world where pretty girls were rewarded with gifts and cash. Despite these tales, Sir Paul chose to support Heather.

Many friends of Sir Paul wondered why the star invested such trust in a self-publicising minor celebrity with a dubious past. One way to look at Paul's relationship with Heather is to consider that, like John Lennon, McCartney had spent his adult life in a situation where almost everybody he met venerated him. John and Paul had chosen as their partners gutsy women who treated them as normal people. Yoko, Linda and Heather were all three a match for their partners. And the senior Beatles were a handful. John and Paul had become so famous, so rich and so powerful that they were inevitably slightly monstrous. They were only comfortable with equally monstrous women.

SIR PAUL FOUND HIMSELF showered with money again when Neil Aspinall gathered together the twenty-seven Beatles singles that had reached number one on a CD titled *Beatles 1*. Although many commentators figured Beatles fans already owned all these songs, *Beatles 1* made number one in thirty-four countries, becoming, amazingly, the best-selling album of the decade in the USA. It seemed there was no end to the public's appetite for the Beatles' music.

Paul took Heather to India for most of January 2001, touring the country, staying in the most exquisite hotels. The couple flew on to the USA. Paul took Heather shopping in Manhattan on Valentine's Day, then to the top of the Empire State Building, where he wrote their names on the stonework. Travelling west to LA, Paul was inspired to record almost a whole album of new music in two weeks. Most of the songs on *Driving Rain* reveal a man befuddled by love, with intimations of disagreements, rifts and doubts. He made it plain in 'About You' that in the wake of Linda's death, he felt he'd fallen into a slump as bad as that he suffered when the Beatles broke up. As Linda saved him then, Heather was pulling him out of his grief now. He was grateful, and terrified he would lose her, besotted and adoring. To top it all, there was 'Heather', a pretty tune with a lyric based on Edward Lear's *The Owl and the Pussycat*, with Paul and Heather sailing away into a dreamy world of magic and love.

While he worked on this album, Sir Paul rented a property on Heather Road, Beverly Hills. They liked their 'Heather House' so well he bought it. Back home, MPL loaned Heather £800,000 to buy and fix up another house, Angel's Rest, part of a terrace of gorgeous, whitewashed houses on a private beach near Hove in Sussex. Paul and Heather were often to be found walking hand in hand by the shore.

IN THE LAST MONTHS of Linda's life, Paul had been offered a commission by Magdalen College, Oxford, to write a choral work for the college's new auditorium. Paul had accepted the commission, which was prestigious but unpaid, and started work shortly before Linda died. Sir Paul came back to Oxford for All Souls' Night in November 1998, when Linda's name was read as part of the service, and resumed work thereafter. Paul began to think of a composition to commemorate his love for Linda, entitled *Ecce Cor Meum* (*Behold My Heart*).

Paul worked on *Ecce Cor Meum* with David Matthews through the summer of 2001, frequently travelling to Oxford to stay with Anthony Smith, the president of Magdalen. When he wasn't working, Paul could slip over to the college bar where, refreshingly, the students were sophisticated enough not to ask for his autograph, but spoke to him in a normal, civilised way. He mixed easily with everybody, from the choirboys he charmed with stories of his own failed career as a chorister ('If I'd been accepted by Liverpool Cathedral, there would have been no Beatles,' he told them) to the dons.

Smith feared that some of his learned colleagues might condescend to Paul, but everybody was respectful of what the musician had achieved in his career, and indeed were quietly thrilled to have him at Magdalen. Says Smith, 'He wants to do something for the world and, as he feels himself growing bigger, his musical work is developing at the same time. He has now established himself as a public person in a way that commands respect, [and] I think he also has a sense of himself as a bit of a national monument.'

Heather Mills made a less favourable impression, showing little interest in Paul's classical projects unless she had suggestions for changes, which she gave freely, in the irritating manner of Yoko Ono. 'I think she felt she knew best about the music as well [as other things],' snorts Smith. There was a sense of the couple not being entirely at one, perhaps because Paul was working on a piece in praise of his past love. 'I didn't get a strong sense that she was in love,' says Smith.

Among Sir Paul's friends and associates, the consensus was that Heather was trouble. Many worrying stories were swirling around. Eric Stewart was so concerned he wrote a letter to Paul: 'I didn't get a reply, but as soon as they got together, the people I knew at MPL got replaced. Suddenly I couldn't ring him there. I could ring him at home or at the studio, but there nobody would put you through. It was like he was trying to sweep out anybody who knew him and Linda together.'

When Paul introduced Heather Mills to another old friend, Tony Bramwell, he immediately remembered Heather. 'She looked at me in horror, knowing I'd been in the clubs when she was slapping around [looking for] a rich man.' Bramwell found Heather to be every bit as horrible as he had always found Yoko Ono.

That summer, Paul took Heather to Liverpool, where he was to preside over the annual LIPA graduation. Beforehand, he introduced his girlfriend to Mark Featherstone-Witty. 'In a normal conversation, you meet somebody—"Tell me a little bit about yourself"—and at some point you expect the favour to be returned,' Featherstone-Witty observes. 'Two and a half hours later she was still talking. I've met self-centred people in my life, but I think she has to get the gold star.'

Yet Paul was smitten. After the ceremony, he drove Heather to the Lake District, checking into the Sharrow Bay Hotel on Ullswater where he dropped down on his knee and said, 'I love you, Heather. Will you marry me?' When the charity worker said she would, the famous widower burst into tears.

10: THAT DIFFICULT SECOND MARRIAGE

On the morning of September 11, 2001, Paul and Heather were sitting in the first-class compartment of an aeroplane at John F. Kennedy Airport, about to fly to London. As their aircraft taxied for takeoff, the couple saw the familiar outline of Manhattan blemished by a pall of smoke. The captain asked everybody to remain calm as he found out what was happening. Shortly afterwards came news of a terrorist attack on the World Trade Center and, as a result, all commercial flights were grounded.

When they had disembarked, Paul and Heather were driven back to Long Island where they sat watching television coverage of those extraordinary events.

Paul and Heather had been in New York so that Heather could collect an award for her charity work. Since getting engaged, she had become more prominent in public life, giving the impression she expected to be taken notice of independently of her fiancé. Linda had been happy to be Paul's consort, never trying to overshadow him; with Heather, there was the sense of a rival ego. Ever since she first sold her story to the British tabloids, she had revelled in media attention. Now she swaggered on an international stage.

Heather suggested to Paul that he 'do a charity concert' for 9/11. Paul wasn't immediately keen. His new album, *Driving Rain*, was due out and he didn't want to give the impression he was using the disaster to sell records. Heather told him not to be so silly. 'Write a song about freedom,' she suggested, picking a touchstone word used repeatedly by President George W. Bush in the aftermath of the terrorist attacks. Empathising with the hurt suffered by the American people, Paul acceded to his fiancée's suggestion and set President Bush's rhetoric to music. The song 'Freedom', co-written with Heather, is one of McCartney's most lumpen compositions.

Producer Harvey Weinstein and the television company VH1 were already planning a concert in aid of the firefighters and other emergency workers who had suffered during the attacks, with the Who committed to perform. Sir Paul was persuaded to join the VH1 event. In doing so, he became the headliner. The show at Madison Square Garden on October 20, 2001 was a highly emotional event featuring appearances by actors, sports stars and political figures, including New York's mayor, Rudolph Giuliani. Roughly half the acts were British, with David Bowie, Eric Clapton, Jagger and Richards, Sir Elton John and the Who all performing before Sir Paul took the stage. The show, which raised millions for charity, naturally overshadowed the release of *Driving Rain*, a weak album that made little impact on the charts. Likewise, 'Freedom' just scraped into *Billboard*'s Hot 100.

The momentous events of 9/11 also overshadowed the last days of George Harrison who, having survived a knife attack by a maniac intruder at Friar Park in 1999, was in the US receiving treatment for cancer. Paul visited his old friend at Staten Island University Hospital in November. Theirs had always been a difficult relationship, but all bickering was now put to one side. Sitting by the hospital bed of his childhood friend, Paul took George's hand and stroked it tenderly.

It was with fast-fading George in mind, and the loss of Linda, that Paul prepared for the first performances of his choral work *Ecce Cor Meum*. Paul and Heather stayed again with Magdalen president Anthony Smith, who found he liked Ms Mills no more now that she was Sir Paul's fiancée. 'You know when a woman loves a man she's with, and there was no love there. Everyone could see it and he didn't, or he had convinced himself that—because he was a good man, which he is—he felt he *ought* to love her. That's my theory.'

The first performance of *Ecce Cor Meum* was under-rehearsed. Perhaps Paul was distracted by his new love. In any event, he got up on stage to excuse *Ecce Cor Meum* as a work in progress. He would make changes before bringing it before an audience again.

Three weeks later, on November 29, 2001, George Harrison died, aged fifty-eight. The death was a momentous loss, the third Beatle to have left the stage before his time (counting Stuart Sutcliffe), and Paul seemed determined not to fumble his public reaction as he had when John died. He spoke to reporters of how George was a brave, beautiful, funny man whose music would live for ever.

In the new year, Paul took Heather back to India, where he bought her more jewellery. He also advanced her £150,000 to decorate her new home near Hove, writing off the original £800,000 loan as a gift, and gave her a joint Coutts credit card—a useful accoutrement as they set out together on tour.

THE DRIVING USA TOUR was a fourteen-month, round-the-world odyssey with a sense that Paul was seeking to demonstrate to his fiancée what a big star he was. Though this may seem unnecessary, Heather professed herself largely ignorant of Paul's history, claiming not to know that classic songs that came on the radio—'Back in the USSR', for example—were by the Beatles. Her favourite group was the Australian heavy rock act AC/DC.

Having associated himself so closely with 9/11, Sir Paul continued to wrap himself in the American flag during his progress across the United States in 2002, literally waving the Stars and Stripes on stage, while subtly encouraging stories about his shows 'healing' America as the Beatles were seen to do in the sixties after the assassination of President Kennedy. Paul's journey was almost regal, in the style of a man who really was the king of pop, whatever Michael Jackson claimed.

Ever since his watershed tour of 1989/90, Paul had increased the Beatles content of his live show. Now he played approximately twenty-three Beatles songs as part of a thirty-six-number set, with an all-Beatles encore. Each night Paul spoke to the audience about his fiancée as an introduction to 'Your Loving Flame'. Other numbers now assumed a memorial purpose: Paul played 'My Love' for Linda, something that seemingly irritated Heather.

During a solo acoustic set, Paul introduced 'Here Today' as a song he'd written 'after my dear friend John passed away'. He then exchanged his guitar for a ukulele, telling the audience how, when he used to go round to George Harrison's house, the ukuleles would come out after dinner, his friend being a George Formby fan. 'I said to him, "I do a little song on ukulele." I played it for him and I'll do it for you tonight as a tribute to George.' Paul proceeded to perform George's most lovely song, 'Something', a touching moment introduced in such a way that audiences might be forgiven for thinking this was the only night Paul had paid this musical tribute. In fact, once he realised how well it worked, Paul gave his ukulele 'Something', with a virtually verbatim prologue, every night. It became as much a fixture of his show as the audience response section of 'Hey Jude' and the explosions in 'Live and Let Die'.

In official pictures, Paul and Heather presented the image of happiness on tour, but away from the cameras there were ugly scenes. In mid-May, the Driving USA tour reached Florida. Paul and Heather checked into the Turnberry Isle Resort and Club in Miami where, on May 18, guests awoke in the early hours of the morning to hear Paul and Heather having a blazing row. Paul was heard shouting, 'The wedding's off!' Heather's engagement ring was then apparently flung—by an unknown hand—from their

hotel window. Staff spent a good part of the following day search-
ing for it. The ring was eventually found and returned to Sir Paul
in England, where he had gone to help celebrate his monarch's
Golden Jubilee.

To mark Queen Elizabeth II's fifty years on the throne, a pop
concert was staged inside the grounds of Buckingham Palace. The
bill included a roll call of British rock stars headed naturally by Sir
Paul. At the end of the show, Paul played a cheeky reprise of 'Her
Majesty', the ditty that concluded *Abbey Road*. When the Queen
came on stage to join Sir Paul and the other artists, McCartney suggested that they might hold a show like this in her back garden
every year, to which she replied tartly that she didn't think so.

The summer break in Paul's tour schedule gave Paul and
Heather an opportunity to get married. The wedding was held in
County Monaghan, the land of Paul's maternal ancestors, where
he hired Castle Leslie, an hour south of Belfast, for his big day.
Paul's Liverpool family were put on a chartered plane to Ireland.
Brother Mike was to be best man again, while Ringo Starr led the
list of celebrity friends. Once again, Yoko Ono was notably absent.
While Paul's daughters Mary and Stella attended, there was no
sight of Heather and James, both of whom were understood to be
against Dad's second marriage.

The ceremony was held in St Salvator's Church on the Leslie
estate at 4.30 p.m. on June 11. The guests assembled inside where
they waited and waited, press helicopters thudding overhead, Sir
Paul pacing up and down nervously. The bride-to-be was missing.

Some say Heather had been delayed putting on her wedding
dress, others that she and Paul had had a last-minute row. In any
event, it was with a sense of relief that the couple emerged from
the church as husband and wife to be showered with confetti.

Six years hence, when this union ended in a divorce court,
telling personal details emerged about the build-up to the wedding, including the fact that Paul continued to wear Linda's
ring until the day itself, and that he and Heather used contracep-
tion until their wedding night. In other words, he didn't seem sure
he was doing the right thing until the last minute.

AFTER A SUMMER BREAK, Paul resumed his North American tour, travelling with Heather, who took the opportunity to promote a revised version of her autobiography, retitled *A Single Step*, from which had been excised the more lurid details of her affair with Milos the ski instructor. In the book, Heather revealed intimate details of her courtship by Paul, as well as making it plain how much she disapproved of his smoking marijuana. Interviewed by the broadcaster Barbara Walters on TV, Heather made further complaints: 'I am married to the most famous person in the world and that is very unfortunate for me,' she said, making it clear she didn't like her charity work being overshadowed by Paul. Indeed, she seemed to find her husband generally annoying.

Then came a series of alleged marital arguments. According to court documents later leaked to the press, when Paul's tour reached Los Angeles, Heather complained to her husband about the Barbara Walters interview, in which the host had tackled her on some of the less flattering stories emerging about her early life. Paul apparently dismissed Heather's concerns, saying she was in a mood, while she decided he was drunk. According to Heather's account later set down in legalese: 'The Petitioner [Sir Paul] grabbed the Respondent [Heather] by the neck and pushed her over a coffee table.'

Heather's experience with Barbara Walters had not put her off American chat shows, however. Indeed, she appeared repeatedly on *Larry King* to talk about her charity work, though she increasingly found herself facing tough questions. 'Did you ever have to prostitute yourself?' King asked Heather directly on November 1, 2002.

'No, never!'

In November, the two surviving Beatles appeared together on stage at the Royal Albert Hall to honour George Harrison a year to the day since his death. In a long, perfectly paced tribute show featuring many old friends—from eighty-two-year-old Ravi Shankar to Eric Clapton—Paul played 'Something' on the ukulele, with Ritchie; Eric and the house band came in halfway through, which proved an even more effective arrangement than Paul's solo version. In future, he'd do the song this way. 'I was choked with emotion when he sang "Something",' comments Ravi Shankar.

'It is amazing to see how much he [still] loves to perform.'

Paul now set out on the European leg of what was becoming a world tour. '[It was] as if we were listening to the best Beatles' tribute band in the world,' wrote Ray Connolly in his *Daily Mail* review of the first night in Paris. A few days later, Sir Paul gave to the *Daily Mirror* what now reads as an ironic comment on his second marriage: 'Heather said to me this morning, "I don't think of you as rich, you know."' Only rich enough to give Heather a cash gift of £250,000 in December, after which he set up a £360,000-a-year allowance for her, paid quarterly.

In May 2003, Channel 4 broadcast *Heather Mills: The Real Mrs McCartney*, which contrasted her account of her life in print with what people who knew her remembered. There appeared to be gaps between the story and the truth: the Clapham jeweller who'd employed Heather as a teenager alleged that she stole far more from him than she had admitted to, including gold chains worth £25,000. 'She virtually plundered the shop.' Most damaging was the testimony of two female associates of Adnan Khashoggi who spoke of Heather enjoying the high life with wealthy Arabs in London and Paris at the time she claimed to be working for a French cosmetics firm. It seemed she had been looked after by a Lebanese businessman for a time, but excelled herself in marrying Sir Paul.

In May, too, McCartney's world tour reached Rome, the star playing two prestige shows at the Colosseum, a relatively small acoustic show inside the ancient amphitheatre, followed by a free rock concert for half a million people outside the stadium the following day. This was the biggest show of Paul's career to date.

Ten days later, Paul played the AOL Stadium in Hamburg, introducing Heather to his old St Pauli friends Horst Fascher and Astrid Kirchherr, who didn't warm to his second wife. Astrid felt Heather had taken advantage of Paul's vulnerability. 'Being handicapped and good-looking, he probably felt sorry [for] this woman with one leg. [But] she turned out a bitch.'

Sir Paul didn't hear any of this. He lived in a world where everybody told him how great he was and every year brought new levels of achievement.

SIR PAUL WAS REACHING a stage in his career where it wasn't enough just to play huge, sold-out shows: his tours had to include special event concerts, such as the Colosseum. So he found the idea of playing in Moscow enticing.

Before the Red Square show, Paul and Heather were granted an audience in the Kremlin with President Vladimir Putin. The McCartneys told him they were campaigning against landmines, a subject he deflected deftly. When Putin said he probably wouldn't be attending the concert itself, Paul treated him to a private performance of 'Let it Be'. In the event, the president did come to the show on May 24, 2003. Never had there been a better place to sing 'Back in the USSR', with its ironic Cold War lyrics.

The couple returned to the UK to attend Stella McCartney's August wedding, on the Isle of Bute, to publisher Alasdhair Willis. Then they flew back down to Sussex.

Since Lin's death, Paul had hardly used Blossom Farm. When he and Heather visited the estate, they stayed on Woodlands Farm, an adjacent property he'd acquired in 1989. As the name suggests, this new part of the estate included extensive woodland, in which was a large, man-made lake. Sir Paul had commissioned a glass-fronted pavilion and two-storey lodge, the Cabin, to be built on the lakeside, in which he intended to live with Heather and their baby for, having suffered one miscarriage, Heather was pregnant.

On October 28, 2003, she gave birth to a baby girl they named Beatrice Milly. The star was a father again at sixty-one.

Paul and Heather began family life with baby Bea in the Cabin in February 2004. Essentially, Sir Paul was seeking to re-create the snug family life he'd enjoyed with Linda, but this was not a comparable marriage.

The union was not *yet* an unremitting Hell. The couple had their good days and could appear very happy together. That Christmas, Sir Paul had given his wife a second £250,000 cash gift, meaning he'd given her £500,000 in the space of twelve months. She used the money to buy a £450,000 apartment at Thames Reach, a new complex on the Thames at Hammersmith. Paul also used his contacts to get Heather a star guest to interview when she filled in as presenter on *Larry King Live* in April 2004. Paul Newman agreed to be quizzed by Heather, who made a poor job of the interview in the opinion of critics. Despite this flop, Heather remained ambitious to establish herself as a media personality in the United States, which was in itself a cause of disagreement in the marriage. Paul didn't want Bea's mother abroad for too much of the year.

SIR PAUL HAD HEARD from his friends what a great gig Glastonbury was — one of the largest and most famous music festivals in the world — so it was arranged that Paul would bring his show to Glastonbury's Pyramid Stage in 2004. The Glastonbury Festival attracted 150,000 people, a vast and muddy medieval army of an audience waving banners and flags under driving rain as Sir Paul began his set. Clearly exhilarated, Paul proceeded to give one of the best shows of his life — two and a half hours of music complete with his greatest hits and choicest Beatles anecdotes. 'Boring!' shouted irreverent young hecklers as Paul rattled on about the 1960s. Turning a deaf ear, Sir Paul continued to deliver a powerhouse set. Even the cheekiest urchins in the crowd were singing along to 'Hey Jude' by the end.

When Paul came off stage, he asked to see Michael Eavis, the festival's founder. 'He was weeping tears of joy. It was such a good show,' says the impresario-farmer. 'The pair of us just hugged each other for a bit. It was lovely.' The men also spoke of having lost their wives to cancer, but then Eavis saw Heather looking daggers at them from across the room and sensed she wanted him to leave. 'She was a bit edgy.'

When Linda McCartney read hurtful things about herself in the press, she wisely chose to turn the other cheek: she would have made it far worse had she moaned. This is the mistake Heather now made. She was increasingly irked by the negative press she received, which grew more hostile as a consensus developed that she was a devious, self-publicising harridan into whose clutches a great man had tragically fallen. When Heather was informed in advance that *The Sunday Times* would be running a story in which it was observed that losing a leg was the best thing that ever happened to her, she allegedly implored Paul to intervene. He was scheduled to play at the forth-coming Super Bowl, which was broadcast by the Fox network owned by Rupert Murdoch, who also owned *The Sunday Times*. According to divorce papers, Heather suggested Paul tell Murdoch he wouldn't play the show unless the press baron pulled the story. Paul refused.

After decades in which he had used hotels when he came to New York, Paul now had his own Manhattan apartment, in a town house on West 54th Street, next door to the offices of Eastman & Eastman. The town house accommodated MPL Communications, the American arm of Sir Paul's publishing company. The star had the upper storeys converted into a penthouse apartment for himself and Heather, who had her eye on space downstairs as a private office. Paul told his wife 'he did not want her to have an office in the same building' and 'agreed to provide her with alter-native office space in the city'. Heather told Paul that the new office—a twenty-minute walk away—was too far and too small. When she refused to use it, Paul called her an 'ungrateful bitch'.

Some might think Paul was speaking the plain truth in calling his wife ungrateful. On top of the large cash gifts, the £360,000-a-year allowance, the joint credit card, the beach house, the London flat at Thames Reach and the New York office, during 2005 he gave Heather jewellery worth £264,000. Yet, like Oliver Twist, Heather always wanted more. In November she emailed Paul Winn, Paul's accountant at MPL in London, asking Winn to pay £480,000 into her bank account so she could clear a mortgage on her Thames Reach property. On March 1, 2006, Paul Winn informed Heather that he would not pay her the money 'without proof that the loans exist . . .' Heather could not provide such proof because there was no mortgage.

It emerged that Paul's new Cabin and its pavilion had been constructed on the Sussex estate without planning permission. When this oversight was noticed, he applied retrospectively. Rother District Council turned him down so Paul launched a planning battle to retain the buildings. While this application pro-ceeded, Paul and Heather campaigned in Canada against the annual seal cull, which they added to a list of causes that included being pro-veggie, anti-poverty and anti-landmines. These predictably safe issues gave Heather endless reasons to expound on television and in print, to the degree that she and Paul started to appear more than a little tiresome. And while they appeared together as a united, loving couple, posing with a cuddly seal pup in Canada in March 2006, they were on the brink of separation.

On April 25, the couple reportedly had a particularly bad row that ended with Sir Paul pouring the remainder of a bottle of red wine over Heather. He then 'threw what remained in his wineglass at the Respondent', as the story went in legal papers. 'The Petitioner then reached to grab [Heather's] wineglass and broke the bowl of the glass from the stem. He then lunged at the Respondent with the broken, sharp stem of the wineglass, which cut and pierced the Respondent's arm just below the elbow. He proceeded to manhandle the Respondent, flung her into her wheelchair and wheeled it outside, screaming at her to apologise for "winding him up".'

The allegations continue: 'On Friday April 28, at 10 p.m. [Sir Paul] returned home staggering drunk, demanding his dinner. The Respondent stated that it was on the stove but that she would not be cooking for him again, as he had no respect for her. The Petitioner called her "a nag" and went to bed. That evening, the Respondent realised the marriage had irretrievably broken down and left, crawling on her hands and knees while dragging her wheelchair, crutches and basic personal possessions to the car.'

They separated the following day, after less than four years of married life.

THE McCARTNEYS announced their separation a month later, blaming the media largely: 'Both of us still care about each other very much but have found it increasingly difficult to maintain a normal relationship with the constant intrusion into our private lives . . .' Paul sought solace with his grown-up children, spending time with Stella and her husband at their country house in Worcestershire. Stelly was now a wealthy and famous woman in her own right, head of the eponymous Stella McCartney fashion house, with boutique stores in London and abroad.

Now it was clear that Sir Paul's ill-starred marriage had failed, the popular British press began to publish sensational stories about his estranged wife. LADY MACCA HARD CORE PORN SHAME screamed the front page of the *Sun* on June 5, 2006. Its journalists had laid their hands on a German sex manual from 1988, in which Heather was pictured nude and seminude, simulating sex acts with an equally bare male model. Heather's lawyers disputed the picture set was pornography, describing the book as 'a lover's guide', which became a moot point when even more explicit pictures of Heather emerged of the model with her legs splayed apart.

The *News of the World* then published HEATHER THE £5K HOOKER, alleging that during the time Heather had supposedly been a legitimate model in Paris, she had actually been working in London and elsewhere as a prostitute. There was no empirical evidence Heather had taken part in group sex with Arabs for £5,000, as alleged: it was all down to the word of denizens of this shadowy world. Heather threatened to sue, but no action came to trial.

Such was the sorry state of Paul's affairs as he reached sixty-four. A lifetime ago, 'When I'm Sixty-Four' had been one of the first tunes McCartney composed at Forthlin Road, putting lyrics to the song in his twenties. He had envisaged life as a grey-haired old man sitting by the fire with his wife: if they scrimped and saved, perhaps they could afford a summer holiday in the Isle of Wight, cheered by visits from their grandkids Vera, Chuck and Dave. Now he'd reached this fabled age, the reality was rather different. Paul's hair might indeed be grey, but he'd dyed out the traces; the wife he expected to live with into old age was gone. As to scrimping and saving, Sir Paul had so much money he didn't have a clear idea how much he was worth. With a divorce settlement looming, he had to hire the accountants Ernst & Young to find out how rich he actually was.

Paul did have three grandchildren, though: Arthur, Elliot and Miller. The first two were Mary's boys, aged seven and three respectively; the third was Stelly's sixteen-month-old son.

In the weeks leading up to Granddad's birthday, Mary and Stella marshalled everybody at Abbey Road Studios to record a family rendition of 'When I'm Sixty-Four' as a surprise gift. The family, including little Bea, greeted him in Sussex with a rousing chorus of 'When I'm Sixty-Four' and gave him their special recording.

A month later, Paul filed for divorce from Heather on the grounds of her unreasonable behaviour. He changed the locks at Cavendish Avenue and the press were on hand to photograph the moment when Heather tried to open the front gate, eventually sending a man over the top to open it from within, whereupon Paul's staff called the police. On August 11, Paul's lawyers offered the other side a quickie divorce, which was rejected.

Ernst & Young now reported on what Sir Paul was worth. It added up to approximately £387 million. In detail, his business assets came to approximately £241 million. In addition, he owned property worth £33.9 million, investments of £34.3 million, and another £15.1 million in various bank accounts. Valuables, including original artwork by de Kooning, Magritte, Matisse, Picasso and Renoir were worth another £32.2 million, with £36 million tucked away in pension funds. In a statement, Paul said that most of this had been accumulated prior to his marriage, though he had added £39 million to his fortune during the marriage. In that time, he had been generous not only to his wife, but also her family, lending Fiona Mills £421,000 to buy a house, and buying another Mills relative a £193,000 property. All these figures were as yet confidential, but this was to be a highly unusual divorce, both in its bitterness and in how much information emerged into the public domain.

The first watershed of information came at lunch time on October 17, 2006 when a fax machine at the Press Association emitted nine of thirteen pages of Heather's 'Answer and Cross-Petition'. Included were all the allegations of cruelty and mistreatment. This fax was a windfall for the press. It was traced to a newsagent's shop in Drury Lane, the proprietor of which said a woman sent it. Heather denied she was behind the leak.

The allegation that Paul had got drunk and pushed Heather around, ultimately stabbing her with a broken glass, was the most astonishing. Friends were outraged by suggestions Paul was an abusive drunk. Eric Stewart, who had written to warn Paul about Heather before they married—and received no reply—now wrote offering himself as a character witness in the divorce. 'I said, "I will speak for you in court and I will say what I knew about her setting you up." [Paul] said, "Thanks. If I need you, I'll let you know."'

Unable to stop the flood of ugly stories, Sir Paul adopted a policy of dignified silence, pressing on with his work as Heather became ever more excitable and vociferous. Her popularity plummeted accordingly, reaching its nadir when, presenting an awards show in London, Jonathan Ross described Heather as such a 'fucking liar [I] wouldn't be surprised if we found out she's actually got two legs'.

NINE YEARS since the president of Magdalen College invited Sir Paul to write a modest choral work for the new college auditorium —and two years since the tryouts in Oxford—*Ecce Cor Meum* finally premiered at the Royal Albert Hall. Commissioned during Linda's last months, the music had been in the works so long that Paul had been widowed, remarried and separated in the meantime. Arranged in four movements, with a melancholy orchestral interlude, it is in many ways a typical example of McCartney music: lovely tunes, beautifully played and orchestrated, yet the result was uneven, bland in places, while the libretto struck the critic from the *Independent* as 'sententious'. A bit of a mess really, reflecting the fact that *Ecce*, like his other classical works, was the result of hired hands trying to express what they thought Sir Paul wanted to hear.

Several relatives were invited to the premiere but there was discord behind the scenes. Word had got about that eighty-year-old Aunt Joan had been chauffeur-driven all the way from the Wirral to the show, leading to younger family members asking MPL to lay on door-to-door cars for them, too. Although the extended McCartney family was close, Paul's wealth had long created dissent in the clan. Paul had been very generous over the years with his family, helping relatives buy homes, lending money and in some instances putting 'relies' on the McCartney Pension so they didn't need to work. Still some weren't satisfied. When reminded by Paul's accountant that a loan to help buy a home had not been repaid, one relative apparently retorted, 'Fuck him, he's got enough money and I don't need to fuckin' pay him back.'

All of a sudden it wasn't as much fun being Paul McCartney. That winter, Sir Paul abandoned his planning battle to keep the Cabin, agreeing to tear the wooden house down. A routine medical examination revealed that Paul had a 'minor heart irregularity'. It turned out to be nothing much to worry about, unlike the news from Heather's lawyers that she wanted £50 million as her divorce settlement.

In the new year, Sir Paul counter-offered with a more reasonable £16.5 million, which, together with assets Heather had accrued during their marriage, meant she would walk away with about £20 million. She turned this offer down as insufficient. Paul also filed an affidavit that revealed how much he had wanted their marriage to work. 'I believed it was for life,' he said, sadly. While the divorce was thrashed out, Sir Paul agreed to pay his wife an interim sum of £5.5 million. She bought a large, secluded property thirteen miles from Peasmarsh so they could take turns ferrying Bea to school.

That autumn Paul was seen with a new girlfriend, Nancy Shevell, a pencil-thin American almost a quarter of a century Paul's junior. Nancy was the daughter of a New Jersey trucking magnate, Myron 'Mike' Shevell, who'd built a small firm, New England Motor Freight, into a huge concern with a $400 million turnover, facing accusations of racketeering in the process. Nancy joined the family firm in 1983 after graduating from Arizona State. Apart from helping run NEMF, Nancy and her husband, Bruce Blakeman, raised a son, Arlen, maintaining homes in New York and the Hamptons, where they first became friendly with Paul and Linda. The Blakemans were separated when Nancy began seeing Paul in October 2007. In many ways, she was similar to Linda: American, Jewish, the moneyed daughter of a tough, self-made man. She had also suffered a bout of breast cancer and was a denizen of New York and Long Island. In romancing Nancy, Paul was retracing his past.

The couple was first photographed together on a beach in the Hamptons in autumn 2007. By now Paul was more exercised about the paparazzi, saying, 'I didn't think they were around. I really didn't expect it.' His reaction was mild compared to that of his estranged wife. On the morning of October 31, Heather invited herself onto the morning television show *GMTV* to rant about the British press. Becoming increasingly worked up, she reminded viewers of the very worst the papers had written: 'They've called me a whore, a gold-digger, a fantasist, a liar, the most unbelievably hurtful things, and I've stayed quiet for my daughter, but I've been close to suicide. I've had worse press than a paedophile or a murderer,' she wailed, 'and I've done nothing but charity for twenty years.' Heather hinted darkly that she was the victim of a conspiracy. 'There is so much fear from a certain party of the truth coming out that lots of things have been put out and done,' she said mysteriously, adding that she'd had death threats. 'That means my daughter's life is at risk, because she's with me all the time. The tabloid media created such a hate campaign against me, they put my life and my daughter's life at risk. And that's why I considered killing myself, because I thought if I'm dead, she's safe, and she can be with her father, and that is the truth.'

Heather was ridiculed for this TV appearance, which, apart from being a hysterical display, seemingly contravened a legal agreement that she wouldn't talk about her divorce in public. As a result, Heather's relationship with her legal advisors broke down and she began representing herself in the case.

Her outburst was also in marked contrast to Sir Paul. A hint of what he was feeling came when he said, in reply to a question about the divorce, 'As Winston Churchill once said, "If you're going through Hell, keep going!"' But he said no more.

On February 11, 2008, proceedings began in the Royal Courts of Justice. Inside Court 34, Heather asked Justice Bennett for a £125 million settlement. She said this sum would enable her to support herself and Bea in the style to which they had become accustomed, allowing her to buy a London home, a New York apartment and an office in Brighton, giving her a total of seven residences, which would have to be staffed. The balance of the divorce payment would be invested to generate an income of £3.25 million a year on which she expected to be able to get by.

Paul's barristers argued in reply that Heather should leave the marriage with total assets of no more than £15 million, on top of which Sir Paul would pay for Beatrice's nanny, education and security. Heather addressed the judge, relating details of Paul's alleged assault on her with a wineglass in April 2006, also claiming her husband had colluded with the press in a hate campaign against her. The arguments went on all week and, when the couple failed to agree, Justice Bennett retired to formulate his own judgment.

Paul and Heather were called back to the High Court on March 17 and Justice Bennett read his fifty-eight-page judgment aloud. The headline result was that Sir Paul should pay Heather a lump sum of £16.5 million, meaning that, with the wealth she had acquired during their marriage, the charity worker would walk away with cash and assets worth £24.3 million, which was £100 million less than she'd asked for and roughly what Paul had offered her two years before. In addition, Paul would pay approximately £35,000 a year for Beatrice's nanny and education. As much as anybody who has to go to court to end their marriage can be said to be victorious, Paul was.

In order to quash press speculation, the judge intended to publish his judgment in full on the court web site, so the press and public could read the true facts of the matter. Although Heather had been warned, she wasn't happy, and tipped a jug of water over the head of Paul's solicitor, Fiona Shackleton.

The next day Justice Bennett's judgment was published in full, giving the public unprecedented detail not only of the divorce but of Sir Paul's personal life. The star had effectively sanctioned the court to tell the world what he was worth, where he lived and what security he had. The rationale, perhaps, was that the document showed him to be an honest man, while Justice Bennett came to highly critical conclusions about Heather Mills McCartney. His words make fascinating reading: 'The husband's evidence was, in my judgment, balanced. He was consistent, accurate and honest. But I regret to have to say I cannot say the same about the wife's evidence . . . I am driven to the conclusion that much of it was not just inconsistent and inaccurate, but also less than candid.'

This was damning, and the subsequent details proved very revealing. During the case, Heather argued that she was 'wealthy and financially independent in her own right' before she met Paul, claiming to have earned approximately £200,000 a year as a model, and up to £25,000 an hour as a celebrity speaker. But the judge decided Heather's claims were 'wholly exaggerated' and lacking corroboration. 'During the hearing she was asked repeatedly to produce bank statements . . . No bank statements were ever produced.' Her tax returns showed her annual earnings were in the more modest range of £11,500 to £112,000 prior to her marriage. Also, there was no paperwork to support her assertion that she gave the rest of her income to charity.

Justice Bennett described Heather's claim that Paul had bought the house in Beverly Hills as a gift for her as 'wishful thinking'. Heather claimed to have passed up business opportunities for Paul's sake. 'I would have made millions,' she said. Yet tax returns showed Heather earned more during her marriage than before it. Heather alleged that Paul frustrated her charitable activities, and failed to make good with his promised donations. On the contrary, the judge found that Paul introduced Heather to the animal welfare organisations she now associated herself with, while his sister-in-law Jody Eastman had introduced Heather to the Adopt-A-Minefield organisation, to which Paul had given an astounding £3.4 million during their marriage.

Heather had taken credit for 'counselling' Paul after his bereavement and said she had helped him write songs, encouraged him to tour, and helped with set design and stage-lighting. Paul agreed that Heather helped him over Linda's death, but denied she encouraged him to get back on the road.

As to Heather's own assets, they were principally due to her husband's generosity. Justice Bennett listed the numerous gifts and loans Sir Paul had given his wife, and addressed the repeated requests Heather had made to MPL for £450,000 to clear a non-existent mortgage. 'It is not an episode that does her any credit whatsoever. In the light of the husband's generosity towards her, I find the wife's behaviour distinctly distasteful.'

Heather was greatly concerned about her personal security, claiming Sir Paul was behind stories about her leaked to the press, which compromised her security. As a result, she claimed to have spent £349,862 on security men. Despite being asked repeatedly by the judge, she failed to produce 'one single invoice or receipt' to substantiate these expenses.

Aside from when he was on tour, Sir Paul said he had never felt the need for full-time security people. He and Linda had brought up their kids largely without protection. 'It is not healthy for a child to have security 24/7. Such children live in gilded cages. I do not want this for Beatrice.' Paul added that Heather's attitude to the press was contradictory: she courted attention, yet complained about what the papers published.

Heather had attempted to bring allegations about Paul's conduct into the divorce case—that is, the lurid allegations leaked to the press in October 2006. In reply, Sir Paul's QC told the court about Heather's conduct *after* the separation. 'First, it is said on June 25, 2006 the wife illegally bugged the husband's telephone, in particular a call between him and his daughter Stella in which Stella made very unflattering comments about the wife,' the judge summarised. 'It is further said the wife subsequently leaked the intercepted material to the press so as to discredit him.' (This had seemingly led to a *Sunday Mirror* story, 'The Maccagate Tapes'.) 'Second, on October 17, 2006 the wife, or someone acting on her behalf, leaked to the media some or all of the contents of her Answer and Cross-Petition, which contained allegations against the husband in order to discredit him. Third, the wife has failed to abide by court orders regarding confidentiality. On October 31, 2007 and November 1, 2007 the wife gave several interviews to UK and US television stations in which she made many false statements about the husband and these proceedings in order to discredit him. Individually and collectively these actions, it is said, represent a deliberate attempt by the wife to ruin the husband's reputation.'

In his closing comments, Justice Bennett said, 'This case is a paradigm example of an applicant failing to put a rational and logical case and thus failing to assist the court in its quasi-inquisitorial role to reach a fair result.' He ordered that neither Paul nor Heather disclose further details to the media. Even Heather learned to be bound by this order and, unable to say anything of substance and with plenty of money to spend, she faded into the semi-obscurity from whence she had come.

MANY OF PAUL'S ASSOCIATES had died prematurely, several worn down by the rigours of the rock 'n' roll lifestyle. Now Neil Aspinall, the backroom boy who had as much claim as anyone to being the 'fifth Beatle', was dying of cancer in New York. Paul went to see him, as he had George, and thanked Nell, as the boys always called their friend, for all he had done for the band, discreetly paid his medical bills, and mourned his passing when he died in March 2008 at the age of sixty-six.

Sir Paul spent a good part of the spring on holiday with Nancy Shevell, his *decree nisi* coming through in May, at the end of which he returned to Liverpool to help his home town celebrate its year as European Capital of Culture, with the city hosting an impressive series of events. The centrepiece was the concert on June 1 at Anfield, iconic home of Liverpool Football Club, headlined by Sir Paul McCartney.

Liverpool was overcast that evening, as 36,000 people streamed towards Anfield for the concert, most of the ticket-holders local people, though others had come from around the world to see Sir Paul play his home town. After the support acts, the Kaiser Chiefs and Zutons, two of whose members had attended LIPA, the comedian Peter Kay appeared on stage to a warm reception. 'It's my job to introduce the star turn tonight,' he said, and proceeded to do so.

Strolling on stage in a silver suit, Paul opened with 'Hippy Hippy Shake', taking his audience back to the Cavern. Next came 'Jet', the audience singing along to the verses in the style of a football crowd at a home fixture. 'Liverpool! I love ya!' exclaimed Paul at the end of the number, and who would doubt him?

In recent years he'd spent more time in the city than at any stage since the early sixties, becoming almost a familiar figure on the streets again.

Paul sang 'My Love' for Linda, whose picture appeared on the huge screens (all images of Heather excised). The audience applauded everything the star said, his every joke and story, and sang along heartily to almost every song, the ukulele tribute to George Harrison having a universal resonance: Olivia was watching. Yoko was beside her. She appeared to approve of Paul's performance of 'Give Peace a Chance' as a tribute to her late husband. Paul signed off with 'I Saw Her Standing There', setting ladies of pensionable age re-creating the dance steps of their youth. With a detonation of fireworks, the home town celebration of the greatest pop band ever was over.

THE MUSICIAN'S LIFE is on the road, and for an artist who loves to perform, tours are a pleasure, an opportunity to cast the happy spell of music over an audience and bask in their appreciation. 'I think it's basically magic,' Paul has said. 'There is such a thing as magic, and the Beatles were magic.'

Later that summer, Paul indulged himself with massive shows in Kiev and Quebec. En route to Canada, he joined Billy Joel on stage at Shea Stadium for the final concert at that famous venue before it was demolished. Afterwards, he motored west with Nancy Shevell on Route 66, via Chicago, St Louis, Flagstaff, Arizona— 2,000 miles and more to LA. It was a road trip he'd always wanted to make.

In the spring of 2009 Paul appeared on stage at Radio City Music Hall in New York with Ringo, in support of transcendental meditation, something the men had carried with them into old age. More North American shows followed. Excluding the Radio City benefit, Paul played a dozen shows across the USA in the year, grossing almost $41 million. Together with the other concerts he'd given recently, the divorce was paid for.

Two old foes died that summer. First was Michael Jackson, aged fifty, never having given Paul a pay rise on Northern Songs, part of which Jackson had sold to Sony to help fund his excessive lifestyle, putting the songs beyond Paul's grasp. It seemed he would never get them back now. Ten days later, a true enemy, Allen Klein, died aged seventy-seven. As old friends and foes alike dropped away, McCartney rolled on, looking spry for a man approaching seventy.

On a frosty night in December 2009, with Christmas in the air, Sir Paul McCartney opened his latest tour in Hamburg. It was way back in 1960 that Paul first drove here with the boys, in Allan Williams's overloaded van, to play the Indra club. A lifetime later, Paul flew back by private jet to play the Color Line sports arena.

Paul's voice sounded thin at first, like an old man's. But as he warmed up his voice strengthened. He spoke about when the Beatles first came to town, 'when we were children', name-checking old friends in the audience. In the first few rows sat Horst Fascher, Astrid Kirchherr and Klaus Voormann, little old people wrapped up warm on a cold December night.

Taking off his jacket and rolling up his sleeves, Sir Paul looked more than ever like a nineteenth-century mill owner. This was not a young artist who needed the audience's approval. He was there because he enjoyed playing music and revisiting the past, and those lucky enough to have a ticket were fortunate to share the moment with him. Between songs he regaled us all with stories, like the night his mate Jimi (Jimi Hendrix, that is) played 'Sgt. Pepper' at the Saville Theatre, and asked Eric (Clapton, you know) to come up and tune his guitar. Everybody listened attentively to an elder telling tales of a vanished age. As he played 'The Long and Winding Road', photos Linda had taken of their Arizona ranch, including the desert trail they rode just before she died, were shown on the screens. 'Here Today' was performed '*für meinen Freund*, John . . . Are you listening?' Paul asked suddenly, glancing up at the roof as if to find his friend's ghost sitting in the rafters. 'Something' was played on the ukulele, and Paul held his arms up in salute to a picture of a young smiling George. When Paul turned back, his face was wet with tears.

With John and George gone, and Ritchie always of lesser importance, it had fallen to Paul to carry the Beatles torch. Along with the sadness, there was a sense that he felt liberated by the fact John and George weren't around to snipe at him any more. He could play whatever he liked now, including 'Ob-La-Di, Ob-La-Da', which went down a storm with the Germans, even if John had mocked it as 'granny music'.

After 'Yesterday' and 'Helter Skelter', Paul informed his audience that it was time for him to go home. The Hamburgers groaned. 'It's time for you to go home, too,' Paul reminded them; it was almost midnight.

He thanked his band and his crew. 'But most of all, tonight, we want to thank *you*,' he said, before playing 'Sgt. Pepper's Lonely Hearts Club Band', segueing into 'The End', pictures of a sun going down on the screens as Paul sang the sublime last lines about the love you take being equal to the love you make, after which everybody exhaled a happy '*Ahhhhh*.'

As one fan remarked, 'The best music—*ever*.'

'*Danke schön*, Hamburg. We'll see you next time!'

HOWARD SOUNES

Howard Sounes is the author of several books including acclaimed biographies of Bob Dylan and Charles Bukowski. Each work is based on lengthy original research, enabling the author to write with a rare sense of authority and to surprise his readers with an abundance of new information.

Howard Sounes lives in London.

For more information, visit www.howardsounes.com

Sue Johnston
Things I Couldn't Tell My Mother

Over the years my mother hadn't been an easy person to deal with—she was someone who, I'm sad to say, found it difficult to show affection or warmth towards me. It is strange to admit this, and yet at the same time she was my mother and I loved her. There were many times when I just wanted her to be proud of me, but it seemed she never was. As close relationships in life often are, ours was complicated.

Sue Johnston in 'Things I Couldn't Tell My Mother'

Prologue

Ena Sharples once famously said of her mother's death, 'She just sat up, broke wind and died.' My mother would have considered herself to be a cut above the fictitious Mrs Sharples and her mother. But as she lay in her bed, in the home where she'd been living for the past year, she did make one last Herculean effort to sit up, reaching out to be helped. Then she sneezed, lay back, and I felt the life leave her, like someone had flicked off a switch.

She was ninety-two. I was sixty-three. These were her final moments, but the preceding weeks and even months had been long and exhausting.

As I reflect now, nearly four years after her death, I miss her. This may seem unsurprising; of course I should miss my mother. But things were far from plain sailing between her and me; our relationship was often difficult and fraught.

MY MOTHER BEGAN to decline sharply when I was filming *Waking the Dead*. Any time that I wasn't filming I would be making my way up the M6 to be with her. Then I received a call early in September 2007 saying that I should get there as soon as I could.

When I arrived in Warrington my mother had rallied and was sitting up in bed, alert and ready for me. She looked me up and down in my on-screen make-up and asked scathingly, 'What have you come as? You look like a bus conductress.'

This used to be quite a common insult when I was younger, as bus conductresses were known to wear thick pan-stick make-up. That I'd arrived to see my mum for what I thought would be the last time, only to be greeted with this, really makes me smile now. It was so typical of her. I stayed with her for a while and then reluctantly returned to filming in London.

A few days later I had another call. The nurses said they were sure this time that this was it. On the way, I got a flat tyre but I didn't stop. Everything and nothing was going through my mind.

When I arrived at the home, my mother was lying in bed, looking helpless and fragile. There was no caustic put-down this time. She was awake and aware that I was there but quiet and restful, slipping in and out of consciousness. I took her hand and vowed to stay by her side. I would remain there for the next four days.

This time to be with my mother was a privilege that I know many people aren't afforded. I was mindful that I had the opportunity to say things to her that I might not normally have said. Over the years my mother hadn't been an easy person to deal with — she was someone who, I'm sad to say, found it difficult to show affection or warmth towards me. It is strange to admit this, and yet at the same time she was my mother and I loved her. There were many times when I just wanted her to be proud of me, but it seemed she never was. As close relationships in life often are, ours was complicated.

But in these, her final days, as I sat in the chair next to her bed, it seemed to be a time for peaceful acceptance. As she became more vulnerable I felt things soften between us. I suppose it was because she needed me and I was happy to be needed and to help.

With all of this time to think, with nursing staff and relatives coming and going, but me as a constant in the room with my mother, I felt I needed her to hear something from me that was from my heart. Something I could say with absolute honesty.

I took her hand and said, 'Mum, I had the best childhood I could ever have had.'

Tears sprang to her eyes. Her hand was gnarled with arthritis, but she had enough strength for me to feel that she was holding on to me. Things changed as I got older, but I really did have the best childhood and I needed her to know that.

SINCE HER DEATH, I have realised that whatever age we are, we all feel like children at times, even when there may be no one there to be a child for. Only last week I found myself hovering near the phone: I had found a recipe that I knew my mother would have liked and I wanted to tell her about it. Grief seemed to hit me all over again when I realised I couldn't have that conversation. It was a small thing, but it made me sad that I couldn't share it with her.

My aim with this book is to look back and explore what it was I couldn't tell my mother, and why that was. But also—and more importantly perhaps—I want to set down a record of all the love and life, loss and laughs: all the big things, and the small things. Everything I wanted to tell my mother but felt I never could.

Chapter One

I was born in my Aunty Millie's house in Warrington during the Second World War. My mother Margaret was staying at Millie's while my dad was away with his regiment. It is fitting that I was born in the thick of my extended family because although I was an only child I always felt part of a large clan.

My mother and her sisters would take turns to stay at each other's houses. The reason they gave was 'to keep the houses aired'. It seemed that everything needed 'airing' in those days. 'No wonder you've got a cold,' my mother would say, 'that top's not even aired.' So the houses were occupied in rotation in order to keep them aired, but I'm sure the real reason was the reassurance of safety in numbers.

My father, Fred, was in the Royal Engineers and was stationed in Portsmouth. At around the same time that my mother found out she was pregnant with me, Dad came down with an illness. He was throwing up every morning and eventually they took him into the field hospital to have him checked over. They couldn't find anything wrong with him, but then he happened to mention that my mother was pregnant. The doctor told him he was suffering from psychological morning sickness. Apparently it was quite common! While my dad was hospitalised his unit flew to Syria, where they were targeted and many of his regiment were killed. Dad always used to say, 'Our Sue saved me.' Thinking about it now, it must have been harrowing for Dad, knowing how close he had come to death and to have lost so many of his comrades.

My mother would tell another story of a time my father was preparing to go back to Portsmouth. He turned to wave goodbye to her, not looking where he was going, and as he did he walloped his head on a lamppost. He staggered back into the house, oozing blood from his head. My mum and her sisters were doubled over laughing. Poor Dad needed stitches and ended up having to stay off for another couple of days. So my dad could say that he was hospitalised twice during the war—once for morning sickness and once for walking into a lamppost!

I often think about those years when I was first in the world and what it must have been like for ordinary people living through that extraordinary time. They were living on the edge in a very real sense. No one knew how events would unfold; all they could do was pull together and hope for a positive outcome. My Aunty Millie would always say about the war, 'Well, we just had to get on with it,' and she was right—what choice did people have?

They were an extraordinary generation; they were never indulgent or self-pitying about what they'd had to face. It does make me think that we're so very nannied now. I don't know how people would survive if they had to face the same thing.

During the war, Liverpool and Warrington were targets for the German bombers. Liverpool because it was a port and hub for industry, and Warrington because, after Pearl Harbor, when the

Americans entered the war, it became an American air base. The place was swarming with GIs, and my mum and her sisters would talk later about getting stockings and chocolates from the American soldiers. They spoke very highly of them, saying they were extremely courteous and generous. They used to go to the dances, but as far as they were concerned it was all very innocent.

I arrived in the world on December 7, 1943. At that time women were expected to stay 'in confinement': they had to rest up in bed for several days and get their strength back after giving birth. While Mum was lying there a few hours after having me, looking at her new baby and minding her own business, the air-raid sirens began to wail. My aunties Millie and Ena came charging in and took me out of my cot, wrapped in my blanket.

'Where are you going?' my mother asked.

'To the shelter, of course,' Millie said, holding me tight. Millie had an Anderson air-raid shelter in her back garden.

'She's a tiny baby, we can't leave her in the house,' Ena added.

'What about me?' my poor mother implored.

'You need to stay there. You're in confinement.'

And with that the sisters were out of the door with me, while my mother had to hope that the bombs that were dropping paid due respect to the notion of confinement and left her alone.

So this was my rather unceremonious introduction to the world, and I was named Susan. It wasn't the name my mother had intended for me. I was to be Margaret Jane after both her and her mother, and my father was duly sent to register the birth. I'm not sure what happened between him leaving the house and getting to the registry office but with uncharacteristic bravery he decided that I should be called Susan. The name didn't have any family connection for either my mother or father; I think he just liked it.

So here I was, Susan Wright. Hearing my first name and my maiden name together always makes me smile. You were only ever addressed by your full name at registration time at school, or if you were in trouble. If someone shouted 'Susan Wright!' at me now I'd still drop everything and wonder what I'd done.

One of my first really vivid memories of my mother is of me playing in the street waiting for her to return from an afternoon in Warrington. She rounded the corner and I saw her and waved excitedly. She had had her hair cropped. In those days most women we knew seemed to have a regulation perm, or their hair was rolled back and pinned round their head. So to see my mum with her short hair made her seem so glamorous and I was really proud of her. She was wearing a suit, a skirt suit, as Mum never wore trousers. In fact, the first pair of trousers I managed to convince her to buy was when she was in her eighties.

Mum had dark, well-shaped eyebrows, which I inherited from her. She had blue eyes and a lovely nose, but I inherited my dad's! My parents made a handsome couple. Dad was five foot ten and very trim; he had a bit of a swagger when he was younger. He was a great swimmer and his physique showed it. He had huge blue eyes and fair hair. Like my mother, he was always very well turned out. He wore a trilby hat and a shirt and tie. I once bought him a Liverpool club tie and he was as proud as punch to wear it.

Dad worked as a plumber before and after the war. Mum had worked before she married Dad, in a box-making factory. She started as a machinist but moved to the assembly line, where she worked alongside her sisters Millie and Ena.

The house where I grew up was ten miles away from my Aunty Millie's in Warrington. It was on the outskirts of Liverpool in a place called Whiston on a newly built estate. The house itself was plain-fronted, with a small front garden, but as my family lived on the corner plot we had a larger back yard, which gave me and my cousins room to play and space for my father to tend to his plants.

It wasn't just the rent collector who knocked on our door every week. The pop man would come on his horse and cart and we would hand back our bottles and get a discount on that week's cream soda or dandelion and burdock. The rag-and-bone man would pass by on his horse and cart shouting 'Any Old Iron!' but to us he just sounded like a strangled donkey shouting 'Eeyore!' The coal man would come round, heaving his sacks of coal on his shoulder. It was so cold in those days, we would wake up with icicles on the inside of the windows. When I was ill my dad would come up and put some coal in the grate of the fire in my room. I still hanker after a fire in my room like the one I had as a child. The milkman was also on a horse and cart and again we would give him back our bottles in return for that day's milk.

We didn't have many toys or things to play with; every family had the same board games—Ludo, Monopoly, Snakes & Ladders, and a pack of cards for the adults. My mother would dye her legs with gravy browning and draw a line up the back of her legs to make it look as if she was wearing stockings.

We had a bath once a week. Heating the water for a bath involved lighting the fire. One of these bath days was the day before Warrington Walking Day, a yearly event that is still held today. It was essentially a parade with a fair afterwards and we would receive a few pennies to go on the rides.

I was very much looking forward to the parade the next day. Mum took some boiling water in a pan, brought it into the bathroom and set it down at the side of the bath. I was faffing around with the plug. As she went to pick up the boiling water, I got in her way and she spilled it all over my foot. I immediately began screaming in pain, my mother panicked and whipped off my shoe and sock, taking the skin with it. I was in agony and absolutely hysterical. Uncle Joe, my friend Valerie's dad and our neighbour, was passing our house and came inside to see what was going on. Seeing me sitting on the mangle, where my mum had plonked me so she could get a better look at my foot, he looked shocked.

'Ring an ambulance, Joe, please!' Mum pleaded.

Poor Joe had only one leg but he turned and hopped to the phone box as quick as that leg could carry him.

An ambulance arrived to take me to hospital. I was bandaged up and sent home, and a nurse came round to our house every day to give me an injection. For a couple of months I had to use a wheelchair to get about. It was very painful and quite traumatic. I missed the walk, of course, and was very sad to have to sit at home ailing while everyone else was enjoying themselves.

I was only little at the time but I could tell that my mother was horrified and blamed herself, even though she would say, 'Why were you messing about like that?' She was right, it was me messing about that had caused it, but she felt guilty. Poor Mum. I still have that scar on my foot. I have the ugliest feet in the world and getting a scar on one seems to me to be adding injury to insult.

MY FONDEST EARLY MEMORY is of sitting on my mother's knee. We were in the living room as *Listen with Mother* came on the radio. I remember it was on just before two in the afternoon and I can hear the tinkling intro clearly. Here comes our story, I would think.

I felt very encircled, very loved, by my parents when I was younger. Although I was an only child I never felt that I was on my own. My dad's family lived nearby and my mother's family were not far off in Warrington and we saw them all the time. My dad was one of six, but that seemed like a small family compared to my mother being part of a massive brood of twelve!

My cousins Pauline and Marjorie, Ena and Millie's daughters, were like sisters to me when I was younger. Although, I have to say, we didn't all scrub up in quite the same way. Pauline and Marjorie were always well turned out. I started out in the same orderly fashion, but as the day progressed I was always the first to get grubby. I think that my tomboy ways may have been a direct reaction to my mother's assertion that she had always wanted a boy. It was something that she would tell me quite often — 'You were meant to be a boy.' She even had a name: Michael. There was also the odd comment that led me to believe I was a 'mistake' and that she had never intended to be a mother. I think the fact that she came from such a large family put her off having children. Also, this was during the war and it was such a time of uncertainty that I'm not sure the idea of bringing a child into the world was something she and my father even considered.

I don't mean to sound melodramatic when I say that comments like this made me feel that I was never quite wanted by my mother. Of course, it was never addressed by us because in our family we just didn't talk about how we felt. I could never have sat my mother down and said, 'So, Mum, you say that you wanted a boy instead of me—do you know how that makes me feel?' She would have told me, in no uncertain terms, that if she had had a boy he wouldn't be trying to have conversations like this with her.

As a child I spent a lot of time at my grandparents' in Warrington. It was a large three-bedroom semidetached which they rented. It had a big bay-fronted window, and the house formed an L-shape round the back yard with the dining room, kitchen and back kitchen overlooking it. We always used the back door, never the front. I'm not sure who would have been allowed through the front door as my grandmother wasn't much for visiting dignitaries.

But as large as it was for a semi I could never quite work out how they had managed to fit twelve children and two adults in there when my mother had been growing up. Eventually I asked my mother how the logistics had worked and she replied, 'The girls were in one bedroom, the boys in another, of course.'

My mother's mother was a large lady, round with ruddy cheeks and a face that reminded me of a toasted bun. Her hair was grey and pulled back into an untidy French pleat. She was a real character who had a healthy disdain for cleaning and didn't care who frowned upon her for it, something I think I have inherited.

She was very capable in other domestic areas, though. A self-taught seamstress, she made everything from coats to wedding dresses for an array of customers who would come to the house. Her children acted as a team, the older ones looked after the babies when they came along, wiping, feeding and cleaning. They would pick up the odds and ends of material that lay discarded round the house and try to keep on top of this industry that my grandmother had created.

My grandmother dressed her own daughters; all six of them were immaculately tailored. She used to buy *Vogue* and copy the designs from there. And when us grandchildren came along she dressed us too. Pauline, Marjorie and I would all be dressed the same. I think we quite liked it—identical until, of course, I got myself covered in dirt.

As well as sewing, my grandma loved to cook and bake. Cooking is also a passion of mine; I love to cook for others but cannot lay claim to my grandmother's prolific abilities. Her house always smelled of apple pie or custard tarts, or mince on cottage pie days. We would be greeted with piles of baking—lemon meringue pies stacked next to huge chocolate éclairs. My grandma seemed to be able to do ten things at once, a skill learned, no doubt, from having to deal with all those kids!

My mum's dad was the strong, silent type. As a small child I found him quite distant, but when he did speak to me he had a knack of making me feel very special. A few years ago I was asked to go on BBC TV's *Who Do You Think You Are?* where you delve into your family history. I knew that my grandfather had been from a well-to-do family and had turned his back on his privately educated upbringing to pursue a life on the railways. But here I learned how his own father had dragged himself up by the bootstraps from a life of poverty in Carlisle to being a hotel owner and a man of considerable means. When my grandfather got married, on the wedding certificate under 'Father of the Groom', my great-grandfather had written 'A Gentleman' as his occupation.

The fact that my grandfather then turned his back on this privileged life no doubt caused ructions within his family, but he went off to do a job that he loved. Anyway, he wasn't just a train driver, I was told as a child: he drove one of the most iconic steam engines in the world, the *Flying Scotsman*. Not so, the *Who Do You Think You Are?* programme informed me. He was indeed a steam-engine driver, but he only ever worked on the west coast and the *Flying Scotsman* went down the east coast. A childhood belief was shattered by this revelation. However, I did receive a kind letter from someone after the programme aired, telling me the *Flying Scotsman* had travelled down the west coast from time to time and may well have been driven by my grandfather. I do hope so— I built any popularity I had at primary school on this connection!

One thing that I clearly remember about my grandmother and grandfather's house was the huge amount of crockery and silver they had, obviously a legacy from the hotel days. The amount of silver was mesmerising and seemed so precious to my young eyes. There were coffeepots and teapots, sugar bowls, cruets, cutlery and trays all with 'Globe Hotel' stamped on them.

My father's mother died just before I was born. Everyone always said what a lovely woman she was and I often felt that I had missed out on meeting someone very special. My father's father lived round the corner from us in Eccleston Park with two of his children, my Uncle Harry and Aunty May. Just along the road from them lived Aunty Reenie, Uncle Alec and my cousin Alec. About a mile away was Uncle John, Aunty Ada and my cousin Lavinia, and round the corner from them was Uncle Bert and his wife Lynne, and their daughters Catherine and Elizabeth. It sounds like we were all living on top of one another, but everyone I knew had his or her families close by.

Aunty May was very much part of my life in Whiston. She was a midwife at Whiston Hospital and during the war had nursed injured soldiers. She had never married but always wore a little diamond engagement ring. Aunty May was the first person in our family to get a television and every Saturday I would go to her house and we would watch *Six-Five Special*, a forerunner of *Top of the Pops*. As we were sitting there I plucked up the courage to ask her where the ring had come from. She said that it was from a Belgian man whom she had met and nursed in the war. When he recovered, he went back overseas with the intention that he would return and they would marry. But he was killed on his return to active service.

I went to see Aunty May three days before she died, shortly after her ninetieth birthday, and she was still wearing that ring. It makes me sad to think that she lost the love of her life at such an early age and then carried a candle for him until her death.

I went to Whiston Infants. My infant school teacher's name was Miss Cross and we would say, 'Cross by name, cross by nature', making sure that she never overheard us as we didn't want to incur any further wrath than she was already more than happy to dish out.

I went happily to school on the first day but the next day I woke up and said to my mother, matter-of-factly, 'I don't think I'll go to school today, thank you.'

My mother, with a look that could curdle milk, said, 'There's no "think" about it. You're going to school, young lady!' With that I was dressed and whisked out of the door.

I wasn't having this, I decided. As all the other children filed through the school gates, I clamped my hands round the railings and clung on for dear life. My mother tried to pull me off but in the end she gave up trying and marched into the school, asking the head teacher if she would be kind enough to come outside and prise me away from the school gates and into the school itself.

The head came out and looked at me. I glared back, my face puce with defiance. 'Come on now, Susan, let's have you inside,' she said. She peeled one finger off and immediately I flipped it back onto the gate. It must have been like wrestling an octopus. Finally the head and my mother managed to prise me away from the gate and the head carried me, kicking, into the school.

After this altercation I was fine, but I like to think that this was a precursor to my future political life—the first of many protests!

I was, I am informed, very bright at infant school. We had little cards that we would write our class exercises on and I'd always be the first up with my card, arm outstretched, 'Finished, Miss!'

One day as I was waiting to be seen by the teacher, I slid my exercise card down the back of a poster on the wall. I'm not sure why I did it: boredom, curiosity; whatever the reason, it resulted in me receiving a good hiding. I was given the ruler—for that! Mind you, at the time, if you had the audacity to go home and say that you'd been smacked you would get smacked again, so I never told my parents.

I had my first acting experience at that school. I'd like to say there was early evidence that it would eventually become my career, but that wasn't the case. I remember seeing my parents come into the room and look around; maybe they were looking for me playing Mary, or even a shepherd or king. But no, there I was, standing on a stool pointing at the words with a stick, under strict instruction that I wasn't allowed to sing. I'm still no use at singing. I might on occasion fancy that I can sing but I'm reminded that I can't as soon as the notes leave my mouth.

We moved from infants to junior school when we were seven. My junior school, Eccleston Park Church of England School, was a mile and a half away and I would walk there and back twice a day, coming home for my lunch. Six miles a day—no wonder we were all beanpoles! One of the tricks of our teachers at junior school was to throw our work out of the window if we were misbehaving. Mr Dean was the worst for it. So we would be standing there, agog as our work frittered through the air. While we were distracted we'd get a great thwack on the back of the legs—not from a ruler this time but a cane; we were seven now, we'd moved on! Then we'd have to hobble into the garden to pick up our ruined work. Thinking back, it's a wonder we learned anything.

Growing up I may not have had any brothers or sisters but I was extremely lucky as there were three other girls in the three houses next door to us who were only children too. We all knocked about together playing on the street and in our garden—my dad had strung up some old netting he'd acquired for us to play badminton, or 'shuttlecock', as we called it. Dad could always be relied upon to make something out of nothing. The four of us would play outside together every day after school and we'd often be joined by a lad called Nigel. I don't remember spending much time inside, unless it was teeming down with rain.

SOME OF THE happiest times in my childhood were during our family holidays. We would rent a seaside chalet in a place called Gronant just outside Rhyl. North Wales was and still is a big draw for people from the Northwest. It's not too far and has some lovely seaside towns. There was a bluebell wood near the campsite and a stream where I played in the water with my cousins, when we weren't on the beach building sandcastles. Of course now as I look back it all seems to have been dappled by sunlight, but I'm pretty sure we also had days, if not weeks, of rain where we sat in the chalet and vowed never to go back to Wales again.

We would sometimes hire a caravan when it was just my parents and me. There was something very comforting about cosying up on a bed that flipped down from an overhead cupboard, while my mother and father turned the table into a double bed. Cosier still was the feeling that we were all together in the same room, playing cards and board games.

Another holiday that sticks in my mind was on a farm in Egremont, Cumbria. It was haymaking time and they had a young lad on the farm who kindly allowed us to get involved in the baling. They would get the hay on the back of the cart and then my cousins and I would climb up and be pulled along, bobbing about on top of the hay, by two cart-horses called Blossom and Biddy. It was one of those holidays that stands out as so much more than just a week away. Again, it seemed to be sunny all the time.

My childhood really was lovely and I am pleased that I got to tell my mother that I felt that way. My memories as a youngster are something that I'll always treasure and I am thankful to both my mum and dad for creating the kind of environment that allowed me to have such a happy time.

MY RELATIONSHIP with my mother began to change when I was a teenager. Although on the one hand she had been encouraging of my progress at school, now that I was growing up, she was beginning to view my enquiring mind with suspicion.

I don't believe my mother's attitude to have been malicious; I just think that she feared losing me, she feared that I was outgrowing our family unit, she feared the inevitable day that I would leave home and make a life for myself. Her ideal situation would have been for me to marry a local lad, settle down nearby and have grandchildren for her. But I had ambitions and a life that I wanted to lead. I wanted to see a bit of the world, or at least travel a bit farther than the end of our road.

My dad was always very encouraging towards my academic success. I think that this is because, in another life, he would have loved to have been a scholar. He had had to leave school aged fourteen because his parents couldn't afford the uniform required. He took an apprenticeship as a plumber and later in life went to night school and worked his way up to become a clerk of works at the Ministry of Defence. My father was a very bright man, and in lieu of any formal education he educated himself. He had a great love of literature and would recite chunks from Shakespeare. It never occurred to me that this was quite unusual; I thought everyone's dad knew whole swathes of *King Lear*.

Dad loved books, or at least loved talking about books. I never saw him read, but he would talk about Dickens, telling me abridged versions of his favourites. He loved *Kidnapped* by Robert Louis Stevenson and I felt I knew that book without ever having read it. So where my mother was unimpressed about any of my academic successes, my father was always very interested.

My mother was encouraging in other areas. In my teens I showed real promise at the high jump, and she thought this might be a good thing to pursue. Mum too had been good at the high jump when she was at school and I knew that she was pleased that we shared a talent. She and Dad wanted me to train and be part of the Liverpool Harriers, and so did I until I realised what a commitment it would be.

One thing I pursued for a number of years was playing the piano. This was another thing that pleased my mother as it was a very ladylike thing to do. I used to attend piano lessons with a lady called Miss Anderson who lived in Prescot, Merseyside. I really enjoyed playing the piano and I even got to play at the Philharmonic in Liverpool.

On reflection, I think my mother was very proud of me that day. I had been put forward by my music teacher to play alongside other young people who in turn had been nominated by their teachers, and I played Mozart's 'Minuet in G'. When I saw my mum after the performance, it was clear she had been crying.

Suddenly Miss Anderson stopped taking piano lessons and my mum and dad found a lady in Thatto Heath, an area of St Helens about three miles from where we lived. I would sit on the bus dreading going to this woman's house. She wasn't as warm and welcoming as Miss Anderson, so my mother found me someone far closer to our house and I went there for four years until I was sixteen and the pull of a social life was proving too great to resist.

I started skipping my piano lessons in favour of spending time in the back room of the nearby pub. Instead of using the half-crown that Mum and Dad gave me to pay the piano teacher, I started spending it on a round of shandies for me and my friends.

One summer there was a church fête and I was there with my parents, but I had wandered off and was standing talking to some friends when I spotted them talking to the piano teacher. She was shaking her head and all three were looking puzzled. By the time I got there my dad had gone silent, something he did only when he was angry or disappointed. My mother took on the admonishment for the two of them and let fly. 'How could you, Susan?' she said, fixing me with a burning glare.

'I'm sorry,' I said, wanting the ground to open up and swallow me.

'If you'd done it for a week then sorry might be good enough, but six months?'

'I know, I don't know what I was thinking . . .' I said weakly.

'Well, you weren't thinking, were you? Otherwise you'd have thought that half a crown is a lot of money for me and your dad.' I had to pay back every penny of it, and I was informed I couldn't have piano lessons again.

I WAS ALWAYS on the lookout for a creative outlet, and my cousin Lavinia recognised this. Lavinia was a total inspiration to me as a teenager. I was fourteen years her junior, a huge gap at that age, and it was through her that I developed a love of the theatre. Each year on my birthday she would take me into Liverpool to see a play and then have a roast chicken dinner at the cafeteria in Lewis's, the famous old department store.

As a family we did manage to get to the theatre and the ballet quite regularly. I find this remarkable now, as at the time money was extremely tight. But somehow my mother and aunts would find the money to troop us off to the ballet, dressed up and buzzing with excitement. What else is amazing is that in the late forties and early fifties these very working-class ladies embraced high culture. But then again, it was just what that generation did, I suppose. At this time Variety was still popular and people went out to the cinema and the music halls for their entertainment.

Although I did like to go to the theatre, the first time I remember being bitten by the drama bug was around the age of fifteen. Until then, acting hadn't been something that I'd thought of as an option. It just wasn't the done thing for someone from my background. I had always enjoyed English, and had won the school prize for spoken English reading from *Alice in Wonderland* when I was in the third form, but it wasn't until I met my teacher Miss Potter that I realised that I wanted to act. Miss Potter was one of those inspirational teachers that everyone hopes they'll have. She was then only in her mid-twenties, so she was young, enthusiastic and full of energy. She decided that we needed to perform a school play. Drama wasn't something that was on the curriculum then so any plays that were put on at school depended on the drive of the teacher. The play she chose was *The Tinderbox*, and she cast me as the witch. From the day we started rehearsals I knew that I loved acting and that this was what I wanted to do.

After the play Miss Potter married and became Mrs Sutton. She continually encouraged me to become an actress and I never forgot about the impact she'd had on me in my school years.

Years later, I was surprised to find myself on *This is Your Life*. My mother had told the producers about Mrs Sutton but they were unable to track her down. I had always wondered where she was and how she was getting on. About twelve months after the programme I was asked to present at the Teaching Awards, and when I went onstage the presenter asked me about teachers who had inspired me as a child. I of course told them about Mrs Sutton. Then a voice that I recognised came over the speakers and I turned round to see an older lady on the screen behind me, sitting at a desk and reading from her diary. 'Today Susan Wright was remarkable in *The Tinderbox* and I hope she'll continue with her acting endeavours . . .' It was Mrs Sutton!

The next minute there she was, up on the stage with me. I was absolutely thrilled. Afterwards we spent all evening in a bar catching up. She said that she'd followed my career but had never known that I was the Susan Wright she had taught. She introduced me to her husband and we talked about the time we had seen Albert Finney understudy for Laurence Olivier in Stratford. She said, 'Well, of course we all had the hots for him . . .' As schoolgirls we'd never thought that our teacher felt the same way about the young actor as we did!

After that I stayed in touch with Mrs Sutton until she sadly passed away two years ago.

I THINK IT IS so important to have figures like Mrs Sutton, outside your family, who can encourage your passions as a child. Parents aren't always the best people to understand why you want to follow a certain path in life. Although my mum did encourage some things that I was interested in, it was in my teenage years that a definite divide appeared between my mother on one side and me and my dad on the other. My mother had always been caught up in what other people might think, as if somehow what mattered most was the opinion of the neighbours five doors down, whom she'd never really met. My mother was quick to judge, and as a result Dad and I forged an alliance as we strived to avoid her scathing criticism. We shared small things, never huge secrets, but it lead to this air of division between my mum and me and my dad.

That said, if my dad thought that I was out of line, especially with regard to my mum, he would tell me. He loved my mother dearly and was fiercely loyal to her. The only reason he kept things from her was so as not to upset her, or to make life easier.

There was a lot that we kept from my mother. My dad would say to me as a teenager 'Don't tell your mother' about the slightest thing. My father liked to smoke, but my mother wouldn't let him so he would go to his shed to do it and only I knew.

We knew that if my mother found out that I was going out into Liverpool or seeing a friend she would have something to say about it, would have put it down in one way or another, so we didn't tell her. We couldn't face the disapproval.

When I was seventeen years old my dad was in charge of my curfew. There were times when he'd know that I'd come in late but would say to my mum, 'Oh, Sue was in in good time,' and then give me a wink. One evening, though, I pushed him too far.

My dad knew what time the last bus back from Liverpool was and that if I missed it then the only other bus dropped me miles away and meant I had a long walk up a dark country lane. One night I had stayed out later than usual, and missed my last bus home. I got off the other bus and ran, my heart pounding in my chest. What would usually happen was that my dad would go to bed, leave the back door on the latch and then I could let myself in and sneak to bed. However, that evening he'd obviously had enough. I got to the back door and pulled but nothing happened; it was locked. I pulled again, still nothing. As I stood there on the step, I heard the bolt being drawn and the door opened. My dad looked at me, with an expression on his face that I dreaded. He was disappointed. He stood back to let me in the house.

'I'm sorry, Dad, I missed the bus and then I had to get the other one; it won't happen again,' I gabbled.

My dad fixed me with a look that still makes my heart sink thinking about it now. 'You'd better go to bed. And we won't tell your mother about any of this.'

At that age I thought that the gap that appeared between my mother and I was all down to me. Something I had done, something that had changed in me. I picked up tension in other people, and thought that if they were upset it was all my fault. It's something I still tend to do now.

A couple of years on from this my mother became really ill. She had always been a bit of a drama queen about her asthma, but this was serious. She developed pneumonia. Eventually the doctors brought in a respirator and my mother was surrounded by tubes and bottles of oxygen. It was a very scary time. Mum was only forty-seven but I felt that there was a possibility we might lose her. Dad would drive all the way back from Liverpool city centre every lunch time to tend to her, and her sisters came round to make sure she was OK when Dad and I weren't there.

One day, the doctor came round, took one look at my mum and said, 'She needs to go into hospital. She's very ill.'

Dad prevaricated. My mother was adamant that she wasn't going anywhere, so Dad comforted her and told her that it was fine, she didn't have to go anywhere. I looked at them both, then went downstairs and called for an ambulance.

As Mum was strapped up and bundled into the back with dad she turned to me and said, 'I'll never forgive you for this!' The idea that the entire street would see her taken to hospital was mortifying to her. Never mind that she was at death's door!

I jumped in my dad's blue Volkswagen Beetle and followed the ambulance to the hospital, where I parked up at the first place I could find and ran inside to A&E. Mum, an oxygen mask covering her nose and mouth, was wheeled past me on a stretcher and taken into a cubicle, leaving Dad and me outside. Feeling terrible, I looked at my dad.

'Don't worry, love, I think she's forgiven you,' he said.

'No, I haven't!' Mum's voice floated out from behind the curtain. Dad and I had to laugh.

I did well at my O levels, but the leap between O levels and A levels was vast, as was the social life that became available. I left school at the end of the first year of sixth form. My dad wanted me to go to university and he was fiercely disappointed when I left, but I knew there was life out there that I had to experience.

Chapter Two

I left sixth form in 1961 and decided that I would get a job and see where things took me. I knew that I wanted to be an actress, but as I had no idea how to go about becoming one, I thought I should earn some money.

My uncle was an inspector of taxes in Manchester and he suggested I might enjoy working in the tax office. My parents were happy as they thought that if I took a job I might relent and think about university in the near future. My mother was thrilled that I was going to be a civil servant. I went to work in the tax office in St Helens for six months and was then transferred to Liverpool.

I loved working in Liverpool. The city has always been full of life and energy. The people there know how to have a laugh and the tax office was no exception. Everyone was very friendly and socialised together. The girls I worked with used to go to a club at lunch time and very soon I was invited along too. This was no ordinary club: this was the Cavern, the place that spawned the Beatles.

Although I enjoyed working with the people there, I hated working in the tax office. The monotonous drudgery of the job drove me nuts—I was literally paper shuffling—I didn't and still don't have a natural administrative bent.

We used to go to the Cavern for our lunch break at twelve and return at one. But soon I wasn't returning at one. It became half one, then two, until I was stretching my lunch well into the afternoon and cheating my time card. I remember seeing one of the tax collectors, Chris Crummy, performing there with his band. I nearly fell off my chair and had to hide in order to watch him, but he soon left the tax office, when his band the Searchers became successful, changing his name to Chris Curtis. That was the thing about the Cavern. It seemed that everyone in Liverpool of a certain age was down there, being part of it. Even the tax officers! But it was only going to be so long before someone found out what I was up to.

About this time I joined a drama group at the Liverpool Institute. We didn't seem to learn much; we were just given different things to perform and instructed to go out and perform them. I seem to remember a lot of time on buses, dragging our props with us. I soon began to drift away. There was no focus in what we were doing and the pull of the Cavern proved too great.

I used to love going there on my own, taking in the sights and sounds of everything that was going on. When I first started going it had just stopped being a jazz club but still had the overhang of that jazz/beatnik fashion—tight black trousers and black polo necks, so my attire had to be black. I would wear a big baggy mohair jumper and leggings; I thought I looked the bee's knees. The Cavern was on Mathew Street, directly off the main shopping street in the city centre. You walked downstairs, and it was as its name suggested: an underground cavern.

Once down there it was very dark. There were brick arches that straddled the two cellars that made up the club. It used to drip moisture from the ceiling, and it wasn't unusual to go to the toilet and find yourself face to face with a rat. I'm not painting the best picture, am I? But there was such a buzz about the place that you just wanted to be there. The stage, if you could call it that, was a slightly raised area at the back of the cellars and there were rows of chairs positioned in front of it. To the side of the stage there was a band room where the bands got changed. Down the side of the cellars there was an area where people would stand and do the Cavern Stomp, the signature dance of the club.

At the back of the club they served tea and pop. It sounds very naive that we all gathered and drank cups of tea, but it wasn't about getting drunk, it was about the music and the atmosphere, and the Cavern had both in spades.

There is a Cavern club still there on Mathew Street but it isn't the real one. The original Cavern was filled in by Liverpool council in 1973 when they bulldozed the building above. Planning and heritage weren't big on the agenda in the early seventies.

I marvel at my confidence back then. I would get on the bus, go into town on my own, and turn up at the Cavern to see if there was anyone I recognised. I was by now hanging out there in the evening as well as at lunch time. If there wasn't anyone I knew, I'd just make friends with whoever was there.

When I came home my mother would say in disgust, 'You've been to that club again!' And she was right, I had, because it had become part of my life and I was in there every day that I possibly could be. I tended not to tell her who I was with or what I was doing, which, when I think of it now, probably added to her feelings that I was drifting away from her.

I remember the first time I saw the Beatles perform. It was 1961. I had gone to see the Swinging Blue Jeans play, and supporting them were a group who would go on to become the biggest band in the world. I have to say, I was mesmerised. There was something so edgy and vital about their performance, which was airbrushed out when they were given their mop-tops and their suits and told to act clean-cut for the teenyboppers' worried parents. Back then they were going between Liverpool and Germany—they spent a lot of time gigging in Hamburg, honing their craft—and they were unbelievably raw and sexy.

I got to know Paul well, and Ringo, who wasn't drumming for them yet; it was still Pete Best. I would see John Lennon there with his first wife, Cynthia, who I felt was treated shoddily by the girls who came to see John and were in love with him from afar. I met Gerry Marsden from Gerry and the Pacemakers, and his girlfriend, whom he later married, and we all became good mates.

The Beatles first appeared on TV on October 17, 1962, on a regional programme called *Scene at 6.30*. At that point my mother knew that they were the reason her daughter spent so much time in the Cavern but she had yet to clap eyes on them. They were dressed in leather biker jackets and looked very sexy. My mum was appalled. After that, when Paul came to our place to drop me off, she'd ask in disgust, 'Has that dirty Beatle been in my house?' She gave me the silent treatment for a while after that.

Paul wrote to me from the Star-Club in Hamburg once—a great letter, it even had doodles on the front of it, which was stolen from me when I was working on *Brookside*. I took it in one time as no one believed that I had this treasured possession, but then it was whizzed from my locker and I was devastated; no one ever owned up to the theft.

Another piece of Beatles history I had, which I have to hold my hands up to losing, was an old reel-to-reel of the Beatles singing 'Love Me Do' in someone's garage when they were first putting it together. I am shamefaced to say that I taped over it with the Max Miller show. Whenever I admit this to anyone there is always a sharp intake of breath—I've yet to meet someone who's said, 'Still, you're the proud owner of a classic Max Miller show.'

While the Beatles were in Hamburg I began seeing the drummer from the Swinging Blue Jeans, who was still a car mechanic at the time. His name was Norman Kuhlke and he was my first serious boyfriend. Strangely enough, my mother took to him. She would make him apple pies to take on tour.

Towards the end of my numbered days at the tax office, Paul McCartney told me there was a job going at NEMS, the record and management company run by the Epstein brothers. When I first started there it wasn't quite the empire it would become; they used to sell a few records and had a furniture shop too.

I was offered a job working for Brian Epstein's personal assistant Peter Brown's personal assistant. I would be his personal assistant. So I was personal assistant to the personal assistant to the personal assistant of Brian Epstein—try putting that on your business card! Epstein would go on to manage the Beatles and give them their signature look. It was great to have a job at the centre of all of the new music that was coming into the country.

One day I had a record land on my desk from America. It was called 'The Hippy Hippy Shake' by Chan Romero. I listened to it and it blew me away. I grabbed the record and went in search of Norman. 'You have to listen to this song,' I told him. 'It's amazing.'

He put it on and his face lit up. The minute the record was finished he went in search of the other band members and that was how the Swinging Blue Jeans came to record their hit single 'The Hippy Hippy Shake'. I also told them about 'You're No Good'. I wish I'd asked for a cut of the royalties!

My parents were glad that I hadn't gallivanted off anywhere farther than Liverpool city centre, but they were keeping a watchful eye on me, wary that if I was daft enough to pack in a job at the tax office I might be daft enough to do anything. When I think about it, I must have been a constant worry to my poor parents. At the time I'm sure they envisaged that I was up to all sorts, but the worst thing we did, I think, was to take something called Purple Hearts. These pills were given to us by our bosses at NEMS to get us through the night when we had a big record launch ahead of us. If someone had suggested to us that we were taking 'drugs' I'm sure we would have been horrified.

By the time I was nineteen I had been seeing Norman for over two years. I was still going to the Cavern as well as to another club called the Mardi Gras. One night I was out with my friend Bah when I bumped into the tour manager for the Swinging Blue Jeans. This was odd, as I thought that they were all away on tour together—or at least that was what Norman had told me.

'Hi,' I said, trying to be as casual as possible. 'I thought you lot were on tour.' My mouth had gone dry.

'Nah,' he said. 'Norman's just gone off on holiday to the Canaries with a friend.'

I knew exactly what 'friend' meant. I was devastated. I looked at Bah dumbly, wanting the ground to open up and swallow me. I turned away and ran from the club; I needed to get out of there. I went home and sobbed uncontrollably all night.

The next morning I woke up and just thought, 'Sod it!' I was still devastated by his betrayal but it had galvanised me somehow. I knew that I had to stop living vicariously through other people and get on with my life and what I wanted to do. Norman came back from his week with his groupie, full of remorse. But I was gone, not interested. I needed to stop literally following the band.

Almost overnight I turned my back on the Liverpool scene. I didn't have any regrets about doing this. The Beatles had moved to London and most of the other bands who had played at the Cavern had also made it big and left. I felt that I had been there for the best part of it. It seemed the right time to move on.

The last time I saw Paul was when the Beatles came back from London to appear at the Cavern. 'She Loves You' had just hit number one. I was with Paul, then George met us and Ringo came later. We were all going to a party but first we met for a drink. They were all nervous. Since they had left for London they had begun to worry that Liverpool would see them as deserters.

'Sod it,' Paul said eventually. 'Shall we go for a drive past the Cavern and see if there's anyone there?' Before the Beatles had left for London, people would queue the day before they played to ensure they had seats.

We all piled into Paul's bottle-green Ford Classic and headed for Mathew Street. We turned the corner and there was a queue snaking along the street.

'Is this for us?' Ringo asked, craning his neck to look.

Mathew Street was so narrow that we couldn't turn round, we had to keep going. We drove on towards the crowd and as people began to realise that the car slowing down had the Beatles in it, I experienced Beatlemania first-hand. Paul wound the window down; girls were screaming, men were shaking his hand. The crowd surged round the car and it began to rock. I hid under the lads' coats in the back and waited for the fuss to die down. Eventually Paul was allowed to wind his window up and we drove on. I came out from under my pile of coats.

'Well, I think they still remember us,' Ringo said drolly.

We went to the party and that night Paul offered to drop me home. His pride-and-joy Ford began spluttering. Eventually it came to a shuddering halt. We both got out and stood for a moment, wondering what to do, until a taxi came our way and we flagged it down. The taxi driver couldn't believe his eyes when he realised he had a real-live Beatle in his cab. Paul accompanied me back home, and we sat up chatting until the early hours—my mum and dad were away and there was no risk of the 'dirty Beatle' being escorted off the premises—and then he went on his way.

That was the last time I saw Paul for many years.

SINCE SCHOOL my only real contact with the world of acting had been with the group from the Liverpool Institute. Now that I was determined to become an actress, I set about looking for somewhere that might give me some direction.

I heard that a new theatre was being built by Pilkington's, or 'Pilks' as it is known locally, a large glass manufacturers in St Helens that was only a bus ride away from Whiston. The owner of the factory, Sir Harry Pilkington, was married to an actress, and their daughter, April Wilding, was an actress too. They were very keen on the arts. The theatre had visiting companies bringing in different shows and I knew that if I could get involved it would be great experience for me. I was also aware that if I got a job at Pilks it would make my parents happy, as the glass factory was seen as a good place to work.

I began work in the Pensions Department and immediately joined the amateur group. Of course, I didn't like my new office job that much, but, as with the tax office in Liverpool, the people I worked with were great. I decided that I needed to tackle this job differently. I was going to approach it as if it were an acting role. Rather than making my discontent known to all and sundry, I took on my new role of clerk with great gusto. One of my responsibilities was paying out weekly pensions to past employees. This was the nicest part of the job. After a few weeks I went along to the first casting for a play that was to be performed at the new theatre and was delighted to be given the role of a cockney maid. All the old people recognised me from pension day and cheered when I came on. I still have the programme from that show, a treasured possession. There was an article in the *Liverpool Echo* about the show, and when my mum died I found it among her possessions. I was really touched that she had cut it out and kept it.

This was a peaceful time for me and for my parents. I had an office job, which pleased them, and I'm sure they thought that once I'd got this acting fad out of my system this job would offer security and a future. For myself, I was involved in the theatre and learning all the time so I was very happy. I began working part-time at the theatre itself as well as in the office. It became my new haunt—I would operate the lights and do the amateur shows and work there at weekends—it was a big part of my life.

Duncan Weldon, the now hugely successful West End producer, was running the Salford Players, and he decided to come to Pilkington's theatre for a season. He'd seen me perform, and he offered me a job. I would be working in weekly rep as an ASM—acting stage manager. I saw this as a great opportunity, so again I gave up a secure job and off I went.

ASM would have been better titled ADB—acting dogsbody! There was a lot of running around involved, but I loved it because, just like when I was working in the NEMS office, I was in the thick of it all. We were performing one show while simultaneously rehearsing another. From the moment I opened my eyes till I fell back in bed at the end of the day I was working, and it felt great.

I got six pounds a week and paid ten bob on my national insurance stamp. My other job had paid eleven pounds a week so it was a big cut in wages, something that greatly worried my parents. Also, it was only for three months so there was no future in it—a thing that would have made anyone's blood run cold in the early sixties, especially my poor despairing mum and dad.

At this time, people in the theatre company began to push me to look into going to drama school. If I was going to pursue acting seriously I needed to learn more about how to act, rather than getting up onstage and hoping my personality would see me through. The only drama school I had heard of was the Royal Academy of Dramatic Art (RADA), but that seemed so posh and unattainable for someone from my background that I didn't think I could apply there. However, I recalled that one of the girls from the course at the Liverpool Institute had applied to Webber Douglas in London and had got in, so I decided to apply there.

My dad didn't want to know and refused even to speak about it, but my mother, surprisingly, was very supportive and she took me to a womenswear shop where we got things on tick and bought me two outfits for my auditions. This really stands out in my mind, as it was so rarely the case that my mother would be the one on my side while my father was the one who voiced his disapproval.

I recall being on the train to London in the pink outfit that Mum had purchased for me and feeling like the bee's knees. I had two speeches that I had learned by heart, a modern piece and a Shakespearean passage. For some unknown reason I decided on the way there that I was going to scrap the modern piece and learn something else. I arrived at Webber Douglas a bag of nerves, shaking like a leaf in front of a stony-faced panel.

'Was the hope drunk. Wherein you dressed yourself?' I began.

I could hear my accent reverberating round the room. I sounded like Cilla Black! Lord only knows what they made of me. I was terribly nervous waiting for their verdict, but I got in!

When I returned home with my news I thought that Dad would come round and be pleased for me, but he didn't. In fact, he refused to sign the forms for my grant. My mother signed the papers, even though she also wasn't happy about me moving to London.

Years later my dad admitted that he was angry because I seemed to flit from one thing to another. 'You get so fixated on things,' he said, 'and then you go cold on the idea and move on to the next. I thought you were going to go the same way with acting.'

Dad finally relented but he still wasn't happy and insisted that I stay in an all-girls' lodging house.

WHEN WE ARRIVED at the hostel in Earl's Court, which would be my home for six long weeks, the woman who ran it looked us over and was friendly to me and my mother, but she eyed my father and said, 'Men are not allowed over the threshold.'

My mother was much comforted by this woman's draconian

approach. Usually, you knew exactly where you were with my mother, as disapproval was her default position. However, since she had been so good in buying clothes for me and signing my papers, I thought that maybe we had reached a turning point.

I was wrong. My mother looked round the room, her eyes brimming with tears, before saying, 'My life has ended now.'

For a long time I was very upset with her for saying this.

My parents said their goodbyes and went on the five-hour journey back to the Northwest. I was left in a shared room with a glamorous art student and a young Australian girl who was working in the City. The room was the size of an average double room but in it were squashed three single beds, three bedside lockers, three wardrobes and a basin. The art student kept herself to herself, but the Australian would bound across my bed every night like a mountain goat when she returned from her evening follies, crushing my legs. I would politely lie there, pretending to be asleep.

Outside our room was a Baby Belling—a hot-plate contraption that was a mainstay of cheap bedsit-living at the time. There was a meter at the side of the oven and I duly put my sixpence in on that first evening there. I was having a boiled egg, such was the glamour of my first night in London. I wandered off for a few minutes and returned only to find a plethora of pans placed strategically on the hot plate to get the most of this free opportunity. From then on, when I put money in the meter I would watch that Baby Belling like a hawk. Depressingly, it was the same story for the bathroom. Sixpence in the meter and you were given a few inches of hot water, hardly enough to wet your feet. The taps were held together with tights, and then if you left the bathroom for any reason someone would run in and steal your water. It was miserable and I vowed to get out of there as quickly as I could.

After six weeks at college I had begun to make some good friends, and two guys on my course told me of a room in their shared house in Notting Hill. I was delighted to be seeing the back of my nocturnal Aussie room-mate and the Baby Belling, not to mention the tap tights. When they offered to help me move out I readily accepted. From then on things got a lot better for me. My grant had arrived and my living situation had improved. Notting Hill was in the heart of trendy London, and I loved every minute of it.

Chapter Three

Webber Douglas was in South Kensington, a well-heeled part of London, in a beautiful old building. It was much smaller than I'd imagined it would be, more intimate, and it was full of extremely beautiful people. There were lots of girls with blonde flowing hair, who were like stick insects with impeccable diction. I would be asked to read and I would burn with embarrassment at anyone hearing my northern accent. I went to classes and was asked to dance—something I dread to this day—and felt clumsy alongside those gazelle-like creatures. I suffered from an inferiority complex, but in those days I think most people from working-class stock thrust into a middle-class environment felt the same.

Once I began to settle in and became familiar with my surroundings I realised there was a slight malaise about the place. A lot of the students weren't taking the course seriously. The principal of the college had been there for years and I felt that his methods were stuck somewhere back when time forgot. But he was about to retire and everything was about to change.

A new principal came in, a man called Ralph Jago. At the same time I was beginning to make more friends: there was Mike, a Brummie, and Val who was from Birkenhead, the other side of the Mersey from me, and we clung to each other, northerners in a sea of posh southerners. Val had a boyfriend, Matt, also from Birkenhead, who was in the year above us, and he had a friend called Neil who would eventually become my first husband.

Our class consisted of only twelve people, which was a good

number because it was enough to have an audience for any performance you gave. One day we were talking to the new principal. He was really inspirational, and when he spoke we all listened. He asked, 'Can anyone who's working class put their hands up?'

The three of us sheepishly put up our hands.

Ralph Jago pointed to myself, Val and Mike. 'These are the ones to watch, because they are the next generation of young actors with angry, working-class voices.'

It was the time of John Osborne and Harold Pinter, and kitchen-sink dramas like *A Taste of Honey*. *Coronation Street* was already on, and suddenly this part of society, my part of society, was being seen and heard in the theatre and on screen. From then on we were laying on our accents and thoroughly enjoying the thought of being at the centre of this new wave of modern theatre.

At the end of first year we were all assessed in order to be allowed through to the second and final year. I didn't expect Ralph Jago's criticism. He said that he thought he might have to let me go. As far as he could see I was just 'a personality'.

Looking me straight in the eye, he said, 'You can leave here and be a poor man's Pat Phoenix. You'll work, don't get me wrong, but I think you could be a good actress if you worked hard.'

I felt my face burning with embarrassment. I stuttered something about really wanting to carry on and he allowed me through to the second year, but I felt that I had to come back and really show him that I deserved my place.

That summer I went to work as a ward orderly in a psychiatric unit — or lunatic asylum, as they were still called in those days. I was staying in Lincoln, where I had gone for the summer with Neil, who by then was my boyfriend. I was just trying to make ends meet, and at the back of my mind I knew that whatever the job was like it wouldn't be dull and it would be grist to the acting mill.

I was charged with varied tasks. I would make up beds, clean, empty bedpans and look after the patients and talk to them. There were three ladies who were in their seventies but had the mental age of toddlers and I loved spending time with them. They viewed the world with such childlike wonder. We would pack them off to 'nursery' every day and they would all hold hands and walk together. They would then amuse themselves with books and toys. When I think about how frightened my own mother could be in her final years, when she was having one of her delusional episodes, it is nice to look back and think how happy these ladies were. Most of the women in there had had nervous breakdowns of some sort but a few had been there for many years, put into a psychiatric ward simply for having a child out of wedlock.

I became close to one woman. She helped me change the beds and we would chat. She asked me if I would teach her the Twist, which I duly did. A few days later something triggered an episode of psychosis in her and she began screaming and grabbed one of the staff, threatening them. The next time I saw her she was heavily sedated, and the whole incident really upset me.

Once back at drama school after the summer break, the new play that we were to perform was announced. By an extraordinary coincidence, it was *Marat/Sade* by Peter Weiss, or to give it its full, not very succinct title: *The Persecution and Assassination of Jean-Paul Marat as Performed by the Inmates of the Asylum of Charenton Under the Direction of the Marquis de Sade*. It is a play within a play, and I was cast as Charlotte Corday, a woman institutionalised for suffering from narcolepsy. It was the perfect role for me to show that I could embody a part — I'd just had a full summer of research to draw from.

The role of Charlotte Corday wasn't one I would have been drawn to in my first year as she was very well spoken. But this was what Ralph Jago had meant when he said that I might just become a character actress. I was avoiding taking on the challenge of speaking with a voice that wasn't my own, or inhabiting a character that wasn't close to my own personality.

In performing this role I proved to myself that I could rise to the challenge. We performed the play and it went down very well. I was pleased with my performance and I felt that I had finally got what it meant to be an actress.

I went to Ralph Jago's office the following day filled with trepidation, but he told me that he had been thrilled by it. I was so relieved; I left the room on a high, convinced that I'd finally arrived, but the very next play we did he shouted at me again for 'just acting', bringing me back down to earth with a bang. He was one of the great teachers in my life, and to this day there are still things he said to me about performing that I try to adhere to.

I had mixed emotions when I left college. I was very excited about getting out in the world and trying to make my way as an actress, but there was also the fear that I might never actually get work. I admit that that fear as an actress has never left me. Every time a job comes to an end I feel sick with worry and am quickly convinced I'll never work again.

Now everyone is in the same boat: work is precarious and there is no guarantee of a job for life. But in the sixties, most people felt that their job and future was secure, yet here I was, flitting around, ready to embark on a career that by its very nature was short term. My poor parents must have wondered what on earth was going to become of me.

I WAS TWENTY-THREE years old when I left drama school. In one respect I was extremely independent. I had forged a life for myself that really wasn't expected for a young woman from my background. But when I went back home the important question was, 'Are you courting?' Getting married and creating a stable family life was still the most valued prize for women, even though some women of my generation were stepping away from this role.

I was still very much influenced by this way of thinking and instinctively wanted someone who would love me and validate me. Someone I could trust implicitly and who would be my ally in life. When I found out that my first boyfriend had cheated on me it had rocked me very badly. After that I didn't know who I could trust and, as a result, I'm sure I became needy. I was insecure and needed reassurance. Neil gave me this reassurance.

I had been going out with him throughout drama school, and

when he moved to Lincoln we still managed to see a lot of one another, even though we were in different cities. I was visiting him as often as possible towards the end of my course, and it was on one of these trips that Neil bought me a beautiful antique pearl and diamond engagement ring. I was absolutely thrilled.

In those days you were supposed to save up to buy a house before getting married. Neil and I had no money, and acting wasn't a career with steady prospects, but we didn't care. Mum and Dad came to visit, and although they smiled and tried to look pleased, I knew they didn't really approve.

WHEN I FINISHED COLLEGE I was offered the role of understudy in the play *Boeing Boeing*. It was to tour, and this meant a lot of time away from Neil, but we both knew that this was the nature of the job and I had to take this opportunity.

I would be working with the comedian Norman Vaughan. He had just finished presenting *Sunday Night at the London Palladium* and was hugely popular. Norman had never acted before but he was a genius at knowing how to get a laugh. He'd say, 'Right, I'm going to stand here and say my first line,' then he'd march over to the other side of the stage. 'Here's where I'll say my second line, then I'll pause'—he would pause for effect—'and then look back at the audience.' And then he'd say with absolute confidence, 'Then they'll laugh.' And sure enough, he was right.

We arrived in Torquay for the summer run, and Yvette, the other understudy, and I hired a little bungalow together. Neil would come to visit with his brother Geoff and his friends and we had a lovely, fun, sun-drenched summer. I remember sunbathing on the theatre roof on our days off. The stage manager at the theatre was also a fisherman and would take us out on his boat. We would catch our tea and come back and cook it on the beach. Afterwards, we would hotfoot it to the local pub, the Devon Dumpling, where we would spend the evening drinking and chatting. If it was a warm night we would return to the beach to go skinny-dipping!

I THINK IF I'M really honest with myself I pushed Neil towards marriage. I wanted him to demonstrate to me how much I meant to him, and I felt that marriage meant a total guarantee of trust. I also wanted to be part of Neil's family. I loved his mother, Peggy. She was such a carefree woman. I remember we would go back to their house and stay up chatting and drinking and Peggy and her husband would be in bed. Neil would shout upstairs, 'It's us!'

His mother would shout back, 'Help yourself to whatever!'

She was so laid-back in her attitude. It was so different to my mother, who would have had a fit if I'd turned up late at night with friends. The next morning Neil's mum and dad would sit around chatting to us about what we'd been up to the night before.

Neil and I moved back to London and got a place in Tufnell Park. It was a flat where the landlady lived above us. It wasn't an ideal situation as we didn't have a front door to our flat, just a curtain, and the landlady would march in whenever she felt like it.

We were married in January 1967. I had just turned twenty-four. I recently found some footage of my wedding day and have had it transferred to DVD. I just marvel at all the people who are on it, who were so important in my life but have since died—to see them brought to life again is amazing. The other thing that strikes me is how happy we all were. I also look at myself and think, 'You're just a girl! What were you doing?'

Back in London I got my second job in the theatre working as deputy stage manager and understudy at the Whitehall Theatre, which is now the Trafalgar Studios.

After a while, the flat in Tufnell Park became very stressful and Neil and I began to argue. I remember one argument particularly well. I had been working all day and then working at the theatre in the evening and I was really spoiling for a fight. There was no privacy and it was a large open flat. Add an intrusive landlady to the mix, and the fact that friends had been staying on the couch for weeks, and it was a recipe for disharmony!

Neil was unwilling to rise to the argument. I had been cooking spaghetti Bolognese and eventually I became so enraged that I threw the entire bowl at him. He just sat there with Bolognese dripping down his front. I stormed out only to return an hour later. Neil was still sitting in the chair with Bolognese all over him. We laughed about it afterwards but it was becoming clear that we had big problems in our relationship.

We both agreed that we needed to get out of there for our own sanity. We found a place in Wimbledon and handed in our notice. By then my contract at the Whitehall Theatre had finished, and I got a job in a toy shop called John Dobbie's in Wimbledon village. However, as we had started arguing in Tufnell Park, Neil and I found it difficult to stop, and a distance had begun to set in that I wasn't sure we could overcome. I didn't feel the need to confide in Neil about anything any more and I'm sure he felt the same. After months of this we both had to admit that things had come to an end. It was very sad but, in hindsight, we had married too young.

I remained very close to Neil's family, and his mother Peggy took me in when the marriage broke up. His brother Geoff and I were great friends for many years, and he was like a brother to me.

I was very nervous about telling my parents that my marriage was over, my mother more so than my dad.

I called home and spoke to my father; I was very upset. 'Dad, Neil and I have split up,' I explained.

There was silence and then he asked, 'Are you all right, love?'

Through my tears, I managed to blurt out, 'What will Mum say?'

'Come home, love. I won't say anything until you get here.'

My mother wasn't thrilled by the notion that her daughter was to be a divorcée. I don't think we even knew anyone else who was divorced at the time. Mum was very upset for me, and was wondering what would become of me. I suppose her concern was that no one else would want to marry me, that I'd be left on the shelf. She was also worried about what other people would think.

There was a family party that weekend. 'Don't say anything when we get there,' Mum warned me. So that evening I had to do the rounds and smile while everyone asked me how Neil was and how life in London was treating me, when all I wanted to do was go home and cry. I came away annoyed and embarrassed.

'I'm not coming back again, Mum, until everyone knows. It's not on,' I informed her.

My poor mother. She didn't want the job of telling everyone I was getting a divorce, but if she wouldn't let *me* tell them the truth, then she would have to.

Not long after the marriage ended, I discovered that I was pregnant. I was very scared and wasn't sure who to turn to, so I called my dad and told him. I said that I didn't know if I could have it; how would I cope? Dad went very quiet on the other end of the phone. The idea of contemplating an abortion in those days was extremely controversial. It must have been very hard for Dad. He eventually said, 'Well, you do what you need to do, love.' I knew that I had my dad's support in whatever happened and this meant the world to me. Then he said quietly, 'Let's not tell your mother.'

I agreed that Mum didn't need to know this right now. A few days later I miscarried. At the time I was relieved. Relieved I'd not had to make a decision, relieved that I didn't have to be a single mother at the age of twenty-five. I felt that I could move on a little now, but these things have a way of staying with you.

I HAD MOVED into Peggy's after the marriage ended. I felt safe there, and still considered myself to be one of the family. I began working at a pub on the Thames in Shepperton called the Red Lion, and the camaraderie there buoyed me up for a time.

I got to know the customers well. One of the regulars was a man in his fifties. He would begin the evening chatting away pleasantly. He would start with beer then move on to spirits and a mixer, then he would dispense with the mixer and drink more and more. I had never known anyone get quite so drunk.

'You know, Sue,' he said to me one day, leaning in and waving his empty glass towards me. 'You've got a lovely face.'

I smiled awkwardly and served the bloke next to him.

'No, really,' he said, as if everyone had disagreed. 'You have! It's such a shame about that nose, though,' he added, waving his finger at his face to indicate where my nose was, should I not have realised. 'Spoils it. You really should get a nose job.'

He plonked himself back on his bar stool and his mind wandered to his next drunken thought.

The man I was serving paid and slunk away, embarrassed. I was devastated. The landlord had been serving someone else nearby and had heard what the drunk had said. He lifted him from the stool and ejected him into the London night. But it was too late; I was in floods of tears.

This man's cruel jibe stayed with me for years and years. I suppose it still does, if I'm honest. In fact, it came back to haunt me last year when I had something written about me that was so hurtful that I felt the same pain again.

Last year I was on steroids for my back and had put on weight. I had gone up to eleven stone, which is very heavy for me. It was during the time I was filming *A Passionate Woman*. I am immensely proud of that drama but I find it hard to look back at it because my face looked so bloated by the steroids.

Then something compounded my self-consciousness to such a point that if I hadn't been working on *Waking the Dead* and had to go into work the next day I might have given up acting altogether.

It was the day of the London Marathon and I had been invited by Ian McKellen to go and watch the race from his place. I had bought the *Observer* that morning and I was having a quick flick through when I came across a picture of me and Alun Armstrong — who played my husband in *A Passionate Woman* — and underneath it was the line: 'Sue Johnston looked confused, but wouldn't anyone with a pair of tennis balls lodged in their cheeks?' The writer then went on to mock how I looked.

I was devastated. I already thought I looked at my worst, but for someone to pick up on it and make such an issue of it was extremely hurtful. I didn't want to leave the house.

Frances Barber, who had played my sister in the drama, had read it too and she was extremely supportive. 'Sue, you have to try to ignore it,' she said. 'They don't think they're writing about a person when they write these things,' she said, trying to comfort me. 'They just think that as you're on the telly you're fair game.'

It didn't feel fair. I didn't want to be fair game to some critic.

Without me asking anyone to do it, people emailed the editor of the *Observer*. My friend Susie emailed the critic in question, telling him in no uncertain terms what she thought. He emailed her a rather curt response back. 'Right!' she said angrily. 'He's going to be getting a little present from me!' And she marched off to buy two tennis balls. She parcelled them up and I saw her writing a note.

'What are you doing?' I asked.

She held up the note that she was about to post along with the balls. It read, 'Shove these up your arse!'

I like to think that I'm made of tougher stuff, that I could weather something like this, but it just makes you feel vulnerable. The critic did issue an apology, and I was very grateful to everyone who complained on my behalf, but I was still very shaken by it.

Attacks on one's appearance are so personal that I think it is hard ever to shake them off. It certainly is for me. The nose comment from the drunk in the bar came at a time when my self-esteem was on the floor. I really needed some help: I felt that the grip I had on myself was getting looser day by day.

One evening, Peggy threw a family party and one of her relations asked rather cuttingly what I was doing there when I was Neil's ex-wife. I felt devastated. I realised it was time I moved out.

I FELT I had failed, that my life was beginning to move off into uncharted territory, and I wasn't quite sure how I'd come to this point. I needed some control, and the one thing I knew that I could control was food. I performed in a drama at a summer school around this time and I was talking to the director about a part that I would quite like to play.

'Oh, you could never play that part,' he said. 'You need to be thin to play that role and you'll never be thin, you're big-boned.'

I was left thinking, Who is he to tell me what size I can be?

After the summer school, I embarked on another theatre tour, and while I was away I stopped eating. When I did eat it was in a very controlled way. I would have a pork pie and a Scotch egg at lunch time and then nothing until lunch the next day. I don't know why I chose those two things, but I don't think that matters; the fact was I had begun to ritualise my eating habits.

This obsession with food, or control of what went in and out of my body, wasn't something that I'd had when I lived at home with my parents. It had crept up on me since college.

It is interesting to think about where the seeds of body consciousness are planted. As a teenager, I'd always been happy with the way I looked. I was an average weight. I never went on a diet. We'd have fry-ups for breakfast, a lunch that consisted of whatever my mother put in front of me, and dinner at night. I was very active, expending energy all the time. Food wasn't something I worried about; it was simply fuel for my body.

My mother would occasionally tell me if I put on weight, and if I lost it she'd say, 'Ooh, you look thin.' She wasn't frightened of telling me that my hair looked a mess, that I could do with putting on some make-up, or that I should stop dressing like a boy. But my mother never fanned the flames of what would eventually become an eating disorder.

I can remember clearly when food became an issue for me. While at college, Neil and Matt had gone away on tour for a few weeks, and Val came in one day waving a piece of paper.

'Look at this!' she said excitedly. 'It's the grapefruit diet. We should do it while the lads are away. We'll look great by the time they get back. Surprise them.'

'What's the grapefruit diet?' I asked. I'd never heard of it.

'Well,' she said, scanning the instructions, 'you have a grapefruit before every meal.'

The look of the moment was led by the likes of Jean Shrimpton and Twiggy, and round the corner from our college Biba had just opened their first shop, which was full of little slip dresses. Skinny seemed a perfectly normal thing to want to be.

'And that's it? I can eat what I want?' I asked, thinking about having grapefruit then pie and chips, yet still managing to slink down the road a size eight.

'No,' Val said, looking downcast. 'You can have an egg for breakfast, some turkey for lunch and a bit of ham for tea. Oh, hang on,' she said, her face brightening. I leaned in—what was it? Crisps? I wondered. 'You can have some veg,' she said flatly. My face fell.

So this was a classic high-protein diet. And having never dieted before in my life, at the age of twenty-two I embarked on the grapefruit diet. Val and I stuck to it religiously and miserably and when the lads came back we had lost over half a stone each.

Of course, after a few weeks of eating normally, I was back to my old size and my Biba dress was confined to the wardrobe. What I hadn't realised was that I had begun the never-ending diet cycle.

THE THEATRE TOUR took us to Gillingham and I had a particularly unhappy time there. We were staying in high-rise blocks near the precinct in the city centre. There was a large municipal swimming pool nearby that would become my haven from the oppressiveness of where we were staying.

One day I had taken myself off to the swimming pool and while I was there a child drowned. It was so awful, and although there was nothing that I could have done about it personally, it hit me really hard. I couldn't stop thinking about this poor child and his poor mother. This event compounded my homesickness and how low I felt. I practically stopped eating and got thinner and thinner, still feeling that it was something that I was in control of in a world where everything else was out of my hands.

When I left Gillingham I went back to the theatre where the director who had said I was big-boned worked. He didn't recognise me. My skinny frame was shrouded in an oversize jumper. The director looked at me in horror but I felt triumphant. 'See, I told you I could be thin.' Like it was some kind of prize.

Even though I was managing to work as an actress, I felt very alone and rudderless. It would be a long time before I felt like I got back to being me again.

Chapter Four

It was the late sixties and the world of theatre was transforming. Politics was seeping into not only the performances but the way that theatre companies were being set up. Small co-ops were springing up that would survive hand to mouth until they proved to the Arts Council that they were worthy of a grant.

The Portable Theatre Company had been set up by David Hare and Tony Bicât. As time has passed it has become part of modern folklore that David was an 'angry young man', one of the new breed of directors, railing at the establishment, which Ralph Jago had referred to back in college. I can't say that I saw much anger, if I'm honest—he was just a genuinely lovely director and writer to work with. But I suppose at the time we were all angry in a sense, if angry means unwilling to accept the place that our class deemed we should take in life.

That said, we were based at Tony's mother's house off Charlotte Street in Fitzrovia. It was a very grand place for an impoverished actor to be renting a room; we were hardly down t'pit!

We managed to get our hands on a clapped-out Volkswagen van to tour in and off we went round the country. My first role was as Madame in Jean Genet's *The Maids*, and after that we performed a number of plays, with David writing some to throw into the mix. We would often find that we struggled to pay ourselves a wage, and the places we played weren't exactly packed to the rafters. On one occasion, in Coventry, we played to an audience of two, which was pretty depressing.

Although David wasn't quite the angry young man everyone would have him be, he was extremely well read and was the first person I'd met who brought an intellectualised way to looking at politics. I was very emotionally driven in my politics; any sense of injustice had me up in arms. David was the first person who showed me that having a strong political opinion didn't mean that

I had to lose my rag, that my political beliefs could be expressed in a methodical and rational way.

At the Portable Theatre Company, I still had one eye on my weight. I was convinced that I was too big, so I went to the doctor's to see if I could procure some slimming tablets. I told myself it was because I was attempting to give up cigarettes and didn't want to put on weight, but as anyone who has had the eating demon in their head will tell you, it wasn't just to manage my weight without cigarettes; I wanted them to make me as thin as possible.

The doctor gave them to me and I went home and popped my pills. I completely lost my appetite, I smoked like a chimney — so much for that — and I cleaned the house from top to bottom. I had been prescribed amphetamines. When my packet of pills ran out I went back to the doctor's like a junkie after their next fix.

I walked into the doctor's room and said breezily, 'Hi, Doctor, I've just come to get some more of the pills you prescribed.'

'I'm sorry,' he said, looking at my notes, 'I've been told that I can't prescribe those tablets any more.'

I felt a stab of anxiety. 'But the thing is, Doctor, I'm an actress and I have to keep an eye on my weight and . . .' I launched into a pathetic story of why I needed these tablets. As my pleas became increasingly desperate, the doctor put his hands up to appease me.

'Just wait here, Susan,' he said, and quickly left the room.

I sat in the chair, wondering where on earth he had gone. After what seemed about ten minutes later he came back clutching a paper bag. 'Here you go,' he said quietly. 'And don't tell anyone you got them from me. You'll have me struck off.'

This is shocking, really, a doctor handing over slimming tablets to a desperate young woman. But there was something very manipulative in my behaviour that day. Something that with hindsight was a warning bell for how gripping my food obsession would become.

AFTER TWO YEARS with the Portable Theatre Company, I met a director called Malcolm Griffiths, who had just been appointed by Farnham Theatre Company. He asked me if I would consider joining him. Malcolm wanted to do great experimental work and he was a fantastic director, so off I went. We were performing plays such as *Look Back in Anger*, where Matt from drama school — now my friend Val's husband — played opposite me.

Malcolm continued to introduce new plays and new ways of directing, but when he decided to stage *Much Ado* with an avant-garde twist, it was too much for the traditional theatre board and they told him that his contract would not be renewed. We were a cooperative and everyone felt that if Malcolm was going to be made to leave, then we would leave too.

Several of us decided to move back to London, and a few of us, including the actors Maev Alexander and Denis Lawson, shared a flat in Chiswick. On the surface I was happy to be moving back to London, but the despondency I'd been feeling throughout my twenties was magnified by the move.

I began to take to my room, getting under the bed covers and not coming out for days. I had started painting everything black: my bedroom was filled with bottles of flowers and I had painted both the bottles and the flowers black. It seemed like a perfectly normal expression of how I felt at the time. But my friends were beginning to worry about me. I finally took myself to the doctor's.

'Is there a history of depression in your family, Sue?' he asked.

Depression? I was shocked. Surely I wasn't depressed. 'No, of course not . . .' I began, but as soon as the words came out I knew that it wasn't true. Depression — or at least a propensity to be despondent — had been with me for as long as I could remember.

Mum would say, 'What have you got that face on for? You need to cheer up, everything you've got, you should think yourself lucky.' My mother belonged to the school of thought that says that everything can be solved by pulling your socks up. But even as a teenager I knew that there was more to it than just tugging at the tops of my socks. I used to write in my diaries about the way I was feeling, but the fear of my mother reading them was so great that I would write in code. Months later, when the black fog of depression descended again, I would go back to my diaries to see how I had felt last time, only to find I couldn't decipher my own code!

I knew that my dad experienced a similar malaise from time to time. When he was upset about something he felt it very deeply. I cannot say for certain that he suffered from depression but I do know that this is how *I* have often reacted to things over the years. We didn't talk about it when I was growing up; it was only as I got older that I realised my feelings of despair were similar to his.

So I told the doctor that, yes, maybe there was depression in my family. He prescribed antidepressants, and I went home feeling I'd somehow let the family cat out of the bag.

I have heard it described as the 'black dog', and over time I came to understand why this is. Depression is a malevolent black presence, always stalking you.

THE TABLETS took the edge off my depression and I now felt up to taking a job in a pub called the City Barge, next to Kew Bridge on the Thames. I quickly got to know the regulars and began to feel at home, but I think my friends still viewed me as something of a lost soul. One of them, Peter, a friend from Farnham, came to me with an offer. I think he wanted to help get me back on track.

There was a new arts centre in Marylebone called the Cockpit and Peter had got the job of running it. He asked me if I'd go along to open a coffee bar for them. It would be a stopgap, I decided, and at least I would be working in a theatre environment, so if any opportunities arose I'd be there to take advantage of them.

One of the groups being run at the Cockpit was headed up by Gordon Wiseman. I was very interested in the work he was doing, using theatre to teach children with special needs. He then went on to set up a Theatre in Education team for all schools. I would sit in the gallery watching as he worked and had lengthy discussions with him about his methods. I let slip that I was an actress and soon he was allowing me to join him in the discussions with the young people he was working with. Eventually there was a vacancy for a new member of the team so I auditioned and got the part. It was the start of an exciting new chapter in my life.

Part of Gordon's brief was to perform set texts that were on the school curriculum for fifth and sixth formers. The funding for this group came from the Local Education Authority, so he wasn't allowed to develop any extracurricular work. Observing how he took the text apart and presented it to young people in a way they could understand it really appealed to me, and it was the beginning of my huge love affair with Theatre in Education, or TIE.

For anyone not familiar with TIE, put simply it brings theatre into schools to use as an educational tool. At a basic level, it is just another way of teaching children, but I think that at its best it is capable of transforming lives. I spent two years at the Cockpit and I learned so much from both the people in the theatre company and the young people we worked with.

But then something was to happen that made my newly regained sunny outlook and love of London come tumbling down.

ONE NIGHT I was heading home on the tube. It was November 7, 1970. I was twenty-seven. I'll always remember the date. I got off at Gunnersbury Park tube station with the usual crowd but had to stop to pick up a prescription.

When I came out of the chemist's, the place was deserted. I opened the gate to take me along the lane, under the bridge — the path I usually took. I felt vulnerable, but I'd committed to taking this way home so I carried on.

I heard a noise behind me that made me turn round. A young man was leaning back against the fence and I realised he was masturbating. I stopped momentarily, shocked by what I was witnessing, then I began to run. I heard him thundering along behind me and I was panic-stricken. I knew he was going to try to attack me. I threw down my bag, thinking that he might just want the contents of my purse and hoping that he'd take it and leave me alone, but he lunged for me, grabbing my throat. He punched me in the side as his fingers squeezed into my neck. I heard screaming; it seemed to be coming from far away and then it came nearer until I realised it was me. I was screaming for my life.

I suddenly began to fight back with every bit of strength in me. I was kicking and clawing at him. At that moment the fact that he might be about to rape me hadn't crossed my mind: I was simply fighting for survival. He stopped and hovered over me, staring straight at me, spitting bile—as if sizing me up. I'm not sure if he heard something that disturbed him or was deterred by the fight I'd put up, but he ran off, leaving me scrabbling to pick myself up.

I picked my bag up and ran. He had punched me everywhere but I didn't feel any pain. I was too terrified he might be waiting round the corner. I had a good friend, Kathy, who lived on the estate next to the station, so I ran to her house.

'Oh, Sue,' she said, pulling me in, shocked to see the state of me.

'I've been attacked,' I said and then burst into tears.

'Come and sit down,' Kathy said, guiding me over to the settee.

Kathy's husband and brother-in-law came in. They took one look at me and knew that I'd been attacked. I couldn't look at them.

'What does he look like?' Kathy's husband asked.

I could only describe my attacker's clothes. They shot off in the car to look for him. Kathy went into the kitchen to make me a cup of tea. I felt something trickling down the leather settee and onto the floor. I looked down and realised I had wet myself.

Kathy came back in. 'Don't worry,' she said kindly and took me upstairs. 'Let's get you cleaned up.'

She put me in the bath and I scrubbed myself clean and changed into some of Kathy's clothes, which of course I shouldn't have done as the police wanted to examine me when they arrived. Kathy's husband had called them. They put me in the back of the panda car and drove me around to see if I could spot the man, but I couldn't see him anywhere. I went home that night terrified.

After this I lost the plot. I couldn't go into work. I began suffering from severe migraines and was prescribed Valium. I had to walk down the middle of the road when I went out, obsessed with being visible to other people should I be attacked again.

My friends tried to get me to talk about what had happened, but their kind words had the reverse effect and I began to close down entirely. I didn't tell my parents what had happened as I didn't want to worry them. I wanted them to think that things were going well for me, even when I was at rock bottom.

FORTUNATELY, my friend Jude, the secretary at the Cockpit, asked me if I'd like to move into a flat with her and her partner in Maida Vale. I was able to start putting what had happened behind me, and living with Jude was one of the happiest and most peaceful times in my life. The apartment was on the top floor of an old Georgian house. It was owned by a designer, so everything about it was well thought out and it was a pleasure to live there. I cycled to work each day and felt that my depression was lifting.

I look back at the attack and the subsequent trauma, and feel that it was one of my darkest times. I came out of it, though, and things changed and improved for me. I have learned that whenever things are really bad something good is always round the corner. It just might not be the first corner that you come to.

I WAS STILL very much in love with TIE, but my love affair with London, for the time being, was over. As a team we would meet up with other TIE companies to find out what people were up to in other parts of the country and to share best practice. At one of these meetings the TIE group Coventry Belgrade put on a demonstration.

Coventry Belgrade was at the forefront of TIE, performing their own original work and breaking new ground as they did so. They performed one of their programmes for infants for us, and a section of a play about the Protectorate period or, as they termed it, the Civil War. Both pieces were thought-provoking, putting events in a social framework and drawing parallels with the modern world, but allowing the children to reach their own conclusions.

The performance and energy of the company inspired me. I left feeling that I would do whatever I needed to move up to Coventry and work with this fantastic theatre group. Coventry Belgrade was

My dad home on leave during the Second World War.

Here I am aged seven.

With my mum.

My cousins, Pauline and Marjorie, and in our matching Warrington Walking I outfits.

e drama student.

Joel with his granddad, who he adored.

Anfield with Joel.

My 'Brookside' family.

Dean Sullivan could always charm my mother.

It was an honour to play Pat Phoenix.

The wonderful 'Royle Family'.

Me as Nurse Sal with the rest of the 'Jam and Jerusalem' cast.

This was the final scene ever of 'Waking the Dead', taken under Waterloo Bridge.

Receiving my OBE—my mother would have been so proud.

And I was so proud to see Joel getting married to the lovely Zoe.

aimed at children of all ages, not just secondary school kids, and they weren't married to the curriculum texts as we were at the Cockpit. I was thrilled when I was offered a job there.

Having the opportunity to start again was a relief. The actress Maggie Steed and I were friends and we both moved to Coventry at the same time, so we rented a house together. During the Second World War, Coventry had been hit hard by the Blitz and was still in the process of being rebuilt in the early seventies. There were amazing new buildings being erected, like Coventry Cathedral, but at the same time there were still streets with craters where the bombs had fallen during the war. I was very hippyish at this time. I wore my hair long, dressed in long, flowing skirts, and I never wore a bra or a pair of shoes. We used to wander round barefoot.

There was a pub called the Town Wall in the city centre that had been left standing in what was now the car park at the back of the theatre. We became regulars there. I was by now very involved with the life of the theatre and loved my new group of friends. We were politically active, we discussed politics, we discussed the world, and we wanted this to be reflected in the work that we performed. After a while a large group of us moved into a house together on the main road into the city.

It was at this time that my friend Margot Leicester came into my life. Before we married, in my early twenties, Neil and I went to visit his friend Mitch in Exeter. Mitch's girlfriend Margot was meant to be there but had gone home to visit her family. After that I heard a lot about this Margot, and from what I heard I would have liked to have met her but never got the chance.

Five years later, when Margot and I first got to know one another, we were out for Sunday lunch one day and it struck me to ask her, 'You didn't go to university in Exeter, did you, and have a boyfriend called Mitch?'

Margot's mouth dropped open. 'You're *that* Sue?'

'And you're *that* Margot?'

What a coincidence! Margot and I became great friends, like the sisters that we'd never had. We are still incredibly close to this day.

I think I was at my most politically active at this time. Ted Heath was the prime minister and we were heading towards the time of the three-day week. The country was gripped by uncertainty. There was a real feeling that the government had no idea what it was like for normal, working people to make ends meet. Sounds familiar, doesn't it? But I think that there seemed to be even less hope for the future then than there is now.

WHEN I FIRST SAW Coventry Belgrade perform back at the TIE conference, the director had given a talk when the demonstration was over. He was extremely charismatic and I thought he looked a little like Che Guevara. A few nights later I went out for dinner with our group, and who should be in the restaurant but this handsome director. That evening we spoke, and I have to say from that moment I was smitten. He was funny and witty and utterly charming, and offered me the place with Coventry TIE.

If I'm honest, I never thought I had a chance with him, but once I moved cities Dave and I got to know one another and started a relationship. I fell hook, line and sinker for him, and for the following four years we had a blissful time together. Dave was very exciting and driven by both the theatre and politics. I found him interesting and challenging but also great fun to be around.

One of Dave's hobbies was restoring old cars. He already had a 1933 Morris Minor sports car with a split windscreen, which he thought was the bee's knees. But then he bought a newer 1950s Morris Minor for eight pounds. We had a lot of fun hand-painting it, and Dave bought an engine and gearbox from a scrapyard.

Once the car was in working order, we decided to take ourselves to Devon. We managed to get all the way there from Coventry and were rather pleased with the capabilities of our new car. As we headed back home, and were less than an hour from Coventry, the car began spluttering. 'What's that?' Dave asked.

'I've no idea,' I said.

The car shuddered to a halt at the side of a country road. Dave popped the bonnet open. He spent a few moments looking at the engine, then he pulled his head out and said, 'It's the fan belt.'

'That doesn't sound great,' I said.

'It's fixable. Give us your tights,' he said, holding out his hand.

'My tights?' I had on a lovely pair of brand-new tights and he wanted me to hand them over for a makeshift fan belt? I huffed and puffed but eventually handed them over. I was glad I did, as my faithful hosiery got us home to Coventry!

There was a pet shop not too far from the garage that Dave used when doing up his cars. I had been to see Dave one day when I walked past and in the window were some beautiful, tiny little puppies. They were a German Shepherd/Collie cross. I fell in love as I looked through the window and went inside and bought one. She was so tiny and adorable that I put her inside my coat to protect her from the outside world. I then caught the bus to the garage.

'Dave, I've got something to show you,' I said when I arrived at the garage, taking this tiny bundle out from my coat.

Dave took the puppy from me and she nestled in his hands, her big brown eyes looking up at him. 'She's gorgeous,' he agreed.

We decided that we should call her Woodbine, as there was a joke that someone had told Dave about a dog called Woodbine and people would ask if they could take it out for a drag. We quite liked that, so the name and the joke stuck.

A few weeks later Dave came home with another bundle. While at the theatre he had seen a little dog in the yard and watched as a caretaker kicked the poor little thing. Dave had gone berserk and asked this man what he thought he was doing. He had picked the dog up and taken it there and then, and that was how we came to have Bugswart, or Bugsy for short. She had a tail that curled tightly round and was a real Heinz 57, a mixture of every breed. We felt like a real family, and in March 1973 Dave and I married.

We would go and visit his friends John and Dot who lived in a place called Whitworth on the outskirts of Rochdale. Their cottage backed on to a nature reserve and was the most idyllic place, ideal for walking Bugsy and Woody. I became good friends with Dot.

One weekend they called to say that they had spotted a house in the area that would be perfect for us, so the next weekend we went up to see it and fell for it. We put in an offer and when it was accepted I was thrilled. A few months later I was offered a job at Bolton Octagon TIE and I decided it was the perfect time for a change. I moved to the house and started to settle in. Dave followed twelve months later when he formed a theatre group in the north.

WHEN I BEGAN WORK at the Octagon, the first play we performed was on the rise of fascism. They'd had a request from a head-master in the area because he was concerned about the children in his school being recruited by the National Front. We decided that we needed to see how the National Front operated, so I went along with another member of the theatre.

I dressed in a twin-set and pearls—a far cry from my usual dun-garees—so that I looked respectable and fitted in with the crowd. The police were guarding the event and we were ushered in and told to take a seat. Someone was handing out leaflets with a crude copy of the progression of man from ape. It was claiming to demonstrate that someone from the West Indies had a brain the size of a chimp. I was outraged.

The meeting got going and I've never heard such a load of clap-trap in my life. But everyone in that room seemed to be in such agreement at this propaganda and racism. In the end I got so angry I shouted something out; I was very emotional. There was unrest in the room at my comments and a policeman came over and said to me, 'For your own good I think you ought to leave.'

After that we felt that we had to do a play that addressed this scapegoating that was going on in the community. We devised a play called *No Pasarán*, which means 'none shall pass'. One of my roles was as a young Jewish violinist who had been forced to play at the gates of the gas chambers at Auschwitz. Mike Kay—who would go on to play a big part in my life along with his wife Veron—portrayed a young Jewish boxer. It was a play that taught about the dangers of complacency against extremism and one that I think is as relevant today as it was in the seventies.

As is happening today, Bolton Octagon was soon affected by governmental cuts. We lost our LEA grant and some of us began to wonder if we might be better setting up on our own. We started looking at places where we could house our new venture. The Gracie Fields Centre had been built in Rochdale and wasn't over-run with people trying to use it, so we decided that if we could set up there and prove we could provide educational theatre for the area, we might be able to qualify for a grant to go into schools.

We left the Octagon and threw all our energies into this new project. We called ourselves M6 because we knew that this venture would involve a lot of touring and that we'd be spending a lot of time on the M6 motorway. We worked in Manchester, London, Bolton, Rochdale, all over the place. We did a lot of stuff for schools for children with severe learning difficulties.

I was with M6 for about three years. But the company is still around and keeps on going from strength to strength. It has been run wonderfully for over thirty years by Dot, the friend who found me the house in Whitworth.

Chapter Five

There's an old Native American saying: 'A child is an arrow from the bow. You let them go, you let them go free.' And that is how I have always felt about my son Joel. I may have brought him into the world but he is his own person with his own thoughts and feel-ings, and I hope that I have always respected that.

I was living in Rochdale and working at M6 when I found out that I was pregnant with Joel. It was late 1978, and I was with Dot when I did the pregnancy test. I remember seeing the little blue line and knowing that my life was about to change. At the time my marriage wasn't as perfect as it had been, but I had a very real sense that my biological clock was ticking and that I really wanted to be a mother. Whatever happened, I would make it work.

I felt sick for the first three months with terrible nausea that saw me crawling to my bed whenever I could. Everyone kept telling me, 'After three months it will just go,' and amazingly they were right—overnight I felt fantastic. After that I just loved being pregnant. I understand why some women become addicted to having babies. I think I could have gone on to have several pregnancies if life had turned out differently.

I had been in the pub the evening before Joel was born when I felt a dull ache. My friend Dave Swap was there and we were talking about the fact that there would be a baby here any time soon. 'Well, I hope it doesn't have your feet, Sue,' he said.

'What's wrong with my feet?' I asked indignantly.

'What's right with your feet?' Dave said, laughing.

That night I tried to sleep but the ache continued and got worse. 'I think the baby's coming,' I told my husband Dave, and he grabbed his coat and bundled me into the car. As I clung to the door handle and tried to breathe through my contractions, we came to a roundabout where a police car was parked. Dave put his foot down and hared round it, not once, but twice. 'What are you doing?' I shouted.

'I want him to follow me,' he said, 'and when he asks why I'm driving like a lunatic, I'll say, "My wife's in labour!"'

I think the look on my face made him realise that he might have to do without the police escort and just get me to the hospital.

The labour was an amazing experience. I zoned out of everything that was going on around me, breathing slowly and deeply. When Joel popped out into the world and was handed to me, I just had this overwhelming rush of love for him. I was smitten. But the first question I asked was, 'Are his feet all right?' Never mind is he healthy but *are his feet all right*?

After the birth I slept, as in those days the midwife would take the baby away to the nursery to give the mum some rest. When I woke I walked down to the nursery to see my lovely little boy, still not believing that it was real—the idea of me, a mum! I walked into the room and all the babies were lined up in little cots. Joel began to cry and I knew straight away that it was him. There was an immediate surge of milk into my breasts; it was the strangest thing to experience for the first time, that my body knew my baby out of all the babies in the room.

One thing having a child does is it makes you look outside yourself. It stops you from obsessing over your own problems and focuses you on this other little being who is relying on you for everything. And no one can make you understand the love that you feel for your child. I still find it quite overwhelming.

On the day I was allowed out of hospital with Joel my parents came to get me. We got back to the house and I wanted my mother and father to stay with me and show me what to do! They stayed for a little while, but of course I had to face the world as a mum and just get on with it. That said, it was lovely to see my parents with Joel. They loved this new baby so much.

It was shortly after I had Joel that my marriage to Dave ended. We had been trying to hold it together but things had been going wrong for some time. I wanted it to work, for us to be a family unit, but I had to admit that we weren't going to be together and adjust to life as a single mother. Because the nature of our work meant that we spent a lot of time apart, I didn't find Dave not being there strange at first. But I soon missed him, and started to blame myself for the breakdown of our marriage.

I really wanted to be a brilliant mum. I hoped that I would be able to breeze it, but anyone who's ever had a child will tell you (and if they don't they're lying!) that it's hard work at first. Back then everyone used towelling nappies, so as well as the sleepless nights, the fretful days and the sheer responsibility of having a child, there was also the relentless washing of bloody nappies!

I wouldn't let anyone smoke in the house — this is the norm now, but at the time everyone smoked willy-nilly. I would also have the heating on and it was paralysingly hot. One day I called Cathy, a retired midwife friend of mine, because I was worried to death about a rash that Joel had.

'Has he got a temperature?' she asked calmly.

'Well, yes, he's hot,' I said, looking at Joel sweltering in his cot.

'Is he lethargic? Is he responding to your voice?' Cathy was being the voice of reason in response to my near hysteria.

'Joel!' I said gently. 'Joel!'

His face was red and hot, but he recognised my voice.

'Yes, yes he is, but he's covered in this rash and lobster red. I think I'll have to take him to the hospital,' I said, panicking.

There was a pause on the other end of the phone, then Cathy asked, 'Sue, have you got the windows shut?'

'Yes,' I answered.

'And the heating?'

'That's on too.'

'And is he in his cot?'

'Yes, all tucked in,' I said.

'Sue, it's the middle of summer; you don't need to take him to the hospital, you just need to cool him down!'

Poor Joel was dressed for an arctic winter, but it was the only way I knew. When we'd been in hospital the wards had been boiling hot and we would be chastised if we so much as went near a window to open it. I unswaddled my poor boy and not very surprisingly his rash went within the hour.

My friends and family really got me through that difficult time. Everybody was so supportive and life began to get back on an even keel. The best advice I got, and that I pass on to any new mums, is sleep when the baby sleeps. Being constantly tired just exacerbates everything that you have to deal with. Although I felt down and unable to cope at times, I feel blessed that I was spared the curse of postnatal depression and that the black dog stayed away at this time in my life.

I had to go back to work after seven weeks. Statutory maternity leave was only about three months then and I'd used some of it up before I had Joel. One of the actors who was in the M6 Theatre Company said that his wife would be able to look after Joel. She could come to our house in the morning to take over and then I could come home at lunch time to breastfeed and then return to work. I knew that Joel would be well cared for.

A few months later the actor's wife got pregnant so I was stuck again, but my mother and father stepped in. I had weaned Joel by this time so my parents used to take him to their house in Warrington, where they'd moved after I left home. I used to hate it when he stayed there overnight; I would come home from work to a babyless house and feel bereft. But I have to say that my mum and dad were always fantastic with Joel; they had such energy for him, and there is no way I could have gone back to work without them.

On Joel's first birthday, I was with him at my parents' house in the morning, but in the afternoon I had to travel to London with M6. It was then that he walked for the first time. I hated the fact that I wasn't there—I still do.

Eventually, the amount of time that I was spending away from Joel wore me down. There were times when a week would go by and I hadn't seen him. I realised I was again at a juncture, of the same significance as when I decided I had to pursue acting. It required a leap of faith. So I took a two-pronged attack. I made enquiries to see if I might be accepted on a teaching course, but I also applied to agencies to try to find an agent who would represent me for TV and radio work. I was lucky enough to find an agent who would take me on.

I HAD BEEN with my Manchester agent only a short time when she put me up for a three-episode role in *Coronation Street* as Mrs Chadwick, the bookie's wife. I got the part and was absolutely thrilled to be given the opportunity to perform in this great British institution.

Nothing prepared me, though, for actually walking onto that set. The street itself looks smaller in real life than you might expect, but it is unmistakably Coronation Street. The new houses had yet to be built at the time, and the extra set of the café and the butcher's wasn't there either. It was just the Rovers Return, the row of terraces, the cobbles and the corner shop.

Meeting the actors who played the characters I had watched for years was an experience. I had been an actor for years myself and

I knew I should be calm and collected, but there was something so iconic about some of those characters that I was as giddy as a kipper. I was washing my hands in the ladies' toilet at Granada when Doris Speed, who played Annie Walker, came in. I stopped in my tracks, face to face with a National Treasure! She came up to the basins, nodded to me, and rummaged in her bag. There was so much that I wanted to say but I just managed a strangled, 'Hello'.

She reached in her bag and pulled out a wig, which she placed on the ledge in front of the mirror. Then she took off her hat and fitted the wig over her own hair, transforming into Annie Walker in front of my very eyes. I stood there, still washing my hands, mesmerised. She put her hat in her bag, smiled politely and went on her way. I smiled back, still wringing my hands under the tap. She must have thought I was a compulsive hand-washer!

I was then called through to rehearsals where I was just awestruck with everyone I was introduced to. They were all very warm and welcoming; there was none of the cliquishness that you might assume goes on with long-running shows like *Corrie*.

Liz Dawn, who played Vera, put me very much at ease. We would go on to become good friends. Then Pat Phoenix came in and she had this amazing charisma about her. She breezed through the room, chatting with everyone. She'd just come back from some time off and had obviously brought with her an unlined face. She claimed it was her second face-lift, and everyone was commenting on how it suited her. I felt like I'd been let into a little club, privy to all this potentially scurrilous information. Years later I would play Pat Phoenix in a TV biopic of her life together with Tony Booth, the actor, and father of Cherie Blair. My mother had a picture of me on the wall dressed as Pat with a pack of Pekinese dogs surrounding me. That she loved that picture was due to her admiration for Pat Phoenix, I'm sure!

IT WAS 1982 and my agent had put me up for a role in a new drama that was going to be set in Liverpool. Phil Redmond, the producer, who had previously created and worked on *Grange Hill*, had bought a cluster of brand-new houses for Mersey Television. Six of these formed what would become Brookside Close and the rest were used for the canteen, the editing suite, production office, make-up and wardrobe. Phil wanted the whole thing to look and feel real to both the viewers and the actors.

This new series was an opportunity to show the world that life might be hard in Liverpool but it wasn't all destitution, unemployment and poverty. It was a city like anywhere else, with people moving up and down the social ladder. This was something that hadn't been seen before in a popular, long-running drama.

My first audition took place at the Liverpool Playhouse studios on Mathew Street, where the Cavern had been. It was strange to return to my old stomping ground, so many years on. I was invited to sit down and was introduced to Phil Redmond and three other people. It wasn't an audition, it was more like an interview. I talked at length about my work in TIE and Phil picked up on my political views and pushed me on them. I realised only later that he was being contrary because he wanted a reaction; he wanted to see what kind of spark I might be able to bring to a character.

The second audition was at the set of *Brookside*. It was still only half built. The houses were up but there was no road as yet. I traipsed through the mud to the house that was to become the canteen. I was interviewed by Phil and the other producer, Colin McKeown, and Chris Clough the director.

I was then called back a third time and this time other auditionees were there. As we were all sitting in reception waiting to be called through to read, a big hairy man came in. Everyone seemed to know him; he was shaking hands with all around and cracking jokes. It was, of course, Ricky Tomlinson. He was in a band that played around Liverpool and people knew him as 'Hobo Rick'. I recognised him from somewhere, and then I realised where from. In 1972, Ricky, who had always been heavily involved in the Labour movement, had gone along to support a strike as a flying picket. He was sentenced to two years after being found guilty of 'conspiracy to intimidate', alongside Des Warren, who was sentenced to three years. There was a countrywide demonstration to free the Shrewsbury Two, as they came to be known. I joined it when it reached Coventry, where I was living at the time. To think that I marched to free someone who would become my future husband, not once but twice!

Eventually, we were all divided into family groups and asked to improvise. It was a very sparky and exciting process, acting as different family members. I went home when we were done and prayed that I would get a role.

I spent the next few days biting my nails down to the quick. My friend Veron was staying at my house with her daughter Gemma.

'Will you sit down?' she said as I paced nervously.

'I haven't got it,' I said, despairing. 'They'd have called by now.'

Suddenly, the phone began to ring. I leapt to answer it.

'Hi, Sue,' my agent said. The pause was agonising. I held my breath, ready for the bad news. But instead I heard, 'You've got it!'

I screamed and dropped the phone, then I picked it back up again, thanking her over and over.

'I've got it!' I shouted at Veron. 'I don't know what it is, but I've got it!'

Veron fell about laughing. 'Well, whatever it is, let's celebrate.'

I went in search of a shop that would sell me a bottle of champagne, not the easiest thing to procure in Rochdale in 1982. I managed it, though, and Veron and I celebrated in style. As we were toasting my success my agent called back. 'I'm not meant to have told you!' she said. 'It's meant to be a surprise. Keep it to yourself.'

So the next day all the successful actors were called back on set, put into our prospective families and asked to perform some more improvisations. Everyone was still wondering what their chances were of getting a job while I was trying hard not to pop with excitement. Then Phil Redmond came in, looked at Ricky, me and the kids and said, 'You're our Grant family.' My jaw fell, then I began to jump around with glee, hugging the others, appearing totally shocked—best bit of acting I've ever done! I was to play Sheila Grant, and Ricky would be my husband Bobby.

WE HAD BEEN WORKING on the show for weeks and it felt like a comfortable family bubble. There was Ricky and me and our on-screen kids—Barry, played by Paul Usher, Damon, played by Simon O'Brien, and Karen, played by Shelagh O'Hara. Then there was everyone else in the cast, rehearsing and filming together and then socialising afterwards when we had the chance.

Because both the show and the channel it was to be aired on were new, we had no preconceptions of what lay ahead. As the transmission date neared, Channel 4 held a press conference. We were to be the second-ever show on Channel 4 after *Countdown*. The press conference seemed to be a big deal, and the fact that we were about to stick our heads above the parapet was beginning to dawn on us all.

Amanda Burton was also an original cast member, playing Heather. We discussed the remote possibility that once the show started we might not be able to swan around shops without being recognised, but quickly dismissed it. We didn't anticipate the popularity and notoriety that *Brookside* would garner. How could we? No one had any idea how this new channel would fare. We didn't even know if anyone would bother watching.

THE DAY FINALLY CAME: November 2, 1982. The cast and crew went to a club in Liverpool. We all stood around, looking at a big screen that had been erected, and then the soon-to-be ubiquitous Channel 4 sign came on, the voice-over guy announced that the new channel was in business and we all cheered.

When the *Brookside* theme tune began to play I got goose bumps. We all watched ourselves in trepidation. When it ended I felt relieved.

I arrived home to pick up Joel, and nervously awaited my parents' verdict. I knew it would, in some ways, represent how other people in the country had viewed the programme.

'We liked it, me and your father, but we didn't like the swearing,' my mother said matter-of-factly.

Nobody liked the swearing. Channel 4 received an avalanche

of complaints, and the writers hastily had to rewrite the future episodes, while the editors took their scissors to the ones already filmed. *Brookside* might have caused controversy on its first outing, but the controversy meant that the show had started with a bang. For the actors, our lives were about to change dramatically.

WHEN THE CONTRACTS for Brookside were renewed it seemed sensible to buy a house near Mum and Dad's. There was six weeks in between selling the house in Rochdale and buying my new house in Warrington, so Joel, Woodbine and I (Bugsy had gone to live with Dave) moved into Mum's dining room.

I don't know how we survived for six weeks without throttling one another. My mother would stay up for me, even if I was on a night shoot. I'd come through the door and she'd be bolt upright in her chair, scaring the living daylights out of me. But once we were in the new house it was comforting to be so close to my parents.

My father's relationship with Joel was very special. Joel called him Gramps and idolised him. They spent so much time together, and I used to watch my dad shower Joel with love and affection, always attentive to him, always on hand to answer his questions or show him how to do something. I have pictures of the wonderful vegetable patch that my father, with Joel's help, put down in the garden at the house in Warrington.

I had weekends off, which would be unusual now working on a soap opera, but that was normal at the time. Life settled down for the first time since I'd had Joel and I was very content. I had a great job, a wonderful son and my family nearby.

AS PUBLICITY for the show, we started being asked to appear in magazines. It wasn't anything like it is now. I didn't run the risk of a photo taken through a long-lens camera popping up on the front of a magazine with me in a swimsuit. It was just the odd *Radio* or *TV Times* appearance and the occasional *Woman's Own*.

One of the first times I was recognised was in Kendals store in

Manchester. I was on the escalators travelling upwards and two women stood at the top, waiting for me to reach them.

'She doesn't look as good off the telly, does she?' one said.

'No,' her friend replied. 'I don't like that suit she's wearing.'

I looked down at the trouser suit I had on. I could feel myself burning with embarrassment. Amazed at their audacity, I concocted what I wanted to say by the time I was level with them. But then I panicked. I can't say anything, I thought. They'll tell people that that woman from *Brookside* was rude to them. I didn't know how to behave. I had been thrust into a new world where I wasn't sure of the rules—these women knew me, or at least thought they did. I didn't know them and they were talking about me as though I wasn't even there. I got to the top and powered past them, casting my eyes to the floor.

'How rude!' one of them said loudly.

I didn't turn round to find out which one. I kept my head down and kept walking.

As the show's popularity grew, I became more and more recognisable to people. I found it odd at first that someone would want my autograph or want to chat to me about the show, or get me confused with Sheila Grant. I think if I had gone into acting because I wanted to be famous, as a lot of young people do now, I would have felt differently. But I had been an actress for eighteen years, and this was all new to me. I did on occasion say, 'It's Sue!' after being called Sheila for the fifteenth time that day. But after a while I got used to the fact that I was in people's living rooms twice a week and couldn't expect everyone to remember that I had a name aside from that of the character.

ONE OF THE BIGGEST storylines during my time at *Brookside*—which happened a few years in—was when my son in the show, Damon, was killed. It even got its own spin-off episodes, *Damon and Debbie*, where we followed the two of them to Yorkshire, where Damon was tragically stabbed. It was a huge hit and teenage girls all over the country mourned his death.

One day I was introduced to an actress who was being brought in to play Marie Jackson. Her name was Anna Keaveney and she was brilliant in the script read-through. I thought, 'My God, she's a proper actress!' To tell the truth, I was a little intimidated.

The Jacksons and the Grants became enemies, rowing over the kids. Barry was having an on–off affair with Marie's sister and all sorts of acrimony ensued. One day it all got out of hand and Sheila and Marie had a fight in the street—hair pulling, fists flying, the lot. As Sheila and Marie grew to hate one another, Anna and I grew closer. She was a great friend.

I was learning on the job, and things that hadn't been a problem when working in theatre were evident now that the camera was on me. In one of the early episodes of *Brookside* I remember a director saying to me that I didn't blink much. He didn't tell me whether this was a good or bad thing so I took it to be a bad thing. After forcing myself to blink my way through a scene the next day he asked me what I was doing. It was then that I discovered that not blinking too much on camera is actually a good thing.

One of the best things about working on *Brookside* was working with some of the great writers and directors who have since gone on to be huge talents in their field. One of them was Jimmy McGovern. He loved writing for the Grants and we loved performing his work. I once asked him how he wrote so well for women. He said in typical droll Jimmy McGovern style, 'Eileen tells me.' Eileen being his wife. But then he went on to say that emotions are emotions in everyone and it's how you react to them and deal with them that sets the sexes apart. I thought that was such an interesting observation. He has since created *Cracker*, *The Street* and *Accused*.

Frank Clarke is another writer who springs to mind. Frank went on to write the excellent film *Letter to Brezhnev*. He wrote an episode for Karen and Sheila where Sheila's Catholic faith was called into question by her daughter. It culminated in Karen throwing a souvenir lighter from Lourdes with a picture of the Virgin Mary at Sheila, asking if this was really what her faith was about. I then had to slap Shelagh O'Hara, who played Karen, across the face. The poor girl. We retook the scene a few times and her face was red raw and covered in finger marks by the time I had finished.

Whenever there is a slap or a punch on TV it is real, or at least that has always been the case in my experience. There was one episode when Sheila had a night out with her friend in town. This was to be the culmination of months of acrimony between Sheila and Bobby. On Sheila's return, Bobby was waiting for her and after an almighty row he went for Sheila. The director was Ken Horn and he promised me that they would do it in one take. But as Ricky thumped me in the face, I saw my earring fly out and hit the floor and I knew that the previous scene and the next scene had me wearing an earring and the continuity would be spoiled. I thought, I'm not saying anything. But someone on production said, 'Sue's earring fell out!' And we had to do it again.

SHEILA BEING RAPED was perhaps the biggest storyline that I undertook at *Brookside*. I was asked to go and see Phil Redmond. I sat down and he looked at me seriously. 'Sue, we're thinking of doing a storyline where Sheila is raped.'

I felt the hairs on the back of my neck stand on end. 'Right,' I said slowly, trying to gather my thoughts.

'I think we can make it work. What do you think?'

Until then I'd never talked to anyone other than close friends about when I had been attacked. I looked at my hands, feeling nervous, guilty and embarrassed about what I was about to say.

'I think you should know, Phil, that I was attacked when I was younger,' I confessed.

Phil was visibly taken aback.

'And if we're going to do it, I need to make sure it's done with the sensitivity it deserves.'

Phil listened as I told him that if we were to go ahead with the story then I was adamant that we shouldn't just produce a sensationalist piece of television. What we screened had to be representative of what women who had been raped went through. I knew the shame and the trauma that stemmed from such a violation.

The day of filming came and I was very nervous. The one thing that bothered me was that the attacker was to come at me from behind, something that was still my biggest fear. We filmed it, and I managed to get through the day without losing control and being overcome. In the end, acting and performing a rape scene allowed me to get rid of a lot of fear I had carried round for years.

After the episode aired, we received hundreds of letters from women who wanted to share their own experiences; many of these women had been raped and had kept silent about it for years. It is not often as an actress that you get to perform something that you feel directly affects people. I felt that this storyline really reached out to women who had first-hand experience of the horror of rape.

Chapter Six

It was during my time on *Brookside* that I became involved with the miners' strike. On March 5, 1984, the Yorkshire miners came out on strike at the proposed closure of Cortonwood Colliery. This sparked the national miners' strike.

Throughout the seventies there had been a number of miners' strikes and we had grown used to power cuts and everyone making a dash for the candles. In the eighties, though, when the miners went on strike to protest against what they saw as the plan to shut down mines systematically across the country, it became a battle of wills: Margaret Thatcher versus the miners. Coal had been stockpiled so that there would be no power cuts and the government and the miners fought a bitter war.

I was incensed at the way these people were being treated. Ricky had always been heavily involved with the trade unions and he wanted to show his support in any way he could, as did I. So the two of us began to make collections from the cast and crew and take the proceeds to Sutton Manor Colliery near St Helens.

From these visits I got to know some of the women whose husbands were striking. I was taken by how strong these women were. It seemed to me that they were the heart of the strike. Without the women making ends meet and holding their families together I felt that the spirit of the miners may have been broken far sooner.

The papers soon got wind that Ricky and I were visiting the striking miners and that we had begun to attend meetings and rallies. It didn't bother me that it was public knowledge, I was proud to be involved. I attended a rally in Manchester with Jimmy McGovern. Dennis Skinner, my political hero, was there, and I watched in awe as he walked past me. He muttered something to the person he was with and the only words I could make out were 'Sheila Grant'. Recognition of sorts from my idol! He went on to speak and it was extremely moving; he was an amazing orator and had been a miner himself so knew exactly how the miners were feeling. It was around this time that I met Neil Kinnock and began to attend Labour Party events with him. I thought it a great shame that he never got to be prime minister.

The miners' strike continued, growing increasingly bitter by the week. Men who were police officers and men who were miners from the same family found themselves pitted against one another on the picket line. After a while, policemen were bussed in from different areas, as feelings were running so high on both sides.

Eventually the miners were returned to work—those who had work to go back to—and the process of closing down the coal industry in this country was begun. It was a very sad time, and there was such an air of defeat among mining communities across the country. But when the miners went back, they did so with their heads held high, displaying a dignity that I feel was never shown by the government of the day.

IT DIDN'T TAKE LONG before people got wind that 'Sheila Grant' lived in my house. Strangers would come and sit on the wall and stare through the windows, so we'd spend most weekends with the curtains drawn. I took to not answering the door when there was a knock. One weekend, however, I was waiting for a friend, so when a knock came at the door I answered it.

'Sheila Grant?' the woman asked, standing there in all her finery.

'Er, yes . . .' I stammered.

She turned to her friend and shouted down the path, 'It is her. Told you. Come and have a look.'

Then she turned back to me and said matter-of-factly, 'We just came to have a look at you.'

They both continued to stand, staring at me. I'm not sure what they expected me to do—invite them in and make them tea, perhaps? After what felt like an eternity of me staring at them and them staring at me, my friend rounded the corner.

Seeing these two women hovering in front of the door, who I obviously wasn't inviting into my home, she ushered me inside and said curtly to the women, 'She's very busy at the moment.'

The two women looked very disappointed.

A couple of weeks later there was a man in my garden late at night staring up at my bedroom window. This might not have had any connection to Sheila Grant—he could have been more interested in my video recorder. I threw the window open. 'What the bloody hell do you want?' I shouted. He looked startled and then asked, thinking on his feet, 'Do you know what time it is?' Like I was the speaking clock. I called my neighbours who rang the police.

After this I began to feel quite vulnerable in the house. I think the straw that broke the camel's back was when I threw a party where a lot of the cast and crew from *Brookside* came along. Word soon got out round the area and kids arrived from miles around. After that I decided that I really needed to move.

Frank was a close family friend who had bought some property at auction. It was in the middle of an estate and surrounded by trees. Years ago there had been a stately home there called Enfield Hall, with a villa, cottages and stables attached. The hall had since burned down, but Frank had bought what remained and had set about refurbishing the houses. He said that he would sell one to me if I was interested.

It was perfect. The house had a footpath that led through the trees to a brook. It felt calm and peaceful and somewhere Joel and I would be happy. So I bought it and went back to my parents' dining room while the building work was completed. This time we had a new dog in tow. Woodbine was still with us but now we also had Ben, a golden retriever I'd bought on Joel's sixth birthday.

Shortly before, Joel had been sitting on his bed and I'd sat next to him and said, 'Do you know what you'd like for your birthday?'

Joel had looked at me and with an earnestness that only a child can muster said, 'A brother, a sister or a dog.'

I nodded as if I was carefully weighing all three options up, 'OK, I'll see what I can do.' As a single mother with two days till his birthday, his chances of getting one of the first two were slim to none, but I was happy to go with the third. So Ben arrived in our lives.

We moved into the new house on December 23, 1986. We hadn't unpacked, but we put some blinds up and a Christmas tree, we made sure the table was in the kitchen and we were ready to have Christmas there. Poor Joel was devastated to leave the old house and his friends behind, but he soon settled in and quickly grew to love our new home. And because it was quite secluded I didn't find myself with visitors having a gawp every weekend.

IT WAS AROUND this time that my eating demon reared its ugly head again. I had begun a relationship with a lovely man but he was very keen on taking the next step and settling down and having children together. I really liked him, but I wasn't sure I needed a husband with all that that entailed. I was happy with my life with Joel. I found the situation very stressful and it is at times of stress that I now know I begin to over or undereat.

There were other things in my life at the time that contributed to me turning my attentions to the rigid control of food. I have never liked seeing myself on screen, but I was on TV all the time now and I became acutely aware of my appearance. Having spent years chasing my ideal weight—although I honestly don't know if I even knew what that was—I hit upon an idea. The Romans had vomitoriums, where they would purge themselves after gorging on food. The Romans were a civilised bunch, I reasoned, surely they knew what they were doing?

I began making myself sick after every meal. I was triumphant, feeling that I could eat what I wanted and with one simple trip to the toilet and my fingers down my throat I wouldn't put on weight. I didn't give any thought to what it was doing to my stomach, my gums and my teeth, which began to decay from all the stomach acid eroding them. And that's not to mention what it was doing to my mind.

Looking back at pictures from that time, I look awful. I started to feel exceptionally low, but I never thought of going to the doctor. Anorexia had begun to be talked about in the media at the time but bulimia wasn't really. So I didn't think of it as an illness. I didn't even have a name for it; it was just what I did.

After a while, though, I became convinced that it was damaging me. I was utterly horrified with what I was doing to myself, but I couldn't stop. I would look in the mirror and cry with shame. I would think to myself, *I'm in my early forties, not some silly teenager!* It took me years to confront my fears. It was a conversation with a friend that finally made me realise that I had a problem so out of control that I needed to seek professional help. She admitted that she had been bulimic for a few years, and as she spoke I just came out with it. So was I. Just saying it out loud helped me. It gave me some relief from the guilt and the shame. I finally went to the doctor and told him how I had been suffering.

The journey from bulimia back to health was a slow process. I was prescribed antidepressants again, and they helped kick-start my recovery and gave me a more positive frame of mind. After that I had to be diligent and honest with myself. I had to acknowledge what triggered the feeling that led me to make myself sick.

An eating disorder is a cruel form of addiction, as the person suffering from it cannot abstain as they can with alcohol or drugs.

You still need to eat. Bulimia not only attacks you physically but mentally too, and I am glad to say I can look back on it and be thankful that it is something that I don't suffer from now, although I will always be mindful of how and what I eat.

WHEN I WAS YOUNGER my dad used to take me to both football and rugby and on occasion Mum would join us to watch the rugby. St Helens was Dad's rugby team and Warrington was my mother's, so there was a good-natured rivalry between them. My dad's football team was Liverpool and football was a huge part of his life. I'm pleased to say that because of his influence it is a huge part of mine.

For me, being a Liverpool fan is as much about the camaraderie and spirit of the club and its supporters as it is about following the team. I love being immersed in the banter that goes on at the match. I think that a lot of this comes from working somewhere that has two teams in one place. When I had worked in the tax office in Liverpool in my teens I had enjoyed the slanging matches that used to go on between the Liverpool and Everton fans.

In April 1989 I was working on a book and I was very behind deadline. I had been at the Grand National the previous week and had met a few of the Liverpool players and their wives. I was invited to the upcoming away game: Liverpool were to play Nottingham Forest at Sheffield Wednesday's home ground, Hillsborough. I readily accepted the offer, only to be told by the editor of the book that she was coming to see me in order to get me to submit the manuscript. I had to relinquish my tickets for the game.

It was April 15, and a beautiful spring day. I'd left the TV on in the house while we worked outside. As the game began I popped my head in to see if there had been an early score. I looked at the TV but couldn't work out what was going on. At the time huge fences had been erected at a number of football grounds and the plan was for them to be installed at all football grounds to prevent pitch invasions. People were scaling the fences and spilling onto the pitch. Bruce Grobbelaar was waving his arms trying to stop the match. I stood with my hand over my mouth. Had some sort of riot gone on? People were penned in behind the fences, desperate to get out to avoid being crushed. Those who could, climbed up the stand and were reaching to the upper stand for help.

I called to my editor and we both watched it unfold. It was a truly terrible day. People were tearing up hoardings to create makeshift stretchers. Fans were being brought out and laid on the pitch; at the time we didn't know that some of them were the bodies of those who had died.

I drove the editor to the train station later; the radio was on and they played 'You'll Never Walk Alone' and 'Eternal Flame', which was number one at the time but seemed very poignant. In between each song the DJ gave out more information about what was happening in Sheffield. Each time, the death toll had risen and the reports from the ground had become more harrowing. In total, 96 people lost their lives and 766 were injured.

My cousin Bob, who had gone to the game, called the following day to say that a service was going to be held in Liverpool Cathedral for the victims. I picked him up and drove to the outskirts of Liverpool city centre and walked into town. The streets were full of people heading in the same direction, heads bowed in silence. Once we got to the cathedral we realised we couldn't get near — there were thousands of people outside.

Knowing that everyone was there to hear the service and that no one wanted to go home until it was finished, priests walked through the crowds holding up transistor radios transmitting the service inside. People were passing their scarves along the crowd to be tied to the railings of the cathedral. An Everton fan standing in front of me passed his scarf forward. It was an extraordinary time for both teams. These rivals were joined in this common bond, a city-wide grief. The service came to an end and everyone drifted off, again in silence.

The club wrapped its arms round the people involved. It was like a home for those who didn't know where to go with their grief. The players all attended funerals but Kenny Dalglish, who was player-manager at the time, went to every single one. You could see the grief weighing in his face as each funeral passed.

A month later we got through to the final of the FA cup and by serendipity we were to play Everton. Gerry Marsden sang 'You'll Never Walk Alone', and it was the first time I had seen the Everton fans join in. It was extremely moving. Fittingly we went on to win. We were glad to win but it was a very subdued celebration.

Every year there is a memorial service and every year the names of each person who died is read out and a candle is lit in their memory. It was my privilege to be asked to read a lesson at a service a few years ago. Outside the ground, a memorial has all the names etched in stone and an everlasting flame burns. It is always festooned in flowers and scarves, and sometimes when I'm walking into the ground I'll see someone kiss their fingers and touch a name, something that I find very moving every time I witness it.

MY MOST TREASURED MEMORY relating to my father and Liverpool was having the opportunity to take Dad to Wembley to a cup final. Liverpool were playing Manchester United and the tickets were like gold dust. I had begged and pleaded round the cast and crew of *Brookside* for two tickets, to no avail. Then Paul Usher wandered over to me and casually asked, 'Still fancy the match at the weekend, Sue?'

My eyes narrowed—of course I did, but was this a wind-up? I thought he was going to laugh and say 'tough!'

'Yes, why?' I asked tentatively.

'Because I can get you two.'

My jaw dropped. 'Who from? I'll have them!' I said immediately, jumping with excitement. Paul was friends with Craig Johnston who played for Liverpool, and later that day Craig dropped the tickets at the set. I called my dad with the news that I knew would make his year: 'Dad, get ready, we're going to Wembley!'

I booked first-class tickets on the train as I wanted to make this a special day for my father. He had his packed lunch with him and we headed off to the final. When we got to the ground it was such a delight to see Dad walk into that hallowed stadium. It was lovely to see him taking in the atmosphere and enjoying himself so much. On the way home on the train Dad realised that opposite us was the legendary footballer Sir Tom Finney sitting with his wife. Tom had been known as the Preston Plumber when he played for Preston North End. Dad began chatting to him and the two whiled away the hours back up north chatting about their shared histories: plumbing and a love of football. It was lovely to see these two men enjoying one another's company–both legends in my eyes.

Chapter Seven

Brookside had been going from strength to strength, and Ricky and I did two great specials together. One was in the Costa Del Sol in Spain. We were staying in the centre of Benidorm and we got a lot of people following us round as we filmed or when we went out at night. In the end someone on the production team suggested we hire a villa in the sticks and drive in for filming. It was a beautiful place, surrounded by orange groves. The owner was extremely kind to us and took us to a restaurant up in the mountains. There was Ricky and me and the director Chris Clough and Ken Horn, who was then the cameraman. We sat down, jugs of sangria were placed on the table, and so began a night of eating, drinking and merriment. At the end of the night, when we were all fit to burst and sozzled, I reached into my bag to get the kitty and realised I didn't have it. By this time the owner of our villa had gone and we were communicating in our pidgin Spanish. In the end, after a number of '*mañanas*' and some pocket-pulling from Ricky, we conveyed that we would be back the following day to pay for our meal. We were. And it became our mountain hideaway for the rest of our time there.

Another time Ricky and I went to film Sheila and Bobby on a second honeymoon in Rome. We were perched on the side of the

Trevi fountain. The fountain is famous for two things: the scene from Fellini's *La Dolce Vita* and for visitors throwing coins in and making a wish. There were hundreds of coins under the water.

Suddenly Ricky started twitching his head and speaking like a ventriloquist.

I leaned in. 'What?' I asked.

'Them fellas, over there,' he said through gritted teeth.

I turned my head slowly to see two men, very smartly dressed, with a carrier bag at their feet. With them they had what could only be a giant magnet, and they were using it to fish in the fountain. They were stealing the coins! Someone must have alerted the police because they were there in moments and the entrepreneurial thieves fled through the streets chased by the *Polizia*.

Brookside was a great programme to work on, but after eight years I began to feel restless. It was at this time that my friend Andy Hay, who was directing at the Octagon Theatre, my old stomping ground in Bolton, contacted me to say that he was developing a play with Jim Cartwright. He said that they thought that John McArdle and I should play the parts if there was any chance we could get a sabbatical from *Brookside*. Phil Redmond agreed to give us two months off and so John and I began workshopping the play with Jim and Andy, and the result was *Two*. *Two* is set in a pub, and the central characters are the landlord and landlady. As the play progresses, a succession of other couples come in and we are given an insight into their lives as well. The play was very simple, with all the characters played by just two actors, hence the name. We loved it and felt that it worked really well, but of course we didn't know what other people would think.

We premiered at the Bolton Octagon in the summer of 1990, and the play was extremely well received. John and I were thrilled. We went on to win the *Manchester Evening News* Theatre Award for best new play. After that, we took it to Edinburgh for the festival. Again we got a great response. We were really pleased with what we'd achieved, and when we went back to *Brookside* things never really felt the same again.

I wanted security for Joel but I wasn't happy. Even the drive to work was getting me down: the same road, the same streets. I knew in my heart that I needed to move on. But the thought of being a jobbing actress again scared me.

A year after we premiered at the Octagon, John and I were approached to revive *Two*, but this time after an initial run in Bolton we would transfer to the Young Vic theatre in London. I knew John had decided to leave *Brookside*. As the character he played was Sheila's love interest I felt that I couldn't bear to see her lose another man, but I also knew that Phil Redmond wouldn't let me take another chunk of time out from *Brookside* to do *Two*, so I decided it was time for me to leave too. John and I left at the same time and had a joint leaving party. *Brookside* had changed my life, and I will always be grateful to Phil for giving me my big TV break.

DURING THIS NEW RUN of *Two*, one of the saddest and hardest things I have ever had to deal with happened. I was very close to a couple named Veron and Mike. I met them when I first worked at the Bolton Octagon, and they had a child, Dominic, who was six. They soon had a daughter, Gemma, who was born six months before Joel. Gemma and Joel used to play together all the time, and had a very special bond. The family had always seemed to be a very solid unit, but later Mike got a job at the Crucible Theatre and they moved to Sheffield, and things started to unravel. Dom did well in his GCSEs but never really settled in his new school. Mike was spending more and more time away from the family at work and Veron was becoming increasingly lonely.

When Dominic went into sixth form he became very unhappy. There were a horrible few days when he went missing. He turned up again, but it transpired that he had been smoking marijuana and then had taken magic mushrooms, which precipitated a breakdown in his mental health. He was later admitted to a mental hospital where he was diagnosed with schizophrenia.

Instead of bringing Mike and Veron together to deal with what was happening with Dom, it drove a wedge between them: Veron felt as though she was having to cope with this on her own, and she began to question their relationship. After much thought, she told Mike she couldn't be with him any more. He was terribly angry, and after one particularly bitter argument Veron went to the psychiatric unit to see Dom. Dom told her that his dad had already been in to see him. He didn't say what Mike had said to him.

Veron was meant to be coming to stay with me the following day, a Friday evening. At about seven that evening I received a phone call from her.

'Sue,' she said flatly, 'I think you'd better sit down. Dom's dead.'

I let out a horrified gasp. She told me that after she had left Dom he had borrowed a pound from one of the other patients and used it to catch the bus into town, leaving a note in his room. He had then gone to the top of a high-rise block of flats and thrown himself off. I closed my eyes, horrified by the violence of his death, horrified by what Veron must be going through.

Veron was staying at her sister Di's in Sheffield, and first thing the next morning I left Joel with my mum and dad and drove over.

Wordlessly, Veron looked at me, and I at her, and I held her. I could not comprehend what she was going through. She was so utterly in shock that it didn't feel like she was actually in the room. I saw Veron walk off; it was all too much for her. She went into the bathroom and then moments later we could hear a banging. She was keening, hitting her head against the wall.

Gemma was eleven at the time, and it was awful for her to witness what was happening to her family. She asked if she could come back and stay with me and of course I said yes, and she came home with me for the week before the funeral.

The funeral was in a beautiful country church. I read the passage 'Footsteps'. I don't know how I kept my voice from cracking. As Veron stood behind the coffin she let out a wail that seemed to come from the bottom of her soul. She was utterly devastated and blamed herself.

A few short weeks after Dom's death I was invited to a party, and Veron said that she would like to go, just to get out and to try to establish some kind of normality in her life again. We hadn't been there long when Veron asked if we could leave. We went back to my house.

That evening was awful; she kept saying that she could see Dom at the end of a tunnel calling for her. The following morning as she walked away from me to leave she cut such a sad figure. That was the last time I saw her.

Less than a month after Dom's death Gemma went to stay with her father for the weekend. That night Veron wrote a letter asking that her sister Di and I would look after Gemma. She then took an overdose. My friend Romy called me the following day to tell me Veron had died. I couldn't take in what I was being told.

A month to the day after Dom's funeral we were all back in the same church for his mother's funeral. Veron was buried in the same grave as Dom.

It was such an awful time for everyone involved, but for Gemma, this poor little girl who was only eleven years old, it was absolutely devastating. I missed Veron but I was so terribly angry with her for leaving Gemma. Gemma went to live with her dad but she would also come and stay with Di and me. She always wanted to talk about her mum. She used to say, 'Didn't she love me as much as Dominic?' Of course she had loved Gemma with all her heart, but that wasn't how it looked to her young daughter. Suicide leaves this huge question that is never answered, which is why it is so hard for the people left behind to get over it.

Gradually, as Gemma has got older and matured, I think that she has come to understand the guilt and shame that her mum carried on her shoulders. Veron blamed herself for the breakdown of her marriage and for Dom's death and didn't have the heart to go on. I've come to terms with that now. And I think Gemma has too.

Despite all she has been through, which also included losing her father at nineteen in a tragic accident, Gemma is an amazing young woman and a real beauty. When she got married I was so proud of her, and I dearly wished that Veron and Mike could have been there to see her and share in her special day. Gemma is pregnant with her first baby, and I wish with all my heart that Veron could have held on, that we could somehow have got her through that pain.

AFTER I LEFT *BROOKSIDE* I felt free to do things that I wouldn't have been allowed to do while I was working on a long-running series. As well as *Two*, one of the other projects I took part in was a Radio 4 play set in a women's prison, using the stories and voices of real women prisoners. This wasn't the first time that I would work in a prison. At M6 we had performed a play about the Peterloo Massacre at Strangeways. Strangeways is a huge Victorian prison in the middle of Manchester. It sits looking out of the north of the city as if as a reminder to the people of what grim fate awaits them if they step out of line. At the time, we were taken inside and into the prison chapel where we were to perform.

Five minutes into our play, a guard blithely breezed past with scant regard for our performance and plonked a number where the hymn numbers should have been. 'Nice one,' a prisoner said, and he hurried past like he couldn't wait to get out of the room. Two minutes later the door opened again and the guard once again heavy-footed across the wooden floor and stuck another number up. Again another prisoner was on his feet, pleased as punch that his number had been put up.

I came offstage and whispered to one of the guards, 'What's going on? What's with the numbers?'

He looked at me. 'When the number goes up it means they've got a phone call. They're just glad to be out, to be honest.' My face must have fallen because he added, 'No offence.'

I don't think my appearance at Strangeways was my finest hour.

The time I would spend with the women in Styal Prison, near Wilmslow in Cheshire, recording the radio play, was a far more sobering experience. I was working with a group of actors including John McArdle again, and the director Kate Rowland.

We were taken through to the secure section where the women we would be interviewing were housed. They were Section 45 prisoners, sex offenders. These women were seen as pariahs by the other prisoners, their crimes such that they couldn't be kept near the others for fear of attack. While she was researching this play, Kate had spent a lot of time with these women. The script centred on a fictitious prisoner who was serving a life sentence, but the women that Kate had interviewed were to play the extras.

We were introduced to the women that we would be working with during the next five days. In their cells were pictures of their children, some that they had been party to the abuse of, or even killed. It was hard, but we had to try to disassociate ourselves from what had brought these women to this place.

The aim was that they would tell us their stories and then we would build this into the play. We wanted to know what being a female 'lifer' in prison was like. What we hadn't thought about was the amount of denial that these woman had about their crimes. A lot of them blamed their partners for the abuse they had been accused of but couldn't accept their part in it.

Anyone who says that prison is an easy option can never have been inside one. The loss of liberty is always there. The clank of keys against locks telling you that someone else is in charge of where you go and what you do. The cells are small and bare. The women had personalised them with pictures from home, but it seemed to me that this only served as a constant reminder of the crimes they had committed.

My lasting memory of working on that project is leaving those women after five days. We looked back and could just see these hands waving out of the cell doors. I found it terribly sad. I still think about them, and the fact that they were in there for life.

LATER, I WAS SENT a script for a TV drama called *Goodbye Cruel World*, written by Tony Marchant. I thought it was fantastic. I went to an interview with the producer, David Snodin, and the director, Adrian Shergold, and read for the part, and when I arrived home my agent had already called to say that I had been offered the role—I was thrilled.

It was about a woman suffering from motor neurone disease, although we never called it that directly. We termed it 'Wey's Disease' — some symptoms we used might not have been experienced by someone with motor neurone disease, and we didn't want to portray anything that wasn't factually correct. Alun Armstrong was to play my husband, with Jonny Lee Miller as my son.

Motor neurone disease is degenerative, aggressive and fatal, attacking the neurones that control the motor function of the body. Alun and I met some amazing people with the disease during our research. One woman lived in a council house outside Oxford. She was very kind and hospitable to us, and I thought it was extremely brave of her to let us in to see how she coped. She showed Alun how to pick her up and how to put her into the bed as I watched her intently, absorbing it all.

We went on to meet someone who told us how people dealt with MND psychologically. And we met the people whose lives had been turned on their heads when their loved ones were diagnosed.

Around this time my dad started to have problems with his health. He had contracted shingles and had been in such distress. One evening as I was sitting in my room, learning my lines, I received a call from my mum. 'Your dad's in hospital, Susan,' Mum said, sounding shocked. 'He's had a stroke.'

I couldn't believe it. It was too late to drive home so the following morning I told the director and the producer, who were very understanding, and I drove from Margate to Warrington and headed for the hospital.

I was shocked when I saw my dad, his face drooping to one side and his arm paralysed. Thankfully, he didn't have to stay long in hospital, and I returned to Margate to finish filming. The next time I returned to Warrington, he was recovering well.

IT SEEMED TO TAKE an age from the filming of *Goodbye Cruel World* to it being aired. During this downtime I threw myself into being with Joel. I would take him to school and pick him up, I'd spend my days cooking — looking through recipes to see what I could make and thinking about who I could invite round to eat it. I spent time with my parents. But after a while the dread that I might never work again crept up on me. The part of me that knew that a few months out of work and I wouldn't be able to pay the mortgage was beginning to take over, and I became increasingly occupied by this concern. I decided that I would take whatever came up, that no part would be too small as it would mean that I could meet new people and hopefully gain work that way.

I had a role in *Inspector Morse*, which I was very pleased to get. I also worked on *A Touch of Frost*, which was in its first series. After this I filmed a play called *Bitter Harvest*, for the ITV series *Screenplay*, which was shot in the Dominican Republic in 1992. To mark the 500th anniversary of Christopher Columbus discovering the Dominican Republic, the government had erected a huge cross on the coastline that could be seen from miles away at sea. It was illuminated, but the only problem was that every night when the cross was switched on, the lights went out across the island.

I returned home, and after a few months *Goodbye Cruel World* finally aired. After the first episode finished the first person to call me was my dad. He told me how wonderful he thought it was and that he loved my performance and that he was very proud of me. I was so thrilled. He also said that my mum had enjoyed it.

The second episode, screened the following week, didn't fare quite so highly in my mother's estimation. I knew that when they didn't call my mother probably wasn't happy. There was a scene in which I was in the bath naked and I thought that must be what had pushed her over the edge. I picked the phone up and called.

'Dad, it's me . . .' I said nervously.

There was a pause and then Dad said gravely, 'I think you had better come and see your mother. It was the swearing, Sue.'

I'd said 'fuck' twice, or rather my character had. A woman with motor neurone disease had said fuck twice as all control over her faculties left her—it seems reasonable enough in the circumstances, but try explaining that to my mother!

I went round to see Mum. She was sitting there, arms crossed, her face set as if she'd just sucked a lemon.

'Well,' she said, with utter disapproval, 'I don't know how you expect me to go into the post office again after that!'

Later that year I was nominated for the *Radio Times* Performance of the Year Award. I called Dad and told him. He went quiet and then said how pleased he was for me. He was a man of few words, my dad, but I could hear it in his voice: he was very proud. Then he said, 'I'll tell your mother, she'll be pleased.'

At least an award might see my mum venturing to the post office again.

I WAS IMMENSELY PLEASED when I was offered some regular work—a part in a series called *Medics*. I played the administrator, Ruth Parry, opposite 'general surgeon' Tom Baker, and it was to film in Manchester, which was great for me as it was near to home and my family. Soon after we began work on *Medics* my dad started to suffer from chest pains. Dad was the opposite of my mother. She had spent much of her life being happy to be indulged because of her asthma. Dad hated being ill and really resisted it, so to hear him complain that he had chest pains I knew that he must be ill.

The doctor referred Dad to the hospital and he was X-rayed to see if they could pick anything up. They found a shadow on his lung. They told my dad he had cancer, and that it had spread to his bones. The consultant explained that he would undergo radiotherapy, with the reassuring words, 'In six weeks, Fred, you'll see a difference.'

I'm not sure if this doctor knew that dad was dying and just wanted to give him some hope or genuinely thought that the treatment would work. Dad was given morphine to ease the pain and I would ferry him to the hospital to receive his radiotherapy.

Towards the end of his six weeks of treatment my dad's condition suddenly deteriorated. We arrived at the hospital but the doctor on admissions insisted that Dad have an X-ray. My father was crying out in pain but this man was keen to tick his procedural boxes. By chance, the doctor who had diagnosed my father with cancer was passing by. I threw myself on his mercy, pleading with him to give my dad some pain relief. He quickly administered some morphine. I was so thankful to him.

I was at my dad's bedside for the last three days of his life. It was close to Christmas and carol singers came on the ward. I cried as I listened to the singers, knowing that Christmas was so near but feeling sure that my dad would not be with us by then. Joel came in to see him but he found it difficult to see his granddad so ill; he had always been more like his father than his grandfather. My mum came in every day but it was overwhelming for her.

On the third day of sitting by my dad's side, my mum and my Aunty Millie came in to see him. Joel had been dropped off at the hospital by a friend and I decided that I would take him home and have a shower. I have no idea why I chose that moment but when I arrived home I received a call saying that Dad had gone into a steep decline. I jumped back in the car with Joel.

When I arrived, I ran to the nurses' station. I could tell by the look on the sister's face that it was bad news. 'I'm sorry, Sue,' she said. 'Your dad has passed away.'

I was distraught; I should have been there.

'We see this a lot, you know,' the nurse explained gently. 'He might not have wanted you to see him die.'

I thought about this and realised that there might be some truth in what she was saying, but I don't think it was me he would have been worried about; it was Joel. Joel was so special to my dad that I think he would have done whatever he could to make sure that Joel wasn't upset in any way.

Dad died on December 21, 1993. I was convinced that we would have to wait until after Christmas for the funeral, but we were told that there was a space on Christmas Eve. I discussed it with my mum and we decided to take it.

Afterwards everyone came back to my mum's; my friends Dean and Janice had put on a wonderful spread and set it all up while we were at the church. After a while I noticed that Joel wasn't around and I went to find out where he'd gone. He was sitting on the edge of my dad's bed.

'Joel, are you all right?' I asked.

He nodded his head, then after a bit of thought said, 'Mum, can we start Christmas now?'

Poor Joel, all this sadness and focus on my dad's funeral had totally taken away from any Christmas preparations. My dad would have agreed with Joel; he loved Christmas and loved to see Joel's face when he opened his presents. I gave my son a hug and a kiss and said, 'Course we can.'

Mum, Joel and I had a quiet, sad Christmas together. We didn't know what to do with ourselves—Dad's death was so recent and we missed him desperately. But my mother and I gave Joel his presents and tried to make sure that he didn't miss out on the day.

I went back to work on *Medics* the following week and Tom Baker gave me a big hug. I felt very lucky to be working on that job in Manchester. All the cast and crew were lovely and very understanding.

Chapter Eight

I didn't feel I had time to grieve for my dad. I missed him dreadfully but I thought my role was just to get on with it, so that's what I tried to do. I know now that grief will always find a way out.

For the next year and a half after my dad's death I was looking after my mother, looking after Joel, and working on *Medics*. I think I was aware that as soon as I stopped, the fragile edifice I had constructed round me in a bid to ignore the grief I felt at my father's death would come crashing down.

It was around this time that I took a step away from the Labour Party—or perhaps it is more correct to say that the Labour Party took a step away from me! I had always been happy to go along to Labour events to speak or just show my support and as such had been approached by the group Arts for Labour, who involved people in the arts and media with the party.

After the shock death of John Smith, the party needed a new leader. It is well known now that a deal was struck between Tony Blair and Gordon Brown and that the job of Leader of the Opposition went to the slicker, New Labour Blair in July 1994. This wasn't common knowledge, but I did think that within the walls of the party it was an acknowledged fact.

Shortly after Blair became leader I was asked by Arts for Labour if I would go along to one of their events. My role would be to make a little speech and then invite Gordon Brown onto the stage to address the party faithful.

I arrived at the venue and there was an air of genuine optimism in the room, and I have to say I felt buoyed by it. Labour seemed to be getting itself into shape for the next general election after the severe bruising it had taken in 1992. Everyone was extremely lovely to me when I arrived, saying how pleased they were that I could make it. Peter Mandelson was there, keeping a beady eye on everything, but I wasn't introduced to him.

I went up on stage, said my little bit, and then I said, 'I'd like to welcome Gordon Brown onto the stage and I'm sure that everyone will join with me in thanking him for stepping aside in the bid for the leadership in order to not cause a rift in the party.'

There was stunned silence in the room. I had obviously said something that no one was supposed to acknowledge. Gordon Brown came on the stage with a tight smile and I was ushered off. After he spoke, everyone in the room literally turned their backs on me. It was the most extraordinary thing. An aide approached me and said simply, 'Your car is ready.'

The following day the woman from Arts for Labour who had asked me to go along to the event called. 'What on earth did you say to Peter Mandelson?' she asked.

'I didn't say anything,' I assured her. 'I didn't even speak to him.'

'Well, he completely lost it,' she informed me. 'He was shouting, "How was that allowed to happen? No one vetted her speech!"'

I was horrified. I suppose I was given a glimpse of what was to come. Up until then I had always seen the Labour Party as somewhere you were encouraged to speak freely, but this was the beginning of the era of 'spin'. After that, I was occasionally asked to go along to Arts for Labour events but I didn't feel that I could. The incident had soured things for me.

My mother was leaning heavily on me. She missed my dad dreadfully. He had done all of the jobs round the house, cleaned the car, scrubbed the floor and tended the garden. He also cooked and used to make a great Sunday roast. Dad had been in the catering corps for some of his time in the army and had learned to cook there. It might have been unusual for a man of his generation, but Dad enjoyed it and was good at it, so it was just normal in our house.

And I can't remember ever seeing my mother look for her own handbag when my dad was around. 'Fred, where's my handbag?' she would demand. Dad would go in search of it for her.

'Here you go, Margaret,' he would say without a note of complaint. He was so used to his role as Chief Handbag Fetcher.

There was no one in my life that I could take any of my own thoughts and feelings to about my dad, so I just bottled them up. There were times when I did try to speak to my mum about it. 'Mum . . .' I'd begin tentatively. 'I've been thinking about Dad . . .'

Mum would immediately be up out of the chair, busying herself so that we didn't have to have a conversation that she didn't want.

'Mum, are you listening?' I would say, trying to persevere.

'Are we having a cup of tea?' she'd ask, making it clear that she wasn't prepared to have a conversation about my father. I found this very sad, but I knew my mother wasn't the sort of person who was going to have a heart-to-heart just because I wanted one.

I began to feel extremely low again, and after eighteen months I slumped back into utter despondency: my depression was back. No one who was working with me at that time would have known, as I was now adept at putting on a mask and pretending that everything was normal. My self-esteem was very low then and I began to feel quite worthless. At the same time I would berate myself, 'You've got a good job, a good home, a lovely son. You haven't anything to be depressed about.'

When *Medics* came to an end it compounded these feelings of worthlessness. I was again waiting at home to see if anyone would call to give me a role. I had moved into a different age group, as far as parts were concerned. I was in my early fifties, and I do think that at this age a lot of women disappear. I went to look at small flats near Joel's school, sure that I wouldn't be able to continue to pay the mortgage on my house.

Mum had begun to bounce back at about the same time that my dad's death was finally hitting me. She was getting out more with her brothers and sisters, and they would go on days out together and fill their time well with activities.

I had begun to avoid calls and to stay in bed when Joel was at school. I didn't feel that I wanted to be part of the world, and eventually I had to admit I needed help. I hauled myself out of the house and went to the doctor's and told him of the bleak time I was having, and I was put on antidepressants again. I finally came out of the blackness and felt a little more like myself again, but of course something was missing, and that something was my dad.

I needed a focus to take me out of myself, and by serendipity I was asked by Comic Relief to go to South Africa to film and see first-hand some of the work they were doing there. I think there is a common misconception that Comic Relief's work is solely focused on Africa, but in fact much of the money supports charities in the UK, and I had visited refuges where women who suffered from domestic violence were given a safe place to stay, counselling and support. On this occasion, though, I would be seeing how the money was spent in Africa. Joel was sixteen, so I took him with me. For both of us it was the most amazing, eye-opening trip.

ON MY RETURN, I was approached regarding a role in a film about a group of miners who played in the colliery brass band as the pit was being forced into closure. After my involvement with the miners' strike, the subject was very close to my heart. The film was *Brassed Off*. It was the first feature film I had been involved in. I went to meet the director, Mark Herman, and was offered the part later that day. I couldn't have been happier.

Pete Postlethwaite had already signed up to be in the film, and I was tremendously excited about having the opportunity to meet him and work with him. Pete and I had been born a few streets apart in Warrington but until now our paths had never crossed.

On the first day of filming I walked into the foyer of the hotel in Doncaster, where we would be staying for the next few weeks, ready to introduce myself to everyone. Pete Poss, Phil Jackson, Jim Carter and Stephen Tompkinson were all sitting there.

'Hi!' I said cheerfully.

'Hi, Sue,' they all said in unison.

I sat down.

'We're just talking about the rugby,' Pete said.

There had been an England game that day. I'd just seen the result. Smashing icebreaker, I thought. 'We did well to win, didn't we?'

There was a collective groan.

'Bloody hell, Sue!' Pete said, laughing.

I looked around, perplexed. What had I done?

They had all been holding off finding out the score and had wanted to watch the match on the TV later. 'Oh no! I'm so sorry,' I said. 'Shall I just go back out, come back in and start again?'

So much for my icebreaker!

We filmed in Grimethorpe, near Doncaster, although in the film the place was called Grimley. On the first day of filming we went into a room where the real colliery band were all waiting for us. We all gathered round and they played for us: the music was magical.

We spent a lot of time in Grimethorpe and met lots of families who had lived through the strikes and the pit closures. A little over ten years on from the first of the eighties' miners' strikes, the fall-out was clear. Unemployment was high; there were drug and drink problems among the youth; buildings that had once thrived with life were derelict, their windows smashed. There was a shiny new uninhabited community centre but it felt like too little too late.

At the end of *Brassed Off*, the colliery band go to the Royal Albert Hall to be in the Band of the Year competition. When it is announced that they have won, Pete's character, Danny, stands up and makes an impassioned speech declining the award. This has become one of the most memorable speeches in British cinema. Before it was filmed, Mark, the director, gathered us all round and said that he wasn't going to do a run-through. Pete was going to do one speech and that was the one he would use in the film.

Pete took to the rostrum and began speaking. The words encapsulated everything I felt about the miners' strike.

> 'In the last ten years this bloody government has systematically destroyed an entire industry. *Our industry*. And not just our industry: our communities, our homes, our lives. All in the name of progress and for a few lousy bob.'

Danny's anger, *Pete's* anger, was palpable. The Grimethorpe band were in the background as extras. I saw their heads bow, it was such a powerful, heartbreaking speech, and I can't think of another actor who could have made it with such force and passion.

We finished filming and all said our goodbyes, off to work on other projects. I never know if something I have been in will be a success—I have no barometer for that sort of thing. I just knew that I'd really enjoyed myself and hoped that it would be well received.

Brassed Off was released in cinemas and was a huge hit. When Pete died I was terribly sad. He was such a lovely man, and it was a great loss not only to his friends and family but to the world of theatre and film when he passed away. I went to his memorial service in Shoreditch. The Grimethorpe Colliery band were there, and when they played 'Danny Boy' it was especially poignant. The service was a beautiful and moving tribute to a truly great man.

WHEN JOEL WAS EIGHTEEN he got a place at college studying graphic design. Having always been sure that when he left home I would not behave the way my own mother had, and declare that my life was over, I was shocked to find how upset I was.

I drove him to Wrexham, which would be his new home, and helped him unpack his belongings. As we sorted out his room, some of the other lads who Joel would share the house with, and who would become his great friends, came in and introduced themselves. I was happy that he was about to embark on a new adventure but I have to admit I was bereft. I drove home in tears.

Once home I took the dogs out for a walk but felt totally despondent. I thought things might improve the next day but I awoke still feeling desolate. I passed a young woman pushing a pram and I began to cry. I was a wreck. Susie called in, and seeing my face all puffed up asked quite reasonably, 'What are you crying for?'

'It's Joel . . .' I said, descending into tears again before I could finish my sentence.

'What's happened?' Susie asked, looking alarmed.

'Nothing, it's just he's gone, hasn't he?' I sobbed.

I think Susie thought I'd gone mad. 'He's back on Friday, isn't he?'

I soon got used to the fact that Joel was at college and would look forward to the times he was home, but I threw myself into work again and was very glad that I had my career.

Suddenly, I began to understand what my mother had gone through. When she was raising me, I was her life. Joel is the most important person to me in the world, but I had a career that I'd maintained throughout his childhood, so when he left home I had something else to be getting on with.

It was around this time that I was asked by Ron Rose, a northern writer who had worked at the Bolton Octagon, if I would play Pat Phoenix in *The Things You Do for Love*. Having met—and been overawed by—the woman herself I readily agreed.

I had never taken on the role of someone real before, and I certainly wasn't an impersonator, so I sat down and watched hours of footage of her, trying to get her manner and her character right. I learned a lot about her that I hadn't known. She had had a tempestuous relationship with Tony Booth, Cherie Blair's father, an actor famous for his role in *Till Death Us Do Part*.

Tony was involved in a terrible accident where he was horribly burned and scarred, and returned to Pat on his uppers. She took him in and looked after him. After this, she herself contracted lung cancer, and we filmed at the hospital where she had been nursed.

She had been a lifelong heavy smoker and even in her hospital bed she'd had an ashtray.

I met one of the nurses who had looked after her in her final weeks. 'Why did you allow her to smoke when she was so ill?' I asked. I wasn't being facetious, I was genuinely interested.

'It was her only pleasure,' she admitted. 'We just thought there was no point in denying her something she enjoyed so much in her final days.'

Pat married Tony Booth on her deathbed. She lasted another eight days and died in her sleep. She had been such a vibrant, strong woman and her love for this man had spanned her life. I thought it was a very moving story.

LATER THAT YEAR Ricky Tomlinson was at the Royal Television Awards in Manchester when he was approached by Caroline Aherne at the bar. Caroline was already well known from her roles in *The Fast Show* and her own show *Mrs Merton*, which had been a huge success. She told Ricky that she was writing a comedy.

'You're going to be my dad, and Sue Johnston's going to be my mum,' she said matter-of-factly.

For a few years after *Brookside* finished Ricky and I hadn't seen one another, but we were reunited in a small film, *Preaching to the Perverted*. It was after this that Ricky called me to tell me about his encounter with Caroline. The idea of playing husband and wife again might seem a strange thing to do after being such well-established characters for years, but the Royles were very different from the Grants so we both agreed to do it.

The scripts arrived and were brilliantly funny but so sparse, and nothing really seemed to happen—it wasn't like any other TV script I'd seen before. I rang Ricky to see what he thought.

'It'll either be a cult hit or they'll be showing it on the graveyard slot because no one gets it. I don't think there'll be an in between,' he said frankly.

We went to the read-through at Granada. There were heads of production from Granada Studios and from the BBC in London, along with the writing team consisting of Caroline, Craig Cash and Henry Normal. I was very excited when I saw the other actors. There was, of course, Liz Smith, a very young Ralf Little, Ricky, Caroline and Craig, who played Dave. We read the scripts and laughed a lot.

Afterwards, the Granada and BBC heads took the writers to one side, and they had a heated discussion while we all sat there wondering what on earth was going on. Eventually Caroline told us to go across to the V&A Hotel over the road from Granada and said she would join us as soon as possible.

She and Craig came over a little later and explained why everything had ground to a halt. The heads of production were worried that without an audience or canned laughter or music—which had been the norm in comedy—then it would just feel too strange. It hadn't been done before and they were concerned. Caroline said that she and Craig were adamant that it should be very naturalistic, as if we were just watching a family in their living room. They came to an uneasy compromise. We filmed the pilot in a studio as if we were performing in front of an audience.

When it was shot it wasn't at all what Caroline or Craig had wanted. Caroline was so embarrassed by the tape that she buried it in her brother's garden. The writers reconvened and rewrote the episodes; they brought in a new director and we reshot it. Now it was filmed like a fly-on-the-wall documentary as Caroline had wanted. There were no obvious gags, no clever put-downs, the pauses were long and natural and the characters were all sitting watching the telly! I remember one direction that jumped out at me when I first read the script: 'They all suck a mint.' Imagine a minute of TV time taken up by a family sucking on mints! I loved it, but I had no idea if anyone else would.

The Royle Family aired for the first time on September 14, 1998. No one anticipated the reaction we received. Overnight it seemed people took the show to their hearts. My family were very impressed. My mother had never been very complimentary about any of the roles I'd played in the past but she loved *The Royle Family*. I think for her it was the same as with most working-class people—she could totally relate to it.

My Aunty Jean was round at my mum's just after it aired. They had been discussing it and she said, 'I think it's very good but I really don't understand why you have to say "fart", Susan. Can't you have a word with someone about that?'

My mum did take issue with some of the storylines.

'Have you been telling them about my cataracts?' she asked when Norma appeared with a patch on her eye after having her cataracts removed.

'No!' I said honestly. 'I haven't said a word.'

'Well, someone's said something. It was on the programme!'

Mum didn't realise that there were thousands of old ladies going through the same thing as her every week.

Then she called me up to say, 'Nana's got a china cup, I drink out of a china cup!' Again, I told Mum that other people up and down the country drink out of a china cup; she wasn't unique.

The final straw came when she called and said, 'She was making gravy this week. You've been telling them about me making gravy, haven't you?' I think she thought I was taking notes when I was with her and feeding them back to Caroline and Craig.

A second series was commissioned, but instead of filming in Manchester we were asked to go to Ealing Studios in London. It was great to be back together. The cast all got along brilliantly. Throughout filming *The Royle Family* I felt I was surrounded by so many funny people that I daren't crack a joke. I felt more comfortable sitting and laughing at their jokes.

The crew built a naughty corner for us. It started off as just a corner of the set where we would have to stand if we laughed when we shouldn't, or forgot our lines, but as the series progressed the naughty corner became more and more elaborate until it was an actual prison cell. By the end of the second series we all ended up in it behind bars!

AT THE END of filming each of the three series we would return home having had a wonderful time together and, without sounding too over the top about it, the love for the show would follow us home. It was great that it chimed with so many people. But *The Royle Family* was not only something that ordinary people enjoyed, critics loved it too. Ricky and I won best performance at the Comedy Awards, the show won the comedy BAFTA a number of times, I was also nominated for a BAFTA, and we picked up gongs at nearly every other TV award show there was. It was very exciting to go along to these award ceremonies.

I also worked on other projects in between *The Royle Family*. One was a series called *Duck Patrol* about the Thames river police, starring Richard Wilson and David Tennant. I'd met Richard before at Labour Party events and I had asked him for his autograph for Joel, who was a huge fan of *One Foot in the Grave*.

My character was the landlady of a pub on the Thames. We filmed near Hampton Court, which is one of my favourite places in London, but more personally it is near Shepperton, where I had lived a lifetime ago with Neil's mother Peggy. I felt very nostalgic revisiting these old haunts.

Richard Wilson had played Victor Meldrew brilliantly, and the expression 'I don't believe it' had become synonymous with Meldrew. He was forever being spotted and asked, 'It's you, isn't it?' He would politely nod and confirm that yes, it was him.

'Go on then, say it,' they would demand, waiting for Richard to say his infamous line.

One day Richard and David, who were both playing river policemen, were filming a scene in a speedboat on the Thames. Richard had a police uniform on with a peaked police cap pulled down over his eyes. He was sitting down low in the boat behind the windscreen. How anyone could have recognised him without actually sitting next to him I have no idea. The director shouted 'action' and as the camera rolled a barge passed in the background. On board was a group of men who were clearly on a stag do. Just as Richard was about to begin speaking his lines, the lads on the boat shouted in unison, 'I don't believe it!' Poor Richard!

In 2000 we filmed the third and final series of *The Royle Family*. The final episode was the Christmas special where it's Baby David's first birthday and we all sit down to Christmas dinner together. Jim gets the best Christmas present anyone could ever have bought him: Sky TV!

After *The Royle Family* ended, Craig went on to make *Early Doors* and Caroline moved to Australia for a while. Any time I meet up with any of them it really does feel like I'm meeting up with family. In fact, Caroline calls me her second mum. They say all good things must come to an end, but on this occasion I wished they didn't have to. I genuinely loved being Barbara Royle.

Chapter Nine

I was at the National Theatre performing in *The Mysteries* and staying with my friend Anna Keaveney and her partner Mark when I was offered a pilot in a new TV drama. It followed a police team who investigate murders that had been closed years before, or 'cold cases'. They used the latest advances in DNA and criminal profiling to reopen these cases and solve the crime. The police had been using these new scientific advances on cold cases for only a few years, so to see it on TV was something very new.

The character I was to play was called Grace Foley, and the new show was *Waking the Dead*. I was very excited because Trevor Eve was to star in the main role of Peter Boyd. I had never met him, but I knew him to be a wonderful actor. Holly Aird, Will Johnson and Claire Goose were all in the cast too. I was drawn to the part because the concept was so interesting and new.

The woman on whom my character was based was a psychological profiler for the Metropolitan Police, and the minute I met her I knew how to play this character. She was warm and friendly and extremely down to earth. She was also very unruffled. I wanted to bring this calmness and confidence to Grace. I also wanted her to appear as though she had a life outside work.

In the pilot a lot of the action took place in a landfill site in southeast London. It was pretty grim and stank to high heaven, and we were all given protective clothing to wear. When it was time to film, the actors were told to hand over their protective clothing and we disrobed and stood knee-deep in muck while the crew all looked on through their white paper suits.

One of the first scenes I filmed with Trevor was of us driving over the site in a 4x4. As we had only just met we were still very much at the pleasantries stage. But as soon as Trevor put his foot on the pedal the pleasantries went out of the window. He shot off at a hundred miles an hour while I clung on like grim death. He drove like a lunatic! When we finished the scene I said, 'Did you think you were on *Top Gear*?' to which he just shrugged, suggesting that it might be something I'd just have to get used to. A few years later Trevor would go on *Top Gear* and fly round the racetrack, swearing and destroying a wheel into the bargain: he clocked a great time though. Looking back I think I got off quite lightly!

A few days later we were filming a scene on the South Bank in London. I had to run across the concourse in heels. As I set off running, one leg went one way and the other went the other. I heard a pop and then suddenly was in absolute agony. I was taken to hospital and informed that I had snapped my hamstring. I was bandaged up and had to stay in overnight.

But not only did I have to finish off filming the pilot for *Waking the Dead*, I had to continue performing in *The Mysteries*. In that role I had to sing and dance and generally jig around on an out-of-action leg. The director at the National decided to work round my damaged leg, so I was able to be on stage, and someone else danced for me. Back on *Waking the Dead*, because of some insurance clause, I was literally lifted from a wheelchair to wherever the action was taking place. I went from being very animated to sitting behind a desk for the last days of filming.

During the pilot we really gelled as a team and we all found Trevor's enthusiasm and passion for his role terribly infectious. When we were told that the BBC wanted to make the series I was very happy to be going to work with this great bunch of people.

From the beginning I realised that working on *Waking the Dead* wasn't going to be an easy ride, but it was all the better for being challenging. Trevor is a perfectionist and he would go over the scripts time and again, asking that things be changed if he thought they could be improved.

One thing that never seemed to get any easier was managing to say the psychology terms that Grace had to pronounce. I would sit in her office and look at the huge tomes and think, Grace has read all of these books! One day I stared at the script — 'counter-transference', 'diathesis stress hypothesis' and 'Electra complex' all stared back at me. I stumbled across the lines like a child trying to get out a particularly difficult tongue twister.

'Come on, Sue!' the director David Thacker said. 'It's got to trip off the tongue! Grace says these things every day.'

'Diathesis stress hypothesis,' I stuttered.

'Trip it off the tongue, trip, trip, trip!'

In the end I went away and learned the lines, and eventually I managed to trip them off the tongue for the camera, but I needed a large glass of wine when I was finished. I would get the scripts and begin learning the lines straight away, scared to death that I was going to come unstuck with the unfamiliar terms.

I was fifty-six when I was cast as Grace, and the role could easily have gone to a younger woman or even a man. But Barbara Machin, who created the series, was adamant that she should be a mature woman. I was very proud to play Grace. All of the female characters in *Waking the Dead* were strong and brilliantly drawn.

I loved the relationship between Boyd and Grace. There was

never any element of romance but they were very close and knew one another extremely well. They often fell out, and he could be dismissive and disrespectful to some of her ideas, but on the whole they were a team. Antagonism between the two was a great way of creating drama and helped to lift the facts off the page.

We would perform scenes where Trevor and I would chat in the office. Over time the writers allowed us to ad-lib them as they trusted us to know what the two characters would talk about. One scene I remember well was when Trevor suggested to the director that he should be doing something in the scene and suggested he wash his feet. There is something quite personal about someone getting their size tens out and scrubbing them in front of a colleague, and I think it said a huge amount about how relaxed the two characters were with each other.

Waking the Dead went on to run for ten series. The crew who worked on it were fantastic. I think the success of the show was down to the chemistry of the team, and that the scripts were brilliant and credited the audience with the intelligence they deserved.

DURING ONE OF the breaks in filming *Waking the Dead* I was in *The Play What I Wrote*, a comical look at the comedy duo Morecambe and Wise and the relationship between comedy duos in general. We started at the Liverpool Playhouse and went on to Wyndham's Theatre in London. In the second half of the play a guest artist would appear to star in 'the play what I wrote'. We did a special performance for the Prince's Trust and I was delighted when Kylie Minogue agreed to be the guest star. She was great fun, very down to earth and sweet. Afterwards I arrived at the party to see her sitting with Dawn French and Jennifer Saunders. It was before *Jam and Jerusalem*, which I would work on with them. Dawn's face dropped when she saw me. She looked horrified; I wondered what I had done.

'What?' I asked.

'We've just spent all day being you,' Dawn replied.

'Being me?' I exclaimed. I couldn't think what she could mean.

'We're doing *Waking the Dead* for the Christmas Special,' she explained. 'I'm you and Jennifer's Boyd.'

I laughed, extremely flattered. I have to say that, in my opinion, to have French and Saunders perform a skit of your show means you've arrived.

'Right,' I said, sitting down next to them. 'Do you want some tips?'

I let them into a few trade secrets, one of which was that when we remove our glasses and put them back on again, it's usually because we were looking at a script. When the sketch came out they had us putting on and taking off the glasses throughout.

The next time I would meet Jennifer would be by pure coincidence, but it would be the start of a new friendship.

Susie and I had gathered a group of us together to stay in a pub-cum-bar in Devon for the New Year. We had discovered it the previous summer. It was on the moors with roaring log fires.

On New Year's Eve, I got dolled up and headed to the bar to meet my friends and family. As I was sitting there, who should be in a corner, with her husband Ade and their children, but Jennifer Saunders. It turned out that the landlord was Jennifer's brother.

I got a drink and went to sit with them, and Jennifer said, 'I'm writing a series for you, Sue.'

I was delighted. I loved *French and Saunders* and *Absolutely Fabulous* and I was thrilled with the idea of being in Jennifer's next show.

'And,' she went on, 'the woman I'm basing it on is over here. Come and meet her.' She took me over to meet her friend Cindy and we had a good chat. And this is how I first heard about *Jam and Jerusalem*.

The evening descended into drunken debauchery and we all had a marvellous time, playing parlour games that none of us could quite keep up with and chatting into the wee small hours.

I woke the next day with a sore head and returned to London hoping that I would hear from Jennifer but putting it to the back of my mind. Eventually, months later, my agent rang to say that a script had arrived. I loved it and was delighted to hear who else was going to be in the cast, among them my friend Maggie Steed, whom I had known since the early seventies.

When I arrived in Devon to begin filming it was to discover that my home for the next couple of months would be Jennifer's brother's pub. My overriding memory of my time on *Jam and Jerusalem* was how much we laughed. As on *The Royle Family*, I was surrounded by funny people. We would have great evenings out after filming, and I remember one evening sitting in the pub getting merrily merry when I got chatting to one of the supporting artists. He was very friendly and asked me if I'd ever considered a tattoo. I hadn't, I told him, but now that he mentioned it . . .

So I sat with him for the rest of the night, carefully planning what my tattoo was going to look like. I was going to mark my dedication to Liverpool for life. I stopped short of suggesting Steven Gerrard's head and decided on a simple Liver Bird, the symbol of the club.

The following day, when I arrived on set, the tattooist was there, ready for me with his equipment. I looked at him in horror. I had to tell him politely that I wouldn't be requiring a tattoo after all.

IT WAS AROUND this time that I noticed a real decline in my mother. Things had been going downhill for the past few years but now it was getting serious. My mum had, of course, always been a forceful character and that extended to telling me her opinion of old people's homes.

'You're not putting me in a home!' she had told me on numerous occasions.

So when the strong, forthright, no-nonsense woman I had grown up with began to be beset by health problems, I, at first, tried to care for her myself. I would head home at the weekend, after filming *Jam and Jerusalem*, to look after her.

Over the past few years her respiratory problems had worsened. She had also begun to suffer falls that were becoming increasingly severe. I had to admit that she was a danger to herself, doing things like leaving the gas on and not realising she had. Her mind was becoming affected by dementia: one day she would be fine, the next she would be imagining things. She began to have an ongoing hallucination about a young boy who lived on the roof, whom she could see through the window.

Sometimes I arrived to find her particularly agitated.

'He's getting wet,' she said anxiously.

I sat down in the chair next to her. 'Who?' I asked.

'The boy on the roof. It's raining and no one's brought him in, poor love. He's feeding them birds but who's feeding him?' She looked worried. 'I'm not sure he's looked after,' Mum added, straining her neck to look at the roof outside.

I strained my neck too, knowing full well that there was no one there. After a good while listening to my mother's tales, I headed into the kitchen to make a cup of tea. On my return she looked much happier. 'Next door have put a telly in the top room for him so he can watch his programmes,' she said, satisfied.

'That's nice of them, isn't it?' I said agreeably, supping my tea.

We used to have these conversations over and over again. At times I did feel as though I was going doolally myself but I didn't want to burst my mother's bubble. The doctor said it would frighten her if she were to be confronted with the truth when she was so convinced of what she imagined.

One day, one of my uncles came to visit. My mother was happily telling him all about the boy on the roof when he snapped at her, pulling back the curtains and gesticulating out of the window. 'For God's sake, Margaret, there's no one there!'

My mother's face crumpled. She looked distraught and went very quiet. When my uncle had gone she became tearful and said to me, 'They think I'm mad, don't they?'

I hated seeing her like this, upset and frightened. It was far better to pretend that what she imagined was actually happening.

But sometimes I had to disillusion her for her own good. She would call me in the middle of the night, confused and distressed. She would have fallen asleep and then woken up, not knowing what time it was, got dressed, put on the TV and fallen asleep again in front of it. Whatever was on the TV so late at night would form the backbone to her confused state.

Once, the phone began to ring at two o'clock in the morning. I jumped out of bed. 'Hello!' I shouted into the receiver.

Although I knew at the back of my mind that it would be my mother, there was always the fear that it was someone else ringing because something had happened to her—if she'd managed to get out of the house and was wandering round, or had had a fall, or something even worse.

'Susan!' she shouted hysterically. 'Your leg! What's happened to your leg?'

'Nothing, Mum,' I reassured her. 'My leg is fine.'

'It's not. It's on the telly now and it's gashed open. There's blood everywhere.'

'Mum, I'm looking at both of my legs and honestly, they're fine.'

'It's hanging off!'

'It isn't, Mum!'

'Have they stopped the bleeding?'

'There isn't any bleeding, Mum, honestly.'

'But it's on the telly, Susan, I can see it.'

Mum sounded so utterly distraught that I was desperate to calm her down. Knowing that there was little I could do to allay her fears from 200 miles away, I put the phone to my legs, stamped on the floor several times and shouted, 'Look, I'm fine, Mother, two legs, in perfect working order.'

There was silence on the other end of the phone as Mum tried to take this in. Then she said quietly, 'Oh well, OK. If you're sure.'

'I'm sure, Mum. Try to get some sleep.'

She eventually believed me and went back to bed. These incidents were so distressing for her because she believed in the reality of them. Throughout my mother's dementia she would see members of the family that had long since died and inform me that they had just been in to visit. But she only ever imagined that she had seen my father once. I arrived one day to find her sitting quietly, looking very displeased.

'You all right, Mum?' I asked.

She nodded towards the bedroom. 'He's in there, sulking.'

'Who is?' I asked.

'Your father,' she said. 'I'm not going in while he's in there.'

I went into the bedroom and came back out again. 'It's all right, Mum, he's gone,' I said, and after that she never claimed to have seen him again.

THE GUILT that I used to feel leaving Joel as a boy when I went to work was now replaced with the guilt of working while my mother was ill. Throughout this time I soldiered on, trying to look after her myself and work at the same time. I was living life on an ad hoc basis, with no time for myself, just work and spending time looking after my mother. My Aunty Jean and other members of my family were brilliant and mucked in constantly, and Susie was always on the other end of the phone ready to help out with my mother while I was away working. My family and Susie lived nearby and were an absolute godsend.

My mother, on the other hand, didn't quite see things the way I did. While everyone else was busy making sure that she was looked after, she made her feelings quite clear. I should give up work and move back to Warrington to look after her. She wanted me near. 'Why couldn't you have married a plumber?' she would still ask with great disappointment.

One day I arrived at my mother's, laden down with shopping, and set about stocking the fridge. She must have felt that she had exhausted the 'Why couldn't you have married a plumber?' line of attack so instead she said, 'I wish you'd never had an education!'

I took a deep breath, bit my tongue and continued filling the fridge. Of course, my mother's disappointment in me was nothing new—she'd been saying things like this all my life—but it was frustrating. I was working flat out, flying up the motorway any time I had a day off, only to be greeted with constant criticism.

As my mother's health began to get worse, I was receiving constant worried phone calls at work. When she had a fall that saw her hospitalised again I knew that I had to do something. I decided that I needed to get some outside carers in to help.

Mum was extremely truculent when presented with these women invading her space, as she saw it. I would no sooner be through the door than she would whisper conspiratorially. 'Them nurses,' she hissed referring to her carers, 'they're taking my tea bags. They stick them in their pockets and go out with them.'

I would tell her that I didn't think that was the case.

'They do!' she would protest, getting upset. 'You don't know what it's like because you're not here to see it.'

I managed to talk my mum round and convince her that the carers were a good thing, but she still kept an eye on her PG Tips.

A FEW MONTHS EARLIER I had received a call from Caroline Aherne. I thought she was calling up for a chat but she said, 'Sue, I'm going to do another *Royle Family*, are you in?'

She explained that she had been to her grandmother's funeral in Ireland and it had made her think that she wanted to do another *Royle Family*. The one thing she would be really sad about was to kill Nana off, but if we were coming back after six years then it had to be for something big.

Meeting up with everyone again was fantastic. Six years on, Anthony was all grown up and we were all back in the house with Nana living in the living room. Caroline had written in the script that Nana picks up a magnifying glass and we see her big magnified eye through it, something she had seen her own grandmother do. I was in hysterics watching Liz do this and it still makes me smile now thinking about it.

It was great to all be back together, but while we were filming I was leaving the set and heading straight to see Mum. There is a scene in the episode where Jim puts down a laminate floor. I'm not in it because I had been called to the hospital. After we filmed the scenes by Nana's bedside as she is dying, I again had to head straight to my mum's bedside in the hospital. It was very sad for me. Liz reminded me of my mother. In her later years Mum had snow-white hair like the wig Liz wore as Nana, and looked quite like her. But it was more than that.

When the 'Queen of Sheba' episode aired later that year I didn't tell my mother it was on. It would have been too upsetting for her, and for me. She identified with Nana, and to see her die would have shocked her.

Everyone seemed pleased that *The Royle Family* had returned, and with such a heart-rending story. I was just very sad for Liz. She loved the Royles—we really were a family for her. Since then we have made three Christmas specials, and Liz has been sadly missed by everyone.

OTHER PEOPLE had begun pointing out to me how ridiculous this situation was with me flying up to be with Mum whenever I had a free moment. Aunty Jean took me in hand one day.

Mum was having a doze in her chair and Jean nodded to the garden, so we both went outside. Jean was thoughtful for a moment, then she said, 'Susan, love, you can't go on like this.'

She was right, of course, but hearing it said out loud made me very upset. I felt slightly underhand, out here in the garden discussing my mother's life when she was only a few feet away.

'I'm going to move home and look after her myself,' I said again, feeling that this was definitely the only option.

Jean shook her head. 'Don't be silly,' she said gently. 'How would you live?'

'Well, I'll find a job,' I replied.

'Where? What else can you do?'

She had a point. I'm not sure there was much call at Warrington Job Centre for someone who could recite Pinter. I shrugged my shoulders, fighting back tears.

'Susan, if you moved back you'd want to kill your mother within five minutes and she'd want to kill you,' Jean reasoned with me. 'You need proper help. Not me, not anyone else we know. Real help from people who know what they're doing.'

I looked at my Aunty Jean and nodded. I couldn't move back

home, it was nonsense. I needed to keep working and mum needed full-time care. But as with everything to do with my mum, it took me a long time and a number of changes in my mother's condition to implement what Jean and I had discussed.

Where my mother lived in Warrington was a great community, with lovely neighbours and people who looked out for her. I felt that if she was to go into a care home it must feel like this. So I began to notice care homes, seeing if they fitted in with the picture in my head of what a care home for my mother should be. Whenever we were out for a drive or a meal I would spot them, having never noticed them before—in the same way when you get a new car you suddenly see that make and model everywhere. I'd think, Did they look inviting? Did they have a sign half hanging off, unloved and uncared for, which immediately made me think 'like my mother would be if she went there?'

One day I was driving through the village of Grappenhall on the outskirts of Warrington when I spotted a care home that looked perfect. It was in a lovely position, just by the side of the canal in a semirural setting. There were two pubs in the cobbled square, which I thought would be handy for people visiting my mother— not that I'm saying she drove everyone to drink but it was nice for people to go for a catch-up after they'd visited. I could imagine us going for walks along the canal. There was a wonderful old church next door; in fact, the old people's home had formerly been the rectory. It looked so inviting that I was a bit worried about going in because I thought it might be a disappointment.

As I walked in a nurse came over and introduced herself and was so warm and welcoming that I felt immediately at ease. She was the sister and introduced herself as Theresa. She said that she understood that the decision I was trying to make was an extremely difficult one. She explained that everyone who came through the door on behalf of their elderly parents had the same choice to make after coming to the same impasse in their lives.

She showed me round and the staff all seemed very jolly and happy to work there. There were some bits of my first trip round the home that were how I had feared it to be—some old people were sitting in the TV room staring into space or sleeping—but of course this came with the territory. The important thing to me was the feeling of industry round the place. There were activities; people were here to interact with the residents and make their days interesting. There was occupational therapy taking place, and there was a group of old ladies having their hair done because, it transpired, the owner was a hairdresser and this was one of the weekly treats. Also I was told that they gave manicures on a regular basis. I couldn't help thinking that my mother would love that, being pampered every week. Food was cooked fresh on the premises. The notice board was full of ongoing activities and photographs of trips and outings that the residents had been on.

I was then shown the bedrooms and they were all bright and spacious and the whole place was light and airy. The gardens were well kept and I could imagine my mother sitting out there on a summer's day. The area too was somewhere that I knew my mother would be happy with, if she could ever be happy about the idea of going into a care home. Grappenhall was near Stockton Heath, 'the posh part of Warrington'.

After my look round, I came away feeling lighter. At the time, though, it still wasn't a decision I was willing to make.

Within weeks of this, however, my mother was in hospital with another bout of illness. The doctor was a constant visitor to her bedside. My mother was on a respirator most of the day and her dementia was getting completely out of control.

It was clear now that she was becoming a danger to herself, and the nurses at the hospital tried to impress upon me the need for more consistent long-term care. I was taken to one side and told that they would not sign her out unless she had somewhere to go where she had night-time care.

I called the home in Grappenhall and asked if there were any places available. There was, in a shared room. I was just relieved that they had a place. So I reluctantly told my mother about the home. I said that it was somewhere she could go to convalesce.

As it happens, this turn of phrase appealed to her. After a severe bout of pneumonia when she was in her forties she had been to a convalescent home in North Wales to recover. She had quite enjoyed the genteel notion of 'convalescence'.

So she went from hospital to the care home. I could see that she liked it from the day she moved in. She shared a room with another lady at first so there wasn't much space to make the place her own. When she moved to her single room I suggested that I should bring more of her own things in. I wanted to be gentle in this as I didn't want her thinking she would never see her own house again. It was all very gradual, just a few bits brought in at a time. Making sure she was settled was most important.

Whenever Mum mentioned her house I was always keen to reassure her that it was still there for her to return to whenever she wished. It often felt like dealing with a child in that I was always negotiating, always giving hope without promising something on which I couldn't deliver. She never did go back, and as time passed she asked for more and more of her things, and made a real home for herself in the care home. But always in the knowledge that she could return to her own house any time she wished.

When I was visiting my mother, I would bring things in to prompt her to chat. If she was in a genial mood she liked to talk about the past. I would gauge how she was feeling and would often bring old photographs for her to look at if I felt she was up to seeing them. She would remember everybody and these old pictures would open up a wealth of stories and memories for her. We often found it hard to chat—we soon ran out of things to say—but having these photos as a memory aid meant that my mother had lots to talk about and I was happy to listen.

MY MOTHER had her ninety-second birthday in the grounds of the home. It was July 2007. It had been a beautiful sunny day and she, who was always smartly turned out, looked lovely in her pearls and the M&S dress I had bought for her. She had been very bright and alert all day, so much so that she got me to one side and said,

'Your Aunty Jean's had two pieces of cake,' and later after a quick recce of who was supping what, said, 'Mind this lot don't drink all the wine; I want to make sure there's some left for the staff.'

Shortly after this my mother began to decline sharply. Not long after, I received the call to say I had to go back for the last time.

I sped back from London and sat next to Mum and took her hand. She was in and out of consciousness but she knew I was there. I told her what a great childhood I had had. Knowing that she had heard this gave me some peace. I settled in next to her bed as visitors and nurses came and went. The days passed and I kept my vigil, chatting to my mum, trying to make sure she was as comfortable as possible. She looked so old and frail. The fact that she wasn't sitting up, immaculately dressed wearing her red lipstick, was still a bit of a shock to me. In fact, it was only a few weeks earlier that Mum had stopped reaching for her red lipstick and I knew then that she had given up. It makes me sad to think of that now. The nurses were wonderful, coming in to make sure I understood when anything was happening why it was happening. They encouraged me to talk to her, reminding me that hearing is one of the last things to go.

As my mother lay in her bed for what would be her final night, her arms, by now tiny and bony, began reaching up in the air, her fingers moving as if plucking the strings of a harp. She seemed compelled to continue, and it became eerily beautiful to watch.

The following day my mother had calmed down. Joel had joined me at her bedside. The nurses changed shift and the new duty nurse came in to say hello to my mother.

'Hello, Margaret.'

My mother opened her eyes.

'You've got Susan and Joel.'

She suddenly became animated. 'Ah,' she said, 'Joel, my favourite person in the world.'

Joel and I looked at one another and laughed — nothing changes! My cousin Pauline arrived and later my Aunty Jean and cousin Elizabeth came in to see Mum and stayed for a while. When they left, my cousin David and his wife Ali arrived. I knew that these were my mother's last hours, but even so you are never truly prepared for it. We were all gathered round the bed. Mum was very peaceful now, and her breathing had become faint and shallow. And then she reached out, we helped her up, she sneezed, and then I felt the life leave her. As she lay back on the bed, her beautiful piercing blue eyes staring at me, I knew that she had gone.

WHEN I THINK BACK on the days after my mother's death it is always with a bit of bewilderment. There was so much to do in those following weeks that the actual activity somehow propelled me through. Unlike my father's funeral, which took place within a matter of days of his death, my mum's had to be held a full two weeks afterwards.

During the weeks between my mother dying and her funeral, I had to go back to the care home to clear out her belongings. Susie came with me. It was very sad and something I found extremely difficult. I packed up her little amount of belongings and took them back to her house, where there was the much larger task ahead of me. Something that has stayed with me about the process of clearing my mum's stuff was that, in the end, what she really wanted with her were just a few photos containing her treasured memories. We spend so much of our lives buying and acquiring things but none of it seems to matter in those final months, certainly not in my mum's case: family was what had mattered.

When I set about clearing her house, Beryl and Peter, my mum's next-door neighbours, and my Aunty Jean and Susie again were all fantastic; all were on hand to help me as I trawled through Mum's belongings. We spent days sorting through them, some of the stuff she had kept for years. There were even wedding presents that were still in their boxes. I tried to throw away as much as I could, but I am a hoarder and my mother's boxed wedding presents are now in my attic and no doubt will end up being passed on to Joel either to throw away or keep in his attic.

But what struck me most were the things of mine that she had kept that I had no idea she even had—programmes from theatre productions I'd been in, cuttings from papers and magazines of shows I'd appeared in—I was ever so touched. She would never in a million years have shared with me the fact that she was keeping these things.

THE DAY OF my mother's funeral finally arrived and we made our way to the church. The lovely thing about it taking place in the church next to the home was that some of the residents could attend, and as we pulled up outside they were all there waiting for her. I thought this was such a lovely thing, such a mark of respect for my mum. Then the staff all came into the service. I think my mother would have really loved this, as she had been so happy in her final months there.

Susie had had the order of service printed with two pictures of my mother on the front, one as a little girl and the other as an old lady, which was such a lovely personal touch. When my cousins entered the church carrying the coffin with the beautiful blue cloud of flowers on top, I knew that we had done my mum proud.

'Nessun Dorma' was sung, as was 'Bring Him Home' from *Les Misérables*, and then as they carried the coffin out the recording of 'Do You Hear the People Sing?', again from *Les Misérables*, was played. Everyone had the words in their song sheet and joined in. It is such a rousing emotional song and I was so pleased; it felt that we left on a high with a real celebration of my mother's life.

I FEEL VERY STRONGLY that those last few years with my mum saw a shift in the dynamic of our relationship. I had spent so many years trying to please my mother without ever feeling I had. But as she became weaker and more vulnerable she turned to me, and it was having her need me that made me realise that we had a very strong bond. She was my mother and I loved her very much. In those final months and days in the home, when she was frightened and needed someone there, it was me that she wanted, me whose hand she held. She looked at me with love and I was transported back to those times on her knee, waiting for *Listen With Mother*, feeling that the world began and ended with my family.

My mother and I had been through a lot over my lifetime, both together and separately, and there were times when I found her utterly exasperating. But she also gave me much to be proud of. She was a strong woman who provided me with a solid family bedrock on which to build my life. She may have struggled to let me go free, as the old proverb said, but she sure as anything gave me somewhere I could always return to.

Chapter Ten

Since my mother died there have been a number of times when I have thought that I would really like her to share something that I know she would have loved. It is the everyday things that I miss the most—not being able just to call her up and tell her about a recipe I've read or something I'm watching on TV that I know she'd have enjoyed. Those small bits of life are the things I really miss sharing with my mother. However, there have also been a few big occasions where I wished both she and my dad were there.

In 2009 I was appointed OBE. It was November 5. When I looked this up in my diary to check the date, the entry for the day says simply '9 a.m.: Palace', as if I am often at Buck House having tea with the Queen! I'm not. And this was to be a big honour.

I had met the Queen once before, some years previously, when she came to Liverpool. Paul McCartney was there and I hadn't seen him for years. It was the year of the Golden Jubilee and the Queen was visiting Liverpool and would reopen the Walker Art Gallery. The great and good of Liverpool had been assembled and my mother had bought a new outfit for the occasion. As we waited to be introduced to Her Majesty, someone said, 'And here's our own member of the Royle Family, Ma'am.'

To which she replied, 'Oh,' in a rather disapproving fashion.

I think I had thought the Queen might chat to my mother but she didn't, and my mum was very disappointed. She didn't say it, but I could tell. A little later Paul McCartney made his way over and made a real fuss of my mother. She was over the moon. When he walked away my mother was beaming from ear to ear. *Not such a dirty Beatle now*, I thought!

In early autumn 2009, I had been standing in the kitchen with Joel, who was visiting, when I received a call from my agent. 'Hi, Sue, are you in? I'm sending something over.'

I needed some milk and the dogs were cross-legged. 'I have to pop out,' I said, 'but if I'm not here they can put it through the letterbox.' I thought it was a script he was sending.

'You'll need to sign for this,' he assured me.

An hour later a courier arrived. I signed for my envelope and opened it to see 'ER' stamped in large letters. I handed the pen back to the courier—he was a normal courier on a bike, not the liveried individual on horseback one might expect to be delivering something from the Palace—so the penny still hadn't dropped.

Joel looked over my shoulder. 'What's that?' he asked.

I read down the page. Slightly stunned, I announced, 'I've been awarded an OBE!'

The hardest thing was keeping it from everybody until the names were released to the press. Then the day itself arrived and I was allowed to take three guests, so I brought Joel, Margot and Susie. It was a strange experience going to Buckingham Palace. There's a familiarity to the place, having seen it a thousand times on TV and in passing. But stepping through the doors was like stepping into another world. The rooms are vast and seemingly endless. The walls are lined with paintings, the soldiers are very straight-backed. There is a real sense of history to it, but it is by no means a museum. In fact, there were so many people going about their business that it felt like a small town.

An equerry came up to us. 'Excuse me,' he said. I looked at him, sure that we had stepped out of line somehow and were about to be told off. He dropped his voice, 'I'm not supposed to say this,' he quickly looked around to check that no one could see him transgressing any professional boundaries, 'but I'm a huge fan.' He smiled and walked off. I was delighted.

'Do you think the Queen watches *The Royle Family*?' Margot asked.

I thought about the Queen and Prince Philip and the gang sitting at Sandringham watching the Christmas special. 'Probably not,' I said.

'I bet the younger ones do, though,' Susie added. 'Prince Harry likes a laugh, doesn't he?'

I said my goodbyes to Joel, Margot and Susie, and another equerry took me through into a room where everyone else who was there to receive an award was gathered. We were divided into categories then put through our paces. I had a hook attached to my lapel so that the Queen could hook the medal on—no faffing with pins as I might have imagined.

'You will be called through,' the equerry told us, 'then as the person in front goes to receive their award you will take four steps forward.'

Four steps, I thought, *four steps*, sure I would forget all of this and collapse in a heap.

'Then when your name is read out,' he continued, 'the Queen is addressed as Your Majesty and then subsequently as Ma'am, as in ham, not Ma'am as in farm.'

Mam not marm; mam not marm. Having spent years remembering long lines of dialogue I was sure all of this was going to leave my head the minute the equerry finished speaking.

'Then she will put her hand out to indicate that it is your time to leave. Take four steps backwards, never turning your back on Her Majesty.'

I was bamboozled. I decided just to follow what the person in front did and hope for the best.

I heard the Queen arrive, and 'God Save the Queen' was played. We were to stay in another room until my name was called to go through. Eventually it was my time, and off I went, with a head full of four steps to the front, four steps to the right; mam, ham, spam. I stood waiting my turn, watching the Queen. For everyone in that room it was such a special occasion, but I couldn't help thinking that for the poor Queen it must be like Groundhog Day. Doing the same thing over and over again.

Then someone read out, 'Sue Johnston, for services to charity and drama.'

And up I went, looking at the Beefeaters who lined the hall and thinking it was all very surreal.

I stood in front of the Queen; it felt very much like being called in front of the head teacher. I approached and stood before her. There was a moment of fumbling as she tried to hook the medal onto my lapel, which made us both smile, and then I stepped back.

The Queen looked at me quizzically as if trying to decide if she knew me. Then she said, 'It must be lovely to be able to combine drama and charity work.'

'Yes, Your Majesty, it is,' I said, thinking, Should I have said Ma'am? 'Yes, it is lovely to combine drama and charity work.'

I had just repeated parrot fashion what she had said to me. What was I talking about? I wanted to say, 'Can I try that again? I must have a better line.' But then the arm shot out and I had to take my four steps backwards.

At the end of the ceremony the Queen came through the hall and nodded to everyone. I'm sure she was thinking, Get me a gin and tonic. In the paper next day it said, 'The Head of the Royal Family meets the Head of the Royle Family.'

I really missed my mum and dad that day. They were great traditionalists and for them to visit the Palace would have been a once-in-a-lifetime opportunity. And I know that I've said that my mother found it hard to say she was proud of me but she would have been as proud as a peacock that day.

THE OTHER and more important big occasion where I sorely missed my parents was Joel's wedding. Joel married his lovely wife Zoe in May 2010. Zoe and Joel had met at the Old Grapes pub in

Manchester. The pub was co-owned by Liz Dawn, and Zoe had worked there from the time she was at college. I always thought this was a great coincidence, as Liz was a good friend of mine. Unlike me, Joel didn't know what he wanted to do when he left school, and it took a while to find his path, but by now he had found his passion as a professional photographer. Zoe was the icing on the cake.

I thought choosing the outfit that I would wear would be fairly straightforward. I had checked with Zoe what the colour of the bridesmaids' dresses was to be, and what colour her mother was wearing, and once I had this established I thought the outfit would buy itself!

I was determined to look my best and do Joel proud without being over the top. I found myself in Vivienne Westwood where I found a blue-spotted dress; it was wonderfully sculptured and would pull me in where necessary. The only problem was that it was sleeveless. So if I was to buy this dress I would need a jacket. They had a perfect jacket to match but they had it in a very small size only. I thought about it for a moment and then decided to buy it anyway. When I got home and tried on the outfit again I realised that the jacket was so tight that once my arms were in I wouldn't be able to raise them or lower them. But why would I need to raise and lower my arms anyway? I thought, conning myself that a jacket I'd poured myself into would be fine.

The week before the wedding I was in Harvey Nichols in Manchester when I walked past the perfect outfit. A muted silver-grey dress with a matching long coat from Calvin Klein. Suddenly my Vivienne Westwood seemed too fussy; I had to have this instead. But the sales assistant informed me they didn't have it in my size. I was devastated. In fear that I might start sobbing, the assistant came to my rescue, locating the suit in my size back in London. I went down to pick it up—and while there I popped into Harrods and bought a matching hat and shoes in a matter of minutes.

The night before the wedding, Susie and I stayed with Joel, his best man and his ushers at Stanneylands Hotel near Wilmslow. We had dinner together and I made sure that the lads were all in bed at a reasonable hour.

The next morning we got up and headed to the Cheshire countryside. The venue was Sandhole Farm in Congleton, a converted barn overlooking a lake. The outhouses round the barn had been converted into cottages, and we were to stay there that evening. It was such a beautiful setting. And unfussy, which really suited Joel and Zoe's laid-back attitude. Once there we felt cocooned; there was no traffic, it was such a tranquil place. It felt like the whole day would focus on Joel and Zoe, just as it should.

I headed to my room. From the window was a wonderful view of the Cheshire countryside and the lake. Once changed, a few of us gathered to have a glass of champagne and calm our nerves—I don't know what I had to be nervous about! When Joel came in I swelled with pride. I had had a bespoke suit made for him and he looked so smart and handsome.

We went through to the barn; the mood was very upbeat, everyone was in great spirits. I knew that Joel was so happy to be getting married to Zoe and we all felt the same for him. Once we entered the room where the ceremony would take place and I saw all those people gathered for them, I began to brim with tears and I had to concentrate on not crying.

We took our seats. Even though I knew that Zoe was in the building there is still that nervous expectation when waiting for the bride to arrive. The bridesmaids came first. Zoe had her sister Gemma, her two friends and Elizabeth, Margot's daughter.

Zoe looked beautiful, like a Grecian goddess. Her dark hair fell loosely on her shoulders. As she walked towards Joel I realised she didn't have any flowers, which I thought must have been something she'd decided against, until I saw her sister running up the aisle later—she'd left them in her room by accident.

For me, all the worries and anxieties of being a single mother were washed away. I had often felt that Joel had missed out by not having a father in his life, being brought up by his mum. But I realised I didn't need to worry any more. Joel is also a very loved man; he is loyal to his friends and has found a wife with a 'proper family'. They have been warm and welcoming to Joel and to me.

Veron's daughter Gemma was there too. It was lovely to see her with her husband Alex, whom she had married the year before. I felt like my family was all grown up. It was such a magical day, and my resounding memory is of a sea of happy faces; I couldn't have wished for more for my son. I can say unequivocally that Joel's wedding day was the happiest and proudest day of my life.

Epilogue

Sitting and thinking about my life has made me realise that, although there have been many ups and downs along the way, I have had a very happy and fulfilled one so far.

I haven't had an actual relationship myself for quite some time but I can honestly say I don't miss it! I spent so much of my early life thinking that I had to be part of a couple for my life to have meaning. But now I am happily alone I realise that there really is more to life than worrying if a man is going to call when he says he will. That's not to say I'm writing men off altogether—I just don't feel that being part of a couple is something I need to define me.

Careerwise, I find myself at another of those 'jumping off' points where I'm not sure what I'll be doing next. *Waking the Dead* has finished, and I'm excited and a little nervous at the prospect of embarking on something new, but I've done it before and I'll do it again. It might be theatre, TV or film, but whatever it is it won't be dull. As long as people are willing to have me in their living rooms I'll keep on acting. Oh, and as long as I can still learn the lines!

Reading over the earlier chapters of this book I can now see that I really must have given my parents sleepless nights as they tried to get their grammar-educated daughter to stay in a good, stable job to no avail. I sometimes think I find it hard to make decisions but I was very single-minded in my desire to be an actress. I pursued it as a career; I didn't just fall into it and hope for the best. And I am very grateful that I did, because I have been given the most amazing opportunities and have played a number of great characters that people have genuinely taken to their hearts.

And so, dear reader, the end of this part of my story is nigh. From beginning writing this book, to penning these final words, I feel like I've come on that much overused term these days: a journey. I began by thinking that my relationship with my mother was difficult and have ended by feeling very much loved and looked after by her, even though she wasn't good at showing it.

From thinking about how she cared for me when I was younger, to remembering how I felt when I discovered she had kept mementos of mine from over the years, I have come to the conclusion that my mum was my mum. She didn't do things the way that I would have liked her to a lot of the time, but she did them her way. And everything she ever did had her family at the heart of it. I did keep parts of my life from her, but that was just our relationship and I have accepted that. It didn't mean I was lying; I was just keeping her happy in the world that she had fought so hard to build round her. She didn't like change and I did. *Vive la différence!*

And as I sit here, coughing from a bad chest I'm just shaking off, wearing red lipstick and eating my lunch from Marks', something has just occurred to me . . . I think I'm turning into my mother!

June 2011

James Corden

May I Have Your Attention, Please?

The truth is, I should never have been this guy. I wasn't the cool, clever, good-looking boy at school. I was never supposed to be the person who writes books or TV shows, hosts award ceremonies or appears in films. Things like that shouldn't happen to someone like me. But I always dreamed of it, hoped for it, longed for it: throughout school when I was disruptive and disinterested, in my teens when I tried to form my own boy band and through hundreds of auditions for parts which were met with constant rejection.

Until finally I co-wrote a TV series called 'Gavin and Stacey'. And my whole life changed. In every single way. Lots of it good and parts of it bad. Some of it funny and bits of it sad.

This is that story. The story of how I found myself here, talking to you.

James Corden in 'May I Have Your Attention, Please?'

INTRODUCTION

I've always thought that the first few lines of any book would be the hardest to write. Where do I start? How do I begin to tell you, someone I don't know, about my life? My life? My story. How do I do this? I'm only thirty-two and, if I'm being completely honest, at least two of those thirty-two years were spent playing PlayStation and eating Crunchy Nut Cornflakes. I could try and be clever and start in the middle and jump back and forth in time. Like *The Social Network*. Though that jumped between various courtrooms and depositions to Harvard University and the creation of a website that changed the way we interact. Mine would jump from my parents' front room to my bedroom and all that would have happened in between is I'd have grabbed a bag of Quavers.

The truth is, my head's a little all over the place. Yesterday was the day I became a father. It's by far the most amazing thing that's ever happened to me. As yet we don't know what to call him. He came a week early, and although that's brilliant, this was my big week for writing this book. So, with a heavy heart, I've left him in his mother's arms and, as I looked back at him, I wondered what might be his earliest memory.

I remember mine clearly. I was four years old and it was so definitive it would shape the rest of my life. It was my younger sister Ruth's christening. Our family was very involved in all aspects of the Salvation Army and my parents wore the uniform. It was a

Sunday morning service and the Salvation Army officer (basically the vicar or priest) asked our family to join him on the platform. I walked up holding Mum's hand and approached the altar. Dad handed Ruth over to the vicar and as a family we formed a semi-circle around him. The vicar grabbed a chair and said, 'Come on, James, stand on here so you can see.' I crawled up onto my knees on it, and then up onto my feet.

I remember this as if it were yesterday. I stood on that chair and looked out at the congregation and saw row after row of people staring back at me. There were probably about forty or fifty people, but to my four-year-old self it looked like a sea of millions. From the moment I saw people looking at me, I don't think I once looked at Ruth or what was happening. Because, in my eyes, this was no longer a platform. This was a stage.

I started to pull faces and a ripple of *oohs* and *ahs* from the people watching turned into giggles, and giggles turned into laughs as I bent over and looked at them through my legs. Even the people on the platform were giggling, as I was by now pretending to sing into a microphone. This felt good. Really good.

As the blessing came to an end, the vicar welcomed Ruth into the church and then turned to me, ruffled my hair and said, 'And thank you, young James. Quite the little performer.' Dad tried to hold my hand as he replied, 'Quite the little show-off, more like.' The congregation started to laugh again, which I took as a signal to raise my hands triumphantly in the air and jump off the chair. I landed on my feet to a healthy round of applause. As I stood there, looking out on the clapping audience, I realised—even at the age of four!—that this was the greatest feeling I had ever had. I walked back to my seat between Mum and Dad, smiling the biggest smile. It felt incredible. My whole body was tingling.

In my head it became simple: if people are looking at me, and only me, it feels amazing. Even though I was only four years old, from that moment I knew exactly what I wanted to do. I wanted to entertain people, to act, sing, dance; everything and anything that would make people look at me and smile.

CHAPTER 1

I was born on August 22, 1978. My full name is James Kimberley Corden. It's OK, you can go ahead and laugh. Kimberley. I mean, seriously. It's a family tradition: the first son in our family will carry the middle name Kimberley. At the moment, I don't know whether my one-day-old son will have it, too. My dad would love it and it would, I'm sure, mean the world to my grandad. But can I really subject my son to the same name-calling that I suffered? Who knows? We've not got a first name for him yet.

My family lived in a small village called Hazlemere, just outside the town of High Wycombe. My mum, Margaret, is a social worker and my dad, Malcolm, used to be a musician in the Royal Air Force, but is now a Christian book salesman. Before we moved to Hazlemere we lived a bit nearer Wycombe town centre, and before that we briefly lived on a military base in Uxbridge.

Dad played saxophone in the RAF band and so he and his young family were allowed to live for free on the military base. But he decided that he wanted us to experience people from different backgrounds, instead of living in what he saw as the very insular, blinkered and barricaded life on an RAF base.

Living off-base meant finding the money to buy their own house, so Mum and Dad scrimped and saved. Dad worked teaching clarinet and saxophone to local kids. But when it came to the crunch and they needed to find money for a deposit, there still wasn't enough there. So Dad sold the one thing he owned of value — his saxophone. It meant he would have to use one of the ones in the band room, which he hated doing. But he did it, for us.

I guess we were a fairly ordinary family. I grew up thinking that nothing we did as a family was particularly different; it's only now that I realise quite how different it was.

You see, every single Sunday we would put on uniforms, go to church in Wycombe town centre and march through the streets playing brass instruments. I know. And I thought this was completely normal. We didn't do it for our own amusement; we were all fully signed-up members of the Salvation Army. Mum grew up in a Salvation Army family, and when she met Dad and they fell in love, Dad found God and joined the Army, too.

So that's what we'd do, as a family, every Sunday. Mum and Dad made it clear that we had to go until we were sixteen and then we could make our own choices. I made some of my best friends there at various music and drama weeks in the school holidays. Three guys in particular—Jason, Anthony and Gavin—still remain a big part of my life.

Sundays were a nightmare: three services—morning, afternoon and evening—with a rushed roast dinner and a march in between. I vividly remember the frantic journeys back and forth into town with Dad picking up various old ladies who needed a lift to get to the afternoon and evening services. But, I suppose, it was a big part of what brought our family together and what made it such a close-knit group.

I'VE ALWAYS BEEN incredibly grateful for the loving and supportive family I grew up in. We were and are still incredibly close. In many ways, I feel closer to my two sisters now than I ever have. Andrea, being the eldest and three years older than I am, was the responsible one, and was often put in charge of looking after me and our younger sister, Rudi, whilst Mum and Dad were at work. (Who's Rudi? I hear you ask. My little sister Ruth is called Rudi, and that's how I'll refer to her in the book.)

Andrea and Rudi are probably more gifted than I am and ever will be. Andrea has an incredible singing voice and Rudi is one of the funniest people you could ever have round a dinner table. But I guess what sets me and them apart is desire. I have this need—a burning ambition—to be in the spotlight. For me, growing up, it was as vital as oxygen. Many hours were spent dreaming of stardom; ridiculous things like taking the final bow on the West End stage, or writing my life story at a crazily young age like thirty-two! Andrea and Ruth have enjoyed the limelight at different times, but it's not something they crave.

Ever since Rudi's christening, I had been first in line to put myself forward for any kind of chance to perform in front of an audience. My big chance came when, for the first time ever, our headmaster decided that the Park County Middle School would put on a summer concert. Children from each year would show-case various talents, and each class would perform a song or dance number. Our class went for a song called 'I Wear a Red Sombrero'. I was put on the back row in a poncho and sombrero. As much fun as it was doing the song, I wanted to be able to do something on my own. Luckily, one of my teachers told me that I'd be reciting a poem called 'Nibble Nibble, Munch Munch'. For an eight-year-old at a school concert it was the best possible thing to be reading. It was all about a guy on a bus who is so hungry that he eats his bus ticket.

I loved performing it. It was both fun and funny—always a good mix—and it brought the house down. The reaction was so good that one of the mums who lived over the road from us, Sonia, suggested to Dad that he try and get me into the Jackie Palmer Stage School, an after-school dance and drama club with an affiliated professional agency that would send kids to auditions.

Sonia's daughter, Laura Sadler, had been going there for a while. I knew Laura really well; she was two years younger than I was but she was the star pupil at Jackie Palmer's. One minute she'd be in an advert for fish fingers, the next she'd be in *Children's Ward* or *Inspector Morse*. She went on to play a regular in *Holby City* until, tragically, in 2003 she fell from a balcony and never recovered. There is not a doubt in my mind that if Laura was still with us today, she would be lighting up stages and screens all over the world. She gave me hope that extraordinary things *could* happen to people from our ordinary little town.

Andrea, Rudi and I all joined Jackie Palmer's at the same time. I was nine years old and stayed there until I was seventeen, whereas Rudi and Andrea didn't last past the first two terms. The afternoon tap classes, filled with pushy mums and screaming stage-school brats, weren't for them. They weren't really for me, either, but I just loved being in those drama classes.

AUDITIONS BECAME a fact of life; getting a part in a show was the reason I was there, after all. I would be auditioning for something every week, sometimes three or four times a week. But although Laura and lots of the other kids at the stage school were getting jobs, no matter how many auditions I went to, no matter how hard I tried, I just couldn't seem to make the breakthrough.

My dad actually remembers that time better than I do. I was a young kid and none of it has really stuck in my memory, probably because I didn't want it to. But for Dad, to have to watch his son being turned down again and again must have affected and wounded him far more deeply than it did me.

There was one particular audition at Sadler's Wells theatre he talks about, where I was going for the part of one of the von Trapp children in *The Sound of Music*. I was twelve then, but I've always looked younger than I am and I was going for a much younger part. Theatre directors often like older kids who look young because they can take direction a bit more easily. A group of about seventy kids had been called back for a second audition.

The kids were split into pools of ten, with two boys or girls from each pool being selected to play one of the children in alternate performances. The director kicked it off by having us sing 'Do-Re-Mi'. We would start together, then he would point at one of us, everyone else would stop and that child would carry on. He pointed to me just as we hit 'Sew, a needle pulling thread . . .' and I sang my heart out. To this day, I wonder if anyone has sung that line with more determination.

I made it through every single cut that day. At the end of each audition round, they would call out the names of the kids who could leave; if you were asked to stay, you were still in with a chance of landing the part. Finally, it got to the point when there were just three of us left. Three boys and two parts.

I walked back into the room, shaking like a leaf. We lined up, and the casting director started reading out the names of the unlucky ones who hadn't made it. And then came the words I'd been longing not to hear: '. . . and James Corden. Thank you very much, everyone, you've been great.'

My shoulders sank and a cloud of disappointment descended. I just ambled out of the rehearsal room. Dad was at the bottom of the stairs waiting for me, and I still remember the cacophony of noise coming from the room above, the director's voice lifting above it all. 'We start in three weeks,' he was saying. 'We're going to have the best time. It's really going to be amazing.'

As we got in the car, Dad sat there with the engine switched off for a moment and then, finally, looked at me.

'James,' he said, 'try not to worry about it. What will be, will be — that's the way life is. You did so well to get to this stage, but . . .' We'd had these chats before but, today, there was something in his tone that I hadn't heard before: a sort of weariness and resignation. 'Why don't you just knock it on the head?' he suggested. 'I don't mean stop going to the lessons or anything, but these auditions. I'm so fed up of seeing you this disappointed all the time. You don't even have to go to Jackie Palmer's any more if you don't want. Why don't you just knock the auditions on the head and call it a day?'

For a long moment I stared out of the windscreen. And then I shook my head. 'I can't do that, Dad,' I said. 'It's just what I've got to do.'

I don't really remember that conversation with Dad. He reminded me of it when I told him I'd be writing about that part of my life. I wonder if he remembers it so well because it was at that moment he realised how serious I was. How, no matter what happened, I wasn't going to give up.

I WAS THIRTEEN and, after the complete non-shock of failing my 12-plus, I had joined Holmer Green Upper School, a pretty ordinary school about fifteen minutes' walk from our house. Most of my friends from middle school came along with me, so it didn't feel that different. The good news was that there were lots of new girls, and girls had recently become much more interesting to me.

The only problem is, if you look like me, girls don't really feel the same way. So I needed to find a way to make myself more attractive. I realised quite quickly that being funny was something girls warmed to; they liked being around someone who would make them laugh, but most of my jokes would have me as the butt and this wasn't going to push me into stud mode.

One day I was walking through the assembly hall when I saw a guy from the year above, Matt Lanchester, playing the piano. He was brilliant. I stood and listened as he played the most beautiful music, gobsmacked by how good he was. I walked nearer to where he was sitting and, as I did, a plan dawned on me—we could form a band! I didn't know it at the time, but I had happened across one of life's great truths: it doesn't matter what you look like, if you're in a band, girls will always fancy you.

I asked Matt what he was playing: it was Queen. I then asked him whether he was up for the challenge of being the first multi-platinum-selling band Holmer Green Upper had ever produced. Kind of weirded out, he said 'Why not?' So, with the two of us on board, we set about finding our other members.

Matt's friend, Richard Morris, played drums. We spoke to him and he was in. So we had Matt on keyboards, Richard on drums and me on vocals. Now I know what you're thinking. What we need now is a lead guitar and bass. You really can't form a band without a bass, can you? Well, you can, and we did. We recruited one other member of the band, Paul Chalwin, who would also be on vocals. Yeah, that's right.

Every lunch hour would be spent rehearsing. It was great; we thought 'we' were great. Before long, we imagined record companies knocking on our door and so we decided we'd better come up with a name. We took this very seriously. This name was going to be on album sleeves and tour posters, possibly around the world, and so it had to send out the right message.

We called ourselves . . . Twice Shy. It was, we thought, the perfect name for a band. It was seamless because, as Paul pointed out, 'We'll call the first album *Once Bitten*.' That sealed it. We were Twice Shy and the whole world was about to hear about us.

Except you didn't. No, after a couple of lunchtime concerts and one set at the school fête, Twice Shy broke up. It wasn't so much due to musical differences as to me realising that I still wasn't getting the attention of girls. If this was really going to take off, and make me an irresistible stud, it needed to be sexy, it needed to be cool, it needed to be . . . a boy band.

FOR AS LONG as I can remember, I've loved Take That. Most days when I came home from school I'd push the sofas and coffee tables in our lounge up against the walls, create my own stage and pretend to be a member of Take That. Sometimes I'd be Robbie, but mostly I'd be Gary. I studied them so much that I knew every single moment of every single routine.

Putting together a boy band became my major ambition. I was still going to auditions fairly regularly and still not getting any acting work, but it didn't matter because I'd started to think that fate was telling me to be the next Gary Barlow.

I knew I had to form the band with way more precision than I had with Twice Shy. What I needed were people who could sing and dance and who, most of all, were good-looking. And where could I find such guys? The Jackie Palmer Stage School.

James Wilson and Tom Goodridge were, and still are, two incredibly good-looking guys. They were good singers and fantastic dancers, and they could both do back flips. They were perfect.

I was determined that we'd be a five-piece just like my favourite group, so I then went to my two oldest friends, Gavin and Jason from the Salvation Army. Jason was a brilliant singer and Gavin was small and cute, with some pretty cool moves of his own. So, between the five of us, I really felt we had something.

We rehearsed every week in a hall at the Salvation Army. We started out doing cover versions, a lot of Take That, obviously, but we'd throw in some other hits to mix it up a little. In the hopes of forming a fan base we played in schools or at local discos. We got the routines incredibly tight, to the point where I truly believed we were going to make it. There wasn't a doubt in my mind. Once again, we had to decide on a name and went for James Wilson's genius suggestion: Insatiable. We would tell everyone who'd listen that the reason we were called Insatiable is ''cos you just can't get enough of us'. (I'm cringing while I type this.)

We broke up after six gigs, one of which was at James Wilson's sister's wedding, while another was at Gavin's family barbecue. So, not really gigs at all—more like favours to us.

NEITHER OF MY BANDS had worked out and I still wasn't getting any of the auditions I was going for. In fact, I wasn't auditioning much at all at this point. I was almost fifteen and school was getting incredibly boring, so much so that I started bunking off. I would head off out of the door to school, saying my goodbyes to Mum and Dad, walk up the road, get to the top and hide between a bush and a tree on the corner. Then I'd watch as Mum left in her car, followed by Dad a few minutes later. I'd wait a good five minutes and then head back home. Once I was back, I'd lie around the house, watch TV, play computer games: anything to pass the time.

It was on one such bunked-off day when I made my first television appearance. I was laid out on our sofa watching *This Morning with Richard and Judy* and eating my third bowl of Coco Pops, when the agony aunt Denise came on and said that today's phone-in would be all about bullying. She went on to say, 'Do you know someone who is being bullied? Are you being bullied and need help? If so, call this number ...'

Without even thinking about it, I went into the kitchen, picked up the phone and dialled the number she had just read out. Within minutes I was telling a researcher about how I was being bullied, and that my parents thought I was at school but I couldn't go in for fear of being beaten up again. I told her my name was Chris and she said someone would call back if I was going to be on the show. Never in a million years did I think I'd get on the show.

The phone rang. I picked it up and it was the researcher I'd spoken to. She asked me some more questions, to which I gave confident answers, every single one of them a lie. And then she said, 'OK, Chris, I'm gonna pass you over to Denise, who'd just like to talk to you before we go on air.' What? Put me on air?

Before I could hang up, I heard a new voice say, 'Hiya, is that Chris?' It was Denise, with her lovely, calming Geordie accent.

'Yes, this is Chris. Hi, Denise,' I answered nervously. We spoke about the atrocities that were happening to me at the school I attended in High Wycombe. How I was too terrified to speak out. How my parents didn't even know that I wasn't at school today. (See? I wasn't completely lying.) And then Denise told me to stay on the line because I would be the first caller on air.

I was starting to get nervous now. Live-television nervous. I had to remember what Denise had told me, that I should just speak calmly and clearly. Denise knew exactly how hard it was for me to call in with everything I was going through . . . Maybe it was the only way I could handle what was about to happen, but I genuinely started to feel as though I was the victim of bullying.

I was waiting on the phone and kept being counted down. 'One minute till we're back on air . . . forty-five seconds . . . thirty seconds . . . ten . . .' And then down the phone I could hear the famous *This Morning* theme music and Richard Madeley welcoming everyone back. Then he turned to the day's phone-in. There I was, standing in the kitchen, about to tell a massive lie on national TV.

After Denise and Richard had introduced the bit, Richard said, 'Well, let's go to our first caller, and it's Chris from High Wycombe. Hi, Chris.'

I paused briefly, took a short breath and said, in a small, shy voice, 'Hi, Richard.' And we were off.

'Chris, you called in to tell us you are being bullied.'

'Yes,' I replied. 'I am.'

'How old are you?'

'Fourteen.'

'And you stayed away from school today because of what's happening to you?'

'Yes,' I said. 'My mum and dad don't know I'm here. But I can't face going into school any more.'

'Can you tell me what's been happening?' Denise asked.

'I'm being bullied. Picked on all the time, you know, by the other boys. I'm bigger than them, fatter. They call me names all the time because of it. Last term one of the kids broke my arm, but I told my teachers I'd slipped over.'

And so it went on, my best performance to date, and I couldn't even hear it because the TV was in the other room. Denise talked to me for a while, advising me about what to do and being very sympathetic, then Richard told me that he really respected me for coming on.

'Thank you,' I said. 'I'll speak to Mum and Dad.'

And then I was off the air. I put the phone down and just stared at it. *That was weird*, I thought. *Was I just on TV?*

I was so swept up in my new television status as Chris the bullied teenager that when the phone rang again, I just presumed that it was *This Morning* calling me back for some reason. So I picked up the phone, only to hear, 'What on earth are you doing at home? Why aren't you at school? And why the hell has Auntie Marilyn just heard you on the television saying you've broken your arm?'

It was my mum. I didn't even think. It's the number one rule: if you're bunking off, you never, ever pick up the phone. Rule number two should be: don't call live television phone-ins and pretend to be someone else while talking in your own voice. But how many people would that apply to?

To this day I have no idea why I did it. When Mum got home, she told Dad and he went mad. Not a little bit cross, but a proper, full-on, red-in-the-face, Malcolm Corden rage. It's never nice being on the end of one of them. But, deep down, I was pleased that people knew. I'd been on television and, even though it was wrong, and even though I'd been lying the whole time, I wanted the whole world to know. The truth is, I loved it.

CHAPTER 2

The only time I ever really enjoyed school was when we were doing the school play. We would rehearse every Tuesday and Thursday after school until suddenly school didn't feel like school any more—it was a theatre. I'm sure it won't come as a shock to hear that when there was a play on, I never bunked off.

We'd often do musicals and I was lucky enough to have a good part for most of the shows. One year, when we did *Zigger Zagger*, a musical about football hooligans, there was a review of our show in the *Bucks Free Press*. It was the first time I'd ever been mentioned in a newspaper of any kind and I remember what it said to this day, word for word: 'James Corden excels as the sergeant major. This lad is a natural and I feel sure he has a future in the acting profession.'

I cut it out of the paper and stuck it on my bedroom wall. I would read it every night before I went to sleep and every morning when I got up. Here's the thing, though—and I've only learnt this in the last two years—the one thing worse than a bad review is believing a good review. If only I'd listened to our drama teacher, Mrs Roberts, when she told me not to let it go to my head. But it was too late for that. I walked around school like I was De Niro. So embarrassing.

It was because of this behaviour and my appalling record of attendance that when the next year's school play came around, Mrs Roberts called me to the school hall. She started by telling me that the show we were going to put on that year was called *Dazzle*, and that it was a musical set on a spaceship. She then informed me that she wanted me to play the lead, the captain of the ship.

When she told me, though, she looked at me in her particular Mrs Roberts way. 'James,' she said, 'don't get too carried away with this because there are some serious conditions. I've talked to other teachers and I have to tell you most of them think I'm making a mistake. You're so disruptive, so utterly disinterested in almost all your other lessons, they—'

'I'm not that bad,' I protested.

'Yes,' she said, 'you are.' She pointed a finger at me. 'I'm sticking my neck out for you here and I promise, if you step out of line in any lesson with any teacher between now and the school play, not only will I take the part away from you, you won't be in it at all.'

She didn't have to say any more. The play was all I lived for and, once warned, I didn't so much as breathe in a lesson without permission. I was the model student.

FOR OUR GCSEs at Holmer Green we had to pick three options to take as well as Maths, English, Science and a language. I made my choices immediately: Drama, of course, Music and Home Economics. No sooner were my options on paper than I was called to see Mr Graham, our head of year.

'James,' he said, 'I've been looking at your GCSE options and I'm rather concerned. You can't do Music, Drama and cooking. What use will Music and Drama be in the outside world?'

I was slightly put out. 'Well, that depends what I do, sir, doesn't it? I'm going to be an actor, I—'

Mr Graham jumped right in. 'James, you're not *going* to be an actor. You'd *like* to be an actor. It's all very well having dreams. We all have dreams, but at some point you have to live in the real world. No, I'm afraid it's out of the question. You can't do both Music and Drama. You simply can't.'

I was wide-eyed now and could feel the heat in my cheeks. 'But—' I spluttered.

'Only three students have chosen Music as an option so we're taking it off the syllabus this year. I'm sorry.'

Mr Graham told me I had to choose something else. I wracked my brains. Then uttered the words, 'Religious Education'.

'And why, exactly, do you want to do RE?' he asked me.

'I don't. I want to do Music. But if I can't do that, I'll do RE instead, 'cos it's easiest.'

Mr Graham informed me that for the exact same reasons that Music wasn't being run as a GCSE, neither was RE. It was ridiculous. I asked Mr Graham which subjects were available and, word for word, this was his reply: 'European Studies and Information Technology, but Mr Longman'—the IT teacher—'has made it clear he doesn't want you in his classroom.'

So that was that, what a waste. Filling out the form, choosing my options, going to 'have a chat' with Mr Graham—the whole thing. What was the point of any of this stuff when the bottom line was I had to suffer European Studies?

From that moment on, school meant nothing to me. I decided I would only focus on the subjects that mattered to me: Drama, English and, of course, Home Economics. The rest was, as far as I was concerned, free time. It was all very silly and I'd like to state that I think my behaviour was foolish. The way I acted meant I was dismissed as stupid, an oaf, someone who didn't care and therefore shouldn't be cared about.

School dragged on until we reached the summer term and, inevitably, exams. I was, of course, completely unprepared for my GCSEs. The thing I'm really embarrassed about is my Drama exam. The only coursework you had to do was keep a diary. Not very difficult. There was no structure, no right and wrong; you merely had to keep a record of what you'd done in the lessons and hand in the diary at the end of the year. But I didn't keep the diary.

'You're an idiot, James.' I can still hear Mrs Roberts's voice and remember wilting under her gaze. 'You're so stupid. All you had to do was hand in a diary and you could have got an A. But you just couldn't do that, could you?'

To this day I can't tell you why I didn't bother.

'I know I should've handed in the coursework,' I told her, 'but I'm going to be an actor, Mrs Roberts. None of my GCSEs is going to matter.'

She looked at me long and hard. 'James,' she said, 'right now you're a big fish in the smallest pond in the world and when you get out there, you'll be a tiny fish in an enormous ocean. You're not going to know what hit you.'

When August came around and the fabled brown envelope flopped through the letterbox, I wasn't there to receive it. I was still in the Salvation Army at the time and a few of us were away at music week. But I didn't even dare to ring home. However, Dad came along to the performance at the end of the week and, with a face etched with real disappointment, asked me if I wanted to know the results. I told him that I doubted it, but he went ahead and delivered the news anyway: a B in Drama, a C in English and the rest, well, all below an E. So that was that . . .

HOLDING MY NEWBORN baby in my arms just now, I couldn't help but wonder what he's going to do, or who he's going to be when he's older. What will he remember as the best day of his life? I remember mine clearly, but to fully tell you about it, I have to fill you in on one of the worst.

I was walking home from school on quite a grey day when, out of the blue, Dad pulled up alongside me in his car and asked if I wanted a lift. We got home, and Dad said he had to tell me something. I went into the lounge where my mum was sitting on the sofa along with Andrea and Rudi.

Dad came in and sat down next to Mum. I wish I could remember exactly what he said, or how he even began to tell us, but I can't remember anything about that moment, except one thing. Dad told us that he'd been called up to fight in the Gulf War: he was going to be a stretcher-bearer and he'd be leaving in three weeks. I remember standing up and dramatically sweeping out of the lounge and up to my room. I did this mostly for effect, but also so my mum wouldn't see me crying.

Three weeks came and went pretty quickly, and the day for Dad to leave arrived. I remember it so vividly. We were all in the kitchen and Dad was standing there, dressed like Action Man, with all this camouflage gear on.

We said goodbye and Dad went down the line, hugging all of us.

There were so many tears. Dad stayed strong but, when he hugged Mum, he was sobbing so much he just held her to his chest and called the three of us over to all put our arms round each other; that cuddle felt as if it went on for ages, the whole family just clinging on to each other.

Dad eventually left, and life kind of got back to normal, but to tell you the truth I was never myself during the time he was away. I couldn't cope with it. He'd ring every couple of days and Andrea, Rudi and Mum would chat to him, but I would just burst into tears if I heard his voice. I couldn't adjust to where he was or what he was doing and pretend it was normal.

Some days were fine—it wouldn't feel too different to any other day, but there were times you'd really notice it. I remember being in the kitchen eating a bowl of Frosties one day, chatting to Mum, when we heard on the news that a Scud missile had been intercepted over the base where Dad was stationed in Bahrain. I just stopped eating and looked at Mum, who had gone pale. She walked over, put her arm around me and said it was good news because it hadn't hit and everyone was fine. I was down all that day; in fact, it got to a point where they were all pretty much down days in our house.

The day we were told that Dad was coming home was an incredible day, totally amazing. Before I knew it, we were in the car on the way to RAF Uxbridge. We got there and there were loads of other families crowding around, all waiting for the return of their loved ones.

There was suddenly a rush of activity, with everyone whooping and cheering, which was then getting drowned out by the noise of an engine and a beeping horn. I ran to the front of the crowd and could see a big blue and white coach pulling into the car park. It drove past us a bit and I ran alongside it, looking up at the windows to see if I could find Dad. I couldn't see him anywhere.

Then, just as the coach slowed to a stop, I saw him. He was right there at the window, looking straight at me. It was as if there was no one else in the world. He was smiling and looking tanned and, in a strange way, he didn't look like Dad. The coach door opened achingly slowly and he was one of the first to get off.

He looked at me and said, 'Hiya, son,' and then threw his arms around me. I remember squeezing him so tight, my face pressing so hard into his shirt. He smelled like the inside of a bag that is full of your wet and musty clothes after a day on the beach. I kept holding on tight as I heard him call out to Mum and Rudi. They came over and, at first, I refused to let go. Then he picked Rudi up in his arms and held a hand out to Mum. I stepped away and Mum put her hands up to his face and just stood there, looking at him. They both smiled and almost began to laugh at the sheer joy of it. Dad pulled Mum closer and kissed her tenderly on the forehead, and she just let out the biggest sigh of relief, as if all her worries had disappeared in that one moment. Then Rudi leant in and gave him a kiss on the cheek. And Dad just pulled them both closer to him, smiling all the time. And that, right there, that moment — that was the best day of my life.

IT DOES FEEL strange, looking back on that day, now that I'm a father. That the things I do and say will have a greater impact on my as-yet-unnamed son's life than I'm sure I can comprehend. I hope, like my father, that I can be a good one. I asked my dad a couple of days ago if he had always believed in me, even when things like my awful exam results happened. Whether he thought that I could do the things I'd dreamt of, the work I'm lucky enough to be doing now. Without even pausing, he said that he always had; he just hoped I would put the work in as he knew how incredibly lazy I could be.

I had already decided I wanted to go to Amersham and Wycombe College to do a BTEC Diploma in Performing Arts, but you had to have four GCSEs or more to get on the course. If you had fewer than that, you'd have to do a sort of access course, before going on to the Diploma. I didn't want to waste a year, but then I didn't have the results to get me in. So I talked to Dad about it and he decided that it would be best if the two of us went to speak to the lady who looked after the admissions.

I was so nervous that I can't remember a lot of that meeting. Dad let me do most of the talking to begin with but, as I started to get more and more desperate, he cut in and told her that whatever my exam results seemed to suggest, I wasn't stupid; it was just that all I cared about was Drama and English. He reminded her that this was a 'Performing Arts' course and that, since the age of eleven, I'd been involved in nothing but that. He was vehement, fighting my corner, asking her what it mattered if I didn't have a C grade or above in Science or French, because it wasn't relevant. And guess what? It worked. She agreed to let me on the course. Dad killed it.

THERE ARE TEACHERS who can really influence your life, for good or for bad. There was one at Amersham who was absolutely amazing: John Keats. John had his own theatre company, which put on some really innovative productions, and his lessons had that same spark: they were like nothing I'd ever known. He had this aura about him, big-time charisma.

In class, we covered all aspects of performance. Every lesson he brought something new and even more groundbreaking to the party. For example, he took a scene from *Guys and Dolls* and made us do it as Nazis. You can only imagine how it was: Sky Masterson and Nicely-Nicely Johnson doing their scenes in stilted German accents. It was definitely different.

I loved that first term. I was learning so much and I was surrounded by so many talented people. It was really magical—until John left. Around about Easter of that first year, his theatre company just took off. We came back from the holidays and he wasn't there. It was a major blow and it wasn't the only one: Julian, another really good teacher, had gone off to study in Russia, and all of a sudden we'd gone from these dynamic, young, freethinking individuals to a guy, Stewart, who would just give us choice morsels like: 'The first rule of theatre is you don't turn your back on the audience.'

October to Easter had been the best few months of study I'd ever experienced, so I felt doubly angry and let down when it started to go wrong. It affected me pretty badly and, to my shame, I have to admit I stopped going to college altogether.

I was living at home with Mum and Dad still, but they were up and out to work before me. Sometimes at college you didn't have to be in until ten, and being home before anyone else wasn't unusual. So when Mum and Dad left for work, I'd say goodbye, pretending to get my stuff ready, and then not bother going in. College would go on without me. I'd stay at home and just laze around the house doing absolutely nothing at all.

This went on for about three weeks before it occurred to me that I probably ought to go back in. Whatever point I was making by staying away—if that's even what I was doing—had been made, and so I knew I had to face the music.

I was in the main corridor looking at the notice board for where my classes were when Stewart came up to me. He looked a little quizzical and then he asked me what I was doing there.

For a moment I just stared at him. 'What do you mean?' I said. 'I've got lessons. Your lesson, actually.'

Arms folded, he shook his head. 'No, you don't. You're not coming to my lesson. You can forget it.'

'What do you mean?' I asked him.

'What I said. You've not been here for three and a half weeks. Your parents didn't write in with any kind of explanation. You just haven't been here. So you're not coming back to my lesson. We're working on a show now and you're not part of it.'

He was so chillingly matter-of-fact about it that I just went cold. I stood there, still staring at him.

'As far as I'm concerned, you're off the course. You'd better go and see the head of year. I'm sure she wants to talk to you.'

He walked off, leaving me staring at his back. What would I tell my dad, who'd fought for my place on the course? Or my mum, who'd always defended me when others had lost faith?

I was all over the shop, so I did exactly as Stewart had told me and went straight to the head of year's office. I waited outside with my head against the wall, trying to think of something I could say that would stop her throwing me off the course altogether.

She came out to fetch me: Karen, the woman whom Dad had persuaded to let me on the course. She was cold and stern, more so even than Stewart.

'Where have you been for the last three and a half weeks?' she demanded.

For a long moment I just looked at her. And then it came to me — I opened my mouth and out it came: one massive, horrible lie. 'I've had family problems.'

'What?' she said. 'What do you mean?'

I'd dug the hole and now I had to fill it: 'It's my parents. They're getting divorced.'

For a moment she didn't say anything, but I noticed her expression starting to soften a little and I latched on to it.

'It's been going on for some time now,' I said, 'arguments, fights in the house. It's been a nightmare.' I was gesturing, my eyes glassy and my voice getting smaller. 'I suppose it blew up over Easter, but it's been going on a lot longer than that. With everything that's been happening, I just couldn't concentrate on my coursework. I've been trying to take care of my sisters. I . . . I . . .' And with that I burst into tears. I've put on some good performances in my life, and that was probably one of the best; it's definitely the one of which I'm least proud.

'All right, James,' she said. 'I'm sorry. I had no idea.'

'I know I should have come in,' I went on. 'I know I should've called or written to explain or something, but —'

'It's all right,' she said, patting my hand. 'It's OK. I understand. Come with me to class and I'll explain it to Stewart.'

So we trooped down the corridor to his class and he had to listen while Karen repeated my lies. There was nothing he could do or say. That was it. I was back. I'd survived after spouting a bunch of really unpleasant crap about my family. To this day my mum and dad don't know about those missing weeks or my lie about their marriage. So here's my chance to say a massive sorry to them and to Karen and, through gritted teeth, to Stewart. *Sorry.*

As it turned out, it didn't really matter as I packed it in that summer, anyway. John and Julian's absence wasn't the only reason for me leaving. Something exciting was on the horizon. I was about to get my first big proper job—a musical in the West End.

CHAPTER 3

Marilyn, my agent, rang and told me about an audition for a new musical that was getting a ton of early buzz—*Martin Guerre*.

Based on real life, the musical had been written by Claude-Michel Schönberg and Alain Boublil, the guys responsible for *Les Misérables* and *Miss Saigon*, two absolutely humongous hits. Just the thought of being in a show written by those two guys blew my mind. I'd never been so excited going for an audition. I was going for the part of one of two young boys in the chorus.

For the audition I chose a song from the musical *Chess* called 'Anthem', a standard song for West End musical auditions. It went well enough that the director asked me back for a dance call, along with twenty other boys of various shapes and sizes. You can imagine them wondering, can't you? Can a guy who looks like that cope with a dance routine?

Please. We all know that I'd been practising for years in the living room, studying and recreating every move Take That ever laid down; they were imprinted on my soul. So I breezed through the dancing and then, later that day, I got a call to tell me that I'd made it to the third stage.

I can still remember that last audition as if it were yesterday. It was at the Criterion Theatre just off Piccadilly Circus. When my turn came, I stepped onto the stage. All I could see was a makeshift desk set up in the middle of the stalls at which sat Cameron Mackintosh, the biggest theatre producer in the country. And next to him were the writers of the show, Claude-Michel Schönberg and Alain Boublil, two of the most successful musical writers in history. Then there was director Declan Donnellan, who ran his own theatre company called Cheek by Jowl and was—and still is—one of the best around. Next to Alain was sitting choreographer Bob Avian, with his assistant, Craig Revel Horwood alongside him. Yup, Craig from *Strictly Come Dancing*. No pressure then.

My nerves were jangling, my palms were sweating and my legs were wobbling. I'm sure it wasn't a pretty sight. I'd prepared 'Stony Ground', a really upbeat song from a Christian musical, but the musical director suggested I sing 'Anthem' again, as I'd done a good job on it last time around and he thought that Claude and Alain would really appreciate my vocal range. I wasn't about to argue with him.

It seemed to go down well and, when I had finished, Declan came up on the stage.

'James,' he said, 'I want you to walk around this stage in a circle. I want you to imagine that an army is standing all around you. They're waiting for orders and, when you decide the time is right, I want you to send them out to war. Send them through the stalls. Send them up to the dress circle and to the upper circle. Send them out until the whole place is full of people and they're all listening to you. It's an army, James. Send them out to war!'

Clearly Declan had his reasons, so I sang the song again, only this time I was in charge; I was in uniform, ordering an army out to war. I was Mel Gibson in *Braveheart*. I went for it, singing with every bit of guts, gusto and passion I could muster. Ten days later, I got the job.

I got £260 a week, so by the time I'd paid my agent, my rail fares and tax, I was barely breaking even. But I couldn't care less. I was so happy to be doing what I'd always dreamt of.

MY FIRST DAY at work, I was so keen that I was one of the first to arrive at the theatre. I just sat in a corner as the minutes ticked by, growing more and more nervous. I had no idea what to expect.

At the beginning of the day, as a bit of a loosener, Declan got everyone singing the trolley song. You know how it goes: *Clang, clang, clang went the trolley. Ding, ding, ding went the bell. Zing, zing, zing went my heartstrings, From the moment I saw him I fell.* We had to sing it jigging around as if we were on a tram. The girls would sing a bit and then the boys would sing a bit and, when we were finished, Declan told us to take five.

I guess you could argue I was only seventeen and this was my first proper job, but I really did feel out of my depth. From time to time, other older members of the cast would crack up at some of the stuff Declan was saying; I never seemed to get the joke. I had no idea what they were laughing about, but I laughed anyway because I thought I'd look stupid if I didn't. Looking back, I wonder if anyone knew what we were laughing about, or if everyone else's nerves were just as frayed as mine, and laughing seemed the best way to hide them.

WE REHEARSED for three months solid. As I only had the one line ('Roast the meats'), most of my time was spent hidden away at the back, watching how the actors in the bigger parts were working.

The longer rehearsals went on, the more I was getting into it. With every day that slipped by, the excitement around the show seemed to grow that bit more. Everyone was saying that this was going to be the biggest thing anyone had ever seen. It was difficult not to believe the hype.

Before we knew it, opening night was upon us. I had my line 'Roast the meats' down to a science and I couldn't wait to get out on stage. And it wasn't just the performance we had to look forward to: there was the after-show party, too. Cameron Mackintosh is renowned for throwing one hell of a first-night party and, for *Martin Guerre*, he hired Bedford Square in London—the entire square. It was done up to look like an eighteenth-century fair. There was an old-fashioned helter-skelter, loads of marquees, goblets instead of glasses of wine and in the middle there was this massive hog roast. The attention to detail was crazy.

So, the first night. How was it? Live up to expectations? Well, *yes*! It was amazing, brilliant, like nothing I'd experienced before. The place was packed and, as the curtain fell, everyone was on their feet, cheering and applauding. It was about as good a reception as you could get.

Walking round to Bedford Square with Mum and Dad was such a special moment. Dad said he couldn't believe what he'd just seen and Mum grasped my hand. The party was incredible. I'd never really been much of a drinker because, growing up in the Salvation Army, you're not allowed to drink. That night, though, I went a bit overboard: I got plastered—the first time in my life I'd ever been blind drunk. Mum and Dad left at around 12.30 a.m. but I stayed on till the bitter end.

THE NEXT MORNING I read the reviews of the show and they were awful. After all the hype, the expectation, last night's party and everything, I was aware of a sinking feeling in the pit of my stomach. I remember calling Dad and telling him that I was mystified because the whole place had been on its feet the night before. Dad's reply was as wise as ever: 'You can never tell a thing from an audience of friends and family.' He was right. Two-thirds of the theatre audience that day were probably connected to the show in some capacity. We'd been seduced by an audience who wanted us to do well. Reviews are very important, and a critic's opinion can literally make or break a show, and these were as bad as anything anyone had ever read. I knew then it was going to be a long, hard slog.

Looking back on that first foray into the West End, I made some good friends and I did enjoy it to some extent, but it was never quite what I'd hoped it would be. I suppose it taught me—even after dreaming about it so much while growing up—that I didn't actually want to be in a West End musical after all. Not just standing at the back, anyway. I also learnt that loads of actors just seemed to move from one West End chorus to the next. I knew how easy it would be to get stuck on that kind of treadmill, so I decided to talk to my agent about the possibilities of doing other things.

To GET THE REALLY good jobs, whether on stage, TV or in films, I knew I needed to have a bigger profile: no one was going to take me seriously as an actor unless I put my head above the parapet. I kept my options as open as I could and, towards the end of that first year of *Martin Guerre*, Marilyn phoned about an audition for a British film called *The Church of Alan Darcy*, by two unknown writers, Shane Meadows and Paul Fraser. The film was set around a failing boxing club in Nottingham, and they were casting boys mostly from that area. Shane wanted lads who hadn't really worked that much before so he could develop what he saw as a raw kind of edge.

Bob Hoskins was playing the lead; the thought of appearing in a film with him was just mindblowing. He was playing the boxing trainer who was desperately trying to set up a gym so that local lads would have somewhere to go and not end up on the streets. Frank Harper was to play the cockney backer who helps out financially on the proviso that his chubby son, Tonka, can train at the club. I was auditioning for the part of Tonka.

The audition was an improvisation with the casting director in London and it went really well. The tape was sent to Shane and, after watching it a few times, he liked it enough to offer me the job. I just couldn't believe it; it felt totally unreal. My second job— a film with Bob Hoskins. However, I was still contracted to *Martin Guerre* and had to get their permission to allow me to shoot the film. After much toing and froing it all got worked out, so I went up to Nottingham to meet everyone and rehearse.

We rehearsed in a cinema called the Scala. A young guy, about twenty-four, and a skinhead, came up to me and just said, 'All right, mate. I'm Shane. Loved your tape by the way. Thanks so much for doing this.'

He introduced me to the other lads: Darren, Johann, Karl and Danny. For the first time I really felt like an actor. I'd been in *Martin Guerre* for months now and at no point had I ever really felt like an actor: I felt more like a warm prop or something, whereas there was a vibe about the film that everyone could feel.

Shane knew exactly what he was doing and exactly what he wanted. He's an incredibly inspiring man to be around, and he made me feel welcome and at ease right from the first moment I walked into the Scala. Working with him was a huge step forward for me.

Being in a West End show and shooting a film at the same time wasn't easy. It felt as if I was never anywhere but on stage or on the set, with barely any time for myself, but it seemed like the most natural thing in the world. In Nottingham, I'd be up at six o'clock in the morning, film all day, then I'd get on the train at half past four and be in London at six thirty that evening. I'd hit the stage at seven thirty, then straight afterwards, around elevenish, get another train back to Nottingham, get up the next day and do it all over again. It was tough, but I wasn't complaining; plus I was pocketing two pay cheques. For the first time in my life, I had some spending money of my own.

The title of the film was changed to *Twenty Four Seven* as the producers thought it would be more commercial. Shane and Paul had written a great script, the first I'd read where the characters actually talked the way my friends and I did. They sounded normal, not fake or filmy, and there was real heart and soul in the writing that I hadn't come across before. Every decision Shane made turned out right—especially filming it in black and white. It really pulled into focus the starkness and rawness of the town, without losing any of the joy or humour in the script.

Bob Hoskins was the experienced old head you need to hold a film like that together but, over time, he became one of the lads. It was a wonderful, wonderful time and I could hardly believe it when the last day of filming came around. Looking back, I was lucky. I still had about three weeks to go in *Martin Guerre* so I never experienced that real low that can happen at the end of a shoot. It's understandable, really: making that kind of film is so personal and, living and working together for weeks on end, the group becomes a tight-knit community. The film becomes your entire world and then, suddenly, it's all over.

But I didn't escape it entirely: the slump for me came when I finished performing in *Martin Guerre*, because I'd decided not to carry on my contract beyond that first year. Most of the cast left at the same time and, though it was sad leaving it, eight shows a week for a year had pretty much taken it out of me. It was time to stop.

I WENT BACK to lazing around at home, playing computer games, eating Quavers and just knocking about. I did have a few auditions, but not many, and I didn't get any of them. Very quickly, the money I'd earned from *Twenty Four Seven* and *Martin Guerre* was gone. I remember being £30 overdrawn and realising that this was it, the life of an actor—feast or famine. It was time to find myself a normal job.

I went into the metropolis that is High Wycombe town centre to see if there were any jobs going. I walked into Bella Pasta (they've changed their name now to Bella Italia). It was just after the lunchtime rush and I spoke to the manager, who was a really lovely woman. 'Have you waited before?'

'I've not, no, but I'm a quick learner.'

'Do you have black trousers, a white shirt and a black tie?'

'Erm . . . yes, I think so.'

'Well, you're in luck. I've just had two people leave—you can start tomorrow.'

So that was that; I was a waiter. Some people say it's only when you've been a waiter that you can actually call yourself an actor. And I have to say of my stint at Bella Pasta, I think I was very lucky. I really enjoyed it, it was always fun, and the people who worked there were great.

The job itself felt like the exact opposite of what I'd been doing in the West End. In *Martin Guerre* it was the same thing every night, but when you're a waiter, no two tables are ever the same. I loved the crack with the customers and I earned way more money than I ever did in *Martin Guerre*, with the tips on top of my basic pay. Whenever we had a hen night in, I'd get put on those tables and do jokes about the size of the pepper grinder and what kind of meat they wanted on the meat pizza — you know, the good stuff. I was so enthusiastic and my repertoire so varied, it almost felt like doing stand-up.

There was another reason Bella Pasta was a really happy time for me, too. It was around this time that I first fell in love.

NOTHING PREPARED me for how completely bowled over I was when I met Shelley. Not only was Shelley the first girl I loved, she was without question the first girl to completely love me back: she was the first girl who wasn't looking over my shoulder to see if someone better walked in.

I met her through my friend Stuart Hay. He introduced us one day and we went for a drink after work and ended up chatting all night. Shelley was doing a degree in Film Studies and we talked for hours about our favourite films and actors. She was beautiful and funny and so bright, and I remember thinking I could talk to her every day for a year and not get bored. I was completely smitten. When the evening came to an end, she offered me a lift home in her Fiesta and, as we pulled up outside my parents' house, I thought for a moment about leaning in to kiss her. But the evening had been so perfect that I didn't want anything to ruin it. I was used to girls just liking me as a friend, so instead I said goodnight and stepped out of the car. I took a few paces towards the front door and stopped dead: what if I never saw her again? What if this was my one chance? I couldn't let this be it.

I turned round, walked back to the car and tapped on Shelley's window. 'Erm . . . could I get your phone number?' I said. 'I'd love to see you again . . . If you'd like to. Only if . . . Don't worry if you don't want to. It's cool. I mean . . . I'm not bothered, just . . . Erm. Whatever. I just think it'd be . . . nice.'

In the time I'd been babbling on, Shelley had reached into her bag, taken out a pen and pad, and scribbled her phone number down. She handed it to me and I held it and looked at it for a moment, just taking it in.

I noticed in the bottom corner some small letters: P.T.O., with an arrow attached. I turned it over and in big letters it said: YOU'RE MAD, BUT I LIKE YOU. I smiled and chuckled a little as I gazed at this amazing girl looking up at me. I didn't even think. I just leant down and kissed her. Like I'd never kissed anyone. And she kissed me back. It was incredible. Romantic, silly, heartfelt and sexy, all rolled into one.

After that first kiss, we immediately became a couple and were completely inseparable. Most nights I would stay at her house, which was about five minutes away from mine. Her mum and dad, Mike and Di, were lovely, and I have the fondest memories of the time I spent at their place. They came from Barry Island in South Wales and it was through them I got to know the area. If I hadn't, then things might have turned out so differently.

I DID SIX MONTHS at Bella Pasta. My acting career seemed to have come to a halt. It was just at that point, feeling pretty low, when *Twenty Four Seven* came out to the most incredible reviews. Everyone who saw it loved the film, and Shane was hailed as the best of his generation.

A year had passed since we'd wrapped the shoot, but here we were, a year on, all us lads having a little reunion in Nottingham doing a photo shoot for *The Face* magazine. It was amazing; none of us had ever done a photo shoot before and there we were, now part of this great British film success.

It was being back in the public eye that made me think about what I was going to do next. I needed to get some acting work. Nathan Harmer, a friend from *Martin Guerre*, was looked after by an agent called Jacquie Drewe at London Management. On his recommendation, Jacquie went to see the film and, a few days later, we met up and got along really well. She seemed to have no hesitation in taking me on.

I was moving on but, having been looked after by Marilyn for so long, it was really traumatic to say goodbye. I'd never really left anyone before, and it was horrible having to let down a friend. Marilyn was upset, but we talked about it and I know that, deep down, she understood my decision. I shall always be grateful to her and to the amazing people at the Jackie Palmer Stage School. Without them, my acting career might still be a far-off dream.

Not long after I signed with Jacquie, she phoned me about a new comedy show called *Boyz Unlimited* that had just been commissioned by Channel 4. It sounded really exciting: it was a mockumentary about a boy band and they were looking for a guy to play a character called Gareth, who was loosely based on Gary Barlow. He was one of the main characters, the one who wrote all the songs. I nearly dropped the phone in shock. Someone had written my dream part.

I met Andy Pryor, the casting director, and he put me through a singing audition followed by an acting audition. I seemed to do well in both. We got along great and I was called back for a dance audition. It was a bit like *Martin Guerre*; with my size and everything, they made no secret of being worried about whether I could pull off the routines without looking foolish.

They had brought in Paul Domaine, the choreographer who at the time was creating the dance routines for all the biggest boy bands in the country. I think he was as sceptical as the rest of them, but then none of them knew that growing up I'd spent hour after hour pretending to be Gary Barlow. He started taking me through my paces, and all the moves he was showing me were ones I already knew in one form or another. I just went for it and, two weeks later, I was told I'd got the job.

The show was written and produced by a great guy called Richard Osman. The script was funny and smart and I loved it; the seven weeks of filming were basically a dream come true as I spent every day either singing or dancing or acting. There were four of us in the band: Billy Worth (the cute one), Adam Sinclair (the manly one), Lee Williams (the model-looking one) and me (the fat one who writes the songs). We thought it was going to make us stars. We were in magazines and posters on the Underground; people were calling it the next big comedy of the autumn. Not for the last time in my career, I believed the hype.

It's an interesting phenomenon, hype—creating expectation, talking something up before it happens. Nothing suffers from that kind of expectation more than comedy: if something is built up to be the funniest thing since Morecambe and Wise, there's only one way it can go. That's what happened with *Boyz Unlimited*: it never really caught on. Right from the start the ratings weren't good, and it became obvious that it wasn't going to get recommissioned. I had really believed I was on my way to superstardom and it had all ended so suddenly.

CHAPTER 4

With no sign of a job, I was kicking my heels again when, out of the blue, Jacquie called me about an audition for *Hollyoaks*.

About thirty boys were asked to read for the part of Wayne, the janitor at the college. Wayne wasn't your typical *Hollyoaks* character. He wasn't meant to be very attractive; he smelled a bit; he was overweight. I auditioned. A week later I was filming in Liverpool.

I wasn't a fan of the show and I remember this being the first time in my career where I was doing something I didn't truly believe in. But the contract was only for two months and, given it was the only thing on offer, I decided it didn't matter.

It's a soap opera, of course, and as soon as you arrive you realise why so many members of the cast stick around for so long. It's great fun, like being a student at university, only with lots of money. Everyone is young, attractive and much richer than they've ever been before. It's pretty intoxicating.

I didn't particularly enjoy the way the show worked, though: neither the atmosphere on the set nor the lack of care that went into the actual shooting of the show. It never really felt professional and, from an acting point of view, it frustrated me. That said, I have huge respect for the actors involved, and I made some really good friends there. I've done some interviews where I slagged the show off and I know I was quite negative. I don't mind admitting I regret that now. I don't think it was very fair, because the show doesn't pretend to be anything other than what it is. I guess I was too young, too naive, maybe, to understand it. The fact is, when I did slag it off, it was at a time where I thought I could say and do what I liked, and that says more about me than it does about *Hollyoaks*, doesn't it?

There are reasons I felt negative towards the show. My character became popular quite quickly, probably because he was the only one who didn't have a six-pack or chiselled jaw. It was refreshing in a way. In one episode, my character, Wayne, moved in with Nick Pickard's character, Tony, so the art department had to build a new set for Wayne's bedroom.

I arrived on set, ready to film about six scenes with Nick, all in the flat, when I saw something that I couldn't believe. Blu-Tacked to the walls, in the same way you would stick up pictures of your favourite band or football player, they had placed pictures of food. Not a scene from a bohemian restaurant—actual food. Pictures of fish and chips, or a cottage pie, the odd individual sausage here and there. I was gobsmacked.

What were they trying to say about the character or, deeper still, what were they saying about anyone who was overweight? That fat people worship food in the same way that the other, 'normal', good-looking characters worship footballers or bands? I was immediately offended, told them it was out of order and refused to begin filming until they took the pictures down. I made a stand and to this day I believe I made the right one. I remember telling the art department guy that if he could find me one teenager in the country with pictures of food on his walls, I would go with it.

One of the producers came down to the set. He told me to stop causing a scene, that it was only a bit of fun, and that time-wise the crew were really up against it and we needed to get on. I told him that the quickest way we'd shoot the scene was if they just removed the pictures and then I'd be happy and get on and do it.

I didn't say another word; I just pretended to write a text on my phone. The silence went on so long that I did actually text Shelley telling her I might be about to get fired.

In the end, the producer backed down and asked the art department to remove the photos. It was a strange atmosphere on set that day. I'm not sure many people ever really say things are wrong on *Hollyoaks*.

MY *HOLLYOAKS* CONTRACT was nearly up and I figured we'd shake hands at the end and go our separate ways. Despite some bad moments, I genuinely had enjoyed my time in Liverpool; it's a great city and I always had fun with the cast.

I only had three more days of actual filming, on the Wednesday, Thursday and Friday. It was Tuesday night, and I was at home when Jacquie called and said that *Hollyoaks* wanted to extend my contract. I told Jacquie that I wasn't sure I wanted to do it and she said we should wait for a bit and see what the offer was. Dad thought that was the right way to go, too.

I'd never been in that position before, knowing an offer was coming and sitting around waiting for it. Previously, they'd always come out of the blue and I'd never been in any doubt as to whether I'd want to do it or not. Eventually, Jacquie called and told me she'd got them to the best money she could get. However, there was a condition: they didn't just want to offer me another couple of months; they wanted to book me for a year. The money — Jacquie paused for effect when she told me — would be £70,000.

What?! *How much?* Vividly, I remember going into the kitchen to see Mum and Dad, having just got off the phone with Jacquie.

'What's happened, then?' Dad asked me.

'They've offered me a year's contract,' I told him. 'Seventy grand, Dad. Seventy thousand quid.'

He took that in his stride. 'So, what do you think?'

I shrugged. 'I'm not sure. It's such a lot of money.'

And then Dad said something I've never forgotten. He said,

'Well, if you want my advice, I reckon if they've offered you seventy thousand pounds for a year, and you're not sure if you want to do it or not, I'd imagine you don't want to do it.'

'Yeah, but . . . seventy—' I replied, before Dad interrupted me.

'You don't need it, James. You don't need that kind of money when you're nineteen and living at home. You need it when you've got a wife and a family. You're not in that position, are you? I think if you take that money and get used to all the things that come with it, then the harder it'll be to leave. So you'll stay, and stay again, and before you know it, you'll be Ken Barlow. [He actually said that, I promise you.] It's totally up to you, mate.'

I turned it down. I told Jacquie I didn't want to get stuck in a soap opera—though, to be honest, when I came off the phone I wasn't sure I'd made the right decision. I worried about it for a week or so, and genuinely felt sad when saying goodbye to the friends I'd made there. I also felt a slight pang when the train pulled out of Liverpool Lime Street Station.

A week or so went by. Just at the moment when I started to wonder if it was too late to go back, Jacquie called me with an audition for a film.

Whatever Happened to Harold Smith? was a film about a middle-aged man who starts to display psychic and telekinetic energy, causing the deaths of three pensioners when it interferes with their pacemakers. It was a comedy and when Jacqui told me the names of the cast, I got seriously excited: Tom Courtenay, Stephen Fry and David Thewlis, to name just a few.

CAREERS CHANGE direction unexpectedly. If I'd taken the offer from *Hollyoaks*, that audition would never have come up. But it did and, three days later, I got the part of Walter, best mate to Harold Smith's son, Vince.

Harold Smith was directed by Peter Hewitt, who made *Bill & Ted's Bogus Journey*, and the thought of working with him and the cast he'd put together was totally excellent. When I first arrived at the audition, I didn't think I stood a chance. Nobody else going for the role looked even vaguely like me. My first thought was that they clearly hadn't realised I was this big from my head shot but, oddly, this was one of those situations where my size really helped me out. I stood out as the only big guy up for the part.

Nina Gold was casting the film. Directors use people like Nina because their expertise is in knowing who is around and who is up-and-coming and who might be best for a certain role. With tight scheduling and budget restrictions, a director might only have one day to sit down and cast a couple of parts.

When I got the job, I remember telling Peter that I hadn't thought for a moment I'd be chosen. He admitted that he hadn't thought of Walter as a big guy either, but that the minute I'd walked in, he realised that a big lad would make the part even better.

Walter was Vince's best mate and Vince was being played by Michael Legge, who had just finished three films back to back. I felt a little out of my depth.

The first day on any acting job is always the read-through. Everyone involved sits around a table and you literally read through the script, each actor delivering his or her lines.

It was all a little mindblowing. I was nineteen, I'd just turned down a year's contract with *Hollyoaks* and I was in London sitting opposite David Thewlis, who was sitting next to Stephen Fry, who was sitting next to Tom Courtenay. Crazy. But I had plenty of time to sit there and stare in awe because my character didn't appear until about fifty pages into the script.

I managed nervously to deliver my lines in the read-through without messing up too much and, afterwards, the producer invited us all to his house in Holland Park for a drinks party. That was the first I'd heard about it; no one had mentioned it before. David Thewlis asked me if I was going to go and I told him that of course I was, I wouldn't miss it, and he offered me a lift (which was a relief, as I had no idea where Holland Park was). He had an old Peugeot 305 and, as I sat next to him in the passenger seat, all I wanted to talk about was Mike Leigh. David had played the lead in *Naked*, one of my favourite Mike Leigh films.

I remember the drinks do for two reasons: one, it was in the biggest house I'd ever been to—it was an amazing, luxurious townhouse, spread over countless floors. And two, it was the first time I'd ever tasted hummus. I didn't really know what to do with it and at first I was eating it with a spoon, piling it high like it was Ready brek. After looking around at other people, I soon found out this was not a good look, and started using it as a dip instead.

Aside from the hummus embarrassment, the whole experience of making that film was great, actually. It was a brilliant bunch of people to work with and be around, and the whole shoot was a really happy and satisfying experience.

So, what did happen to *Harold Smith*? When the film wrapped I was really hopeful it would be a success. It was quite a big British production; it wasn't a huge budget or anything, but it was big enough. I'd almost forgotten that when the film came out there was going to be a Leicester Square premiere. It was my first one. I remember walking down the red carpet with the TV cameras looking on and all the gathered press and photographers: people wanted to interview me. Me! I've got to admit that I loved all the attention.

Unfortunately, for whatever reason, the film didn't set the world on fire. Often, that's just the way it is—*Harold Smith* didn't quite hit the mark as we'd hoped, but that's not to say it was a complete disaster. There was a silver lining: because of the calibre of the cast and crew, a lot of influential people in the industry went to see the film and, soon after its release, I noticed a change in the kind of auditions I was going for.

ONE WEEK I went for six different auditions for six different films. One of them was for a film called *Dead Babies*, an adaptation of a Martin Amis novel. It was going to be the new *Trainspotting*, and every young actor was dying to get a part in it. Initially, I was reading for the role of an American but, when I got there, both the director and the producer told me they didn't think I was right for it and asked me to read for another character instead.

OK, that was fine. They told me to go away for an hour, familiarise myself with the new character and come back. I checked through the script and found the new part they wanted me to read for. Here's the description of him: 'The ugliest, vilest man you've ever seen. Less than five feet tall, his hair was falling out, he had boils on his face. A disgusting little creature.' Thanks, guys. I guess I could have been offended that they took one look at me and thought I was right for the 'ugliest, vilest man' part, but it didn't cross my mind at the time. I was just concentrating on the script. I wanted to be in this film no matter what, and it didn't matter that much what part I'd be playing.

I auditioned three times for the film and I eventually got the part. The offer came through on my twenty-first birthday and I remember thinking that I was going to be in the film that everyone was calling the new *Trainspotting*, albeit playing the least attractive man in human history. Olivia Williams was already cast and she'd worked on massive Hollywood movies, and Paul Bettany was another of the leads. Paul is an incredible actor and at that moment was right on the cusp of making it huge both here and in America. I was excited about working with them both, and also with the rest of the brilliant cast that had been assembled.

I'VE GOT TO ADMIT right here and now that I didn't really like the script. I didn't say anything to anyone and maybe I should have, but I never quite got it. The story was about a group of people spending a weekend in a country house, doing loads of drugs, drinking loads of booze and having lots and lots of sex. A killer is stalking the house at the same time and, one by one, the party-goers are all killed off. The premise is great, but there was a tone to the script, a harshness, that I didn't really like. But I'd agreed to be in it, and I was still quite inexperienced at this point, so I didn't have the nerve to tell anyone what I was thinking.

We started rehearsing. My character wasn't short of scenes; he was just short. And all he wanted was to be tall. He made himself a pair of shoes with elevated heels and prayed for an *Alice in*

Wonderland-style drug that would give him the extra inches. That was fine, except I'm not that short. In fact, I was taller than a couple of the actors I was sharing scenes with, so the director would get frustrated because I had to be seated all the time. It got pretty tense at times, and it all came to a head when the production team told me of their plans for my character's hair.

The designer took me to one side and told me that what they wanted to do was bleach my hair to the point where my scalp would turn red. And that, in turn, would make parts of my hair snap off so it would look as if it was falling out. Then, after that, they would shave big clumps out of my hair in various places all over my head.

Wow, I thought, *that sounds a little dodgy—and painful*. But it was for the film, it was in the script, so it had to be done. It only then occurred to me to think about what might happen when the film was over: I wouldn't be able to work. I would be unemployable. I mean, how many parts were there going to be for a guy with clumps of hair missing and a bleached scalp? They weren't paying me much for the film, and definitely not enough to live on for the time it took for my hair to grow back.

I spoke to Jacquie about it, told her I wasn't refusing to do it or anything, but that I was worried about what was going to happen afterwards. Jacquie had reservations as well, so she called the producer, Richard, mentioning our concerns and suggesting we come to some sort of arrangement whereby they compensated me in some way for the hair wreckage.

The phone calls went back and forth between Jacquie and the producer, but the bottom line was they said they couldn't afford to pay me any more money. Ultimately, we reached a compromise where we agreed to try and achieve the same effects with prosthetics. They'd still dye and thin out my hair, but not to the point where it snapped off, and they could colour my scalp with make-up instead of bleaching it red. So, not total carnage, just a radical new look. I agreed to that happily.

My make-up artist was an Australian girl who had just moved

to London. I was aware that what they were planning was no easy task and so, a little nervously, I asked her what she'd been working on before she left Australia. *Home and Away*, she said happily.

Home and Away? It occurred to me, as I'm sure it does to you, that on a soap there wouldn't be that much call for crazy red scalp and fally-outy hair. I was a little worried, to say the least. She did her best, though, and started by thinning my hair out to the point where you could see my scalp. I sat there watching in the mirror as she cut away, my beautiful locks floating unhappily to the floor.

When she had thinned it enough, some other make-up artists took over and started slapping on the red stuff. This was the part that needed to look good. Only it didn't. They kept on trying really hard to make it right, but it became pretty clear that the only way it was going to work was by going the whole hog and shaving the clumps out like they'd originally wanted.

Bill, the writer, director, co-producer and star, entered the room and stood behind me. We were looking at each other in the mirror and we both knew it didn't look right.

'Bill,' I said, 'I don't think this is going to work.'

For a moment he didn't say anything. Then he turned on his heel as if to leave.

'Shall we just go for it?' I said quickly, not wanting to disappoint. 'Just shave and bleach it. Shall we?'

'I tell you what,' he said on his way out, 'I think we should just hold off for a moment. Right now, let's not do anything.'

A moment later, one of the runners came in and told me that Richard the producer wanted to see me, so I left Make-up and walked over to the makeshift office he was using. I went in and sat down at his desk.

'So, James,' he said, 'how's it going?'

'Good, I think.' I'd been smiling when I came in, happy to tell him I'd decided we should go ahead and shave my hair. But there was something about his expression that put me on edge. Coupled with the way Bill had been in Make-up and the way the runner had summoned me, I knew something was up.

Richard was looking everywhere except at me. His eyes glanced all around the room—above my head, to my left, then to my right, down to the ground; anywhere but me. Finally he sighed really heavily. 'Look, James,' he said, 'we're having problems with the way the character is going.'

'Yeah, I know. It's not really clicking yet, but we'll get there.'

'We're quite worried about it, actually,' he went on, 'what with your hair; all that hassle we had with your agent.' He pursed his lips. 'You know, we're wondering whether you're completely committed to this film.'

I didn't say anything. I was unsure as to where this was leading. I'm not committed? I've just looked the director, writer, co-producer and, we must never forget, star, in the eyes and told him to go ahead and shave lumps out of my hair.

Richard was still talking. 'The thing is, I have to make up my mind whether we're going to stick with you or look for another actor, and I've got to decide that by the end of the day.'

I sat there staring at him, completely gobsmacked. He was talking about firing me from what was rumoured to be the next big thing in British film. I didn't know what to say. I just sort of sat there, squirming. He was talking about chemistry and passion for the project and much else besides—it's a bit of a blur and I can't remember exactly what he was saying. All I remember is how he finished. 'So that's why I'm going to have to fire you, James. I'm sorry, you're off this movie.'

I felt as if I'd been punched in the stomach. I took a few moments to try and get my wits together.

'Richard,' I said, 'hang on a minute; you just told me you had until the end of the day.'

'Yeah,' he said, sitting back. 'I don't know why I said that.'

'You don't know why you said that?'

'No,' he replied. 'Sorry, James. I have to let you go.'

We went back and forth for what seemed like ages. I was so upset. I told him I thought his decision sucked and how could anyone accuse me of not being committed? Then he brought up my height as an issue and I reminded him that I hadn't actually grown since they'd given me the job. But nothing I said was going to make any difference. No matter how hard I tried, there was nothing I could do to change his mind.

At the end of it, I left the office and went outside to the car park. I think I stood there for a moment, not quite knowing what do to; then I called Shelley and bawled my eyes out.

I called Jacquie after and she told me to come straight over to the office, but that first she would speak to the producer. I stood there in the car park, my hair thinned out and tears rolling down my face, waiting for Jacquie to call back. The worst part in all of it was that right at that moment the rest of the cast were having lunch at some picnic tables across the way. It was a glorious hot August day and they were shouting and beckoning me over to them. I waved back, but I knew that if I went over to tell them what had happened, I'd find it impossible not to cry. Then Jacquie called me back and told me what I'd known all along: Richard wasn't changing his mind. It was over.

I had no choice but to head for the car they had provided to take me home. I used it to take me into London, and had it wait while I saw Jacquie (I was getting my money's worth). We spoke for a while and she told me I'd still get paid, which was a massive relief, and then she also told me that in all her years as an actors' agent, no client of hers had ever been fired from a film. So I was the first, then. That was nice. What a day! As I took the car back to Shelley's, I felt beaten down—totally and utterly dejected.

At home that night my family kept trying to cheer me up, but the fact remained that I'd been fired from a film set. I had no idea what it might mean for my career. It really worried me because, deep down, I knew my attitude hadn't been right. The bottom line was, I had never liked the character and I suppose, eventually, it showed. It was scarily familiar. It reminded me of how I'd been at school: if something didn't float my boat, I'd react flippantly; be uninterested to the point of disruption. Was that how I'd come across to the crew?

I THOUGHT ABOUT THAT film every day for a year—the endless, painful possibilities. What if this film is the biggest British film ever? What if every member of the cast is catapulted to stardom? It was a horrible feeling that never really went away until the film was released a year or so after I'd left, and made next to no impact in the cinema. I'm not gloating, truly. I just felt relieved. I hadn't missed the boat. For all its efforts, the film just sank without trace. For months I'd been preparing to be the guy who had to admit that he'd been fired from the movie that scooped all the awards and broke all box-office records.

I learnt a lot from the experience. I decided that I'd never be on the outside of anything again; that if I was lucky enough to be offered a part—any part—and accept it, then I had to go for it hook, line and sinker.

I was out of work for four months after *Dead Babies*. I'm not sure it had anything to do with being fired; it may have done, but I think it's unlikely. Most actors are out of work for long stretches.

It's hard when you're just sitting there waiting for the phone to ring for an opportunity to do things, totally at the mercy of your agent or a casting director. It's a frustrating, soul-sapping time. However, the next time the phone did ring, it was a big call. It was the call I'd been longing for.

Jacquie got in touch about a prime-time series called *Fat Friends* that ITV had commissioned. It had been written by Kay Mellor, who already had *Band of Gold* under her belt, a ground-breaking piece of TV about prostitution in Yorkshire.

The series focused on the lives of a group of chubsters who attended the same slimming class in Leeds. There were six hour-long episodes, each driven by a different character. The character I was going for appeared in five of the six, and the fourth episode centred on his story. His name was Jamie; he was an overweight schoolboy with problems at home. I've never wanted a part so badly. I remember reading it, lying on the floor in Shelley's parents' front room, ripping through the script, not putting it down until I'd finished the last page.

As soon as I was done with it, I rolled over on my back and stared at the ceiling for what must have been twenty minutes, and let my mind run away. This part was everything I'd waited for. There is no other way I can describe it. I mean, if you're a big guy, you're not going to be offered James Bond, are you? If it's a rom-com or a bittersweet love story, you're going to be the funny mate of the lead guy who gets the girl rather than the guy who gets the girl. I knew that when I started out. And yet, there I was reading this brilliant story that focused on an overweight schoolboy. His mum had been left by his dad and was depressed to the point where she was taking pills, so Jamie had basically assumed the role of a parent. He had a home life from hell and, at the same time, he was being bullied at school. His story carried the whole episode — all the attention was on him. And though it might sound depressing, there was fun and laughter to go along with the tears. I'm sure you know that I'm fond of a laugh, but there's also a side of me that loves serious acting, getting into the meaty roles that really challenge you. Jamie's character had that rare mix of both.

I remember talking about it to Shelley and telling her that if I couldn't get this part, I might as well give up. It could've been written for me — I don't mean that in a bigheaded way; I just really *felt* the part.

I thought the audition in Leeds went pretty well. Each production has a different way of doing things, and this time they said they would call back the people they wanted for a second reading. On the way back to the station I shared a cab with Richard Ridings, who had been reading for the part of a guy called Alan. We chatted about the day and my heart plummeted when he told me he'd been offered all six episodes, right then and there in the room.

What did that mean? Was I out already? I didn't know what to think. They'd told me they were doing call-backs, but if they'd already offered a role to Richard, then maybe they were just being polite. I must have missed out. I couldn't believe it. I'd been convinced I could make that part my own. It was a long, lonely journey back to London.

The next week went by slowly and, just as I'd got to the point where I'd abandoned all hope, I got a call from Jacquie. Kay Mellor had been in touch: she wanted me to meet her at the Groucho Club in Soho. I was still in with a shot.

I GOT INTO SOHO an hour and a half before the meeting. In the Groucho Club, I went over to where Kay was sitting in the corner with one of the directors, Audrey Cooke, and one of the producers. We talked for an hour or so about the series, about Jamie's character and how they viewed him and how I viewed him, and about what I thought I could bring to the role. I suppose we reached a natural pause and they said they needed to have a chat, just the three of them together. Fine, I said, you guys do that. I'm off to the loo.

I left them alone, and in the toilets I stood looking at myself in the mirror. This was my first time in the Groucho Club. I knew it was where famous people went and so being there kind of felt important, as though I was on the right track. I was feeling pretty confident: I just had a feeling they were going to offer me the role.

Giving them what I hoped was a decent amount of time, I walked back to the table. My heart was fluttering a little as I sat down. For a long moment they all just looked at me and then, with a smile, the producer said they would love to offer me the role. *Yes!* There is no feeling like it: thinking you've missed out on something only to be offered it is the most amazing sensation. I sat there tingling with excitement. I had a lead role in an hour of prime-time television to look forward to, and I couldn't wait to get started.

THE READ-THROUGH was back up in Leeds. As I got off the train, I spotted a woman standing in the middle of the station holding up a massive sign with the words 'Fat Friends' scrawled across it. Spotting Richard Ridings making his way over, I was keeping an eye peeled for anyone else I might recognise or who might fit the bill. There was nobody immediately obvious but, as I headed over,

I found myself walking alongside a lady carrying a heavy suitcase. I asked if she needed a hand and she gratefully let me take it.

And then it hit me. Oh my God, it was Alison Steadman. Alison *Life Is Sweet*, *Nuts in May*, *Abigail's Party* Steadman. And I was carrying her case. Not only had Alison appeared in three of my favourite Mike Leigh films, she'd been married to the guy.

A sudden thought struck me. There was no way she could be in the same TV series as me, right? No way. It was just coincidence, nothing more. I was happy enough that I'd bumped into her at all and that she'd allowed me to carry her suitcase. But, as we walked together towards the lady holding the sign, Alison was matching me step for step. Still, it was only as we both climbed into the people-carrier and sat next to each other that I was prepared to believe the truth: I was going to be in a TV series with one of the all-time greats of British television.

I WON'T GO into all the details of how the shoot went—it was wonderful, amazing, life-changing—apart from to say that the first time Ruth Jones and I really got talking was after we'd finished the first read-through. Ruth, who was playing Kelly, had some big emotional scenes and had tears in her eyes as we came to the end. We had a chat about it afterwards and there was something, right then, that just seemed to click between the two of us. I'm happy to say that click has never gone away.

I couldn't wait for the series to air and, when it did, about ten million people tuned in. I think everyone involved was pretty bowled over by the reaction. Four weeks into the series and my episode came around—my first leading role and the first time I'd held down an hour of prime-time television. I was at home watching with Mum, Dad and Rudi. By the time it was over, all three of them were in tears. Almost immediately after it ended, the phone started ringing: aunts and uncles, cousins, friends from previous shows, schoolmates—it was absolutely amazing.

The show was a runaway success. By the end of the run, there were rumours flying about that it might be up for some awards.

Not for a moment did I think I'd be up for anything, so I had to be picked off the floor when Kay Mellor phoned and told me I'd been nominated in the 'Best Newcomer' category for the Royal Television Society Awards.

And so it was that Shelley and I went along to our first awards ceremony. Shell looked resplendent in her evening gown, and I think I looked all right in my rented tux. We floated around drinking in the atmosphere (and the free drinks). This was a major TV awards do, and I still couldn't believe that I'd been nominated.

It occurs to me now that I had no idea who I was up against until we actually sat down at the table. The other nominees turned out to be Dom Joly for *Trigger Happy TV* and Rob Brydon for *Marion and Geoff*. As soon as I saw his name on the paper, I knew Rob would win. I mean, the guy created a whole series around a guy sitting in a taxi. I certainly didn't mind losing to Rob, and I wouldn't have minded losing to Dom either. As I saw it, to be nominated along with two guys who had written and created their own shows was an achievement in itself.

Finally, the 'Best Newcomer' category came around. I remember holding Shelley's hand as the names were called and a clip from each of the shows was played to the audience. And the winner was . . . Rob Brydon, of course. The two of us spoke briefly together afterwards, and that's when I discovered that he and Ruth had gone to school together. Rob admitted he hadn't seen the show, but Ruth had told him I'd been great in it, which was very nice to hear.

I also got to speak to Graham Norton, who hosted the awards. He came over, introduced himself, and told me that the clip they'd showed of me crying had silenced the room and that that, in a roomful of television people, was a real achievement. I was so happy just to be talking to him, let alone receiving compliments from him. The whole night, everything about it, was so different to anything I'd experienced, and yet, at the same time, had some bizarre sense of familiarity, which must have come from having dreamt of it for so long.

CHAPTER 5

So much of acting is about luck, being in the right place at the right time and knowing the right people. And it's definitely true that the more you work, the more people you meet, and the more likely you are to get opportunities to work.

Tiger Aspect is a big production company making many television shows, from documentaries and comedies to dramas like *Fat Friends*. Because I'd worked with them on that show, they asked me if I'd like to audition for a new Channel 4 series called *Teachers*. It starred Andrew Lincoln of *This Life* fame and was centred around the lives of a group of young teachers in Bristol.

Once again, the fact that I had experience yet still looked like I was a schoolboy played into my hands, and I was offered the part of Jeremy, the class geek. Working with Andrew was a real joy. So encouraging, with the perfect balance of fun and professionalism.

I made lasting friendships on that job—not just with Andrew but also with the runner, a young guy called Ben Winston. There's a runner on every production and, for my money, they have the hardest job on the set. It's utterly thankless: they are the first to arrive on set and are the last to leave; they do everything, for everyone, and yet they're often treated as irrelevant. They are the worst-paid member of the film crew, but they're vitally important to the smooth running of the production and, the truth is, anyone who is anyone in film will at one point or another have been a runner. The best way to discover whether you're cut out for a life in TV—the shitty hours, the time away from home, the unpredictability of where your next job will be—is to become a runner. If you can hack that, then there's a good chance you'll be all right. And Ben could hack it—I've never known anyone light up a film set the way he did. Everyone fell in love with him—nobody more than me.

But more about Ben later, because right now I want to tell you about a call I got that very nearly killed me stone dead. I'd just come off the set of *Teachers* when my mobile started ringing. It was Jacquie and she was phoning to tell me that she'd arranged an audition with someone I was a fan of.

'Who? Who is it?' I asked.

'Mike Leigh.'

I just stood there holding the phone.

'What?' I said. 'You mean actually with Leigh. You're talking about *the* Mike Leigh? My favourite film-maker of all time?'

'That Mike Leigh, James. Yes.'

How to explain? If you ever passed Mike in the street, you'd barely notice the little guy with dark, smiley eyes, cropped hair and a smallish, Father Christmas-style white beard. He's so unassuming he looks like a cross between a good-natured hobbit and a monk. The reality is that Mike is probably the purest film-maker on the planet. I know that sounds a bit wanky, but it's the truth. Acting in his films is the most original, fundamental and raw experience you can have professionally. For months on end you soak yourself in the character you're about to play and get to learn them inside and out: their thoughts, their instincts, their hopes and aspirations, what they'd eat for breakfast — everything. You essentially become the author of a person.

Jacquie told me that she'd taken a call from Nina Gold, who had cast me in *Whatever Happened to Harold Smith?* Nina was casting Mike's new film and she wanted me to meet him.

THE USUAL THING you do when you're going for an audition is to read through the script and familiarise yourself with the part so you can really do it justice when the time comes. But that's not how it works with Mike. There is no script at the 'audition'; at that point, I don't think Mike even knows exactly what he's looking for. It's the kind of thing that, if you over-think too much, can get very daunting; that sense of a blank page and having nothing to work from but your instincts. But if you look at it another way, it can really free you: you're not constrained by lines that must be

Me, aged three, just taking it easy on the beach.

My sisters and I. Andrea (left) and Ruth (middle).

Just a young guy in buckled shoes, leaning against a tree.

Mummy's boy.

ge school agency photo. I had asked the
rber to cut my hair like Gary Barlow's in
'Pray' video.

The cast of 'Fat Friends' and, yes, I am
wearing a woman's coat.

e History Boys': Russell Tovey, Sam
derson. Me, Andrew Knott, Dominic
er, Sam Barnet, Jamie Parker and
ha Dhawan.

Me, Mat, Joanna and Ruth. The first photo
shoot the four of us ever did.

And there she is, my best friend in the whole wide world, on a night neither of us will ever forget.

David and I. Putting towels on our heads was his idea.

Smithy and the England Team.

On the high board with Tom Daley. Tom's the one on the left.

Me and Jules in the Maldives, jumping into the rest of our lives!

Me and my Bubba. She is the best person I've ever met.

Oh, and by the way, we've decided on a name for him. Oh yes. His name is . . . Max McCartney Kimberley Corden.

said in such-and-such a way or dealing with someone else's creation—the character is entirely yours.

Mike's office, in the middle of Soho, was on the first floor of a Georgian townhouse and the bell you rang from the street had two other bells alongside it. One was for the place downstairs and the other was for the lady of the night's pad on the top floor. By the time I got upstairs, the nerves had overtaken me a little and I sat down in front of him, still not quite believing I was actually there, and that he was Mike Leigh.

'So,' he said, in his quietly considered way, peering out from his hooded eyes. 'You were in this programme *Fat Friends*, then?'

'Yes,' I said, 'I was.'

'Well, I don't think it was very good.' He studied me. 'What do you think?'

Mike is renowned for his no-nonsense honesty, but to be hit with that from the get-go was a little alarming. I didn't jump right in. I considered my answer for a bit and told him I could see why he might not like it, but that I was very proud of my bits.

'Really,' he said. 'I haven't seen your bits. I'll have to look them up.'

I chilled a little after that. We talked about acting and films, about my career and the kind of films I liked. I told him how important I thought films were and that I didn't have anything more valuable than my DVD collection. A lot of the films in it had been made by him, and I had to make a big effort to stop myself from telling him again and again what kind of influence he'd had on my life.

I can tell him now, though: the two greatest influences on my working life have been Mike Leigh's films and *The Royle Family* series on TV. In different ways they show you that, no matter what you might think or feel about this world, nothing is ordinary. Mike has the ability and talent to show you how people actually live, and make incredibly moving drama and comedy from it. He doesn't shy away from everyday concerns, or hardship, or even boredom; he manages to find drama and emotion in very normal places. I'm not criticising other films for their lack of realness—every movie has its place and I love my Hollywood as much as any man—but it's the genuine, challenging stuff that has always moved me the most.

It was an audition, of sorts. I was with Mike for about an hour and we did a bit of background work on a character and then Nina came in. Mike told her that he thought I ought to come back again the following Thursday, when I had a day free from filming.

Travelling back down to Bristol, I couldn't get over the fact that I'd just spent the best part of an hour sitting and working with one of my heroes, and now he wanted to see me again. This was the guy I'd admired all my life, the director I most wanted to work with.

WHEN I WENT BACK to Soho again the following week, the nerves had gone. It helped that, as I walked up the stairs, I passed an Australian guy who was tucking his shirt in his trousers. 'Oh strewth, mate!' he said. 'Get yourself up there. She's a ripper!'

Mike was standing in the doorway on the first floor chuckling to himself at the exchange. We sat down on the sofa in his office and he told me that he'd watched my episode of *Fat Friends* and, though he thought I was right to be proud of it, he still thought it was an awful show. I wasn't offended.

Mike's films are entirely about the characters. Prior to their creation nothing exists at all—no story, no plot, no locations; everything takes shape as the characters develop. On that second visit he asked me to think of someone I knew who wasn't a relation and wasn't an actor either. Anyone. For whatever reason, Luke Smythson popped into my head, a guy from school who was a massive Leeds United fan. Mike told me he was going to go out of the room for a while and, in my own time, he wanted me to become Luke. He didn't tell me to do anything specifically, just to 'become'.

'All I'm going to do is step back into the room and observe,' he said. 'All right?'

So for forty minutes I did absolutely nothing. I read a newspaper;

I looked out of the window; I stared into space; because that's what Luke would have done. When we finished, Mike asked me to tell him about what had been going on for the last forty minutes. I amazed myself by what I started to say. I explained that I (as Luke) was reading the newspaper because a Leeds fan had just been stabbed in Turkey and the truth of it was that if I'd had more money, I'd have been there for that match, no question. He was nodding, asking a few questions, probing a little deeper, but there wasn't much more to it than that.

We talked a little more and then I left. I didn't really know what to think other than that I'd really enjoyed the process. I'd had a taste of what it would be like to work with Mike Leigh and, difficult as it could be, the organic nature of the work was even more stimulating than I'd imagined.

It was just before Christmas when I got the phone call telling me Thin Man Films, who make all Mike Leigh's films, was booking me for eight months. I was absolutely ecstatic; it was a moment I will never forget. I was on the set of *Teachers* and I remember telling Andrew Lincoln and him giving me the biggest hug. Ben Winston was there and he was jumping around too, celebrating with me.

IT TURNED OUT that working with Mike was both brilliant and brutal. It was incredibly hard work, but also extremely rewarding. The truth is, I could write a whole book on the experience and still wouldn't be able to get across exactly what it was like. It was the most challenging, difficult, lonely, yet fulfilling work I've ever done as an actor.

You start with nothing. Absolutely nothing. Then you and Mike get together in a room and, over time, you fashion this character from birth to the age they're at in the film. It's kind of a gamble because you sign up not knowing what you're going to be doing at all, or how big your part will be. I've heard endless stories of actors signing to do a film and ending up with three lines or, worse still, being cut altogether. Fortunately, in my case that didn't happen. The film was called *All or Nothing*, and I played Rory, an overweight, angry boy who lives in a high-rise on a council estate.

If you asked me what Mike Leigh is like, I'd describe him as the nicest, warmest, funniest, most generous arsehole in the world. It's very, very hard doing his films. You never get any praise. The best you could hope for was a slight purse of the lips and maybe a quiet 'That was good acting.'

Ironically, given it was my dream job, I look back on that time with a lot of regrets. I was so in awe of Mike that I found it hard to do my best work. When you're so desperate not to mess something up, that's all that occupies your mind, and you find yourself second-guessing your instincts and constantly questioning yourself. I find that my best work comes when I'm totally open to screwing a few things up: you accept the mistakes and learn from them. Anyway, whatever it was, I was never myself on that set. I felt out of my depth with the other actors. I didn't feel intelligent. In fact, compared to everyone else, I felt really stupid; most of the time when we'd sit round a table at lunch, they'd all be talking about things I had no clue about.

For the first time in my life, the fact that I hadn't trained professionally suddenly bothered me. Mike would tell us to warm up and send us off into a room on our own so we could get into character. I wouldn't know what to do. The really stupid thing is that if I'd swallowed my pride and told Mike that I needed his help, he'd have given it to me. I lost something out of the experience because I was so uptight about getting it right (or at least being seen to be able to get it right). But saying that, I'm incredibly proud of the film. It's beautiful. Incredibly bleak, but very beautiful.

I remember one day—actually, 'remember' is the wrong word; it's a day that's tattooed on my mind for all eternity. It was only my second day of actual filming, and we were doing a scene between Rory and his mother, Penny, played by Lesley Manville. Rory was an angry kid. I mean really, bitterly angry. So angry that he kicked out at every opportunity. Overweight, friendless, living on a council estate, he was a victim of his own loneliness. And the lonelier he was, the angrier he got, and vice versa. He was big, ungainly and clumsy. Finally, in the second half of the film, he suffers a heart attack.

We were doing a scene in which Rory and his mum come out of a lift in the high-rise block of flats they live in. This was a real block on a disused estate. The art department managed to create the feeling that the entire block was lived in; every flat we used was fully functional so they all felt like real homes. Everything worked, from the plumbing to the lights to the cookers.

Rory and his mum had to walk along an open walkway to their front door. Rory goes to open the door, finds it locked and then just loses it. He starts banging his fist against the door, banging and banging, then yelling at his sister inside to open it. We had rehearsed this over and over again, the improvisation gradually being scaled down until we all knew exactly how the scene worked. Every gesture and every expression had been practised to the point where they felt as natural as possible and had the sense of authenticity that is the hallmark of all Mike's films. Only, in my case, it wasn't quite as authentic as I thought.

The line I had was simple: 'What's she doing?' The words were supposed to spill from my mouth like stones—angry, frustrated, totally raw.

Mike led us into the scene in his usual fashion, which is completely unlike any other: he'll quietly tell you to get into character and then actually give you the time to do so. Then, after that preparation time, comes the measured sound of 'Turn over the camera, cameras at speed and . . . action.' By the time you start rolling, the entire crew is absolutely focused.

So, I'm hammering on the door and Lesley's telling me to stop but I keep on banging, ignoring her, and then I spit out my line. 'Well,' I said, 'what she's doing?'

'Cut.' Mike stopped the cameras. And then he laid into me. Day two of filming and he's tearing this massive strip off me in front of the whole crew.

'Well?' he said. 'What's "well"? Where does that fit? *Well*'s not right. *Well*'s not motivated.' He shook his head and told me to concentrate. Then he turned to the crew. 'Sorry, everyone, we're going to have to go again.'

The ground could've opened up and swallowed me. Please God, let me not be here suffering this bollocking from Mike Leigh of all people. I don't know if he meant to humiliate me that badly, or if he was turning my mistake into an advantage, thinking that a dressing-down would only make me — and thus Rory — angrier. If that was his motivation, he was spot on. By the time we did the next take I was really angry.

You might be wondering what the difference is between 'What's she doing?' and 'Well, what's she doing?' In the context of the film it was massive. The word 'well' sounded as if Rory was apologising for his actions, and Rory didn't apologise for anything. By the time I'd finished working with Mike, those kind of subtleties were becoming much clearer to me. In fact, it was the best education as an actor that I ever had.

When they showed the film at Cannes, it received a five-minute standing ovation that sent shivers down my spine. I remember Sting coming up to me afterwards and telling me he thought my performance had been amazing. I couldn't believe it. I was so shocked I don't even think I said thank you; I just stood there open-mouthed.

Critically, the film polarised opinion. There was nothing lukewarm about anyone's reaction: they either loved or hated it. But that's often how it is with Mike's films and I'd wanted to be part of it for the experience, not for where the film might take me.

He's such a phenomenal director that everyone who works with him yearns for another opportunity. There are a chosen few who get invited back: Alison Steadman, Timothy Spall, Ruth Sheen, Lesley Manville, people like that. I've got a feeling that *All or Nothing* might've been my one and only shot, though. The way my career has gone since, I'm not sure I'm what Mike's looking for.

Mike doesn't want people who pussyfoot around him and laugh at his jokes all the time — I did both. He wants actors who challenge him and I don't know that I did that.

CHAPTER 6

On the whole, I got good reviews for my part in *All or Nothing*. A month or so after it came out, I went for an audition for a TV film called *Cruise of the Gods*. It was written by Tim Firth and starred Steve Coogan and Rob Brydon. Steve is one of my comedy heroes, so this was a big deal for me.

The premise of the show revolved around two stars of a hit eighties TV show called *The Children of Castor*. Rob was playing the guy who'd been the lead, while Steve's character had played second fiddle. But, since the show ended, Steve's character had gone to LA and become a massive star; by contrast, Rob's had ended up working as a doorman in a hotel. He was broke, depressed and living on his own in a bedsit. Out of the blue, he's asked to be the guest of honour on an Adriatic cruise organised by the fan club. The part I was going for was a boy called Russell who was the fan club's chairman's assistant and, unbeknown to anyone, Rob's long-lost son.

I think they had been looking for an actor who was a bit better known than me, but I wanted the part so badly that my enthusiasm must have shone through. Here was a chance to work with Rob and Steve, and with David Walliams, who was playing the chairman of the fan club. Three of the best comedy actors in Britain. Finally, they did call to say I'd got it.

I was totally over the moon. (I realise at this point I've said this a few times, but truly, every job I get, I still can't believe that people are prepared to pay me for something I enjoy so much.)

THIS JOB, MORE than any other, felt like a new chapter of my career. It was the first time I'd ever had to go abroad to work. The whole shoot would take place on a cruise ship that would be sailing around the Greek Islands. I kissed Shelley goodbye and headed off to the airport. The shoot would be the longest time we'd ever spent apart since we'd been together, and I felt incredibly sad at the thought of being away for so long. This was the first time I realised that I'm someone who gets quite homesick. I love travelling, don't get me wrong, so maybe homesick isn't the right way to describe it. I get people-sick, I guess. I miss my family and my friends a lot when I'm away.

My sadness at leaving Shelley was soon at the back of my mind, though, as I was seated next to David Walliams on the plane. Pretty much instantly, I thought he was one of the funniest people I'd ever met. Within minutes, he had me in stitches.

When we landed, we headed to Baggage Reclaim. I remember, as we all stood there waiting, watching David, Steve and Rob stand around together, bouncing off one another hilariously. It was pretty obvious that they shared an easy rapport and a similar mindset and had real respect for each other. I so wanted to be a part of that. I was standing about fifteen feet away from them, but it might as well have been fifteen miles. I had a burning desire to be included in this special band of comedy musketeers about to take to the seas.

We collected our bags and then walked over to the coach for the three-hour trip to the port. My bag had been the last off, so I was trailing a little behind everyone else. I was the last to board the bus and, after putting my bag in the hold, I walked up the steps. I immediately felt as if I was back at school. Steve, Rob and David had taken the back seat—of course they had, they were the cool gang. But where was my place? I stood at the front and looked down the aisle. I started taking some tentative steps down the centre of the coach and then thought to myself, *Screw it. Just go and sit with them.*

I had to let them know that I wanted to be in their gang; I couldn't wait for an invite that might never come. So I strode right up and sat down on the seats just in front of the back row, and from that moment on, and for the whole three-hour journey, all I did was laugh. I don't think I offered a single word to the conversation; I was more than happy to be their audience. They all seemed so confident and I remember thinking that this is what it's about—performing your own stuff. All three of them had created and starred in their own shows and so they weren't at the mercy of casting directors or agents if they didn't want to be. Just being around people like that made it all seem so much easier, and so much more achievable.

WE SET SAIL on the ship and began filming the very next day. It was a great shoot. We filmed as we sailed, in and out of dock, down the coast and all around the islands. Whenever we had a day off I'd spend it with David or Rob, or both. Steve was only in the film sporadically, so he came and went quite a lot.

I don't remember a time when I've laughed that much. In fact, the whole job was like that, just laughing all the time. Working with those guys really made me want to be part of British comedy. The way they talked about getting television shows off the ground, commissioning pilots, investing in new talent; all that had a huge and lasting impression on me.

The time I spent with David and Rob was totally invaluable, and I remember one conversation in particular that I had with Rob. One evening we were on our way to grab some dinner at a taverna as the sun set over the sea. We were talking about our careers and what each of us was aiming to do in the future.

'I know you've done lots of different stuff already,' Rob said, 'but what do you really want to do? Where do you want your career to go?'

I had to think about that. Nobody had ever asked me as directly. 'I don't really know,' I said. 'I suppose comedy is something I'd like to do more of. I want to do something that people are going to remember.'

He was nodding. 'I heard Ruth wrote an episode of *Fat Friends*. Why don't you take a leaf out of her book and have a go at something yourself?'

He was right. Ruth *was* writing an episode, and there was nothing to stop me thinking about doing something off my own bat.

'The thing is,' Rob went on, 'you can't just sit around thinking that you want to be part of British comedy. You have to *be* part of it. Take David,' he said, pointing to Walliams, who was wandering up behind us. 'He's writing his own sketch show with Matt Lucas. They came up with an idea, put together a treatment and now they're making it for the BBC.'

Little Britain was about to hit our screens, the series that would catapult David and Matt into the stratosphere. Steve Coogan had created Alan Partridge and Rob had built his career with *Marion and Geoff*. He was right. British comedy wasn't going to come calling for me. If I wanted in, I would have to gatecrash the party.

WITH THE IDEA of doing my own stuff firmly planted, I returned to Leeds to film the new series of *Fat Friends*. I was buzzing after those weeks on the ship. And after that inspiring chat with Rob, I was looking at the future in an ultra-positive light. I'd never felt so energised. The realisation that I didn't have to wait for parts completely changed the way I thought about work. I started actively looking for stories and dreaming up ideas for shows. No matter where I went, I would see something that intrigued me—I'd catch sight of an interesting-looking character in a shop or waiting at a bus stop, or in a café or on the train plat-form, and start thinking about what kind of life they led, how you could make a character out of them. I tried to take in as much as I could of the world around me and then write it all down in a journal I always carried around. It's a tried and tested method; who was I to muck around with it?

I suppose things began to take some proper shape when Shelley took me to a family wedding down on Barry Island. We were invited to just the evening reception rather than the whole cere-mony, so we spent the day walking along the beach and soaking up that special kind of atmosphere you only get from a seaside town. You know what I mean—Skegness, Cromer, Eastbourne, all those old Victorian holiday destinations: there's something unique about them. They have a kind of era-defying Britishness that you don't find anywhere else: donkey rides, teeth-breaking rock, wind-breakers all down the beach. I love those towns out of season, too. They become so bleak so quickly, all shut up and empty, forgotten until the next time.

We went to the evening do as arranged, and Shelley spent some time catching up with a few friends she hadn't seen in a while. Rather than crowd her, I sat myself down at a table on my own. I wasn't fed up or bored or anything; in fact, I was just the opposite. I was more than happy to sit there quietly and take it all in. Weddings are strange occasions, aren't they? I mean, the way two groups of people who don't know each are thrown together, forced to get along, and by the end of the night, hopefully, they're all doing the conga.

Every now and then I'd pick up the odd word, or a line or two here and there, that would make me chuckle. Sitting there, with my attention switching from one group to the next, it occurred to me that I'd never, ever seen a 'proper' wedding on a TV show. TV weddings are heated, theatrical affairs—someone busts in halfway through to stop it going ahead—and there's all this dramatic tension that doesn't exist in real life. In my experience, 99 per cent of weddings go off without a fight or a massive family fall out.

I didn't know the couple getting married; I didn't know anyone at all, actually. But I did know the girl was from Barry and the guy she was marrying was from Runcorn in Cheshire, so there were two different families and two different sets of friends from two very different parts of the UK, all thrown together in this room. That got me thinking, and I began to wonder whether a wedding like this could be a pretty nifty setting for a comedy.

Now I really started to look around and listen. Two middle-aged men at the next table, one local, the other from Runcorn, were chatting away, a couple of pints between them. They clearly didn't know each other. I started eavesdropping and, at first, I thought they were talking about cars. You know, what they drive, what they'd like to drive, good motorway routes—it was a solid man chat. But the more I heard, I realised that they weren't talking about the cars themselves; they were using them as metaphors to describe the kind of people they were, or at least the guy from Barry was.

'The thing with me is,' he was saying in his deep Welsh accent, 'I'm a Mondeo. That's what I am. I'm not a Ferrari. I'm not a Porsche. Of course, I'd love to be an Audi, but I'm not. I'm a Mondeo and I'm fine with that. That's who I am, see.'

With the kind of solemn, knowing nod you get in church, the man from Runcorn seemed to understand.

'I'm better than a Vauxhall,' Mondeo man continued, 'or a Volkswagen.'

Now Runcorn man sat forward, his eyebrows arched.

'So you think a Mondeo is better than a Volkswagen then, do you?' he said.

'Well, yeah,' Mondeo man went on. 'It's better than a Polo, isn't it, or a Golf? A Mondeo is better than a Golf.'

Runcorn man nodded. 'Aye,' he said, 'fair enough. It's better than a Polo or a Golf maybe. But it's not better than a Passat, though, is it?'

'No,' Mondeo man admitted, 'not a Passat. I'll give you that. It's not better than a Passat. But it's better than a Golf, and a Mondeo is what I am. I'm right in the middle, see. I'm a Mondeo man.'

I could feel the hairs lifting on the back of my neck. This was great; this was real life in a way I understood it—a conversation about everything these two men actually were, told through Mondeos and Golfs. *A wedding*, I thought, *a wedding*. Nobody had written a wedding like this. The way the small sideline events unfold, the insignificant conversations, the nonsenses. Suddenly, I could visualise a whole set of sequences that were as crazy and hilarious as this one.

You know when you've had a good idea because it stays with you. We've all been there. You think of something, get really excited about it, then go to sleep that night and, when you wake up, you're delighted to find that the idea still feels as good as when you first thought of it. And that idea of a wedding stayed with me.

BACK IN LEEDS for the *Fat Friends* shoot, there was this one evening when Ruth Jones and I were sitting on our own at the hotel bar. I started telling her about Mondeo man and Runcorn man, and all the other people I'd spotted at the wedding. She got the characters immediately; they just clicked with her in the same way they'd clicked with me. Also, Ruth sort of knew them herself. I mean, she's from Cardiff and she'd known lots of Mondeo men; she'd met them at countless weddings.

Ruth and I are really like-minded in the way we see situations and think about scenarios and characters. It's hard to explain it exactly—there's no real science to it—but there are certain people you get, and who get you. I'd felt it with Ruth since we'd first met, but sitting there in the bar, that connection between us developed into something really exciting.

We started riffing, improvising, working out different characters, playing out little scenes. We got talking about two families at a fictional wedding: who they were and where they came from, who was marrying whom, who was the Mondeo and who was the Golf. Before we knew it, we came up with Barry Island and Billericay. We imagined their relatives and friends, old and young, their mannerisms, their accents, the way they spoke, the different phrases they might come out with. We decided the girl would be from Barry and the man from Billericay, and then we worked back to figure out who would be at the reception, why they were there, who'd arrived with whom and who was going to get off with whom. We improvised scene after scene: the drunk, the girl crying in the corner, the loudmouth and the overbearing uncle who can't tell you enough about his latest gadget.

In this case it had to be the digital camera. At the wedding on Barry Island, Shelley's uncle had sat me down and told me all about his new camera, as if he was the only man in the world to have owned one.

'See this,' he'd said, showing me the screen on the back. 'There's no film in there, no film at all. You just take a photo and if you don't like it, you delete it. See? You just delete it. No need for a film at all. The film is the camera: it's a chip, a microchip inside, and if you don't like a picture, you just delete it.'

This was 2002! I already had a digital camera. My dad had a digital camera. Most people I knew had digital cameras. I even told Shelley's uncle that I had one, but that didn't stop him talking about it as if he'd lifted it from a NASA lab. Ruth and I named him Uncle Bryn.

The hours slipped by as we went from one scene to another, one character to the next. Later on, a bunch of office workers came into the bar, and we used them as substitutes for our wedding guests, picking out who was from Essex and who was from Barry Island. Then we got them involved a bit and got them laughing and joking around with us. The whole of it felt so natural and organic: pure, like the comedy I'd talked about with Rob back in Greece.

IT WAS INCREDIBLY exciting. The original idea of the wedding had developed into something solid now, with depth and layers and, with Ruth's involvement, the scope was endless; but we both knew that a few hours of improvisation did not a TV show make—we had to write it down.

Thinking back on it, that evening was the only time Ruth and I were ever in the bar on our own. We were in the middle of filming the series and there would normally be other members of the cast hanging around, having a drink and a chat. But that day it was only us. Had anyone come along, the flow might have been interrupted and, who knows, maybe the whole thing would have fizzled into nothing. But for whatever reason—fate, luck, coincidence; call it what you want—nobody did come, and we both left with the same belief that we had the beginnings of something special, and the promise that we wouldn't let it end there.

So much of life is about being in the right place at the right time. Had Mondeo man been down the other end of the room instead of on the table next to me, maybe none of what came after would ever have happened.

Even with all our enthusiasm, we never got round to putting anything down on paper over the remainder of the *Fat Friends* shoot. We were both very conscious of it, though, and both equally determined not to let it slide into being just another good idea that never went anywhere. On the last day of the shoot, we agreed that we must get together and put something down on paper.

AFTER *FAT FRIENDS* had finished shooting, I was out of work again and looking for my next gig. A few months before, I'd been having conversations with Jacquie about trying to get back into theatre, as I was becoming increasingly aware that my CV had a big hole in it: a proper play.

In theatreland, the difference in attitude towards doing a play and doing a musical is massive. There's an old prejudice that some people still cling on to: proper actors do plays, 'turns' do musicals. A 'turn' is a performer who sings and dances, but isn't seen as having the necessary depth to play the straighter, more challenging roles. ('Turn' comes from people calling such actors 'twirly turns'.) It's not something I agree with, not in the slightest; it's just another form of snobbery. Why should an actor who's giving a brilliant performance in a West End musical be held in any less regard than someone who's working at the RSC? I've known lots of important people who make the assumption that, just because someone can do one thing well, that's all they can and should do for the rest of their career. I wonder how many brilliant actors have never been able to show the world what they're truly capable of because they've been dismissed as one thing or another.

I was determined that I wasn't going to be one of those guys who did the same thing over and over, and I knew a good way of ringing the changes was to land a part in a decent play at a respected London theatre. I just had to be patient.

In fact, I had just been offered a guest lead in a BBC drama called *Messiah*, which was really exciting. Ken Stott was in it, and he'd done a lot of work I admired so I was really looking forward to working with him.

But, only a week or so afterwards, Jacquie phoned to say that we might have to stall because I had an audition coming up at the National Theatre. She was going to send the script straight over.

To MY MIND, the National Theatre is the greatest theatre in the world: all the greats have worked there at some point. What's so special and unique about the National is that it's home to three individual theatres: the Cottesloe, the Lyttelton and the Olivier. Each varies in size and each theatre houses two different productions that play in repertory (which means that they alternate back and forth). With six different productions, all either rehearsing or performing at any one time, it means the whole place is constantly buzzing with an incredible creative energy.

As soon as I'd spoken to Jacquie, I started to daydream about what it would be like to work there, but I knew I had to be realistic. I'd auditioned there once before when I was about fourteen but, as you haven't come across the chapter about my big break as a child working for Trevor Nunn, you'll have worked out that I didn't get the job.

As I prepared for another audition, Dad made sure that I kept my feet on the ground: 'James,' he said, 'the part probably has one line said off-stage and the rest of the time you'll be standing at the back wearing a mask.' Truth is, he was right: I couldn't get too excited before I'd read the script.

It arrived the next day. As I opened the envelope, I needed both hands to pull out the giant stack of pages. It was the biggest script I'd ever seen: dense and heavy, hundreds and hundreds of pages full of dialogue. But there, on the front, were six words that any young actor (in fact, forget 'young' — just any actor) dreams of seeing: 'A new play by Alan Bennett.'

I couldn't believe it. Not just 'a play' by Alan Bennett: 'a *new* play'. There must only have been a handful of people in the world who had read it, and I was soon to be one of them. I felt lucky to be holding it; it didn't even register at that moment that I might have a shot of actually being in it. But first I had to read it.

It was called *The History Boys* and was about eight young sixth-formers in the eighties being prepped and groomed to get into Oxford and Cambridge. Here's a confession: I found it really hard to understand the first time I read it through. I got totally lost: there were references to Auden, a whole scene entirely in French and lots of details about historical events that I knew very little about. I found it frustrating, and I got annoyed at myself for not working harder at school. At the end of it, I put the script down, clasped my hands behind my head and let out a long sigh. *Oh well,* I thought. *That was nice. Getting to read that. Shame I don't understand a word of it.*

I relayed my frustration to Jacquie, but she brushed right over it and instead concentrated on which part I could play. But even though she was really upbeat, she was still unsure about where I might fit in. There was Dakin, the good-looking, cool kid; Posner, a young, effete Jewish boy who lusted after Dakin; Scripps, Dakin's friend and the narrator for much of the play; and Rudge, the really athletic captain of the rugby team, who wasn't the brightest. There were four other boys listed but, at that point, their parts weren't properly defined: they had character names, but many of the lines were just written as Boy 1, Boy 2, etc.

Jacquie told me not to get too downhearted and that, however I might feel about the play, I should still go and meet Toby Whale, the casting director. If he liked what I did, then I'd most likely be called back to meet Nicholas Hytner, the director, and maybe even Alan himself.

IN THE DAYS that followed I worked as hard as I could to get to grips with the scenes where lots of the boys spoke—they were brilliantly written, snappy back and forths between a teacher and his class of eight boys. I didn't want to count myself out of any role at that point, so I learnt as much as I possibly could of all of them. I've never worked so hard for an audition.

The week after the script came, I was in the casting rooms of the National Theatre, sitting down in front of Toby Whale. (Toby is one of the most brilliant and lovely casting directors in the country. So brilliant and lovely, in fact, that he would go on to cast a TV show you may have heard of called *Gavin & Stacey*.) The first thing he asked me was whether or not I liked the script. Like it? I said. I *loved* it.

It's normally at this point that the casting director will suggest reading some scenes through, with him or her playing the other parts. If it's a television or film casting, they'll press record on the video camera and away you go. Toby stood up and said, 'OK, James. Let's go through, shall we?'

I looked up in surprise. 'Go through to where?'

Now it was Toby's turn to be confused. 'Through to meet Nick and Alan. Where else?'

It took me a couple of seconds to register the information. Toby was already heading off down the corridor, but he turned and stopped when he heard me call out, in a squeaky voice, 'Nick Hytner and Alan Bennett?' He just nodded, smiled and carried on walking.

The look on my face must've been pretty familiar to Toby by then. All day, I imagine, a stream of young actors must have been coming in thinking they were there for a general meeting with Toby before the real auditions began, and then having the rug pulled out from under them as they realised this *was* the audition, and it was now or never.

I've realised in the last few years that something happens to me when I get nervous. Basically, when I'm at my most nervous, I act my most supremely confident. When everything inside me is turning to jelly, my outer shell seems to harden and I exude this aura of confidence. Occasionally—and I hate it when this happens, believe me—those nerves turn into the kind of overconfidence that unfortunately comes across as arrogance.

Now, I don't know which level of nervousness my audition with Alan and Nick would be gauged at. I don't even remember much of the meeting—I wish I could. All I know is that when Alan wrote about our meeting in his book *Untold Stories*, he said that

I walked into the room and immediately took over the audition. The one thing that did stick with me was that they both laughed a lot during the read-through, which I guess couldn't have been a bad thing. But, walking away, I didn't know if I'd done enough (I still didn't even know what part I was auditioning for); all I knew was that I'd tried my best.

I left the theatre and called Dad straight away. As he often does, he managed to sum up exactly what I was feeling. 'Well, if you've not got it, at least you've met Alan Bennett.' He was totally right; at the very worst I'd met a living legend. That was all I was thinking as I stood waiting on the platform for my train home. And then my phone started ringing.

It was Jacquie. 'Have you got on the train yet?'

'No, I'm on the platform. Why?'

'You should come into the office. You've been offered the play, but *Messiah* need an answer today, and *Fat Friends* has been recommissioned. They all clash; we have some decisions to make.'

WHEN I GOT TO THE OFFICE, Jacquie told me that I'd been offered the part of a boy called Timms. I picked up the script and flicked through it as fast as I could. I then did it again, only this time much more slowly, because I was finding it hard to find any of Timms's lines. It slowly and painfully dawned on me that Timms only had four lines in the whole play, and one of them was, 'Yes, sir.' Talk about back to earth with a bump.

I told Jacquie that it was my dream to work at the National Theatre, but to turn down two well-paid parts in successful TV dramas seemed silly for a part with four lines. But Jacquie was adamant that I should do the play. She got on the phone, trying to work out a way I could do all three. I sat in her office for three hours that day, waiting for this merry-go-round of phone calls to come full circle, when, out of the blue, Alan called her. He spoke to Jacquie for a few minutes before she handed the phone to me.

'Hello?' I said, in a croaky, nervous-schoolboy type of voice.

'Hello, James,' said Alan, in his lovely northern lilt. That was basically enough for me right there. I would have dropped every-thing else at that point, because Alan Bennett had made the effort to call me personally. But, amazingly, he went on to say that he knew that the character of Timms wasn't written up as much as the others, but that if I were to commit to doing the play, he would write the part up and give me something I could have fun with. He ended by telling me that I would have to trust him, because he would only change it with me in mind.

My jaw nearly hit the floor. I couldn't believe what I was hear-ing, and who I was hearing it from. I looked at Jacquie and she, too, had the biggest smile on her face. I told Alan that I was totally overwhelmed and that I couldn't wait to be involved; then I kept saying thank you, and he told me to stop being so silly.

I put the phone down and smiled, and didn't stop smiling for about two weeks. I was going to act at the National Theatre, work with Alan Bennett and be directed by Nicholas Hytner.

CHAPTER 7

I stood on the station platform gripping the revised script that Alan had sent over. He'd been good to his word and Timms's part was now way more substantial, but—and you'll like this—a lot of his new lines were in French. Why did it have to be French? Was this some kind of karmic retribution for all those hours I'd messed around in European Studies?

Alan seemed to have written the part as a sort of class clown. It was basically me at school: attention-seeking, boisterous, up for constant fun, but not thick or nasty in any way. I knew I could do this. Throughout the journey I flicked back and forth over my lines, hoping my northern accent was good enough and praying that I'd have the courage to just be myself and not be crippled by wanting to impress like I had when I worked with Mike.

I was so determined not to be late that I was the first one of the cast outside the stage door. I checked myself in on the sign-in sheet and then glanced down at the other names. Other than Frances de la Tour and Richard Griffiths, whose involvement had been announced some time before, there were no names I recognised. Richard was one of my favourite actors, who'd been Uncle Monty in one of my all-time best-loved films, *Withnail and I*, and Frances was an almost god-like figure who'd been a massive part of the success of one of the country's favourite sitcoms, *Rising Damp*. I wondered what it'd be like working with them. Generally, when you're spending time day in, day out alongside such brilliant actors, you can only ever learn from them. I hoped this would be the case with them.

Underneath those two, there was a list of unfamiliar names; among them the seven other guys who would be playing my classmates. The dynamic between the group of boys would be so vital to the play's success that I couldn't help but dread what the other guys would be like. Would they be a group of theatrical darlings who would look down on me for not having trained professionally? Or laugh behind my back because this was the first play I'd been in? I sat outside the theatre stressing over all the possible scenarios for so long that when I next looked at my watch, it was 9.58 a.m., two minutes before I had to be inside. I rushed down the maze of corridors that run underneath the theatre until I got to Rehearsal Room Two. I stood outside for a moment, took a deep breath, closed my eyes and gave myself a pep talk: just be yourself, James. Don't be how you were with Mike.

I opened my eyes to find a really good-looking young guy standing in front of me. 'You all right, mate?' he said, in a sort of posh cockney accent.

'Yeah, I'm fine, thanks. Just a bit . . . y'know?'

He smiled, chuckled a bit, then said, 'Oh, don't be nervous. It's gonna be a laugh, this. I loved you in *All or Nothing*—it's my favourite Mike Leigh film. I grew up round where it was shot. You made me cry in that film. Amazing piece of work.'

It turned out that the young, good-looking, posh cockney was

Dominic Cooper. I still don't think he'll ever really understand how those few words he said to me then so completely put me at my ease. My shoulders relaxed, my nerves vanished, my tummy unknotted itself and, as Dominic and I walked through the door into the vast rehearsal room, I felt calm, excited, confident and relieved, all at the same time.

The cast and stage management were standing around drinking cups of tea, being polite to each other, when Nick called everyone to sit round a long table in the middle of the room. We sat down and then, one by one, went round the table introducing ourselves and telling each other what parts we were playing. After that, we read through the entire play.

The other actors were brilliant: Stephen Campbell-Moore was already amazing as Irwin, the young supply teacher; Samuel Barnett was Posner and he read the part as if it had been written for him; Jamie Parker played Scripps and I remember him having the most incredible voice that made him sound as if he'd been born on stage. In fact, everyone was incredible—Dominic was Dakin, Russell Tovey was Rudge, Andrew Knott played Lockwood, Samuel Anderson was Crowther, and the youngest of the bunch, Sacha Dhawan, played Akthar.

The read-through went really well (even the French was all right because no one, it turned out, was particularly fluent) and at the end everyone applauded. The stage-management crew went back to the business of building the set, which left us—the twelve cast members, Nick and Alan—all alone in the rehearsal room.

I RECKON THIS is always the trickiest moment for a director. Where do you actually start? How do you begin the process of 'putting on a play'? Do you just stick the whole cast on the makeshift set and start ordering them on from stage left and stage right? Or do you insist on spending hours playing theatrical games, chucking imaginary beanbags to each other whilst pretending that the floor is on fire? Believe me, this stuff happens all the time. But luckily not in Rehearsal Room Two when Nick is in charge.

Many people regard Nick as one of, if not the best, theatre directors in the world. And they think this because of his brilliantly received spectrum of work, from opera at Glyndebourne to Shakespeare to *Miss Saigon*, and the fact that most of his productions end each night with a standing ovation.

Personally, I think Nick is the best in the world for different reasons: one of the main ones being that when he was sitting round a table with a group of young, mostly inexperienced actors, some of whom had trained, some of whom had not, some of whom he knew and most of whom he didn't, he said this: 'There's a lot going on in this play and I think the best thing to do is for all of us to take a vow of stupidity. We must all agree that no one in here knows more about certain things than others. That way we can all learn together and nobody should ever have to feel stupid or be made to feel stupid about putting their hand up and saying they don't understand something. So we're going to just sit here for a couple of days, and together we'll go through everything. OK?'

In that one moment he put everyone in the room on a level playing field. I know, from having spoken to the other guys, that all eight of us felt relieved that he'd said it. Feeling much more relaxed, we sat and chatted about school and poetry, but mostly we talked about history. There were times when some of us didn't completely understand certain aspects of what was written, and on those occasions we'd turn to Alan who, in his own wonderful words, would explain it in such a way that anyone could understand. Suddenly, dense mountains of words that had previously been closed off came alive and had meaning. We would laugh at each other's stories from school—I told some myself and, occasionally, if he liked a phrase, or found something touching or amusing, Alan jotted it down in his notebook.

There was one unforgettable afternoon when Alan read to just us eight boys, on our own in the rehearsal room, for an hour. You could've heard a pin drop. He read different poems and then talked about why or where they were written, and what he thought they meant.

ALAN HAS SPOKEN many times of how rude all of us boys were. About how, even on day one of rehearsals, he overheard Dominic on the phone to a friend, talking loudly enough for Alan to hear every word: 'Oh, I'm doing a play by some bloke called Alan. Not Ayckbourn, the other one.' Alan said he found it refreshing and liked that we were making him one of the gang.

For all his accolades and awards, the most important thing about Alan is that he still lives in the world he cares and writes about. He has seen and done it all, and yet he couldn't be more approachable and encouraging to others. There is no establishing status, no enjoyment at the fact you might feel slightly uncomfortable in his presence. He, like so many of his brilliantly written words, reaches out to you and makes you feel at home. As far as he's concerned, whether you're an actor or the security man on the stage door, you are valid and will have something to say, or something worth listening to.

I asked him once why he had never accepted a knighthood or something similar, and his answer wasn't anything to do with a statement about the monarchy or a deeply held political view. He simply said that as a writer he felt he should still be a person in the world that normal people live in. Believe me, I could fill chapter after chapter of stories and conversations we had with Alan. They are his stories, though, and not mine to tell here. But, I'm sure he wouldn't mind if I sneaked in just this one. (Bear with me on this, as some of it happens a few years away from the rehearsal rooms of *The History Boys*.)

Alan had been incredibly encouraging when it came to me writing comedy. He would often tell me that I was funny and that he believed I could write. I'd told him I was working on a script with Ruth and he would always ask about it, and we'd talk about the characters and possible scenarios. He was incredibly supportive, and said that he would always be on the end of the phone should I need any help or advice.

Fast forward a few years to the night when the first episode of *Gavin & Stacey* eventually aired on BBC3. As the end credits rolled, I was sitting there waiting for him to call. I knew he would've watched it—he'd told me he was looking forward to it—but nothing came. *Maybe he'll call tomorrow*, I thought. But no, episode after episode, I heard nothing from Alan. I resigned myself to the fact that he must hate the show and would rather not call if he had nothing nice to say about it. It got me down a bit, to be honest. Alan was one of the people I really wanted to like it.

And then, as the final episode finished, the phone rang.

It was Alan. 'Hello, James.' I tingled at the sound of his voice. 'I've just watched the last episode and I enjoyed it so much, I feel a little sad that it's over. You both wrote it with such love that it made me care about every single character. You should be very proud tonight.'

You would not believe how happy that made me. I told Alan how relieved I was that he'd called and how I'd been worried he didn't like the show because I hadn't heard from him, and he said simply, 'Well, I wanted to watch the whole show. It's a series and I wanted to call when I'd watched it until the end.'

And that's the thing about Alan—he just makes sense. He has a way of saying things and holding himself that is so together and so precise, and yet he is completely unaware of how profound he's being. He'll be so embarrassed if he ever reads that.

(And we're back.) As we got nearer to the opening of the show, we moved out of the rehearsal room to begin the tech rehearsal on stage. This is one of the most exciting times when you're putting on a play. It suddenly becomes much more real, and you start to imagine all the possible outcomes, both good and bad—the fear of everything that could go wrong, along with the excitement of everything going right.

When you've been rehearsing for six weeks, you more or less lose all judgement as to whether what you're doing is any good or not: the play, your part in the play, the set, the lighting, everything. After that long, you just can't tell. Eventually, though, all you're longing for is to get out in front of an audience.

We were doing ten preview shows before press night. Nick says, to this day, that *The History Boys* had the best first preview he's ever seen. It was absolutely electric. Waves and waves of laughter in response to jokes we didn't even realise were jokes. The French scene was such a hit that Richard had to stop and wait for the laughs to die down before repeating a line that had been lost amongst the noise.

The play was a hit with the audience, no question, but, as happy as we all were with how it had gone, there was that nagging thought at the back of my mind — *Martin Guerre* had been a smash with the audience, too, and look what had happened there. We just had to hope the critics liked it.

PRESS NIGHT CAME. Both Alan and Nick wrote lovely cards to every cast member, and there were flowers and champagne and hundreds of notes from well-wishers all over the backstage area. The nerves were setting in. The funny thing is, the show was already sold out for the entire run, so I'm not entirely sure why we were all so nervous. Well, I do kind of know — the critics.

A couple of nights before we opened, I asked Nick what he thought the reviews might be like. Taking each one in turn, he went through the eight or nine critics who were coming and said who would like it, who would enjoy it but find negatives and who would be the one to hate it.

The show opened to the most sensational reviews you could possibly imagine. One critic described it as Alan's finest work, another picked out Richard's performance as being the best on the London stage. Just one critic, the one Nick had been so sure would hate it, said it was awful and boring. I found it astounding that Nick could be so on the money with his predictions; then again, he had called it right every single step of the way.

The show was a sure-fire hit. It's so rare to be part of something that both critics and audiences enjoy in equal measure: so often it's one or the other. But here we were, twelve actors: us eight boys and the four teachers, having the time of our lives.

The only real challenge in a long run is keeping the boredom at bay. The routine can get pretty monotonous: the same words, the same action, passing people in the wings at exactly the same point, every single night. It can sometimes feel as though you're getting stuck on a treadmill—except, that is, when you're working with seven other boys who are rapidly becoming your best friends. If you happen to be doing that, well, then you embrace the boredom.

IT's FAIR TO SAY that for every person who enjoyed having us at the National that summer, there were probably two others who hated it. I can understand why—we took over the place. The canteen, the bar but, most of all, the dressing rooms. The dressing rooms at the National are all in a quadrant, with the windows facing in on each other; at various points throughout the day, actors from different companies will be leaning out of windows talking to each other, or walking around having a cigarette.

I shared a room with Andy, Sam Anderson and Sacha. Dominic was next door and Russell, Sam Barnett and Jamie were directly below us. Our room became the hub of all things *History Boys*. We would eat there together, play darts (until the dartboard was confiscated), play indoor football (until the football was confiscated), play indoor squash (you get the idea) and generally hang out.

As the play became more and more successful, the eight history boys also became more and more in demand. Every day, Dominic was coming into work with a different film script, Sam Barnett was constantly out being wined and dined by sexy new American agents and Sacha was auditioning for epic TV dramas. Everyone, in fact, was having a good time professionally and looked as if they had a bright future after the play. Everyone, that was, except me. I just wasn't being seen for any of the big jobs.

I remember one day Andy, Russell and I all came into work with the same script. It was a film about two young British guys who go travelling in Thailand and end up with a girl who subsequently gets kidnapped; then they're accused of her murder. It was a decent script and all three of us wanted to land one of the two lead parts. We started reading the script through together, bouncing off each other, and it was only then that we realised there weren't just the two main boys (the funny, charismatic leads in the film); there was also the 'newsagent', who had three lines on page six. I had a proper look at the note that had come with the script that told me which part I should prepare. I'm sure it's not hard to guess which one it was . . .

I tried to brush it off as being funny, but Andy and Russell must have known how much it upset me. Why wasn't I being seen for the proper parts in any of these films? Why was I near the bottom of the casting ladder when I thought, after all the success the show was having, I'd be nearer the top? As I've said earlier, I knew that my size would make some roles difficult to get, but it surely couldn't keep me from every decent part out there.

IT SEEMED PRETTY clear what I needed to do if I was ever going to achieve anything close to the dreams I had—I was going to have to start putting the hours in and make stuff happen myself: scripts weren't going to just land on my doorstep with wonderful parts to play. Every night, Dominic and Stephen would have their big dramatic scene near the end of Act Two and I would stand watching in the wings, wishing that it was me out there. I knew their lines by heart. I still feel like that now, to be honest: it hasn't gone away, that desire to have a go at playing the more dramatic roles—not in Hollywood or even the West End, just . . . somewhere. I'd love someone to see that potential in me again. I'm not sure it's going to happen anytime soon, as currently I'm not sure people even think of me as an actor at all. These days, I'm a comedian (despite never having done stand-up or ever having professed to be one) or a 'tawdry celebrity', which was the pleasant way a journalist described me the other day.

So, I was on a mission and the first thing I did was call Ruth Jones to speak more about writing together and fix times when we'd both be in London. We believed in the idea we had, and the more we talked about the characters and scenarios, the more we felt we really had something.

It was around this time that I parted company with Jacquie. I think we both recognised that, although I was in this hit play, I was also in something of a rut, and that a change wouldn't be a bad thing. She was incredibly honest about the time her bigger clients were taking up and told me that she didn't want that to be a negative for me. Generously, she agreed that she'd look after me until I found someone new. We hugged and said our goodbyes.

I met with a few different agents, and got along with them all, but then someone suggested I should meet Ruth Young at United Agents. She had—and still has—an incredible reputation, and the list of names the agency represented read like a *Who's Who* of British acting talent.

I went to meet Ruth at her offices. I was immediately taken by how large the agency was. Walking down the long corridors, all I could see were film posters and endless awards.

I got to Ruth's office and waited for her to come in. Her assistant, Heloise, asked if I'd like anything to drink and I said thanks, but I was fine, which was stupid because I was really thirsty. In fact, I was so thirsty that when I was walking from the Tube to the office, I remember thinking that I wouldn't buy a drink to quench my thirst because the chances were that I'd be offered a drink once I got there. They were a big swanky agency with loads of huge stars and they'd probably have posh juices and iced teas, or iced mochaccinos. 'I really want an iced mochaccino,' I distinctly remember saying to myself.

This whole being-thirsty-and-not-drinking thing was only making me more parched. And then Ruth walked in. 'Hi, James,' she said in her lovely Scottish accent that immediately puts you at your ease. 'Have you been offered a drink or anything?'

'No,' I replied. *What?! Why did I just say that?*

Ruth looked concerned and pressed her hand down on the intercom next to her telephone. 'Heloise, can you come in here, please?'

What had I done? This was the only agent in London I wanted to be represented by. I'd been in her office two minutes and I'd already lied to her face.

Heloise came in. 'Heloise,' Ruth said, 'why haven't you offered James a drink?' I could feel my whole face going red.

Heloise turned to look at me. 'I think I did? Didn't I?'

'No . . . no, I don't think so,' I said, in a way-too-high-pitched voice. Heloise kept on looking at me, *through* me.

'Would you like a drink?'

I looked at Ruth. 'Are you having one?' I said, hoping Ruth would order an iced mochaccino so I could just simply say, 'Make that two.'

'I've actually got a coffee here,' said Ruth, pointing at an over-sized mug she was holding that I hadn't noticed.

And then I looked back at Heloise. 'No, I'm fine, honestly. I had a drink on the way here. Thanks.' She gave me one more long, bemused look and left the room.

Luckily, the meeting got better from there. I loved Ruth. She spoke so passionately about actors and how she represents them — and all in all we got on great. Just as the meeting was wrapping up, Ruth told me that she'd love to represent me, that she saw me as a good challenge and that, if I was up for it, then she was. We celebrated with an awkward half-handshake, half-hug and I left the room feeling as if I could walk on water — until I saw Heloise sitting outside, glaring at me.

'You sure you don't want a drink?'

I shook my head, walked speedily over to the lift and got the hell out of there as quickly as I could.

CHAPTER 8

So far, this whole 'taking control of my own career' thing seemed to be working out. There was still one person I had to call, though: Ruth Jones. We'd been swapping texts with little quotes and character ideas for some time, but we hadn't actually met and written anything down. I was walking back to the tube station, about to press 'Call' on my phone, when it starting ringing in my hand. It was Ruth Jones.

'I was just about to call you. Literally this second!' I said, incredibly excited.

Ruth wasn't quite as moved by that as I was; there were bigger things on her mind. 'Listen, I really think we need to write this treatment. If we don't do it soon, we'll lose the momentum and it'll just disappear 'cos we'll have both moved on.'

Amazing. She was feeling exactly the same as I was. That, coupled with the whole phone-ringing thing, was enough to make me go bananas. I tried to keep it together. 'But when?' I said. 'When can we meet? I've got eight shows a week for the next month before we have a six-day break. I won't be able to come to Cardiff. Are you going to be in London at all?' As it turned out, Ruth's schedule was just as busy as mine, if not busier: she was filming the second series of *Nighty Night* on the south coast.

We then realised we'd both agreed to do an early morning breakfast television show in ten days' time to promote the fourth series of *Fat Friends*. (We'd shot another series of *Fat Friends* shortly after *The History Boys* play opened. They worked around the play's dates and we filmed it in Leeds. The reason I didn't tell you any of this is because it was more of the same. Seemed silly to keep going on about it.) So, on this breakfast show, we would be done by 8.30 a.m., and we could go off somewhere and write for a few hours, and try to get as much done as we could before Ruth had to leave London. The plan was set.

THE BREAKFAST SHOW was fine. Ruth and I got wheeled on, talked about *Fat Friends*, made sure we mentioned at least twice what time it was on and then were promptly wheeled off again.

Once out of the studio, it was a short walk to the hotel where Ruth had stayed the night before. We got into the room and Ruth pulled out her laptop. Stephen Fry once said that in all good writing partnerships, there is someone who sits and types while the other tends to pace around, shouting his or her thoughts aloud, occasionally looking over the shoulder of the person who's typing. Guess which one I was?

I think one of the biggest strengths we had in the writing process was that we never specifically talked about jokes. As both of us were actors, I think it was easier for us to focus on the characters — what they'd be wearing and how they'd speak, their backgrounds. The jokes, we thought, would arrive naturally once we'd got the personalities nailed down.

First off, we needed to think of a reason why the majority of the guests at the wedding hadn't met before. Lots of the scenes we'd worked out relied on people meeting each other for the first time. I told Ruth a story about my best mate, Gavin, and how he met his wife, Sara, on the phone at work. She was working in Accounts and he was a buyer; they flirted on the phone, a lot, until one day they decided to meet. They fell in love immediately. Gavin proposed soon after, and they got married straight away after that.

Ruth agreed it could make a good backstory for our characters. We knew that we weren't ever going to use it, but it was an exercise to help us plot out who was going to be there. At this point, Ruth was going to be the bride, and I was going to play the best man. We decided that we'd call the bride Stacey and, in honour of my mate Gav, we'd keep the groom's name as Gavin.

My cousin Lee had a best mate who was a builder called Smithy. I told Ruth about him, his mannerisms, the way he pronounced words, how he was always 'up for it', whatever 'it' was. We thought he'd make the perfect best man. Then we talked about their families and friends and fleshed out the backstories so it felt as if all these characters had real lives, that they actually existed.

As we sat there, I kept thinking back to working with Mike Leigh and how it was his attention to detail that made his characters so real. It was vital to get to the point where we felt we could answer any question that the characters might throw up once we started improvising.

So, we had Gavin and Stacey, we had Smithy, and now we started to sketch out the bride's best friend, whom we called

Vanessa. We worked everything a few more times through and began writing properly.

As this was still just a pitch, we wanted any TV executives who were reading to get the style of the show straight away so, right at the top, we explained how we envisaged the style and pacing of the show being like *The Royle Family* meets *Marion and Geoff*. We wrote small snippets of dialogue to show the sort of tone we envisaged and, right in the centre of the page, we wrote in bold: **This is a wedding where nothing happens.**

We were trying to get across what we believed to be the show's greatest asset—the fact that nothing obviously dramatic happened: it would simply show real people with real lives.

Before we knew it, we'd finished the treatment. It came in at about ten pages. We hoped it was good, that we'd done enough and that the TV people would understand what we were trying to do. It was in the envelope, ready to be sealed, when Ruth suggested, 'Shall we put the backstory in? You know, just to give them a feel of how Gavin and Stacey met?'

I thought about it for a moment. I wish I could make this seem more dramatic, but the truth is, it wasn't. I just sort of shrugged my shoulders and went, 'OK, yeah. Let's put it in the envelope.'

And that was that. We sent it off to ITV and waited. Ruth got on a train to the south coast to carry on filming *Nighty Night*, and I walked the few hundred yards back to the National Theatre.

I DON'T KNOW WHY, but I used to love getting to the theatre before anyone else. It probably has something to do with my constant need to feel in some way dramatic. I liked being the first in the dressing room; I liked being the one to turn on all the spotlights round the mirrors; I liked walking down to the stage and looking over the empty wings, which in a few short hours would be full of people bustling, whispering and running around; I liked walking out onto the stage, seeing the empty seats, taking in the silence. I liked all the anticipation.

That morning I followed my routine and ended up sitting down on the empty stage at the National. I remember thinking how much I'd enjoyed the morning with Ruth—more than I ever thought I would. Even if no one went for our idea, I thought that we should definitely try to do something else.

But as I sat on the edge of the stage, as fun and positive as that morning had been, I started to feel quite down.

For as long as I can remember, I've always had an inability to see the bigger picture. Rather than focusing on the good, I seek out and find the bad in me, or my career. Now, I was sitting on an empty stage in one of London's greatest theatres, having appeared on breakfast television that morning to publicise a BAFTA-nominated drama I was starring in, having just spent a great morning writing something new and exciting with an actress and friend I really loved and admired. And yet, all I could see was a fat boy who was never going to amount to anything. It's my worst trait, the thing I can't stand in myself—the inability to see any positives. Looking back, I can see I was the luckiest guy in the world.

Something I used to do a lot back then, and still do now from time to time, is judge my success against other people's. So, for example, just the other day someone was being incredibly kind and encouraging about my career, telling me how well they thought I was doing, and all I could think inside was, *Andrew Garfield is at the Golden Globes. He's a success. If I was that good, I'd be there, too.* It's a ridiculous way to behave and I'm embarrassed that I'm even telling you. I wish I didn't feel like that, but I also wonder where I'd be without it. Would I have bothered to write *Gavin & Stacey*? Would I have bothered to do anything at all if I didn't feel so driven to be the biggest and best?

I'm happy to say that the jealousy and constant comparisons happen less frequently these days. I hope this is because I've grown up, not because I'm more successful. The truth is, I doubt whether all the success in the world would change how I feel at certain times. It's a part of my personality that I've struggled long and hard to change: it doesn't help anyone to judge their happiness or career by looking at where others may or may not be.

Dad said it best: 'All the time you're looking left and right at other people, you're neglecting what's in front of you. If you focus on looking straight ahead, you can take the odd glance at the future.' He's got a wonderful way of saying something that just puts everything into perspective.

Even with all my self-doubt, things were still going really well on *The History Boys*—so well, in fact, that Nick had called a meeting with the whole cast to put to bed various rumours about what was going to happen after our run at the National ended.

We were sitting in the theatre stalls when Nick and Alan came in. 'All right, A.B.!' came the cry from the boys. A.B. was now Alan's nickname. Yep, we gave Alan Bennett a nickname. Actually, by this point in the run, pretty much everyone in the play had a nickname: Richard Griffiths was 'Rizzo'. I came up with that one, though I'm not sure he ever really warmed to it as much as we wanted him to.

Andrew Knott ended up being known as 'Moon' and this came about organically—his first nickname was 'Anders', which then became 'Andeye', which then became 'Andeye Moon', and then simply 'Moon'. Makes sense.

Jamie Parker was known as 'Scripps', which was his character name in the play. Unoriginal, maybe, but it fitted him.

Sacha was 'Sachgelia'. I've no idea why.

Russell was 'Rusty', except to me. To me he was 'My Russ', and to him I became 'My Jim'. Beautiful.

Sam Barnett was, I think, 'Sam'. That's disappointing.

Sam Anderson was, and always will be, 'Zammo'.

Frances de la Tour was either 'Frankie' or 'J-Lo', on account of her occasionally wearing velour tracksuits similar to, um, J-Lo.

Clive Merrison, who played the head teacher in the play, was 'Clive-O'.

Stephen Campbell-Moore became known to all as 'Steve-Ex'.

Dominic Cooper became lovingly known as 'Dirtbox'. I wish I could tell you why, but I'm worried about how young some of you reading this may be.

And my nickname, which has stuck better than any nickname I've ever been given, was, and very much still is, 'Levine'. Or, to give it its correct parlance, 'Jimmy Levine'. I picked it up halfway through the run. Here's how it happened: I was at home one day and I called up Dominic. As he picked up the phone he simply said, 'Jimmy Levine! How's it going?' Granted, it's not the most exciting nickname-giving story. Apparently Dominic had seen some post in his house from someone by the name of 'Jimmy Levine' and then, because he's a strange and wonderful man, decided to call me that. The name stuck. Actually, it stuck so well that we have both, over time, become 'Levine'.

In the theatre, Nick stood up in front of us all and told us that the play was about to go on a world tour! It would travel to the Hong Kong Arts Festival, then to New Zealand, then spend six weeks in Sydney, Australia, before embarking on a possible six-month run on Broadway in New York.

WE WERE absolutely gobsmacked. No one knew what to say. Then, just as it was beginning to sink in, Alan Bennett said, 'But before all that, we need to shoot the movie.'

What? What movie? Nick told us there had been several offers to turn the play into a film and that Alan was working on the screenplay. And he'd only agreed to write it on the proviso that everyone from the play would be in it. It was a very touching and very classy stance that Alan took. It's that sort of loyalty that makes both Nick and Alan loved by everyone they work with.

It took a while for it all to sink in. So that was the next step then—a movie of the play and then a world tour with the chance of six months or more on Broadway. Exciting as that was, there were some big implications—it meant a long time away from the people we most cared about.

For me, that meant Shelley. For a while now, things had been a little hard for us. We were living together in a flat I'd bought in Beaconsfield. We still loved each other lots but I was working every evening while Shell was working days. We'd not been spending enough time together to make the relationship work.

Shelley was delighted for me when I told her about the tour—she couldn't have been more supportive. She told me that I would regret it for the rest of my life if I didn't go. So that was that. The next year or so of my life was all laid out in front of me. It seemed as if it couldn't get any sweeter—and then, ITV called.

Ruth and I had sent our early treatment off to Sioned William, the head of comedy at ITV, because she was Welsh and we thought she'd get the dialogue and understand the characters.

We'd heard nothing back and so we'd thought they hadn't liked it. But then, out of the blue, we got a call asking us to come to Sioned's office on Gray's Inn Road to have a chat.

The meet with Sioned went better than we could have imagined. As soon as we sat down, she told us she loved it, that the characters were spot on and that it would be perfect as a one-off, hour-long film. She went as far as asking us if we had any cast in mind, and we talked loosely about Rob Brydon and Alison Steadman. The vibe in the room was so positive that it felt as if there was a good possibility of it getting made.

But—and here's the kicker—nothing got greenlit in that meeting. At ITV, and it's the same with every other TV station I know of, that first meeting is only the beginning of a very long road. After the initial stages, they have what they call 'commissioning rounds', which is when a potential new show is taken to the other commissioners and controllers who decide whether it's something that they think could work.

As Sioned took it off to do the rounds, we were very hopeful but, a couple of weeks later, she came back and told us they wouldn't be doing it. It was tough to hear. She told us that everybody appreciated there was something there, that they all really liked the characters, but the bottom line was they didn't think it was quite right for them.

It was a setback, without a doubt, but it wasn't enough to knock our belief in what we had. So we sent it out again, to Stuart Murphy, a friend of Ruth's, who was the controller of BBC3. Stuart is an ultra-sharp, very talented guy and was renowned for taking risks. He also has the ability sometimes to see even beyond the writers' vision—he was a godsend.

Stuart had had the treatment about a week and we'd not heard anything when one evening I happened to bump into him in a bar. Rather sheepishly, I mentioned our treatment and he told me it was on his desk and he was going to look at it the next day. He seemed very genuine so I nipped outside and phoned Ruth.

Ruth told me that if that's what he said, then that's what he meant. So, for the next few days we waited. We waited and we waited and we waited. I know it was only a few days—I've waited longer for a hair appointment—but this was big. Anyway, we waited some more and then, finally, my phone rang. It was Ruth.

'James,' she said, 'are you sitting down?'

'No.'

'Sit down.'

I sat.

'OK,' she said, 'listen to this email I just got from Stuart Murphy.' Then she began to read:

Dear Ruth and James,

I've just finished reading your treatment and I have to tell you I think it's absolutely brilliant. I do have some reservations, however. The truth is we don't really have a slot for an hour-long, one-off comedy like this. I also think it would be a waste of what is clearly a brilliant story with well-rounded characters and insightful dialogue. I think this could be a series. The backstory you've written is as interesting as everything else. Have you thought about that? Forgive me if I'm speaking out of turn, but if you're interested in doing this as a series, I'm really keen to discuss it.

Regards,

Stuart.

And then came the killer line, the line that when we were having a bad day writing would always keep us on track:

PS I believe this could be the best thing BBC3 ever makes.

Stuart's enthusiasm and confidence were a massive help to us throughout the writing and filming process. Right from the beginning, he saw something that nobody else did. The truth is that the treatment wasn't actually that good, but Stuart managed to see past that and grasp what *Gavin & Stacey* could become. We were commissioned to write the first episode. Boom!

RUTH REALLY CAME into her own now. When there's stuff that needs doing, there is no one better than Ruth Jones to do it. When we got that email, she was shooting *Nighty Night* for Baby Cow, the same production company that had made *Cruise of the Gods*, as well as loads of other brilliant stuff. We had a chat and decided to give the treatment to Henry Normal, the head of Baby Cow. They were exactly the kind of people who would understand the show and, if a series was greenlit, we wanted them to make it.

Henry had a read of the material, got us in for a meeting and we pretty quickly sorted out all the arrangements: Ruth and I would write the scripts (with lots of helpful suggestions from Henry), Henry and the lovely Lindsay Hughes would be the executive producers, and Ted Dowd would produce it. We would all work together on crew, cast, locations, script supervision and everything else, then deliver the finished product to the BBC.

It's important to remember that at this point all we really had was Stuart's enthusiasm; we were still miles away from any guarantee of a series. The BBC commissions lots and lots of scripts, with maybe two in ten actually being made. The odds were against us, but with the crack team we'd sorted, we felt we had a pretty good shot.

So Ruth and I had to write a script that would make the BBC want to commission a series. And because of all the other stuff going on—the play, and Ruth's TV commitments—we only had two full days to do it: a Tuesday morning, a Thursday afternoon and all day Sunday. If we didn't get an episode written in that time, it would be six weeks until we could sit down again, and we'd lose the momentum. The heat was on.

We didn't start well. By the end of the Thursday afternoon, we'd only written seven pages. A BBC half-hour is about thirty-seven pages in length: we had to write thirty more on Sunday.

I got to Ruth's hotel at 9 a.m. and we both knew neither of us would be leaving until that first episode was not only finished but written to a very high, so-good-the-BBC-will-commission-it standard. We got completely into the zone and the material started to flow, just as it had done back at the bar in Leeds. We'd already worked out the main characters: Gavin, Stacey, Smithy and Vanessa, but we now decided that Ruth would play Nessa instead of Stacey because she was a no-nonsense, straight-talking kind of woman of considerable experience.

We wanted the characters to be identifiable. They had to walk and talk the way we did, say and do stupid things, make mistakes, be like normal, regular people. We wanted the show to feel as natural as possible.

Once we'd established the ground rules, we started sketching out the families: Gavin's mum and dad should be this outgoing, flirty couple whom we called Pam and Mick; Stacey had lost her father but she was looked after by her uncle, Bryn, and her mum, Gwen. Once we had all the core characters, we started writing. Or rather, Ruth did. I paced up and down, lay on the floor, sat on the windowsill—I just couldn't stay still.

One of the first things we wrote was Smithy's introduction, when he walks in on Pam, Mick and Gavin all having dinner. Ruth suggested he should come in with a bit of a bang. I thought about it for a moment and then just opened my mouth: 'Gavlar!' I said. 'Pam-la! Mick!' I'm not sure why I said it, but Ruth liked it so we put it in the scene. It never crossed my mind that those few words might one day sort of define me. Rarely does a day go by when someone doesn't shout that line at me across the street. It's even printed on T-shirts and mugs. I have no idea what part of my brain it jumped from.

I didn't leave Ruth's room until nearly midnight. By the time we finally finished, we were totally exhausted, but we were pretty sure that we'd written a good episode. We sent out the two copies to Henry and Stuart, and went our separate ways—I went off to *The History Boys* shoot and Ruth went back to the *Little Britain* set. We'd done all we could—we were back to waiting.

THE HISTORY BOYS was filmed over the summer at some grammar schools in Watford, as well as on location in Harrogate. Escaping from the confines of the National Theatre seemed to reinvigorate us all. All the old jokes and nicknames were still there—Dirtbox was still 'Dirtbox' (and I still can't tell you why)—only now we had more room to spread our wings, and our friendships became even deeper. The laughs we had on set were perfect for taking my mind off the *Gavin & Stacey* script.

Right at the end of the shoot, when I'd almost given up again, Ruth, Henry and I all got called into the BBC to have a chat about the first episode. It was the first time I'd been to Television Centre. Since then I've been loads of times, but nothing changes—I still get that tingle of excitement walking through the doors.

Cheryl Taylor and Lucy Lumsden, the two comedy commissioners we met with, told us from the very start how much they loved the material and that they were really keen for us to write more. Initially, they asked us just to do another couple of episodes, but Henry managed to persuade them to commit to us writing a full series. Six episodes. That meant a lot of work. Then, for the first time, they mentioned shooting it, which made it much more real. We were no longer just talking about words on a page: this was gonna be a TV show—*our* TV show. But with that came the problem: they wanted us to think about filming it in April or May of the following year.

'Ah,' I said, 'in January I'm going away for an eight-month tour with *The History Boys*.'

Silence. I waited for their answer, biting my lip. Surely my schedule wasn't going to screw us now?

'Well,' said Lucy, 'let's just see how it goes. Go ahead and write the series and we'll take it from there.'

WE LEFT THAT meeting totally elated, and with a whole lot of work to do. This was the end of October and, in roughly four months' time, I'd be on my way to Hong Kong. We quickly got a routine together. Ruth would come up to my place in Beaconsfield for two and a half days; she'd sleep on our sofa bed and we'd write in the kitchen. Then she'd go home, we'd give it a day and then I'd drive down to Cardiff and we'd do another couple of days at her house. It worked. We would spend entire days just laughing together. There were the big landmark moments, like when we decided that Stacey had been engaged five times already before Gavin popped the question, or when we first thought up the fishing-trip subplot. Those days were some of the best. As time went on, we built up such a deep affection for the characters that we more or less fell in love with them. And Ruth and I kind of did the same. (Whoa, not like that.) The more time we spent together, the more we became part of each other's lives. There was an openness and honesty to our relationship that was absolutely vital to making the show as good as it could be. If you think something doesn't work, especially in comedy, you have to be allowed to say so, and Ruth and I never felt as if there were any no-go areas with each other.

We worked solidly for those two months but, by the turn of the year, and with me off on tour in a couple of months, we hadn't quite finished episode six. And that was the one we'd been working towards — that the whole series had been working towards — the wedding. Christmas came and went and luckily, when we spoke to Henry about the last episode, he thought that what we were delivering would be enough for the BBC to make the call on whether they wanted to shoot it or not. So we sent everything in and, before I knew it, it was time to go on tour.

LOOKING BACK, the build-up to leaving was a very emotional time. I was going away for eight months — maybe more — and I had no idea what that would do to Shelley and me. That was the big downside of the tour: it meant having to leave behind the girl I'd fallen in love with. By this point, Shelley and I had been together for almost eight years. We'd never been apart from each other for that long before.

To say goodbye, we had a meal together at the little pullout table in our kitchen, the table where I'd been writing *Gavin & Stacey*. It was so romantic, but heartbreaking at the same time. Shelley was absolutely wonderful. She'd put together a playlist of songs that meant a lot to both of us and created a photo album with pictures of us together, along with pictures of my family, my sisters and my nephew. She fell asleep before me, so I slipped quietly out of bed and wrote hundreds and hundreds of little 'I love you' Post-it notes and hid them all over the flat, in every nook and cranny. I hoped that as the months rolled by, she'd still be finding them and be reminded of how I felt.

CHAPTER 9

The car came to pick me up; after wrestling my enormous suitcase into the boot, I turned to say goodbye to Shelley. We held on to each other for as long as we could, tears rolling down our faces, both of us shaking like leaves. I cried all the way to Heathrow. I cried because I knew how much I'd miss her but also because, deep down, there was a part of me that knew things would never be the same again.

When I got to the airport, I found that I wasn't the only one struggling to hold it together: all the other guys were just as upset as I was. We saw each other in a completely different light that day; as we were all standing around glumly waiting to check in, it seemed as if we'd lost a layer or two of skin.

Things calmed down as we boarded the night flight to Hong Kong. I was in a row of three together with Dominic and Stephen Campbell-Moore in economy (this was a play, not a Hollywood movie). We decided that the best way to deal with our emotions and the long flight ahead of us was to get totally hammered. When we touched down in Hong Kong, we were all wearing high-altitude hangovers.

Hong Kong was a difficult place to kick off the tour. In a way, we weren't properly prepared for it. The problem was that the play was subtitled into both Mandarin and Cantonese, and so, as a consequence, it lost some of its spontaneity. There were two giant screens on either side of the stage translating all our lines as we spoke them. We'd say our words and, instead of that instant feedback of a big laugh, there would be this stony silence. Then, moments later, when the translation came through, the audience would get the joke and start cracking up, but by that point we were on to the next line. It was no one's fault, but it meant it didn't flow as it normally would have done.

Hong Kong was more about what happened after the show than what happened during it. Most nights—OK, every night—after the show was over, four of us would pile into Jo-Bananas, the nearest bar, and get the party started. I don't recall seeing Hong Kong at all in the daylight. We'd do the play, be out all night, then crawl into bed at nine the next morning. Then do it all over again. The whole place just passed me by. It was kind of a relief to get out of there, to be honest.

New Zealand had real appeal. For starters, it just seemed much healthier with the amazing waterfalls and mountains—wide open, beautiful countryside compared to the densely packed high-rises of Hong Kong.

Landing in Wellington, I made my way to Baggage Reclaim, switched on my phone and a text from Ruth popped up. I hadn't heard from her for a while, so this must be something big.

'Oi, Smithy,' it said. 'We've got a green light, a'righ'.' Written as Nessa—nice touch.

Not even thinking of the time difference, I phoned her right away. It was late morning in Wellington and almost midnight in the UK. Ruth was just about to go to bed when she picked up.

'What's this?' I asked her excitedly. 'I just landed in New Zealand and I got your text. What green light?'

'We've got the green light, James,' she told me. 'The BBC are going for it. They want the whole lot. The whole six episodes. They want us to start shooting as soon as you get home.'

Ruth and I shouted at each other for a bit down the phone, then I let her get off to bed. I hung up and stood fixed on the spot by the baggage carousel, my mouth hanging wide open. Jamie Parker was standing next to me, looking a little concerned.

'Levine,' he said, 'you all right? What's up?'

I stared at him for a while before answering. 'The show's been picked up,' I mumbled. 'Our show. *Gavin & Stacey*. The BBC's picked it up.'

'You're joking,' he said, beginning to smile.

'No.' I shook my head. 'That was Ruth on the phone. They've given us the green light.'

Telling Jamie made it real and—boom!—like that, suddenly it hit me. I was gonna make my own TV show! Jamie grabbed me, hugged me, slapped me and kissed me and then the two of us started jumping up and down and round and round.

Hearing that fantastic news really chilled me out. We had three days to ourselves before the play opened, and we decided to hire a camper van to check out some of the countryside. If you've seen *The Lord of the Rings* movies, then you'll know what it's like, so I won't bore you with all the details. All right . . . quickly, though. It is really, really beautiful. There, said it.

FROM NEW ZEALAND we moved on to Sydney for a six-week run, which meant renting apartments. I shared with Dom. Our place was massive: twin balconies overlooking the city centre, and only a few minutes down to the waterfront. There wasn't a lot not to like about our time there: the theatre was great, the show got a fantastic reception, and on our days off we'd hire a catamaran and sail under the Harbour Bridge or just lie on the beach.

The night before we were due to leave for New York, Dom and I went out for an all-nighter, which made the flight very rough. We had a brief stopover in LA but, before that, there was a painful fourteen hours of being squeezed in with no legroom. Happily, on the connecting flight to New York, I managed to wangle three seats to myself and, within seconds of taking off, I was out for the count. I've been lucky enough to have been on some pretty expensive flights since but, I promise you, nothing has ever compared to the relief of stretching out over that row of seats and passing out.

So, New York. Broadway . . . it was totally awesome. It's New York. When we landed, Richard Griffiths told us that we had no idea how brilliant this was going to be, and he couldn't have been more right. We were staying in some serviced apartments in Midtown to begin with as we had no idea how long we'd be staying there. We were booked in for six months, but that was only if we made it past the critics.

We were playing at the Broadhurst Theatre on 44th Street between Eighth and Broadway. That first day is one I will never forget. We all came out of the subway at Times Square and there, right in front of us, was a *History Boys* poster the size of a London bus—it was of all eight of us, and I still get a tingle down my spine just thinking about it.

As it turned out, the play was a *major* hit. It went down as well in New York as it had in London, maybe even better. The reviews were great and, a couple of days later, we were told that we'd definitely be on for the full six months. Amazing! You can imagine how it was. You're in your mid-twenties; you're in a hit play on Broadway; you're living and working with your best mates in one of the greatest cities in the world. If that isn't living the dream, I don't know what is.

THE PLAY WENT on to win six Tony Awards in the United States, more than any play had ever won until then. That whole time in New York was magical; I just loved being there. Six incredible months living in an uptown apartment with Russell next door and Central Park just over the road. Being neighbours, Russell and I became very close. On matinée days, we'd walk the thirty-odd blocks to the theatre and afterwards the eight of us boys would go for a drink somewhere. We'd sit down and, before we could order, the waiter would bring a tray of drinks that somebody had already bought for us. It was nuts. A fan site started up on the internet and every night when we'd finished a show there would be more and more people crowding around the stage door. It was my first real taste of fame and, being someone who likes a spot of attention (check out the title), I revelled in it.

As THE MONTHS rolled by, I found myself thinking more and more about that last episode of *Gavin & Stacey*. Ruth and I still hadn't finished it. We were always chatting on the phone, discussing it with each other, but we both knew we needed to be in the same room together to get it done. Ruth had some time in between TV stuff, so I suggested she come out and stay with me to finish it off, which she did.

We had five days to complete that last episode. Just as we had done back home, we'd sit in my apartment and start riffing, improvising and getting into character. We'd write all day, then I'd go and do the show; when I got back, we'd plough on into the night. It was hard, energy-sapping work and I was nowhere near getting enough sleep. To compensate, I started taking a sneaky little nap at work.

There was around a thirty-minute gap between the last scene of Act One and the second scene of Act Two where I wasn't on stage at all, and I used it to catch up on the sleep I was missing out on. Normally, I'd have been watching that final scene of Act One from the wings because it was my favourite of the whole play. It's a really poignant moment where 'Drummer Hodge', a poem by Thomas Hardy, is being discussed by Richard Griffiths's Hector and Sam Barnett's Posner. Hector is talking about writing; how there are times when you think you might be the only person ever to have experienced a particular kind of emotion, only to discover it has been written down, word for word, by someone long ago. Someone you don't know, even long dead, had experienced every single feeling you were going through and, in writing it down, had reached out across time to clasp your hand in theirs.

It's one of the play's most moving moments but, when Ruth was in town, I was so tired that I'd roll up my blazer to use as a pillow, lie down, close my eyes and nap right through it. Act Two started with this loud burst of music so I wasn't afraid of not waking up, and there'd be enough time before I was on stage to get my head back in the game.

But this one Thursday matinée it didn't quite pan out as I'd hoped: I was so far gone that I slept right through the music. I woke up to hear someone else speaking my lines: I'd missed my cue. Worse than that, I'd missed the entire scene. I felt horrible; I'd let everyone down. There was nothing I could do but wait in the wings until I could apologise to Richard.

Earlier I told you he played Uncle Monty in *Withnail and I*, one of my favourite films. I'd never stop asking him questions about it: what it was like filming it, who he'd based his character on — anything you can think of.

When I went up to him at the end of the scene, full of apologies, he put his hands on my shoulders and studied me for a long moment. Then, in his best Uncle Monty, he said, 'I'm preparing myself to forgive you, boy. I'm preparing myself to forgive you.' After that, I kept the sleeping to my bed.

Ruth and I were halfway through the week and making great progress with that final episode, but it was hot in New York that summer, so we ended up writing a fair bit over the road in Central Park. Together we would sit on a bench with Ruth's laptop, do some people-watching and get the last bit down. That's where we wrote the wedding scene in which Uncle Bryn gives Stacey a letter her dad had written just days before he died. It's one of the scenes I'm most proud of.

AFTER SIX MONTHS in New York, plus a one-month extension, the play was finally coming to a close. What we hadn't realised was that *The History Boys* film was coming out on the day we got back to London. There was going to be a royal premiere, and we were flying out literally after the curtain came down on our last show.

It was an incredible way to end the run on Broadway. The rush was perfect, too. If we'd had time to sit there thinking about it and discussing it, we'd probably never have left the theatre. We'd been together off and on for so long it was agonising to think it was almost over.

Our bags were packed, we'd checked out of the apartments, and our dressing rooms had been cleared of all the bits and pieces we'd acquired over the last months: the good-luck cards, the photos, all the other mementoes. Walking into the theatre for the last time, the barren spaces felt completely alien, as if we'd never been there in the first place.

We were determined to make that last show the best we'd ever done. And it was a very special night. We were sure that most of the audience had seen the play at least once before, but just wanted to be there for the last performance. Their energy and laughter and sheer positivity were totally infectious and pushed our performances up one more notch.

In the last scene, after Hector is killed, the boys all sit at the front of the stage and sing 'Bye Bye Blackbird'. If you've seen the play or the film, you'll know that Frances de la Tour's character also explains what happens to the boys after going to university. One of us is a journalist; another is a property developer; my character owns a chain of dry cleaners and takes drugs on the weekend. Finally, as she gets to Posner, Richard's character appears at the back of the stage. 'Pass it on, boys,' he says, 'pass it on.'

That Sunday, that last ever performance, the last time he spoke those words, Richard's voice cracked. This was an actor who had been on stages all around the world, yet he was so moved his voice just started to go. *Pass it on, boys.* That line and, specifically, that moment, just seemed to capture the spirit of the whole production, and an incredibly special time in our lives. This wonderful, momentous, brilliant play, which had taken us all on such a journey, was finally coming to a close.

When the lights came up, Russell started crying and then we all started crying. We did the curtain calls, three or four of them, but the audience just refused to leave. The house lights came up and they were still out there, screaming for more. The stage manager told us that we couldn't leave them like that and had to go out again, so we ambled back on stage. We didn't bow; we just stood there, taking it all in. Everyone was on their feet. Most of us were in bits; I know I was a total mess.

Then Richard, ever the professional, stepped forward, put his hand up and eventually the audience quietened down. 'Thank you,' he said. 'Thank you so much for having us in your incredible city. We've been blessed to be part of this play, and to do it in your city has been amazing. Thank you for taking us to your hearts. We have to go and get a plane now. We have to be back in London for the premiere of our film. Thank you, New York. Thank you.'

Zammo did a back flip. I ripped off my tie and, like a pop star, jumped down into the aisle, where I gave it to a girl who must've come to see us at least fifty times. Sacha was running up and down like a crazy person high-fiving everyone and, by the time we finally pulled ourselves away, we were all so overcome with emotion, we could barely see straight. I'm never going to forget that night; thinking about it still gives me goose pimples.

It was time to go, so we grabbed our bags and bundled into cabs to JFK Airport. We'd flown in from Sydney in economy, but we were flying out first class, courtesy of the film's distributor, Twentieth Century Fox.

WE TOUCHED DOWN in London and were driven straight to the Dorchester Hotel, where we caught up on a little sleep for an hour or two. Then we slipped into the Giorgio Armani suits that had been made specially for us and then went out to where a pair of limos were waiting to take us off to Leicester Square. Less than twenty-four hours previously we'd performed for the last time on Broadway, and now we were on our way to meet Prince Charles. This was totally ridiculous.

As the *Gavin & Stacey* scripts had developed, I'd asked a few of the boys to play various parts in the show. At the premiere, we did that thing where you line up and Prince Charles walks along, being introduced one by one, shaking hands and asking questions. He asked Zammo what he was up to next, and Zammo told him that he was going to be in my TV show. So, when the prince got to me, he said he'd heard I was making a programme set in Wales.

'That's right, sir,' I said. 'We've not cast all the parts yet so there's a part for you if you want it. We'd love you to join us if you're available.'

'Really?' he said. 'Well, if this job ever goes wrong, it's good to know there's something to fall back on.' I liked him, and Camilla. I told her that the dress she was wearing was a triumph and she seemed to like that.

We watched the film and then headed off to the after-show party, which turned into this wonderful reunion with all our families and friends. It felt so good to be home.

WITH THE FILM now out, work-wise I was concentrating all my energies on *Gavin & Stacey*. While I'd been in New York, Ruth and Henry had been sending over casting tapes of various people to start filling the roles. As soon as I saw their tapes, I knew that Mat Horne and Joanna Page would be perfect as Gavin and Stacey.

Ruth had phoned to tell me about Christine Gernon, who she thought would be good as our director. So, while I was in New York, I'd caught a night flight one Sunday that got me to London on Monday morning to grab an hour or two with Christine. She was great, really enthusiastic and full of ideas about how she saw the show. We had offered her the job there and then, and then I had gone straight to the airport and back to New York.

We cast Larry Lamb as Gavin's dad. Alison Steadman had agreed to play Pam, Gavin's mum, which we were over the moon about: Alison playing that part was all we'd ever wanted. We had already worked out that Ruth was Nessa, I was Smithy, and we got Rob Brydon to complete the set as Stacey's Uncle Bryn.

A couple of weeks after *The History Boys'* premiere, we organised a read-through with all the cast. It's still one of the best I've ever been to. I am, of course, incredibly biased, but it was a magical day, particularly for Ruth and me. People at the BBC told us afterwards that they were taken aback by the laughter in the room, that the way all the personalities had just clicked was incredible—and pretty unusual. Ruth and I kept glancing at each other, neither of us quite believing that it was actually going so well. There were all kinds of indicators and little moments to let us know we were on the right path; jokes that we'd thought might be a touch subtle, but which worked in the room. The read-through honestly couldn't have gone any better.

More or less as soon as it was over, we all went off to Cardiff to begin shooting. So I'd barely been back a couple of weeks—one of them spent travelling all over the country promoting *The History Boys* film—and I was already leaving again to go off working. Eventually, it took its toll on my and Shelley's relationship.

To this day that break-up with Shelley makes me feel so sad. Since I'd got home it had become clear that the relationship had nowhere else to go. There's no question it was absolutely the right thing to do, but that didn't change how difficult or painful it was. We'd been together since we were eighteen. I was twenty-seven now, and the emptiness I felt after she was gone was just awful. To be honest, I was so busy that it wasn't for quite some time afterwards that I actually grieved for what had happened to us. I threw myself into work and it became my entire focus. All I can say is, Shelley, if you're reading this, I'd like to take this moment to say thank you. Thank you for being the first person I ever loved and the first person to love me. You are one of the best people I've ever known. Your love, support, friendship and care have in no small way shaped the man I am today. I'm sorry if there were times I wasn't a good enough boyfriend, if I put work before you. I have so many fond memories of our time together. You will always have a special place in my heart.

IT WAS SUCH a strange time, with so much going on, and I used all the distractions to take my mind off what was happening with me and Shelley. And one of those distractions was Mat Horne.

I'd seen Mat on tape back in New York, and then we'd met for the first time at the read-through; after that, we had our first phone call, which lasted for an hour. It was a beautiful thing.

Mat and I got each other immediately and, as we got deeper into filming the first series, we became absolutely inseparable. By about week four we'd got so close that we were finishing each other's sentences. Prior to *Gavin & Stacey*, Mat had been part of a double act called Mat and Mackinnon, so he was a natural when it came to riffing ideas and scenarios. As the shoot went on, we started doing little improvised sketches together in our downtime, which got us thinking about working together on another project, maybe some kind of sketch show. In the meantime, though, filming was going well and we were getting some really good stuff in the can. Within a couple of months the shoot wrapped, we began the edit and, before we knew it, the first show was ready to air.

CHAPTER 10

Gavin & Stacey by James Corden and Ruth Jones. It was such a proud moment—probably the proudest I've ever had—sitting with Mum and Dad on Sunday night at our family home in Hazlemere. It felt like my very own opening night. The next day, I got down to the newsagent's first thing to read the reviews: it seemed as if everyone was talking about the show with affection, and that never really disappeared. In fact, from the moment the first episode aired in May 2007, the show just took on a life of its own: the ratings started at 500,000 viewers and, by the time the last episode of the last series went out on New Year's Day 2010, the figures were over 12.5 million. It still takes my breath away.

The people at the BBC were so excited that, before the first episode had gone out, they'd commissioned a second series. I was staggered that they could have that kind of faith. And so, weirdly, Ruth and I ended up writing the second series while the first one was still being shown on TV. In some ways, that was actually quite difficult. It's very hard to emulate success, especially when that success is happening at the same time as you're trying to emulate it. It wasn't a position either of us had been in before.

When we'd written the first series, there had been no comparisons and nobody was telling us how good we were. This time round, the pressure was really on. *Gavin & Stacey* seemed to be growing into something special; the characters had struck a real chord with lots of people, so Ruth and I didn't want to disappoint anyone who'd taken the show to their heart.

With all those thoughts whirling around my head, all that pressure Ruth and I were putting on ourselves and each other, writing that second series was bloody difficult. I'd drive down to Cardiff and we'd sit for five or six hours at a time, trying things out but often coming up empty. Writer's block: up until that point I hadn't believed it really existed, but I became pretty familiar with it during that time.

On the other hand, everything else seemed to be going along well. I was about to fall for a new girl I'd met while filming *Fat Friends* a few years back, an actress called Sheridan Smith. She had been in *The Royle Family* and *Two Pints of Lager and a Packet of Crisps* as well as loads of other things. She is an incredible actress. Funny, and absolutely intoxicating to be around. I loved her more than I ever knew was possible. I was head over heels in love with her and, for the next two years, on and off, off and on, we were together.

With the first series doing well, more auditions started rolling in, and Mat and I found ourselves up for a British film called *Lesbian Vampire Killers*. I don't think either of us could believe that we were being considered for the two leads in a film.

It was such a strange time for me. Professionally, it couldn't have been better and yet, personally, I was starting to feel quite lost. My relationship with Sheridan was seesawing—true love or the deepest heartbreak—and so I lost that stability that I'd known for most of my life. Everything that I knew, everything that was familiar, seemed as if it was drifting away. The next couple of years went by in a bit of a blur. *Gavin & Stacey* was swiftly becoming the kind of success Ruth and I could only have dreamt of, but the reality is, I don't remember a lot about it.

BY THE TIME Ruth and I were writing the second series, in the summer of 2007, Shelley had long since moved out of the flat in Beaconsfield. From the day she left, the place had a lingering air of emptiness: the home that we'd worked so hard to create together had lost its heart. For some time I'd been in this turbulent relationship with Sheridan. When we were on, we spent a lot of time together in London, and when we were off, I had no desire to be on my own in Beaconsfield, so I'd crash wherever I could.

Dominic Cooper had recently broken up with his girlfriend, and we spent a lot of time together. He was living in a self-contained studio at the top of Nick Hytner's house. My car boot was always full of clothes because I never knew where I was going to end up. I'd either stay with Dom or I'd wind up in beds I'd never slept in before, with girls I'd never met before. I was single at the time, so I wasn't doing anything outrageous, but I'd never been a womaniser, and the longer it went on, the emptier my soul felt.

Success can be giddying, if you know what I mean. I was a young guy, in the public eye for the first time, and I no longer had the stability of a settled home life as back-up. In terms of the show, the good news just kept on coming. It had been nominated for seven different British comedy awards, which was not only a record, it also added more media interest about the people in it. In the end we won three of the seven: Best New Comedy for the show, and both Ruth and I won Best Newcomer. We were named the Writers' Guild of Great Britain's Comedy Writers of the Year. The Critics' Choice, *The South Bank Show* Award for Comedy. The plaudits and praise just kept rolling in. Ruth took it all in her stride. She enjoyed it and found the fun in it. I, too, relished it. But the difference was, I started to believe the hype. I'm not saying I regret all the experiences I had because I don't. I definitely regret certain things I said and did, but it was a wild time.

I was on and off with Sheridan throughout most of 2008. Each time we got back together the love would be more intense, and then, of course, the break-up would be all the more heartbreaking. When I was single, I would go out all the time. And I mean, all the time: I couldn't really see the point of staying in.

The night that *Gavin & Stacey* won *The South Bank Show* Award for Comedy sticks out in particular. The ceremony took place on a late January afternoon at the Dorchester Hotel. It's an amazing buzz to be in a room with a whole mix of people, from Tracey Emin to Ken Loach. Art and artists everywhere. I celebrated by having a glass of champagne on my own. And when I say a glass, I mean a bottle. And when I say on my own, I mean On My Own. I'd lost Ruth, who I think had gone to the bar with Alison Steadman, and I couldn't get hold of anyone I knew, so I just sort of wandered around the room drinking. Sooner or later the realisation hit me that I didn't know any of the people in the room—or any of the people I was climbing into a taxi with later. (I didn't know where we were going, either.)

This was not a one-off; it was happening almost every single night. Parties after parties after after-parties. House parties of people I didn't know; back rooms of pubs and other crappy dives. I wish I could remember more about it so I could better understand why I was behaving like that. Every single one of my dreams was coming true and yet I couldn't have been more miserable. I think most of all I felt lonely, which is why I wanted to surround myself with people. In one sense, I must have appeared supremely confident, but I was crumbling inside. The woman I thought I loved was with someone else at this point and it was killing me. Everything I did—all the showing off, all the partying and drinking—was just compensation.

They say you should never believe your own publicity, and

they—whoever they are—are absolutely right. But the truth is it's really, really hard not to absorb some of it, at least when your picture is being plastered across the covers of major magazines and when everyone and their uncle is lining up to tell you how great you are. I'm sure that if I'd been more grounded and surrounded myself with the people who really cared about me, I might have behaved differently. I'd gone from talking to my dad almost every day to not speaking to him for weeks. I was ignoring the people who had known me growing up, who had been such a huge part of my life before all the fame stuff. Why didn't I just stop and look around at what I had and see how lucky I was?

This was the spring of 2008. I was coming up to thirty and my career was going as well as I could have dared hope. The second series of *Gavin & Stacey* was running and the viewing figures were better than the first series and growing.

I SAID EARLIER about how well Mat and I bounced off each other on set. Well, after the success of the second series, we began talking with the BBC about the possibility of doing a sketch show. Originally, I thought we should try and make a pilot. We'd not made one for *Gavin & Stacey*, but then Ruth and I had lived with the characters for so long, and we were working with such experienced actors, that it didn't feel as if we needed one. This was different, though: this wasn't a sitcom with a developing story; this was a series of sketches. Time was a big factor, however. Mat and I had just been offered the leads in *Lesbian Vampire Killers* and so we, the BBC and the producers decided to push on without a pilot. So, we had to write and shoot the sketch show, shoot the movie, and Ruth and I had a BBC1 Christmas special of *Gavin & Stacey* to write.

But the cherry on top of the cake was about to arrive. I awoke one morning in March to a few voicemails and text messages, all saying congratulations. I didn't know what they were for until I scrolled further down to find one from our producer, Lindsay Hughes, which said, 'Well done. You've been nominated for a BAFTA!' I honestly nearly fell out of bed. The first thing I did was call Ruth

Jones. I couldn't wait to share the excitement of it all with her (and I also just wanted to check that this wasn't a massive wind-up). Some people had predicted we might get nominated after doing well at other awards dos, but I never thought it would actually happen. I found it hard to believe that our show had been nominated for 'Best Comedy' at the BAFTAs.

Except it wasn't. Ruth told me that the show was up for the Audience Award for Television Programme of the Year, and *I* had been nominated for Comedy Performance. It never even crossed my mind that I might have received a nomination for my performance. I always felt that if anyone from our show was going to be nominated, it would be Ruth. Her performance as Nessa is, in my opinion, astounding. So understated and yet rich to its very core. It couldn't be further away from who she is as a person and, when I catch moments of the show now, I am still in awe of what she did with the character. It felt strange to have been nominated when she wasn't. The only slight disappointment was that we hadn't been nominated in the 'Best Comedy' category.

WHEN THE NIGHT came around, it was tremendously exciting. It started off with Ruth and me walking down the red carpet and all the fans screaming our names, which was a very weird experience. Then, when we got inside, I was sitting behind Piers Morgan, who I didn't know at the time. I kept leaning forward, tapping him on the shoulder and saying, 'This is huge. This is bigger than all of us. Tonight. Tonight is huge.' Piers and his lovely partner (now wife) Celia kept looking round. I'm sure they were both thinking, *Who the hell is this guy?*

The ceremony started and quickly came to the award for Comedy Performance. I was up against three incredible actors in Peter Capaldi, David Mitchell and Stephen Merchant, so I never, even for a second, contemplated winning. Simon Pegg was giving the award. He read out the nominees and then they played the clips. (Mine finished with a shot of my bare bum, which made Piers turn round to me and say, 'Now that's huge!') As Simon said the words

'And the BAFTA goes to ...' I was getting ready to clap the winner up onto the stage. And then ... I heard my name. I sat there in such a state of shock.

I was sitting next to Rob Brydon, who had his hand on my arm, and I vaguely remember him telling me that I'd done it. Suddenly, I was on my feet and hugging Ruth, and then I was making my way up to the stage to collect the award. I was trying to keep my nerve. I was about to receive a BAFTA! Even now I can't quite get my head around the fact that it actually happened.

I think my speech was good. It went exactly how I hoped an acceptance speech might go, when I was dreaming of giving speeches back when I was a kid. I thanked my mum and dad, I thanked my sisters, and then I thanked Ruth, for not only being a brilliant actress and writer, but also for being the best friend I could wish for. I said that I was sharing the award with her, and meant every single word. There'd be nothing without Ruth, and I really do think of that award as half hers and half mine.

Normally, when you win, you then go off the side of the stage and you're taken to the press room where you do a short interview and they take a few pictures. But when I came off, they ushered me straight back to my seat. That got me suspicious. Why were they rushing me back? Unless, unless ...

Sitting down, I remember my palms were tingling. I waited nervously until it came to the Audience Award. I can still hear them announcing it. 'The Audience Award for Television Programme of the Year goes to — *Gavin & Stacey*.' I clean jumped out of my seat. I hugged Ruth and Rob. None of us could believe it. We'd won. We'd won a second BAFTA.

What happened next ... No, I'll rephrase that: what *I did next* I will regret as long as I live. We walked up to collect the award and, as we got on stage, I opened my gob. Instead of being gracious, or delighting in the fact that we'd won a second BAFTA, I asked a question: 'How can what is apparently the best comedy performance and the television programme of the year not even be nominated as a comedy?'

Instead of applause or nods of agreement, I was met with silence, shock and disbelief. Now, of course, I can see why, and how it must have looked—ungracious, ungrateful and brattish. Rather than using my speech to thank everyone who'd helped on the show, I'd ruined the moment and belittled myself in the process. I was so full of my own importance that I thought I could stand up there and ask why our show hadn't been nominated for Best Comedy. The two awards had given me this huge sense of entitlement and I'd acted like a fool. Who on earth did I think I was?

I WILL ALWAYS regret it—but it's only now, a couple of years down the line, that I can look back and see what a prat I was. Back then, I honestly couldn't see the problem everyone had with me asking the question. I wish I could tell you that this was a wake-up call for me, that I immediately saw what a fool I had become. The truth is, my behaviour probably got worse. As 2008 wore on, it got so bad I was being rude to my agent, and I even started being rude to Ruth. If I was in company and the conversation wasn't revolving around me, I would just switch off. I was the youngest person on The *Guardian*'s Media Power List, I had a new sketch show lined up, I had the lead in an upcoming film and, on top of that, I'd been asked to host the Brits with Mat and Kylie Minogue. I had everything I'd ever dreamt of and yet I was behaving like an oaf. Deep down, I was the unhappiest I think I've ever been.

What happens to the dream part of a dream when it becomes a reality? What happens to the bit of you that had the capacity to dream the dream in the first place? It seemed to me that all my life I'd been looking at these goalposts; they'd dominated the horizon for so long that I hadn't been able to see beyond them. My dreams had come true. I'd kicked that goal, but when I ventured beyond the posts to retrieve the ball, not only could I not find it, it was foggy out there and I sort of lost my way.

I was in a very bad place. I had an entire sketch show to write but instead of knuckling down and focusing on it, I put in probably a third of the work, effort and time as I should've done. Once you've had success, you have to go to ground, dig really deep — deeper than you ever did before — because that's the only chance you'll have of beating or even emulating what you achieved the last time. I just assumed we could put a show together without too much thought and we'd be the toast of the town all over again.

I TRULY BELIEVED in what Mat and I were trying to do. But to form a double act, to stand up there with the greats, the thing you need most is time. You need to find out what it is that makes you tick, what is unique about you as a duo, a twosome. Most great double acts have been together for years, experiencing triumph and disaster together, working comedy clubs night after night. Ours was a friendship where there were sparks showing we could have the kind of chemistry to make something great together.

Instead of testing the material unannounced at comedy clubs like we should've done, we took the show to a handful of students' unions where our audiences were people who wanted to see a couple of blokes from off the telly. They loved it. We went down a storm, but it was no yardstick. I was complacent. I can't speak for Mat, I only know how I was, and I was far more interested in how many girls I could get back to my hotel room than I was in making sure we had a show we could be proud of.

Lesbian Vampire Killers was directed by a talented man called Phil Claydon. The film had a budget of about £2 million so everyone felt fairly confident that it was going to do good business. Mat and I were now doing almost all of our work together for the next year or so. I had secured an American agent and just been offered my first part in a Hollywood film: *Gulliver's Travels* starring Jack Black, so professionally things couldn't have been better.

In many respects, however, it still felt hollow. I had once again been on and off in my relationship. I felt further and further away from my friends and family, and was still continuing to go out like my life depended on it. Christmas came and went and in January, Mat and I were told that the Brit Awards, the sketch show and the film were all going to come out within the same month.

THE BRIT AWARDS came first. To host it alongside Mat and Kylie Minogue was a dream come true. We did the show and thought it went well. People were coming up to us afterwards and saying it was great. We went off and danced and drank well into the night. Mum and Dad came to the show and were crying throughout—it had been a momentous night.

The next day the reviews were awful. We were called the worst hosts of all time. Not Kylie—she didn't really get mentioned, which was probably fair as she hadn't written the script. It was the first time I'd ever been on the end of criticism like that and it was strange. The truth is, I was bad, really bad. I've no idea what we were thinking. We were under the illusion that people cared that we were hosting the Brits, when the truth is the host should be almost invisible, just ushering the show from one performance to the next. I was, however, lucky enough to be asked back in 2011 and, thankfully, I got good reviews second time around.

The sketch show aired on Tuesday nights on BBC3 and had the most phenomenal ratings. It is still, as I write this, the highest debut comedy in the history of that channel. In fact, more people watched the first series of *Horne & Corden* than ever watched series one of *Gavin & Stacey*. But none of that mattered, because when it came to reviews, we had the worst. From broadsheet to tabloid it was open season. It was awful. 'The worst show that's ever been made,' said one. 'Puerile and disgusting,' said another. It was endless. We were called homophobic and talentless and, from there, it just kept getting worse.

The film then came out a week or so after and brought with it another round of awful coverage. The most embarrassing film since whatever the last awful film was seemed to be the gist of most of the write-ups. In three weeks, we'd seemingly gone from heroes to zeroes. It hurt. It really did. It was a huge wake-up call. Day after day, another piece would be written. I remember going to meet Mat one day and he was reading an article in the *Telegraph* that said: 'The backlash begins for the cocky princes of comedy.' It went on to say that we were basically awful, our careers were finished, that I was arrogant, and mentioned my BAFTA speech. Mark Lawson, a broadcaster and journalist whom I really respect, wrote a piece in the *Guardian* titled: 'Catch a Falling Star. How can Mathew Horne and James Corden rescue their nosediving careers?' This was probably the fifth or sixth of these articles that had been written in the few weeks since the film had been released.

The truth is — and it's taken a while for me to realise this — that the reviewers and other journalists writing these things were right. Unkind? Sure. Enjoying our fall from grace a little too much? Absolutely. But most of all, they were right. The Brits, the sketch show and the film. Not one of those things was good enough. The show lacked vision; it lacked heart and soul. Mostly, though, it wasn't funny enough.

It's difficult writing this. But, ultimately, I know that all of those reviews were right and, worse than that, I know that I was to blame. The person I had become wasn't the person I had wanted to be. I was lost and I needed to find myself again.

I thought it would blow over more quickly than it did, but it seemed to go on and on. The easiest thing to do in these circumstances is not to read any of the papers, but there was so much being written that if I tried to ignore them, it wasn't long before someone would come to me and say, 'That piece in the such-and-such newspaper is horrible. Just ignore it.'

All I'd want to do was say, 'I'm trying to ignore it. I didn't even know it existed, but now I do. Thank you.'

It was a testing time, to put it mildly. I was now back with Sheridan and was only staying at the flat in Beaconsfield occasionally. One day, when I was sitting in the kitchen going through a mound of bills and bank statements, I found a postcard with a beautiful picture of an old seat on the front. On the back was written: '*I'm sorry to read that you've been going through a tough time. I've no advice other than to say, "Screw 'em." It's always stood me in good stead. All my love, Alan Bennett.*'

I sat staring at it and was touched that he'd bothered to do such a thing. Over the next couple of weeks lots of people called and sent messages telling me to keep some perspective on this.

Piers Morgan sent me texts with wonderful nuggets of wisdom from his days on Fleet Street. He told me I was due a kicking, that this was how the press roundabout worked. He called me a few days later to talk the whole thing over.

So I became totally focused on the third series of *Gavin & Stacey*. Ruth and I had to make the best series we ever had. The show had become bigger than we'd ever dreamt possible and the reviews for the sketch show had told us that the knives would be out again if series three wasn't up to scratch. My agent and I agreed that I shouldn't be on television for a while, so we said no to any offers that were coming in.

However, there was one TV appearance I just couldn't say no to and that I was very passionate about.

CHAPTER 11

For as long as I can remember, I've loved Comic Relief. I'd been involved in some small way ever since I was a kid. Red Nose Days were always a laugh at school—you'd be allowed to wear your home clothes and there was inevitably some kind of mad fundraising event that involved getting wet or really messy. There was one time when my band Twice Shy charged a pound a head for a lunchtime concert, with all the money going to Comic Relief. (That was the most we ever made from a gig, and we didn't even get to keep it.)

Richard Curtis had been in touch about doing something, and Ruth and I were thinking of doing a *Gavin & Stacey* special. We had this idea where all of the characters were heading to BBC Television Centre in White City to watch Uncle Bryn hand over a cheque for £45 that he'd raised from doing a sponsored swim. All the characters would be there, but in one way or another they would all get lost whilst walking around TV Centre. This is easily done, I might add: I've been lost in there for hours before. The idea was that Bryn would end up on the set of *Strictly Come Dancing*, Gwen would show Jamie Oliver how to cook the perfect omelette, Gavin and Stacey would try and have a quickie in the Blue Peter garden, Nessa would keep bumping into famous old flames and Smithy would walk onto the *Match of the Day* set, meet the England team and give them a team talk.

Richard loved the idea but it soon became clear that getting everyone together in the same place at the same time would be impossible. So I suggested we concentrate on Smithy and the England team: Smithy could say to the England team what every fan would dream of saying if they were ever face to face with them.

I remember Richard shaking his head. 'James,' he said, 'I've got to tell you there's no chance of getting anywhere near the England team. We've tried to do stuff with the FA before and got absolutely nowhere. It's a bit like trying to do something with the Royal Family — it just never happens.'

I was insistent, and Richard came around to the idea that asking wouldn't do any harm. He also asked if I had any preference about who should direct it. I knew instantly. Remember the runner from *Teachers*, Ben Winston? Well, we had stayed friends and he'd since gone on to become one of the most exciting directors/producers you could wish to meet. I told him about the idea for the sketch and he got it immediately, but he too had his doubts over whether the FA would go for it.

I GUESS IT WAS a matter of timing. Just as we were asking the Smithy question, the FA was trying to think of ideas to reconnect the England team with the fans. They felt the gap between the players and the average supporter had been getting too big, and it wasn't healthy for the country as a whole. So, amazingly, and without much prodding, they said yes to the sketch idea and told us they'd guarantee us a minimum of four players.

Richard, Ben and I were stunned. We had to strike while the iron was hot. It's not often the England squad is together and, when they are, their time is precious. Ben brought in the legend that is his producing partner, Gabe Turner, and we all worked together on trying to find the time to do it.

It was the perfect production team with the perfect opportunity, and all we had to do now was come up with the perfect sketch. The truth is, we had plenty of ideas, but had nothing written down, which was largely because we didn't know which players were going to do it. We had to deal with the fact that it was probably going to remain that way right up to the last minute, so the sketch would have to be fluid and flexible.

The day got nearer and the guys from the FA were being very supportive, but we still didn't know who the players would be. We arrived at the hotel on the day of the shoot and the FA told us that the players would, at most, have twenty minutes to spare after a team meeting and before dinner. That was it, which, with the faffing around and sitting down when they got there, meant more like eighteen minutes if we were lucky.

Eighteen minutes is not a lot of time to shoot anything. With an episode of *Gavin & Stacey*, for example, it takes six days to shoot the twenty-eight minutes that end up on the TV. Still, that's what we had, so we got busy: we filmed the background stuff—Smithy arriving in the car, lying on his back fixing pipes in the corridor before hunting down the toilet—and, when that was done, Gabe, Ben and I worked on the lines we had about different players, hoping as many as possible would show up.

The big problem was we'd had no access to them beforehand. Fortunately, Rio Ferdinand had become a bit of a mate. A couple of years before, he'd got in touch with me to say he was a fan of *Gavin & Stacey* and we'd stayed in touch off and on. So I was texting him, trying to get an idea of who was going to show up; he was instrumental in persuading lots of the players who eventually did come along. He told me that he'd be there, together with John Terry and Ashley Cole, and one other who he thought was going to be Shaun Wright-Phillips, but he couldn't say for sure. At least I knew who three of them would be, so I got working on the script. But I was desperately hoping Rio could come up with a few more, because the sketch would be hard to do if there were only the four of them.

As the time drew closer, he sent me another text telling me that Peter Crouch was coming now as well. Then he mentioned that some of the players were coming down to Reception where there was a stack of shirts to be signed. That was my chance to grab a word with a few of them, and see if I couldn't persuade a couple more of the squad to join in.

The problem was that we'd been told under no circumstances were we allowed to approach any of the players, or even talk to them beforehand. This came from the team management, and Franco Baldini (Capello's number two, and the second scariest man I've ever met after Capello) was making sure that was how it was. You know Franco, the grey-haired, good-looking guy who sits next to Capello and looks like he might be a mob-enforcer—not the kind of man you want to cheese off.

But this was Comic Relief, so I hung around Reception as the players came downstairs for the shirt signing. Franco was there, too, watching like an angry hawk. I kind of hoped that one or two of them would recognise me from *Gavin & Stacey* and, maybe, just wander over to say hello. But no one did. I was getting a little desperate when I saw Frank Lampard come down. Frank was a big name and I knew that if we got him, a couple of others might come along, too. So, risking Franco's wrath, I walked over to where he was standing on the other side of the table.

'Frank,' I called. 'Frank!'

He looked up and smiled.

'Hi, Frank,' I said, shaking hands. 'I'm James.'

'Nice to meet you, James,' he said.

'Listen, have you heard about this sketch we're doing today?'

'Yeah,' he said. 'Rio's trying to get some of the lads down.'

'Great,' I said. 'Are you going to be in it, then?'

'No,' he said. 'It's not my thing really. I'd feel a bit silly.'

'Frank,' I said, 'I promise you, mate, we're not going to make you look silly.'

Still he was shaking his head. 'It's not about you making me look silly. I'm no good at that kind of thing. I wouldn't be any good in a sketch.'

'Look,' I said, 'you don't have to worry about that. You don't have to do anything. You just need to sit there and listen.'

'I don't know,' he said.

'Frank,' I said, 'this sketch will save people's lives and your involvement will help us raise so much more money. People love you, Frank, they love you. It won't be the same without you.'

It was real, savage, emotional blackmail. I didn't want to go there, but this was Comic Relief. 'Frank,' I said, 'I promise you, if you come down, you won't be asked to do anything stupid.' And then I shut up. I didn't say another word. I just kept on looking at Frank, and he stood there with a kind of half-smile that told me he knew just how badly I was guilt-tripping him.

'OK,' he said finally. 'If it's for Comic Relief, of course I'll come.'

'Thank you, Frank,' I said. 'That's great. And please, do me a favour and just bring as many of the other players as you can.'

SO WE HAD Frank, which was huge, but there was still the one name we wanted to get: Beckham. Becks was in the squad, but he'd played for Milan the day before, flown in late and had been training all morning. We'd asked about him, of course, but they told us his schedule was really hectic so we would just have to wait and see when the time came whether he was up for it.

So we waited and, finally, word came down that the players were on their way: John Terry followed by Frank and Rio. Peter Crouch and Shaun Wright-Phillips. Michael Carrick took a seat, as did David James. Ashley Cole came in and then last—and I couldn't believe it—the door opened and in walked David Beckham. As soon as they were all in, the clock started running. Twenty minutes and counting.

So we got into it. The only bit that worried me came at the very end of the sketch when hopefully Smithy had the players all fired up. We hadn't told them about that bit, as we really needed them to be spontaneous and just go with it.

What I wasn't prepared for was how amused the other players were when one of their team mates was getting laid into. It was hard to concentrate with Ashley Cole trying not to crack up as I ripped David James about his hair.

Apart from that, the whole thing just flowed. Each player took whatever Smithy dished out on the chin and then, at the end, when we really needed them to get up for it, all I can say is, God bless Peter Crouch. As I finished the rap, Crouchy went with it and was the first to shout, 'Go on, Smithy!' The others followed his lead, clapping, cheering and punching the air.

The sketch went down brilliantly when it aired. I had been totally unprepared for the reaction to it. People were calling it the highlight of the night. I know, me making a good sketch. Who would have thought?

THE NEXT THING I had to do was write the third series of *Gavin & Stacey* with Ruth. As before, we would often write in hotels so we could basically just lock ourselves away and concentrate. Being back in a room with Ruth was just what I needed at the time. It was good for the soul to be laughing with her again.

We knew before we started writing that this was going to be the last series we'd make and, when it came to us writing the last ever line of our last ever script, it was around midnight in the Soho Hotel. We both stopped, stood up and hugged each other. That was it. This series that had meant so much to us, that had been such a big part of our lives—we'd finished it. Ruth and David, her husband, had been my only real constants over the last topsy-turvy couple of years. Ruth, in particular, had always been there for me, and was the first person I'd pick up the phone to speak to in times of triumph or despair. As I left her that night, I couldn't help but wonder who, or what, would be my constant now.

After finishing writing, I shot *Gulliver's Travels* for seven weeks in the late spring of 2009, which was a fun experience. Working on something with such a huge budget was so different to anything I'd ever done before, and I had the added bonus of doing all of my scenes with Billy Connolly—a real dream come true. But however much I was enjoying the shoot, the turbulent relationship I was in still hampered my mood. In fact, it dominated me. I was so preoccupied with myself that it can't have been fun to work with, or be around, me.

After *Gulliver's Travels* I went back to Cardiff to shoot *Gavin & Stacey*. As with the other two series, I loved every single minute of it. Well, almost every minute. During the last week of filming, my relationship with Sheridan finally ended, in a manner that meant there'd be no going back. Once and for all, it was over. Only a couple of days after that came the last day of shooting.

I was incredibly upset, both for the end of the relationship and for the loss of the show. The last scene we ever shot was the scene in the final episode when Smithy meets Nessa at a service station. It has one of my favourite moments in all three series—it's Nessa's line when she says to Smithy, 'There's only one of you, isn't there?' Ruth delivers it perfectly. With everything that was happening personally, filming that last scene took it out of me. I cried my eyes out all day long.

I GOT BACK to London and, within a few days, Dominic and I began renting a flat together in Primrose Hill. Dominic has always been an incredible friend to me and I remember our time together in that flat with great fondness. We had the top two floors of a five-storey house and, to my shame, I have to tell you that we were probably the worst neighbours you could ever wish for. That flat could have been lovely, but we never made it a home.

We rented it furnished—which meant it had one tiny, two-seater sofa in a corner, Dominic's black velour chaise longue (don't ask) in another room, two beds and that was it. In a way, it was handy that we never really furnished it properly because it meant there was more room for all the dancing that would regularly take place.

I once got dropped in a cab four or five streets away from our place and, as I was paying the cab driver, I could hear the thud of a dull beating bass coming through the air.

'God, someone's having a party,' said the driver.

'Yeah!' I said, taking my change. As I walked up and over the hill towards our flat, the bass just kept getting heavier and heavier. As I arrived outside the front door, it was clear the party was in our flat and all of the windows were wide open. I walked up through the house, up the small staircase, passing people on every other stair, to the open-plan top floor. There, in the middle of the room, was Dom playing a drum kit. An electric drum kit that he'd threatened to buy for a long time.

Dominic looked up at me. 'LEVINE!' he shouted as he went round the tom-toms for the thirtieth time in as many seconds.

I couldn't help but smile. I went over to him and said, 'Who are all these people?'

For some reason he chose to reply in an Australian accent. 'I've no idea, mate. Now grab ya'self a beer and loosen up, me old mucker!' So I did, and we went on to have a great night. I woke up in bed the next morning with someone I'd only just met.

I wish I could tell you that nights like this were once in a blue moon but they were probably once or twice a week. This went on for a good couple of months, so I'd like to take this moment to apologise to our neighbours (although I'd be amazed if they are reading this book), who would regularly ask us to keep the noise down.

THERE WERE PLENTY of times when Dom went to America for work, and it was at those moments, sitting in the barely furnished flat on my own, that the reality of my situation would start to hit home. I just wasn't moving on.

I'd been living there for a couple of months and Mum and Dad had been keen to visit. They'd never been to the flat and I'd not been in regular contact with them for a while. Then, one morning, Dad called out of the blue and told me that they were in Primrose Hill and they were coming over. I was hung over and feeling really rough, but I knew I couldn't put them off, especially when they were only round the corner. I tried my best to tidy the flat but within minutes the buzzer was sounding. When I saw Mum, though, I couldn't help but give a big smile; she came in and squeezed me so tight, just like she always had. Mum and Dad were on the sofa, me on the floor—and, sadly, I had nothing to say to them. The conversation went from pause to even longer pause. Dad would ask about this thing or that, but I had no real answers, certainly none of any worth. I felt distant from them, so far away from the person they expected me to be, from the boy they had so lovingly raised. I hated them seeing me like this and I could barely lift my eyes to look them in the face. Then, all of a sudden, Dad came over to where I was sitting on the floor, knelt down and put his arms around me. I can't begin to tell you how it felt. I couldn't help but cry.

I felt so embarrassed at the way I'd been living my life, the arrogance and lack of respect I'd shown myself and my work. Every tear that left my eyes made me feel a little lighter. Dad said a prayer as he kissed my forehead and Mum came over and joined the hug. I've no idea how long we stayed there, but it felt like a lifetime. When they left later on, Dad turned to me and said, 'You've so much to be thankful for, James. I know it's been a tricky year, but you can't carry on like this.'

Mum told me only last week that after they'd left the house they drove the car round the corner and had to pull in because Dad had got so upset. They didn't know how to help me and were worried I wouldn't help myself. It's only now, after having a child of my own, that I can even begin to comprehend how hard it must've been for my parents: journalists turning up on their doorstep asking about this and that, pictures of me falling out of clubs and bars, me never answering their phone calls. I knew that I was on a roller coaster, but it never crossed my mind to look behind me and realise that my family and some of my closest friends were riding it with me, hoping I would get off.

I needed a change of scenery. I got a call from Andrew, my American agent, about an audition for a film over in the US. It was the perfect opportunity to get away from everything.

Normally, with early auditions like this, you record yourself on video, send it via email, and if they like what they see, you go out and meet them in person. I made a snap decision—nothing was going to change as long as I stayed in this cycle of going out and feeling sorry for myself, so I told Andrew that if it was OK, I'd fly out the next day and do the audition there.

Although the weather and new environment helped my disposition, I'm not sure LA's the best place to lick emotional wounds, and I only lasted a couple of days before I phoned home and asked my little sister Rudi if she wanted to come out and join me.

We had a wonderful time. Or I did, anyway. That holiday mended me. I poured my heart out and Rudi just listened to it all and never once complained. During those few days she was much more than just my sister—she became one of my closest friends. I'd never have got through it all without her. There was a song she played for me over and over again. The lyrics were: 'I am my brother's keeper and I will always be; as long as there's a need for him there'll be a need for me.'

Daily, hourly, she told me I was going to get through the pain of Sheridan, of Shelley, and of everything else that had made me feel this way. She would talk about the fact that I was at a crossroads and that I had a choice: I could carry on the way I was going or I could go back to who I really was. It was all up to me.

Rudi reminded me of who I'd been before all the success and that, far from having arrived, I had only just got to the point where the real work began.

HOME IN LONDON, I was beginning to get a little faith back. I was sick and tired of the way I'd cheapened everything. I was determined to be the person I once was again. I knew I could get over the slump: the criticism I'd had in the papers had wounded me but had never really hurt; it was the emotional state I was in that had really dragged me down.

I began to work on new ideas for stuff. I stopped going out so much and made a conscious effort to be a little more selective about who I brought home. I felt a difference in my mood almost instantly. I had a clearer head, a more positive outlook. I got together with old friends and, for the first time in my life (at the age of thirty-one), I even stayed in a few times on my own. Once you get over the initial fear, it actually becomes something you really enjoy. At first, it felt so strange to be going to sleep at ten o'clock in complete silence, without a drink in my system or a stranger in my bed. But, within a few days, it became the most natural thing in the world.

ON THE PROFESSIONAL front, there was a decision to be made about the future of the sketch show. The ratings had been so good that the BBC were keen for Mat and I to make another series. We understandably had been reluctant after having such a wave of negativity come our way in the aftermath of series one. In the end, after a lot of discussion, we decided not to carry on. It seemed like too big a risk to try again. It's still the biggest creative decision of my career. The way I see it, all that would've happened is that the old reviews would have been rehashed and the pressure on the show to deliver would have been too great. What critic was suddenly now going to proclaim our show as the greatest show ever? Sketch shows by their very nature are always hit and miss. What one person loves, another person may hate.

Both Mat and I had offers to do other things, and it seemed like the right decision to try out different opportunities. We moved on. The strangest thing about us making this decision was that suddenly Mat and I weren't going to be spending as much time together. I loved every single second of working with him, though, and I hope that one day, in some form or another, we'll be able to do something together again. He is a wonderful friend, actor and writer, and will always have a special place in my heart.

As Christmas got nearer, the third series of *Gavin & Stacey* aired to some pretty amazing figures. On Christmas Day itself, some twelve million people tuned in to watch the penultimate episode, and even more watched the last show on New Year's Day. It was an incredible way to end the series. A month later, we won Best Comedy at the National Television Awards and Ruth and I were named as the Writers' Guild Comedy Writers of the Year.

Looking back on it, 2009 was a really strange year. I'd been as down as I'd ever been, become someone I barely even recognised, and then ended the year on a huge professional high. Happily, as 2010 came round, things were looking up.

CHAPTER 12

I was feeling so much more positive about myself and the future. All I know is the huge relief I felt to be reconnecting with family and friends who I had taken for granted or abandoned somewhere over the last couple of years. I was still living in the flat, but was there mostly on my own as Dominic had been spending a lot of time working in the US. I had been staying in more, and finding time to work on a new television-show idea with Mathew Baynton—who played Deano in *Gavin & Stacey*—called *The Wrong Mans*. It was great getting back in the writing groove again after being away from it for a while.

When Dominic was in town, things weren't quite so quiet. I remember one day when Dominic had flown in after a while away. He burst into the flat like a tornado. 'LEVINE!' he shouted up to me as he crashed through the door downstairs; once again, and for reasons still unknown, in an Australian accent. 'Get your best strides on, mate, 'cos we're going out. Got a big night planned and you'd be a dag to miss it.'

We hugged and he told me that we'd been invited to a Bulgari party that night and that it was gonna be incredible. I told him I hadn't really been going out that much recently. He wasn't having it: 'All the more reason, then. This not going out is fair dinkum, mate, but you can't live like a monk. Let's get our glad rags on and have a bloody good time!'

Dom can be pretty persuasive and, much as I didn't feel like going out that night, part of me knew that it'd be fun.

I didn't really know where this party was or what it was about; I just knew that we'd been invited by an old friend of Dominic's.

We'd been there for about ten minutes when Dom tapped me on my shoulder. 'Levine, I've got someone I want to introduce you to. This is Jules.' I turned round and in front of me stood Miss Julia Carey. She was smiling.

'Hi, Jules,' I said, before looking away at Dominic and staring at him open-mouthed, talking to him with my eyes in the way that only close friends can. We chatted for a while and she told me she worked for Save the Children and that the party was an event she had organised with Bulgari. After a while, she went off to carry on with her work and I immediately set about questioning Dom on who she was and, more importantly, whether she was single. Dominic giggled, 'Hmmmm, I thought you'd like Jules.'

They had known each other for about fifteen years and, although I'd met many of Dom's old friends, I'd never met her. Thank God! I mean, thank God I was meeting her *now*, at this moment, when I felt good about myself and positive about who I was and who I wanted to be. Another way of putting it is that for the first time in a while, I felt ready to be in a proper relationship; one that had all the things that had been lacking before.

When Jules came back, I suggested we go over to the bar together. After we'd picked up some drinks we found a seat in the corner of the room, in a quiet spot, and talked. And we talked and talked for the rest of the party. We spoke about our families, about her work and how much she was enjoying it; we laughed about the benefits of staying in and about how exhausting it was going out all the time. It felt like the most normal and natural thing in the world to be talking to her. I didn't feel on edge or as if I had to pretend to be anyone else—I was just being me.

Once Jules had got the last of her work done, Dom told us about an after-party near Berkeley Square. Jules came with us in the car and, again, we chatted the whole way there. It was during this conversation that Jules told me she had never seen *Gavin & Stacey*. She said she didn't watch a lot of television and didn't really know what it was. I was so happy. I remember thinking to myself, *Wow, this really intelligent, beautiful, lovely lady wants to talk to me, just me.*

We got to the exclusive after-party, which seemed like the same party with the same people but just in a different venue, and we set about finding another quiet little corner to carry on our chat. We talked about places we'd been, things we wanted to see and do in the future; hour after hour ticked by. Julia's outlook and her views on life were so refreshing. She told me about the places she'd travelled to with Save the Children, the array of things she'd seen and how it had given her a perspective on life. I listened, transfixed. She was perfect in every single way.

And, that night, as we were saying our goodbyes, I turned to Jules and said, 'You know how you said you were tired of going out and how exhausting it is? Well, I was wondering, would you like to stay in with me on Friday night? I'll cook and we'll do nothing. In fact, anytime you want to do nothing, I'd like to be there with you. That nothing could really turn into something.' We kissed and it was perfect. And pretty much from that moment on, we've been inseparable.

I loved her instantly. I felt more relaxed, stronger, happier in my skin. I introduced her to two of my closest friends, Ben and Gabe, and they immediately loved her. When we went to meet my family, within minutes it felt as if she had always been there.

I was In Love. I had been in love before, but never like this. Never a love that felt so free, so honest. I felt that Jules allowed me to become the man I'd always wanted to be.

A friend of mine told me the other day that Jules completed

me, but I don't think that's even the half of it. It's hard to put into words quite how much I love her. Meeting her for the first time felt like the moment I started to find my way out of the fog, or the forest, or the labyrinth, or whatever analogy you'd like to use. She was there, waiting on the other side to make me whole again.

The only time we were apart was when Julia had to go on trips for work. She went to Haiti and India within the first couple of months after we met, but from the minute she returned we would stay at each other's houses. We went on our first holiday together to the Maldives and it was the best time of my life. I came back so refreshed and, no sooner had I landed, I got a call from Ben and Gabe, who said they had a new idea.

When Ben and Gabe have an idea, it's always exciting. You never know quite when they're going to come, but when they do they're always worth listening to.

They had two ideas that day. I went to meet them in a café near their offices of their company, though it turned out it wasn't just them: Clyde Holcroft, a writer and producer, was there, too. At the time, he was working as a senior producer for Sport Relief.

After the success of the last Smithy sketch for Comic Relief, there had been lots of interest in doing another one for a different charity. I was interested to hear what the boys had come up with, as the idea of doing another charity sketch could be fun.

I could tell they thought they had something big. Ben and Clyde both looked at Gabe and smiled. 'Tell him,' Ben said.

'*Sports Personality of the Year*. Smithy wins Coach of the Year,' Gabe said with a smile. I thought about it for a second. *Yes!* This could be huge.

As far as I was concerned, the only glitch was that *Sports Personality of the Year* was held in a quiet, controllable television studio, so how would we get the impact and the laughs we wanted? It had to be bigger. And then Clyde put me right—it was actually now held in an arena that would be full of 12,000 people.

Logistically, it was going to be a nightmare, but before we could even think about the speech, we had to work out exactly what form the sketch would take. We watched old videos of *Sports Personality* evenings and realised that often, before giving the winner his or her award, they would show an edited summary of exactly why they were winning. We figured that this was as good a template as any to copy but, rather than Smithy just winning the award for the speech he'd given the England team, perhaps it would be funnier if he was shown being involved in all aspects of British sport. We immediately set about putting requests in with the biggest names: Jenson Button, Andy Murray, the Manchester United team, Tom Daley, David Beckham and Freddie Flintoff. Not one person we approached said no. All of them gave us their time and bought in to the idea.

WE FOUND TIME to film with them over the next few months and every single one of them was amazing: receiving a serve from Andy Murray, who is without question one of the warmest and funniest people I've had the pleasure to meet; jumping off a high board with Tom Daley—an unforgettable experience, though it's an odd feeling having your nerves calmed by a fifteen-year-old when you're both wearing Speedos; the fitness class with Man United—great fun, and Rio Ferdinand once again came through and made sure we got enough players to make it worthwhile.

To film with Jenson Button, Ben and I had to fly out to Abu Dhabi. At first we were told we'd have twenty minutes to film in the pit lane; by the time we arrived at the racetrack, it was down to ten. The F1 officials were pretty strict about the time as the pit lane had to be opened for the practice laps to start. So we flew for eight hours, filmed for ten minutes and then turned round and had another eight-hour flight back.

Everything was really hinging on the big speech. It is, without question, one of the most nerve-racking things I've ever done. Because *Sports Personality* is filmed live, we were going to have to shoot our bit just before the actual show happened, when everyone was in their seats. Once the schedule had been finalised, it became clear we had just eleven minutes to shoot a ten-minute speech.

We got to the arena and all day my nerves were all over the place. I had to start the speech at 6.45 p.m. and be finished by 6.56 p.m. and it was made very clear that I couldn't overrun by even half a minute. As the time ticked down, I called Jules to try and steady myself, then left the dressing room and stood by the stage, taking long, deep, nervous breaths. Then, in what seemed like no time, I was up on stage. As quickly as I could, I explained to the audience what we were doing, then I went to take my seat.

Sue Barker started, then threw to Gary Lineker, who was standing with Sir Steve Redgrave. I, or rather Smithy, was sitting in the auditorium between Joe Calzaghe and Chris Eubank. In no time Sir Steve was calling Smithy's name. I stood up, gave Chris Eubank a big kiss and strode down the aisle. Everybody was on their feet, applauding, and then, when I got on stage, I shared another long and tender kiss with Sue Barker. The speech went better than I could ever have dreamt and was one of the best experiences I've ever had on stage. I came off and felt elated. Ben gave me a look that told me we had it in the bag.

I've never felt more fortunate than the times when I've been able to work alongside my closest friends. It's not lost on me how lucky I've been to do such things. And the next trip we had planned showed just what a bunch of lucky bastards we were.

David Beckham had agreed to shoot something for the sketch, but we didn't know what or where or when. We found out the where was in Milan, the when was in a couple of weeks, and we had to come up with a list of possible whats for David and his agent Simon to look at. We decided that we'd put a few outlandish suggestions at the top and then, by the time they'd said 'no' to a few things, the next batch would seem more realistic. So, top of our list we put: share a bed with Smithy watching a film, have a bath together, have Smithy re-styling David's hair, and flower arranging.

We waited for the response and, an hour later, Simon called to say David was happy to do everything we'd asked. We could not believe it. A week later we were on the plane to Milan.

We'd been told we could only shoot for an hour but, four hours after we started, the cameras were still rolling. David was incredible. He brought so much to the sketch. All of the dialogue was improvised and, I've got to say, his acting really surprised me. It was his idea that we both wear towels on our heads like women. We could barely keep a straight face. And then, the bath.

Now, getting in the bath with David Beckham is still up there as one of the most bizarre things I've ever done. We were both sitting there, just having a chat about anything and everything, and all the time I was thinking about the times I'd watched England play, how he'd made me jump out of my seat for joy. And here I was, in my pants, in the bath with him.

After the filming had finished, David asked everyone to join him for dinner at his favourite restaurant in town. Not just us, the cameraman and soundman, too. Being around him was a lesson in how to behave professionally and courteously. It made me think of my behaviour over the last couple of years, and how being nice is so much easier than being arrogant or trying to be seen as one thing or another.

When the sketch went out a few months later at Sports Relief, it was received better than any of us could've dared imagine. Ben, Gabe and I stood at the back of the studio at the BBC when they played it live to the audience, and hearing the roars of laughter is something I'll never forget.

REMEMBER I SAID that at the café all those months ago there had been two ideas? Well, the other was just as exciting, and it came from Clyde. The 2010 World Cup was on the horizon and Clyde had been thinking about a TV show that could broadcast live post-match. I've never really considered myself a TV presenter, but it's something I've always enjoyed doing, which is more than enough reason to do it.

So, Ben and I went to the BBC with the idea of *James Corden's World Cup Live*, selling it to them on the basis that, although we couldn't guarantee access to the England team, since we'd worked with them before, we had a good shot at getting it. We told them it would be live, unpredictable, would have big guests and discuss all the big stories that happened at the World Cup. Unfortunately, the BBC turned it down. They liked the idea of the show but thought it would be expensive to make. Plus, they'd already decided they'd do all their post-show stuff from South Africa so they didn't have a slot for it.

We were gutted. We'd been sure they would go for it. Actually, we'd been so confident that we'd set up a meeting with Adrian Bevington, the communications director of the FA, only an hour after our meeting with the BBC, to talk about access to the team.

We couldn't back out of the meeting with the FA so we sat in their offices pitching a show we knew wasn't going to happen. And here's the irony: they loved it. As far as access to the players was concerned, they would help us as much as they could. If anything, the good news from the FA made us more depressed. We had access to film the players, but no TV show to put them on. But, what we also had was an incredible executive producer in Suzi Aplin. As Ben and I made our way out of the swanky offices of the FA, dejected and barely talking, Ben stopped and started reading an email on his phone. It was from Suzi and it simply said, 'I've told Peter Fincham at ITV about the show and he wants us to come in and pitch . . . tomorrow!'

Peter Fincham really got the idea and, once we'd calmed a few of his nerves about my lack of presenting experience, he told us he was up for it. We came up with an idea that we'd try and film an activity with each of the England team. It was a tricky one to navigate as we didn't know who was going to make the final squad, but we had to get as many in the can as possible. We cooked with Rio Ferdinand, golfed with Steven Gerrard, boxed with Jermain Defoe, bowled with Michael Carrick, practised Pilates with Rob Green, and did loads of other crazy things with the rest of the squad. The players were brilliant. They all wanted to be involved and the only demand they made was that their appearance fee would be donated to a charity of their choice.

They were all fantastic company, and really warm, genuine nice guys: I can't tell you how many times I saw them helping members of the crew move filming equipment from one location to the next. They are often painted as money-grabbing mercenaries who couldn't care less about the game or the fans but, from where I've been standing, that couldn't be further from the truth.

IN TWO HOURS' TIME I shall be picking up Jules and my newborn son from the hospital to bring them home and, for the first time, we'll be here as a family. I'm so nervous about it. It does make me wonder about the future and quite how it's all going to change. The last year has been really good to me. As well as the things I've already told you about, I've shot another three series of *A League of Their Own*, which keeps getting bigger and better and remains the same brilliant fun. Oh yeah, and I've had a number one single in the charts with Dizzee Rascal—I know, ridiculous! Who would ever've thought?

Here's how it happened: at the National Television Awards, Simon Cowell came over and talked to me about the idea of doing a World Cup song. Simon is incredibly difficult to say 'No' to. We talked some more on the phone and he told me he had a song that he'd like his A&R guy Nick Raymond to come over and play to me. I agreed and, a couple of days later, I was in my kitchen listening to the song with Nick. It was a catchy little tune—a mix of samples from Blackstreet's 'No Diggity' with 'Shout' by Tears for Fears. In between there was this rap—nothing to do with football, just a rap laid down on the track.

'So what do you want me to do?' I asked him.

'The rap,' Nick said. 'We want you to do the rap.'

'You're joking. Are you mad? I can't rap.'

'Sure you can. We've seen you do it on *Gavin & Stacey*.'

'Yeah, but come on,' I said, 'that's a very different thing. I mean, a character rapping on a TV show is one thing, but releasing a record—I can't do that, I just can't.'

'James'—he was looking hard at me now—'Simon told me I'm not allowed to leave here until you agree.'

I got up to make a cup of tea. 'Nick,' I said, 'you have to understand, I know we're talking about Simon Cowell, but I will never rap on your record. It would be awful for you. It would be awful for me. It would be awful for music, generally. I like Simon, I do, but it's just not going to happen.'

'OK,' he said, 'but what if I get a rapper to do it with you?'

'I'll tell you what,' I said. 'The only rapper you could get would be Dizzee Rascal. He's the only person with the right sense of humour, the only one who could pull it off and the only guy I'd do it with.' I'd met Dizzee a few times and really liked him.

'All right then,' Nick said, as I guided him to the door. 'So if we get Dizzee, you're in. I can tell Simon that, can I?'

'Yeah, you can tell him that,' I said, shaking his hand. 'Good luck, Nick. You'll never get him.'

TWO WEEKS LATER I was in a studio with Dizzee Rascal, recording Simon's song for the World Cup. The power of the Cowell.

The record came out and, before I knew it, I was performing on *Britain's Got Talent* with Dizzee. I'd been reluctant at first—with good reason: I ain't no rapper—but once we agreed to give the money to Great Ormond Street Hospital, it was a no-brainer.

After *World Cup Live* was finished, I went out to shoot another big-budget film, *The Three Musketeers*, which, at the time of writing, I've yet to see, but the trailer looks good and it was great filming it. I play the musketeers' servant, so I basically walked behind some really good-looking guys carrying their bags.

I also filmed two episodes of *Doctor Who*, which is something I'm incredibly proud to have been part of. If I had my way, I'd work with Matt Smith every day of the week. He is the most splendid company. I hosted the Brits again and have been asked back to do it in 2012. And, as I write this, I'm about to go back to the National Theatre to do a play for six months. It's called *One Man, Two Guvnors* and Nicholas Hytner—who is now actually Sir

Nicholas Hytner—is going to direct it. He called me whilst I was doing *World Cup Live* and the conversation went like this:

'Hi, James,' he said.

'Hi, Sir Nicholas,' I replied, respectfully.

'Ha!' He laughed. 'Listen, would you like to do a play next year at the National Theatre?'

I thought for half a second. 'Are you directing it?'

'If you do it, then I most probably will—'

I didn't even wait for him to carry on speaking. 'YES,' I said.

'Do you not want to know what play it is?'

'I don't care. If it's with you at the National Theatre, then I would love to do it.'

Some people have said that I was mad to commit to something I'd not read, or crazy to not take more time about the decision. But I think all eight of the history boys have a romantic attachment to Nick and that building, and would bite someone's arm off to be back there, working with him again. The play is a new adaptation of an Italian farce called *The Servant of Two Masters*. I hope it's going to be funny.

IN MY PERSONAL LIFE, I couldn't be happier. A few months ago, on a cold, icy Christmas Day morning, I asked Jules to marry me. It was a moment I will never forget. I knelt down, looking up at her, my eyes filling with tears, with a ring I'd designed myself in my shaking left hand. She said yes! I cannot wait to marry her. I already see her as my wife and it'll be lush to make it official.

Now, if you don't mind, if you have time, I'd just like to share one more story with you. It's something else I get asked about a lot, so it would feel odd not to include it in this book.

A couple of months ago, I made one more sketch for Comic Relief. Ben, Gabe and I felt as though we'd possibly peaked with the last Sports Relief one, and to make another seemed risky. Clyde, however, felt we should definitely give it a try so, although we wouldn't fully commit to doing it, we said we'd certainly explore the possibilities of making one.

We'd been lucky before, because Smithy had essentially walked into rooms that were full of the people we wanted to film with. Now we wanted to do something where we had as impressive a cast list, but didn't know how we could get them all together at the same time. Whichever way we imagined it, we couldn't make it work, and I felt as though we should probably put it to bed. And then Suzi Aplin had a brainwave.

She was producing Comic Relief, and she sent us over a video link of a sketch from an American TV show. It was Jimmy Kimmel's post-Oscar-night sketch called 'The Handsome Men's Club'. It featured a really impressive cast list and was shot round a table where they had made it appear as if everyone was sitting together. This showed us how technically it was possible to shoot the biggest and best cast we could assemble and still make it work round everyone's schedules.

We set about trying to write a script and decided, as we had before, that we'd write it for the biggest people that we could think of, and if they said no, we'd adjust the script accordingly. The main premise for the script was a group of celebrities seated round a table at Comic Relief HQ, arguing about who they thought should go to Africa and shoot the appeal film. They all wanted to do it, but each time they put themselves forward, they'd be gazumped by the opinions of a more famous person sitting at the table with them. We decided that the biggest and best person we could approach had to be Sir Paul McCartney.

We chose to ask him first as I had already been lucky enough to have some contact with him. When we were doing *World Cup Live* the summer before, I'd got a phone call telling me that Paul McCartney wanted to speak to me.

At first I had thought it was a wind-up. I soon realised it was real when I got a call from one of his people telling me that Paul would be calling at 11.30 a.m. I had no idea why he would want to speak to me.

At 11.10 a.m. the phone rang; it was another of Paul's people asking me if I was near the phone. 'Erm . . . yeah. I'm holding it in my hand now. That's how I'm able to speak to you,' I said to the polite young lady.

'No, I know,' she said. 'I know you're near it now. I just wanted to check that you're not about to go into a tunnel or lose signal.'

'No. I'll be right here. I'm looking forward to it.'

'Even if you need the toilet, you'll still take the phone with you, right?' she added.

'Yes.' I chuckled. 'In fact, I'm waiting till I get on the phone to the legend that is Sir Paul McCartney so that I can be sitting on the toilet when I speak to him.'

'Good. Well, that's great. Just wanted to check.' Not sure she got the gag.

I waited by the phone and, as it turned eleven thirty, it rang.

'Hello?' I said tentatively.

'Hi, James, it's Paul,' said Paul McCartney in the soft Liverpudlian lilt you've heard a million times but never, ever expect to hear over the phone.

'Hello, sir, how are you?' I said, and then Paul went on to tell me how much he'd enjoyed the Sports Relief sketch and had watched and liked various other things I'd done and that he wanted me, as Smithy, to introduce him on stage at the Isle of Wight Festival in a couple of weeks' time.

I couldn't believe what I was hearing. Paul McCartney wanted me to introduce him on stage? I told him I was blown away that he had even seen anything I had done and promised that I would do everything in my power to make it happen.

Once I was off the phone, I skipped straight into Ben's office and told him the news. He was as shocked as I was. While I was excitedly pacing around, Ben took a moment to look at the diary and delivered the bombshell: 'We've got a show that night, James. You can't do it. Sorry, dude.'

He was right, I couldn't do it. I called up Paul's people and delivered the news and told them how upset I was that I couldn't do it, but if Paul was still looking for an intro, I could film something that he could play on the screens. Paul said that would be great, so I filmed a big build-up for him. When I saw him at an event a week or so later, he thanked me and told me it had gone down well with the crowd.

With a favour in the bag, I thought we had a good shot at trying to get Sir Paul. We knew he liked the last Comic Relief sketch; plus we'd got on well when we met before. Clyde got in touch with his people, who told me I was to call Paul at midday.

When I was put through, I explained the rough outline of the script. I told him the names of some of the people we were hoping would be involved, and then I launched into full charity-grovel mode. I told him that we would make the whole experience as fun and painless as possible, that we'd shoot it whenever was good for him and that, because now the sketches could be bought as digital downloads, it could make a decent chunk of money that would go towards people all over the world who desperately needed it. I then played the trump card: the simple fact of his involvement in the sketch would, without question, change people's lives.

He paused and I could hear the smile come into his voice. 'Well,' he said, 'I've gotta tell you, James. I've heard some grovelling in my time, but that was the best yet. Have you got that written down?'

I laughed and told him that he hadn't heard anything yet. I told him that if he said no, I was going to offer to name my unborn child after him. Down the phone I could hear Paul burst out laughing. 'You're on. That's it. If you name your child after me, I'll do your sketch.' We both had a giggle and then, very graciously, he went on to say that, all joking aside, he would love to be involved. 'Count me in!' were his exact words.

I WAS CHUFFED to bits and so were the boys. But Paul was just the first. The next person on our list of hopefuls was George Michael. From the moment we started the script, I was sure that music would be the magic ingredient the sketch needed at the start and at the end to really lift it. The thought of Smithy and George acting like old mates in the same tracksuit tops was an image

I couldn't—and didn't want to—shake. George was away in Australia but, after two or three 4 a.m. calls, he said he was up for doing the sketch. Just as we predicted, once we had those two, everyone else started wanting to be a part of it: Rupert Grint, Tom Felton, Lord Winston, Tom Daley, Lord Coe, Rio Ferdinand, Keira Knightley, JLS, Dermot O'Leary, Clare Balding. Ringo Starr amazingly said yes as well, and filmed his stuff down the line from America; the former prime minister Gordon Brown even agreed to be in it (and was the most fantastic sport), as did Davina McCall, Richard Madeley, Roger Lloyd-Pack, Justin Bieber, Lenny Henry and Richard Curtis. Phew. Think that's everyone.

It was the cast list we'd dreamt of and, over the next couple of months, we filmed and filmed and filmed again. Technically it was a nightmare, and I take my hat off to Ben for making it happen so smoothly. Everyone was fantastic.

When the sketch finally aired, the response was bigger than for the other two sketches put together. The next day, people were calling it the greatest sketch ever made on a Comic Relief night. I'm not saying this is true, but it was nice that somebody thought it was. I'm incredibly proud of it. I'm proud of Ben, Gabe and Clyde, and will for ever be thankful to all the people in front of and behind the scenes who made it happen.

I'm thankful for all of it, really. All of the stuff that I've mentioned in this book—the ups and the downs. I'm grateful for every single moment. Just the fact that you, whoever you are, are even reading this is enough to blow my mind. The truth is, often I'm not sure what I've done to deserve all this. To have so many great memories.

IN JUST A FEW moments I will walk out of my front door and when I return I'll have my son and fiancée with me, all three of us together at home for the first time. We will, from now, start to become a family. My whole world is going to change, and I'm incredibly excited about it. And, as I look back on the boy I wrote about at the start of this book, the boy who needed all that constant attention, who craved the limelight like oxygen, well, I realise I don't feel that any more—not as much, anyway. I still have ambition, lots of it, and there are still plenty of things I dream of achieving. But 'attention' is perhaps not the right word for it any more. The flame is still there; it just doesn't burn quite as brightly. Now everything I need I get from Jules and my son. It's their love and their attention that's the most important thing to me now.

So, finally, it's time for me to go and bring him home. Here we go. Have I got everything Jules put on the list? Car seat? Yes. Thing to attach the car seat to the back seat of the car? Yes. Hat for the baby? Yes. Cardigan for the baby? Yes. Baby wipes? Yes. Bib? Yes. Endless lists of stuff. This is only going to intensify.

Here goes ... Wish me luck!

Oh, and by the way, we've decided on a name for him. His name is ... Max McCartney Kimberley Corden.